The Real Good News

David Eells

© 2014 David Eells. All Rights Reserved. Permission is given to copy and quote portions of this book, provided the context is given, along with copyright notice and contact details.

ISBN: 978-1-942008-07-1
First Printing – Large Print Edition – 2014

Download this book and others freely from www.ubmbooks.com.

In order to make this book broadly available, we also offer it through online book sellers. We have taken the lowest percentage permitted by their systems, so income from these sales is negligible and is offset by the thousands we give away to those who cannot afford to pay for it. We do this to be obedient to our Lord, Who said, "freely ye received, freely give."

IMPORTANT NOTES:

Scriptures are taken from the *American Standard Version (ASV)* of the Holy Bible because of its faithfulness to the ancient manuscripts and Bible Numerics.

Numerics is a system designed into the Bible by God to prove authenticity. The Greeks and Hebrews used their letters for numbers. Therefore, the whole Bible is also written in numbers which show perfect patterns as long as the God-inspired original words are not departed from. It mathematically proves the original text and where it has been added to or taken away from. The *Numeric English New Testament (NENT)* is based on the numeric pattern and is quoted from when necessary.

We have departed from the *ASV* only in the name Jehovah and Lord Jehovah which we replaced with Lord and Lord God, respectively. Neither represents the original YHWH but Lord is less confusing to many and we did not want this to distract from the teaching. The vowels were added by men to make the name "Jehovah." We apologize for sometimes using partial texts but this book would have been much larger had we not. Rarely, where italicized words were added to the text and changed the original meaning, we left them out.

Acknowledgements

May our Father bless those whom He used to create this book from transcriptions of David Eells' teachings:
- Eric Tagg, who did a great job of editing the initial transcription.
- Dwora Jawer, who took the manuscript from there and refined it.
- Brad Moyers, who then proofread the manuscript.
- Kevin Rea, who did the typsetting/formatting.
- Michael Duncan, who created the artwork and the book cover.
- Many brothers and sisters who have worked on this book but do not wish any credit.

Dear friends,

Jesus taught that we must believe we receive everything we pray for in order to receive in the physical realm. ***(Mar.11:24) Therefore I say unto you, All things whatsoever ye pray and ask for, believe that ye receive them, and ye shall have them.*** What you will see from this book is that according to the scriptures we received all our prayers answered at the cross. All provision for all prayers was guaranteed there for those who repent and believe. Being convinced of this gives us a foundation of faith that makes answered prayer the normal Christian life. This revelation has brought miraculous answers to multitudes. Many are waiting for answers, not realizing that this is not faith which is the very substance of the thing hoped for. Once a person sees that God speaks the end from the beginning and He teaches His children to walk in His steps, they have the main key to the Kingdom. Please go with us and see what God Himself teaches: that He has already provided for all our prayers to be answered. Then we can quit spending all of our energy trying to get God to answer and begin receiving what He has already given in every area of our life.

Love from your servant in Christ,
David Eells

Table of Contents

1. It Is Finished! 7
2. Healed and Provided For! 21
3. His Power in Weakness! 34
4. Enter His Rest! 47
5. Healing By Scripture! 59
6. The Curse Is Taken Away! 72
7. Endurance! 86
8. Forgiveness! 97
9. Renewed Imaginations and Miracles! 109
10. They Cast Out Demons! 123
11. Christians and Demons! 136
12. Authority and Demons! 150
13. Act on Faith! 167
14. Demons Fear the Gospel! 182
15. All Needs Supplied in Christ! 196
16. Treasures in Heaven! 211
17. Tithing: Renounce Ownership! 228
18. Provision: Receiving it Multiplied! 244
19. Provision: Receiving it in the Wilderness! 257
20. Assurance, Not Insurance! 271
21. Protection! 284
22. Safety in Zion! 300
23. God's Disclaimer and Ours! 314
24. Beware of Condemnation! 328

Books of the Bible - Abbreviation List

Old Testament

Gen.	Genesis
Exo.	Exodus
Lev.	Leviticus
Num.	Numbers
Deu.	Deuteronomy
Jos.	Joshua
Jdg.	Judges
Rth.	Ruth
1Sa.	1 Samuel
2Sa.	2 Samuel
1Ki.	1 Kings
2Ki.	2 Kings
1Ch.	1 Chronicles
2Ch.	2 Chronicles
Ezr.	Ezra
Neh.	Nehemiah
Est.	Esther
Job.	Job
Psa.	Psalms
Pro.	Proverbs
Ecc.	Ecclesiastes
Son.	The Song of Solomon
Isa.	Isaiah
Jer.	Jeremiah
Lam.	Lamentations
Eze.	Ezekiel
Dan.	Daniel
Hos.	Hosea
Joe.	Joel
Amo.	Amos
Oba.	Obadiah
Jon.	Jonah
Mic.	Micah
Nah.	Nahum
Hab.	Habakkuk
Zep.	Zephaniah
Hag.	Haggai
Zec.	Zechariah
Mal.	Malachi

New Testament

Mat.	Matthew
Mar.	Mark
Luk.	Luke
Joh.	John
Act.	Acts
Rom.	Romans
1Co.	1 Corinthians
2Co.	2 Corinthians
Gal.	Galatians
Eph.	Ephesians
Php.	Philippians
Col.	Colossians
1Th.	1 Thessalonians
2Th.	2 Thessalonians
1Ti.	1 Timothy
2Ti.	2 Timothy
Tit.	Titus
Phm.	Philemon
Heb.	Hebrews
Jas.	James
1Pe.	1 Peter
2Pe.	2 Peter
1Jn.	1 John
2Jn.	2 John
3Jn.	3 John
Jud.	Jude
Rev.	Revelation

CHAPTER ONE

It Is finished!

Greetings, saints! The Lord bless you and keep you in His loving will. Dear Father, in the name of Jesus, we ask Your grace today, Lord. We ask Your grace to get a very, very important message, one of the most important messages, across to Your precious people, Lord. We're asking Your mercy and Your grace to do this. Lord, Your Good News is the very best and it saddens me to know that so many of Your people don't have the revelation of the Good News. We think that's a basic foundation, but not these days, Lord, and people do need desperately, Lord, to know that You've provided all things for them, that it's already done; it's finished. Lord, we're just asking for Your mercy today, Lord, to get this revelation across, to fill Your people's hearts with faith and boldness to be able to apprehend everything that You have provided for them. In the name of Jesus, Father, thank You, thank You.

O Lord, we thank You for this precious Word through Paul. **(Rom.1:16) For I am not ashamed of the gospel** (the "Good News")**: for it is the <u>power of God unto salvation</u> to every one that believeth....** Well then, why do so many of God's people not have any power? It's because they <u>are</u> ashamed of the Good News. The Good News is a powerful revelation and when we exercise faith in it, God imparts His power to us, to save in all things. Notice, the Gospel "is the power of God unto salvation." The word "salvation" in the New Testament is generally the Greek noun *soteria* and the verb of that is *sozo*. It actually has a wonderful meaning of deliverance, salvation, preservation, healing and provision. God has already provided our every need, according to Scripture. **(Php.4:19) And my God shall supply every need of yours according to his <u>riches in glory</u> in Christ Jesus.** Many people limit salvation to such a very narrow band of revelation, but salvation is very, very big. This word *soteria*, which is generally translated as "salvation," is very broad and as we study that, we'll see that the Good News, the Gospel, provides us everything we need. <u>The Gospel is the power of God unto salvation.</u> We once asked a local man, who was Greek, what *soteria* meant to him and he said, "It means, all of my needs supplied, like a little baby." I've never forgotten that and as I researched the Scriptures, I found out that's exactly what it means – "all of our needs supplied." But it's "all of our needs supplied" to the believers. The Gospel is the power of God unto salvation to every one that believes, not necessarily to what we loosely call "Christians," but to the believers.

(Rom.1:16) For I am not ashamed of the gospel: for it is the power of God unto salvation to every one that believeth; to the Jew first, and also to the Greek. (17) For therein is revealed a righteousness.... This is because we are counted righteous by our faith. In the New Testament, the people who walk by faith are the ones who are justified because "counted righteous" means "justified." **(Rom.1:17) For therein is revealed a righteousness of God from faith unto faith: as it is**

written, *But the righteous shall live from faith.* The literal translation there is "from faith" and not "by faith." God puts a high premium on people who believe and act upon His Word. *(Jas.2:17) Even so faith, if it have not works, is dead in itself. (18) Yea, a man will say, Thou hast faith, and I have works: show me thy faith apart from [thy] works, and I by my works will show thee [my] faith.* People who act on what the Word says will see results. They will receive power from God. *(Heb.10:38) But my righteous one shall live from faith....* The numeric pattern again proves that the correct translation is "from faith" and not "by faith." Our spiritual, heavenly life comes from faith. *(Heb.10:38) But my righteous one shall live from faith: And if he shrink back, my soul hath no pleasure in him. (39) But we are not of them that shrink back unto perdition....* "Perdition" is "destruction" and everyone who shrinks back from the walk of faith is being destroyed. They're under the curse; they're subject to all the things that faith delivers us from. *(Heb.10:39) But we are not of them that shrink back unto perdition; but of them that have faith unto the saving of the soul.* When you first receive salvation, it's not your soul that gets saved; it's your spirit that is saved and as you continue to walk after the Spirit, you bear fruit in your soul. Walking by faith brings us the manifestation of God's salvation in our soul, which is our mind, will and emotions. And having our mind, will and emotions in tune with Jesus Christ is what this salvation is all about.

(Heb.11:1) Now faith is assurance of [things] hoped for, a conviction of things not seen. Some translations say, "Faith is the substance of things hoped for." The power of God to save you in every circumstance and every situation, which is the Gospel, the really Good News, comes because of faith. It comes when you believe that you have already received these things. That's what I want to prove to you today. I want to prove to you and encourage you that you don't have to talk God into anything. He has already made provision for you. It's a free gift that He puts into your hand. He gave it to you 2000 years ago and He will not take it back. You can give it up by not walking by faith, but He won't take it back. Our faith stands in as the "substance" of the thing that we need and the thing that we need in every circumstance is salvation. I'm going to prove that to you because many of you have a very narrow idea of what salvation is. *(Heb.11:2) For therein the elders had witness borne to them. (3) By faith we understand that the worlds have been framed by the word of God, so that what is seen hath not been made out of things which appear.* The Word of God has framed the world by the faith of God. God Himself creates through faith and, if we are going to be a son of God, we have to do the same thing. Our words will bring forth the creating power of God through us into every situation and every circumstance, but we need to use the "substance" of the thing hoped for and that's our faith. We need to give God the substance, if we want the thing hoped for, because *(Heb.11:6) ... without faith it is impossible to be well-pleasing [unto him]; for he that cometh to God must believe that he is, and [that] he is a rewarder of them that seek after him.* Also, Jesus said, *(Mat.9:29) ... According to your faith be it done unto you,* and

(Mat.8:13) ... As thou hast believed, [so] be it done unto thee. <u>He constantly made faith the requirement</u>.

And now we see the things that God is creating are not made of things which appear in this world. The things which appear in this world are things that are made by man, but Jesus said, *(Luk.17:20) The kingdom of God cometh not with observation.* The Kingdom of God is a spiritual Kingdom that God is building and He is building it only by faith. The works of man could not be heard in God's Temple. *(1Ki.6:7) And the house, when it was in building, was built of stone made ready at the quarry; and there was neither hammer nor axe nor any tool of iron heard in the house, while it was in building.* The temple that God is building is, of course, His people. No tool could be heard in there and that's a symbol to show that the works of man cannot build this. We also know that all of those things made by man are going to pass away. *(Heb.12:27) And this [word], Yet once more, signifieth the removing of those things that are shaken, as of things that have been made, that those things which are not shaken may remain.* Aha! All the things made by man will be shaken: the works of man, the religions of man, the organizations of man. All these things will be shaken until the only things that are left are the things that are created through faith. We, like God, learn to *(Rom.4:17) ... calleth the things that are not, as though they were*, and our faith has the power to create all of our needs. In other words, it's our faith that is used to create whatever is needed. *(Heb.12:28) Wherefore, receiving a kingdom that cannot be shaken, let us have grace, whereby we may offer service well-pleasing to God with reverence and awe: (29) for our God is a consuming fire.* Yes, and one thing He loves to consume is the flesh of the beast on the altar. We need to cooperate with Him in burning up the beastly nature of our flesh, our old man, and one way we can do that is by believing the Good News, and I'm going to share that with you, too. But first, let me share with you the revelation of just how great and broad the salvation of the real Good News is.

(Eph.2:8) For by grace.... We know that grace is unmerited and unearned. It's a free gift, so you can't work for it. It can only come by faith. *(Eph.2:8) For by grace have ye been saved through faith....* Some versions say, "are you saved," but the numeric pattern and the *Nestle-Aland* text, which is comprised of the three ancient manuscripts, say, "have you <u>been</u> saved" because salvation was accomplished at the cross. The word "saved" here is again the word *sozo* and it's the verb of the noun *soteria*, which covers everything. It covers all of your needs supplied, just like for a baby, and all your needs were supplied at the cross. That is what salvation is. Many people think that salvation is only the salvation of your spirit, but no, we're going to see that it's not just your spirit. Salvation includes not just your spirit; it also includes your soul, your body and your circumstances, so that all your needs are met, completely. *(Eph.2:8) For by grace have ye been saved through faith; and that not of yourselves, [it is] the gift of God; (9) not of works, that no <u>man</u> should glory.* There it is. Man's works are not going to be preserved through this time. Your works will ultimately fail

you. We have a wilderness coming in which man's works won't preserve us. They won't work and it will have to be the supernatural power of God out of Heaven that meets the needs of God's people in the days to come. God is not going to permit our flesh to save us in the days to come; it's going to be faith. ***(Eph.2:9) Not of works, that no man should glory. (10) For we are his workmanship, created in Christ Jesus for good works*** (And, of course, that's the works of the Lord, not the works of the flesh.)***, which God afore prepared that we should walk in them.*** Keep Ephesians 2:8 in mind as we study this word "saved" in other places in the Bible because we're going to see that whatever salvation is, it has already been done and it's only going to come through faith. "By grace have ye been saved." God wants us to believe something in order for us to have the manifestation of our salvation in our life.

If we look at how this word "saved" is used, we'll know that whatever God is speaking about with this word, it has already been given to us. ***(Luk.7:48) And he said unto her, Thy sins are forgiven.*** Obviously, He is talking about salvation of her spirit here. ***(49) And they that sat at meat with him began to say within themselves, Who is this that even forgiveth sins? (50) And he said unto the woman, Thy faith hath saved thee; go in peace.*** This is the common understanding of what salvation is all about and here it used the word "saved" for the word *sozo*, which we saw in Ephesians 2:8. In other words, "By grace have you been *sozo*'d through faith." So we see here that our *sozo* in this case was already provided and now I'm going to apply this to other things. Some people say "Healing is not a part of salvation," or, "Deliverance is not a part of salvation," and they go on and on with what's not a part of salvation, but all of that's a lie. It's not Scriptural and I'm going to prove that to you. We see that your sins being forgiven is the initial step of salvation, of receiving a new spirit from God. "Thy faith hath saved thee; go in peace." "Thy faith" is what gives you the initial salvation, before it bears fruit in the rest of your life. And the word for "saved" here is the word *sozo*, but *sozo* is also used in many other places. ***(Luk.8:43) And a woman having an issue of blood twelve years, who had spent all her living upon physicians, and could not be healed of any, (44) came behind him, and touched the border of his garment: and immediately the issue of her blood stanched. (45) And Jesus said, Who is it that touched me?*** Well, that's very interesting. ***And when all denied, Peter said, and they that were with him, Master, the multitudes press thee and crush [thee]. (46) But Jesus said, Some one did touch me; for I perceived that power had gone forth from me.*** Can you imagine? Here is the Son of God and here is a woman in need who touched Him by faith. One thing we can see here very plainly is that God wants us to understand you don't have to talk Jesus into this. Why? Because it has already been provided. You don't have to convince Him. Don't waste hours trying to get God to do something for you. You're deceived if you're doing that because before we get through with this study, you're going to see that God has already given these things to you. Don't waste your time; accept it by faith.

(Luk.8:47) And when the woman saw that she was not hid, she came

trembling, and falling down before him declared in the presence of all the people for what cause she touched him, and how she was healed immediately. (48) And he said unto her, Daughter, thy faith hath <u>made thee whole; go in peace.</u> "Made thee whole" here is obviously talking about a healing and it was a healing that Jesus did not even know about until it had already happened because of this woman's faith. It was not a matter of Him saying "yes" or "no"; it was a matter of her faith touching God and the answer came because it has already been provided. "And he said unto her, Daughter, <u>thy</u> faith hath made thee whole." He said this constantly: "thy faith." What are you waiting for? Are you waiting for God's faith? Don't wait. She didn't wait. She touched God by faith and she was healed. The word translated "made thee whole" is the word *sozo*. Remember, "By grace have ye <u>been</u> saved (*sozo*'d) through faith." In this case, salvation is a healing. You've been healed by grace, by unmerited favor, through faith. *Sozo* is being used as a healing here and even though the translation is "made whole," it's the same word! It's the same word as in Ephesians 2:8, so what does that tell you? It tells you that you can translate it the same way. It also tells you in this text that *sozo* is a healing, praise be to God! This word is used quite often and we see here that healing is a part of salvation. *Sozo* is the word "saved" and healing is a part of salvation, so don't forget that. Don't let people deceive you about that.

Here's another example: *(Luk.8:36) And they that saw it told them how he that was possessed with demons was <u>made whole</u>.* This was the demoniac with the legion of demons in him. He was "made whole," he was "saved." When you have demons, you need to be saved and that's the word right there, *sozo*. It's the same exact word being used everywhere else as "saved" or "made whole," etc. *(Eph.2:8) For by grace have ye been <u>delivered</u>* (*sozo*'d) *through faith....* In the case of this demoniac, *sozo* is being used as a mighty, powerful deliverance, which the overwhelming majority of mankind doesn't need because most people don't have legions of demons. So we see that salvation has to do with deliverance, too. And then we have this instance: *(Mat.8:23) And when he was entered into a boat, his disciples followed him. (24) And behold, there arose a great tempest in the sea, insomuch that the boat was covered with the waves: but he was asleep.* He was totally entered in the rest and wasn't worried about a thing. He knew He was in the Father's hands. Fear is one of the biggest destructions in our lives. When we react to what we see or feel around us, then we give the devil permission to execute the curse upon us. Fear is faith; it's just faith in reverse. *(Mat.8:25) And they came to him, and awoke him, saying, <u>Save</u>, Lord; we perish.* Again, that's the word *sozo*, but in this case it refers to being saved from destruction and includes the idea of protection. *(Mat.8:26) And he saith unto them, <u>Why are ye fearful</u>, <u>O ye of little faith</u>? Then he arose, and rebuked the winds and the sea; and there was a great calm. (27) And the men marvelled, saying, What manner of man is this, that even the winds and the sea obey him?* "Why are you fearful?" In other words, "Why didn't you take care of this yourself?" Fear did not permit them to partake of the benefit of God. It's a good thing

Jesus woke up! "By grace have ye been <u>saved</u> through faith," but they didn't have faith. They were not claiming the benefits of God, of His deliverance, of His provision, of His safety from destruction. They weren't claiming these benefits because they weren't exercising any faith and then Jesus woke up with His faith and saved the day!

There are also "catch-all" verses, such as Mark 11:24. When you receive this revelation and start acting upon it, you have a miraculous life. It is basically saying the same thing I've said so far, that salvation covers everything you need. Salvation has already been done and all of it has been provided, as Jesus said. ***(Mar.11:24) Therefore I say unto you, All things whatsoever....*** That covers it all, doesn't it? Most of the church doesn't believe this verse; they just jump right over it and ignore it, which they've been taught to do. They don't believe the power of God is available to us today and that's because they don't believe the Gospel. This is a revelation of the Gospel, the real Good News. ***(Mar.11:24) Therefore I say unto you, All things whatsoever ye pray and ask for, believe that ye have <u>received</u> them....*** Here it is again. "By grace have ye <u>been saved</u>." Notice what he's saying: "Believe that ye have <u>received</u> them." It's past tense. The numeric pattern proves that it's past tense and both the *Nestle-Aland* and *Textus Receptus* say that the Greek word is "received." ***(Mar.11:24) Therefore I say unto you, All things whatsoever ye pray and ask for, believe that <u>ye have received them</u>, and ye shall have them.*** Note that you are supposed to believe you have received it in the physical realm. And why is it that we are to believe we have received? Because Ephesians 2:8 says "by grace have ye <u>been</u> saved," and "saved" covers everything that we need, through faith. We have a complete agreement here. So "all things whatsoever" have been provided because He tells you, no matter what it is, believe you received. And He tells you that because it was all provided at the cross, turn around and look behind you. Most of you are looking in the wrong direction. You're looking forward; you're praying, "Provide this, provide that, meet this need, heal me, deliver me." God says, "Read the Word. You will find that I already did that." Don't waste a lot of time without faith. This is what faith is. ***(Rom.4:16) For this cause [it is] of faith, that [it may be] according to grace... (17) [even] God who ... calleth the things that are not, as though they <u>were</u>.*** Past tense. It has already been done. Everything about salvation has been completed. If you're waiting for God to do it, you have <u>no faith</u> and you're not claiming the promise. That's why many people are not growing up in the Lord.

If you really believed that you have received it all back there at the cross, what do you think you would say? What do you think you would do? What do you think your imagination would be like? This is a really good exercise. Practice meditating on what you would say and do if you have already received a healing, a deliverance, a provision, a protection, or so on. In other words, practice believing that it's already yours! How would you act? What would your mouth be saying? What would your thoughts be doing? Faith without works is dead. ***(Jas.2:26) For as the body apart from the spirit is dead, even so faith apart from works is dead.*** Many people say, "I believe I received," but everything else about them is totally backward to what they would be doing if they really believed. Their imagination is only imagining the things of this world, which is the curse and everything negative, and yet they are trying to believe they have received. But a whole part of their being is warring with them because we are kind of a schizophrenic being. We're flesh and we're spirit. However, because we are born-again, we have the power to cast down vain imaginations. ***(2Co.10:5) Casting down imaginations, and every high thing that is exalted against the knowledge of God, and bringing every thought into captivity to the obedience of Christ.*** We cast down these vain imaginations, we begin to speak in agreement with the fact we have received, we act as if we have received, we imagine we have received. We have been made in the image of our Father and our imagination is very powerful when mixed with our faith to do miracles. Believing you have received should take over your whole being from your mouth to your eyes to your feet. Everything that you do should be in agreement with the fact that you have already received.

If you're trying to apprehend, to go after, <u>to buy</u> salvation in any form, it's because you don't believe you have already received it. Believing we have received causes us to cease from doing our own works, so that God may do His. God does not start His works until we cease from ours; our works are what keep God from doing His. When we let God do His works, it's called the rest and we're to enter into His rest. If you believe you have received, what do you do? You rest. The first thing you do is rest. You cease from struggling, striving after this thing that you need or want. You enter into this rest, which is our spiritual New Testament Sabbath of ceasing from our works on His holy day. Notice that everything we've talked about so far is past tense; it's all in the past and this is the really Good News, folks. This is the thing that takes away all of your efforts and let's you keep all of your paycheck in many cases because it's not necessary. God is going to give it to you. He's going to just give you whatever the salvation is that you need. Another good example is found here: ***(1Pe.2:24) Who his own self <u>bare</u>....*** There it is again! It's past tense; it's already accomplished, already finished. "By grace have ye <u>been</u> saved through faith." ***(1Pe.2:24) Who his own self <u>bare</u> our sins in his body upon the tree, that we, having died unto sins, might live unto righteousness; by whose stripes ye <u>were</u> healed.*** We've already seen *sozo* is used as a word that identifies healing and here it's being used the same way. You were already healed at the cross. "By whose stripes ye <u>were</u> healed," you <u>were</u> *sozo*'d.

If we believe that we were healed, then how are we going to react to the bad news that we hear around us? People walk by sight and all the professional people, all the doctors and hireling theologians walk by sight. They don't know how to get a hold on the power of God for salvation. They don't know the Gospel, the Good News that all of this has already been accomplished by Christ. They don't know that the Gospel is the power of God to save you. They can't get a hold of that power because they walk by sight and don't walk by faith, so they receive the bad news. They receive the bad report <u>because they walk by physical sight</u> and they don't receive the Good News, <u>which is walking by faith</u>. There is a big difference. Of the spies who went into the Promised Land, only two came out with the Good News, the good report, because they repeated what God said and the rest of the spies came out with the bad news, the bad report, because of what they saw and what they felt and what they heard. ***(Num.13:1) And the Lord spake unto Moses, saying, (2) Send thou men, that they may spy out the land of Canaan, which I give unto the children of Israel: of every tribe of their fathers shall ye send a man, every one a prince among them. (17) And Moses sent them to spy out the land of Canaan... (25) And they returned from spying out the land at the end of forty days. (27) And they told him, and said, We came unto the land whither thou sentest us; and surely it floweth with milk and honey... (28) Howbeit the people that dwell in the land are strong, and the cities are fortified, [and] very great: and moreover we saw the children of Anak there. (29) Amalek dwelleth in the land of the South: and the Hittite, and the Jebusite, and the Amorite, dwell in the hill-country; and the Canaanite dwelleth by the sea, and along by the side of the Jordan. (30) And Caleb stilled the people before Moses, and said, Let us go up at once, and possess it; for we are well able to overcome it. (31) But the men that went up with him said, We are not able to go up against the people; for they are stronger than we. (32) And they brought up an evil report of the land which they had spied out unto the children of Israel... (14:2) And all the children of Israel murmured against Moses and against Aaron... (6) And Joshua the son of Nun and Caleb the son of Jephunneh, who were of them that spied out the land, rent their clothes: (7) and they spake unto all the congregation of the children of Israel, saying, The land, which we passed through to spy it out, is an exceeding good land. (8) If the Lord delight in us, then he will bring us into this land, and give it unto us; a land which floweth with milk and honey. (9) Only rebel not against the Lord, neither fear ye the people of the land; for they are bread for us: their defence is removed from over them, and the Lord is with us: fear them not. (26) And the Lord spake unto Moses and unto Aaron, saying... (27) ... I have heard the murmurings of the children of Israel, which they murmur against me. (28) ... As I live, saith the Lord, surely as ye have spoken in mine ears, so will I do to you: (29) your dead bodies shall fall in this wilderness; and all that were numbered of you, according to your whole number, from twenty years old and upward, that have murmured against me, (30) surely ye shall not come into the land, concerning which I sware that I would make you dwell therein, save Caleb the son of Jephunneh, and Joshua the son of Nun.*** So the bad news people fell in the wilderness, but the Good News people lived all the way through it and entered into the Promised Land <u>in their bodies</u>. That's very important; that's the power of the Gospel that we're talking about here.

(Col.1:12) Giving thanks unto the Father, who made us meet (or "able")....

We can thank the Father that He made us able through His gift of faith that He has given to us. *(2Th.3:2) ... For all have not faith*, but He has given to each one of us, that is, to God's elect, the measure of faith. *(Rom.12:3) For I say, through the grace that was given me, to every man that is among you, not to think of himself more highly than he ought to think; but so to think as to think soberly, according as <u>God hath dealt to each man a measure of faith</u>.* So He made us able. *(Col.1:12) Giving thanks unto the Father, who made us meet to be partakers of the inheritance of the <u>saints in light</u>.* "The saints in light" means the saints who walk in light. We are able to partake of everything that the saints who walk in light are capable of partaking. *(Col.1:13) Who <u>delivered</u>* (it's past tense again) *us out of the power of darkness....* He has already delivered us, folks. It has already been accomplished. When the devil tells you he has you in bondage, just remember you were already delivered and don't buy the lie. Accept the Good News that sets free. Accept the Good News, which is the power of God to save you. If you do not agree with the Good News, God cannot bring it to pass. People live under the curse all their life, thinking it's the normal Christian life, but the Lord delivered us. You're not under the power of the devil. The devil has deceived many people into believing that he has legal power over them, but he doesn't have any power because Jesus told us, *(Mat.28:18) All authority hath been given unto me in heaven and on earth. (19) Go ye therefore....* So He sent out His disciples to exercise that same authority over the devil's kingdom. *(Col.1:13) Who delivered* (past tense) *us out of the power of darkness, and <u>translated</u>* (past tense) *us into the kingdom of the Son of his love; (14) in whom <u>we have our redemption, the forgiveness of our sins</u>.* We already <u>have</u> our redemption.

What is "redemption"? "Redemption" is the Greek word *apolutrosis* and it means "a release on payment of a ransom." A ransom is paid when a person is being held captive, when they're being kept in bondage. The ransom sets them free. Folks, this has already been done. The price has been paid for us to be set free from bondage to the devil, set free from bondage to the flesh, set free from bondage to the curse. The price has already been paid by our Lord Jesus Christ. You can't earn your redemption. *(Eph.2:8) for by grace have ye been saved through faith; and that not of yourselves, [it is] the gift of God; (9) not of works, that no man should glory.* So redemption, *apolutrosis*, our release from bondage and the forgiveness of our sins, has already been accomplished at the cross. Praise be to God!

But there's something even greater that we should know about. *(2Co.5:16) Wherefore we henceforth know no man after the flesh: even though we have known Christ after the flesh, yet now we know [him so] no more.* And why is that? It's because "after the flesh" is like walking by sight. Now, instead, we know people by faith; we know ourselves by faith; we know the people for whom we have prayed by faith. *(2Co.5:17) Wherefore if any man is in Christ, [he is] a new creature: the old things <u>are</u> passed away....* They are gone; everything that we have known ourselves as, in the flesh, is gone. All that we have known about ourselves in the flesh is over. We know no man after the flesh anymore. *(2Co.5:17) Wherefore if any man is in Christ, [he is] a new creature: the old things <u>are passed away</u>; behold, <u>they are become new</u>. (18) But all things are of God, who reconciled us to himself....* So everything has become new because of what Jesus did at the cross. That was when He provided everything new for us. He provided our life, our deliverance, our healing, our provision, our protection and on and on. We should see ourselves in the light of what the Bible says about us, which is that <u>all things are new</u>. *(2Co.5:18) But all things are of God, who <u>reconciled us</u>....* Now "reconciled" there is the Greek word *katallasso* and it means Jesus made an <u>exchange</u> at the cross. He took all of our curse and gave us all of His blessing. He took all of our lack and gave us all of His provision. *(Php.4:19) My God shall supply every need of yours according to his riches in glory in Christ Jesus.* He has already given us all of our needs because He made an exchange at the cross. And what He took from us is everything we don't want and that we can't enter the Kingdom of Heaven with. Everything has already been accomplished. This is the Good News. This is the real Good News, that we don't have to strive and struggle and fight for what God has given to us. *(2Co.5:19) ... That God was in Christ reconciling the world unto himself, <u>not reckoning unto them their trespasses</u>, and <u>having committed unto us the word of reconciliation</u>.* The Lord is not reckoning to us, not attributing our trespasses to us, and He has given us the opportunity to share with other people that God has reconciled them, too. When we give them this Good News of reconciliation and when they become believers in what God has already accomplished, then they can start having miracles, also! That's our ministry that the Lord has called us to.

Here's another awesome revelation: *(Gal.2:20) I <u>have been</u> crucified with Christ; and it is no longer I that live, but Christ liveth in me: and that [life] which I now live in the flesh I live in faith, [the faith] which is in the Son of God, who loved me, and gave himself up for me.* You don't have to worry about your "old man" anymore. Many people talk so much about, "We have to walk in the crucified life"; "we have to be crucified"; "we have to do this or that." But think more like this: <u>You have already been crucified</u>. The old you doesn't live anymore. *(Rom.6:11) Reckon ye also yourselves to be dead unto sin, but alive unto God in Christ Jesus.* This is because it was accomplished at the cross. If you exercise faith in that, <u>the Lord will bring your crucifixion to pass</u>. If you try to do it yourself, you'll be trying to pick yourself up by your bootstraps and you will constantly fail. You will fall short of the glory of God. "I have been crucified with Christ; and it is no longer I that live, but Christ liveth in me ..." Wow! Since you're dead and He lives, the reconciliation, the exchange, was accomplished at the cross. You were crucified and Christ is now given to you as the gift of God. Christ is manifesting in you and you are entering into the rest, by resting from your own works through your faith in this promise. *(Heb.4:3) For we who have believed do enter into that rest....* You are entering into that rest; God is giving you the promise. The Land of Rest, by the way, was also called the Promised Land because that's where the promises are fulfilled. Now He's given us the real Good News here, that we've been crucified with Christ and we don't live anymore. He lives in us and we're justified by faith in this promise.

(Gal.2:16) Yet knowing that a man is not justified by the works of the law but through faith in Christ Jesus, even we believed on Christ Jesus, that we might be justified by faith in Christ.... "Justified" means "accounted righteous." When you believe these promises that are contrary to your senses, contrary to your eyes, contrary to the things around you, that is when God says you're righteous. Otherwise, you're seeking to be justified by the Law. Do you know what that is? It's self-works. ***(Gal.2:16) Yet knowing that a man is not justified by the works of the law but through faith in Christ Jesus, even we believed on Christ Jesus, that we might be justified by faith in Christ, and not by works of the law: because by the works of the law shall no flesh be justified. (Gal.3:6) Even as Abraham believed God, and it was reckoned unto him for righteousness.*** In other words, Abraham was justified; he believed God and he was reckoned righteous. So when we believe the Good News, we are reckoned righteous and we receive this benefit because we are righteous. It's the unearned favor of God. ***(Gal.3:11) Now that no man is justified by the law before God, is evident: for, The righteous shall live by*** (literally, "from") ***faith....*** Our life is going to proceed from the gift of faith which God has given to us. It's not that many saints don't have faith. It's that they don't know how to exercise faith, or they don't know what faith is, or they don't know that faith is demanded, or they don't know that faith is important. But as you can see, faith is very important. ***(Gal.3:12) And the law is not of faith; but, He that doeth them shall live in them.*** In other words, if you're going to try to obtain righteousness by your own works, by doing the works of the Law, then have at it, but God is not going to be in it. ***(Gal.3:13) Christ redeemed us ....*** "Redeemed" is again past tense. It's the Greek word *exagorazo* and it means "to buy out" or "to purchase a slave with a mind to set him free." What are we slaves of? We're slaves of the curse, slaves of the devil, slaves of the flesh and slaves of our circumstances, but the Lord redeemed us. He set us free from that. Do we believe it? Well, if you do, you're accounted righteous. And if you do, then that's the power of God unto salvation and God will bring it to pass for you. ***(Gal.3:13) Christ redeemed us from the curse of the law....*** The curse of the Law is everything that happened contrary to man's well-being because he was in rebellion against God's will and you can read it in Deuteronomy 28. ***(Gal.3:13) Christ redeemed us from the curse of the law, having become a curse for us; for it is written, Cursed is every one that hangeth on a tree: (14) that upon the Gentiles might come the blessing of Abraham in Christ Jesus; that we might receive the promise of the Spirit through faith.*** Glory be to God!

(1Pe.1:3) Blessed [be] the God and Father of our Lord Jesus Christ, who according to his great mercy begat us again unto a living hope by the resurrection of Jesus Christ from the dead. "Begat us again" means born-again. Being born-again is much deeper and broader than just accepting Jesus Christ as your Savior and receiving a new spirit because He says, *(1Pe.1:5) ... unto a salvation ready to be revealed in the last time* and *(1Pe.1:9) receiving <u>the end of your faith</u>, [even] the salvation of [your] souls*. It's not the beginning of your faith that is the salvation of your soul. The beginning of your faith is the salvation of your spirit. It's by faith that we are born-again at the cross, first spirit, then soul, then body. *(1Pe.1:21) Who through him are believers in God, that raised him from the dead, and gave him glory; <u>so that your faith and hope might be in God</u>. (22) Seeing* (When the word "seeing" is used like this in the Scriptures, it's talking about <u>accepting something by faith</u>.) *ye <u>have purified</u>* (This is past tense because it's already done.) *your souls in your obedience to the truth unto unfeigned love of the brethren, love one another from the heart fervently: (23) having been begotten again* (Remember, He "begat us again."), *not of corruptible seed, but of incorruptible, through the word of God, which liveth and abideth.* So here's born-again of soul and those who walk in bearing the 30-, 60- and 100-fold fruit of a born-again soul will also have a born-again body. Notice your soul is purified through "your obedience to the truth." How do you get obedience? You get obedience by giving faith to God because then He gives you grace to obey. And it's all His works, not your works. *(Eph.2:10) For we are his workmanship, created* ("Created" is past tense.) *in Christ Jesus for good works, which God afore prepared that we should walk in them.* If it's your works, it doesn't get you anywhere; salvation is not by your works.

(Heb.10:10) By [God's] will <u>we have been</u> sanctified through the offering of the body of Jesus Christ once for all. "Sanctified" means "set apart." We have been set apart from sin, set apart from the curse, set apart unto God. It's *(Heb.12:14) the sanctification without which no man shall see the Lord* and we are manifesting our sanctification more and more, as we walk in Him. Here we're told that this has been done at the cross: *(Heb.10:14) For by one offering he <u>hath perfected</u>* ("hath" is past tense) *for ever them that <u>are sanctified</u>.* He perfected you at the cross. I know some people say, "Perfection is not possible," but they don't know what the Bible says because we're not talking about our power; we're talking about God's power. "He hath perfected" us; salvation in every form has already been accomplished. And that's why Jesus said, *(Mar.11:24) Therefore I say unto you, All things whatsoever ye pray and ask for, believe that ye <u>received</u> them, and ye shall have them.* Wow! Think about that. It's an awesome promise.

(Eph.1:3) Blessed [be] the God and Father of our Lord Jesus Christ, who <u>hath blessed us</u> (past tense) *with every spiritual blessing in the heavenly [places] in Christ.* He has already blessed us with every thing in Christ, which is where heavenly places are. He has blessed us with every spiritual blessing in Christ. Of course, it's our faith which justifies this and our faith is what causes God to turn and empower us, and to provide for us everything that we need. *(Eph.1:4) Even as he chose us in him before the foundation of the world, that we should be holy and without*

blemish before him in love. He chose us to be holy and without blemish, and this is the way to be holy and without blemish: we are to exercise faith for it because He has already provided this for us. ***(2Pe.1:2) Grace to you and peace be multiplied in the knowledge of God and of Jesus our Lord; (3)*** <u>***seeing***</u> (We see this by faith through the eyes of the spirit and not through the eyes of the flesh.) ***that his divine power*** <u>***hath granted***</u>***....*** You have to see that it has been done; this is the Good News of the Gospel. Use your imagination, see that it has been done and confess that it has been done. Thank God that it has been done because this is the Gospel that saves. ***(2Pe.1:3) Seeing that his divine power hath granted unto us all things that pertain unto life and godliness, through the*** <u>***knowledge***</u> ***of him that called us by his own glory and virtue.*** You won't do this without knowledge, folks. You have to know what we're looking at right now; this is knowledge. How do you know what to exercise faith in without knowledge? You have to know what has been given to you so that you know how to exercise faith. It's so that you can know how to believe God. Can you do that? Can you practice seeing that God has already given to you everything you need?

God has already given to you everything you need; that's the real Gospel and that's why it's called the Good News. And the Gospel, ***(Rom.1:16) is the power of God unto salvation to everyone that believeth***. Wow! This is why living by faith is so important. Everything that you need from God has already been provided; you don't have to beg Him. Jesus said, ***(Mat.6:7) And in praying use not vain repetitions, as the Gentiles do:*** <u>***for they think that they shall be heard for their much speaking***</u>***. (8) Be not therefore like unto them: for your Father knoweth what things ye have need of, before ye ask him.*** Many people think a simple prayer is not enough. Well, if you have faith, it is! Now, there is the "prayer of importunity." When you don't have any faith, you pray and you pray and you pray until God gives you the faith, and then you can receive. But there is the "prayer of faith," which ***(Rom.4:17) calleth the things that are not, as though they were. (Heb.11:1 KJV) Now faith is the substance of things hoped for, the evidence of things not seen.*** That is what faith is; you believe you have <u>received</u>. And God says, "For that, you are righteous." He wants to see people who have faith. He was discouraged with the people who did not have any faith in the wilderness. ***(Num.14:11) And the Lord said unto Moses, How long will this people despise me? and*** <u>***how long will they not believe in me***</u>***, for all the signs which I have wrought among them. (12) I will smite them with the pestilence, and disinherit them, and will make of thee a nation greater and mightier than they.*** God wanted to wipe them out and make of Moses another people! ***(2Pe.1:3) Seeing that his divine power hath granted unto us all things that pertain unto life and godliness, through the knowledge of him that called us by his own glory and virtue; (4) whereby he*** <u>***hath granted unto us his precious and exceeding great promises***</u>***; that through these ye may become partakers of the*** <u>***divine nature***</u>***, having escaped from the corruption that is in the world by lust.*** These divine promises are for the purpose of giving us the divine nature of God and causing us to escape the corrupt old nature of the old man. And you are a righteous person, so God will do it for you. Why are you righteous? You're righteous because you believe what the Word says.

Do you think you have any problems? ***(Joh.12:31) <u>Now</u> is the judgment of this world: <u>now</u> shall the prince of this world be cast out.*** Some people might say, "Jesus made a mistake there because the devil's still around. I know it; I talked to him this morning." No. The devil was cast out and his power was broken at the cross. That's why Jesus said "now." It's because it was happening right there; the devil was conquered. Don't worry, folks. Your enemies have been destroyed by the cross. ***(Joh.16:33) These things have I spoken unto you, that <u>in me</u> ye may have peace. In the world ye have tribulation: but be of good cheer; <u>I have overcome the world</u>.*** Now maybe you can understand that He actually did overcome the whole world. Everything in our life that is contrary to godliness, Jesus has taken care of it already. He conquered the devil, the world, the flesh, everything. Jesus said when He was on the cross, ***(Joh.19:30) It is finished.*** Glory be to God, folks! It is finished! He conquered everything. He provided all, all of our needs supplied, like a little baby, *soteria*. It has been taken care of. Now you know why Paul said, "And my God shall supply every need of yours according to his <u>riches in glory</u> in Christ Jesus." He has already provided it. He's already given it to you. It is yours, so He's not going to withhold it from you. All you have to do is go to Him by faith, believing you have received.

CHAPTER TWO

Healed and Provided For!

Greetings, saints, and God bless you. Let's go to the Father and ask for His grace, so we can have a good study that we can understand. Father, in the name of the Lord Jesus, we come to You boldly before Your throne to receive Your grace today, to be encouraged in the Word of God, to have ears to hear and eyes to see, to have discernment that will stay with us forever. Lord, we ask that You will bring Your Words to our remembrance by Your Holy Spirit as You have promised. We ask, Lord, that You would raise this standard against the enemies of our lives, that Your Word would come to our mind and our understanding in a time that would defend us in these days. We are thanking You for that grace, Lord, to have a good memory of Your Word. We desire that Your Holy Spirit would help us to remember Your Word, to defend us. Lord, help us today to understand the authority You have given us through Your Gospel. Lord, help us to grow in wisdom and in stature and in favor with God and man, as the Word says about our Lord Jesus. Help us today to understand. We praise You, in Jesus' name, amen.

Well, before I continue on with the real Good News of what the Lord has done for us, I'd like to refresh your memory a little. We discovered this awesome revelation in the Scriptures. **(Eph.2:8) For by grace have ye <u>been saved</u> through faith; and that not of yourselves, [it is] the gift of God; (9) not of works, that no man should glory.** And we discovered that while the Greek word *sozo* used there for "saved" is used all through the Scriptures, in other places it is translated into different words, such as "made whole," "healed," "preserved" and "delivered." It is used throughout the Scriptures for salvation, healing, deliverance, provision and saved from danger, etc; it's all these things. When we apply Ephesians 2:8, we can see "by grace <u>have you been</u> saved, healed, delivered, provided for, protected," and so on, "through faith." We discover that this has all been done. In other words, the only way that we can take advantage of our benefits is through faith. We also discovered that the promises of God all through the Scriptures concerning the sacrifice of Jesus are past tense! And not only that, but the Lord Jesus told us, **(Mar.11:24) Therefore I say unto you, All things whatsoever ye pray and ask for, believe that ye <u>received</u> them, and ye shall have them.** It is literally past tense. "All things whatsoever," everything that you could pray for, according to Jesus has already been provided. We saw in verses like these from 1 Peter and Romans that we <u>were</u> healed and we <u>were</u> delivered from our sins. **(1Pe.2:24) Who his own self <u>bare</u>** (past tense) **our sins in his body upon the tree, that we, having died unto sins, might live unto righteousness; by whose stripes ye <u>were</u>** (past tense) **healed. (Rom.6:22) But now being made free from sin....**

What we're coming to understand is that we need to see ourselves in the light of what the Scripture says <u>has already happened</u>! We need to see ourselves as people who have already been saved, already been delivered, already been healed, already been provided for, already been protected by God's Hand. And, if we do that, we learn to enter into God's rest. We learn that God has already provided all these things for us. It only remains for us to enter into those works which He has done from the foundation of the world and we do that through our faith. **(2Pe.1:3) Seeing that his divine power <u>hath granted</u>** (again, this is past tense) **<u>unto us all things</u> that pertain unto life and godliness, <u>through the knowledge of him</u> that called us by his own glory and virtue.** Notice that this is what we need to be seeing in the spirit, not what we can see in the flesh. This is what it is to "walk in the spirit" and to have "the eyes of the dove," as Song of Solomon 4:1 says, which is to see things the way God commands us to see things. If we did this, we would be full of God's holy boldness, power and His dominion in this earth. "Through the knowledge" is how we gain this spiritual sight of seeing that all things have been provided already and the knowledge is these verses that we've been looking at. It's these past tense verses describing the dominion that the Lord has given us concerning the healing and the deliverance, the provision and the protection, and all these things the Lord has already given to us, already accomplished for us at the cross. **(2Pe.1:4) Whereby he hath granted unto us his precious and exceeding great promises; that through these ye may become partakers of the <u>divine nature</u>, having escaped from the corruption that is in the world by lust.** The divine nature of Jesus Christ is imparted to those people who are serious about taking hold on these precious and exceedingly great promises, those people who realize through the eyes of the spirit that they have already been given everything that is necessary for this life.

Finally, we discovered that, because of these past tense promises like those found in Hebrews 3 and 4, we could enter into what the Bible calls the "rest." Why? It's because we don't have to struggle, we don't have to strive, we don't have to earn or even convince God of our needs. All we have to do is accept what the Bible says, which is that He has already provided them, <u>so now any prayer you pray is a prayer of agreement with what God has already said is ours</u>. **(Heb.4:1) Let us fear therefore, lest haply, <u>a promise being left</u> of <u>entering into his rest</u>, any one of you should seem to have come short of it.** Why should we have any fear of entering into the rest? It's because all the promises together corporately are there to cause us to <u>enter fully into all of God's rest</u> and we don't want "a promise being left" out that would prevent us from doing that.

The Sabbath was a type and a shadow of this rest. **(Heb.3:7) Wherefore, even as the Holy Spirit saith, To-day if ye shall hear his voice, (8) Harden not your hearts, as in the provocation, Like as in the day of the trial in the wilderness, (9) Where your fathers tried [me] by proving [me], And saw my works forty years. (10) Wherefore I was displeased with this generation, And said, They do always err in their heart: But they did not know my ways; (11) As I sware in my wrath, They shall not enter into my rest. (12) Take heed, brethren, lest haply there shall be in any one of you <u>an evil heart of unbelief</u>, in falling away from the living God.** Our fear should be that we would not enter into this rest because He called not entering into His rest "an evil heart of unbelief" that causes us to fall away from the living God. Why is that? If you look at Exodus, the penalty for not entering into the rest is that we have to live under the curse of death. ***(Exo.31:14) Ye shall keep the sabbath therefore; for it is holy unto you: every one that profaneth it shall surely be put to death; for whosoever doeth <u>any work therein</u>, that soul shall be cut off from among his people.*** Well, why is it that all these promises are given to us in a past tense form? It is because if you believe them, you are restrained from doing your own works to bring them to pass. If we believe, for instance, that "by whose stripes ye <u>were</u> healed," then anything we do to receive healing proves that we don't believe that <u>it was done</u> at the cross. If we believe that when we pray, we have received, then what happens? What happens to a person who believes they have received? That person can stop; they can cease, they can rest from their own efforts. If we believe that "by grace have ye <u>been</u> saved through faith" and if we believe that "saved" represents all of the needs of God's people, then we can cease, we can rest. You can enter fully into this rest through the promises of God.

The Bible warns us, too: ***(Heb.4:2) For indeed we have had good tidings*** (This is the real Good News that we have been talking about.) ***preached unto us, even as also they: <u>but the word of hearing did not profit them</u>, <u>because it was not united by faith with them that heard</u>.*** So these promises do you absolutely no good until you believe them by faith, <u>then</u> they cause you to rest. ***(Heb.4:3) For we who have believed do enter into that <u>rest</u>....*** Which is what? <u>It's ceasing from your works</u>, <u>ceasing from your self works to try to save yourself</u>, <u>heal yourself</u>, <u>deliver yourself</u> and so on. We enter into this rest by faith and <u>the penalty for not entering into the rest is to put up with the curse of death</u>. ***(Heb.4:3) For we who have believed do enter into that rest; even as he hath said, As I sware in my wrath, They shall not enter into my rest: although the works were finished from the foundation of the world.*** Notice the works are past. He has already healed us, already delivered us, already provided for us, already protected us. All these things were accomplished through the sacrifice of Jesus and yet <u>people are not entering in because of unbelief</u>. They have to live under the curse of sin and of death because of a lack of faith. ***(Heb.3:12) Take heed, brethren, lest haply there shall be in any one of you an <u>evil heart of unbelief</u>, in falling away from the living God: (13) but exhort one another day by day, so long as it is called <u>To-day</u>; lest any one of you be hardened by the deceitfulness of sin: (14) for we are become partakers of Christ, <u>if we hold fast the beginning of our confidence firm unto the end</u>: (15) while it is said, To-day if ye shall hear his voice, Harden not your hearts, as in the provocation.*** We have to be confident in these promises; we have to stay firm in our confidence until the end. Jesus said, ***(Mat.10:22) he that endureth to the end, the same shall be saved***.

So we are told, ***(Heb.4:9) There remaineth therefore a sabbath rest for the people of God.*** The word "sabbath" in this verse is mentioned only <u>once</u> in the New

Testament. It is the Greek word *sabbatismos* and it means "a continual rest," or in other words, a continual ceasing from your works. This is the only Sabbath that is commanded for the people of God in the New Testament. **(Heb.4:10) For he that is entered into his rest hath himself also rested from his works, as God did from his.** Because these promises are past tense, we can't continue to work or we are proving that we are not believing the promise. That's the whole point. The promises cause us to rest from our works when we discover that the Lord has already healed us, already delivered us, already protected us and already provided for us in every form. We come to this awesome rest through these awesome promises of God.

There's something else I'd like to mention concerning this rest. **(1Co.1:26) For behold your calling, brethren, that not many wise after the flesh, not many mighty, not many noble, [are called]....** You see, God does not want strong, able, wise people. He does not need that. No. He needs a people who are a faithful people, who will believe in His power, in His ability. He needs a people who will believe in what He's already accomplished and not in what they can accomplish. This is the important thing to God. **(1Co.1:26) For behold your calling, brethren, that not many wise after the flesh, not many mighty, not many noble, [are called]: (27) but God chose the foolish things of the world, that he might put to shame them that are wise; and God chose the weak things of the world, that he might put to shame the things that are strong....** Things that are weak to the world are strong to God. Things that are strong to the world are weak to God. God did not choose for His methods the things that the world calls "strong" or that the world thinks is strong because He wanted to shame the world. **(1Co.1:28) And the base things of the world, and the things that are despised, did God choose, [yea] and <u>the things that are not, that he might bring to nought the things that are</u>** (This is a key to exactly what we have been talking about here.)**: (29) that no flesh should glory before God.** God does not want man to be able to take any credit for His methods for His salvation or His provision in any form. He did not want that. So instead of choosing the things that are, God chose the things that are not to bring to nothing the things that are.

The things that Jesus came to destroy were the works of the devil, whether they were manifested through people or not. **(1Jn.3:8) He that doeth sin is of the devil; for the devil sinneth from the beginning. To this end was the Son of God manifested, that he might destroy the works of the devil.** The curse that we see around us is "the things that are." It's the sickness, the death, the destruction, the depravity, the lack. Jesus came to destroy these things that are and the method He chose is to use "the things that are not." Now when you look at all the many, many past tense promises, the past tense provisions, that the Lord has given to us (1 Peter 2:24; Mark 11:24; 1 Peter 1:3; Colossians 1:13; Galatians 3:13; etc), you say, "I don't see that in the physical realm." They are not things that are; they are something that is not. If you look in the natural around you, you see the need, you see the lack, you see the sickness, you see the curse being manifested everywhere. And you look at those promises and you say,

"That is a thing that is not." Well, those promises are the only method that God has given to us to bring to nothing the curse around us, no matter what form it's in. Why has He only given that one method? He tells you right here. It's because with this method, "no flesh should glory before God." Nobody can take credit for what God has done because it has already been done.

And when we cease from our works, when we enter into our rest by believing these promises, that is what brings the promises into the natural realm. ***(Heb.4:2) For indeed we have had good tidings preached unto us, even as also they: but the word of hearing did not profit them, because it was not united by <u>faith</u> with them that heard.*** We have to learn to exercise faith in a promise that is totally outside of our natural sight; we have to learn to walk in the spirit and see these things as having already been done. ***(2Pe.1:3) <u>Seeing</u> that his divine power <u>hath granted</u> unto us all things that pertain unto life and godliness, through the knowledge of him that called us by his own glory and virtue.*** Since all this has already been done, we have to see it to imagine it as done. If you can't imagine yourself <u>having been</u> healed, then how can you expect to exercise faith in this? How can you exercise faith if you can't imagine yourself delivered, if you can't imagine that what the Scripture says about you is true and that you were perfected at the cross? ***(Heb.10:14) For by one offering he hath perfected for ever them that are sanctified.*** Can you imagine ***(2Co.3:18) beholding as in a mirror the glory of the Lord***, and that you ***are transformed into the same image from glory to glory***? Faith is to see the end from the beginning. God is demonstrating to us that He ***(Rom.4:17) calleth the things that are not, as though they were*** and that He chose ***(1Co.1:28) the things that are not, that he might bring to nought the things that are***. How do we bring this to pass? How do we bring to naught the curse around us? We do that by using these promises that are not.

Now notice this: ***(Rom.4:16) For this cause [it is] of faith, that [it may be] according to grace; to the end that <u>the promise may be sure to all</u>....*** Why is that? It's because everybody does not have the same strength, everybody does not have the same opportunity, everybody does not have the same resources. However, everybody in the Kingdom of God, no matter where they live, no matter what their resources are, can have faith and therefore they can have all the benefits of salvation. They can have all the benefits of Jesus Christ. Some people think that their health comes through health food, herbs, vitamins and all these things that people think that they can use to heal them, but that's not an equal opportunity that everybody in the world has. Those are "things that are"; they are not "things that are not." God chose the things that <u>are not</u> to bring to nothing the things that are, so that nobody could brag. No man could take credit because of their great wisdom or whatever. ***(Rom.4:16) For this cause [it is] of faith, that [it may be] according to grace; to the end that the promise may be sure to <u>all the seed</u>; not to that only which is of the <u>law</u>, but to that also which is <u>of the faith of Abraham</u>, <u>who is the father of us all</u>....*** What makes Abraham our father? It's not according to the things that are, but according to the promise. We are the seed of the promise. We are Abraham's seed according to faith. ***(Rom.4:17) (As it is written, A father of many nations have I made thee) before him whom he believed, [even] God, who giveth life to the dead, and <u>calleth the things that are not</u>, <u>as though they were</u>.*** We are children of Abraham by right because God calls the things that are not as though they were and because He's giving life to the dead. We were dead in our sins, yet through faith we have the life of Christ and we are now sons of Abraham.

Just as God calls the things that are not as though they were, so also must we. By what right are we sons of Abraham, unless we claim that right, unless we accept that by faith we are sons of Abraham? You see, it's not just God Who calls the things that are not as though they were. We also call things that are not as though they were. How do we claim God's method to use "the things that are not, that he might bring to nought the things that are"? First of all, we have to give up our works and all our worldly methods in order to bring this to pass. Man chooses to use the things that <u>are</u> to bring to naught the things that are. Man does this because man gets the glory. Man creates things out of things, out of that which does appear, but Hebrews 11 says that faith does not use that method. What Jesus said is different from what man says today. Man says, "Now God uses methods of the world to bring to pass His healing" or "Now God uses methods of the world to bring to pass His deliverance." But <u>where</u> in the Scriptures did Jesus demonstrate that? Jesus used the things that are not to bring to pass the healing; He just spoke the Word. He did not use the things that are or any of the methods of man. He did not use the doctors. He did not use the medicines. He just spoke the Word of faith. What about "psychiatric" problems, as people define them today? The truth is He did not use psychiatrists to bring to pass the deliverance of men from the curse; He spoke their deliverance. He commanded the demons to loose their minds. He brought salvation into their life and restored them from their corrupt thinking and their corrupt ways. ***(Rom.12:2) And be not fashioned according to this world: but be ye transformed by the renewing of your mind, that ye may prove what is the good and acceptable and perfect will of God.*** Men always love to use the things that are to try to attempt to do away with the curse, which they cannot; it is a dismal failure.

Let's take another look at the method God uses. ***(Heb.11:1) Now faith is assurance*** (or "the giving substance to") ***of [things] hoped for, a conviction of things not seen.*** We are using the things that are not and calling them as though they were. ***(Heb.11:2) For therein the elders had witness borne to them. (3) By faith we understand that the worlds have been framed by the word of God, <u>so that what is seen</u> hath <u>not been made</u> out of things which appear.*** That is God's method and now He is training His sons to walk in that method. Our using the things that are not, the promises that are past tense, are God's method of bringing to naught the curse that is and creating His creation. Man does not use that method. Man uses things to bring to naught the curse, to bring to naught sickness and all these other things. But God tells us that everything that can be shaken will be shaken. And what does He say about the things that are made by man? *(Heb.12:27) And this [word,] Yet once more, signifieth the removing* (talking about the shaking of all things) *of those things that are shaken, as of things that have been made, that those things which are not shaken may remain.* Man's works and methods are going to fail. The shaking that is coming is going to prove them fruitless. The only thing that is really going to work in the wilderness experience to come is when God's people call the things that be not as though they were, when they hold fast to these promises that proclaim clearly that we have already received all these things and that they are ours now.

(2Co.4:16) Wherefore we faint not; but though our outward man is decaying, yet our inward man is renewed day by day. So the spiritual man, the one that is the Son of God, is growing up while the old, outer man is decaying. And here is what brings this to pass: *(2Co.4:17) For our light affliction, which is for the moment, worketh for us more and more exceedingly an eternal weight of glory; (18) while we look not at the things which are seen, but at the things which are not seen: for the things which are seen are temporal; but the things which are not seen are eternal.* Many people have their eyes on the things that are seen. They see what they think is the Kingdom of God, but Jesus said, *(Luk.17:20) The kingdom of God cometh not with observation.* What is the Kingdom of God is not observed by the flesh. When we look at the things that are not seen, we are looking at these promises that tell us what we've been given. We see that we are *(2Co.5:17) a new creature: the old things are passed away; behold, they are become new. (Heb.10:14) For by one offering he hath perfected for ever them that are sanctified. (2Co.7:1) Having therefore these promises, beloved, let us cleanse ourselves from all defilement of flesh and spirit, perfecting holiness in the fear of God.* What do we use? He tells us here: *(2Co.4:18) While we look not at the things which are seen, but at the things which are not seen: for the things which are seen are temporal....* They are temporary and are passing away. The shaking of the whole world is going to prove these things worthless and not up to the task of destroying the curse or sickness or bringing salvation in any form to man. *(2Co.4:18) While we look not at the things which are seen, but at the things which are not seen: for the things which are seen are temporal; but the things which are not seen are eternal.*

So the outer man is decaying and this inner man is coming to life only while we walk in the spirit, when we see things the way God commands us to see things and accept these promises that proclaim that we have received all these things through the reconciliation of Jesus Christ. We have already received our healing, deliverance, provision, blessing, protection, maturity and perfection, according to the verses of God. Most people say, "That is a thing that is not; I can't see it." Well, it is true. You can't see it in the natural but we claim it by faith. That's the power of faith, the power of the sons of God. We are to walk in the spirit, as our Lord taught us to walk in the spirit, and we can only do it if we have eyes to see and ears to hear – spiritual eyes and ears. *(Col.3:1) If then ye were raised together with Christ.o..* Why does it say that? *(Eph.2:5) Even when we were dead through our trespasses, made us alive together with Christ (by grace have ye been saved), (6) and raised us up with him, and made us to sit with him in the heavenly [places], in Christ Jesus* (There it is again! We are already made to sit with Him. We are seeing the end from the beginning and calling the things that are not as though they were, just as God is doing in this verse.)*: (Eph.2:7) that in the ages to come he might show the exceeding riches of his grace in kindness toward us in Christ Jesus: (8) for by grace have ye been saved through faith....* The people who walk by faith in verses 5 and 6 are going to see this come to pass. People talk about the rapture a lot, but they don't say much about Enoch being raptured, or translated, by faith.

What is faith? *(Heb.11:1 KJV) Faith is the substance of the things hoped for, the evidence of things not seen.* So it's you claiming something while there is no evidence seen. You're claiming something that you can't see and calling the things that are not as though they were. And now we can go back to Colossians. *(Col.3:1) If then ye were raised together with Christ, seek the things that are above, where Christ is, seated on the right hand of God.* What did Jesus teach us to pray? *(Mat.6:10) Thy kingdom come. Thy will be done, as in heaven, so on earth.* What do we have up there, seated next to Christ? Is there any sickness there? Are there any demon-possessed Christians there? Is there any lack there? Is there any poverty there? None of these things are there. God's will is done in Heaven and He tells us to command His will on Earth. What did Jesus say? "Thy kingdom come. Thy will be done ... on earth." It does not sound much like a prayer, does it? It sounds like He's telling us to exercise authority to bring the Kingdom of God on earth. And Who else is going to bring it? The Lord through us, through the renewed mind, is going to bring the Kingdom. *(Rev.11:15) ... The kingdom of the world is become [the kingdom] of our Lord, and of his Christ: and he shall reign for ever and ever. (Col.3:1) If then ye were raised together with Christ, seek the things that are above, where Christ is, seated on the right hand of God. (2) Set your mind on the things that are above, not on the things that are upon the earth. (3) For ye died, and your life is hid with Christ in God. (4) When Christ, [who is] our life, shall be manifested* (Greek: "to make visible" or "cause to shine forth")*, then shall ye also with him be manifested in glory.* He is talking about *(Col.1:27) Christ in you, the hope of glory.* Here He says, "Seek the things that are above, where Christ is" because you are seated with Christ in heavenly places.

I also like, *(Col.3:9) Lie not one to another; seeing that ye have put off the old man with his doings.* I once had a lady tell me that to claim my healing according to *(1Pe.2:24) by whose stripes ye were healed* was a lie. She said, "I just can't lie. I can't say I am healed when I am not." Notice it says right here, "Lie not one to another" and then it says, "seeing that ye have put off the old man with his doings." In the natural, folks, that would be a lie. This would be a schizophrenic verse. First he tells you, "Don't lie," then he speaks something that is not true in the natural. But remember, the things that are not seen are eternal. They are more truthful than the things that are temporal, which we can see. The people of the world lie; we tell the truth when we speak the Gospel, the eternal truth. The old man has passed away and all things have become new. That old man was crucified. ***(Rom.6:11) Even so reckon ye also yourselves to be dead unto sin, but alive unto God in Christ Jesus.*** We're told, "He made you free from sin" (Romans 6:18,22) and that's the truth, not in the natural realm, but in the eternal realm and that is what counts, folks, forever and ever. ***(Col.3:10) And have put on the new man, that is being <u>renewed unto knowledge</u> after the <u>image of him that created him</u>.*** Without the knowledge of these spiritual things that are not, without believing them or mixing faith with them, we are not coming into the "image of Him that created"; we are just walking in the flesh. Now you can walk in the natural or you can walk in the spirit. To walk in the spirit is to have the eyes that He commands us to have, to have the faith to speak those things that He commands us to speak.

I am going to give you an example, one of the first ones that ever happened to my wife and me. We were reading the Bible diligently as baby Christians and we honestly did not know much of anything. Though my wife and I had been studying the Scriptures and we had seen Scriptures about healing, we hadn't been to a church that really believed in it. At that time, I loved motorcycle riding. I had two dirt bikes, one for myself and one for my wife. I was teaching her how to ride a dirt bike and, well, I made a dumb mistake. I took her to the hills of Mississippi after I had taught her only the basics. So there we were, riding over these hills and, of course, you know it takes a little more expertise than a beginner has to be able to negotiate hills.

Now, in dirt biking, you ride into the air when you go over a hill and that day, when we rode over the top of this hill, I peeled off one way and my wife peeled off another, but her side of the hill went almost straight down. I heard her screaming, "MOMMA!" all the way to the bottom, where she was finally stopped by slamming into the woods. She had bounced off several trees, so I scraped her up out of there and got her to the hospital. We learned she had bruised her kidneys and they made an appointment to operate on her the following month, but first they wanted to clear up an infection she had. In the meantime, we went to a Pentecostal church and we had them pray over her, according to the verses that we saw as we continued to study the Word.

I think we were home for probably a week when my wife was complaining to the Lord. She said, "Lord, we did what you said there in James 5. We called for the elders. They prayed over us and, Lord, I just don't understand why I have not been healed." And the first time the Lord ever spoke to my wife, He said to her loud and clear in her spirit, "If you believe that I have healed you, then why are you taking all that medicine?" It did not make one bit of sense to us because we had <u>not</u> discovered the fact that we have already been healed, but she acted on it. This was a revelation straight from the throne room! But that, right there, is heresy to most Christians. In other words, why weren't we acting as though the Word of God is true? Why didn't we believe that by His stripes we were already healed? Why were we trying to use "the things that are" to heal her? Of course, men would have received great credit for it or maybe even the drugs would have received the credit, but the Lord would not have received the credit. The Lord is a jealous God (Exodus 34:14). He does not want to share His glory with man. The methods that Jesus gave us are the same methods He uses today and they're contrary to most Babylonish doctrine. The Lord Jesus was careful not to use the methods of man so nobody would receive credit but the Father. He jealously guarded the glory of the Father and, of course, we should, too.

Well, when my wife understood that the Lord was saying she was already healed and realized that she was putting her trust in the medicine, she took her medicine and ran into the bathroom. As she was flushing her medicine down the toilet, she was healed right there! She felt a warmth go from her feet up to her head and back down to her feet again, and she knew she was healed. Glory to God! She was healed not just from the damage of the dirt bike accident but also from kidney problems that she'd had since she was a little girl. Her mom and dad would take her back and forth to the doctors for this inherited weakness that had been genetically passed on to her. When that warmth came over her body, she <u>knew</u> that she was healed and the pain and symptoms went away. Do you know when the symptoms came back? They returned <u>on the day</u> that she had an appointment to go back to the hospital, but we had been studying the Word. We had discovered that we were healed at the cross and it had nothing to do with what we saw with our eyes or felt with our body. We were healed at the cross and we are to call the things that are not as though they were. When these symptoms came back on that particular day, she knew that there was some evil intelligence behind this. She immediately rebuked those symptoms in the name of Jesus Christ and they went away.

How many of you have received a healing from God? Or a deliverance? Or a provision? Or a victory in your life and in your soul, and then lost it? Don't walk by sight. Remember it has nothing to do with what you see. It is "calling the things that are not as though they were." So don't be double-minded; continue to see things the way God tells you to see things. **(Mar.11:24) *All things whatsoever ye pray and ask for, believe that ye receive them, and ye shall have them. (2Pe.1:3) Seeing that his divine power <u>hath granted unto us all things</u> that pertain unto life and godliness, through the knowledge of him....*** Seek knowledge, brethren; seek the Word of God. Find out what is yours and claim it. Well, the devil was obviously trying to steal what God had given my wife and Jesus clearly said that the devil comes immediately to steal the seed that was sown in your heart. **(Luk.8:11) *Now the parable is this: The seed is the word of God. (12) And those by the way side are they that have heard; then cometh the devil, and taketh away the word from their heart, that they may not believe and be saved.*** How does he do that? He puts his thoughts in your mind; he puts his symptoms on your body; he gets you to walking by sight, rather than walking by faith in what "thus saith the Lord." She won that battle, by the grace of

God, by the wisdom of God. She rebuked the devil. She rebuked the symptoms and they left and have never returned. She has no more of that weakness that she inherited; it's gone. God is faithful. We need to be faithful to what He said and we need to abide by His methods.

We learned from that first lesson the Lord gave us that the Lord can speak to us even outside the Word, but it will be in the Word if it is truly Him. We searched the Scriptures and we discovered what He meant by, "If you believe that I have healed you." So many people are suffering but they won't do their homework. They suffer and suffer and think that this is normal. Do your homework; get into the Word of God because that is where salvation and victory come from. Well, some years after this, a similar thing happened to me whereby I broke my arm and I needed a healing from God. To make a long story short, I had received a vision in my mind several times that I was about to hit a car. The car turned sideways in front of me and there I was on my motorcycle, about to hit this car. You would not have called it an "open vision," but it was a vision I saw in my mind three times. It was like a warning the Lord was giving me of something that was coming. And there came a day, those many years ago, that I was going to work and the Lord decided to chasten me because I was speeding on my motorcycle. As I came up to the bottom of this interstate ramp that went over another highway, the car in front of me was in the middle lane and I was on the inside lane. That car in front of me suddenly slammed on its brakes and quickly turned sideways. Because it was turned sideways, it was covering two lanes and, of course, because it was sideways, it stopped very quickly. I couldn't stop. I knew I was going to hit him and it was as if my mind had been programmed for me to stand up on my motorcycle because that was what I had seen in my visions. I saw myself about to hit this car and suddenly I stood up on the foot-pegs. I did it automatically, just like the Lord had programmed me. I was traveling at probably 65 miles an hour (100km/h) and there was nothing that I could do; that car stopped right there in front of me and I stood up. And at the last possible moment, I steered the bike away from the driver and the front wheel to kind of in-between. When I plowed into the car, my trajectory was pointed up because I had just started on this overpass ramp and I literally flew over the front of that car because I was standing up.

If I was not standing up, I am sure I would have been dead or if I laid the bike down and let the bike slide up under the car, which I didn't have time to do, I think I would have been dead, too. But since I was standing up instead and my bike suddenly stopped and I didn't, I flew over the hood of the car and completed my trajectory by landing on top of the overpass. I've thought many times since then that I would have loved to have a picture of that, of me flying through the air, because it was a pretty long flight. I landed quite far away from the car that I hit. So there I was, on top of the overpass, and my sight was gone from hitting the concrete, but when I started praising the Lord, my sight started coming back. An ambulance came and took me to the hospital, for the first time I had ever been to a hospital or even been to a doctor since shortly after becoming a Christian. I was witnessing to the nurses. I had the joy of the Lord all over me and I was worshiping and praising God. It was like the Spirit of the Lord came down on me while I was on top of that interstate ramp. They X-rayed my arm at the hospital and found my arm was broken. I told the doctor who was going to set my arm and put it in a cast, "I don't want you to do it. Don't touch my arm." Basically, I told him that the Lord has always healed me and He was going to heal me this time, too. So he didn't set my arm and when my wife came with the car, they had to wheel me over and put me in the car because I had stretched out all my ligaments in my flight. I think maybe one foot actually hung on the handlebars and it pulled my shoe off.

When I got home, my next-door neighbor actually carried me into the house and laid me into my bed. We prayed the prayer of faith, he and I, and I accepted my healing. As soon as I could, I think in a day or two, I was up and hobbling around. I walked around my neighbor's yard, where I had been helping to clear off some of the trees and brush. He had a backhoe and we were cutting the limbs off the trees and burning the trunks and brush. Anyway, I walked around his house and was on the way back to my house. There was a tree trunk, maybe eight inches in diameter and fairly long, lying on the ground next to the fire, waiting to be burned. It was a pretty good load, even if I did not have a broken arm. I thought to myself, "I'd love to pick up that trunk and heave it over on the fire and burn it in half so that the next time it would be easier to handle." That's the way I think. I do try to do things efficiently. The next thought that came into my mind was, "Yeah, if you pick up that trunk, what's going to happen to your arm?" There was just flesh holding it; it was broken. And then the next thought I knew was from the Lord because the next thought that came into my mind was, "If you were healed, you could pick that log up." I knew that was what the Bible said. I had studied my Word. I knew that, "By the stripes of Jesus" I was healed. This is something that has already been accomplished and we can act upon what God says, much like Peter, who walked on the water when the Lord said, "Come." He was walking on the Word of God. Water does not hold people up, but the Word of God does. I thought, "That's right! I agree! I am healed!" When I reached down and picked up that log and heaved it over on the fire, I never felt a thing. I did not feel any pain, not anything, and I knew I was healed.

The next day I was back out at the plant, wanting my job back. I worked at Exxon at the time and they had a pretty nice hospital where they could send people if they had any problems at work, or to make sure people returning to work were fit to do their job. They sent me to the infirmary. They would not let me come back to work. The doctor said, "Well, Mr. Eells, it takes at least 12 weeks for a break like this to heal." I told him, "Doctor, I am healed. By the stripes of Jesus, I was healed." He said, "You will have to go prove it. You go get this X-ray." And I went and they took the X-ray and the X-ray proved my broken arm was healed. The doctor was very confused. He didn't understand how this was possible. I asked him, "What religion are you?" and he told me whatever denomination it was. I said, "Don't you people believe that the Lord heals?" He answered, "Yes, we believe that the Lord uses doctors to heal." I replied, "Well, He didn't do it this time." Then I did calisthenics for him to prove that my arm was healed and they finally had to let me go back to work.

God does not want to use the methods of man. He wants to use the methods of Jesus. He wants to bring it to pass for the glory of God. Praise God that He is faithful to His Word! Praise God that we can stand and act on that Word, even though we don't see it in the physical realm. If you need a miracle, act on what "Thus saith the Lord" because He is faithful every time to bring it to pass. People think that would be a dangerous thing to do because what if God didn't answer? That's like asking, "What if God fell off His throne?" The Lord knows that He has given us these promises so that we can be partakers in His divine nature, power, dominion and of His blessings. And He's going to bring it to pass when we act upon it. That's why so many people don't ever see the answers. It's because they don't act upon the Word of God. So, brethren, act on the Word of God. <u>Imagine that these promises are true</u>. Imagine yourself as healed, just like the Bible says, and walk by faith. God bless you, in Jesus' name.

CHAPTER THREE

His Power in Weakness!

As we discovered in our previous study, the real Good News is that the Lord has already provided everything we could possibly need in this life. As a matter of fact, He says, ***(2Pe.1:3) seeing that his divine power <u>hath granted</u> unto us <u>all things</u> that pertain unto life and godliness.*** It has already been given, folks. That's the really, really Good News. We don't have to convince Him of it or beg Him into it. It's His will to give it to us and all we have to do to have the benefits, to have what has already been given to us, is to walk by faith. We have been told that ***(Mar.11:24) All things whatsoever ye pray and ask for, believe that ye receive them, and ye shall have them.*** And we have been told that He has already ***(Col.1:13) deliver<u>ed</u> us out of the power of darkness*** and that ***(Gal.2:20) I have been crucified with Christ; and it is no longer I that live, but Christ liveth in me.*** We don't have a problem with sin; it's all been solved. We don't have a problem with this old man. We don't have a problem with demon possession or oppression; it's all been solved. It's the Good News. ***(Eph.2:8) For by grace have ye been saved through faith; and that not of yourselves, [it is] the gift of God; (9) not of works, that no man should glory.*** Our problems have been solved. ***(1Pe.2:24) Who his own self <u>bare</u> our sins in his body upon the tree, that we, having died unto sins, might live unto righteousness; by whose stripes ye <u>were</u> healed.*** It's all been solved. Sin problems have been dealt with, sickness problems have been dealt with and now, as we understood from our prior teachings, we can enter into the rest. We don't have to worry about a thing. We can ***(Php.4:6) In nothing be anxious; but in everything by prayer and supplication with thanksgiving let your requests be made known unto God.*** We can give Him thanks that it is done.

So we can enter into this rest. We can keep our spiritual New Testament Sabbath by ceasing from all of our works to try to save ourselves (Hebrews 4:1-11), since God's already done it. He has already healed us, delivered us, provided for us, protected for us, all of these things. And since He has already done all these things, then the only thing that remains is for us to enter into that rest through faith. ***(Heb.4:3) For we who have believed do enter into that rest....*** Whatever problem you have, the Lord has solved. This helps us to be able to enter into faith because, as you know, ***(Rom.4:16) For this cause [it is] of faith, that [it may be] according to grace ... (17) [even] God, who ... calleth the things that are not, as though they <u>were</u>.*** It's all past tense. It was all taken care of at the cross and now we get to enter into this by faith. One thing we discovered about these past tense promises is that they exclude our works. Since it all has been accomplished already, there is nothing we can do to bring it to pass, except believe. ***(Heb.4:3) For we who have believed do enter into that rest... (9) There remaineth therefore a sabbath rest for the people of God.***

(10) For he that is entered into his rest hath himself also rested from his works, as God did from his. God purposely gave us all these promises in the past tense so that, when we believed Him, we would have to cease from our works, enter into the rest and receive this wonderful free gift from Him by grace.

All these past tense promises not only exclude our works and cause us to rest, they bring us to a place of weakness. That's what apostle Paul's story speaks about. **(2Co.12:7) And by reason of the exceeding greatness of the revelations, that I should not be exalted overmuch, there was given to me a thorn in the flesh, a messenger of Satan to buffet me, that I should not be exalted overmuch.** There has been a great deal of deception taught concerning this. Paul wanted and needed to be seen, not as "the great man of God," but as "the man in whom a great God lives." He said he was given this thorn in the flesh so that he would not be exalted overmuch. The Bible mentions "thorn in the flesh" three times in the Old Testament and not one time is it a sickness or infirmity. In every case, the "thorn in the flesh" was the enemies of God's people persecuting them and bringing judgments on them. Paul plainly tells you here what the "thorn in the flesh" is: it is a messenger of satan. The Greek word *angelos* appears in the Bible 188 times. It's translated "angel" 181 times and the rest it's translated "messenger." If it's the same Greek word, it can be translated the same way and it should be. This is talking about an angel of Satan. Some people say, "Satan's messengers are demons and they were never angels." I've heard that doctrine but it's false. **(Psa.79:49) He cast upon them the fierceness of his anger, Wrath, and indignation, and trouble, A band of angels of evil.** Yes, there are demons, but they are also the fallen angels of Satan. So Paul was given an angel of Satan "to buffet" him. "Buffet" means "to hit many times, many strikes, many blows," and Paul was buffeted by a "thorn in his flesh" many times. Again, when we look at the Old Testament, these are the enemies of God's people persecuting and bringing judgment upon them. Paul mentions his buffetings in 2 Corinthians 11 but we'll look at that more closely later on. **(2Co.12:8) Concerning this thing I besought the Lord thrice, that it might depart from me. (9) And he hath said unto me, My grace is sufficient for thee: for [my] power is made perfect in weakness....** This messenger of Satan kept bringing him into many persecutions, troubles and trials in which Paul needed God's power. And in the place of his weakness, in his inability to save himself, the Lord became his savior.

The Lord did this with Israel. He brought Israel into traps where they were not able to save themselves (Exodus 14). He brought them past the Red Sea and then the Lord said for them to go back and camp between Migdol and the Red Sea. Then the Lord brought Pharaoh's army in behind them, putting the Israelites into a perfect trap. They couldn't go one way or the other; they had to go across the Red Sea. Then God did a miracle to save them. He deliberately brought them to the place where they could do nothing so He could save them. Then He brought them to a place where there was nothing but bitter water and he brought them to the place where there was no food. He sweetened the waters with the tree and brought them manna out of Heaven. He brought them water out of the rock. God brought them to places where they could not save themselves because that was what the wilderness was all about. The wilderness was that place of weakness.

Well, folks, these promises are the wilderness. Every Christian can walk into their wilderness because these promises automatically take away your ability to save yourself by the very fact that all of them are past tense. "You have already <u>been</u> saved." "You have already <u>been</u> delivered." "You have already <u>been</u> provided for." "You have already <u>been</u> delivered out of the power of darkness." "You have already <u>been</u> delivered from sin." "You have already <u>been</u> delivered from sickness." Since it is already done, what can you do to bring it to pass? If you say you believe the Bible, "For he that is entered into his rest hath himself also rested from his works, as God did from his," then you have automatically come to a wilderness, a place of weakness like Paul is speaking about here. And just as Paul was buffeted by a messenger of Satan, many times we are buffeted to humble us, just like it was to humble him. It is not something that God says that He is not going to save you from; it is to bring you to the place of weakness so that God can be your Savior. He wants to prove His power to you. **(2Co.12:9) And he hath said unto me, My grace is sufficient for thee: for [my] power is made perfect in <u>weakness</u>.** That means <u>your</u> weakness. These past tense promises make us weak because when we believe them, God can be the only Savior. He is the only One Who can bring it to pass. **Most gladly therefore will I rather glory in my weaknesses, that the power of Christ may rest upon me.** And I think that's still a good idea.

Some people don't understand why we would glory in our weaknesses or why God would pick a weak vessel, like myself, to speak through. But why did He pick those ignorant fishermen, instead of the "Bible school graduates" of His day? He picked them because they were trainable, because they were weak and had to depend on God. **(1Co.1:27) <u>But God chose the foolish things of the world</u>, <u>that he might put to shame them that are wise</u>; and God chose the weak things of the world, that he might put to shame the things that are strong; (28) and the base things of the world, and the things that are despised, did God choose, [yea] and <u>the things that are not</u>, <u>that he might bring to nought the things that are</u>**. "The things that are not" are these promises that we have been looking at. He chose <u>the promises</u> as His method to bring the curse to nothing. When we believe those promises, we cease from our works and enter into our wilderness of our weakness. That is where God's power falls.

(2Co.12:10) Wherefore I take pleasure in <u>weaknesses</u>.... Yes, I know that some of your Bible versions say "infirmities" or "sicknesses." Those versions in other places translate the same Greek word as "weaknesses." You cannot have it both ways. The word is *astheneia*, which means "want of strength" or "weakness." It doesn't mean "infirmity." A simple proof for that is to look where the word is used in other places and you will see that <u>they had to translate it correctly</u>. For instance, in Corinthians where it speaks about Christ being crucified, it reads, **(2Co.13:4) For <u>he was crucified through weakness</u>, yet he liveth through the power of God**. Christ was not crucified through infirmity. He was crucified because He was weak in that He refused to defend Himself before Pilate and the accusers. Another example is, **(1Co.1:25) ... and the weakness of God is stronger than men**. It's not "the infirmity of God." Nobody has ever known God to be infirm or sick. That's just ridiculous, so the word "weakness" is the word that should be translated all the way through. The theologians, who don't believe in divine health or healing, had to put their doctrine in there and that's why they used the word "infirmity."

(2Co.12:9) And he hath said unto me, My grace is sufficient for thee: for [my] power is made perfect in weakness. Most gladly therefore will I rather glory in my weaknesses (This is the same word as above, *astheneia*.)**, that the power of Christ may rest upon me. (10) Wherefore I take pleasure in weaknesses** (same word as above)**, in injuries, in necessities, in persecutions, in distresses, for Christ's sake: for when I am weak, then am I strong.** When *we* are weak, then God is strong, so we can see it is not just faith. If you do believe and have faith in those promises, you are automatically weak. That's part of faith. "Weak" means you don't try to save yourself in those instances. You believe God has already done it. It's just as Jesus said, **(Mar.11:24) All things whatsoever ye pray and ask for, believe that ye received** (it's past tense) **them, and ye shall have them**. Well, these weaknesses are listed in the previous chapter, where Paul was buffeted by this angel of Satan and brought into circumstances where he could not save himself. He was weak in every one of them. **(2Co.11:23) Are they ministers of Christ? (I speak as one beside himself) I more; in labors more abundantly, in prisons more abundantly, in stripes above measure, in deaths oft. (24) Of the Jews five times received I forty [stripes] save one. (25) Thrice was I beaten with rods, once was I stoned, thrice I suffered shipwreck, a night and a day have I been in the deep; (26) [in] journeyings often, [in] perils of rivers, [in] perils of robbers, [in] perils from [my] countrymen, [in] perils from the Gentiles** (those "thorns in the flesh" here)**, [in] perils in the city, [in] perils in the wilderness, [in] perils in the sea, [in] perils among false brethren; (27) [in] labor and travail, in watchings often, in hunger and thirst, in fastings often, in cold and nakedness. (28) Besides those things that are without, there is that which presseth upon me daily, anxiety for all the churches. (29) Who is weak, and I am not weak?** (There's the word *astheneo*, or "weak"; *astheneia* is "weakness" and neither word means "infirm.") **who is caused to stumble, and I burn not? (30) If I must needs glory, I will glory of the things that concern my weakness.** And then Paul goes on to talk about how that the Lord enabled him to escape from Damascus in a basket. All of these were times of being buffeted by this demon that was bringing judgment upon him, that was humbling him.

We have to be humbled because we want to save ourselves. We would love to be our own savior. We like to help out God, but the Lord does not want any kind of salvation outside of grace. Grace is unmerited, unearned, nothing done by the flesh. That's why

He designed His salvation in this way. We discovered that "salvation," *soteria*, is "all my needs supplied, like a little baby." The word for "savior" is *soter*. The *soteria* is everything the *soter* supplied. The Savior supplied all of our needs, and that's what salvation is all about. It has already been supplied, so therefore we can do nothing to bring it to pass. It is by grace. It is unmerited. It is unearned. If you want to pay for it, if you want to go out and earn it by your self-effort and your works, then that's not what the Lord provided; that's just your works, your flesh. It has nothing to do with the Kingdom of God. You would think the Lord could have failed Paul somewhere in all of these things but, you see, Paul knew the secret of faith, which is to "call the things that are not, as though they were." Paul understood the really Good News and he was the one who spoke many of these promises that we're talking about.

Look at what Paul said about his buffetings: ***(2Ti.3:10) But thou didst follow my teaching, conduct, purpose, faith, longsuffering, love, patience, (11) persecutions, sufferings; what things befell me at Antioch, at Iconium, at Lystra; what persecutions I endured: and out of them all the Lord delivered me.*** In Paul's weakness, in having been put in a circumstance where he could not save himself, the Lord became his Savior. Who put the Israelites in that place in the wilderness? The Lord did. Who gave Paul this angel of Satan to buffet him? The Lord did. The Lord purposely wanted to weaken the old man, who likes to take a lot of credit for anything God does. But when you do things in the Kingdom God's way, with God's methods, the old man cannot get any credit for it. That's why the Lord has finished all the works from the foundation of the world (Hebrews 4:3) and the only thing that remains is for us to enter into those works, not by our works, but by faith. The works were finished, therefore we can't do anything to bring it to pass. We just enter in through faith and so Paul says, "Out of all these buffetings, the Lord delivered me." He says it again in the next chapter. ***(2Ti.4:16) At my first defence no one took my part, but all forsook me*** (That was from the Lord, too.)***: may it not be laid to their account. (17) But the Lord stood by me, and strengthened me*** (You and the Lord are a majority.)***; that through me the message might be fully proclaimed, and that all the Gentiles might hear: and I was delivered out of the mouth of the lion. (18) The Lord will deliver me from every evil work, and will save me unto his heavenly kingdom: to whom [be] the glory for ever and ever. Amen.*** The Lord received the glory because the salvation came in Paul's weakness; he couldn't claim any credit for his salvation by grace. Again, all of this is talking about his salvation by unmerited and unearned grace.

Here's another good example: ***(Psa.34:17) [The righteous] cried, and the Lord heard, And delivered them out of all their troubles.*** Do you think that sometimes the Lord wants to leave us these troubles? It's true that the Lord wants to bring us through these troubles because through these troubles we learn that self-effort is worthless in the Kingdom of God, but the Lord is there. He delivered them out of all their troubles. ***(Psa.34:19) Many are the afflictions of the righteous*** (As we can see in Paul's life.); ***But the Lord delivereth him <u>out of them all</u>.*** Here we see that "all" over and over. The Lord told us, "for [my] power is made perfect in weakness." Our weakness brings God's power and our correct faith in the promises brings our weakness because when we believe that God has already provided, we have to cease from our works. Any efforts of our own prove that we are not believing as the Scripture has said. ***(Joh.7:38) He that believeth on me, as the scripture hath said, from within him shall flow rivers of living water. (39) But this spake he of the Spirit, which they that believed on him were to receive....*** By His Spirit, God's power will be manifested through the people who believe on Him "as the scripture hath said." Don't add to God's Word. Don't make this a "future" thing that God will provide. Make it a "past" thing that He <u>has</u> provided everything and that makes our works worthless. So our faith leads us to weakness and that weakness leads us to God's power.

<u>The works of self-righteousness</u>, <u>the works of self-salvation</u>, <u>those works are crucified by the promises of God</u>. They are totally useless and, if we do them, it is unbelief. If, in our self-effort, we try to save ourselves after we have all these promises that we've already been saved, it is unbelief. However, there is a work that is in <u>agreement</u> with <u>faith</u>. How do you act when you believe you have received? Think on that. "How should I act, what should I say, if I believe I have received? If I call the things that are not as though they <u>were</u>? If I am seeing that His divine power has already granted to me <u>everything</u> that pertains to life and godliness? If I have asked God for something and I see that it is promised in His Word, how would I act? What would I say? What would be my works that <u>agree</u> with faith?" There are works that agree with faith and there are works against faith. Works that are against faith prove that you don't have any faith; they're self-works of the flesh and they're forbidden in our Sabbath. The works that agree with faith and prove that you have faith, these are the works of God. If we're going to cease from our works, we have to cease from our works of flesh. We have to stop being like the Pharisees and cease from trying to have <u>justification</u> by works of the Law.

But there are works that <u>agree</u> with faith. ***(Jas.2:14) What doth it profit, my brethren, if a man <u>say</u> he hath faith, but have not works? can that faith save him?*** Obviously not. ***(17) Even so faith, if it have not works, is dead in itself. (18) Yea, a man will say, Thou hast faith, and I have works: show me thy faith apart from [thy] works, and I by my works will show thee [my] faith.*** The only way we can show that we have faith is by our works. What are the actions of a person who believes they have received healing, deliverance, deliverance from the curse (Galatians 3:13), deliverance from sin (Galatians 2:20)? They are joyous, they are rested because they know God has already taken care of it. <u>Their actions are those of ceasing from their own works</u>. <u>Their actions are their confession of what God has already done</u>. The Lord said, ***(Mat.10:32) Every one therefore who shall confess me before men, him will I also confess before my Father who is in heaven.*** "Confess" here means "to speak the same as." Are you speaking what these promises say has already been given unto you? Are your feet walking out your confession? Your confession is a work that completes and proves your faith. Jesus told the lepers, *(Luk.17:14)* ***Go and show yourselves unto the priests***. Well, they were still lepers when they walked away. It was an act of faith that they did in walking to go and be inspected by the priest, to see if any leprosy was still on them so they could make their sacrifice. Their walks were the good works of God and not works of men. Those are the works that prove faith, not works that negate faith, not self-effort. They were not running to a doctor, they were not running to somebody to try to get healed. They <u>knew that the Lord was telling them</u>, "<u>You are healed</u>, so go and show yourself to the priest."

(Jas.2:20) ***But wilt thou know, O vain man, that faith apart from works is <u>barren</u>?*** The word "barren" means "unfruitful." *(21) **Was not Abraham our father <u>justified by works</u>, in that he offered up Isaac his son upon the altar?*** Abraham did something, but what he did was in agreement with his faith. He knew if he obeyed God, that God would have to resurrect Isaac from the dead for God to bring to pass the promised seed that was going to be a multitude of nations. Abraham had such faith he knew that "God will do it" and he went on to obey God. ***(Jas.2:22) Thou seest that faith wrought with his works, and by works was faith made perfect*** (or "complete")***; (24) Ye see that by works a man is justified, and not only by faith. (25) And in like manner was not also Rahab the harlot justified by works, in that she received the messengers, and sent them out another way? (26) <u>For as the body apart from the spirit is dead</u>, even so faith apart from works is dead.*** So you see, there is a work that you need to give up and forsake, and there is a work that is a part of our faith. That work completes our faith. It is necessary. If you do not have this corresponding action to your faith, you don't have faith. Believing in your mind is not enough, as many who receive miracles from God will proclaim, because they have proven it.

Myself, I've had a very miraculous life. I shared with you previously how the Lord tried my faith when I broke my arm in a motorcycle accident. I believed that "by whose stripes ye were healed." I believed that I was already healed at the cross and that we can actually <u>act</u> on that faith. I refused to let the doctors set my arm. I claimed that I was already healed. When the doctor told me it was going to take about 12 weeks for it to heal but that he'd had to set it first, I didn't accept it. So when I was walking in the yard with my broken arm and I passed by this tree trunk, the thought came into my head to pick it up and heave it onto the fire to burn it in half. That way it would be easier to move the next time. Well, the thought came to me, "If you pick the log up with your broken arm, there's nothing but meat holding your arm." But the next thought that came into my mind was, "If you were healed, then you can pick that log up," and I acted on that thought of faith. I reached down and picked that log up and never felt a thing. You would have thought there would have been a lot of pain and I would have put the arm very badly out of joint, but I did not feel a thing because I acted on my faith and God manifested the healing miracle. God's power was made perfect in my weakness (2 Corinthians 12:9). My weakness was I refused to try to heal it myself. I refused to go to the "arm of the flesh"

(Jeremiah 17:5), so to speak. My <u>faith</u> was proven by my <u>work</u> of picking up the log. My works were negated when I refused to try to bring to pass something God's Word says has already been accomplished. If you're going to believe that, your actions have to agree with it.

I shared with you how my wife's kidneys were damaged in a dirt bike wreck and we had taken her to be prayed for. And when it was now a week or two later, she was complaining to the Lord about why she hadn't been healed. She was saying, "We obeyed, we called for the elders, we did just what You said in the Book." God answered her, "If you believe that I have healed you, why are you taking all that medicine?" This was a new thought to us, but we found the verses and discovered, "Aha! That is exactly what it says!" My wife had been trying to heal herself. She hadn't entered into the rest. She wasn't keeping the Sabbath because it was self-works. She immediately ran into the bathroom, poured the medicine down the toilet and God healed her standing right there. We received a revelation from that and we began to understand what faith really is. Faith is not hope. <u>Faith is looking back</u>. <u>Hope is looking forward</u>. Hope is hoping you will see the healing, but faith is what saves and faith is what heals. Faith looks back at the cross: that is where you <u>were</u> healed; that is where you <u>were</u> delivered from sin; that is where <u>everything was already provided</u> for you. You have to be looking in the right direction.

There's a story I like to tell about a woman from Louisiana because it points that out. This woman had two inoperable tumors and she had been going all over the country to be prayed for by many people who believed in divine healing, except she was not exercising any faith. She said, "I just don't know, David, why I have not been healed." I said, "You just told me why you have not been healed; you don't believe the Gospel." I explained to her the Gospel is the Good News that "by whose stripes <u>ye were healed</u>," and I began to share with her these past tense promises. It was just like a light bulb went on in her head. I saw her eyes light up when the revelation hit her and she understood. Then I said, "Now I am going to pray for you one more time, but this time we are going to believe we have received, like Mark 11:24 says." She agreed and we prayed and she received. She felt the change in her body. She felt it when those cancer demons, which is what it was, left her body and she was healed. I said to her, "Any one of those men you went to could have been useful in your healing, but this is the first time you have ever believed." I knew her for a long time after that and she never had any problem with it again.

It is not mental assent. It is "believing as the scripture hath said." You believe that your sickness was put upon Jesus Christ when He sacrificed Himself for you on the cross. You don't have to bear it anymore and you can joyfully go on about your business. Don't pay any attention to walking by sight. Don't pay any attention to feelings. Pay attention to what the Lord has said. <u>We are to be reacting to what the Word says</u>, <u>not to what the world says</u>, nor to the physical things in the world. They will line-up with the Scriptures if we will line-up with the Scriptures.

I remember one of the first healings I received as a baby Christian. I was going to a "full Gospel"-type church, but it was not very full Gospel because they did not understand these things and they weren't getting any miracles, but I was. I was helping them build an addition on their church. We were in a hurry and I stepped on a nail that went through my foot. The interesting thing was that a few days before this happened, while I worked at a machine shop at Exxon, one of the apprentices there had done the same thing. He stepped on a nail sticking through a board. He had the doctor wrap-up his foot and he was on crutches, so as not to put any weight on that foot; it was that bad for him. So a few days later, the same thing happens to me. You know all the thoughts that come through your mind about tetanus, and you know the devil loves to assail you with all the "what-ifs." But I just began to cast down all those vain reasonings that exalt themselves against the Word of God (2 Corinthians 10:4-6). The next night we had a prayer meeting in the church and since it was a bunch of Pentecostals, people were walking around praying, and in the pews praying, and I was kind of hobbling around praying because my foot was painful. The preacher walked up to me at the back of the church where I was praying. I was a baby Christian and didn't know it at the time, but this preacher didn't have any faith of his own. He never really walked by faith in these promises himself, but he came up to me and asked, "David, how is your foot?"

That was my first opportunity to be tried. You are going to have somebody come and ask you, to see if you are going to agree with the Gospel or not and this is the whole point. **(Luk.12:8) And I say unto you, Every one who shall confess** (Greek: *homologeo*, meaning "to speak the same as") **me before men, him shall the Son of man also confess before the angels of God: (9) but he that denieth me in the presence of men shall be denied in the presence of the angels of God.** You don't want to be denied by the Lord. You want to <u>confess</u> Him, you want "to speak the same as." Well, I knew what the Bible said and I just told him, "My foot's healed." I knew he could see me hobbling around over there and of course, that thought's always in the back of your mind, but if you're going to be a fool for Christ, you may as well go whole-hog (1 Corinthians 4:10). So I just said, "My foot's healed" and right when I said that, the power of God hit my foot and all the pain totally left it. It was as if I never had stepped on a nail. I told the preacher, "Man! The power of God just hit me!" and he kind of looked at me strangely. I don't remember what he said but I just started walking normally, started jogging a little down the aisle, feeling no pain. I was so joyful.

These little things started me on a life of discovering what faith really is and how to get a hold of the power of God, and it is very simple. He does not want our help. He wants our faith. He wants salvation to be by grace. He wants salvation to be unmerited and unearned. He wants to give us a free gift. He won't share His glory with your flesh and my flesh. He wants to give us a free gift. No matter what your need is, it was supplied at the cross already and He just wants to give it to us freely. As a matter of fact, <u>He will harden Pharaoh's heart just to make it impossible for you to do anything yourself</u>, so He has to do a <u>miracle</u> for you, to make His power known. This kind of thing continued to happen to us because I realized this simple little key to power: it's faith and weakness. Many people preach the faith part, but it is faith and weakness. When you believe as the Scripture says, you must be weak. You must cease from your works because it's already accomplished. *(Php.4:19) And my God shall supply every need of yours according to his riches in glory in Christ Jesus. (2Pe.1:3) Seeing that his divine power **hath** granted unto us **all things** that pertain unto life and godliness....* This is the way we have to see it. Remember that your faith has to be proven by your works. Many of you are determined to believe in your heart that God is faithful, that He will keep His promises, but make sure that you are agreeing with your mouth and that you are agreeing with your heart because *(Jas.2:17) faith, if it have not works, is dead in itself.*

I want to share another little story with you. Twenty-two years ago, as I was moving to Florida after I had been living in the wilderness for some time, I crossed over the River Jourdan, which is pronounced "Jordan." So I said, "Praise the Lord! I am going to the Promised Land!" And the Lord spoke to me. He said, "No you're not. You are going into a wilderness, so you can tell My people that I still supply there." The wilderness is a place where man cannot supply, where man is not the savior. You don't have all the accoutrements that the world insulates themselves with, in order to save themselves. That's where God was sending me. I did not have a job. He sent me without any visible means of support. He just said, "Go," and so I went and when I passed over the Jourdan, He spoke that to me. If you haven't been in the wilderness, you really can't tell people that God supplies there because you have no experience behind you; it might just be theology in your head. Anyway, we came over here and before long we had run out of almost everything we needed, but God richly supplied our needs because His power is made perfect in our weakness. And we were definitely weak. Sometimes God forces you into a position of weakness; sometimes He expects you to go there. See, when you take these promises that you are receiving from God, you just make yourself weak because you know that this need has already been met. There's nothing else you can do to bring it to pass. God did that with my family and me several times, and those times are when we got to see wonderful miracles. This particular time we had run out of everything in the house to eat. There was nothing left and we were out of money and we were at the end of our rope. Have you ever heard the saying, "Man's extremity is God's opportunity"? Well, it's certainly true because when you come to the end of your rope, that's where the Lord is waiting. He is not going to share His glory with you. He wants you to give up and get out of the way. All He wants is your faith to believe in Him as Savior.

So that's where we were; we had run out of everything. Even though my wife was a genius in mixing-up and cooking the last few things, the last couple of meals weren't very good. We finally came to the place where we couldn't go any further. My wife asked, "What are we going to do?" I said, "Set the table," so she did and she and our five children and I sat down around the table with our plates in front of us. Then I prayed a rather simple prayer; it was just whatever came out of my mouth. I said, "Lord, You sent us here and you promised to supply our every need. You promised it was done, so here we are and we are asking you to either fill our plates or fill our tummies." That was what came to me at the moment. And I'm going to tell you the truth: The first one to get up was my oldest boy. He said, "Dad, I'm full. I don't need to eat." Now it had been a while since his last meal and that just never would have been anything that would have come out of his mouth. I looked at him kind of strangely and pretty soon, another one said the same thing and then another one said the same thing, and they were all getting up from the table because they were all full. My attention had been focused on them, but then I realized, "I'm full, too!" I didn't have any hunger whatsoever. I was full, as if I had just eaten a meal." So we all got up and picked up the plates and that was the end of it. Of course, the Lord came through for the next meal and He came through for many, many more meals. We learned to walk by faith, but we also learned that in the wilderness, the place where man (or Egypt) cannot supply, God will supply. And He did and He has up until this day.

You can't get anywhere where God can't supply if He can put food in your stomach, folks. Would you rather pack it on your back into the wilderness or would you rather see God do a miracle? He said, "My God shall supply your <u>every need</u> according to his riches in glory." What does "every need" leave out? If you really believe Him, what would you act like? Would you be frantically trying to store up enough food for the Tribulation to come? Wouldn't it be a whole lot easier to believe what He said? Remember, the Israelites went out into that wilderness with every thing they could pack on their carts and their donkeys, but in just a few days they started running out and this was what God was waiting for! Even their gold that they had stored up and made into a golden calf, God made them grind it to powder, put it into the water and drink it. It was an idol. Christians are doing the same thing today because history just keeps repeating. ***(Ecc.1:9) That which hath been is that which shall be; and that which hath been done is that which shall be done: and there is no new thing under the sun.*** They're still storing up their gold and they don't realize that it's going to be an idol to them. They'll put their trust in that, instead of God's Word.

If God "shall supply your every need according to his riches in glory," why do you have to worry about the future? ***(Mat.6:34) Be not therefore anxious for the morrow: for the morrow will be anxious for itself. Sufficient unto the day is the evil thereof.*** But people aren't acting that way. They're fearful and they're troubled, and it's because they have no faith. They're full of unbelief when they look at the things that are coming upon the world. If we would get our eyes off the problem and on to the promise, and let that promise be in our hearts, we would realize that is why He calls it "the rest." When that promise is in your heart, you are rested, you are not worried about a thing. You know you are in God's hands. You know He's the One Who's bringing you into the wilderness in the first place. He's planning on bringing water out of a rock and manna out of the sky. What do we have to worry about? ***(Php.4:6) In nothing be anxious; but in everything by prayer and supplication with thanksgiving let your requests be made known unto God. (7) And the peace of God, which passeth all understanding, shall guard your hearts and your thoughts in Christ Je-***

sus. We need to train our thinking. ***(8) Finally, brethren, whatsoever things are true, whatsoever things are honorable, whatsoever things are just, whatsoever things are pure, whatsoever things are lovely, whatsoever things are of good report; if there be any virtue, and if there be any praise, think on these things.*** But instead, we like to think on the things that <u>might</u> happen. That is a real fearful thing that gets into the hearts of people and drives them to do things in the flesh that they would never do otherwise.

The devil always tells you what <u>might</u> happen. Sometimes the answers to our needs are not as instantaneous as my previous example; sometimes we have to endure a trial of our faith. I've done it with my eyes. My family has had bad eyes, glaucoma, diabetes and such, and the devil tried to tell me, "It's passed on to you!" A few years ago, I actually had a problem with my eyes where one of them went far-sighted and one of them went near-sighted, and it was very painful for me to read. Well, reading was the most important thing in my life because I spend hours and hours in the Word everyday. It became so painful to read that it felt like it was splitting my head in half. The devil would tell me, "This is glaucoma and this is this, and this is that," but I would always say, "It's not possible for my eyes to have any problems because the Bible says 'by whose stripes ye were healed.' It's just not possible." Start thinking that way, saints. <u>It's not possible for you to be sick when the Bible says you are healed</u>! ***(Gal.5:16) But I say, Walk by the Spirit, and ye shall not fulfil the lust of the flesh.*** "Walking in the Spirit" is not walking after these eyes of flesh and these feelings of flesh. Walking in the Spirit is walking by "thus saith the Lord." Start thinking this way: it's not possible for you to be in bondage to Satan, it's not possible for him to have dominion over you. It's not possible for you to be sick when the Bible says you were healed. God's Word is <u>law</u>. Consider that. Hold fast to that.

Start thinking the way a person would think if they believed that all these promises have already been accomplished. Start thinking that way and start speaking that way and start walking that way. ***(Jas.2:17) Even so faith, if it have not works, is dead in itself.*** So start walking in the spirit and start confessing the Word of God <u>before men</u>, as I did before that pastor. When I believed, my eyes got better and then a month or two later, they got worse again, but I rebuked it. I accepted only what the Word of God says. I endured another trial of my faith and again my eyes got better for a few months before they got worse. I endured this for quite some time, then it got to be months where my eyes didn't give me any problems. Now, every once in a while, I get tried by that. The devil has tried to take me with quite a few other things but, you know what? He only gets the power that we give him. ***(Mat.18:18) Verily I say unto you, What things soever ye shall bind on earth shall be bound in heaven; and what things soever ye shall loose on earth shall be loosed in heaven. (28:18) And Jesus came to them and spake unto them, saying, <u>All authority hath been given unto me in heaven and on earth</u>. (19) Go ye therefore....*** That doesn't leave any for the devil. Jesus has it all and He gave it to us! So how does the devil get it? If Jesus had it all and if He delegated His authority to us, how does the devil get it? <u>We give it to him</u>. We exercise faith in the devil. We believe what the devil says and he takes dominion over us, but we can take away his dominion by believing what God says. We are ordained to rule over him. ***(Luk.10:19) Behold, I have given you authority ... over all the power of the enemy: and nothing shall in any wise hurt you.*** God bless you, saints.

CHAPTER FOUR

Enter His Rest!

Greetings, folks, and God bless you in Jesus' name. I'd like to begin our study here by letting Paul's awesome prayer in Ephesians be our prayer today. ***(Eph.1:16) Cease not to give thanks for you, making mention [of you] in my prayers; (17) that the God of our Lord Jesus Christ, the Father of glory, may give unto you a spirit of wisdom and revelation in the knowledge of him; (18) having the eyes of your heart enlightened, that ye may know what is the hope of his calling, what the riches of the glory of his inheritance in the saints, (19) and what the exceeding greatness of his power to us-ward who believe, according to that working of the strength of his might (20) which he wrought in Christ, when he raised him from the dead, and made him to sit at his right hand in the heavenly [places].*** Wow! Father, that's what we ask, that You would give us <u>a spirit of wisdom and revelation in the knowledge of You</u>, and that we would have our spiritual eyes enlightened to know what is <u>the hope of our calling</u>, the all-inclusive salvation that You have given unto us. Open our understanding today and make us to know this, Lord. We thank You, Lord. This is our prayer today, that You would give us these gifts. Thank You, Father, in Jesus' name. Amen.

We need for the Lord to help us to understand how deep and broad His precious promises of the real Good News are, and what His power is to those who believe them. Jesus said, ***(Mat.9:29) According to your faith*** and ***(8:13) As thou hast believed, [so] be it done unto thee***. It's important what we believe and know because faith is based on knowledge and you can't believe for something that you don't know about. So we've been looking at how deep and broad this river of salvation is. We discovered the promises of God concerning salvation in personal (soul) salvation, healing (body) salvation and also deliverance, protection and provision. And we learned that all these promises are past tense. ***(1Pe.2:24) Who his own self <u>bare</u> our sins in his body upon the tree ... by whose stripes ye <u>were</u> healed. (Col.1:13) Who <u>delivered</u> us out of the power of darkness.... (Rom.6:18) And being <u>made free from sin</u>, ye <u>became</u> servants of righteousness. (22) But now being <u>made free from sin</u> and become servants to God...*** They are all past tense so that we can enter into His all-inclusive, New Testament rest. The rest mentioned in Hebrews speaks of ceasing from our own works through faith in His promises. We need to walk in that rest and in that peace so that we are not condemned of the devil, separated from the faith of God, separated from the things that God wants to do through us. All provision has been made in our New Testament Sabbath rest and we need to walk in that rest. Our *sabbatismos*, as it is called in Hebrews 4, means "a <u>continual</u> rest." The Sabbath is no longer one day that we rest; we have to cease from our works and enter into His rest through faith every day. That's His promise. The Lord is about to bring the Church into the wilderness and

He's even now bringing individuals in the Church through their own personal wilderness so that they can come to know how to live by faith. *(Heb.10:38) But my righteous one shall live by faith: And if he shrink back, my soul hath no pleasure in him. (39) But we are not of them that shrink back unto perdition; but of them that have faith unto the saving of the soul.* Do you know what your soul is? It's your mind, will and emotions. In other words, it's your nature, your character. Jesus Christ is an example of a saved soul and walking in His steps is something that He has provided for us to do. *(1Jn.2:6) He that saith he abideth in him ought himself also to walk even as he walked.* And we can see from His life that Jesus walked in His Own wilderness by faith, completely trusting the Father in everything. The Lord is going to use our time in the wilderness to work the same thing in us in these latter days.

Now we know that there have been other "latter days," but we ought to at least understand that we are living in the latter days, too, so what Jeremiah said here has to be a type and a shadow for us: *(Jer.30:23) Behold, the tempest of the Lord, [even his] wrath, is gone forth, a sweeping tempest: it shall burst upon the head of the wicked. (24) the fierce anger of the Lord shall not return until he have executed, and till he have performed the intents of his heart: in the latter days ye shall understand it.* Jeremiah did not write in chapters; he just went right on. *(31:1) At that time* (still talking about the latter days), *saith the Lord, will I be the God of <u>all the families of Israel</u>, and they shall be my people.* We have studied about the families of Israel in the end times. Romans 11 tells us about those who are grafted into the olive tree, which is called "all Israel." The Lord broke off the unbelieving Jews concerning the new Kingdom and He grafted in the Gentiles as the Church, and then He said, *(Rom.11:26) And so all Israel shall be saved.* "All the families of Israel" is a very large group of people around the world, not just natural Israel. *(Jer.31:2) Thus saith the Lord, The people that were left of the sword <u>found favor in the wilderness</u>; even Israel, when I went to <u>cause him to rest</u>.* What does the wilderness have to do with the rest? We know that the wilderness is a sparse place with very little worldly provision there for man. In the wilderness, the Israelites had to have their salvation, provision and protection from God. God was bringing them to a perfect place for them to learn to trust in Him, if they would have, because *(Rom.1:17) the righteous shall live by faith.* He made this as an opportunity for them. In that wilderness, they were at the mercy of God. God Himself had to ultimately save them after they ran out of all their provision from Egypt (a type of the world) and there was no natural provision around them.

What we've shared already in this series of studies is that when you believe these past tense promises, because the promises are past tense, you automatically enter into a wilderness because there is no help from man. God's already delivered you, healed you, provided for you, already protected you and saved your soul. He's already done all these things so, therefore, you can't do anything to bring them to pass because He's already done them and you just have to rest. *(Heb.4:3) For we who have believed* *do enter into that rest.... * What are we resting from? We're resting from our own works to bring to pass what God said has already been done. *(Heb.4:3) For we who have believed do enter into that rest even as he hath said, As I sware in my wrath, They shall not enter into my rest: <u>although the works were finished from the foundation of the world</u>.* In other words, God is saying, "Why shouldn't you rest? The works are already finished." The problem is that people don't walk by faith and the promises are quickly dragged away from them. Here's one instance: *(Heb.3:18) And to whom sware he that they should not enter into his rest, but to them that were disobedient? (19) And we see that they were not able to enter in <u>because of unbelief</u>.* So if you want to know where disobedience comes from, it comes from unbelief because when you believe the promises you are at rest. You are at peace. You are trusting in God to bring it to pass and you are ceasing from your works. What are your works? Your works of the flesh are disobedience and they're sin. Your works of the Law, which is of the Old Testament, are sin in the New Covenant.

So you see, unbelief brings disobedience and, as a matter of fact, the Greek word *apeitheia* means both "disobedience" and "unbelief." It can be translated either way. How can that be? *(Heb.4:11) Let us therefore give diligence to enter into that rest, that no man fall after the same example of <u>disobedience</u>* (*apeitheia* or "unbelief"). *(6) Seeing therefore it remaineth that some should enter thereinto, and they to whom the good tidings were before preached failed to enter in because of <u>disobedience</u>* (*apeitheia* or "unbelief"). If you have unbelief, you will be disobedient and one reason is you <u>cannot</u> cease from your own works when you don't believe God's already done it. <u>You always want to help Him out or you get your eyes on the world and on your problems.</u> <u>You fall victim to fear and doubt and discouragement, and all those things that happen when people live by what they see with their physical eyes, rather than what they see in the Bible.</u> If you walk by sight, you will not walk by faith. You'll be like Israel in the wilderness. They looked around and saw lack on every side. They didn't believe that God was able to meet their every need out there and the devil agreed with them, so they became full of fear, discouragement and disobedience, and they spoke against the Lord. It's the only thing you have left, if you don't have faith. Let's read some of that story and look at a few points. *(Num.21:4) And they journeyed from mount Hor by the way to the Red Sea, to compass the land of Edom: and the soul of the people was much discouraged because of the way. (5) And the people spake against God, and against Moses, Wherefore have ye brought us up out of Egypt to die in the wilderness? for there is no bread, and there is no water; and our soul loatheth this light* (or "vile") *bread.* And what were they speaking about? They were speaking about the manna and calling it "this vile bread." The bread of life is sweet to the taste but is bitter in the belly. In other words, the flesh does not like it because it demands your life; it demands you give up your thinking, your ways. It demands submission.

Well, these people were walking by sight, having their eyes on the problems around them, instead of on the promise, so they became discouraged and they spoke against the Lord. That's all you can do when you walk by sight and fill your mind with what you see around you. But, as we've studied and seen, God has already taken care of every problem that you could imagine and every problem that you could possibly have. It's all been covered by the blood. It's already been covered by the Lord on the cross. He's already taken it away; it's already solved. **(Joh.19:30) It is finished.** Jesus told His disciples, **(16:33) Be of good cheer; I have overcome the world.** It's already solved. If we keep our eyes on those promises, they bring us rest. If we get our eyes on the problem, we stumble and fall. I remember a lady we knew some time back, with whom we had really struggled for years. We would minister to her and bring the Gospel to her, trying to stabilize her in the Word, but she would always go back to walking by sight and speaking against the Lord. Do you know what speaking against the Lord can be? <u>It can be anything that is contrary to the Word</u>, anything that is not confessing the good confession in the sight of many witnesses. **(Rom.10:10) For with the heart man believeth unto righteousness; and with the mouth confession is made unto salvation.** Our salvation in every form comes not only by faith, but the works that come from that faith, and <u>the biggest work that comes from faith is what we say</u>.

So we were ministering to this lady and the Lord would constantly talk to us with dreams and visions for her. One time, my wife had a dream that she was in the top bed of a bunk bed and this lady was on the lower bunk. They were supposed to be resting, except for one thing: while my wife was resting, this lady was just tossing and turning and all her covers were twisted up. She couldn't seem to get comfortable. And then my wife kept hearing her say things like, "I'm just so afraid," and "I just can't do it," and a lot of negative things were coming out of her mouth. In the dream, my wife knew that this place where they were was called "Holiness" and she also knew that the only way you could stay there was to confess the Lord. My wife looked down over the end of the bunk at this lady, who was saying all these negative things, and told her, "Nope; that's not what the Bible says. Nope, that's not what the Bible says." My wife kept correcting her, but this lady kept on saying things against the Lord and against the Bible. Then, finally, the lady said, "I just don't know if I want to stay here." Well, you can't stay in the place of "Holiness" unless you are going to agree with the Word of God. **(Amo.3:3) Shall two walk together, except they have agreed?** We have to learn to confess the Lord in the midst of the situations around us.

The Israelites in the wilderness were in what appeared to be a desperate situation, but the Lord had already solved this problem. He brought them there on purpose to try them, to see if they would walk by sight or by faith. Jesus tells us this, too. **(Mat.10:32) Every one therefore who shall confess me before men, him will I also confess before my Father who is in heaven. (33) But whosoever shall deny me before men, him will I also deny before my Father who is in heaven.** We believe His promises and they give us rest, and then what naturally comes out of our mouth is in agreement with the Word of God. And when you confess Him before men, He confesses you before the Father. Again, the word "confess" here is the Greek *homologeo* and it means "to speak the same as." When we are in the tribulations of our wilderness experiences, we see our need, we see our lack, we see our sickness, we see our sin, we see our problems, which we have discovered the Lord has already taken care of. Are we going to agree with the Good News? "For with the heart man believeth unto righteousness; and with the mouth confession is made unto salvation." It's very important that we confess in order to bring the salvation that we're believing for. With our confession, we're "calling the things that are not as though they were." It's very important that we confess Him before men, that we say before men what His Word says. **(Heb.3:1) Wherefore, holy brethren, partakers of a heavenly calling, consider the Apostle and <u>High Priest of our confession</u>, [even] Jesus.** Jesus is the "High Priest of our confession" Who offers an offering before the Father and that offering is what we say; it's the words of our mouth. And if we speak the same as Jesus, then He confesses us before the Father and before the holy angels. **(Luk.12:8) And I say unto you, Every one who shall confess me before men, him shall the Son of man also confess before the angels of God: (9) but he that denieth me in the presence of men shall be denied in the presence of the angels of God.**

I also like this verse: **(Mat.12:36) And I say unto you, that <u>every idle word</u> that men shall speak, they shall give account thereof in the <u>day of judgment</u>.** Thank God that we come into days of judgment so that we don't have to come into *the* Day of Judgment! The Greek word translated as "idle" here means "unfruitful." There are unfruitful words that don't give us any help in the day of judgment. **(Mat.12:37) For by thy words thou shalt be <u>justified</u>** (that means "accounted righteous"), **and by thy words thou shalt be condemned.** When you come into judgment, do you want to be condemned? Or do you want to be justified, so that you come through and overcome it? Well, He tells us in order for that to happen, we have to confess Him before men. **(Mat.15:18) But the things which proceed out of the mouth come forth out of the heart; and <u>they defile the man</u>. (19) For out of the heart come forth evil thoughts, murders, adulteries, fornications, thefts, false witness, railings: (20) these are the things which defile the man; but to eat with unwashen hands defileth not the man.** When we think thoughts that are contrary to God, when we speak what we see, feel and hear, we're like the spies who went into the Promised Land and brought back a bad report. They reported what they saw, what they felt and what they heard, so they were condemned by God. They made the hearts of the people fearful and that made the people fall away (Numbers 13,14). The spies died in the wilderness because they brought a bad report and the rest died because they believed what they heard.

Our report, the good witness that we're supposed to give before men, has to be what "thus saith the Lord." What did the Lord say about this circumstance and what did the Lord say about this situation? By your words you are going to be justified, or accounted righteous, and by your words you are going to be condemned. When these Israelites in the wilderness began to look at the problems around them and became discouraged because they didn't have their mind on the promise, they spoke against the Lord. What did they do? They spoke about what they saw, what they felt, what they heard and <u>what their fears told them would happen</u>. They cried the whole time to go back to Egypt because they loved the fleshly rest of trusting in the world to supply their needs. And yet God wanted to take away any kind of fleshly rest. He wanted them to rest in the promises in the wilderness and He had to bring them through the wilderness to get them to the Promised Land. Of course, they were not worthy to live in the Promised Land unless they went through the wilderness and confessed Him in the midst of those trials. We see here that the people "spake against the Lord" and that's what comes from the disobedience caused by unbelief. They spoke against the Lord, saying that He was going to cause them to die in the wilderness and they spoke of how much they hated the bread. What did that bring? It brought a curse upon them. ***(Num.21:6) And the Lord sent fiery serpents among the people, and they bit the people; and much people of Israel died.*** They said they hated the "light bread." They hated the Lord! Did you know that if you don't love the Word, you don't love the Lord?

Many people say they love the Lord, but what did the Lord Himself say? ***(Joh.14:15) If ye love me, ye will keep my commandments.*** If you love the Lord, you will love the Word. Now the "light bread" that they reviled was the manna, but what was the manna? ***(Exo.16:31) And the house of Israel called the name thereof Manna: and it was like coriander seed, white; and the taste of it was like wafers [made] with honey.*** Some Bible versions have a footnote that the word "manna" is actually the Hebrew word "man." Wow! They called the name of it "man"! And Who is the Man? The Man is Jesus. ***(Joh.6:33)*** <u>***For the bread of God is that which cometh down out of heaven***</u>***, and giveth life unto the world. (34) They said therefore unto him, Lord, evermore give us this bread. (35)*** <u>***Jesus said unto them, I am the bread of life***</u>***: he that cometh to me shall not hunger, and he that believeth on me shall never thirst.*** They hated the manna, which represented the Word of life. It represented He Who is the Word, Jesus Christ. They hated the Lord, but <u>the Lord is these promises</u>. ***(Joh.1:14)*** <u>***And the Word became flesh***</u>***, and dwelt among us (and we beheld his glory, glory as of the only begotten from the Father), full of grace and truth.*** "The Word became flesh," or to state it another way, the Word manifested in flesh. The Word became flesh in order for us to be like Him, bearing His fruit, because we, too, have to be the Word become flesh. God's plan is that He might reveal Himself through the body of Christ today, like He revealed Himself through the first body of Christ.

The Israelites in the wilderness hated the Lord because they had their eyes on the problems, instead of the promises, and they became discouraged. They hadn't entered into the rest. They hadn't ceased from their works and so they were under the curse. ***(Num.21:6) And the Lord sent fiery serpents among the people, and they bit the people; and*** <u>***much people of Israel died***</u>***.*** When I was growing up, I remember my daddy had an old saying that I never really understood until I read the Bible. He would talk about people who just always had problems; the world would call them "jinxed" but my dad would call them "snake bit." After I read the Bible, I realized that "snake bit" represents somebody who is under the curse. They fall into it everywhere they go and the main reason for that is because they don't believe the Word of God. They don't have their eyes on the Savior. They have their eyes on the problem and because of that, their heart just melts. Their heart is not strong before the Lord and they become discouraged, they become fearful and they are full of doubt. **(2Co.7:1) Having therefore these promises, beloved, let us cleanse ourselves from all defilement of flesh and spirit, <u>perfecting holiness</u> in the fear of God.** The promises give us power over the flesh and power to change things. **(Num.21:6) And the Lord sent fiery serpents among the people, and they bit the people; and much people of Israel died. (7) And the people came to Moses, and said, We have sinned, because we have spoken against the Lord, and against thee; pray unto the Lord, that he take away the serpents from us. And Moses prayed for the people.** They sinned because they spoke against the Lord.

Do you know it's overwhelmingly common for God's people to speak against Him? That's because their tongue is connected to their physical sight and their physical hearing, and what they see in the physical realm is not according to the Word of God. It's also common that God's people live under the curse, but the Lord did not ordain us to live under the curse. He ordained us to live <u>above</u> the curse. Do you know what God told Joshua? **(Jos.1:8) This book of the law <u>shall not depart out of thy mouth</u>, but thou shalt meditate thereon day and night, that thou mayest observe to do according to <u>all</u> that is written therein: for then thou shalt make thy way prosperous** (Hebrew: "to push forward"; this has nothing to do with the "prosperity" doctrine.)**, and then thou shalt have good success** (Hebrew: "to be circumspect and hence, intelligent" or "to deal wisely"; so, again, this has nothing to do with the "prosperity" doctrine.)**.** To state it another way, when we speak in agreement with the Word, although not necessarily quoting the Word, "then thou shalt make thy way prosperous." This is how we "prosper" in going to the Promised Land and what else did He say? "That thou mayest observe <u>to do</u> according to all that is written therein." You see, faith makes us obedient; unbelief makes us disobedient. If we never cease from our works, then we will never enter into the rest. That's what the Lord exhorted. **(Heb.3:11) As I sware in my wrath, They shall not enter into my rest.** Why? **(12) Take heed, brethren, lest haply there shall be in any one of you <u>an evil heart of unbelief</u>, in falling away from the living God.** They couldn't enter into the rest because they had "an evil heart of unbelief" that made them speak against the Lord. When they realized this was sin, they asked Moses to pray for them and Moses prayed for the people. **(Num.21:8) And the Lord said unto Moses, Make thee a fiery serpent, and set it upon a standard: and it shall come to pass, that every one that is bitten, when he seeth it, shall live.**

What does the serpent represent? We came out of this world and into the Kingdom of God, into what is called "the body of Christ." So what body were we a part of before we came to the body of Christ? Jesus said, *(Mat.12:30) He that is not with me is against me....* He talked to the Pharisees and said, *(Joh.8:44) Ye are of [your] father the devil....* They were members of the body of the devil! And we used to be in his body, too. We were created in his image and we were actually full of the poison of the serpent. We had that poison in our heads, just like the serpent does. Remember what Revelation says. *(Rev.12:9) And the great dragon was cast down, <u>the old serpent</u>, he that is <u>called the Devil</u> and Satan, the deceiver of the whole world....* And yet the Lord called us to be a part of His body. The Bible says that Jesus became like that serpent on the pole. *(Joh.3:14) And as Moses lifted up the serpent in the wilderness, even so must the Son of man be lifted up.* From now on, when we look at Jesus upon the cross, what we can see is our curse put there upon Him. We can see our sin put there upon Him. We can see our sickness put there upon Him. We can see our lack put there upon Him. We can see whatever our problem is put there upon Him because of this. *(Gal.3:13) Christ <u>redeemed</u> us from the <u>curse of the law</u>....* "Redeemed" is the Greek word *exagorazo* and it means "to buy out or to purchase a slave with a mind to set him free." Christ bought us. He delivered us from the bondage of slavery to the devil and to the curse. The "curse of the law" is all of the evil things that came upon mankind for disobeying God's Law (Deuteronomy 28).

(Gal.3:13) Christ redeemed us from the curse of the law, <u>having become a curse for us</u>.... Jesus became the curse! Well, who is it that administers the curse? It's the devil and he has been given that authority by God to do it so that people would repent and turn to Him. *(13) Christ redeemed us from the curse of the law, having become a curse for us; for it is written, <u>Cursed is every one that hangeth on a tree</u>* (Now we see that Jesus became cursed; He became like the serpent, like us.)*: (14) that upon the Gentiles might come the <u>blessing of Abraham</u> in Christ Jesus; that we might receive the promise of the Spirit through faith.* The Bible says that Abraham was blessed in all things. *(16) Now to Abraham were the promises spoken, and to his seed. He saith not, And to seeds, as of many; but as of one, And to thy seed, which is Christ.* God made all these promises to Christ. He made all these promises to just one seed and now we must abide in Him. How do we do that? We abide in Him by accepting the same promises, by speaking the same promises, by walking in faith in the same promises. That's how we abide in Him. And we receive the benefit of Abraham because Jesus became cursed for us. God put our curse, the whole curse that's enumerated in Deuteronomy 28, upon Jesus. No matter what problem you have, you should be able to see this problem upon Jesus. *(Num.21:8) And the Lord said unto Moses, Make thee a fiery serpent, and set it upon a standard: and it shall come to pass, that every one that is bitten, <u>when he seeth it</u>, <u>shall live</u>.*

I'd like to point out something else: *(2Co.5:21) Him who knew no sin he made*

[to be] sin (Jesus became the curse and He became the sin.) ***on our behalf; that we might become the righteousness of God in him.*** Do you have a problem with sin? Do you have a problem with the curse that comes from sin? We see here the serpent on the cross. We see here that the Lord has put all of this upon Jesus. Now what are we to confess, if we get our eyes on the serpent on the pole, if we get our eyes on the fact the Lord Jesus has borne all of this? We confess what the Bible says: ***(2Co.5:17) Wherefore if any man is in Christ, [he is] a new creature: the old things are passed away; behold, they are become new.*** All of that curse and sin has completely passed away. We are new creatures. When you look at the serpent on the pole, you're supposed to see your curse, your sin, upon Him. The curse is very broad. If you read Deuteronomy 28, you'll find it's all sickness, it's all lack, it's all bondage to your enemies, etc. The curse is all these negative things and the curse has all been put upon Jesus Christ; therefore, what are we to confess? Do we confess what we see in the world or do we confess what we see on the cross? We're speaking against God if we're not speaking in agreement with His promises. We must repent. We must "change our mind," which is what "repent" means. We are new creatures in Christ. Christ has been raised up on the pole for our salvation and we are to get our eyes upon Him because Moses said, ***(Num.21:8) ... every one that is bitten, when he seeth it, shall live. (9) And Moses made a serpent of brass, and set it upon the standard: and it came to pass, that if a serpent had bitten any man, when he looked unto the serpent of brass, he lived.*** So when the Israelites got their eyes on the Son, which in this case is represented by the serpent, and on what the Son had accomplished, they were healed.

The American Medical Association has claimed the serpent on the pole, the caduceus, as their symbol ever since the late 19th and early 20th centuries, but the serpent on the pole represents the fact that God already healed you, not that God is going to use some modern method to heal you. The AMA cannot claim that as God's method. God's method is to "calleth the things that are not as though they were" and "for by grace have ye been saved through faith." It's unearned, it's unmerited and you don't have to pay for it. The serpent on the pole is the fact that we can look at Jesus and see that our sickness has already been put upon Him. We don't have to accept it. That's the really Good News. Jesus and His disciples used that method all through the Scriptures. They did not use the things that are to put to nothing the things that are; they used the things that are not. They used the promises which claim that we are already healed.

Many years ago, I had a vision in which I saw myself walking to a stream and when I got into the stream, I received a revelation that, as long as I laid on my back and looked at the sun, I could stay floating up the stream. As I meditated on that, the Lord gave me the answer to it. I realized that this stream represents the Word of God. God told Moses, ***(Deu.11:26) Behold I set before you this day a blessing and a curse.*** He was talking about His commandments because they represent both a blessing and a curse. They represent the blessing of God's Good News and they represent the curse of death. It all depends on how you deal with these promises as to what you're going to meet in your future. So I realized that the water represented the Word of God, ***(Eph.5:26) having cleansed [the church] by the washing of water with the word***, and that it could either kill me or give me life. I could go upstream, contrary to nature, if I kept my eyes on the sun and I would always stay afloat; in other words, I would always stay above the curse. Water will kill you, if you go beneath it, but if you stay on top, it's a blessing. Noah, of course, stayed on top and the curse went beneath; the rest of the world died underneath the waters of that flood. We have to keep our eyes on the Son in order to stay above the curse that's upon this world. Why? Because He's the One Who promised and He's the One Who bore the curse. We should be able to see our curse upon Him. What problem do you have right now? Can you see that as having been put upon the Lord Jesus? If you can, then you can be free of it; that's His method. It's very, very simple. It's so simple that a babe can do it. That's what faith is all about; faith is believing that you have already received on account of the promises that God has already given.

As I was laying on my back with my face to the sun, I was floating upstream, contrary to nature, contrary to the laws of this world. Everybody wants things to be natural, but I tell you, if you keep your eyes on the Son, it's supernatural. It's above the laws of this world. The supernatural takes precedence over the laws of this world. For instance, healing comes to people who believe that they have received it, but it's very hard to come to people who are seeking for it all the time. It's the same thing for deliverance from sins and every other curse. It works the same way. ***(Mar.11:24) All things whatsoever ye pray and ask for, believe that ye <u>received</u> them, and ye shall have them.*** That's very simple and very cheap, too! It's an awesome benefit that the Lord has given to us. So I'm floating upstream and I looked around me and saw that there were a few others who were doing the same thing. As we floated away, I noticed that there were people on the left side of the stream who floated up under a tent that was stretched over about half the stream. Whenever any of these people who were floating with me went under the tent and the shadow fell upon them, they sank to the bottom of the stream. I quickly got out onto the bank and cut the ropes that were holding the tent up. It fell into the water and the water carried it away. Then I made these floats to float the people up off the bottom. As soon as they saw the sun again, they started floating once more. Then I realized that the tent represented man's religion. The religions of man like to take credit for what God has already done. They like to tell men, "God does not do it that way anymore." They like to have their fleshly ideas and basically how they're leading people is, "Let's go back to Egypt and do it the way of the world. Let's have God's salvation through man's provision. Let's go back by the fleshpots." They don't teach people to walk by faith with their eyes on the Son, but they bring them into darkness. They block the light of the Son and the people sink. They're under the curse and they think it's normal to live under the curse of this world because everybody around them is living that way. God did not ordain us to do that. If we keep our eyes on the Son, we will stay above the curse; that's what the Lord revealed to me about this.

Another vision I received years ago was about moving to Pensacola. In that vision, my wife and I were sitting in lawn chairs on our front lawn, just resting and taking it easy. We looked out front and saw that the power lines running up the street were sagging until they almost touched the ground between the poles. We were just looking at this scene when a tornado came and picked us up out of our chairs and carried us away. I saw all this very clearly and the Lord interpreted it for me. As we ceased from our own works and entered into the rest, represented by the lawn chairs, the power of man was coming to an end in our life, represented by the sagging power line. Our efforts, our ability to save ourselves, was coming to an end and the power of God, which is likened to the whirlwind in many Scriptures, picked us up out of our chairs and carried us away. And the interpretation literally happened when the Lord moved us from where we were over to Pensacola. He provided everything: He bought our house, He bought our car, He opened doors for ministry, everything. He did it all. It was supernatural.

There was another part to the vision. That tornado set me down by a church. It wasn't any particular church but it was like a lot of churches, like the tent over the water. As I walked through the door, I saw an old man standing in the foyer of the church and I knew he was dangerous, so I just hugged the wall to get around him, like he was a rattlesnake. I knew this old man was the preacher. Well, I went into the sanctuary and saw a big double-sink in the middle of it. The sink was full of water and the water was full of babies, all face down. I ran over to this sink and started pulling these babies up out of the water, but most of them were dead. Finally, one of the babies I pulled out of the water and held face up said, "Thank God! We knew He was going to send someone." The Lord pointed out to me that "face down" in the water is people who have their eyes on the world. They're seeing the curse and they're dying because of it. But "face up" toward the Son is facing what the Lord has provided. The Lord became a curse for us. He became sin for us. He made reconciliation and our curse was put upon Him, while His blessing was put upon us. "Reconciliation" means He made "an exchange." So in the vision, most of the babies were already dead and I knew the preacher was the one who was guilty of this. He was using the water to try to clear up the babies, but he had their eyes on the world and not on the Son. One was spared because he had his eyes on the Son. That's what this story is all about. If we keep our eyes on the Son, the Lord Jesus, on the Word of God, on the promises, we will enter into the rest, which is ceasing from our works. If not, then we're going to be looking at the problems in the world and we're going to be <u>forced through fear</u>, <u>doubt and unbelief</u> to align with the world, which is not sanctification.

If we get our eyes on Jesus, then we can walk out from the world. **(Joh.19:34) Howbeit one of the soldiers with a spear pierced his side, and straightway there came out <u>blood and water</u>.** The water is the pale yellowish liquid that separates from the blood when the blood is clotting and it's called "serum." What is serum used for? If you take the serum from an animal that is immune to a snake bite or other toxin and give it to a person who is under the curse, it delivers them. It's an antitoxin. Jesus showed His immunity to the curse of sin and death. He was the spotless and blemishless Lamb, Whom we have to eat (1 Peter 1:19) in order to partake of the Passover! The Passover was the passing over of the curse which fell upon the Egyptians. Because the Israelites had the blood on their doorposts, they walked under the blood of Jesus Christ (Exodus 12). Jesus is immune from the snakebite and, therefore, His serum, which is passed on to us, gives us immunity. It's our antitoxin. He is the serpent on the pole because He bore the curse. An animal has to be sacrificed in order to obtain the serum to save someone and Jesus was the Lamb Who was sacrificed so that we could have immunity.

Why don't we come into this world with immunity in the first place? Well, there's another thing called an antidote. An antidote is when they give you a little bit of the poison so that your own system fights against it and builds up an immunity to the poison. It's kind of like temptation. The more you overcome it, the more immune you become to it. The Lord wanted a people who were overcomers. The Lamb slain from the foundation of the world was a Lamb that was sacrificed for people who had fallen, even from the foundation of the world (Revelation 13:8). This tells us He knew from the very beginning that Adam was going to fall. He knew we would be born into a fallen creation, but He chose us to be overcomers. We've taken the antidote; we've taken the serum. It is Jesus Who became sin for us as the cursed serpent. If we get our eyes on Him, He's going to make us immune. He's going to deliver us from this curse.

We can walk out from under this curse by coming into agreement with Him. Adam and Eve fell under the curse because they came out of agreement with Him. Now He's teaching us through faith to come into agreement with promises that are contrary to this world and our sight. He's teaching us to say that "by whose stripes ye were healed." That is contrary to what we see in this world, but if we "calleth the things that are not as though they were," we become immune. If we find that God gave to us deliverance from the curse, that He gave to us divine health, then we can deny what we see with our eyes and agree with what we see in the Book. We can claim these promises, the manna that they hated so much. If we come into agreement with that, we are walking with the Lord, in His steps, in His immunity. Exodus 12:13 is very plain. He delivered us from every plague; nothing was left out. He set us free through Jesus Christ, our sacrifice. We have no problem that is not covered. We can rejoice and we can praise God. We just need to get our eyes on the Savior. God bless you.

CHAPTER FIVE

Healing By Scripture!

We've been studying the real Good News and it is the Real Good News. It's the cure for what ails you and it's the answer to any problem you could possibly have. *(Rom.1:16) For I am not ashamed of the gospel: for it is the power of God unto salvation <u>to every one that believeth</u>....* The Gospel is the power of God to every one who believes and that's the key: "to every one that believeth." We've been looking at faith and faith in the promises, so now I'd like to share with you some common contradictions a person who thinks they are of the Lord might have.

The first one I want us to look at is, "Well, sometimes God heals and sometimes He doesn't." What's wrong with that statement? I'm going to show you what's wrong with it. To begin with, even from the letter, it's just not true; it's not Scriptural at all. *(Mat.4:23) And Jesus went about in all Galilee, teaching in their synagogues, and preaching the gospel of the kingdom, and healing <u>all manner</u> of disease and <u>all manner</u> of sickness among the people. (24) And the report of him went forth into all Syria: and they brought unto him <u>all that were sick</u>, holden with divers diseases and torments, possessed with demons, and epileptic, and palsied; <u>and he healed them</u>.* They brought to Him all who were sick and had all these curses upon their lives and He healed them. Well, you know, nothing has changed since then. *(Heb.13:8) Jesus Christ [is] the same yesterday and today, [yea] and for ever.* They brought Him all these people and, as you can imagine, some of them had serious problems, but I can tell you that because they had a Covenant with God, God was having favor upon them. Matthew 13 speaks about the hardness, the blindness, the deafness of these people and how Jesus spoke in parables to them because they could not see and could not hear, according to the Scriptures.

These were some hard-hearted people and yet the Father and the Lord Jesus, because of His Covenant, wanted to prove His love for them, so He healed everyone who came to Him. And that precedent is found all through the Scriptures. *(Mat.8:16) And when even was come, they brought unto him many possessed with demons: and he cast out the spirits with a word, and <u>healed all that were sick</u>.* Where do we get this theology that Jesus heals some and He doesn't heal others? We can see here that it's at least His will to heal all of His Covenant people because they have the benefits of the Covenant, the benefits of the Good News of the Kingdom. *(Mat.8:17) That it might be fulfilled which was spoken through Isaiah the prophet, saying: Himself took our infirmities, and bare our diseases.* I know that there's a high percentage of Christianity here who believes what Isaiah spoke about was only spiritual healing. Even when they look at *(1Pe.2:24) by whose stripes <u>ye were healed</u>*, they insist, "That's only talking about spiritual healing." But here we can see the same text from Isaiah being quoted and it plainly refers to physical healing. *(Mat.8:16) And when* *even was come, they brought unto him many possessed with demons: and he cast out the spirits with a word, and healed <u>all that were sick</u>: (17) that it might be fulfilled which was spoken through Isaiah the prophet, saying: <u>Himself took our infirmities, and bare our diseases</u>.* That sounds pretty physical, so why would anyone say such a thing? It's because their leaders taught them to do that as an excuse for the fact that they don't have the power that Jesus offered to us.

(9:35) And Jesus went about all the cities and the villages, teaching in their synagogues, and preaching the gospel of the kingdom, and <u>healing all manner of disease and all manner of sickness</u>. There it is again, only this time it's not just all people, but every kind of disease and every kind of problem. *(12:15) And Jesus perceiving [it] withdrew from thence: and many followed him; <u>and he healed them all</u>.* Is Jesus a respecter of persons? We know that in the New Testament He's not a respecter of race or nationality or any such thing. In the Old Testament, God's people were literal Jews, but in the New Testament, anyone who is born-again has the benefits of the Kingdom. So, no, Jesus is not a respecter of persons, but He is a respecter of faith and the Bible says He healed all from among His people. And yet today people have that doctrine of, "Well, sometimes God heals and sometimes He doesn't." It's not Him, folks; it's us. He healed everyone who came to Him in all of these verses. *(14:35) And when the men of that place knew him, they sent into all that region round about, and brought unto him <u>all that were sick</u>, (36) and they besought him that they might only touch the border of his garment: and as many as touched were made whole.* Wow! And you know, it didn't stop there. It continues to this day among people who believe the Word of God and have decided they're not going to <u>change</u> the Word of God for their own ideas or for their own theology, or to please men.

As a matter of fact, we know that healing continued through the disciples. *(Act.5:12) And by the hands of the apostles were many signs and wonders wrought among the people; and they were all with one accord in Solomon's porch. (13) But of the rest durst no man join himself to them: howbeit the people magnified them; (14) and believers were the more added to the Lord, multitudes both of men and women; (15) insomuch that they even carried out the sick into the streets, and laid them on beds and couches, that, as Peter came by, at the least his shadow might overshadow some one of them.* Jesus said, *(Joh.14:12) and greater [works] than these shall he do.* We don't see an example of Jesus' shadow healing people, but do you know who Peter was here? He was Jesus manifested in the flesh because the Word of God, Who is Jesus Christ, lived in this same Peter, just as He lives in those today who believe His Words. Jesus said, *(6:63) The words that I have spoken unto you are spirit, and are life.* Those words go into you and recreate Himself in you. *(Act.5:16) And there also came together the multitudes from the cities round about Jerusalem, bringing sick folk, and them that were vexed with unclean spirits: and they were healed <u>every</u>*

one. The doctrine that sometimes the Lord heals and sometimes He doesn't just isn't Scriptural. We're commanded not to add to or take away from the Words of Scripture. **(Rev.22:18) *I testify unto every man that heareth the words of the prophecy of this book, If any man shall add unto them, God shall add unto him the plagues which are written in this book: (19) and if any man shall take away from the words of the book of this prophecy, God shall take away his part from the tree of life, and out of the holy city, which are written in this book.*** The Lord is not a respecter of persons (Romans 2:11) and what He'll do for others, He'll do for you. All He wants from you is your faith and your trust in Him.

If I didn't believe that God healed all every time, how could I ever trust Him? I've put my trust in the Lord as my healer and my Savior in all things for many years. I've raised five children and they also put their trust in the Lord and the Lord consistently healed my children. Whenever they were sick at home, I just prayed for them. I knew I had authority over my children. When they were young, I could just exercise faith for them and God would heal them. I love my children so much that if I didn't feel I could trust God, I would not have stepped out by faith in something I wasn't sure of. We had some pretty good trials of our faith, but the Lord endured us through them because He saw that we desired to be pleasing to Him and to walk by faith. **(Heb.10:38) *But my righteous one shall live by faith***, and so the Lord gave us continual grace.

One time, when my two oldest sons and a cousin of theirs were riding motocross bikes in some woods, they stopped for a few minutes to speak with a man by a campfire. Then my oldest boy, Corban, and the cousin got on their bikes and took off down the road, while my next oldest boy, Nathan, stayed to talk for a few more minutes. And then Nathan decided he would catch up to the others, so he jumped on his motocrosser and took off. Well, when he reached the point down the road where it made a sharp left turn, it was too late for him to make the turn because he was going so fast. He wound up going off the road and into a ravine. And after he bounced off some of the trees, he was knocked out cold. After a while, the first two boys started riding up and down, looking for Nathan, and couldn't find him. Finally, a lady who was on the other side of the ravine, riding a four-wheeler on the sand, looked across the water and saw Nathan over there, out cold, laying on the ground. She noticed Corban and his cousin looking around on the hill, so she called to them and asked, "Hey, are you looking for him?" Sure enough, they saw Nathan was out cold and his bike was all smashed to pieces down there. Well, Corban got his pickup truck and they pulled Nathan up out of there, still unconscious, laid him in the back of the truck and headed for the local hospital.

At that point, they called me to tell me what had happened. I asked, "Where's Nathan?" Corban said, "He's here. They don't have an MRI machine and they want to scan his brain," because they said his brain was swelling. I said, "Okay. Can I talk to someone over there?" and he said, "Call this number." So I called and asked, "Where's my son?" and they told me, "We don't have an MRI machine, so they sent him down to Pensacola," which was where I lived at the time. Anyway, I went over to the Emergency Room at the hospital and found my son behind a curtain there. He wasn't unconscious but he was talking a bit irrationally. He would say a sentence, then a few minutes later, he would say the same thing again, like he didn't remember he'd said it, and then a few minutes later he would do it again. I looked at his arm and it was obvious that his arm was broken because the bone was poking up underneath the flesh. I felt around a little bit and it was kind of painful to him. I asked Nathan, "Son, do you believe Jesus healed you?" He said, "Oh, yeah, I believe He healed me." I asked, "Do you want to get out of here?" And he said, "Yeah, Dad, I want to get out of here," but he was still kind of mumbling and a little incoherent. I said, "Well, let's pray then," and we did what Jesus told us to do.

In the Scriptures, they didn't pray for healing for one another. They commanded it to be done in the name of Jesus. The reason they commanded it was the same reason we've been looking at in our study and that is <u>because it has already been done</u>. We are just those who administer the benefits of the Kingdom. The Lord Jesus already paid for it. We don't question Him; we just administer the gift to one another. We do what the apostles did. We just command it to be done in the name of Jesus. So I just commanded my son to be healed in Jesus' name. I didn't know what was wrong with his head but I could tell by the way he was talking that there was something wrong with his head. When I asked him if he wanted to get out of there, he told me, "Yeah." My son was old enough to make his own decisions and I don't believe in legalism. I don't believe in putting people under the Law and I don't believe in peer pressure. And I don't believe that we ought to do things just because someone else has enough faith. People should do what they have faith to do. The Bible says that if you have faith, have it unto yourselves. ***(Mat.9:29) ... According to your faith be it done unto you.*** Don't put your faith on someone else. You can give faith to people by preaching the Word to them. ***(Rom.10:17) So belief [cometh] of hearing, and hearing by the word of Christ.*** But to impress your faith on someone or to use peer pressure to cause someone to do something that they don't have faith for, is just legalism. It's dangerous and it hurts people.

The people who believe act differently than the people who don't believe. The people who believe act in agreement with their faith, as we've already studied. ***(Rom.10:10) For with the heart man believeth unto righteousness; and with the mouth confession is made unto salvation.*** So my son was in agreement with me and I said, "Okay, let's get out of here." I called the nurse and I told her, "Ma'am, we want to go home." She said, "Oh, you can't do that. His brain is swelling and that's why he is talking like this. And his arm is broken ..." I said, "Ma'am, we know the Lord Jesus Christ. He heals and He has always healed us, and this is not a problem. Believe me." She told us, "Wait right here. Don't do anything," and she went and talked to the doctor. Then the doctor came over to us and basically brought us through the same spiel of, "You know you can't do that," but I said, "We're ready to leave." So the doctor told us, "You will have to sign some papers to deliver us from any responsibility here," and I just said, "Bring your papers and we'll sign them." Then, before we left, the doctor warned me, "Be sure you don't feed him anything." I didn't know what that was about but I do know one thing, that when you claim God's deliverance, you don't have to trust in what men say. You don't have to worry; you don't have to be anxious. You can just continue to walk in faith, believing that you have received and acting as though you have received. Nathan got up and he leaned on my shoulder as he hobbled out to the car and we got in.

We hadn't made it very far before my son said, "Dad, I'm starving! I have to have something to eat!" So we stopped and I bought him a hamburger and fries on the way home, and he gobbled that up. When we got home, he had trouble taking his clothes off because of his arm and he was still occasionally repeating phrases over and over, like "What happened to my bike? Did anybody get my bike? Is it okay?" He was more worried about his bike than he was about his body. We would give him the answers and answer him again the next time. That night, he managed to take a shower, although it wasn't easy, and then he got into bed. The next day, Nathan got up and was very proud of himself because he was able to get his shirt on and do everything. I noticed, too, that the bone that had been sticking up about an inch high underneath the flesh was now very low and we hadn't done anything to set it. About this time, the doorbell rang. I went to answer the door and here was this lady standing there, with some books in her hand and she looks at me and says, "I'm *so-and-so* from HRS." I smiled at her and said, "That's fine." She said, "You don't look surprised to see me," and I replied, "No, I am not surprised to see you. Come in."

So she came in and sat down on the couch, and then she began to ask a lot of questions. "Do you not believe in doctors?" But I said, "Oh, no, ma'am, I believe in doctors. I don't have any problem with doctors, but I also believe that Jesus Christ is a healer and He has shown us this over the years. He's been consistent to heal my family. My children have been healed all of their life by the Lord, by faith, by the Word of God." She was skeptical of that and asked, "Do you mind if I examine Nathan?" And I said, "Not at all!" When I called Nathan, he came into the room just grinning and he wasn't repeating himself anymore. The bone had gone down quite a bit, too. She looked at him and questioned him some, and then she said, "He really does not look that bad, but since they called us, this is going to be on your record for ...," and she told us a number of years that I don't remember; maybe three or five. Well, I said, "That's fine; no problem." And by the time she left, she said, "I really don't see anything to worry about." In only a few more days, you couldn't tell if that boy had ever broken an arm or ever banged his head. The Lord just healed him.

I had gone through many trials with all five of my children and God had always been faithful to His Word. We have had to be diligent to be dogmatically determined not to depart from what the Word says, which is "by whose stripes ye were healed." It's not a matter of convincing God to heal us; it's a matter of us believing that He has already done it, and so I was convinced that He always healed. I had cleared up these questions long ago by a diligent study of the Scriptures and by understanding that God had already done this for us. So those problems were already cleared up for this trial with Nathan and many others like it. God is faithful. He is just as diligent to bring the healing as we have read in the Gospel of Matthew, and the other Gospels say the same thing. God was just as diligent to heal those stiff-necked Jews as He does for a lot of stiff-necked Christians nowadays. We all have our problems and God is merciful; it's by grace that He gives us this. It's not because we're perfect. We do want to be on the right side of God, so it's good to confess your sins. ***(1Jn.1:9) If we confess our sins, he is faithful and righteous to forgive us our sins, and to cleanse us from all unrighteousness. (Jas.5:16) <u>Confess therefore your sins</u> one to another, and pray one for another, <u>that ye may be healed</u>.*** It's good to confess your sins and make sure that there's no condemnation in your heart, and to make sure there's nothing between you and God.

The thing about "Sometimes God heals and sometimes He doesn't" is that it becomes a moot point after "by whose stripes ye were healed." It's a moot point about whether God wants to heal you or doesn't want to heal you, or if He will or if He won't in the future. The fact is, He's already done it. Study the Scriptures and, without adding one jot or one tittle, without adding one word or taking away one word, make up your mind that, "I am going to believe exactly what the Word says. I am not going to add to or take away from the Word under penalty of a curse." We're told, ***(1Pe.4:11) If any man speaketh, [speaking] as it were oracles of God.*** In other words, say what the Bible says and the Bible says you were healed. Think it, speak it, act it. Don't believe that God heals sometimes and sometimes He doesn't. He already healed everybody who belongs to His Kingdom at the cross. He already delivered us from every curse. The Bible says, ***(Psa.119:89) For ever, O Lord, Thy word is settled in heaven.*** God is not going to change His mind. It's in the Book. He can't change His mind or He's a liar! And we know that God can't lie. ***(Heb.6:18) That by two immutable things, in which <u>it is impossible for God to lie</u>, we may have a strong encouragement, who have fled for refuge to lay hold of the hope set before us.***

(Gal.3:13) Christ redeemed us from the curse of the law, having become a curse for us: for it is written, Cursed is every one that hangeth on a tree: (14) that upon the Gentiles might come the blessing of Abraham in Christ Jesus; that we might receive the promise of the Spirit through faith. So on the one hand, He has taken away the curse and on the other hand, He has given us the blessing. Do you understand that every time God didn't keep His Word, He would be sinning twice? He would be lying at least twice because we have these positive and negative promises. Here's one instance: ***(Heb.6:13) For when God made promise to Abraham*** (Who has Abraham's blessing now? We do.), ***since he could swear by none greater, he sware by himself, (14) saying, Surely blessing I will bless thee, and multiplying I will multiply thee. (15) And thus, <u>having patiently endured</u>, he obtained the promise.*** We need to patiently endure, holding fast to what the Word of God says, because the devil is going to try to talk us out of it. He does not want us to have a testimony before the people. ***(16) For men swear by the greater*** (Notice it says "men swear." We're commanded not to swear, but men swear by the greater.)***: and in every dispute of theirs the oath is final for confirmation. (17) Wherein God, being minded to show more abundantly unto the <u>heirs</u> of the promise....*** Christ is the heir of the promise. ***(Gal.3:16) Now to Abraham were the promises spoken, and to his seed. He saith not, And to seeds, as of many; <u>but as of one</u>, <u>And to thy seed</u>, <u>which is Christ</u>.*** But as we abide in Christ, we are heirs. ***(Eph.1:3) Blessed [be] the God and Father of our Lord Jesus Christ, who hath blessed us with every spiritual blessing in the heavenly [places] <u>in</u> Christ.*** When you abide in Him by faith in His Word, you are an heir to the promises and the blessings of Abraham. ***(Heb.6:17) Wherein God, being minded to show more abundantly unto the <u>heirs</u> of the promise the immutability*** ("unchangeableness" of what He says in His Word) ***of his counsel, interposed with an oath.*** God can swear and make oaths; we cannot. ***(Mat.5:34) But I say unto you, <u>Swear not at all</u>; neither by the heaven, for it is the throne of God; (35) nor by the earth, for it is the footstool of his feet; nor by Jerusalem, for it is the city of the great King. (36) Neither shalt thou swear by thy head, for <u>thou canst not make one hair white or black</u>.*** We don't have the ability to bring to pass anything that we might swear or promise. Only God has that ability and if He gives us grace to, we will, but if not, we won't. ***(Heb.6:17) Wherein God, being minded to show more abundantly unto the heirs of the promise the immutability of his counsel, interposed with an oath: (18) that by two immutable*** ("unchangeable") ***things, in which it is impossible for God to lie, we may have a strong encouragement, who have fled for refuge to lay hold of the hope set before us.*** In other words, God made a promise to bless Abraham and, to that promise, He added His oath to do so.

Now we have all these promises, plus we have the promise of the blessing of Abraham, plus we have the promise that Jesus bore the curse (sickness and so forth). We've looked at all these promises. How many times would God have to lie in each of our instances in order to not keep His Word? The problem is not, "Sometimes God heals and sometimes He doesn't." It really comes down to, "Is God a liar or not?" Did He tell the truth when He said He healed every one of us, or did He not tell the truth? So, if we change that statement a little bit to, "Christians sometimes receive healing and sometimes not," you'd have to say, "Yes; that's right. That's the truth." But that's not the fault of God; that's our fault. And the Lord Jesus taught us, too, that this is our problem, not God's. ***(Heb.11:6) And without faith it is <u>impossible to be well-pleasing</u> [unto him]; for he that cometh to God must <u>believe that he is</u>, <u>and</u> [that] <u>he is a rewarder of them that seek after him</u>.*** Do you believe that He will reward you and meet your needs? Do you believe that He cannot lie? The problem is responsibility. The statement that, "Sometimes God heals and sometimes He doesn't," puts the responsibility on God, but God says He's already healed everyone. He has already delivered us from the curse. He's already fulfilled His responsibility and we know that this Good News "is the power of God unto salvation to every one that believeth." So now we have to fulfill <u>our</u> responsibility; that's the problem.

It's not, "Sometimes God heals and sometimes He doesn't." It's actually, "We sometimes receive healing and sometimes we don't." The truth is, once you make up your mind that God is always faithful and that He always heals, the devil won't get a foothold in you to bring doubt and unbelief to cause you to miss out on the blessing. Jesus made it plain that this responsibility is <u>ours</u>. Do you remember the story of the centurion and what he said to Jesus? ***(Mat.8:5) And when he was entered into Capernaum, there came unto him a centurion, beseeching him, (6) and saying, Lord, my servant lieth in the house sick of the palsy, grievously tormented. (7) And he saith unto him, I will come and heal him. (8) And the centurion answered and said, Lord, I am not worthy that thou shouldest come under my roof; but only say the word, and my servant shall be healed. (9) For I also am a man under authority, having under myself soldiers: and I say to this one, Go, and he goeth; and to another, Come, and he cometh; and to my servant, Do this, and he doeth it.*** Do you know what he was saying? "I know you are a man under authority and whatever you say goes, so you just say the word and I will believe it." The truth is we have the Word that has been given to us that this centurion never had. We have words that tell us that this has already been accomplished for all of us at the cross. So he said, "Only say the word and my servant shall be healed," and now the Lord has said the word. ***(Mat.8:10) And when Jesus heard it, he marvelled, and said to them that followed, Verily I say unto you, I have not found so great faith, no, not in Israel. (13) And Jesus said unto the centurion, Go thy way; <u>as thou hast believed</u>, [so] <u>be it done unto thee</u>. And the servant was healed in that hour.*** Notice that Jesus was saying that the centurion is the one who is setting the parameters of this healing, this deliverance, this blessing. He put the responsibility on the centurion for bringing this miracle to pass.

Jesus always had faith but the centurion had to believe, too. Jesus said, ***(Mat.18:19) Again I say unto you, that if two of you shall agree on earth as touching anything that they shall ask, it shall be done for them of my Father who is in heaven.*** The centurion was definitely exercising his faith and that's what Jesus always looked for in people before He gave them the benefits of the Kingdom. Now when we look at where He healed multitudes of people, we aren't given any particular instances of that, but when we look at specific instances, we see that first Jesus always tried to get them to express their faith so that He could give them this wonderful gift. He said, "As thou hast believed, [so] be it done unto thee." Or, ***(Mat.9:29) Then touched he their eyes, saying, <u>According to your faith</u> be it done unto you.*** "According to your faith, be it done unto you." See, it's very important what we believe. It's very important that we're agreeing exactly with what the Scripture says. You know, fear and doubt are beliefs; they're just negative beliefs. They are a belief that we still have the curse and that we're still under the penalties of our sins. Fear, doubt, discouragement, all of those are faith; they're just negative faith. Jesus said, "According to your faith, be it done unto you"; that's why doubt and unbelief keep us from receiving. Look at what happened to Jesus in His hometown: *(Mat.13:58) **And he did not many mighty works there because of their unbelief.*** He could not do many mighty works. Why not? Because He knew that the benefits were conditional upon our faith. That's why it's very important that we agree with exactly what the Scripture says. If you want the benefits of God, you have to agree with what the Word says and not add to or take away from the words of this book, or what did He say would happen? *(Rev.22:18) **I testify unto every man that heareth the words of the prophecy of this book, If any man shall add unto them, God shall add unto him the plagues which are written in this book: (19) and if any man shall take away from the words of the book of this prophecy, God shall take away his part from the tree of life, and out of the holy city, which are written in this book.*** Don't change the Word or you will be under the curse.

So the Lord, by bringing us into agreement with Him, is bringing us out from under the curse. We don't belong there. We've been delivered from it and we shouldn't stay there. *(Mar.2:5) **And Jesus seeing their faith saith unto the sick of the palsy, Son, thy sins are forgiven.*** And, of course, the scribes and Pharisees objected. *(Mar.2:7) **Why doth this man thus speak? he blasphemeth: who can forgive sins but one, [even] God?*** But we should understand when God wants to heal you, it's because He has forgiven your sins. Jesus saw their faith. People say today that it's all the faith of the one doing the praying. Jesus didn't agree with that and the Word doesn't agree with that. *(Jas.5:14) **Is any among you sick? Let him call for the elders of the church; and let them pray over him, anointing him with oil in the name of the Lord: (15) and the prayer of faith shall save him that is sick, and the Lord shall raise him up; and if he have committed sins, it shall be forgiven him.*** So when God heals you, it's because He has forgiven you and that's why, when you want a healing, you should repent and confess your sins. *(1Jn.1:9) **If we confess our sins, he is faithful and righteous to forgive us our sins, and to cleanse us from all unrighteousness.*** He has to forgive you before He gives you the benefit. And by faith, we accept our forgiveness from sin and the benefits of the Kingdom.

*(Mar.9:23) **And Jesus said unto him, If thou canst! All things are possible to him that believeth. (24) Straightway the father of the child cried out, and said, I believe; help thou mine unbelief.*** "All things are possible" to whom? To the one who believes. Everything is possible to the one who believes. Nothing is possible to the people who walk in doubt and in unbelief. Some of you probably know these next verses by heart: *(Mar.16:17) **And these signs shall accompany them that believe: in my name shall they cast out demons; they shall speak with new tongues; (18) they shall take up serpents, and if they drink any deadly thing, it shall in no wise hurt them; they shall lay hands on the sick, and they shall recover.*** What was the condition there? Believe. Be perfect? No. Believe. *(Rom.4:5) **... His faith is reckoned for righteousness.*** Do you believe Jesus took

away your sins? Then that faith is accounted as righteousness. We see here that Jesus put the responsibility upon us to receive the benefits of His Kingdom, but it's not just for healing. We're looking at a principle for healing, but it's true for every other benefit, too. The Lord is not a respecter of persons; anything that He has promised to you is yours. The whole problem is not, "Is it the <u>will</u> of God?" Some people are so adamant about, "Is it the will of God to heal me?" or "Is it the will of God to provide my needs?" etc. That's not the problem. **(Heb.4:2) For indeed we have had good tidings** (the Good News) **preached unto us, even as also they: but the word of hearing did not profit them, because it was not united by faith with them that heard.** We are responsible to take the promise that God has spoken and mix our faith with it, so that it comes into the physical realm. Our responsibility is to bring the Kingdom by our faith. **(Mat.6:10) Thy kingdom come. Thy will be done, as in heaven, so on earth.** The Lord has already spoken the promise. He has already spoken the end from the beginning. **(Isa.46:10) <u>Declaring the end from the beginning</u>, and from ancient times things that are not [yet] done; saying, My counsel shall stand, and I will do all my pleasure.** The very fact that God spoke it means it's going to come to pass for anyone who believes.

Another statement that seems to be a hang-up that you hear in a lot of churches and from a lot of people who never get anything from God is, "If it be Thy will." The people who use this phrase to ask God for things never receive anything from God because they never exercise faith. There's no faith involved in this, "If it be Thy will." They point at these verses: **(Luk.22:41) And he was parted from them about a stone's cast; and he kneeled down and prayed, (42) saying, Father, <u>if thou be willing</u>, remove this cup from me: nevertheless not my will, but thine.** Well, let me ask you, did the Father remove the cup of going to the cross from Jesus? No, He didn't, did He? And Jesus was willing to accept that cup. The cup of the curse of all mankind came upon Jesus on that cross. He accepted it when He said, "If it be Thy will." It wasn't the Father's will for that cup to pass away and Jesus received it. Now what's the difference between this and what the Father has promised? Jesus said, **(Joh.12:27) Now is my soul troubled; and what shall I say? Father, save me from this hour. <u>But for this cause came I unto this hour</u>.** In other words, "For this reason have I come into the world." He knew that He had come here for that purpose and God fulfilled that purpose. So what's wrong with using this verse on something like healing, where we have a clear definition of what the will of God is and a clear demonstration of what the will of God is? What's the difference here? The difference is, if you use this verse when you have so much evidence of what the will of God is, then that's just unbelief. That means you're not adding faith to the promise and the promise will not become effectual until you add faith to it. Your unbelief is negative faith; it's faith in the curse, faith in the devil and it's misusing this verse.

Nowhere in Scripture did Jesus, or anyone else, use this verse for healing, except possibly for one man, so let's look at that instance. **(Mat.8:1) And when he was come** *down from the mountain, great multitudes followed him. (2) And behold, there came to him a leper and worshipped him, saying, Lord, <u>if thou wilt</u>, thou canst make me clean.* Notice that it wasn't Jesus Who believed this, nor did He use this, but He did correct the man. *(3) And he stretched forth his hand, and touched him, saying, <u>I will</u>; be thou made clean.* That's about as close as anyone ever came in attempting to use this and Jesus corrected his thinking immediately. It's like what happened with Jairus (Mark 5:21-43). When the people came from his house to try to convince him that his daughter was dead, Jesus jumped in very quickly. *(Mar.5:36) But Jesus, not heeding the word spoken, saith unto the ruler of the synagogue, <u>Fear not</u>, <u>only believe</u>.* He didn't want Jairus to depart from the faith because of what he saw or what he heard. Here He wanted this man's mind to be renewed. "I will." Why was it always the will of God to heal His people in all these verses that we've looked at? It's because God made an agreement and He's not a liar and He gave these benefits to <u>all believers</u>. Notice it's <u>all believers</u>. We enter in to the benefits of the Covenant through faith. We abide in Christ, Who is the beneficiary of the benefits of Abraham's blessing; we abide in Him by faith. When we believe the promise, we're in Him. When we don't believe the promise, we're out of Him. *(1Co.6:18) ... Every sin that a man doeth is without the body.... (1Jn.3:5) ... And in him is no sin.* So we abide in Him by faith. We believe the promise. We accept that He took away our sin. We accept that He took away the penalty for our sin, which is sickness and the curse and so on. We accept this. Now we're in Christ. We're in heavenly places in Christ Jesus where we can receive every spiritual blessing (Ephesians 1:3).

Well, you can see that we don't have an example of anyone using this verse in the Scriptures for something that's clearly delineated as a benefit of the Kingdom. As a matter of fact, you could pray the same thing to the Father yourself: "Lord, if it is Your will, let this cup pass from me." Do you know what He's going to say? "It's not My will; I'm not going to do that." Do you know why? Jesus was going to the cross. Can we pray to get out of our cross? If you do, you'll pray to get out of the Kingdom because with no cross, there's no crown. Jesus said, *(Luk.14:27) Whosoever doth not bear his own cross, and come after me, cannot be my disciple.* There's no prayer, there's no faith that will work against your own cross. We came here to die to self, although that doesn't necessarily mean physical death, but to die to self. *(Luk.17:33) Whosoever shall seek to gain his life shall lose it: but <u>whosoever shall lose</u> [his life] <u>shall preserve it</u>.* So, "Lord, if it is Your will, let this cup pass from me," is a good prayer for that situation, but I can already tell you what God's answer is. Your flesh might want to get out of the cross. Don't believe that Jesus didn't have flesh; He had flesh and He was *(Heb.4:15) in all points tempted like as [we are, yet] without sin.* He had the flesh of David (Romans 1:3) but the Son of God lived inside. Jesus was tempted to want to get out of His cross, and we are, too, but we have to have the same determination He had that the will of the Lord be done. If you said that concerning the benefits of the Kingdom and you believe the will of the Lord is exactly what the Bible says, that by the stripes of Jesus you were healed, then, once again, you need to <u>agree</u> that you were healed. That's the only thing that causes you to be reconciled to God, exchanged to God. Jesus bore your curse and your sickness, and He gave you His health, He gave you His blessings. "Faith is reckoned for righteousness," and so when we agree with the Word of God that the Lord has given us this blessing, it's ours.

The Bible says that we should be, ***(2Co.10:5) casting down imaginations, and every high thing that is exalted against the knowledge of God, and bringing every thought into captivity to the obedience of Christ***. Well, these statements that people make of, "Sometimes God heals and sometimes He doesn't," or that we should pray, "If it be Thy will, Lord," instead of finding out what God's will is and exercising faith, are just vain imaginations. They confuse us and cause us to lose faith in what God says He's already done. Are the promises of God negotiable? What does the Bible say? ***(2Co.1:19) For the Son of God, Jesus Christ, who was preached among you by us, [even] by me and Silvanus and Timothy, was not yea and nay, but in him is yea.*** Jesus gave them a promise and it wasn't "maybe"; it wasn't "His will" or "yes and no" that counted. It was their benefit. ***(Mat.15:24) But he answered and said, I was not sent but unto the lost sheep of the house of Israel.*** Why? Because by Covenant they had a right to the benefits of God. Even as stiff-necked as they were, Jesus was not "yes and no" or "yea and nay" but in Him is "<u>yes</u>"! ***(2Co.1:20) For how many soever be the promises of God, in him is the yea.*** Is God going to say "no"? That's something else that people like to say. "Sometimes God says 'no.'" Well, we call that being a liar when once He said "yes" and when once He has made a promise, and then turns around and says, "no." We call that a liar and God can't lie. ***(2Co.1:20) For how many soever be the promises of God, in him is the yea:*** (and it says here very plainly) ***wherefore also <u>through him</u> is the <u>Amen</u>, unto the glory of God through us.*** That means "also through Him" there will be the fulfillment of it. "Amen" means "so be it." So we know that God's promises are always "yes." He's not going to ever change His mind. Our heart may condemn us and we might not have boldness toward God to be able to receive the things that have been promised, but that's our fault and not the Lord's fault.

We should always make things right between us and God, so we can have the benefits of the Kingdom. ***(1Jn.3:21) Beloved, if our heart condemn us not, we have boldness toward God; (22) and <u>whatsoever we ask</u> we receive of him, because we keep his commandments and do the things that are pleasing in his sight.*** And again, we're not talking about perfect people. The promises of God are all "yes"; He's not going to say, "no." The promises are all "yes" and God is consistent about all of His promises. Healing is just an example I'm using here, but we've been studying the real Good News and the promises cover every area of your life! We need to cast down these vain imaginations because God is consistent. We need to have the renewed mind of Christ, so that we will speak in agreement with the Word of God. We need to diligently study the Word of God because the emphasis that the Lord has on healing all and delivering all is found all through the New Testament. His disciples also believed that God's people should always have the benefits of the Kingdom. We need to endure in our faith, holding fast to these promises. *(Heb.6:11) And we desire that each one of you may show the <u>same diligence unto the fulness of hope even to the end</u>: (12) that ye <u>be not sluggish</u>, but <u>imitators of them</u> who through <u>faith and patience inherit the promises</u>.* So we see that we want to believe the promise until we inherit the promise through faith and patience.

We want to be diligent to endure the trial of our faith, believing what is ours and not letting the devil steal it from us. Jesus said, *(Mat.10:22) But he that endureth to the end, the same shall be saved.* And I especially like, *(Heb.10:23) Let us <u>hold fast</u> the confession of our hope that it waver not; <u>for he is faithful that promised</u>*. Now what is your hope? The Biblical Greek word for "hope" means "a firm expectation." We need to hold fast the firm expectation of what the Bible says about our situation. We need to do this all the way to the end without wavering. *(Heb.10:36) For ye have need of patience, that, having done the will of God, ye may receive the promise.* The Lord is saying that there will be trials of your faith, even though you boldly confess your hope before God, and you're going to need patience to go through this trial of your faith. *(Heb.10:38) But my righteous one shall live by faith: And if he shrink back, my soul hath no pleasure in him. But we are not of them that shrink back unto perdition* (or "destruction")*; (39) but of them that have <u>faith unto the saving of the soul</u>. (11:1) Now faith is assurance* ("the giving substance to") *of [things] hoped for, a conviction of things not seen.* Hold fast to your substance, saints! God bless you.

CHAPTER SIX

The Curse Is Taken Away!

We've been having a good time studying the real Good News. It's just so encouraging to know what the Lord has really done for us. I'm saddened that so many people don't understand what the Lord has already accomplished for us and that we just enter into this freely by faith. It's already accomplished but so many people are spending so much of their time trying to convince God to do something that the Bible says He's already done, when we should just rejoice and give thanks!

Let's start here by taking a deeper look at the curse. ***(Gal.3:13) Christ redeemed us from the curse of the law, having become a curse for us; for it is written, Cursed is every one that hangeth on a tree: (14) that upon the Gentiles might come the blessing of Abraham in Christ Jesus; that we might receive the promise of the Spirit through faith.*** Now I'm sure some people think that this is a prosperity-type Word, but I believe in the prosperity that is spoken of in the Scriptures. ***(3Jn.2) Beloved, I pray that in all things thou mayest prosper and be in health, even as thy soul prospereth.*** "That thou mayest prosper (Greek: *euodoo*, meaning "to help on the road" or "to succeed in reaching") ... even as thy soul prospereth." Prosperity in the Kingdom of God is not the same thing as prosperity in the world. To prosper in the Kingdom of God is to grow up in Him and to be useful in everything that we do. It's not to be burdened down by the curse that's upon this world and upon everybody in this world, unless they begin to walk by faith. So we have to learn to walk by faith in order for the Lord Jesus to walk in us and do His works in us. We have to learn to walk by faith in order to live out from under this curse and that's not something that comes naturally to us; it's supernatural. We do know that the Lord is saying that God put our curse of the Law upon Jesus so that we might have the blessing; and the word "blessing" in the Scripture is the opposite of the word "cursing." We know that from Deuteronomy 28 where the blessings and the cursings are pronounced. ***(Deu.28:1) And it shall come to pass, if thou shalt <u>hearken</u> diligently unto the voice of the Lord thy God, <u>to observe to do all his commandments</u> which I command thee this day, that the Lord thy God will set thee on high above all the nations of the earth: (2) and all these blessings shall come upon thee, and overtake thee, if thou shalt hearken unto the voice of the Lord thy God.*** Recently, we've been seeing a real rash of people who claim to be hearing the voice of the Lord and I ran into people like that when I was young in the Lord. They heard the "voice" of the "Lord" very clearly alright, but the only thing wrong was that what the "voice" would say to them was <u>not according to His commandments</u>.

We have to be careful about what voice we hear and especially so when we begin to deny the Word of the Lord for some other voice because we know it's another "Jesus" and a false gospel. The Hebrew word for "hearken" means to "hear and obey." "Hear and obey

... the voice of the Lord thy God, to observe to do all his commandments." That sounds pretty heavy, doesn't it? How can you have the blessings of God, unless you observe to do all of His commandments? Well, I'm going to point out a couple of things to you here. Do you know the difference between the Law and grace? Do you know that all of God's commandments in the Old Testament mean one thing, but all of His commandments in the New Testament mean quite another thing? That's one reason it's called the Good News. Did you know that the Israelites were held accountable to <u>every</u> commandment in the Old Testament? Even if they were ignorant, it made no difference whatsoever. If they found out later that they had disobeyed one, they had to pay the penalty because they had offended God. ***(Lev.5:17) And if any one sin, and do <u>any</u> of the things which the Lord hath commanded not to be done*** (That's a lot when you're talking about the Old Testament. Nobody can remember all those rules and regulations.); ***though he knew it not*** (Ignorance was no excuse under the Law.), ***yet is he guilty, and shall bear his iniquity.*** In other words, the curse was upon them. ***(Lev.5:18) And he shall bring a ram without blemish out of the flock, according to thy estimation, for a trespass-offering, unto the priest; and the priest shall make atonement for him concerning the thing wherein he erred unwittingly and knew it not, and he shall be forgiven. (19) It is a trespass-offering: he is certainly guilty before the Lord.***

One of the complaints that Paul had about the Old Covenant was that it couldn't make perfect (Hebrews 10:1-4). It forgave sins, looking forward to the time of Christ and His sacrifice, but it could not take away sins. We know in the New Testament that is exactly why Christ came; He was ***(Joh.1:29) the Lamb of God, that taketh away the sin of the world!*** In other words, He came to take away the very nature of sin itself, something the Law could not do. Here we see that ignorance was no excuse under the Law. You were guilty if you broke one of these commandments, even if you didn't know where it was or what it was. I suppose that most people probably didn't even bother to try to figure out which one it was; they just had their sacrifice every year for a blood atonement. The word "atonement" means "to cover." Their sacrifice was a blood covering for their sin. We know that we don't have to go get a ram out of the flock; that's already been solved for us. The Lord Jesus has already been our sacrifice and has already borne our curse. The great thing about the New Testament is that God raises us up the same way we raise our children. We consider that it's normal for a child in innocency and in ignorance to do foolish things. In the New Testament, God does the same thing. He considers your maturity and the Word that's in your heart, but the Law didn't do that. So when it says in Deuteronomy that you had to keep all of His commandments in order to have these blessings of God, that was almost impossible, unless you made the sacrifice as an atonement or "covering." Well, guess what? We have that covering consistently by faith because our Ram has already been sacrificed.

The reason it's called the "Good News" in the New Testament is because of the way God deals with us in sin. ***(Jas.4:17) To him therefore that knoweth to do good,*** *and doeth it not, to him it is sin.* Why is that? It's because the difference between the Old Testament and the New Testament is that when God promised the New Covenant, He said, *(Heb.8:10) I will put my laws into their mind, And on their heart also will I write them.* So what He held us accountable to in the Old Covenant was the Law that was written on the pages, but in the New Testament, what He holds us accountable to is the Law that is written upon our heart. In other words, we're held accountable to any transgression against our knowledge of God, but the deeds that we're ignorant of, like those finer points of the Law, have a covering. I'm certainly not saying that outward immorality is ignorance. Everybody knows that fornication, lying and stealing are sins. I hear so many saints say that they're living under some kind of curse. They've come to God, they've accepted that Jesus became accursed for them, but the thought that the devil always brings into their mind is, "Maybe this healing isn't being manifested in my life because of something I don't know about." Or, "Maybe this deliverance isn't being manifested in my life because of something I did that I've forgotten." But now we see that's not what God is holding against you, according to what the Scriptures say. You can probably just push that aside and start dealing with your faith because that's probably what's causing you to not be able to partake of these benefits. That's why we're stressing this so much. You have to have faith to partake of these benefits. *(Rom.4:15) For the law worketh wrath; but <u>where there is no law</u>, <u>neither is there transgression</u>.* Wow! That's a really good deal and nothing like what we just read in Leviticus 5, is it? *(16) For this cause [it is] of faith, that [it may be] according to grace; to the end that the promise may be sure to all the seed; not to that only which is of the law, but to that also which is of the faith of Abraham, who is the father of us all.* Paul said if a person is seeking to be justified by the Law, they have to keep the whole Law (Galatians 3:10). That's impossible, so it's better to be justified by faith in Jesus Christ, which gives us this New Testament blood covering.

(Rom.4:4) Now to him that worketh, the reward is not reckoned as of grace, but as of debt. In other words, this is a person who tries by their works to be perfect enough before God to be accepted, healed or delivered, but you can't be good enough to receive these blessings from God, not under grace. You are trying to make God owe you something and it won't happen because you can never keep all of the Law. *(Rom.4:5) But to him that <u>worketh not</u>, but believeth on him that justifieth the <u>ungodly</u>....* He's speaking of all of our ignorance of God's ways and His teachings. We're just like a little child. We're ignorant, small, immature and God reckons that to us. He does not impute iniquity to someone who is not grown into righteousness yet. *(Rom.4:5) But to him that worketh not, but believeth on him that justifieth the ungodly, his faith is reckoned for righteousness. (6) Even as David also pronounceth blessing upon the man, unto whom God <u>reckoneth righteousness apart from</u> (his) <u>works</u>....* God reckons us to be His righteous, pure sons by <u>faith</u>. We accept the fact that, *(Gal.2:20) I have been crucified with Christ; and it is no longer I that live, but Christ living in me....* And we, *(Rom.6:11)*

Even so reckon ye also yourselves to be dead unto sin, but alive unto God in Christ Jesus. And that faith causes God to impute righteousness to us. *(Rom.4:7) [Saying,] Blessed are they whose iniquities are forgiven, And whose sins are <u>covered</u>. (8) Blessed is the man to whom the Lord <u>will not reckon sin</u>.* So you see the really good deal we have in the New Covenant is that "where there is no law, neither is there transgression."

We can read that again here: *(Rom.5:13) For until the law sin was in the world....* What does that mean? Well, transgression against the will of God was in the world before the Law. *(Rom.5:13) For until the law sin was in the world; but sin is not imputed when there is no law.* In the New Testament, when there is no law written in our mind or in our heart, sin is not reckoned unto us. So no matter what age we are in the Lord, we can walk perfectly before our God because at every age, we are ignorant of some things that would be pleasing to God. In the New Testament, our heavenly Father is a Father Who looks upon His child and is pleased, even when they are stumbling in their feeble attempts to get up and walk. And sometimes we fail a little less this time than last time. That's a normal relationship, whereas the Law was not at all a normal relationship. Sometimes children condemn themselves because they stumble and can't get upright, but the Lord doesn't want you to condemn yourself. He wants you to have faith for something better. He wants you to have faith in Him to, *(Php.2:13) Work in you both to will and to work, for his good pleasure*. That's what salvation in the New Testament is all about.

The Lord doesn't want you to condemn yourself because you cannot have condemnation and faith at the same time, and faith *(1Jn.5:4) Is the victory that hath overcome the world*. The Lord knows that you have to have faith to overcome. He does not want you to waste time with condemnation when it's not necessary. Condemnation does come from willful disobedience, but not for ignorance or for failure. *(Rom.7:7) What shall we say then? Is the law sin? <u>God forbid</u>. Howbeit, I had not known sin, except through the law....* So the Law is the Law, whether it is on the pages of the Old Testament for them, or upon our mind and upon our heart for us. Through the commandments of God in the New Testament, we come to a revelation of what sin is and now we start being held accountable for it. *(Rom.7:7) What shall we say then? Is the law sin? God forbid. Howbeit, I had not known sin, except through the law: for I had not known coveting, except the law had said, Thou shalt not covet: (8) but sin, finding occasion, wrought in me through the commandment all manner of coveting....* So the Word of God caused us to be sinners. You may say, "Hey! I have a solution for that; I just won't read the Book!" But if you do that, you won't bear fruit. If you remember, Jesus was the Sower Who sowed the seed, or *sperma*, and the *sperma* was the Word of God. And the Word of God goes into the hearts of men and it brings forth fruit, 30-, 60- and 100-fold. *(Mar.4:14) The sower soweth the word. (15) And these are they by the way side, where the word is sown; and when they have heard, straightway cometh Satan, and taketh away the* *word which hath been sown in them. (16) And these in like manner are they that are sown upon the rocky places, who, when they have heard the word, straightway receive it with joy; (17) and they have no root in themselves, but endure for a while; then, when tribulation or persecution ariseth because of the word, straightway they stumble. (18) And others are they that are sown among the thorns; these are they that have heard the word, (19) and the cares of the world, and the deceitfulness of riches, and the lusts of other things entering in, choke the word, and it becometh unfruitful. (20) And those are they that were sown upon the good ground; such as hear the word, and accept it, and bear fruit, thirtyfold, and sixtyfold, and a hundredfold.* Notice, that last group was the only one out of the four He spoke about that entered the Kingdom.

So you're really in a "Catch-22." You <u>have</u> to read the Word of God, but God will work in you to do of His good pleasure, so long as you walk by faith in what Jesus did (Philippians 2:13). You are reckoned righteous because of your faith in what Jesus did for you (Romans 4:5). And since you're reckoned righteous, you're now eligible for the benefits of God. He gives you the gift to walk in His steps and as you walk by faith, God fulfills it in you. Some people try to turn this around by condemning you into obedience, but that's the Law. They're trying to put the cart before the horse. You're not going to be justified in that way. It's the other way around. *(Rom.7:8) ... For apart from the law sin [is] dead. (9) And I was alive apart from the law once: but when the commandment came, sin revived, and I died.* We have no choice but to go on and study the Word, and put the Word in our heart so that we bear fruit. At the same time, we're becoming more responsible, just as any child becomes more responsible as they're growing up. We attribute more responsibility to them, just as the Father does to us. But it's also a growth of grace because the more knowledge you get, the more grace you receive. *(Eph.2:8) For by grace have ye been saved <u>through faith</u>; and that not of yourselves, [it is] the gift of God; (9) not of works, that no man should glory.* The more knowledge you have, the more grace you can receive because grace is based on <u>faith in the knowledge that you have</u>, so it's not as though you're going to get in more trouble if you read the Word of God more. Of course, if you read it and you're a hearer of the Word and not a doer of the Word, you will be judged. *(Jas.1:22) But be ye doers of the word, and not hearers only, deluding your own selves.* You will be proving yourself not to be who you proclaim to be and that is a Christian.

(Gal.3:13) Christ redeemed us from the curse of the law, having become a curse for us; for it is written, Cursed is every on that hangeth on a tree. "Having become a curse for us." Does that cover everybody? Does it cover everything? Does it cover every sin? No. Remember that in the New Testament, it has to do with your knowledge. *(Jas.4:17) To him therefore that knoweth to do good, and doeth it not, to him it is sin.* So the Bible says, *(Heb.10:26) For if we sin wilfully after that we have received the knowledge of the truth, there remaineth no*

more a sacrifice for sins, (27) but a certain fearful expectation of judgment, and a fierceness of fire which shall devour the adversaries. In other words, if you premeditatedly sin with your will, the sacrifice of Jesus in Galatians 3:13 to deliver you from the curse does not apply to you. The atonement does not cover that type of sin. The atonement covers ignorance and failure, like the child who falls due to not rightly applying the Word because of not having wisdom, but it does not cover willful disobedience. I wish all Christians understood this. I hear people say, "It's all under the blood," but that's not true. Jesus did not pay the penalty for that kind of sin and if Jesus did not pay the penalty, guess what? That means you have to pay the penalty. A great example is when David sinned with Bath-sheba. Yes, he repented when he was faced with Nathan the prophet. *(2Sa.12:7) And Nathan said to David, Thou art the man … (9) Wherefore hast thou despised the word of the Lord, to do that which is evil in his sight? (10) Now therefore <u>the sword shall never depart from thy house</u>, because thou hast despised me….* Yes, he repented. *(13) And David said unto Nathan, I have sinned against the Lord. And Nathan said unto David, the Lord also hath put away thy sin; thou shalt not die*, but now he was going to have to pay the penalty with this heavy judgment on his house for his willful disobedience.

Some of you out there have also committed willful disobedience in ignorance and have brought a judgment upon yourself or upon your house, and you're thinking, "I just have to put up with it. There's nothing that I can do." But there is an end to every judgment and the only means to the end is through faith in what Jesus accomplished at the cross. When you repent, the Lord will forgive your sin, but He's going to spank you. "For if we sin wilfully … there remaineth no more a sacrifice for sins." In other words, Jesus did not bear the penalty, so you have to bear it. "But a certain fearful expectation of judgment," so you should fear God. You need to cease immediately because you're bringing a curse on your life, since you know what the Bible says and you're willfully disobeying it. However, some things aren't willful (Romans 7:15-25). *(Rom.7:19) For the good which I would I do not: but the evil which I would not, that I practise.* Paul was saying, "The evil that <u>I will not</u> to do, that I do." He cried out to the Lord to deliver him from these impulsive, or compulsive, behaviors. *(Rom.7:20) But if what I would not, that I do, it is no more I that do it, but sin which dwelleth in me.* He's lamenting here, "I am failing God! But since my will is to do good, it's not me doing it; it's the sin that lives in me." So he had a will to please God, but his flesh was warring against the spirit-man who willed to please God. *(Rom.7:24) Wretched man that I am! who will deliver me out of the body of this death? (25) <u>I thank God through Jesus Christ</u> our Lord. So then I of myself with the mind, indeed, serve the law of God; but with the flesh the law of sin.* So Paul received the revelation that the Lord Jesus has delivered us from the power of the flesh and the curse ruling over us. At first, he didn't know what to do because he wanted to please God, but he was failing; his flesh was overruling him. And God said, "It's not you doing it, since you don't will to do it. It's that flesh. You and I will get together against this flesh; it's <u>our</u> enemy now."

Well, how do you cooperate with God in this war against the flesh? You give God faith. ***(6:11) Even so reckon ye also yourselves to be dead unto sin but alive unto God in Christ Jesus.*** You consider it done and God joins with you in your war against the flesh. Of course, you could waste an awful lot of time in condemnation in a situation like that. Condemnation is right and it is just for willful disobedience because you are sinning with the will. But condemnation is not right for merely failing or for presumptuous sin. Presumptuous sins presume to take authority over you when they don't have it since the cross; we're not under sin anymore. That's the Great News! If you want to be delivered from the curse, Jesus already delivered us from the curse (Galatians 3:13), but not when the curse comes because the sin is from willful disobedience. So with that in mind, let's look at Deuteronomy 28 again. Basically, what it says is that if we hearken diligently to the voice of the Lord and keep His commandments, which in the New Testament He has written upon our hearts and upon our minds, He will bless us. We'll be blessed in our health, provision, protection, family, and on and on; everything is included in the blessings.

The very opposite is the list of cursings and I'd like to point out some things to you about this. ***(Deu.28:15) But it shall come to pass, if thou <u>wilt not</u> hearken unto the voice of the Lord thy God, <u>to observe to do all his commandments</u> and his statutes which I command thee this day, that all these curses shall come upon thee, and overtake thee.*** You are only held accountable for the light that you have. ***(1Jn.1:7) But <u>if we walk in the light</u>, as he is in the light, we have fellowship one with another, and the blood of Jesus his Son <u>cleanseth us from all sin</u>.*** Walking in the light is walking in the knowledge of what we know of God's commandments about righteousness and sin, that we have written upon our mind and on our heart. If we walk in that, He said, "The blood of Jesus his Son cleanseth us from all sin." That's an awesome deal, folks! When we walk by faith, we're not under these curses. ***(Pro.4:18) But the path of the righteous is as the dawning light, That shineth more and more unto the perfect day.*** In other words, we're walking in more and more light, until it's midday and the sun is straight overhead and there are no shadows left. There's nothing but sunlight, so we're walking in pure light. It doesn't start out that way. There are some shadows behind us when the sun starts coming up, but as we walk in the light that God gives us, God puts more light in front of us. And as we take one step at a time in the light we do have, we have a <u>path</u> to walk down; otherwise, we're condemned for all of the light, instead of just the light we have in front of us. That's the wonderful thing about the New Testament.

(Deu.28:15) But it shall come to pass, if thou <u>wilt not</u> hearken unto the voice of the Lord thy God, <u>to observe to do all his commandments</u> and his statutes which I command thee this day, that all these curses shall come upon thee, and overtake thee. (16) Cursed shalt thou be in the city, and cursed shalt thou be in the field. (17) Cursed shall be thy basket and thy

kneading-trough. (Deu.28:18) Cursed shall be the fruit of thy body (meaning your children)*, and the fruit of thy ground* (meaning your crops, your income and provision)*, the increase of thy cattle, and the young of thy flock. (19) Cursed shalt thou be when thou comest in, and cursed shalt thou be when thou goest out.* In other words, everywhere we go, there's going to be a curse. And here's something that most Christians don't believe: *(Deu.28:20)* <u>*The Lord will send upon thee cursing, discomfiture, and rebuke, in all that thou puttest thy hand unto to do, until thou be destroyed, and until thou*</u> <u>perish quickly</u>*; because of the evil of thy doings, whereby thou hast forsaken me.* The Lord will send the curse. There's a lot of prosperity teaching nowadays that says everything good comes from God and everything bad comes from the devil, but we know that a parent sometimes has to use something bad to motivate a child to do right. They will take a switch and chasten a child in order to give them a reason to turn away from their sins and to do right. *(Psa.111:10) The fear of the Lord is the beginning of wisdom....* It's better to love the Lord and obey Him because of love, but the beginning of wisdom is not love -- it's fear. If you need fear to obey the Lord, then you'd better get the fear of the Lord! *(Pro.3:7) Fear the Lord, and depart from evil....* The Lord sends the curse. He wants to motivate us to turn us away from our sins and do what's right before the end of our pilgrimage or we'll fall off this earth into Hell. It's not the devil's will to turn us away from our sins. The devil just hates us but it's the Lord's love that sends chastening to His children. *(Heb.12:6) For whom the Lord loveth he chasteneth, And scourgeth every son whom he receiveth.* Some children are stubborn and need more whippings than others.

The truth is that the Lord ordained, spoke and sent the curse. *(Deu.28:21) The Lord will make the pestilence cleave unto thee, until he have consumed thee from off the land, whither thou goest in to possess it. (22) The Lord will smite thee with consumption, and with fever, and with inflammation, and with fiery heat, and with the sword, and with blasting, and with mildew; and they shall pursue thee until thou perish. (24) The Lord will make the rain of thy land powder and dust: from heaven shall it come down upon thee, until thou be destroyed. (25) The Lord will cause thee to be smitten before thine enemies; thou shalt go out one way against them, and shalt flee seven ways before them: and thou shalt be tossed to and from among all the kingdoms of the earth. (27) The Lord will smite thee with the boil of Egypt, and with the emerods, and with the scurvy, and with the itch, whereof thou canst not be healed. (28) The Lord will smite thee with madness, and with blindness, and with astonishment of heart. (35) The Lord will smite thee in the knees, and in the legs, with a sore boil, whereof thou canst not be healed, from the sole of thy foot unto the crown of thy head. (36) The Lord will bring thee, and thy king whom thou shalt set over thee, unto a nation that thou hast not known, thou nor thy fathers; and there shalt thou serve other gods, wood and stone.* He will bring you into bondage. *(Deu.28:37) And thou shalt become an astonishment, a proverb, and a byword, among all the peoples whither the Lord shall lead thee away.* And on and on goes the curse of God upon man to turn man from his sins. Some people might say that the devil is trying to turn man from his sins because the curse only comes from the devil, but we've just read that the curse doesn't come from the devil. The curse comes from God, through the devil.

(Deu.28:47) Because thou servedst not the Lord thy God with joyfulness, and with gladness of heart, by reason of the <u>abundance of all things</u> (The blessings are the abundance of all things.)*; (48) therefore shalt thou <u>serve thine enemies</u> that <u>the Lord shall send against thee</u>* (Wow! The Lord is sending our enemies.)*, in <u>hunger</u>, and in <u>thirst</u>, and in <u>nakedness</u>, and <u>in want of all things</u>....* Does that sound familiar? The Lord probably had not eaten for at least 24 hours before He was crucified. We know He said, "I thirst." We know He was naked. We know He was in want of all things. He became all of that on the cross for us, so that we could have these blessings, but if we walk in willful disobedience and stubborn rebellion, we cannot avoid these cursings. We can't avoid the curse that He is sending upon the world because He's sending it for the purpose of turning us from our sins. If you're thinking, "Oh, no; the Lord would not do such a thing," the Bible says that the Lord *(Eph.1:11) worketh all things after the counsel of his will.* What does "all" leave out? Only one mind wrote the Bible and there's not another perfectly free will anywhere but God's, or else these types and shadows wouldn't be so perfectly fulfilled in the New Testament. If you want a free will, you have to have His will in you. *(Php.2:13) For it is God who worketh in you both to will and to work, for his good pleasure.* Otherwise, you are bound in sin and "shapen in iniquity" (KJV) and you don't have a free will. *(Psa.51:5) Behold, I was brought forth in iniquity; And in sin did my mother conceive me.* God is not trusting in the devil to raise His children. God hasn't fallen off the throne; He's in control, even of the devil.

Job is a good example. It was the Lord Who pointed out Job to the devil. *(Job1:8) And the Lord said unto Satan, Hast thou considered my servant Job? for there is none like him in the earth, <u>a perfect and an upright man</u>, one that feareth God, and turneth away from evil.* A "perfect and an upright man"? Well, if you read the rest of the Book of Job, you wouldn't believe that, so why is God calling him a perfect and upright man? It's because He *(Rom.4:17) calleth the things that are not, as though they were.* God lives by faith. That's His nature. He sees the end from the beginning and He declares the end from the beginning. *(Isa.46:10) Declaring the end from the beginning, and from ancient times things that are not [yet] done; saying, My counsel shall stand, and I will do all my pleasure.* We come into agreement with His Words, which speak the end from the beginning, and we find the supernatural power to bring us there. So here God is speaking by faith about Job. Then the devil said, *(Job1:10) Hast not thou made a hedge* *about him, and about his house, and about all that he hath on every side?* (That certainly sounds as if the devil can't get to Job without the permission of God.) *thou hast blessed the work of his hands, and his substance is increased in the land. (Job 1:11) But put forth thy hand now, and touch all that he hath, and he will renounce thee to thy face. (12) And the Lord said unto Satan, Behold, all that he hath is in thy power....* The word translated as "power" in this verse is literally "hand." The devil said, "Put forth thy hand now," and here we have the Lord putting Job in the devil's hand. *(Job 1:12) And the Lord said unto Satan, Behold, all that he hath is in thy power; only upon himself put not forth thy hand. So Satan went forth from the presence of the Lord.*

And what did Satan do? *(Job 1:13) And it fell on a day when his sons and his daughters were eating and drinking wine in their eldest brother's house, (14) that there came a messenger unto Job, and said, The oxen were plowing, and the asses feeding beside them; (15) and the Sabeans fell upon them, and took them away: yea, they have slain the servants with the edge of the sword; and I only am escaped alone to tell thee. (16) While he was yet speaking, there came also another, and said, The fire of God is fallen from heaven, and hath burned up the sheep and the servants, and consumed them; and I only am escaped alone to tell thee. (17) While he was yet speaking, there came also another, and said, The Chaldeans made three bands, and fell upon the camels, and have taken them away, yea, and slain the servants with the edge of the sword; and I only am escaped alone to tell thee. (18) While he was yet speaking, there came also another, and said, Thy sons and thy daughters were eating and drinking wine in their eldest brother's house; (19) and, behold, there came a great wind from the wilderness, and smote the four corners of the house, and it fell upon the young men, and they are dead; and I only am escaped alone to tell thee.* And what did Job say about this? Did he give any credit to the devil? No, Job believed in a sovereign God. Scripture never attributes sovereignty to the devil. *(Job 1:21) And he said, Naked came I out of my mother's womb, and naked shall I return thither: Jehovah gave, and Jehovah hath taken away; blessed be the name of Jehovah. (22) In all this Job sinned not, nor charged God foolishly.* God knew there would be people today who believe, "Uh-uh. That wasn't the Lord; that was the devil." So He had this written in the Bible just for those people.

And when God permitted the devil to afflict the body of Job with boils, what did Job say about that? *(Job. 2:10) ... What? shall we receive good at the hand of God, and shall we not receive evil? In all this did not Job sin with his lips.* "Shall we receive good at the hand of God and not receive evil?" When you use a switch to spank your child in order to cause them to repent and turn away from evil, is that good or is that evil? Or is that using evil to do good? That's the whole point: God uses the devil. The devil knows he has a legal right to afflict those who are in willful rebellion and the Lord gave him that legal right for their good. The Lord makes *(Rom.8:28) **all things work together for good, [even] to them that are called according to [his] purpose***. Even the negative things, the chastenings, the curses, everything in this world is working for our good. If you say, "Job must have been a perfect man because God said he was a perfect man," one look at chapter 32 will prove that Job was not a perfect man. However, he was perfect in the eyes of faith of God because that was what God believed Job was going to be! *(Job32:1) **So these three men ceased to answer Job, because <u>he was righteous in his own eyes</u>***. The three friends of Job couldn't find out what was wrong, although they made a lot of guesses.

But the Lord Himself, Who wrote the book of Job, says, "Because he was righteous in his own eyes." This wasn't their opinion; this was God's opinion. *(Job32:2) **Then was kindled the wrath of Elihu*** (Elihu was not one of the three; he was the fourth.) ***the son of Barachel the Buzite, of the family of Ram: against Job was his wrath kindled, because <u>he justified himself rather than God</u>***. It doesn't sound like Job was doing such a good job of being perfect right there, does it? Do you suppose that was one of the reasons all these judgments came upon him? I tell you, if you don't hearken to the voice of the Lord and you justify yourself instead as you continue walking on in your stubbornness, the curse will come upon you. It will come upon you to motivate you to have a reason to turn to God and repent. That's what the curse is good for. *(Job32:3) **Also against his three friends was his wrath kindled, because <u>they had found no answer</u>, <u>and yet had condemned Job</u>***. It's very interesting that God's wrath was kindled against these three friends, too, but not in one place did God ever speak negatively of Elihu, who for six chapters corrected Job for his self-righteousness. And then Elihu is followed-up for four more chapters by God, Who agrees with him. God shows Job how ignorant he is and how he shouldn't be speaking the self-righteous judgments he was.

There are many people today who are living under a curse and if they come to the repentance and faith that Job came to, they'll come out from under that curse. "Hearken unto the voice" is repentance and faith is believing what He said. "Hearken" is changing your mind and saying, "Okay, God, You're right." You cannot "hearken," you cannot "hear and obey," without believing what He said. The only way to the blessings of God is repentance and faith. Now Job was doing a pretty bad job of that, but God brought him to repentance. *(Job.42:6) **Wherefore I abhor [myself], And repent in dust and ashes***. Job realized that he said some things that were too high for him to say in his ignorance and God restored Job and blessed him abundantly. And what God spoke about Job in the beginning was in the process of coming to pass; that is, "a perfect and upright man." God says the same thing about us. *(Heb.10:14) **For by one offering he hath perfected for ever them that are sanctified***. We were perfected at the cross. Our sins were taken away and we were given the nature of Jesus Christ. God is speaking the end from the beginning. Now we have to prove whether we are one of those elect about whom God is speaking. *(Mat.22:14) **For many are called, but few chosen***. "Chosen" is the word "elect."

Many are called but they won't come. They're stubborn and rebellious. They think that it's "all under the blood." They justify themselves when they read the Word of God, instead of humbly submitting and saying, "Yes, Lord, I was wrong." And so they live under the curse and they wonder, "Why?" Well, it's because they are willfully disobedient. You can make it easier on yourself if you decide to believe and to speak what God says in the New Testament. Don't justify yourself because you'll continue to live under the curse and never come out from under it. The Gospel, the Good News, *(Rom.1:16) is the power of God unto salvation to every one that believeth.* We repent and we say, "Yes, Lord! What You say is what I believe. You are right. I've been doing this wrong and I don't accept it. I renounce my sin and choose righteousness. I humbly submit to You. I thank You that this was taken away at the cross. I am not going to do it anymore. I know it is by Your grace and by Your power, and not by my works, that I would depart from evil. I believe that I have been delivered at the cross. I believe that Jesus was the Lamb of God Who took away my sin." The Lord took away the very nature of sin that causes you to sin in the first place, not just the action of sin. He nailed it to the cross. *(Gal.2:20) I have been crucified with Christ* (That is the old "I.")*; and it is no longer I that live, but Christ liveth in me* (Who is that? That is the new "I," Who is Christ in you.)*: and that [life] which I now live in the flesh I live in faith, [the faith] which is in the Son of God, who loved me, and gave himself up for me.* So we walk by faith and we accept the fact that we don't live, but Christ lives in us. Every time we read the Scriptures, we have to be in repentance mode, which means we have to be willing to change our mind because how else are we able to come out from under the curse, unless we are "hearkening and obeying"?

When we walk in failure or ignorance, we have a blood covering because of what Jesus did at the cross, but if we're stubborn and self-willed, the Bible calls it sinning with a "high hand." *(Num.15:30) But the soul that doeth aught <u>with a high hand</u>, whether he be home-born or a sojourner, the same blasphemeth the Lord; and <u>that soul shall be cut off</u> from among his people.* Ultimately, the end of walking in willful disobedience is destruction. There is "a certain fearful expectation of judgment" or, in other words, you are surely guaranteed to get a whipping if you're walking in willful rebellion against the Lord. *(Jas.4:17) To him therefore that knoweth to do good, and doeth it not, to him it is sin.* So you know it's sin, but you're going to do it anyway, thinking, "Oh, He'll forgive me; I'll just confess it." Yes, if you confess it and you mean it, He will forgive you, just as He forgave David, but the sword did not depart from David's house. He paid a terrible penalty. Jesus said, *(Mat.18:34) And his lord was wroth, and delivered him to the tormentors, till <u>he</u> should pay all that was due. (35) So shall also my heavenly Father do unto you, if ye forgive not every one his brother from your hearts.* In other words, "If you don't forgive your fellow servant, My father will turn you over to the tormenters until <u>you</u> pay what was due." *(Mat.5:25) Agree with thine adversary quickly, while thou* *art with him in the way; lest haply the adversary deliver thee to the judge, and the judge deliver thee to the officer, and thou be cast into prison. (26) Verily I say unto thee, Thou shalt by no means come out thence, till <u>thou</u> have paid the last farthing.* You're supposed to make things right with your fellow servant while you are with him in the way; otherwise, you are turned over to the judge and cast into prison until you pay what is due.

We don't want to pay the penalty for our sins, folks. We want it to be covered by the blood, but if you're in willful and stubborn rebellion, or if you're twisting the Scriptures and perverting them to justify yourself, then you're going to have some Job experiences. We need to be softened up through chastening in order to motivate us to humbly submit to God, even though sometimes it feels like we're going under one of those mallets they call a "meat tenderizer." We will make it so much easier on ourselves, if we just repent and say, "Yes, Lord." We will make it so much easier, if we will hear and obey. We will make it so much easier, if we will believe that the Lord Jesus has taken away that curse at the cross and we don't have to walk under it anymore. The curse is everything negative that has ever happened to mankind because of rebelling against the Word and the Lord took the penalty for all of that, but multitudes of God's people are still living under a curse. They've prayed and asked God to deliver them. They know that the Bible says, *(Mar.11:24) All things whatsoever ye pray and ask for, believe that ye receive them, and ye shall have them*, but it won't come to pass because some of them are in stubborn rebellion against God. In other cases, people are tempted by the devil into believing that there's something they're doing (or have done) that they don't know about and it's bringing this curse upon them, and therefore they can't be delivered. Well, we've just discovered that's a lie, too, because it's what you know that you're held accountable to.

The devil will do anything to rob your faith so that you can't accept that Jesus bore your curse. He'll tell you all kinds of things and we have to study the Word to find out what our rights are. The devil is a crooked lawyer. He perverts the Word of God to deceive us so that we'll give up our rights and blessings because *(Mat.18:18) Whatsoever ye shall bind on earth shall be bound in heaven; and whatsoever ye shall loose on earth shall be loosed in heaven*. The devil knows that all authority has been given to us. When Jesus sent out His disciples, He said, *(Mat.28:18) All authority hath been given unto me in heaven and on earth. (19) Go ye therefore....* And how did He send them? *(Joh.20:21) As the Father hath sent me, even so send I you.* He sent them with authority. We have to watch out for those loopholes. We have to close all those "But this!" and "But that!" that the devil brings into our minds, so that we can stand firmly upon the Word and accept deliverance from the curse. Jesus already paid the penalty and the Father does not want us to pay the penalty His Son died for. He certainly does not want us to bear it because it does not honor Him and it does not honor the death of His Son. He's on our side against the old man, against the sin. He wants us to humbly submit to His Word so that we can be delivered from the curse. Take your authority, saints! God bless you.

CHAPTER SEVEN

Endurance!

    We've been studying the real Good News and it's very encouraging to know what the Lord has done for us as we learn to enter into discipleship and walk as He walked. Praise be to God! We discovered that Deuteronomy 28 lists both the blessings and cursings that will come upon us, based on our obedience to the Word. ***(Deu.28:1) And it shall come to pass, if thou shalt <u>hearken diligently</u> unto the voice of the Lord thy God, to observe to do all his commandments which I command thee this day, that the Lord thy God will set thee on high above all the nations of the earth: (2) and all these blessings shall come upon thee, and overtake thee, if thou shalt hearken unto the voice of the Lord thy God.*** And, of course, the opposite is true: ***(15) But it shall come to pass, if thou <u>wilt not hearken</u> unto the voice of the Lord thy God, to observe to do all his commandments and his statues which I command thee this day, that all these curses shall come upon thee, and overtake thee.*** The key here is, "if thou shalt hearken diligently ... to do all his commandments." "Hearken" means to "hear and obey." When we first come to the Lord, we have a problem with "hearing" the right "voices." Jesus said, ***(Joh.10:27) My sheep hear my voice, and I know them, and they follow me.*** This is how God knows His sheep. Many times, we have a problem of hearing the voice of men or the voice of the devil, but the Bible makes us familiar with our Master's voice because He is the Word. And as we become familiar with the Word, we become familiar with His voice. As He said, ***(Joh.10:3) ... And the sheep hear his voice: and he calleth his own sheep by name, and leadeth them out***, because they know His voice. I pray that would be your heart and your desire.

    The Bible has a very important point in regard to hearing the voice of the Lord: ***(2Co.10:4) (For the weapons of <u>our warfare</u> are <u>not of the flesh</u>, but mighty before God to the casting down of strongholds), (5) casting down imaginations, and every high thing that is exalted against the knowledge of God, and bringing every thought into captivity to the obedience of Christ.*** So this is what our warfare is; it's bringing every thought into captivity and obedience to Christ. We do that by casting down every imagination and every other voice that comes into our mind, trying to impersonate the Lord Jesus Christ. We do that by casting down our own reasonings that lead us astray, even though our reason rails against us and even though well-meaning Christians are used of the devil against us, to put thoughts that are very reasonable to our flesh into our mind. We have to learn to ***(Pro.3:5) Trust in the Lord with all thy heart, And lean not upon thine own understanding.*** We have to learn to cast down everything that is contrary to His Word and, if we're doing that, then we're casting down those strongholds of the devil in our mind that keep us captive. ***(2Co.4:4) In whom the god of this world hath <u>blinded the minds of</u>***

__the unbelieving__, that the light of the gospel of the glory of Christ, who is the image of God, should not dawn [upon them]. Not everybody believes the words of the Lord Jesus Christ. They don't hearken to the voice of the Shepherd and don't come out from under the curse and into the blessings of God. We have this warfare to fight of casting down all the imaginations that seem so reasonable and coming to the Lord to learn to be a disciple of His and humbly submit to Him.

I've heard people say many times, "Well, I believed God, but I didn't get my healing. I know I had faith, yet God did not answer." We hear that all the time and yet we know for a fact that our Lord made some very positive statements to the contrary, so we know what men say __is false__. *(Mar.11:24) Therefore I say unto you, All things whatsoever ye pray and ask for, believe that ye received them, and ye shall have them.* This is very clear that what you believe, you receive. *(Mat.21:22) And all things, whatsoever ye shall ask in prayer, believing, ye shall receive.* Now we know our Lord and He's not a liar. And no one who is a Christian would believe that He is a liar, but people will make statements totally contrary to the Word of God, like, "I believed but I didn't receive." It's pretty obvious that a lot of people don't know what faith is! But if you were at least humble to the Lord, you would have to admit that, "The fault would have to be with me," because Jesus said, "When you believe, you receive," and, "All things whatsoever, you will receive." So we have to admit with the Lord Jesus that the Word of God is true and not permit ourselves to accept something in our mind that is just a lie. People who say those things don't realize the devil is using them to cast down other people's faith. They don't get into the Word enough to renew their minds in order for them to speak only the Word of God. *(1Pe.4:11) If any man speaketh, [Let him speak] as it were oracles of God.* And I especially like, *(Rom.3:4) ... Let God be found true, but every man a liar; as it is written, That thou mightest be justified in thy words, And mightest prevail when thou comest into judgment.* We know that the judgment of this world is the curse and we want to prevail every time we come under the judgment of curse, no matter what the cause.

Whether it comes as a trial to build our faith, whether it comes as a chastening, or whatever, we want to prevail when we come under the curse. And God says that there's only one way to prevail: we have to "Let God be found true, but every man a liar." "Man" in the Scriptures is used negatively because, obviously, God is not birthing men. God is birthing sons of God, the spiritual, born-again man on the inside who is being created in the likeness of Jesus Christ. This is the man who speaks the words and believes the thoughts of the Lord Jesus Christ. This is the righteous man before God, the Israelite. The old Egyptian, the old man who died in the Red Sea, is the __man__ who speaks things contrary to God. This is the __man__ who has "reasonable" thoughts that are contrary to God. So He says, "Let God be found true, but every man a liar; as it is written, That thou mightest be justified in thy words." It's very important that we are justified in our words. "Justified" means being "accounted righteous," and without being accounted righteous, we are not able to partake of the benefits of the Kingdom. *(Jas.5:16) Confess therefore your sins one to another ... that ye may be healed.* We have to be accounted righteous from God's side. We have to renounce the old man. We have to renounce the old life and repent of it, if we want to have the benefits of the Kingdom of God. In every case, when you want to prevail in the midst of judgment, you need to be justified in your words.

Jesus said, *(Mat.12:37) For by thy words thou shalt be justified, and by thy words thou shalt be condemned.* Wow! I wish everybody would think about that for a minute; it lets you know just how important what we say is. If we claim to be Christians but we let that old man speak, he can bring us into an awful lot of judgment and wrath because we are not justified. We have to be careful that we are agreeing with God's Word and trusting in what He says, so that we can be justified in our words. *(Rom.5:1) Being therefore justified by faith....* So we see here that it's not just words; it's words that agree with God. It is words of faith because *(Rom.1:17) the righteous shall live by faith.* When our words agree with God's Words and we confess our faith in every situation, then we're coming into a renewed mind, the mind of Jesus Christ, and we are being transformed by that renewed mind. We are coming into His image and we're prevailing when we come into judgment. *(Rom.5:1) Being therefore justified by faith, we have peace with God through our Lord Jesus Christ; (2) through whom also we have had our access by faith into this grace wherein we stand....* Now that's very clear. Our words of faith and actions of faith give us access to the grace and favor of God. We stand in the favor, benefits and blessings all because our faith gives us access.

So how does God judge your faith? In the Scriptures, we are told many times that it is God *(Rom.2:6) Who will render to every man according to his works.* Your works are proof of your faith because *(Jas.2:17) faith, if it have not works, is dead in itself.* And one of your major works is the tongue. Jesus Himself said, *(Mat.12:37) For by thy words thou shalt be justified, and by thy words thou shalt be condemned.* So we see that words of faith give us access to the unmerited favor of God. *(Rom.5:2) Through whom also we have had our access by faith into this grace wherein we stand; and let us* (In the original, it reads, "let us rejoice," not "we rejoice.") *rejoice in hope of the glory of God. (3) And not only so, but let us also rejoice in our tribulations: knowing that tribulation worketh stedfastness....* The word here for "stedfastness" is also translated as "patience." Many times we don't want to wait and trust in God or we don't want to endure the struggle or the pain in order to see the manifestation. This is an "instant gratification" society. We want to believe and then see something happen immediately. But if we stand in faith, we have access to His grace, His grace enables us to stand and we eventually receive the thing we are believing for. *(Rom.5:3) And not only so, but let us also rejoice in our tribulations: knowing that tribulation worketh patience; (4) and patience, approvedness....* The word "approvedness" is a word for "character." What character is that? It's the character of the Lord Jesus Christ. We are called to come into His Image. *(Rom.8:29) For whom he foreknew, he also foreordained [to be]*

conformed to the image of his Son, that he might be the firstborn among many brethren. If we want His character, we have to walk patiently in our faith.

Don't give up! Most people do and it's sad that this is the major problem among Christians. They don't keep the Word of God before their eyes and the Word of God in their thoughts; they do not pray to God for mercy to write this Word upon their hearts. They are just useless in their faith. We're called to be warriors for the Lord Jesus Christ and warriors for our brethren around us who need the benefits of God's Kingdom. In order to do that, we have to be like Jesus and His disciples were and that is a warrior through faith. We have to be someone who walks justified before God because they speak faith in agreement with the Word of God.

(Rom.5:4) And patience, approvedness; and approvedness, hope: (5) and hope putteth not to shame; because <u>the love of God hath been shed abroad in our hearts</u> through the Holy Spirit which was given unto us. How do we know we have the love of God in our hearts? According to this, those who are patient in their faith have hope and that hope does not put them to shame. Some people think that "the love of God hath been shed abroad in our hearts" means "the love that God has for people," but I think it's talking primarily about "the love that <u>we have</u> for God." That's because those people who are only living to be seen of men are not interested in walking by faith. They don't see the reason or benefit of it, since they can get their needs met by other means, but what pleases God is ***(Rom.1:17) the righteous shall live from faith***. A person who wants to please God walks by faith because we know ***(Heb.11:6) without faith it is impossible to be well-pleasing [unto him]***. So the people who want to please God are the people who love God. These are the people who are struggling to be patient in their faith. They are justified because it is important to them to endure the trial of their faith, not to show off to anyone else. We have a proof about the meaning of "the love of God" in verse 5 because it's also found here: ***(Jas.1:12) Blessed is the man that <u>endureth temptation</u>....*** See, we're back to Deuteronomy 28, where the one who is blessed is the one who "hearkens unto" the voice of the Lord, the one who hears and acts upon the voice of the Lord. The people of faith hear the voice and they act upon it, they speak in agreement with it and their feet prove it. ***(Jas.1:12) Blessed is the man that endureth temptation; for when he hath been <u>approved</u>*** (There's that "approvedness" again; we endure temptation in order to be approved of the Lord.), ***he shall receive the crown of life, which [the Lord] promised <u>to them that love him</u>.*** Notice that the people who endure temptation are the people who love Him and want to be well-pleasing to Him. They want to be called "righteous" because they walk by faith and faith is submitting humbly to the Word of God, agreeing with the Word of God, speaking the Word of God. They are learning to walk as sons of God in the Kingdom of God.

(Jas.1:2) Count it all joy, my brethren, when ye fall into manifold temptations (or "trials"); ***(3) knowing that the proving of your faith worketh <u>patience</u>. (4) And let patience*** (which is so well-pleasing to God) ***have [its] perfect***

work, that ye may be perfect and entire, lacking in nothing. The person who patiently endures the trial of their faith lacks nothing. Most people will not endure to the end. They endure to somewhere down the trial and then they decide that God's not quite right about this, that He really hasn't answered their prayers. They decide that they can't believe that they have received because their eyes tell them the truth and that God's Word has not told them the truth. They're proving themselves to be unbelievers. They have an "evil heart of unbelief" (Hebrews 3:12) which we all war against. The person who is patient in their faith will be perfect in their entirety, lacking nothing, so you see how important it is to endure the trial of our faith.

(Jas.1:5) But if any of you <u>lacketh</u> wisdom, let him ask of God, who giveth to all liberally and upbraideth not; and it shall be given him. (6) But let him <u>ask in faith</u>, <u>nothing doubting</u>: for he that doubteth is like the surge of the sea driven by the wind and tossed. (7) For let not that man think that <u>he shall receive anything of the Lord; (8) a doubleminded man, unstable in all his ways</u>. You can feel the Lord's feelings about people who are double-minded, who cannot ask without doubting. Now we all have thoughts that come <u>through</u> our mind that are of doubt, although those are not necessarily <u>our</u> thoughts, but if we give into them and act upon them, <u>then we have doubted</u>. ***(Heb.10:36) For ye have need of <u>patience</u>, that, having done the will of God, ye <u>may receive the promise</u>.*** Everyone starts out asking God and believing, but they don't all endure in their patience to receive the promise. The people who have learned patience are people who have lived miracles. They see answers from God and they awe everybody with their faith. It's not necessarily that their faith is any stronger, but it's that they don't give in to doubts or unbelief. They cast these imaginations down when they come into their mind. They're well-pleasing to God and accounted righteous because they are patient in their faith and they will receive the reward. ***(Heb.6:11) And we desire that each one of you may show the same diligence unto the <u>fulness of hope</u>*** (The word "hope" here means "firm expectation.") ***even to the end: (12) that ye be not sluggish, but imitators of them who through <u>faith and patience inherit the promises</u>.*** Obviously, if God speaks so much about this, it must be what is dear to His heart because it is His joy to see His people receive the benefits of the Kingdom.

I've had many trials of my faith that I can share with others and I know that the Lord brought me through these things so that I, myself, would learn patience and faith. Some of these were enduring trials that took a while and a lot of wrestling to receive answers. They were a warfare of casting down reasonings, imaginations, dreams and revelations. One trial was an experience many years ago with cancer. Now I didn't go to a doctor, so I can't prove exactly what this problem was from men's words, but there came a time when I was receiving a lot of pain and I was passing a lot of blood. When I went to the Lord about it, the word "cancer" came to my mind. Well, I cast that down. Though the Lord might be telling me that this is what I am wrestling with, the Lord also told me, "by whose stripes ye were healed," and so I cast those thoughts down. I didn't accept those thoughts, even though that might be the manifest problem that I was wrestling with and I'm sure it was. That's because shortly after this started, I traveled across town to a Christian bookstore that I didn't usually visit, since it was a lot farther away than the closest one. I knew some sisters there who were faithful servants of the Lord and sometimes I went over there just to give them the business and say hello. Of course, I hadn't told anybody what the Lord had revealed to me, not even my wife.

That day, as I came in the door, these two sisters had their eyes on me and I knew they had something to say, since they immediately walked over to me. They told me that they'd been in prayer for various ministers they knew and that they were praying for me because the Lord had spoken to them very plainly that I was having a battle against the spirit of cancer but that I would win. I told them this was a confirmation of what the Lord spoke to me and spent a few minutes sharing a good word of faith with them. Then I thanked them very much and left, but on my way home, I did something that I wouldn't have done if I'd thought about it. I said to the Lord, "Lord, when I get home, I am going to ask You to give me a Word out of the Bible, as You have done so many times for me, concerning this situation." But I'd already been living by faith for many years and I already knew what the Bible had to say about this situation. It was like Balaam in Numbers 22:19 asking the Lord a second time for His opinion because he wanted to hear something else from the Lord, but Balaam already had a Word; he just wasn't sticking to it. Anyway, when I got home, I flipped my Bible open by random and I put my finger down on, *(Isa.38:1) In those days was Hezekiah sick unto death. And Isaiah the prophet the son of Amoz came to him, and said unto him, Thus saith the Lord, Set thy house in order; for thou shalt die, and not live.* My finger came down exactly in the middle of the phrase, "thou shalt die, and not live." So when I read that, I thought, "Whoa! Look at that!" There's only one other place in all of the Bible that has this phrase and that's in 2 Kings 20 where the same story is told.

I tell you the honest truth, from the moment that I received this revelation of what the problem was, I never feared one time because it's not that important to me to stay on this earth. I'll be so happy when my job is done here and I can go and be with the Lord. I don't fear death. I think of it the way Jesus spoke of it. *(Joh.5:24) Verily, verily, I say unto you, He that heareth my word, and believeth him that sent me, hath eternal life, and cometh not into judgment, but hath passed out of death into life.* Fear never really tried to attack me concerning this, but I knew it was true and I knew that I was having to wrestle with the spirit of cancer. From shortly after I became a Christian, I had been exercising my faith in the Lord as my healer and He had always done it faithfully. I learned that I had to fight a battle to take my benefit from the devil because, *(Mat.11:12) ... the kingdom of heaven suffereth violence, and men of violence take it by force.* It's a battle to take our benefits away from the devil because he tries to resist us with his words, his minions and the people around us, sometimes even Christians. And the devil uses our flesh, too. *(Rom.3:4) ... let God be found true, but every man be a liar....* So the old man in you can be a liar when he speaks to you.

    Well, when I saw the Isaiah text, I thought on it for a few minutes and then I said to the Lord, "Lord, this is not according to Your covenant that You made with me and I believe that You don't want me to accept this." And I didn't accept it because the Word of God says that "by whose stripes ye were healed," and it was obvious that Jesus healed everyone who came to Him by faith. I'm convinced that many people have left before their time because they're not totally confirmed in their thinking that the Lord Jesus is a consistent Savior, including Savior of our body. He desires to heal every one of us. We don't have to die of diseases; that's the curse and Galatians 3:13 says that Jesus bore the curse. You can just leave this life and people do just leave this life and not die of curses. Before I continue, I want to point out that the Lord gave Hezekiah 15 more years because that's a part of this story I'm sharing here. ***(Isa.38:2) Then Hezekiah turned his face to the wall, and prayed unto Jehovah, (3) and said, Remember now, O Jehovah, I beseech thee, how I have walked before thee in truth and with a perfect heart, and have done that which is good in thy sight. And Hezekiah wept sore. (4) Then came the word of Jehovah to Isaiah, saying, (5) Go, and say to Hezekiah, Thus saith Jehovah, the God of David thy father, I have heard thy prayer, I have seen thy tears: behold, <u>I will add unto thy days fifteen years</u>.***

    "Thou shalt die, and not live." I said, "Lord, I don't accept that, so I am asking You to give me something that is according to Your covenant." Understand, if even the Lord God speaks to you anything contrary to the covenant, you are not to accept it. You say, "What?! David, what are you talking about?" ***(Psa.11:5) The Lord trieth the righteous....*** God tried father Abraham, did He not? And we're spiritual sons of Abraham, only if we walk by faith (Galatians 3:7). He tried Abraham and He tries us in the same way. God is going to see if we will depart from His Word or if we will be steadfast and patient, and endure whatever comes our way, even if we think it is a Word from the Lord. It's awesome how many very specific answers I've gotten from the Lord in this way, so I was confident I was getting an answer from the Lord when He gave me, "Thou shalt die, and not live." And after I'd thought on it for just a minute, my training supported me in helping me to realize that I was not to give in to this. This was a trial. The Lord was trying me and I was to hold steadfast to the Word of God. We know what the Bible says about healing and you should be totally convinced by now that God wants you healed. It's just as consistent as salvation of the soul. So I told the Lord, "I don't accept that word and I don't think it pleases You for me to accept that. So I am asking You to give me another word." Then I flipped my Bible open and put my finger down right in the middle of the phrase, ***(Psa.118:17) I shall not die, but live***, the exact opposite of the first word I received! That text is in only one place in the Bible, too. I said, "Lord, I accept that one. I accept it because it is what You have taught me the Word of the Lord is," and I know that I was accounted righteous for being steadfast in my faith and holding on to what the Word of God says. I also know that I could have died if I wanted to. I could have gone on to be with the Lord because I failed the trial.

Many people do fail and go on to be with the Lord or miss the Lord one way or the other because they fail in these trials. **_(Mat.9:29) ... According to your faith be it done unto you._** Jesus did not overrule their unbelief. He said, **_(Mat.8:13) ... As thou hast believed, [so] be it done unto thee...._** He did not exercise His faith over their faith. He exercised His faith when they agreed with His faith and He's still doing that with us. We need to walk in agreement with the Lord. The Lord has spoken to me enough over the years of the things that I still want to see happen on this earth. I still want to see people saved and healed. I still want to see the Man-child's ministry through the latter rain. I don't want to miss the great thing that God is getting ready to do on this earth and I think there will be plenty of time to rest with the Lord afterward.

Well, as I continued to endure the trial of my faith, I had one person pray for me. I had to take a trip to Louisiana to visit family and stopped in to visit an old friend. While I was there, I just had him pray over me for this healing. I didn't receive a manifest answer at that time. I didn't feel anything different, either, but you're not supposed to walk by feelings. God is trying to cause us to walk by faith in what the Word says and be stable, instead of going up and down with the circumstances that we see. The feelings and emotions that we have are stirred up because of the thoughts that we think. If you don't humble yourself to the Word, you'll become a victim to your own emotions. They will conquer you and that's why you must cast them down. Thoughts can stir up emotions and emotions can get stirred up to where you just can't put that fire out. And so I endured that for a while longer, until the symptoms eventually went away and I accepted the full manifestation of my healing.

Then, 15 years later, although I did not realize it had been 15 years, I started to receive other symptoms. This time my heart was giving me pain and I knew I was having a cardiovascular problem because my whole right side was getting cold. It didn't have to be too cold outside and I would be cold on my right side. My circulation was having problems. I lead a pretty sedentary life. I do a lot of studying and I sit at a computer, so I don't get a lot of exercise. You know, the devil will start reasoning with you, telling you that you've caused this because of the way you live your life. He wants to tell you that you need to exercise, or do this and do that, to do all these things in the natural in order to get rid of your problem. I wasn't totally without exercise because I would get up and run or walk around a few blocks every once in a while and I really did not change anything when these symptoms appeared, but I knew that the devil was definitely threatening me with the end of my life through this circulatory problem. I lost a very good friend in the same way. His arteries all clogged-up and he died. But when this started happening, I called the devil's bluff. I just told the devil, "I don't accept this. This is not the Word of the Lord."

How I found out that it was 15 years later was that several people in our assembly had dreams I had died of a heart attack and some of these people were gifted by the Lord with very consistent, accurate dreams. When my wife was sharing a couple of the dreams with me, she said, "It's been 15 years since you had the problem with that cancer." It didn't register with her, but it immediately registered with me. I said, "15 years? God gave Hezekiah 15 years and that's the verse He gave me." I went to the Lord immediately and asked, "Lord, are You saying that the rest of that was true for me, too, that You were only giving me 15 more years, like Hezekiah?" And the Lord said in my spirit, "Yes, that's true," so I thought on that and I thought on these dreams. I said, "I didn't accept something contrary to Your Covenant last time and I don't believe that I am supposed to accept it contrary to Your covenant now, so I don't accept this either. I accept 'by whose stripes, ye were healed.' I accept only what the Word of God says." By the grace of God (I am not taking any credit), I was able to hold diligently to the Word of God and not be moved, even by what appeared to be words from God that I was going to die. Obviously, the first Word that I had received out of Isaiah 38 was true and the word given to Hezekiah was very prophetic, and now God was using the rest of that on me. Again it was, "The Lord trieth the righteous." Like He tried Abraham, He was trying me. So I cast down all these things, even these dreams, thoughts and revelations. I cast them all down. I accepted nothing but what the Word of God says.

I didn't receive the answer immediately. As a matter of fact, the devil was speaking to me that I was going to drop any minute with a heart attack because my arteries were all clogged-up and, of course, the symptoms were telling me that was true. I would still get out and walk, and it came to me one day while I was walking that, "Devil, I am not accepting this. I am a healthy man and healthy men can run." So I ran and I would run and run, just to call the devil's bluff. The devil would tell me, "You're going to fall on the side of the road and you're not going to make it home." Sometimes I would feel that was true and I didn't have the stamina that I had when I was younger, but I ran anyway because **(Jas.2:17) faith, if it have not works, is dead in itself.** If we believe the promise, we will act on it. We are "justified by faith" (Romans 3:20). James proclaimed that actions prove faith, saying, **(Jas.2:18) I by my works will show thee [my] faith**. We are justified, or "accounted righteous," by words of faith and/or corresponding actions of faith. Understand that I am not talking about legalism here. Legalism is very dangerous. We are not accounted righteous by the works of the Law. <u>When we get our works ahead of our faith</u>, it's like putting the cart ahead of the horse and <u>that's legalism</u>. Some people hear words of faith and they think, "Okay, in order for me to get healed, I have to throw away my medicine," or act contrary to the physical laws of nature, but <u>they're</u> trying to pay for something that has already been paid for.

The correct attitude is the reverse of this: "Since I'm already healed, I can continue to live in the presence of God. I can continue to walk in the ways of someone who is healed." It's like the testimony I shared with you previously, when I realized, "If I am healed, I can pick up this log." This was true faith and my broken arm was healed when I picked up that log. That was one of those instant manifestations but for these two manifestations, I had to endure a trial of my faith. I had to fight the devil and come out victorious. Beware of legalism and peer-pressure. Don't do anything in order to be esteemed by men and don't try to put your faith on someone else. Our attitude should be like that of Jesus when He said, "According to your faith be it done unto you." He wasn't demanding that this person exercise their faith because He Himself had faith, so we should not do that, either. We should not demand people to act as though they had faith, when we're not sure that they do. This is how people get hurt because they would be seeking to be justified by works and not by faith, so we have to be very careful when dealing with other people in this regard.

Something else that we need to do consistently is, *(Jas.5:16) Confess therefore your sins one to another, and pray one for another, that ye may be healed....* Now we know that Jesus said, *(Mar.11:24) All things whatsoever ye pray and ask for, believe that ye received them, and ye shall have them*, and that's exactly right, but we also know that if our sins are against us, then we're not going to be bold toward God. *(1Jn.3:21) Beloved, if our heart condemn us not, we have boldness toward God; (22) and whatsoever we ask we receive of him, because we keep his commandments and do the things that are pleasing in his sight.* Confession is a way to get rid of your unbelief because your conscience is right with God. It's not that God wouldn't heal you. Did you notice in the Scriptures that Jesus healed every single one of those Jews who came to Him? They came to Him and He healed them because it was a benefit; Jesus called it "the children's bread" in Matthew 15:26. In cases where He wasn't sure if the people had faith, He tried to draw faith out of them, such as with the Syrophoenician woman and with the centurion. Jesus said things to make them speak words of faith because He knew that this person had to agree with Him. In His own hometown, *(Mat.13:58) ... He did not many mighty works there because of their unbelief*, so we know that Jesus didn't heal because of people's unbelief. Confessing our sins is very important. It's humbling before God and it's necessary in order to get rid of double-mindedness, which is caused by a conscience that's not right before God.

We don't know how much we suffer in our faith because of our conscience. *(Psa.32:1) Blessed is he whose transgression is forgiven, Whose sin is covered.* Here's that Deuteronomy 28 blessing again. *(2) Blessed is the man unto whom the Lord imputeth not iniquity, And in whose spirit there is no guile. (3) When I kept silence, my bones wasted away* (I don't know if they knew back then that a person's blood which, according to Leviticus 17:11, is "the life of the flesh," is created in your bones.) *Through my groaning all the day long. (Psa.32:4) For day and night thy hand was heavy upon me* (Notice it was God Who sent the curse in order to motivate man to repentance, as we saw in Deuteronomy 28.)*: My moisture was changed [as] with the drought of summer.*

(Psa.32:5) I acknowledged my sin unto thee, And mine iniquity did I not hide: I said, I will confess my transgressions unto the Lord; And thou forgavest the iniquity of my sin. (6) For this let every one that is godly pray unto thee in a time when thou mayest be found (Or, in other words, before it's

too late. Confessing your sin quickly will keep you out of a lot of the curse.)**: Surely when the great waters overflow they shall not reach unto him.** The waters, which represent the curse of the world, will not reach unto this person because he has confessed his sin and so he is accounted righteous and entitled to the benefits of the Kingdom. ***(1Jn.1:7) But if we walk in the light, as he is in the light, we have fellowship one with another, and the blood of Jesus his Son cleanseth us from all sin. (8) If we say that we have no sin, we deceive ourselves, and the truth is not in us. (9) If we confess our sins, he is faithful and righteous to forgive us our sins, and to cleanse us from all unrighteousness.*** Here is a person who has confessed his sin and is entitled to the benefits of the Kingdom.

Another favorite of mine concerning this is, ***(Psa.66:18) If I regard iniquity in my heart, The Lord will not hear.*** I'm surprised at how many people don't realize that self-justification is simply regarding iniquity in your heart. They're not being honest with themselves or with God about their sins and so they're bringing themselves under a curse. They don't admit what they're doing is wrong. Their heart is not bold and they cannot have faith toward God. They cannot endure in patience to see the manifestation and sometimes they don't even know why they don't have faith. ***(Pro.28:13) He that covereth his transgressions shall not prosper: But whoso confesseth and forsaketh them shall obtain mercy.*** Everything that the Lord does for us, folks, is mercy, but we don't always get mercy; sometimes we get justice. Justice will come upon those who will not be honest with God about their sins, so that they can have a conscience "washed with pure water" (Hebrews 10:22). Only when a person's conscience is clean can they exercise faith toward God for everything. We need to walk as faithful servants of the Lord, especially in the days to come, but we can't do that unless we're very honest with the Lord and His Word. ***(Rom.3:4) ... Yea, let God be found true, but every man a liar....*** That means, let even the flesh-man be a liar, but you speak what the Word says. Hear and obey His voice. Don't justify yourself but humbly submit to the Lord.

As we continue studying the real Good News, we'll see that the principles we've been looking at concerning healing also apply to every other benefit of the Kingdom because faith works in that way. We'll find out what it is to walk righteously and purely before the Lord. Many of God's people don't comprehend the absolute purity that God wants to put in us and the overcoming power that God has given us over sin. They don't realize nor understand that the Lord took away our sins. We have been totally delivered. ***(Heb.10:14) For by one offering he hath perfected for ever them that are sanctified.*** Instead, many people believe they're always going to be sinners and they're just saved by grace, but we're no longer sinners. We are saints. We are sanctified ones. The Lord gave us that gift and we should receive it by faith. We should just humbly submit to it. This is one of the keys to healing, too, and it gives you a clear conscience; it gives you a holy life. Obviously, coming into agreement with God is the way that we can walk with God. ***(Amo.3:3) Shall two walk together, except they have agreed?*** God bless you.

CHAPTER EIGHT

Forgiveness!

Well, brethren, we've talked about faith and about learning to abide in and hold fast to the Word. Now I'd like to look at something that I consider just as important. It's something that's washing over the world right now, something that will ultimately destroy the world as we know it and that something is unforgiveness. We studied in the previous chapter about confessing our sins. We learned how important it is to have a clear conscience before God, so that we can be bold before Him and so that we can have our prayers answered. In the days ahead, there's going to be nothing more important than being able to connect with God and having your prayers answered.

Jesus told us, ***(Mar.11:24) Therefore I say unto you, <u>All things whatsoever ye pray and ask for, believe that ye received them, and ye shall have them</u>.*** Now that's an awesome gift to be taking into the terrible times ahead. Most people would think, "Yes, if I had that kind of a gift to be able to believe and receive anything I needed, I would be pretty safe." Well, this is the true Word of God that we've been studying, folks, and the Lord is not going to back away from His promises. He has guaranteed them to us; however, He adds a condition to this that many people don't continue on to read and it's just as important as this verse: ***(Mar.11:25) And whensoever ye stand praying, <u>forgive</u>, if ye have aught against any one; that your Father also who is in heaven may forgive you your trespasses.*** Obviously, when we stand praying for "all things whatsoever," we need to be forgiven so that we're entitled to the benefits of the Kingdom, but we also need to forgive in order to be entitled to the benefits of the Kingdom. Jesus said, ***(Mat.9:5) For which is easier, to say, Thy sins are forgiven; or to say, Arise, and walk? (6) But that ye may know that the Son of man hath authority on earth to forgive sins (then saith he to the sick of the palsy), Arise, and take up thy bed, and go up unto thy house.*** In other words, when a person receives the answer to their prayer, when they are healed or delivered, this is a sign that God has forgiven them. That means we need to be forgiven in order to have the benefits of God.

Forgiveness is not hard to obtain from Him and we need the forgiveness of God in order to have the benefits of God. ***(1Jn.1:9) If we confess our sins, he is faithful and righteous to forgive us our sins, and to cleanse us from all unrighteousness.*** The Lord said, "I am going to prove to you that the Son of man has authority on earth to forgive sins," so He says, "Be healed" and, of course, the man is healed. The Lord is saying to us that this is proof that the Lord has forgiven. Therefore, if we want God's benefits, we should make real sure that we are forgiven. ***(Jas.5:16) Confess therefore your sins one to another, and pray one for another, that ye may be healed.... (1Jn.1:9) If we confess our sins, he is faithful and righteous to forgive us our sins, and to cleanse us from all unrighteousness.*** That puts you in right standing with God, so that you may receive the benefits of the Kingdom, no matter what they are, whether healing or anything else. We're nearing a time when we need to be in right standing with God because we're going to need the benefits of the Kingdom just to live through the things that are coming.

According to Jesus, we know that we have to forgive in order to be forgiven. ***(Mat.6:14) For if ye forgive men their trespasses, your heavenly Father will also forgive you. (15) But if ye forgive not men their trespasses, neither will your Father forgive your trespasses.*** We need our sins covered so that we can have all the benefits of grace in the New Testament. I believe that many people read over this, but they haven't really forgiven down in their hearts. Many times people go on for years and years living under the curse because they haven't forgiven others; they have "aught against their brother." Jesus told a parable to explain how we're delivered over to the curse because of our holding on to unforgiveness. The King, representing God, forgave his servant of a great debt, but then that servant went out and took his fellow servant by the throat and threatened him because of a much smaller debt. This greatly angered his lord. ***(Mat.18:32) Then his lord called him unto him, and saith to him, Thou wicked servant, I forgave thee all that debt, because thou besoughtest me: (33) shouldest not thou also have had mercy on thy fellow-servant, even as I had mercy on thee? (34) And his lord was wroth, and delivered him to the tormentors, till he should pay all that was due. (35) So shall also my heavenly Father do unto you, if ye forgive not every one his brother <u>from your hearts</u>.*** The key here is "from your hearts." Many people give lip-service of forgiveness to others while their actions prove that they do not forgive others. They're not turning the other cheek. They're not resisting evil and they go to war with their enemies, instead of loving and forgiving their enemies.

We as Christians are called to be "peculiar" (KJV) people. We're not called to join with the world in wars against the world because we have a "peculiar" Kingdom, the Kingdom of God, which has a different set of rules. The being "delivered over to the tormentors" is something that many, many Christians live under because they don't have a blood covering. They are not forgiven by God, since they themselves are unforgiving toward others. Their actions prove that. They may give lip-service to it but they meditate on their angers against other people. The Lord taught me years ago that sins come in "threes." You have a thought; the thought stirs up an emotion; then the emotion stirs up your actions. For instance, a very common thought could be unforgiveness. As you meditate on your unforgiveness of the wrongdoing that this person has done to you, your emotions are stirred up and you become angry. As you continue to think on these things and meditate on your anger, the next demon that's let in is wrath. So this initial thought gives way to actions and demons are let into our life in this way. If not demons, it doesn't make any difference because when we give in to evil spirits; we allow them to sow their seed in us and we become like them. Jesus spoke to the Pharisees as though they were sons of the devil. ***(Joh.8:44) Ye are of [your] father the devil, and the lusts of your fa-***

ther it is your will to do. He was a murderer from the beginning, and standeth not in the truth, because there is no truth in him. When he speaketh a lie, he speaketh of his own: for he is a liar, and the father thereof. They were sons of the devil because he had recreated his nature in them. They gave in to the thoughts he gave them, they came into agreement with him and they were recreated in his image. Although very religious, they were still sons of the devil.

Many people have told me, "David, I don't really know how to forgive from my heart" or "I just don't know if I've really done that." Well, I understand and I've thought on it, and I felt that the Lord has shown me that we are to make the <u>decision</u> to forgive. God is the only One Who can take the emotion out of us and we know that He has done that. Through our study of the real Good News, we understand that He has already solved this problem by taking away the nature of sin. ***(1Pe.2:24) Who his own self bare our sins in his body upon the tree....*** But first He wants this decision from us. We can't do anything about the emotions, other than, if you do not think on these things, the emotions aren't going to be stirred up. They're going to be starved, if you cast down imaginations that are contrary to the Word of God (2 Corinthians 10:5). They're going to be starved, if you cast down these illegal thoughts about unforgiveness toward other people. You can make the decision. God will cleanse you because you make that decision. ***(1Jn.1:7) But if we walk in the light, as he is in the light*** (the light of His Word), ***we have fellowship one with another, and the blood of Jesus his Son cleanseth us from all sin.*** That's a really good deal, folks! If you have for years wanted to experience <u>real</u> forgiveness down in your heart or "from" the heart, the first thing you have to do is refuse illegal thoughts -- thoughts that are contrary to the Word of God -- against a person. Since you are commanded to forgive, you make that decision. You decide, "Okay. I am not going to think this way. I cast down these imaginations that are against the Word of God. I bring every thought into subjection to Jesus Christ." When you do that, you're starving these emotions and you won't act in disagreement with the Word of God.

Let's look at Esau as one example of a man who had a root of bitterness. ***(Heb.12:14) Follow after peace with all men, and the sanctification*** (Or "holiness"; it's the same Greek word.) ***without which no man shall see the Lord.*** He tells us to follow after this sanctification, which means "separation from the world unto God," and that without this, you won't see the Lord. Many people are deceived because they think they'll see the Lord, but they're worldly, just like these Pharisees and Sadducees, who thought for sure that they knew the Lord. Even though they were sons of the devil, they still thought they would see Him. But Jesus said, "Ye are of your father the devil." Jesus told Nicodemus, a very religious man and probably the most righteous among the Pharisees because he recognized that Jesus was a righteous man, ***(Joh.3:3) ... Verily, verily, I say unto thee, Except one be born anew, he cannot see the kingdom of God.*** And Jesus told him, "You have to be <u>born from above</u> or you will never see the Kingdom." Being born "from above" is receiving the Word of God into your heart so that it begets you unto Jesus Christ. That's a continual process. You first receive a new spirit, which is what everybody calls "born again," but that's only a part of it. As you follow and submit to the born-again spirit and you let the Word of God put to death your old life and bring forth your new life, then your soul becomes begotten-again unto God. And, if you have been faithful in that, then you will have a born-again body. This is the process that Scripture teaches and "sanctification" is the process in your soul. ***(Heb.12:15) Looking carefully lest [there be] <u>any man that falleth short</u> of the grace of God; lest any root of bitterness springing up trouble [you,] and thereby the <u>many be defiled</u>.*** Notice he's saying that a root of bitterness would cause you to fall short of the grace of God. We don't want to come short of any of the grace of God because it sanctifies us in the first place. The grace of God brings healing, deliverance and provision. The grace of God brings all of the benefits of the Kingdom but, if we're not forgiven, we don't have grace. If we don't forgive, we don't have forgiveness. So a root of bitterness will cause us to fall short of the grace because, if you have unforgiveness, you will not have the grace of God.

He says the "root of bitterness springing up will trouble you and thereby the many be defiled." In what way does a root of bitterness defile many? ***(1Co.5:6) ... Know ye not that a little leaven leaveneth the whole lump?*** Just through your association with other people you sow seeds in their life. You leave an impression on them. You cause them to give in to the same temptations that you do. You are a temptation to them. ***(1Co.15:33) Be not deceived: Evil companionships corrupt good morals.*** You may think you can get around evil people and they won't rub off on you, but the Bible says, "<u>Be not deceived</u>: Evil companionships corrupt good morals." That's why the Bible says, ***(1Co.5:7) Purge out the old leaven, that ye may be a new lump....*** "Don't you know a little leaven leavens the whole lump?" If you have a root of bitterness, you're corrupting the people around you by sowing your thoughts into their life. The opposite is also true. If you're around a real Christian who sows seed in your life, they're sanctifying you, they're washing your feet, they're cleaning up your walk and separating you from this old, dirty world. But all a corrupt person can bring forth is corruption.

There's another way that a root of bitterness can defile a man. ***(Lev.17:11) For the life*** (or "soul"; it's the same word) ***of the flesh is in the blood.*** We pass on our nature to our children through the blood. The sins of the parents are passed to the children of the third and fourth generation. ***(Exo.20:5) ... For I, the Lord thy God am a jealous God, visiting the iniquity of the fathers upon the children, upon the children, upon the third and upon the fourth generation of them that hate me, (6) and showing lovingkindness unto thousands of them that love me and keep my commandments.*** Your life that you have walked in and corrupted is passed on to your children; you can't stop it. There's only one thing that can stop it and that is walking in a sanctified life so that you don't enter into anymore sin. Truly, we pass on our natural characteristics to our children but you don't have to continue to walk in more sin that's multiplied by your steps. A root of bitterness has been passed on from generation to generation in many families and it's all passed on by associations when other people do you wrong but you don't turn the other cheek, you don't resist not the evil (Matthew 5:39). Jesus told us, *(Mat.5:44) But I say unto you, Love your enemies, and pray for them that persecute you.*

So we see that many can be defiled when a root of bitterness that gets into one person is passed on. The root of bitterness can become a generational curse through a person's bloodline and it can also infect others with whom they associate. *(Heb.12:15) Looking carefully lest [there be] any man that falleth short of the grace of God; lest any root of bitterness springing up trouble [you,] and thereby the many be defiled; (16) lest [there be] any fornicator, or profane person, as Esau, who for one mess of meat sold his own birthright.* Esau, our example here, definitely had a root of bitterness. His mother didn't cater to him at all because he wasn't her favorite. Jacob was her favorite. And then his father Isaac gave away Esau's blessing to Jacob. Esau became bitter enough to want to kill his brother. *(Gen.27:41) And Esau hated Jacob because of the blessing wherewith his father blessed him: and Esau said in his heart, The days of mourning for my father are at hand; then will I slay my brother Jacob.* If Jacob had not left at his father's instigation, Esau might have done just that. Well, after years of Jacob being away from his brother, Esau managed to have some semblance of forgiveness and when Jacob came back, he told his brother that he was going to settle in the land of Esau with his sheep and cattle. But Jacob stopped short of there and I'm thinking he knew that absence makes the heart grow only temporarily fonder. I believe that Jacob understood that if he lived around his brother Esau for very long, that old demon would have risen up in him again, so Jacob decided to separate himself from Esau and I think it was a wise decision. We know that Esau's descendants are still walking in his steps today.

Ishmael is another good example. You probably know the story. God had prophesied to Abram and Sarai (this was before their names were changed) that Abram would have seed like the stars of heaven for multitude and that they would be blessed. So they waited for a time but then they got in the flesh and decided to help the Lord out. *(Gen.16:1) Now Sarai, Abram's wife, bare him no children: and she had a handmaid, an Egyptian, whose name was Hagar. (2) And Sarai said unto Abram, Behold now, Jehovah hath restrained me from bearing; go in, I pray thee, unto my handmaid; it may be that I shall obtain children by her. And Abram hearkened to the voice of Sarai. (3) And Sarai, Abram's wife, took Hagar the Egyptian, her handmaid, after Abram had dwelt ten years in the land of Canaan, and gave her to Abram her husband to be his wife.* What Sarai did to carry on the bloodline was common in those days, but as you might expect, when Hagar conceived, she was a little rebellious against her mistress. I'm sure Hagar considered herself to be the real wife of Abraham, but Sarai saw it differently and complained to Abram. *(Gen.16:5) And Sarai said unto Abram, My wrong be upon thee: I gave my handmaid into thy bosom; and when she saw that she had conceived, I was despised in her eyes: the Lord judge between me and thee. (6) But Abram said unto Sarai, Behold, thy maid is in thy hand; do to her that which is good in thine eyes. And Sarai dealt hardly with her, and she fled from her face.*

Basically, Hagar had bitterness toward Sarai and she fled into the wilderness, where the Word of the Lord came to her. *(Gen.16:7) And the angel of the Lord found her by a fountain of water in the wilderness, by the fountain in the way to Shur. (8) And he said, Hagar, Sarai's handmaid, whence camest thou? and whither goest thou? And she said, I am fleeing from the face of my mistress Sarai. (9) And the angel of the Lord said unto her, Return to thy mistress, and submit thyself under her hands. (10) And the angel of the Lord said unto her, I will greatly multiply thy seed, that it shall not be numbered for multitude.* That's very interesting because God had told Abram this and now God was saying this about Ishmael, or at least about Hagar's seed, which would be through Ishmael. There are many Arabs and Muslims who believe that Ishmael was the true promised seed and it could be because God spoke this to Hagar. As a matter of fact, God said it to Abraham again in the next chapter. *(Gen.17:20) And as for Ishmael, I have heard thee: behold, I have blessed him, and will make him fruitful, and will multiply him exceedingly; twelve princes shall he beget, and I will make him a great nation.* And so they replaced the promised seed of Isaac with Ishmael. There's just one problem with that. We know that the Scriptures have a perfect numeric pattern going through them and that the testimony that's written here is the correct testimony because every Hebrew letter has to be in its place to sustain the numeric pattern.

However, Hagar was bitter toward Sarah, and no doubt some of this bitterness got into her son Ishmael. In fact, she is told, *(Gen.16:12) And he shall be [as] a wild ass* (The KJV says "wild man" but the literal translation is "wild ass.") *among men; his hand [shall be] against every man, and every man's hand against him; and he shall dwell over against all his brethren.* What would have caused this to happen and for it to be fulfilled over almost the last 4,000 years? It's because "the life of the flesh is in the blood," so the sin is passed on from generation to generation and, of course, each generation adds to that sin. Man is degenerating more and more all the time, even to the point of becoming the most bitter, most unforgiving generation that does not mind destroying most of humanity, and some of that bitterness is due to this situation we're reading about right here. Millions of people can be killed merely by someone pushing a button. The only hope we have is Jesus Christ. As Christians, we are to "know no man after the flesh" (2 Corinthians 5:16). As Christians, we are forbidden to have respect of persons (James 2:1-9). A lot of Christians prefer the Jews over the Ishmaelites, but the Jews that they prefer, in most cases, are lost Jews. They don't know God, they're not born-again and they look with disrespect upon the name of Jesus. Remember that Jesus told one of the most respectful Jews, Nicodemus, "You must be born again or you will never see the Kingdom of God" (John 3:3). That's still true today. We are to know no man after the flesh. Let me tell you, a lost man is a lost man. In the New Covenant, it makes no difference what nationality he is. You're to preach the Gospel to one just as quickly as you would preach it to another. That's what the Scriptures command and yet many don't see it that way. They prefer the Jews but, **(Rom.9:27) ... If the number of the children of Israel be as the sand of the sea, it is the remnant that shall be saved.**

Well, what happened through his mother's experience all by itself would have caused bitterness to enter into Ishmael; however, there was more to come. **(Gen.17:24) And Abraham was ninety years old and nine, when he was circumcised in the flesh of his foreskin. (25) And Ishmael his son was thirteen years old, when he was circumcised in the flesh of his foreskin.** Many people think that Ishmael was a baby when Hagar was driven out of the camp, but the truth is he was an older teenager and he recognized Abraham as his father. In the next chapter, the angel of the Lord tells Abraham that when the season comes around, meaning another year, Sarah will have a son. Then we go to chapter 21 where we see that Abraham was 100 years old when his son Isaac was born and that would have made Ishmael 14 years old. **(Gen.21:8) And the child grew, and was weaned. And Abraham made a great feast on the day that Isaac was weaned.** So Ishmael could have been 16 years old, at a wild guess, but we're talking about a teenager who saw Abraham as his father. **(Gen.21:9) And Sarah saw the son of Hagar the Egyptian, whom she had borne unto Abraham, mocking.** Of course, Sarah was offended and she went to Abraham. **(Gen.21:10) Wherefore she said unto Abraham, Cast out this handmaid and her son. For the son of this handmaid shall not be heir with my son, even with Isaac. (11) And the thing was very grievous in Abraham's sight on account of his son.** Abraham was hurt about this and he went to the Lord. **(Gen.21:12) And God said unto Abraham, Let it not be grievous in thy sight because of the lad, and because of thy handmaid. In all that Sarah saith unto thee, hearken unto her voice. For in Isaac shall thy seed be called.** In other words, God was saying, "Yes. Cast out the handmaid and her son."

What did Ishmael feel? His father was casting him out! He wouldn't have been mocking, except he already had some feelings of rejection. Here this baby comes along and now suddenly he wasn't important anymore. "I'm not the son of the father." Suddenly Sarah's a little jealous and she is wanting Abraham to cast his son away. You can just imagine the bitterness and rejection that entered into his heart, not to mention what his mother experienced in this situation. If you and I were not prejudiced for the Jews and we read this not knowing, we might have said, "That really seems unjust to me." But, first of all, we need to bear in mind that God is the One Who told Abraham to do this. And I'd like to make another point: **(Joh.3:27) ... A man can receive nothing, except it have been given him from heaven.** Did you know that God has commanded everything that happens in your life? **(Rom.8:28) And we know that to them that love God all things work together for good, [even] to them that are called according to [his] purpose.** It is God Who **(Eph.1:11) worketh all things after** *the counsel of his will. (Dan.4:35) And all the inhabitants of the earth are reputed as nothing; and he doeth according to his will in the army of heaven, and among the inhabitants of the earth; and none can stay his hand, or say unto him, What doest thou?* Everything we receive comes from God. When we become angry and bitter, who are we actually angry and bitter against? God! We look at people and we see them as the culprits, yet God is the ultimate Sovereign in all of creation. He's the One ultimately behind things, even the devil. If you read the Book of Job, you find out that even behind the devil is God. The devil is restrained from doing things that he would do; he can only do what he's permitted to do because he's not sovereign. And so here God has told Abraham to obey Sarah and, yes, cast this son out.

Did God not know that this lad would be full of anger and bitterness, and become a persecution against His chosen people? Of course He knew; God has raised up many beast kingdoms throughout the world. The Bible says God hardened pharaoh's heart (Exodus 4:21; 7:3) in order to cause him to restrain Israel's ability to leave Egypt. God did this for the purpose that He would have to do signs and wonders to show His power to save. We were put here for a purpose, but a lot of people don't know their purpose. If they knew, they would be more likely to cooperate with God. *(1Pe.4:1) Forasmuch then as Christ suffered in the flesh, <u>arm ye yourselves also with the same mind; for he that hath suffered in the flesh hath ceased from sin; (2) that ye no longer should live the rest of your time in flesh to the lusts of men</u>, but to the will of God.* We came here to suffer in the flesh and we may suffer at the hands of other people, as Ishmael did. If we understand that God is sovereign and that we're actually being angry and unforgiving toward Him, if we understand that's foolishness and we begin to cooperate with God, we'll have far less room in our heart for bitterness and resentment toward other people when we suffer rejection from them. If we would just have our relationship with God and not wrestle with flesh and blood, we wouldn't fall into these traps. But Ishmael permitted bitterness and anger in his heart against his father, who was obeying God. And everyone around us is, in one form or another, fulfilling the will of God, even if it's to bring us to our cross. When we permit bitterness and anger to enter into us, not only our offspring, but many people around us are going to become defiled because they're partaking of our nature through the words that we speak.

Jesus said, *(Joh.6:63) ... The words that I have spoken unto you are spirit, are life.* Well, I have news for you: everybody's words are spirit and life, but they're just not all good spirit and good life. Jesus' Words went into His disciples and changed them. His Words recreated Himself in them and everyone does that. People put their lives into other people through the things that they say. So God is telling us here what Ishmael passed on to his seed and the people around him was a root of bitterness that caused many people to be defiled over the next almost 4,000 years. We're heading toward Armageddon and terrible judgments of man against man even before that. God is proving what the liberal theologians have been saying about man, that "He's basically good," is hogwash. Man is not basically good. He has a capacity to do evil far worse than the animals do. *(Gen.6:5) And the Lord saw that the wickedness of man was great in the earth, and that every imagination of the thoughts of his heart was only evil continually.* One thing that has been passed down from generation to generation is these animosities, unforgiveness and a root of bitterness that will cause the whole world to rise up and fight against one another. "His hand shall be against every man, and every man's hand against him; and he shall dwell over against all his brethren." That's proven true, hasn't it?

Am I faulting Ishmael any more than Isaac? No, because there are roots of bitterness in every culture and people. I'm making a point here that everyone needs forgiveness. No matter what their sins, if they go to Jesus Christ and accept His sacrifice, if they accept that He took away their sins and they walk by faith, He is going to deliver them. It doesn't matter what nationality you are, so I'm not playing favorites here. I'm just pointing out the fact that we can either pass it on or bring an end to it. First of all, if we walk by faith in Jesus Christ, we don't have to continue in our sins. And second, if we forgive from the heart, if we cast down these imaginations, the Lord can cleanse our emotions and our actions. Jesus gives us these commands: *(Mat.5:21) Ye have heard that it was said to them of old time, Thou shalt not kill; and whosoever shall kill shall be in danger of the judgment: (22) but I say unto you, that every one who is <u>angry with his brother</u> shall be in danger of the judgment; and whosoever shall say to his brother, Raca, shall be in danger of the council; and whosoever shall say, Thou fool, shall be in danger of the hell of fire. (23) If therefore thou art offering thy gift at the altar, and there rememberest that thy brother hath aught against thee* (not that you have aught against him, but he has aught against you)*, (24) leave there thy gift before the altar, and go thy way, first be reconciled to thy brother, and then come and offer thy gift.* In other words, God is saying, "I don't want what you can do for the Kingdom, or anything from you, until you make this right." There's no use in this thing being passed on from generation to generation and to the people around you. There's no use in you being a pollution to the Kingdom of God because "a little leaven leaveneth the whole lump." Go take care of this first.

(Mat.5:25) Agree with thine adversary <u>quickly</u>, while thou art with him in the way.... Isn't that interesting? It's almost like a disease. Somebody with a disease walks in the midst of other people and one person passes it on to another. Then that person walks off and passes it on to three more. It's a geometric progression and pretty soon you have a plague. Sin is the same way. That's why God says, "Deal with it now." Don't meditate on it and don't pollute other people, who will then become leaven, too, and go on to spread the pollution even more. *(Mat.5:25) Agree with thine adversary <u>quickly</u>, while thou art with him in the way; lest haply the adversary deliver thee to the judge, and the judge deliver thee to the officer, and thou be cast into <u>prison</u>. (26) Verily I say unto thee, thou shalt by no means come out thence, till thou have paid the last farthing.* We know Jesus

came, *(Isa.61:1) **To proclaim liberty to the captives, and the opening [of the prison] to them that are bound***. This isn't referring to physical prisons, but prisons of bondage to these demonic hordes, the prison of bondage to your old, fallen flesh. A bondage is that you are not able to be and do what you think is right because of our fallen human nature, and the demons that take advantage of it. Notice that if you find out that your brother has aught against you, you go to him. If you have aught against him, you need to give it up. If he has done something against you, you need to go to him and make it right. God taught me a long time ago that, if you ask someone to forgive you, it's not always an admission of guilt. It's something that you need to do in order to cleanse their life and put forgiveness in their heart. God is saying, "We want to cut this off completely, as quickly as possible." If you've offended somebody, learn to say, "I'm sorry; please forgive me." Ask them to forgive you, whether you're guilty or not. Jesus said that you'll be thrown into the prison until you pay the last farthing or, in other words, you're going to pay the debt for your own sins. If you don't forgive others or if you're not useful in them forgiving you, you're going back into prison.

I once knew a family and, for the sake of telling their story, I'm going to call their son "Pete." I was used by the Lord in his life. I shared and prayed with him about receiving the Holy Spirit and he did. Pete enjoyed our teachings and he was here in our meetings regularly. One of the first experiences I had with Pete was that his wife had left him because she was an unfaithful woman. She was also very dishonest and doing anything she could to corrupt his children, about which Pete was heartbroken. Then she decided to retaliate against him by coaxing the kids into saying that their dad molested them. I knew it was a lie when I heard about it, but the kids were barred from going to their dad's house by the courts. However, their kids would come over and play with my kids, so one day I talked with his son and asked him, "Why is it that you are lying against your dad? I would like to know." And he answered, "Well, it wasn't my idea," and he broke down and started telling me things. I said, "Just wait right here," and I went and got a tape recorder. So I came back in and sat down with him and said, "Let's talk about this again." I asked him a bunch of questions and we went back through it and put it on tape. He knew what I was doing. Then I sent that tape to the lawyers and they dropped the boy's case, but they never thought, "Let's see ... he lied and he said the momma caused him to lie ... maybe she's lying about the two girls' cases we have here." No, they went to court anyway, even knowing she had lied once already.

So I ended up going to court and was out in the lobby with his family and some friends. I got them all together and said, "Let's pray. The Bible says that, *(Mat.18:19) **If two of you shall agree on earth as touching anything that they shall ask, it shall be done for them of my Father who is in heaven***. Let's pray that the jury will immediately see through this woman." And that was really asking a lot because this woman was a professional liar. She beat a lie detector test. Now most of those people in the lobby with me didn't have very much faith and they didn't know much about the Lord. All they had were very shallow religious experiences but I shared for a few minutes and then we came into agreement. I said, "Let's put our faith together and agree that Pete will get released very quickly." Well, that jury wasn't out 15 minutes before they came back and Pete's lawyer thought they'd lost the case because this lady was very convincing and the jury had been so quick to reach a decision, but Pete was released. When we talked with some of the jurors afterward, they told us, "I just knew that woman was lying" and "I just knew that was not the truth." The people who needed to understand did.

Something else is that Pete's family had an arguing spirit. They would argue constantly. Even the mailman, who was a Christian preacher, said, "Sometimes I would be going up to their door and I would hear all that arguing and fussing, and instead of going to their door to give them the mail, I would turn around and leave. I'd come back the next day, so sometimes they got their mail late." They'd argue, fuss and fight, yet they still stayed around each other. One day, I went over there with my Bible and sat down at the kitchen table with them. I said, "I would like to share something with you," and I started talking to them about unforgiveness, about how this was really hurting them. I pointed out to them what the Bible says about the tormentors, and so forth, and they were polite but it only went in skin deep. A while after that, I was walking around in Pete's yard when the Lord spoke to me and said, "I've warned them; now I am going to take one of them." I think I told Pete that and just a few days later, Pete's grandfather, who lived with Pete, was called to the phone. His daughter had called to ask him for money. He was furious about that and he left the phone cursing and screaming. Within a minute, he was dead. A few days later, although I really didn't want to do it, the Lord made me talk to Pete's dad. I told him, "When I was in your yard the other day, the Lord told me that, 'I have warned them and now I am going to take one of them.' That's why your dad is dead." Then I left. It wasn't long, though, before Pete's dad was dead, too.

This root of bitterness that defiles many can be passed on from generation to generation. It has to be fought against because you don't have the forgiveness of God while you have that garbage in your heart. You have to repent and deal with it quickly. And the way to get it out of your heart, or to get it out of other people's hearts toward you, is to pray for one another. **(Jas.5:16) Confess therefore your sins one to another, and pray one for another, that ye may be healed. The supplication of a righteous man availeth much in its working.** Unforgiveness is destroying multitudes of families, whole generations of people, and in these end times, millions of people are going to be destroyed because of this. We fall short of the grace of God if we don't deal with all offenses, even going back to our childhood. It might be somebody who has been dead for years who we've not forgiven and, because of that, we're not able to walk in the grace of God as we should. Many people teach faith and faith is necessary, but you'll never have faith, as long as you have this sin in your life. Your heart will condemn you. **(Eph.2:8) For by grace have ye been saved through faith; and that not of yourselves, [it is] the gift of God.** God is the One Who gives faith. He grants faith to those who have a relationship with Him (Romans 12:3). He puts that faith in our heart. If you have bitterness and unforgiveness, you don't have a relationship with God. You don't have the forgiveness of God, so you are not entitled to the benefits of God and therefore you are not entitled to the faith of God.

Some people say that they don't have that kind of faith. Well, sometimes there's a reason that they don't. We need to fight the good fight of faith and cast down illegal thoughts and imaginations that come into our heart to stir up our emotions. Then those emotions will cause us to destroy ourselves. They will cause us to walk in actions that are contrary to the will of God. I've had quite a few experiences with people like that. There was a lady here who had offended an awful lot of people. She was one of those who "possessed" her friends and she would drive away anyone else who came around. So she kind of claimed my wife and me and we would find out after the fact that she was offending people to drive them away from us. We kept trying to reason with her, to put Scriptures in her, until one day the Lord told me, "I want you to turn her over to Satan for the destruction of her flesh" (1 Corinthians 5:5). Don't be shocked because God uses Satan to chasten people and bring them to repentance all the time. ***(Mat.12:25) Every kingdom divided against itself shall not stand.*** Do you know that Satan's kingdom won't stand? That's because the very thing that he does to Christians to torment them is the very thing that causes them to come to repentance. They know they've been delivered over to the devil and they come to repentance.

Anyway, I turned her over to Satan in obedience to the Lord. I would never do that any other way and she became deathly sick <u>immediately</u>. She was so sick, she couldn't get out of her bed and she was vomiting and everything like that. And when she talked to the Lord about it, the Lord said, "I want you to go back and get in front of that congregation, and I want you to tell them that you are sorry that you have done this thing to them. I want you to repent in front of them." And she protested, "Lord, I can't get up!" So the Lord lifted the sickness off of her and she came and stood in our assembly. She confessed her sin, but when she went back home, she became deathly sick again. She called out to the Lord again, "Lord! How does this happen? I confessed my sin!" He replied, "You have been turned over to the devil," and she said, "What?" She called me right away and said, "David, the Lord just said that I've been turned over to the devil!" I'd never told that to anybody. I said, "That's right. The Lord told me to do that, but you've confessed your sins and I don't see any reason not to release you. You are healed in the name of Jesus," and the Lord healed her right then! She received a respect for God's authority in the Church. The reason for her root of bitterness was that she had been molested as a child and she needed deliverance. Make sure that something from your childhood is not a stumblingblock and causing you to mistreat others. Come to the Lord and repent. God bless you.

CHAPTER NINE

Renewed Imaginations and Miracles!

As we've been studying the real Good News that's the power of God unto salvation, we've looked at the role that faith plays in salvation, but I discovered a number of years ago something that was missing. And when I shared it with the saints, we instantly began to see more miracles. The something that was missing is imagination. Imagination is the link between faith and putting things into action. People don't generally connect imagination with faith and some people don't see anything positive about imagination in the Bible because when man fell, his imagination fell. The Lord wants to renew our imagination to be able to see things with our mind's eye before they come to pass. I discovered this is a real key to connecting your mind and your heart with the promises of God. ***(Gen.6:5) And the Lord saw that the wickedness of man was great in the earth, and that every imagination of the thoughts of his heart was only evil continually.*** Well, obviously, God expected more from man. He expected the imaginations of the thoughts of his heart to fulfill His will and yet that wasn't happening.

I remember how the Lord helped me to see and understand this about imagination years ago when I worked for Exxon as a machinist. They would move apprentices around from first class mechanic to first class mechanic, so I had a lot of apprentices pass through. Now I was a Christian and I talked about the Lord a lot, but I didn't know that I had really left much of an impression on any of them. It was quite a few years later when I had the opportunity to speak with one of them who had gone on to become a mechanic. That particular young man shared with me some things I didn't know that he had seen years before when he apprenticed with me and I was witnessing to him. He told me, "David, I remember back when I first worked with you and you were walking across the unit, I saw this glow around you; I really saw it. And I wasn't saved and I didn't know the Lord, but I really saw this thing." Well, I'd been raised a Catholic, so I'd seen these pictures of a halo around people. Anyway, he went on, "With all the mechanics I worked with in those days, you were the only one I knew who could go and pick up all the tools that were necessary to finish the job without going back to the tool box." And I told him, "That's because I would do the whole job in my mind and I knew the equipment pretty well, so as I thought through the job, I would pick up every tool I needed and put it into my tool bag and would take off." You see, it was usual for the apprentices to be run crazy by the mechanics. They'd say, "Oops! I forgot this or that. Go and get it." And the apprentices would run back and forth, so he really appreciated that I didn't do that to him. I learned that this is what God has for us, that we're to see things in our mind before they happen because God's told us in His Word that they've already been accomplished.

God destroyed man because his imaginations brought his own destruction, but at the same time, God was preparing to save an elect group of people in the ark. God told Noah, ***(Gen.6:14) Make thee an ark of gopher wood; rooms shalt thou make in the*** *ark, and shalt pitch it within and without with pitch. (15) And this is how thou shalt make it: the length of the ark three hundred cubits, the breadth of it fifty cubits, and the height of it thirty cubits. (16) A light shalt thou make to the ark, and to a cubit shalt thou finish it upward; and the door of the ark shalt thou set in the side thereof; with lower, second, and third stories shalt thou make it.* God gave a complete description of how He wanted the ark built and that was put into Noah's mind. It was the Word of the Lord that gave Noah the picture in his mind of what had to be built in order to save the saints in what was then the latter days. And, of course, *(Mat.24:37) As [were] the days of Noah, so shall be the coming of the Son of man.* The Lord, through His Word, puts these things into our mind, so we know what God is building because of His promise and His Words. We know that the eye of the mind is this imagination, the drawing board of man's creation. We were created in the image of God and, as such, we were created to be His vessels through whom He creates. He does that by programming our mind with His Word. *(Rom.12:2) And be not fashioned according to this world: but be ye transformed by the renewing of your mind, that ye may prove what is the good and acceptable and perfect will of God.* You are "transformed by the renewing of your mind."

When man is left alone to his own devices, his imagination is corrupt. The pictures in his mind that he uses to create with become corrupted. We can see that principle in Scripture. *(Gen.11:1) And the whole earth was of one language and of one speech.* Man, who was created in the image of God, has certain powers that he has lost through the fall. You can imagine the great wisdom that Adam had to name all the animals and to rule over God's creation; he was no caveman. But, through the fall, and especially on our end of the fall, man has lost much of this natural gift that God has given him. We were created in the image of God, which means that we have some of God's power within our own soul. There's a very interesting book, *The Latent Power of the Soul*, by Watchman Nee. I don't know if Watchman Nee came up with this idea, but it occurred to me that what the devil really wants to do is harness the power of all humanity to use it for his own evil ends. Of course, this was a good example of that here in Genesis, where man had been left to his own devices: *(Gen.11:4) And they said, Come, let us build us a city, and a tower, whose top [may reach] unto heaven, and let us make us a name; lest we be scattered abroad upon the face of the whole earth.* "We're going to build us a tower to Heaven. We're going to build us a name." In other words, it was going to be our own nature, character and authority, and not the name of Jesus. Man left to his own devices falls into corruption and even one of the most powerful things that God has given him, his imagination that can be used by his faith, is corrupted. In fact, I don't think God disagreed with that because of what He did. *(Gen.11:6) And the Lord said, Behold, they are one people, and they have all one language; and this is what they begin to do: and now nothing will be withholden from them, which they purpose to do. (7) Come, let us go down, and there confound their language, that they may not understand one another's speech. (8) So the Lord scattered them abroad from thence upon the face of all the earth.* And now here we are once again, seeing that through the problems that are coming upon the world, men are about to build another Babel, another one world government. "We'll build us a name. We don't want to be scattered. We don't want to be at war with one another. We'll come together in peace," and so on, but God's not going to permit it. He's going to cause division and scatter them again. They're not going to see eye-to-eye or speak the same speech of destruction any more.

So God speaks a little of what He has for us and I want you to notice that He speaks three times here of remembering what He has to say: *(Isa.46:8) <u>Remember this</u>, and show yourselves men; <u>bring it again to mind</u>, O ye transgressors. (9) <u>Remember</u> the former things of old....* "Remember, remember, remember the former things of old." As we're reading this today, we think about the former things of old that were spoken in our Covenant. We go back to the time of Jesus and the apostles when those things were spoken. He says, "the former things of old." As a matter of fact, we go back to the time of the former rain when the promises of our Covenant were given. In the former rain, God would say to us, "Remember, remember what I said. Remember, let this come into your mind again." *(Isa.46:9) Remember the former things of old: for I am God, and there is none else; [I am] God, and there is none like me; (10) <u>declaring the end from the beginning</u>, and from ancient times things that are not [yet] done; saying, My counsel shall stand, and I will do all my pleasure.* God does speak "the end from the beginning," just like He spoke it to Noah when He described the ark to him. Of course, God sees everything from the beginning and He knows everyone from the beginning, even those who have never been born and never lived on Earth. *(Mat.7:22) Many will say to me in that day, Lord, Lord, did we not prophesy by thy name, and by thy name cast out demons, and by thy name do many mighty works? (23) And then will I profess unto them, <u>I never knew you</u>: depart from me, ye that work iniquity.* But He knew those whom He chose from the foundation of the world to be in Christ, Who was the Savior from the foundation of the world. *(Eph.1:4) Even as he chose us in him before the foundation of the world, that we should be holy and without blemish before him in love: (5) having foreordained us unto adoption as sons through Jesus Christ unto himself, according to the good pleasure of his will.* God knows you, even though you never existed. He knew you in His imagination; He saw the end from the beginning, and anyone who sets their mind to build something does that. Noah had an idea in his mind, in his imagination, of what was being built.

We are God's sons, through whom He is going to do what He's going to do in these end times. It's very important that we renew our mind with the Word of God because then our imagination can be used by God to build what He's going to build. Think about all the motion pictures that have come to pass many years after they were filmed. Each one began as an imagination in the mind of the person who put that motion picture together.

When I was a just a boy watching the *Flash Gordon* series, the technology of the future shown there didn't yet exist, but it wasn't long until it came to pass. And even today, when I hear about some of the motion pictures made by lost men, I think, "How prophetic! That's going to happen because we see it in the Bible." Yet these people weren't necessarily drawing any conclusion from what they read in the Bible because they don't read the Bible.

Some people read what God spoke in the beginning of our Covenant, **(Isa.48:3) I have declared the <u>former things from of old</u>**, and they wonder, "Why don't I see that happening?" Well, God is doing the same thing with you that He would do if He gave you a dream or a vision of something that is to come to pass in your life. He's giving you something in which you can exercise faith. Many times when God speaks to us in dreams or visions, it's for the purpose of keeping those in mind, remembering them, exercising faith in what God has spoken to us. **(Isa.48:3) I have declared the former things from of old; yea, they went forth out of my mouth, and I showed them: suddenly I <u>did</u> them, and they came to pass.** Notice that doing them is different from showing them or even knowing them. Doing them comes later and sometimes God shows what He's going to do thousands of years before it actually manifests, before it actually comes to pass. He knew you before the foundation of the world, but we've only come on the scene in just the last few years. What God speaks into existence, He knows first in His imagination and He exercises faith in that. We are created in His image and we do the same thing.

(Isa.48:4) Because I knew that thou art obstinate, and thy neck is an iron sinew, and thy brow brass; (5) therefore <u>I have declared it to thee from of old</u>; <u>before it came to pass I showed it thee</u>; lest thou shouldest say, Mine idol hath done them, and my graven <u>image</u> (There's an "image," there's an "imagination."), **and my molten image, hath commanded them.** That sounds like the Tower of Babel, doesn't it? What was in their mind as lost men, not having guidance or input from the Word of God, as Noah had, just led them to destruction. The same will happen in our day, except for those elect who are putting the Word of God into their mind and heart. **(Isa.48:6) Thou hast heard it; behold all this; and ye, will <u>ye</u> not declare it?** That's very interesting. He says in verse 5, "I have declared it to thee from of old," and now He says, "Will <u>you</u> not declare it?" Isn't that our job as servants of the living God? It's our job to hearken unto His Words, to let them sit in our mind, to meditate upon them. It's our job to imagine them as true. If you can't imagine something is true, can you actually exercise faith that it is true? By faith, we are to **(Rom.4:17) calleth the things that are not, as thought they were**, but if you can't even imagine this thing coming true, what kind of faith could you have? You see, the connection between your faith and your mind is this imagination. We're to imagine them as having come true.

(Isa.48:6) Thou hast heard it; behold all this; and ye, will ye not declare it? I have showed thee new things from this time, even hidden things, which

thou hast not known. (7) They are <u>created now</u>, and not from of old; and before this day thou heardest them not; lest thou shouldest say, Behold, I knew them. He spoke them then, but they're created and coming to pass now. It's the same with us. *(Lam.3:37) Who is he that saith, and it cometh to pass, when the Lord commandeth it not?* Doesn't that mean that we need to be in agreement with Him? *(Amo.3:3) Shall two walk together, except they have agreed?* We have to come into agreement with God. We have to sow His Word into our hearts and minds. We have to think on these things and see the picture of these things so that God can bring them to pass. Obviously, not just our feet, mouth and faith need to be in agreement with the Word of God, but our whole being needs to be in agreement, and that includes our imagination. The connection between our faith and our actions seems to be our imagination. The Lord proved this to us with signs and wonders many years ago, right after I first taught this. *(Lam.3:38) Out of the mouth of the Most High cometh there not evil and good?* On the earth, God uses men to speak His Words; we are His mouth and hands here, and He acts through His body.

See if you can imagine this: *(Col.1:22) Yet <u>now</u> hath he reconciled in the body of his flesh through death, to present you holy and without blemish and unreproveable before him: (23) <u>if</u> so be that ye continue in the faith, grounded and stedfast, and not moved away from the hope of the gospel which ye heard, which was preached in all creation under heaven; whereof I Paul was made a minister.* He says <u>right now</u> it's done: you are reconciled and holy and without blemish, <u>if</u> you continue in the faith. We have to stay grounded in the faith and continue to believe what God said from the very beginning. *(Heb.10:23) Let us hold fast the confession of our hope that it waver not; for he is faithful that promised.* We need to meditate on these things, as though they are done. We need to use our imagination, which is the connection between our faith and our actions, to see them as done. "Yet now hath he reconciled." The Greek word here for "reconciled" is *apokatallasso* and it means "to exchange completely." What was "exchanged completely" in the Body of Christ when He died on the cross? *(Gal.2:20) I have been crucified with Christ; and it is no longer I that live, but Christ liveth in me: and that [life] which I now live in the flesh I live in faith, [the faith] which is in the Son of God, who loved me, and gave himself up for me.* Can you stop and imagine that? Can you imagine that when you were born again, you received of His Spirit? Can you imagine that when you accepted the baptism of the Holy Spirit, that the Holy Spirit came to dwell in you? *(1Jn.4:17) Herein is love made perfect with us, that we may have boldness in the day of judgment; because <u>as he is</u>, <u>even so are we in this world</u>.* Wow! Can you imagine that Jesus lives in you? John says, "As he is, even so <u>are we</u> in this world." How can you express faith to walk as He walked, or how can you express faith to do the "greater works," unless you can imagine in your heart that this is true? *(Joh.14:12) Verily, verily, I say unto you, he that believeth on me, the works that I do shall he do also; and greater works than these shall he do;*

because I go unto the Father.

I often hear people say, "I believe the Bible from cover to cover." Well, that's a pretty neat trick! I don't even know that I do, but I'm looking for it and I'm steadily attempting to do that. I'm diligently asking God to put it all in me because saying you "believe the Bible from cover to cover" is just words. Until we can imagine that God has actually done this, it's just words. Stop for a minute and meditate on the fact that <u>Jesus lives in you</u>, the same Jesus Who did the mighty miracles and spoke the Word of God, the same Jesus Who wasn't sick or under any curse. Reconciliation, an exchange, has already been made, which means that Jesus became accursed for us so that we might have Abraham's blessings. **(Gal.3:13) *Christ redeemed us from the curse of the law, having become a curse for us; for it is written, Cursed is every one that hangeth on a tree: (14) that upon the Gentiles might come the blessing of Abraham in Christ Jesus; that we might receive the promise of the Spirit through faith.*** Can you imagine that this exchange is now done? Imagine it when you're being tempted to believe in your sickness. Imagine it when you're tempted to believe that the devil has power over you. Imagine it when you're tempted to believe that your sin is stronger than Christ. Imagine it concerning all of the curse of sin and of death that has come upon this world. Imagine that Jesus lives in you, the Jesus Who said, **(Joh.10:17) *Therefore doth the Father love me, because <u>I lay down my life</u>, <u>that I may take it again</u>. (18) No one taketh it away from me, but I lay it down of myself. I have power to lay it down, and I have power to take it again....*** That same Jesus lives in you and I believe in the days to come, that because of the outpouring of the Holy Spirit, people are going to begin to believe this again. **(2Th.1:10) *When he shall come to be glorified in his saints, and to be marvelled at in all them that believed <u>(because our testimony unto you was believed)</u> <u>in that day</u>.*** Wow! That's our day he's talking about! By the power and grace of the Holy Spirit, in our day that God's people are not just going to imagine these things are so, but are going to exercise faith and walk in the steps of Jesus Christ.

This world is going to be shaken! The sons of God are going to be manifested and, more importantly, <u>the</u> Son of God is going to be manifested in His people who believe and who are partaking of this latter rain. It's very important to imagine that Jesus Christ now lives in us. Begin to meditate on that and believe it, and you'll see the power of God. Use your imagination, use those pictures in your mind, to see that this gift God has given you is true and has happened in your life. You can see an imagination that was given to us here: **(2Co.3:18) *But we all, with unveiled face*** (those who are unveiled) ***beholding as in a mirror the glory of the Lord, are transformed into the same image....*** That's an imagination because we can't see this in any physical mirror; we see the image in our mind. We imagine that God's Word is true. Some people think that using imagination is of the occult, but we know the devil likes to copy anything that God does. There's nothing wrong with imagining that this is true and you can't really believe it unless you can imagine that it's true. **(2Co.3:18) *But we all, with unveiled face beholding*** *as in a mirror the glory of the Lord, are transformed* (this is the power of imagination) *into the same image from glory to glory, even as from the Lord the Spirit.* Practice imagining that this reconciliation has been accomplished, that the exchange is total and complete, that you don't live anymore but Christ lives in you.

(2Co.4:3) And even if our gospel is veiled, it is veiled in them that perish: (4) in whom the god of this world hath blinded the minds of the unbelieving, that the light of the gospel of the glory of Christ, who is the image of God.... In other words, if you're "beholding as in a mirror the glory of the Lord" and you "are transformed into the same image," then it's the image of God that you're coming into as sons of God. *(Rom.8:19) For the earnest expectation of the creation waiteth for the revealing of the sons of God.* And that's going to happen in these days, folks. It's the clear, written Word of God. *(2Co.4:4) In whom the god of this world hath blinded the minds of the unbelieving, that the light of the gospel of the glory of Christ, who is the image of God, should not dawn [upon them].* These are people who are blinded by the devil, whether they be religious, whether they claim to be born-again or whether they're just lost sinners in the world. Unless they can accept the fact that this reconciliation, this exchange, has been made, as well as walk in that and act it out, how could they possibly believe the Gospel Paul's talking about here? Your imagination is important and you need to begin to exercise it because in our imagination, just as in every other part of our being, we struggle against the curse, the fall of man. The Lord is giving us a renewed imagination when we read the Word. We use our imagination to see things that are not so in the physical. The only way they can be so is in our imagination first and, after that, God will use the renewed imagination of our transformed mind to bring it to pass. *(2Co.4:5) For we preach not ourselves, but Christ Jesus as Lord, and ourselves as your servants for Jesus' sake.* The Lord wants to use us and, in order to do that, two need to walk together in agreement. "Shall two walk together, except they have agreed?" When we walk by faith in what the Lord says, we're coming into agreement with Him because we're calling "the things that are not, as though they were."

(2Co.4:6) Seeing it is God, that said, Light shall shine out of darkness, who shined in our hearts, to give the light of the knowledge of the glory of God in the face of Jesus Christ. So now we behold in a mirror the glory of the Lord. We're looking into the face of Jesus Christ. We see ourselves as gone and Christ taking our place because reconciliation, the complete exchange, has already happened and we accept it as done. Jesus has already borne our curse. *(Gal.3:13) Christ redeemed us from the curse of the law, having become a curse for us; for it is written, Cursed is every one that hangeth on a tree.* He became like the serpent on the pole in the wilderness. *(Num.21:4) And they journeyed from mount Hor by the way to the Red Sea, to compass the land of Edom: and the soul of the people was much discouraged because of the way. (5) And the people spake against God, and against Moses, Wherefore have ye brought us up out of*

Egypt to die in the wilderness? for there is no bread, and there is no water; and our soul loatheth this light bread. (6) And the Lord sent fiery serpents among the people, and they bit the people; and much people of Israel died. (7) And the people came to Moses, and said, We have sinned, because we have spoken against the Lord, and against thee; pray unto the Lord, that he take away the serpents from us. And Moses prayed for the people. (8) And the Lord said unto Moses, Make thee a fiery serpent, and set it upon a standard: and it shall come to pass, that every one that is bitten, when he seeth it, shall live. (9) And Moses made a serpent of brass, and set it upon the standard: and it came to pass, that if a serpent had bitten any man, when he looked unto the serpent of brass, he lived. What God did was to give them something they could exercise their imagination in. When they looked at the serpent on the pole, they could see that the curse was upon the serpent and suddenly they would be healed of the snake bite, which represents the curse upon us in this world. As they began to see that in their imagination, they were healed and delivered. It's the same today. We have to get our eyes off the problem and on the Savior because God put our sin and curse upon Jesus.

Do you remember what happened when Jesus went to Jerusalem to cleanse the Temple? *(Mar.11:12) And on the morrow, when they were come out from Bethany, he hungered. (13) And seeing a fig tree afar off having leaves, he came, if haply he might find anything thereon: and when he came to it, he found nothing but leaves; for it was not the season of figs. (14) And he answered and said unto it, No man eat fruit from thee henceforward for ever.* (This was the Word of God going forth out of Jesus Christ. God desires in these days that we, as the Body of Jesus Christ, would walk in His steps and God would be able to manifest His faith, works and wonders through us.) *And his disciples heard it* (But they didn't see it; they only heard it.). *(Mar.11:15) And they come to Jerusalem: and he entered into the temple, and began to cast out them that sold and them that bought in the temple, and overthrew the tables of the money-changers, and the seats of them that sold the doves; (16) and he would not suffer that any man should carry a vessel through the temple. (17) And he taught, and said unto them, Is it not written, My house shall be called a house of prayer for all the nations? but ye have made it a den of robbers. (18) And the chief priests and the scribes heard it, and sought how they might destroy him: for they feared him, for all the multitude was astonished at his teaching. (19) And every evening he went forth out of the city. (20) And as they passed by in the morning, they saw the fig tree withered away from the roots.* Those roots probably began to die the minute Jesus spoke that, but what could have been seen would have been beneath the earth. When they came back by the next day and saw the fig tree totally withered, the disciples were awed at the power of God. Jesus saw it (in His imagination). He spoke it. They heard Him speak it but they didn't see it, and then later they saw it.

Some people think that everything that Jesus did just happened automatically, but He was walking by faith. I know that we're coming to a time when the latter rain is going to manifest many things miraculously very quickly, there's no doubt in my mind about that, but right now many of us are having to walk by faith to see these things. And I can tell you that the missing link is the imagination; men just can't even imagine that these things are so. We have to call "the things that are not, as thought they were." We need to be in cooperation with God in our whole being. ***(Mar.11:21) And Peter calling to remembrance saith unto him, Rabbi, behold, the fig tree which thou cursedst is withered away. (22) And Jesus answering saith unto them, Have faith in God. (23) Verily I say unto you, Whosoever shall say unto this mountain, Be thou taken up and cast into the sea; and shall not doubt in his heart, but shall believe that what he saith cometh to pass; he shall have it.*** "Not doubt in his heart"? What is part of your heart and mind? Your imagination. Some people think that it's all mechanical: you believe it and you speak it. But can you truly believe it, unless you can imagine it?

I'm not talking here about imagining just any old vain thing. We're to imagine what God says is so! "Who is he that saith and it cometh to pass, when the Lord commandeth it not?" How could He use us, how could He use our faith, unless we believe it with all of our heart? And part of your heart is your imagination. ***(Mar.11:24) Therefore I say unto you, All things whatsoever ye pray and ask for, believe that ye receive them, and ye shall have them.*** Believing that you received them can be greatly helped by imagining them as done and we should practice doing this. When I first taught this some years ago, we had an example literally that very night. Pauline, who was one of the ladies who usually came to the meeting, told us, "Jackie was going to come but she has a terrible abscessed tooth and the whole side of her face is swollen and puffed out." Well, I shared this message about imagination and then I suggested to the brethren in the room, "Let's see Jackie in our imagination. Let's see her suffering and with her face all swollen, with her cheek all puffed out. Then let's just command that to be healed in the name of Jesus Christ and watch the swelling go down in the name of Jesus." So that's what we did. We imagined seeing poor Jackie with her suffering. We rebuked that pain in the name of Jesus and we commanded her tooth to be totally healed. Then, in our imagination, we just watched that swelling go down. The next morning, I received a call from Jackie. She said, "Last night while you all were at the Bible study and I was at home, just suffering with this thing and in a lot of pain, suddenly the whole swelling in the side of my face went down. It was gone and my tooth was healed!" I replied, "Jackie, this is what we did ..." and she became excited as I explained the teaching on using our imagination.

Right after that, we had another example of God demonstrating the power of using our imagination. Brother Bob Aicardi shared with us that somehow a leak had developed in his pool after a hurricane. He thought it was possibly in the underground piping because thousands of gallons of water were pouring out and he couldn't locate what was leaking.

So he wanted us to pray the prayer of agreement, which is very powerful. Just as at Babel, where the prayer of agreement in the negative was very powerful and God scattered them across the face of the earth, the prayers of faith of the saints are powerful. ***(Deu.32:20) How should one chase a thousand, And two put ten thousand to flight, Except their Rock had sold them, And the Lord had delivered them up?*** One will chase 1,000, but two will chase 10,000; it's more powerful than double! Well, as we were getting ready to come in agreement in prayer, I said, "Why don't we practice what we did the other day when we stood in faith for Jackie and got a miracle? Let's see Bob's pool leaking and then let's just command it to be restored in Jesus' name and imagine in our mind that it's stopped leaking." I think most everybody said their prayer out loud and I remember that I said, "I command you, pool, in the name of the Lord Jesus Christ, that you will not leak one more drop of water." Then I told Bob, "You can go home and look at that pool and make a mark where the water is because it's not going to lose any more water." So Bob went home and made that mark and, sure enough, his pool didn't lose any more water. Some months later, Bob had a technician over to work on the pump and the man asked him, "Did you know you have a hole about the size of a quarter in the side of your pool liner?" It seems the ladder had poked a hole through the side of the pool and water was pouring out of that hole up until the time we said not one more drop was going to leak out of that pool.

God Almighty is behind His Word that goes forth from us and He said, "All things whatsoever ye pray and ask for, believe that ye receive them and ye shall have them." God wants to be glorified in what He does through His sons and how can He do it, unless we agree with Him and are a pure channel that He can move through? Another instance is when Bob was walking by faith for his lawn, while all of his neighbors were putting down poison because of a plague of mole crickets. Mole crickets, in case you don't know, burrow underneath the ground and eat the grass roots, which kills the grass and pretty much plows up the yard. The ground becomes mushy and your feet sink in. Bob was struggling, fighting the good fight of faith to get rid of these mole crickets, and all his neighbors were asking him, "Aren't you going to do something about these mole crickets?" Of course, Bob was becoming a little nervous because he really didn't want to displease his neighbors but here these mole crickets were marching across his yard and wiping out his nice green St. Augustine lawn. Bob told us, "They're passing across my front yard, almost in a line, wiping out my grass, and I want you guys to come into agreement with me in the name of Jesus." And we did that, but I also said, "Let's do the same thing we did for Bob's leaking pool. Let's use our imagination again to see this curse and then see it stopped in its tracks. Bob, you describe it for us." So Bob described what he saw, looking off from his front porch, how the mole crickets were coming from the right and making almost a straight line going across his front yard. When we all prayed, I said, "I command these mole crickets, in the name of the Lord Jesus Christ, to die where they are and not take one more inch of that property." Then I told Bob, "Bob, when you go home, I suggest you stand on your front porch and get a sight off your porch where they are right now because they're not going to take any more of your yard."

Now Bob was a man of faith (several years later, the Lord took him home). He was standing in faith all this time. He was agreeing with God and it's easy to agree with somebody who's believing God already, but it's very hard to give a gift to someone who won't believe. Jesus tried to bring the gifts of God to His Own hometown but couldn't. **(Mat.13:58) And he did not many mighty works there because of their unbelief.** So it's easy to give any kind of deliverance from the curse to people who are believing. I'm not saying the manifestation happens instantly; sometimes we do endure a trial of our faith and it's good that we learn to endure a trial of our faith. Jesus said, **(Mat.10:22) And ye shall be hated of all men for my name's sake: but <u>he that endureth to the end</u>, <u>the same shall be saved</u>**. Just because you don't receive an instantaneous answer, don't think that God hasn't heard. That's what faith is all about. **(1Pe.1:7) that <u>the proof</u>** (or "trial") **<u>of your faith, being more precious than gold</u> that perisheth though it is proved** (or "tried") **by fire, may be found unto praise and glory and honor at the revelation of Jesus Christ**. It's very important that we learn not to give in to the thoughts of the flesh, the imagination of the fallen mind. Instead, we can renew our minds, we can see a picture in our minds of the thing we've asked of God. He said, "All things whatsoever ye pray and ask for, believe that ye receive them and ye shall have them." How can you believe that you have received these things you've prayed for? You do that by seeing them in your mind as done.

Some people have this idea that you're offending God by using your imagination because fallen man uses their imagination. But they're in sin and their mind is corrupt; it's not renewed with the Word of God. They believe and do what they want. Fallen men created nuclear bombs. Is this the perfect will of God? No, not for a vessel of honor. The thoughts and imaginations of fallen man are only evil continually. All a lost man can really do is choose which sin he wants to commit, but everything he does is sin and corruption. Nuclear bombs aren't the perfect will of God but they are the permissive will of God and I know He will use them to bring judgment upon mankind. Oh, the devil is very wise and intelligent. He has wisdom and knowledge that we don't have, but it's all corrupted. In our simplicity, we're just like children. We believe the Word of God; we renew our mind with the Word of God. We begin to speak it, act, think and meditate on it. We imagine it as done.

Well, to make a long story short, Bob did go home and he took a mark off of his front porch. The next day when he went outside, he saw that the line hadn't moved, so he walked out in his yard and dug around in the grass. All the mole crickets were dead! They didn't take another inch of that property and that was a testimony to his neighbors. Those neighbors were worried about Bob's mole crickets getting on their lawns, but this was a trial for Bob and he overcame it. For years afterward, whenever Bob had ants, moles or mole crickets in his yard, he would run them out of there by faith. Each victory builds on the previous one and we just keep on going from glory to glory. "Beholding as in a mirror the glory of the Lord, are transformed into the same image from glory to glory, even as from the Lord the Spirit." We're growing in our faith as we come together. We meet with the brethren. They share their experiences with us and we think, "Wow! I never thought about exercising my faith for that!" Folk, this link between faith and imagination is very, very powerful, if we would only catch onto it.

I don't put anything past God. Years ago, I was teaching in an assembly that was in a mission for the homeless when this young girl and her common-law husband received salvation. We prayed for her and she confessed her sin before the pastor, myself and some other people in the room. She told us that she had killed her baby in the womb three days prior. Then she had gone to the public health unit and they told her that the baby was dead. They wanted to schedule a D&C, but during this time, she was running into the Lord everywhere, which was how she came to the meeting and got saved. And now it was three days later and the baby was still dead. Well, after she confessed her sins, it came into my mind to ask her, "Is there anybody that you need to forgive?" She confessed that there was a doctor whom she thought had purposely aborted one of her children, but here she was coming to us with the same thing. I told her, "You've done the very same thing that you have judged him for and you need to forgive and pray for him," so she did. She forgave him and prayed that the Lord would save and deliver him. When she was done, we prayed for her to receive the Holy Spirit. She had a very quiet, reserved nature, but when the Holy Spirit fell upon her, she started jumping around and praising God; she was just so full of the joy of the Lord.

When she slowed down for a minute, I said, "It's obvious that the Lord has forgiven you and I don't see any reason why the Lord won't resurrect your baby." So she came over and sat down in front of me and I explained how faith worked. I told her how we "calleth the things that are not, as though they were," and "All things whatsoever ye pray and ask for, believe that ye receive them, and ye shall have them." I explained that we don't accept anybody's words of doubt or any words contrary to the things that we pray for. **(Mar.11:25) And whensoever ye stand praying, forgive, if ye have aught against any one; that your Father also who is in heaven may forgive you your trespasses**. Since we had met that condition, I called my wife over to put her hand on the girl's tummy and I commanded the spirit of life to come back into that baby in the name of Jesus Christ. When we were done, we noticed that there was nobody left in the room, except for the three of us. The pastor and the others there had cleared out like a covey of quails, but when we left there and I started down the hall, the door beside me opened and the pastor reached out to snatch me into the room. He said, "David, the Lord isn't going to do that for her. You're just giving her hope that she shouldn't have." But I answered him, "If I am believing this, why do you want to attack my faith? Just let me believe it!" And I walked out and left him standing there.

The next morning, the girl called me and said, "David, I want to go down to the public health unit, but none of these people want to take me." I told her, "I'll take you," and went over there and picked her up. I reminded her about our prayer and what the Bible says about faith. I went over Mark 11:24 again and told her **(Mat.18:19) ... if two of you**

shall agree on earth as touching anything that they shall ask, it shall be done for them of my Father who is in heaven. I also reminded her about enduring the trial of her faith. So we arrived at the public health unit and she told the doctor that she wanted to be checked again. He told her that she should have done something by now since it had been over three days, and sent her back with the technician for another sonogram and heartbeat monitor check. After the technician had run the tests, she told the girl, "Ma'am, your baby is dead and we have to do a D&C or you're going to have blood poisoning." Now, remember, this young girl had only known the Lord for hours; she was a brand new baby Christian, but she answered, "I don't accept that," and the heartbeat monitor kicked on and that baby came to life! And that unbelieving technician turned to her and said, "That's a miracle!" So they came out and told me the good news. Glory to God, folks! We just need to give God a chance. He just needs a little bit of faith from us, just a mustard seed of our faith. ***(Mat.17:20) And he saith unto them, Because of your little faith: for verily I say unto you, If ye have faith as a grain of mustard see, ye shall say unto this mountain, Remove hence to yonder place; and it shall remove; and nothing shall be impossible unto you.***

This baby Christian had more faith than people who had been with the Lord for 60 years! They should have been renewing their mind all that time, but instead they were looking at one another's failure. They were comparing themselves with themselves. ***(2Co.10:12) For we are not bold to number or compare ourselves with certain of them that commend themselves: but they themselves, measuring themselves by themselves, and comparing themselves with themselves, are without understanding.*** The childlike faith of this baby Christian would put almost all of us to shame. ***(Mat.18:3) ... Verily I say unto you, Except ye turn, and become as little children, ye shall in no wise enter into the kingdom of heaven.*** This child-like faith is what we need. We need to boldly imagine these things with our mind. We need to be happy when we pray the prayer and not wait until we see the answer to rejoice. ***(Php.4:6) In nothing be anxious; but in everything by prayer and supplication with thanksgiving let your requests be made known unto God.*** Thank the Father when you pray. Believe you have received. Just see it as done and thank Him. ***(2Pe.1:3) <u>Seeing</u> that his divine power <u>hath granted</u> unto us <u>all things</u> that pertain unto <u>life</u>*** (This is the Greek word *zoe* and it means "God's life.") ***and godliness, through the knowledge of him that called us by his own glory and virtue.*** Where do we see that? Do we see it in the physical, in the flesh? No, we don't see it there until it is manifest.

First, we have to see it in our imagination. We have to look in the mirror and see Jesus. Jesus isn't under the curse. Jesus is holy. Jesus is not under sin; He's separated from sin. He's not under the power of darkness. ***(Col.1:13) <u>Who delivered us out of the power of darkness</u>, and translated us into the kingdom of the Son of his love.*** The devil has no more authority or power over us. It's we who have been given authority and power over him. ***(Luk.10:19) Behold, I have given you authority*** *to tread upon serpents and scorpions, and over <u>all the power of the enemy</u>: and nothing shall in any wise hurt you.* Do you think the devil has power? Sure, the devil has power, but we have the authority, the *exousia*, over his power, over his *dunamis*. That means we can tell the devil what to do with that power, but most of the time, we just give that power back to the devil because *(Mat.18:18) Verily I say unto you, what things soever ye shall bind on earth shall be bound in heaven; and what things soever ye shall loose on earth shall be loosed in heaven.* When we disagree with the Word of God, when we don't have the Word of God in our imaginations, then the devil is able to take advantage of us because we're giving him all the faith he needs to do what he does. *(Mat.28:18) And Jesus came to them and spake unto them, saying, <u>All authority hath been given unto me in heaven and on earth.</u> (19) <u>Go ye therefore</u>, and make disciples of all the nations, baptizing them into the name of the Father and of the Son and of the Holy Spirit: (20) teaching them to observe all things whatsoever I commanded you: and lo, I am with you always, even unto the end of the world.* The Lord has delegated His authority to us, but we spend too much time in the imaginations of our heart giving that authority to the devil. If the Lord says, "All authority hath been given unto me," then that does not leave any for the devil. Jesus has delegated it to you and me, and we give it to the devil through unbelief. Did you know that unbelief is faith in the devil and the curse? Unbelief gives the devil authority over us.

When Adam disagreed with God, he gave authority to the devil and fell under the curse. *(Rom.6:16) Know ye not, that to whom ye present yourselves [as] servants unto obedience, <u>his servants ye are whom ye obey</u>; whether of sin unto death, or of obedience unto righteousness?* Adam had been given authority over all of God's creation, but Adam obeyed the devil and became a servant to the devil. He made the devil his lord. When we agree with the curse, which is "the things that are," instead of calling "the things that are not, as though they were," we're giving the devil authority. I believe if you will practice imagining that this Word is true, God will use that to empower your faith to manifest signs and wonders. Can there be anything wrong with that? Father, we thank You for Your gifts. Lord, we thank You for the Word that You're putting in our heart. Father, please finish the good work that You have started in us. Let us walk in the steps of our Lord Jesus. Let us be vessels through whom He can flow. Let us manifest our sonship. God, we praise You for this. We trust You and we believe You, and we know that the greater works are going to be fulfilled through us. God bless you, saints!

CHAPTER 10

They Cast Out Demons!

Let's go to the Lord and ask His mercy and grace upon our study. Father, in the name of our Lord Jesus Christ, we ask Your anointing, Your wisdom, Your understanding to be upon us, Lord. Lord, let Your Words go into our heart and let them manifest in us the life of Christ. Lord, we know that Jesus can do all that's necessary in us and through us, that once again, He chooses to speak and do His works in the world. Lord, what He did in that first body, He is once again going to do in His second body. He is going to manifest Himself to the world. And Lord, today we ask You to give us eyes to see and ears to hear. Thank You, Lord. Thank You, in Jesus' name. Amen! Praise be to God!

Well, we're going to continue talking about something that we could probably talk about forever and that's the real Good News. It's the Good News of what has already been accomplished and that we're just entering into the works that were finished from the foundation of the world. Glory be to God! ***(Heb.4:3) For we who have believed do enter into that rest; even as he hath said, As I sware in my wrath, They shall not enter into my rest: although the works were finished from the foundation of the world.*** I'd like to change direction a little here and take another look at something we've read previously. ***(Luk.1:68) Blessed [be] the Lord, the God of Israel; For he hath visited and wrought redemption for his people.*** And this redemption is described as ***(71) Salvation from our enemies*** (Notice, this is for His people.)***, and from the hand of all that hate us. (74) To grant unto us that we being delivered out of the hand of our enemies Should serve him without fear.*** Glory be to God! We've been delivered, folks! Now it only remains for us to enter into those works through faith in what He said about us.

These statements right here are power: ***(Rom.1:16) For I am not ashamed of the gospel: for it*** (the Gospel) ***is the power of God unto salvation to every one that believeth; to the Jew first, and also to the Greek.*** "The Gospel is the power of God unto salvation to every one that believeth." When God makes a statement that seems to be so contrary to what is naturally going on in the world, so contrary to what our senses are telling us, it's because He wants us to mix our faith with the Word to see it come to pass. Only believers can do that. Only we, who have a gift from God to believe, can do that. ***(Col.1:13) Who delivered us out of the power of darkness, and translated us into the kingdom of the Son of his love.*** He has "delivered us out of the power of darkness." We're no longer under the dominion of the devil and his forces. You may be thinking, "David, that's contrary to a lot of things that I see in Christianity and a lot of the situations that God's people are living under." Well, that's true, but you see, our faith is what changes those things. ***(Rom.4:17) ... Even God, who giveth life to the dead, and calleth the things that are not, as though they were.*** Our calling the promises, which are "the things that are not, as though they were," is what brings them to pass. And the Lord says that one of those promises He's given to us is authority over our enemies. **(Luk.10:19) Behold, I have given you <u>authority to tread upon serpents and scorpions</u>** (Serpents and scorpions represent different kinds of demons.)**, and <u>over all the power of the enemy</u>: and nothing shall in any wise hurt you.** So the Lord has delivered us out of the power of our enemies and He's given us authority over that power. Do we have to be very wise to use that authority? No, but there is one condition: **(Mar.16:17) <u>And these signs shall accompany them that believe</u>: in my name shall they cast out demons; they shall speak with new tongues; (18) they shall take up serpents, and if they drink any deadly thing, it shall in no wise hurt them; they shall lay hands on the sick, and they shall recover.** The only condition for being able to do this is to be a believer; the authority is to "them that believe."

You don't have to go to a "deliverance" ministry to cast out demons. All you need to do is hear the voice of the Spirit. It's actually very simple. Now I know that there are people out there who have more experience, but I want to talk to you who are just young in the Lord: you young Christians have authority. I've been casting out demons since shortly after I became a Christian. I was reading the Word of God and I was putting what I read to work in the world around me. I learned a lot through doing that. Folks, the Lord knows that we make some stumbling steps as we're growing, but He teaches us through the things that we go through, if we're willing to be obedient. "In my name shall they cast out demons." Don't think that you can't do it because this list is for every Christian. "These signs shall accompany them that believe." That's the only condition. All you have to be is a believer!

(Mat.8:16) And when even was come, they brought unto him many possessed with demons: and he cast out the spirits with a word, and healed <u>all</u> that were sick. Well, if you listen to a lot of people today, you'd think, "Jesus has already gotten rid of all the demons and we don't have to worry about that." I don't think those people are experiencing what's really going on around them because there are no fewer demons today than there were in Jesus' day. And although I haven't worked it out myself, supposedly, a third of Jesus' ministry was spent casting out demons, yet you see very few Christians doing that today. Let me tell you, though, that demons are still a real problem. The more that God gives you a discerning of spirits, the more you understand and see that we're wrestling with principalities and powers all around us, folks. **(Eph.6:12) For <u>our wrestling is not against flesh and blood</u>, but against the principalities, against the powers, against the world-rulers of this darkness, against the spiritual hosts of wickedness in the heavenly places.** We're not called to wrestle with flesh and blood. Notice "he cast out the spirits with a <u>word</u>." With a word! Wow! Maybe you're thinking, "Aha! There must be a magic word out there somewhere and I'm looking for that word but I can't find it." Wouldn't you really like to know what that word was? Well, what did we just read? "Behold, I have given you <u>authority</u>." The Lord just exercised authority and the Lord has given us authority over all the power of the enemy. You know, if He cast out demons with a word, there's no hint there that He used anything else but authority.

The Lord Jesus Christ didn't wrestle with those demon-possessed people, as I've seen many Christians do. The seven sons of Sceva are a good example of that. ***(Act.19:13) But certain also of the strolling Jews, exorcists, took upon them to name over them that had the evil spirits the name of the Lord Jesus, saying, I adjure you by Jesus whom Paul preacheth. (14) And there were seven sons of one Sceva, a Jew, a chief priest, who did this. (15) And the evil spirit answered and said unto them, Jesus I know, and Paul I know, but who are ye? (16) And the man in whom the evil spirit was leaped on them, and mastered both of them, and prevailed against them, so that they fled out of that house naked and wounded.*** We're taught not to wrestle with flesh and blood, but with principalities and powers, and they can be a whole lot stronger than you and me. I've never physically wrestled with anybody, or held anybody down, or tried to force anything on them that the authority of the Lord wouldn't do. In fact, when you exercise your authority and the demons obey, I believe that's one sure sign that God is with you. If you need to get in the flesh and physically wrestle with anybody to give them a deliverance, then God's not with you and there must be a reason for that. So we see that Jesus didn't wrestle with the demons; He just cast them out with a word. I had a very good learning experience years ago when I became involved with a church that also operated a mission. I had been casting out demons since shortly after I became a Christian, but here there were more demons in one spot than I had ever seen. There's a reason a lot of people are out there on the road, folks. They need some deliverance and these missions are filled with a lot of people who are dysfunctional. And that's the way it was in this mission; there was a desperate need for deliverance.

The pastor hadn't even baptized anybody and he knew nothing about deliverance, so I preached the first baptism sermon they ever had and then baptized most of the church. After I taught the pastor how to do it, he started baptizing people, too, but it was just a ceremony to them. It wasn't an act of faith. They weren't casting out demons, either, and they were having lots of trouble because of that, so I started casting out demons. Now I'm not one of those guys who believes in casting out demons behind every bush, but I have had a discerning of spirits since not too long after becoming a Christian. The most common way I began to see demons was in people's eyes. Well, one day I was talking to a deacon from this church who had been asking to be filled with the Holy Spirit and that was a good thing because he really needed it. He was a little carnal and he needed the power of the Spirit in his life. He told me that some of the people in the mission needed deliverance and asked if I thought he should go over there to cast out demons. I told him, "Brother, it would be a real good idea for you to get filled with the Holy Spirit. I don't even suggest that you go over there until you have His guidance." It was similar to what happened to the disciples. ***(Act.1:4) And, being assembled together with them, he charged them not to depart from Jerusalem, but to wait for the promise***

of the Father, which, [said he,] ye heard from me: (5) For John indeed baptized with water; but <u>ye shall be baptized in the Holy Spirit</u> not many days hence. Jesus told the disciples to wait for the baptism of the Holy Spirit before they went. But, this brother didn't pay a bit of attention to what I said and, of course, I don't ever become offended if people don't take my advice.

The next day or so, that deacon went over to the mission looking for demons and, lo and behold, the Lord had some demons waiting for him and they were mean. A man named Jim had come into the assembly drunk two days earlier and he received salvation and was miraculously sobered. He really was greatly blessed. But some people need guidance, even after they receive salvation, because they do dumb things that turn them back over to the devil. Well, that deacon walked down the hallway into this long room where Jim had been watching television and demons manifested in Jim, even to the point where his features changed. I know that because I got to see it later. I've cast out a lot of demons but I never saw anything like this in my life. This guy stood up like a big old bear, taller than what he was in normal life, and began to go after the deacon, who took off running through the building with Jim right behind him. Then Jim slammed the deacon through the thick plate glass door of the mission, as if he had supernatural strength. You wouldn't think you could ever break one of those doors; they were about 5/8ths of an inch, or 16 millimeters, thick. So there was the deacon, lying out on the street all cut up and crying out for somebody, anybody, to come get the demons off him because now the demons were on him, instead. He told me later that a very young Christian came by, who had never done anything like that before in his life, and just said, "Come out in the name of Jesus!" And the demons left him. And then they hauled the deacon off to the hospital. After that, the pastor was called over to the mission and the pastor's secretary came with him because they always traveled around together. So the pastor, not knowing much about what had happened, went in there to talk to Jim and the demons manifested again. Jim jumped up, about to swallow the pastor alive and the pastor and his secretary took off running out of the building. There's no doubt in my mind that if Jim had caught them, he probably would have torn them limb from limb because he was mean. He wasn't the guy we knew at all.

Let me backtrack a little here and tell you how the Lord arranged it so the pastor respected me. The first time I ever walked into that building, a woman I never knew and he never knew stood up, turned around and pointed her finger at me on the other end of the building. Then she started prophesying about me, with the pastor listening. She said, "I see the Word of God living in that man," and she went on in that vein, and that made me an expert to these people. So I didn't know it, but the Lord was setting me up. And this pastor started asking me questions. As he preached, he would turn to me with, "Isn't that right, David?" He was looking for a confirmation, but he didn't know much about the Word. I was doing my best to be honest and I would say quietly, "No," and he would look at me and march off. He really liked to march around. Then, a few minutes later, he would march back and ask again about something else, "Isn't that right, David?" And once again I would quietly say, "No." Finally, the guy sitting behind me tapped me on the shoulder and asked, "Did you say, 'No'?" And I told him, "That's right. And if he doesn't want a truthful answer, he should quit asking me questions." Anyway, the Lord set me up as an "expert" through that and also through some preaching I did there.

Well, the pastor called me right after being run out of the building. He said, "David, we have a real problem over here at the mission. It's Jim, who was saved the other night when you were preaching. He has demons! Do you think you can come and do something about this?" And I answered, "I don't know about me, but I believe the Lord can." So I went over there and met him and the secretary at the door, and we all walked down the long hall into a room that led to the very long room where Jim was. When I turned into the room, I saw Jim down at the other end. I didn't see anything abnormal and I didn't know that I was walking into an ambush, but I did notice when I was about halfway down the room that the pastor, who had been right behind me up to that point, had stopped at the doorway. I turned to look back and saw him and his secretary peeking around the corner. So I thought, "That's strange," and kept walking further into the room, until I realized just why they were peeking around the corner. As I got closer to Jim, he saw me and jumped up and started manifesting those demons! Boy-o-boy! Even his features were changed and I'd never seen anything like that before. I never did become fearful, but out of my mouth came the command, "Sit!" I had to say it quickly because he was bearing down on me. And as big as he was, Jim immediately plopped down like a little puppy and sat there, completely docile. I could just imagine having to wrestle with this guy; I don't believe I could have overcome him in his normal mind, let alone with the demons. I'm quite sure I would have been torn to shreds.

The Lord's given us authority, folks, and the devil knows that. We don't have to wrestle with flesh and blood. The key is to act in His name. **(Mar.16:17) And these signs shall accompany them that believe: <u>in my name</u>....** "In my name" means "representing" Him and that's why we study the Scriptures. We want to be sure that we're not representing ourselves, that we're not doing it on our own, but that we're trusting in Him, as we are His representative authority here on Earth. We are the body of Christ and the youngest Christian out there has this authority. "And when even was come, they brought unto him many possessed with demons: and he cast out the spirits with a word." The body of Christ cast out those demons in Matthew 8 and now Christ is being manifested in us through His Word. He's called us to be His body through whom He can continue to cast out these demons.

So I began to command demons to come out of Jim. Some of their names came to me through a Word of knowledge and in some cases when a demon was speaking, I would ask its name. Well, when the pastor saw that Jim was under control, he and his secretary slipped in alongside me and the pastor started to command demons to come out, too, in the name of Jesus. Now when the demons were talking to me through Jim, they didn't like me one little bit at all. They were real derogatory, but they dearly loved the pastor and I thought, "Uh-oh; something's wrong here," and not only because he initially stopped at the door. There was something else. I came to find out later that the pastor and his secretary were having an affair. Anyway, as I continued to cast out the demons, at one point they asked permission to enter into the dog. I thought, "Dog?" I looked around and I didn't see or hear any dogs, but after we left, I learned that there was a dog on the other side of the wall. It belonged to a woman in the next room who was visiting her husband at the mission. But I never saw or heard a dog and when the demons asked permission to enter into the dog, I said what came to me, "No. You can just find the nearest cockroach and enter into him." And that was that.

I had cast out about 10 demons, when the Lord spoke to me and He said, "They entered in through that TV set." I thought, "They entered in through the TV set?" And I asked Jim, who was now much more in his right mind and was much more in control of himself, "Jim, what were you watching on this TV set?" And he showed me that he'd been watching pornography. It was just amazing to me that here was a guy who had just come to the Lord and the Lord sobered him up and he was gloriously saved, but he didn't have any better sense than to go and do something like that. But, you know, the Lord gave him a swift lesson. When you're saved, you're under the Lord and He doesn't treat you like He treats the world. He loves you so much that He'll do something drastic sometimes to turn you around and that's what happened with Jim. You say, "It was to turn him around?" Yes. This was a real strong lesson for Jim. Then the Lord told me, "There are two more demons. Leave them in there." I'd never heard the Lord say that before, but I knew it was the Lord, so I said, "Okay." Jim was in his right mind and I left.

At the next assembly of God's people at the mission, Jim was there and he was doing pretty well and able to function. After I gave the teaching, Jim came forward for prayer because he wanted some more deliverance. I knew the Lord was teaching me something in this particular aspect. The Lord has been teaching me for decades, as I've been diligently seeking Him, and He's still teaching me. I don't think we should ever be unteachable. Anyway, Jim came forward and, just as I was getting ready to pray for him, the pastor, who was standing beside me, reached out his hand to "slay" him in the spirit, so to speak. The Holy Spirit rose up in me when the pastor did that and I did something that I would never do normally. I'm a pretty meek and quiet person, not very domineering over people. I try to keep my place with the Lord and so on. But when the pastor laid his hand on Jim's forehead and Jim began to fall backwards, right then the Holy Spirit just rose up in me. I quickly stepped to the side and put my hand behind Jim's back to stand him back up, so he fell only a little bit. And I just commenced to command the demons to come out of him, which was what he came down there for in the first place. And I realized that the devil wanted Jim out on the floor. The devil didn't want us to exercise dominion over those demons. As I learned later, this pastor had been part of a very famous rock band. He came to the Lord, but he didn't come all the way. He still had a lot of demons in him and that was proven to me over the time I ministered there. When the Lord dried him up, I found myself doing all the teaching for some time and I even took over his radio ministry for a short while. When I asked him, "Aren't you going to preach anymore?" he said, "No, I feel kind of dried up," and I thought to myself that was a good thing for the Lord to do. Anyway, Jim got his deliverance and I realized the devil was using that "slain in the spirit" thing to try and keep Jim from receiving deliverance.

I tell you, we need to recognize our authority in the Lord and not get in the flesh like the seven sons of Sceva did when they preached a "Jesus whom Paul preacheth." Those demons said they didn't know these men. They jumped on them and bested them so that they fled out of there naked and wounded. God told His disciples, ***(Mat.11:12) And from the days of John the Baptist until now <u>the kingdom of heaven suffereth violence, and men of violence take it by force</u>***. And He told them, ***(11) Verily I say unto you, Among them that are born of women there hath not arisen a greater than John the Baptist: <u>yet he that is but little in the kingdom of heaven is greater than he</u>.*** In the New Testament, this born-again experience gives us the authority to act in the name of Jesus Christ. A baby Christian cast those demons out of the deacon and I was casting out demons when I was very young in the Lord. I had a lot of faith because the Lord gave me a gift to love the Word and get filled with the Word. ***(Rom.10:17 KJV) So then faith [cometh] by hearing, and hearing by the word of God.*** My faith was just a natural byproduct of staying in the Word. I really believed in God as my Savior and that God is the One Who wants to live through me, speak through me and do works through me. And I believed that we are the body of Christ for the purpose of Jesus Christ living in this body. In casting out those demons in Jim, the Lord showed me that we have to exercise our dominion and not wrestle with flesh and blood.

You know, I made a little joke earlier about "casts out spirits with <u>a word</u>." And I asked, "What could that word be? I'd like to find out what that powerful word is." Well, now I'm going to tell you. First, let's back up in the chapter. ***(Mat.8:5) And when he was entered into Capernaum, there came unto him a centurion, beseeching him, (6) and saying, Lord, my servant lieth in the house sick of the palsy*** ("paralytic"), ***grievously tormented.*** That sounds like demons, doesn't it? ***(7) And he saith unto him, I will come and heal him. (8) And the centurion answered and said, Lord, I am not worthy that thou shouldest come under my roof; but only <u>say the word</u>, and my servant shall be healed. (9) For I also am a man under authority, having under myself soldiers: and I say to this one, Go, and he goeth; and to another, Come, and he cometh; and to my servant, Do this, and he doeth it.*** Why was the centurion talking about authority to rule over his servants? What does that have to do with this situation? The centurion recognized that Jesus was a person of authority. He knew Jesus had authority, but authority to do what? Was it authority to rule the angels? Was it authority to rule the demons that were in this paralytic boy? Yes, I would say that the centurion recognized Jesus as an authority in the spiritual world and in the spiritual Kingdom. Jesus had authority over the forces of darkness and He also ruled over the angels who go forth and serve those who are heirs of salvation. Jesus overcame to rule over the principalities and powers.

(Eph.1:20) Which he wrought in Christ, when he raised him from the dead, and made him to sit at his right hand in the heavenly places, (21) far above all rule, and authority, and power, and dominion, and every name that is named, not only in this world, but also in that which is to come: (22) and he put all things in subjection under his feet, and gave him to be head over all things to the church.

So the centurion was seeing this authority that Jesus was able to exercise and he knew that nothing could stand before that. He told Jesus, "only say the word." There's that "word" again! "You just say the word and my servant shall be healed." Wow! What is that word that he's talking about? We can read on down and see that the centurion recognized the great authority of Jesus in this situation, the great authority of Jesus in the spiritual realm. ***(Mat.8:10) And when Jesus heard it, he marvelled, and said to them that followed, Verily I say unto you, I have not found so great faith, no, not in Israel. (11) And I say unto you, that many shall come from the east and the west, and shall sit down with Abraham, and Isaac, and Jacob, in the kingdom of heaven: (12) but the sons of the kingdom shall be cast forth into the outer darkness: there shall be the weeping and the gnashing of teeth.*** But He still hasn't said what that word is! Well, it's the same Greek word for "word" in both Matthew 8:8 ("say the word") and Matthew 8:16 ("with a word"). The word in both places is *logos* and it just means "a communication" or "something that is said." Jesus was something that God said. ***(Joh.1:1) In the beginning was the Word, and the Word was with God, and the Word was God.*** And "the Word" there is, of course, *logos* because God spoke to us through Jesus, not just through the words that Jesus spoke, but through His life. He is the living Word of God. You ask, "So what is the word?" Jesus finally comes with the word that the centurion was looking for and, once again, it was not a single word, but it was a communication. It was a group of words, but it was a word from God. ***(Mat.8:13) And Jesus said unto the centurion, Go thy way; as thou hast believed, [so] be it done unto thee. And the servant was healed in that hour.*** Notice Jesus didn't say, "Come out in the name of Jesus," or "I command you, paralytic spirit, to come out in My name," although that would work quite well. He didn't give a name; He just exercised authority. What was the word? "As thou hast believed, so be it done unto thee." In other words, "You said it; you got it. You believed it; it's yours."

You see, there is no "magic" in the words. People study diligently to find out what you say to demons, how you talk to them and cast them out. It's really simple: we're just exercising the authority that the Lord gave us. ***(Joh.20:21) Jesus therefore said to them again, Peace be unto you: as the Father hath sent me, even so send I you.*** He delegated His authority. Just as the Father sent the first body of Christ, He sent the second body of Christ and Jesus did, too. We have that authority. Jesus said, "As thou hast believed, so be it done unto thee," and that's not at all what we think of as the normal deliverance ministry. Jesus was exercising authority. He knew He had authority. He didn't get red in the face wrestling with anybody because He just knew He had authority.

The devil is involved in every sickness, but everything is not a demon possession; even spirits of infirmity don't have to be a possession. ***(Act.10:38) Even Jesus of Nazareth, how God anointed him with the Holy Spirit and with power: who went about doing good, and healing <u>all</u> that were <u>oppressed</u> of the devil; for God was with him.*** Jesus "went about doing good and healing <u>all</u> that were <u>oppressed</u> of the devil; for God was with him." What does that mean? It means that all the people Jesus healed were oppressed of the devil. An oppression can be a possession. The devil can oppress you from within and he can oppress you from without, but it's still an oppression. It's the devil's job to administer the Deuteronomy 28 curse on humanity and he does it very well. He does it according to the Law of the Word, believe it or not. When Jesus spoke, His faith, His agreement with the Word, bound the devil and broke his power over the paralytic boy. Remember, "And these signs shall accompany them that <u>believe</u>: in my name shall they cast out demons." All you have to do is believe. Now I agree that there are believers in some things who are not believers in other things, but a person does have to believe that they have authority. "I have given you authority ... over all the power of the enemy." A lot of people brush that off and say, "Jesus was just talking to those first disciples; He wasn't talking to us." Then how is it that some people are going around casting out demons? I'm sure some of those nay-sayers probably wouldn't agree people are doing that, but the testimonies are abundant. People are being delivered of demons and sometimes just by baby Christians because the only condition is to believe that you have authority.

Jesus believed He had authority. He exercised it and He spoke it. And Jesus gave authority to the words of the centurion because, even though the centurion wasn't a Jew according to the Old Covenant, he was a man of faith. When the Jews didn't believe Jesus, God broke them off the olive tree and He grafted in the Gentiles who believed. ***(Rom.11:17) But if some of the branches were broken off, and thou, being a wild olive, wast grafted in among them, and didst become partaker with them of the root of the fatness of the olive tree; (18) glory not over the branches: but if thou gloriest, it is not thou that bearest the root, but the root thee. (19) Thou wilt say then, Branches were broken off, that I might be grafted in. (20) Well; by their unbelief they were broken off, and thou standest by thy faith. Be not highminded, but fear: (21) for if God spared not the natural branches, neither will he spare thee. (22) Behold then the goodness and severity of God: toward them that fell, severity; but toward thee, God's goodness, if thou continue in his goodness: otherwise thou also shalt be cut off. (23) And they also, if they continue not in their unbelief, shall be grafted in: for God is able to graft them in again. (24) For if thou wast cut out of that which is by nature a wild olive tree, and wast grafted contrary to nature into a good olive tree; how much more shall these, which are the natural branches, be grafted into their own olive tree? (25)***

For I would not, brethren, have you ignorant of this mystery, lest ye be wise in your own conceits, that a hardening in part hath befallen Israel, until the fulness of the Gentiles be come in; (26) and so all Israel shall be saved: even as it is written, There shall come out of Zion the Deliverer; He shall turn away ungodliness from Jacob. Jesus was willing to go to this man's house to cast the demons out, but the centurion exercised authority and faith. "Hey, I am not even worthy for you to come to my house. You just say the word and my servant will be healed." And the servant was healed, but notice that, since it was the centurion who exercised authority for the servant, God permitted the centurion to exercise his responsibility in the spiritual areas, too. He accepted this man as responsible and He accepted this man's faith.

Jesus had the authority to cast out demons, but He put responsibility upon the people who needed the deliverance, either for themselves or for those under their authority. Jesus didn't say, "According to My faith"; He said, "According to your faith." *(Mat.9:27) And as Jesus passed by from thence, two blind men followed him, crying out, and saying, Have mercy on us, thou son of David. (28) And when he was come into the house, the blind men came to him: and Jesus saith unto them, Believe ye that I am able to do this? They say unto him, Yea, Lord. (29) Then touched he their eyes, saying, According to your faith be it done unto you. (30) And their eyes were opened. And Jesus strictly charged them, saying, See that no man know it. (31) But they went forth, and spread abroad his fame in all that land.*

Who is entitled to deliverance? "For [the gospel] is the power of God unto salvation to every one that believeth." That's talking about the person who needs the salvation. So we see here that Jesus had authority when a person was entitled to the benefits, but the devil also has rights and the Kingdom of God gives him those rights. *(Heb.10:26) For if we sin wilfully after that we have received the knowledge of the truth, there remaineth no more a sacrifice for sins, (27) but a certain fearful expectation of judgment, and a fierceness of fire which shall devour the adversaries.* God says, if you walk in willful disobedience, there is no sacrifice for your deliverance. You're going to pay the price; you're going to go through judgment, in order to bring you to repentance. You can't take away the devil's authority, if he has authority given to him by God. We have authority over the devil only when we are dealing with someone who is entitled to the benefits, like the centurion, who was entitled to the benefits because he believed.

So not everybody is entitled to the benefits and, as a matter of fact, Jesus told the disciples, *(Mat.10:5) These twelve Jesus sent forth, and charged them, saying, Go not into [any] way of the Gentiles, and enter not into any city of the Samaritans: (6) but go rather to the lost sheep of the house of Israel.* He told them that because the Jews had a Covenant and Jesus was going to the people of the Covenant. Jesus Himself said, *(Mat.15:24) ... I was not sent but unto the lost*

sheep of the house of Israel. Romans 11 speaks of the faithful Jews who stayed in the olive tree and the believers who were grafted into that olive tree. "And so all Israel shall be saved," meaning those in the olive tree of "all Israel" are believers in the Lord Jesus Christ. Even the Old Testament saints, who were born again when Jesus preached to the souls in prison, are believers in the Lord Jesus Christ. ***(1Pe.3:18) Because Christ also suffered for sins once, the righteous for the unrighteous, that he might bring us to God; being put to death in the flesh, but made alive in the spirit; (19) in which also he went and preached unto the spirits in prison, (20) that aforetime were disobedient, when the longsuffering of God waited in the days of Noah, while the ark was a preparing, wherein few, that is, eight souls, were saved through water.*** Those faithful Jews who came and followed Him were believers and they were entitled to the benefits. Jesus went forth to share the Gospel with the Covenant people to see who was entitled to these benefits. The centurion happened to be a Covenant person by faith, not because he was a Jew according to the Old Covenant, but because he was a Jew according to the coming New Covenant and Jesus accepted that. He said, "Go not into [any] way of the Gentiles" because these Covenant people were entitled to the benefits.

What were the benefits? ***(Mat.10:8) Heal the sick, raise the dead, cleanse the lepers, <u>cast out demons</u>: freely ye received, freely give.*** Jesus was saying, "Don't go to the lost. Go to the <u>Covenant people</u> and <u>cast out their demons</u>." A fairly large portion of Christianity today doesn't believe that God's people can have demons, but Jesus was casting demons out of God's people. He and His disciples were going to the lost sheep of the house of Israel and casting demons out of them before God turned to the Gentiles. Wow! Here's another proof of that: ***(Mat.8:16) And when even was come, they brought unto him many possessed with demons: and he cast out the spirits with a word, and healed all that were sick: (17) that it <u>might be fulfilled</u> which was spoken through Isaiah the prophet, saying: Himself took <u>our infirmities</u>, and <u>bare our diseases</u>.*** Who was Isaiah speaking to? He was addressing the Jews; he was addressing Israel. We have the benefits of the Kingdom. They belong to us. And not only are they ours, notice they're past tense. Jesus "took our infirmities." Jesus "bare our diseases." It's already been done. Therefore, since it's already been done, we have authority to cast out demons.

Also notice that the sacrifice was effectually for God's people. You say, "But David, I thought it was for whosoever will?" Well, there isn't anybody who wills except those people who have a gift of faith from God and are drawn of the Father. That's what the Bible says. ***(Joh.15:16) <u>Ye did not choose me</u>, <u>but I chose you</u>, and appointed you, that ye should go and bear fruit, and that your fruit should abide: that whatsoever ye shall ask of the Father in my name, he may give it you.*** "Ye did not choose me, but I chose you," so therefore the Covenant people are the people who "will." ***(Php.2:13) For it is <u>God who worketh in you</u> both <u>to will</u> and to work, for his good pleasure.*** Effectually, Jesus died for "whosoever will" because these are the ones who have faith and so have a right to the benefits of the Covenant. The Syrophoenician woman is another proof of this. ***(Mar.7:25) But straightway a woman, whose little daughter had an unclean spirit, having heard of him, came and fell down at his feet. (26) Now the woman was a Greek, a Syrophoenician by race. And she besought him that he would cast forth the demon out of her daughter. (27) And he said unto her, Let the children first be filled: for it is not meet to take the children's bread and cast it to the dogs.*** So here you have a Gentile woman with a daughter who has a spirit of infirmity and Jesus said it's not right to take the children's bread and cast it to the dogs. In other words, the children of God have a right to the benefit of deliverance. ***(Col.1:13) Who delivered us out of the power of darkness, and translated us into the kingdom of the Son of his love.*** The meaning is that the people of the Kingdom have this deliverance but the world does not. We would love to cast demons out of everybody out there and sometimes God speaks to us and says, "Cast out that demon," concerning one of His elect who hasn't come into the Kingdom yet. God can do that because He knows the elect before we do, so don't say we can't cast demons out of somebody who is not a Christian.

However, we know without a doubt that people are entitled to the benefits of the Kingdom, if they are a child of God, and so we can freely give them those benefits. The benefits are guaranteed to them because Jesus cast out all of their demons. However, we know the devil has rights. If we cast the demons out of somebody who is walking in willful disobedience, the demons will just come back. As long as the person won't repent, they're still under the penalty of their sin and the demons will come back. They returned, even after Jesus was the One Who had cast them out. ***(Mat.12:43) But the unclean spirit, when he is gone out of the man, passeth through waterless places, seeking rest, and findeth it not. (44) Then he saith, I will return into my house whence I came out; and when he is come, he findeth it empty, swept, and garnished. (45) Then goeth he, and taketh with himself seven other spirits more evil than himself, and they enter in and dwell there: and the last state of that man becometh worse than the first. Even so shall it be also unto this evil generation.*** So Jesus cast demons out and He healed the sick, but they wouldn't turn from their sins and they wouldn't turn from their rebellious ways, and guess what? It all came back on them, but it came back on them seven times worse. It happens today, too. Many people don't keep their healing or their deliverance and it's because they won't repent.

We need to appreciate what God does for us. We need to appreciate His grace, mercy and love so much that we'll decide to live for Him. Many don't do that. They go right back and end up worse than before. Oh, yes, they're so happy to be free because now they can go sin some more. It doesn't work that way, folks. The devil has rights and he knows it. He's a good lawyer. He knows the Bible and the Word of God gives him his rights. The apostle Paul even turned a man over to Satan in order to save him. ***(1Co.5:5) To deliver such a one unto Satan for the destruction of the flesh, that the spirit***

may be saved in the day of the Lord Jesus. When people are in rebellion and living under the curse of the devil because of their sins, you may be able to give them some temporary deliverance, but it won't be permanent until they repent. The curse in Deuteronomy 28 is God's chastening upon the wicked to bring them to repentance. God sent the curse and God sent a Savior to deliver us from the chastening. That deliverance is for those not in willful rebellion who believe Jesus bore the chastening and the demonic oppression. Jesus came to show us that. He "went about doing good and healing all that were oppressed of the devil; for God was with him." If you want to repent of your sins and serve God, deliverance will do you very well, but if you don't want to repent, deliverance will just be a bigger curse on you. Be sure you appreciate God's precious gift.

The Syrophoenician woman expressed her faith. ***(Mar.7:28) But she answered and saith unto him, Yea, Lord; even the dogs under the table eat of the children's crumbs. (29) And he said unto her, <u>For this saying</u> go thy way; the demon is gone out of thy daughter. (30) And she went away unto her house, and found the child laid upon the bed, and the demon gone out.*** Jesus certainly didn't argue with the demons or get red in the face, or anything else. He spoke it and He knew it had to come to pass. The demons have to obey you. There is the word, the *logos*, right here in that text. "For this saying go thy way; the demon is gone out of thy daughter." There's the "communication" and the "something that is said." Glory be to God! Thank You, Father, for the Word of faith. We have that authority. We're not doing anything of our own power and we have authority over the power of the devil when we find people who are entitled to the benefits of the Kingdom. Jesus found this woman, who expressed her faith, so she was entitled and He gave it to her because she, too, was a child of the Kingdom. Through faith, she became Abraham's seed and her circumcision was a circumcision of heart and not of flesh. ***(Rom.2:28) For he is not a Jew who is one outwardly; neither is that circumcision which is outward in the flesh: (29) but he is a Jew who is one inwardly; and circumcision is that of the heart, in the spirit not in the letter; whose praise is not of men, but of God.*** We have that authority as well when we preach the Gospel to the people who believe it and receive it. Then we <u>know</u> we're standing on firm ground and that they're entitled to the benefits. Jesus gave us the demonstration and we walk in His steps. If you're a believer, you don't have to bring anybody to the preacher and you don't have to know the names of the demons. You don't have to get red in the face, wrestle with anybody or hold anybody down. All you have to do is exercise your authority over the devil.

Glory be to God! Thank You, Father, for the brethren who are studying with us. I ask that You bless them with the authority and wisdom that You have spoken in Your Word. And thank You so much for bringing to pass in them the life of Christ. Amen.

CHAPTER 11

Christians and Demons!

God bless you and thank you so much for joining us in this study. I do pray that the Lord will be with you and give you wisdom to prepare you for the great things that God is about to do. Glory be to God! Thank You, Father. Thank You for being with us, Father. Thank You for Your precious promises, Father. Thank You for drawing us, Lord, and giving us a hunger and a thirst for righteousness. Thank You, Lord, that everything You're working in these coming days is for our good and to bring us into the glory of God that was ordained for us through the sacrifice of Jesus Christ. Thank You, Father.

Well, saints, we've been learning about the real Good News of what the Lord has accomplished for us and how we can cooperate with Him in bringing this to pass. I'd like to back up just a little bit to the previous teaching. ***(Mat.10:5) These twelve Jesus sent forth, and charged them, saying, Go not into [any] way of the Gentiles, and enter not into any city of the Samaritans: (6) but go rather to the lost sheep of the house of Israel. (7) And as ye go, preach, saying, The kingdom of heaven is at hand. (8) Heal the sick, raise the dead, cleanse the lepers, cast out demons: freely ye received, freely give.*** We see that the Lord sent His disciples to cast the demons out of the Covenant people of God and we've noticed that everything that happens to Israel is a type and a shadow for the Church: ***(1Co.10:5) Howbeit with most of them God was not well pleased: for they were overthrown in the wilderness. (6) Now these things were our examples, to the intent we should not lust after evil things, as they also lusted. (7) Neither be ye idolaters, as were some of them; as it is written, The people sat down to eat and drink, and rose up to play. (8) Neither let us commit fornication, as some of them committed, and fell in one day three and twenty thousand. (9) Neither let us make trial of the Lord, as some of them made trial, and perished by the serpents. (10) Neither murmur ye, as some of them murmured, and perished by the destroyer. (11) Now these things happened unto them by way of example; and they were written for our admonition, upon whom the ends of the ages are come.***

The Lord gave authority only for those who were Covenant people because, obviously, the promises were given for God's people. The promises are not made for the world. What causes the world to enter in is that they have to be believers. Jesus said, ***(Mat.9:29) According to your faith be it done unto you***, and ***(Rom.1:16) for [the gospel]*** (the Good News) ***is the power of God unto salvation to every one that believeth***. There's the condition and it's all the way through the Scriptures. You have to be a believer. Now we looked at some examples in the previous chapter of people who were not Covenant people, according to the Old Testament, but they were Covenant people, according to the New Testament. They entered in through their faith. We're sons of Abraham through faith and those who are born from above, born again, are circumcised in heart. *(Rom.2:28) For he is not a Jew who is one outwardly; neither is that circumcision which is outward in the flesh: (29) but he is a Jew who is one inwardly; and circumcision is that of the heart.* And so, just as Jesus sent forth His disciples to cast the demons out of His Covenant people, in these days there's going to be a perfect fulfillment of this in the Man-child ministry sending forth disciples to cast demons out of the lost sheep of New Testament, spiritual Israel. Some of you reading this are thinking, "No, it's not possible. Christians can't have demons." But it was God's people out of whom Jesus and the disciples cast the demons! Jesus sent forth the disciples to the lost sheep of the house of Israel. *(Mat.10:5) These twelve Jesus sent forth, and charged them, saying, Go not into any way of the Gentiles, and enter not into any city of the Samaritans: (6) but go rather to the lost sheep of the <u>house of Israel</u>. (7) And as ye go, preach, saying, The kingdom of heaven is at hand. (8) Heal the sick, raise the dead, cleanse the lepers, <u>cast out demons</u>: freely ye received, freely give.*

I've been casting out demons since I was a very young Christian. After I read the Book, after I was born again, I just read, read, read the Word and I decided I was going to pay attention to what I read. I didn't have a lot of religious experience, so I just read it and acted upon it. And almost all of the people that the Lord used me to cast demons out of were Christians. Folks, don't say it can't happen. It's just not the experience of people who have the gift of discerning of spirits. Do you know what discerning of spirits is? It's a supernatural gift that God gives to people to see demons, not just discern them, but the discernment many times is seeing them and I'm telling you that I see them in Christians. You know, it was a sad situation when we had a "revival" of sorts in this area because the devil picked a church that doesn't believe Christians can have demons to bring in all sorts of religious deception. Well, just as His first Covenant people could have demons, His second Covenant people can and do have demons. We need to be wary, folks.

(Luk.13:10) And he was teaching in one of the synagogues on the sabbath day. (11) And behold, a woman that had a <u>spirit of infirmity</u> eighteen years; and she was bowed together, and could in no wise lift herself up. (12) And when Jesus saw her, he called her, and said to her, Woman, thou art loosed from thine infirmity. He called this a "spirit of infirmity," a demon spirit that causes a sickness. *(Luk.13:13) And he laid his hands upon her: and immediately she was made straight, and glorified God.* Now that's deliverance! And what did He say? "Woman, thou art loosed from thine infirmity." He just exercised authority. There were no magic words, like, "Come out in the name of Jesus." The Lord just exercised His authority over these demons and they knew what He said went. It's the same with us, folks, because Jesus said, *(Joh.20:21) As the Father hath sent me, even so send I you.* He sent out His disciples to exercise that same authority and we have that same authority today. *(Mar.16:17) And these signs shall accompany them that believe: in my name shall they cast out demons.* We just need to

believe the Word of God and start acting upon it. *(Luk.13:13) And he laid his hands upon her: and immediately she was made straight, and glorified God. (14) And the ruler of the synagogue, being moved with indignation because Jesus had healed on the sabbath, answered and said to the multitude, There are six days in which men ought to work: in them therefore come and be healed, and not on the day of the sabbath. (15) But the Lord answered him, and said, Ye hypocrites, doth not each one of you on the sabbath loose his ox or his ass from the stall, and lead him away to watering? (16) And ought not this woman, <u>being a daughter of Abraham</u>, whom Satan had bound, lo, [these] eighteen years, to have been loosed from this bond on the day of the sabbath?* One of the conditions He pointed out there was that she was a daughter of Abraham. Isn't it quite legal for a daughter of Abraham to be loosed from demons on the Sabbath? She has a covenant with God, a guaranteed right to deliverance from God. Nobody in the world has that but a child of God; in this case, a daughter of Abraham.

In the New Testament, for instance in the Book of John, Jesus was speaking with the Jews concerning their status in the Kingdom. *(Joh.8:31) Jesus therefore said to those Jews that had believed him* (So you can believe Him in some ways and not in others.), *If ye abide in my word, [then] are ye truly my disciples; (32) and ye shall know the truth, <u>and the truth shall make you free</u>.* As in our day, folks, the truth is what sets us free from bondage. Jesus received that Isaiah 61 anointing to open the prison to those who were bound and to set the captives free. *(Isa.61:1) The Spirit of the Lord God is upon me; because the Lord hath anointed me to preach good tidings unto the meek; he hath sent me to bind up the broken-hearted, to proclaim liberty to the captives, and the opening of the prison to them that are bound, (2) to proclaim the year of the Lord's favor....* This is also prophesied in the New Testament: *(Luk.4:14) And Jesus returned in the power of the Spirit into Galilee: and a fame went out concerning him through all the region round about. (15) And he taught in their synagogues, being glorified of all. (16) And he came to Nazareth, where he had been brought up: and he entered, as his custom was, into the synagogue on the sabbath day, and stood up to read. (17) And there was delivered unto him the book of the prophet Isaiah. And he opened the book, and found the place where it was written, (18) The Spirit of the Lord is upon me, Because he anointed me to preach good tidings to the poor: He hath sent me to proclaim release to the captives, And recovering of sight to the blind, To set at liberty them that are bruised, (19) To proclaim the acceptable year of the Lord.* That applies to us, also, folks; we're to set the captives free, too.

But whom did Jesus choose to set free? It was only those who were Covenant people, whether Old Covenant or New Covenant. Jesus came in a time when He was leading people out of the Old Covenant and into the New, and both were in effect. He had to come first to the Jews, who were the Covenant people at that time, and offer them this benefit of the

Kingdom. And, of course, when they rebuked Him and renounced His Words, when they turned away from Him and His disciples, then the Jews were reprobated and God offered this gift to the Gentiles. What was the Jews' argument with what Jesus said? *(Joh.8:33)* ***They answered unto him, We are Abraham's seed, and have never yet been in bondage to any man: how sayest thou, Ye shall be made free?*** Well, there are a lot of people who believe that today, folks. They think because they're Christians that they don't need to be set free. They think because they're Christians that they don't need any deliverance, but the truth will set you free and a lie will keep you in bondage. Jesus understood this. But then those Jews said to Jesus, *(Joh.8:39)* ***They answered and said unto him, Our father is Abraham. Jesus saith unto them, If ye were Abraham's children, ye would do the works of Abraham.*** In the New Testament, what causes you be a child of someone is that you walk in their steps. In the New Testament, it's what the spiritual seed brings forth that counts and not the physical seed, so what is it to be a child of the Kingdom? *(1Jn.2:6)* ***He that saith he abideth in him ought himself also to walk even as he walked.*** The only proof that you are a child of someone in the New Testament is, do you walk as they walked? And, of course, Jesus was pointing out that, if they were true children of Abraham, they would do the works of Abraham. But instead, He said, *(Joh.8:44)* ***Ye are of <u>your father the devil</u>*** (Why? Because they were walking in <u>his</u> steps, right?), ***<u>and the lusts of your father it is your will to do</u>. He was a murderer from the beginning, and standeth not in the truth, because there is no truth in him. When he speaketh a lie, he speaketh of his own: for he is a liar, and the father thereof.*** So, in the New Testament, genealogy isn't reckoned according to the flesh because the seed is passed on through the Word and believing the Word. We give fertile ground to the seed when we believe and act on the Word of God, which is the seed or the *sperma* of the Kingdom in the Parable of the Sower (Matthew 13:1-23).

Also, let me point this out to you: *(Gal.3:6)* ***Even as Abraham believed God, and it was <u>reckoned unto him for righteousness</u>. (7) Know therefore that they that are of faith, the same are sons of Abraham.*** You see, we inherit the benefits of the Kingdom, just like that woman in Luke, because of our <u>faith</u>. We are walking in the steps of Abraham. *(Gal.3:8)* ***And the scripture, foreseeing that <u>God would justify the Gentiles by faith</u>, preached the gospel beforehand unto Abraham, [saying,] <u>In thee shall all the nations be blessed</u>.*** "In thee shall all the nations be blessed." An elect group of all nations is abiding in their father Abraham. *(Gal.3:29)* ***And if ye are Christ's, then are ye Abraham's seed, heirs according to promise.*** And Paul said, *(Gal.4:28)* ***Now we, brethren, as Isaac was, <u>are children of promise</u>***. Do you believe the promise? Then you're a child of Abraham and a child of God, and you have the benefits of the Kingdom. You have the benefits of the Covenant and one of those benefits is that you have the right to be delivered of demons, and you have the right to cast out demons (Matthew 10:8; Mark 16:17). All believers can do that. There are people out there who specialize in this, but Mark just makes one condition and that is <u>believe</u>. "These signs shall accompany them that <u>believe</u>." A baby Christian can cast out demons and should be doing it. It's been spoken unto us, so we should be doing it.

Now I'd like to go a little further with something we looked at last time. ***(Mat.12:38) Then certain of the scribes and Pharisees answered him, saying, Teacher, we would see a sign from thee. (39) But he answered and said unto them, An evil and adulterous generation seeketh after a sign; and there shall no sign be given it but the sign of Jonah the prophet.*** Jesus was speaking to the Pharisees and the Scribes. It was the Jews who were "an evil and adulterous generation." And Jesus tried to warn them. ***(Mat.12:43) But the unclean spirit, <u>when he is gone out of the man</u>, <u>passeth through waterless places</u>, seeking rest, and findeth it not. (44) Then he saith, I will return into my house whence I came out; and when he is come, he findeth it empty, swept, and garnished. (45) Then goeth he, and taketh with himself <u>seven other spirits more evil than himself</u>, and they enter in and dwell there: <u>and the last state of that man becometh worse than the first</u>. Even so shall it be also unto this evil generation.*** Jesus said that when the demon is cast out, it passes through waterless places and returns, and brings seven worse than himself; even so shall it be unto this generation. Well, folks, there's no difference between <u>that</u> end-time generation at the end of their Covenant and this end-time generation at the end of <u>our</u> Covenant. As you know, the former rain came at the end of their Covenant and the latter rain is coming at the end of our Covenant because history just repeats. And I want to tell you that many demons will be cast out in the days ahead from <u>Covenant</u> people and because they will not repent, the demons will return much worse. This is a sad but true thing. Now some of you may still be asking, "Can Christians really have demons? How is it that Christians can have demons?" Well, for years people have quoted this *verse* to me. "My Spirit will not dwell in an unclean temple." If you've ever heard that *verse*, guess what? It's not to be found in the Scriptures, folks. It's become very popular but it's like one of those old wive's tales. There's no verse in the Bible that actually says that, but I do agree with it in a way because where the Spirit of God dwells, it's a holy place. So the problem is, how is it that Christians can have demons and yet have the Holy Spirit?

I'll tell you what the Lord told me many, many years ago, that I think fits perfectly. He showed me that the Tabernacle in the wilderness was not only a type of the Lord Himself, but it was a type of His body because in the midst of our very heart and spirit, God dwells, like He dwelt in the Holy of Holies in the Tabernacle in the Wilderness. The Tabernacle was just a portable Temple, like we are. This body is a tabernacle, you see, and people say God and the devil, or God and demons, can't dwell in the same temple. Well, that's not quite true. Let me point out just a few things to you. The Holy of Holies represents our spirit. Only the High Priest could go into the Holy of Holies and, if he hadn't been sanctified, he would not live through that experience. As a matter of fact, the High Priest went into the Holy of Holies with a rope tied around his ankle, just in case he was going in there unsanctified, according to the Law. That way, they could just drag them out dead, which was always a possibility. So nothing evil could enter into the Tabernacle, which was the place of the Ark of the Covenant, the place of the Presence of God. That was where God would speak to His people from between the cherubim over the Mercy Seat. No one could go into the presence of God, except the holy. And the High Priest, of course, represented our High Priest, the Lord Jesus Christ. The shekinah glory was there in the Holy of Holies. Then, the next place, just outside the Holy of Holies, was the Holy Place and it represented the soul. Over them both was the Tent of Meeting. The covering over the tent represented this covering over the place of God's presence and an interesting thing was that the outside of the tent was covered with ram's skins that were dyed red. **(Isa.1:18) Come now, and let us reason together, saith the Lord: though your sins be as scarlet, they shall be as white as snow; though they be <u>red</u> like crimson, they shall be as wool.** And here we have ram's skin and what would a ram represent but a stubborn beast? By the way, rams were <u>sacrificed</u>, just as we, as Christians, have a continual burnt offering. **(Rom.12:1) I beseech you therefore, brethren, by the mercies of God, to present your bodies a living sacrifice, holy, acceptable to God, which is your spiritual service.** We are to sacrifice this old beast. So now we can see that there is a Holy Temple of the Lord and a temple that's not so holy. Lastly, on the outside of the Holy Place, not the Holy of Holies but the Holy Place, was the Outer Court and it represented our physical body.

Well, in the Old Testament, many an unholy person entered into the outer court and many an unholy person entered even into the Holy Place. We have instances of wicked kings and wicked queens entering, taking hold of the horns of the altar and asking for the mercy of God, and they didn't immediately die. It's true about us, too, folks. Things that are unholy can enter into our soul. Did you know that when we are born again and we are given a new spirit, that we have that Tabernacle of the presence of God in our spirit? That's our Holy of Holies and nothing unclean can enter there; no demon can enter there. What God desires to do is control your soul through your spirit. He desires to take possession of us. Your soul represents your mind, will and emotions, and what God desires is, through the spirit, to control <u>all</u> of the soul: all of our mind, will and emotions. But, at the same time, the devil or demons can enter into the Outer Court because there's nothing holy about the flesh. **(1Co.15:50) Now this I say, brethren, that <u>flesh and blood cannot inherit the kingdom of God</u>; neither doth corruption inherit incorruption.** The flesh cannot even enter the Kingdom, but the demons in the flesh also want to take control of the mind, the will and the emotions of the Christian. There's a battle going on between flesh and spirit, between the carnal man and the spiritual man. **(Rom.8:13) For if ye live after the flesh, ye must die; but if by the Spirit ye put to death the deeds of the body, ye shall live.** We are in the midst of a situation where we're ministered to by angels and by demons, by God and the devil, by the flesh and by the spirit. You know, everywhere we turn, there's a decision for our soul to make. And, since we're in this position, let me tell you that Christians <u>can</u> have demons in their flesh because, once again, there's nothing really holy about the flesh.

As a matter of fact, God won't renew, God won't regenerate, the flesh. He wants it to die. The mind of the flesh is the mind that's been taken over by the flesh, or the soul and the mind that's been taken over by the flesh, by the lusts of man. ***(Rom.8:5) For they that are after the flesh <u>mind</u> the things of the flesh; but they that are after the Spirit the things of the Spirit.*** And, of course, the mind is a part of the soul. You see, the flesh is constantly seeking to have its way with the mind, in order to cause you to give in to the lusts. ***(Rom.8:6) For the <u>mind</u> of the flesh is death; but the mind of the Spirit is life and peace*** (The mind of the flesh cannot enter the Kingdom of God. It's the enemy of God.)***: (7) because the mind of the flesh is enmity against God; for it is not subject to the law of God, neither indeed can it be: (8) and they that are in the flesh <u>cannot please God</u>.*** The reason that's so is because the mind of the flesh is an offspring of the devil. Think about the lusts of the flesh, the works of the flesh. ***(Gal.5:19) Now the works of the flesh are manifest, which are these: fornication, uncleanness, lasciviousness, (20) idolatry, sorcery, enmities, strife, jealousies, wraths, factions, divisions, parties, (21) envyings, drunkenness, revellings, and such like; of which I forewarn you, even as I did forewarn you, that they who practise such things shall not inherit the kingdom of God.*** There are demons that have the same names as those lusts of the flesh. Why is that? It's because the demons are the fathers of the lusts of the flesh, just as God is the Father of the fruits of the Spirit. The flesh is created in the image of the devil, folks; that's why it has to die, so that we might be renewed. ***(Rom.8:7) Because the mind of the flesh is enmity against God; for it is not subject to the law of God, neither indeed can it be*** (So, it's the enemy of God and do you think that the devil can enter into the enemy of God? Of course he can!)***: (Rom.8:8) and they that are in the flesh <u>cannot please God</u>. (9) But ye are not in the flesh but in the Spirit, if so be that the Spirit of God dwelleth in you. But if any man hath not the Spirit of Christ, he is none of his.*** God's anointing, by His Holy Spirit, <u>empowers</u> us to overcome the strong desires of the lusts of the flesh.

I'd like for us to take a closer look at those verses in Galatians. ***(Gal.5:17) For the flesh lusteth against the Spirit, and the Spirit against the flesh; for these are <u>contrary</u> the one to the other; that ye may not do the things that ye would.*** The word "lust" here just means "desire"; it's not imputing any evil to the Spirit of God. ***(Gal.5:18) But if ye are led by the Spirit, ye are not under the law. (19) Now the works of the flesh are manifest, which are these....*** By the way, the "works" of the Spirit are called the "fruits" of the Spirit. The list here is also the "fruit" of the flesh, but they call it the "works" of the flesh. It's bad fruit, but it's fruit. ***(Gal.5:19) Now the works of the flesh are manifest, which are these: fornication, uncleanness, lasciviousness, (20) idolatry, sorcery, enmities, strife, jealousies, wraths, factions, divisions, parties, (21) envyings, drunkenness, revellings, and such like; of which I forewarn you, even as I did forewarn you,***

that they who practise such things shall <u>not</u> inherit the kingdom of God. In other words, that old man who does these things is never going to Heaven. The old man, the old life, the one that's created in the image of the devil with his fruit that we're reading about here, is not entering the Kingdom. He is <u>against</u> God. ***(Gal.5:22) But the fruit of the Spirit is love, joy, peace, longsuffering, kindness, goodness, faithfulness, (23) meekness, self-control; against such there is no law. (24) <u>And they that are of Christ Jesus have crucified the flesh with the passions and the lusts thereof.</u>*** What does that mean? Does that mean that they're perfect? No. It means that their old man is on the cross and they're just not letting him down to rule.

You know, when flesh is on the cross, it doesn't have ability to do its own will and the Christian who walks in the Spirit doesn't permit their flesh to do its will. And, of course, the more you permit the flesh to do its will, the more the devil is invited in and permitted to take over control of your soul. Ultimately, a person becomes, in that case, twice dead and plucked up by the roots. ***(Jud.12) These are they who are hidden rocks in your love-feasts when they feast with you, shepherds that without fear feed themselves; clouds without water, carried along by winds; autumn leaves without fruit, <u>twice dead</u>, <u>plucked up by the roots</u>.*** Now, you can't be twice dead unless you're twice born, can you? So, if you believe that a person can't be born-again and yet have a demonic spirit, I ask, then how can a person be twice dead? The truth is, the old man has to die. As a matter of fact, Jesus made that a condition for entering the Kingdom. ***(Mat.10:39) Except you lose your life, you will not gain your life. He that findeth his life shall lose it; and he that loseth his life for my sake shall find it.*** So this old man has to die and we have to cooperate with God in this crucifixion of the old life because the devil can use you as long as you give in to your lusts. He can take you over and, in some cases, people can become totally possessed.

There are people who say Christians can't be possessed, that they can only be oppressed. They say oppression is from the outside and possession is from the inside. There's no truth to that, folks. A person can be oppressed from the inside and not possessed. The Lord showed me that the demons go in and out of the soul. When a demon is in your body and he reaches into your soul and takes possession of your mind, your will and your emotions, that's possession, but the demon's been on the inside the whole time, you see. And he can back out, by the way. Have you ever noticed that a person can be quite normal one moment and the next moment they act as though they're possessed? It's because the demons go in and out of the soul. They go in, they take control; they back out, they sit dormant. Sometimes they can be very quiet for years and you will never know that they're there until something happens to cause them to manifest. Many times when children pass through puberty, the demons will start manifesting in them. And people will wonder, "Where did <u>that</u> come from?" Well, probably all they have to do is look back in their heritage and they'll be able to figure it out. After all, what did you inherit from <u>your</u> parents? We're all wrestling with what we inherited from our parents. ***(Lev.17:11) For the life of the flesh is in the blood....*** It's been passed on. But we know that we've been given a transfusion at the cross. We know that we've been given the blood of Jesus Christ and it's been passed on to us, glory be to God! We have a new heritage now, a new Father and we give thanks to God for that. But we all wrestle with what was passed on from our parents and, in some cases, not only the <u>nature of the flesh</u> is passed on, but the <u>demons</u> that the parents have had are passed on and we have to wrestle with those and cast them down.

The really, really Good News is that the Lord has already done this for us. He's already accomplished it. ***(Joh.16:33) These things have I spoken unto you, that in me ye may have peace. In the world ye have tribulation: but be of good cheer; I have overcome the world.*** He's already overcome the world. ***(Gal.2:20) I have been crucified with Christ; and it is no longer I that live, but Christ living in me: and that life which I now live in the flesh I live in faith, the faith which is in the Son of God, who loved me, and gave himself up for me.*** He's already overcome the flesh and we were crucified with Christ. ***(Heb.10:14) For by one offering he hath perfected for ever them that are sanctified.*** By one offering the old man was crucified and the new man was given to us, so we have been perfected. Our faith imputes righteousness to us from God and our faith in what the Lord has already done is the only thing we need to conquer the demons, to conquer the flesh and to conquer the world because the Lord's already accomplished this for us. That's why we can boldly exercise faith to come against demons concerning someone who is a child of God, concerning someone who is in Covenant, every time. Jesus never turned away Covenant people who had demons anymore than He turned away Covenant people who were sick. The Bible says He healed them <u>all</u>. Now, we just saw that, even though He healed them all and He cast out their spirits of infirmity and their demons, those demons came back because the people didn't appreciate their gift from God (Matthew 12:43-45). As a matter of fact, the demons came back worse because the heavy penalty of the curse causes many people to repent.

Of course, we all need to repent. We all need to turn away from this old flesh and, if we give in to the flesh, we are opening a door for the demons to take advantage of us. Remember what Jesus said: ***(Joh.14:30) The prince of the world cometh: and <u>he hath nothing in me</u>.*** That's the key: "He hath nothing in me." In other words, the Lord hadn't been catering to His flesh. He hadn't been giving in to His flesh. He hadn't been making a door for the devil or demons to enter in and take any kind of possession or take any kind of rights. Glory be to God! That's the great thing about this spirit, soul and body sanctification that the Lord has given us. If you're wise concerning these things, you can cut the devil off. You can use your shield of faith. ***(2Co.7:1) Having therefore these promises, beloved, <u>let us cleanse ourselves from all defilement of flesh and spirit</u>, perfecting holiness in the fear of God.*** Notice who's getting this deliverance here: "Having therefore these promises." Who is it who believes these promises? It's only the Covenant people. "Let <u>us</u> cleanse <u>ourselves</u>," He didn't say, "the wicked world." We have a right to cleanse ourselves. We have a Covenant with God, a guarantee with God. "Of all defilement of flesh and spirit"; that is speaking about defilement of your soul by your flesh and by demon spirits. We have a Covenant right; we are guaranteed this cleansing.

Not everyone has a right to these benefits because not everyone is not delivered from the curse. *(Gal.3:13) Christ redeemed <u>us</u>....* Who's Paul speaking to? He's talking to the Galatian <u>Christians</u>. And, by the way, they were Gentile Christians. *(13) Christ redeemed <u>us</u> from the curse of the law, having become a curse for <u>us</u>; for it is written, Cursed is every one that hangeth on a tree: (14) that upon the <u>Gentiles</u> might come the blessing of Abraham <u>in Christ Jesus</u>; that we might receive the promise of the Spirit through faith.* Where do you get the blessing of Abraham? Abiding <u>in</u> Christ Jesus; that's the only place you can find it, folks. The *unconditional eternal security* people are wrong. You have to abide in Christ. And what does the Bible say about that? *(1Jn.2:6) He that saith he <u>abideth in him</u> ought himself also <u>to walk even as he walked</u>. (24) As for you, let that abide in you which ye heard from the beginning. <u>If that which ye heard from the beginning abide in you</u>, <u>ye also shall abide in the Son</u>, and in the Father.* In other words, the doctrine that was given unto us is what we must abide in, is what we must have in our heart. This causes us to abide in the Son because He is the Word. So we see here, "that <u>we</u> might receive the <u>promise of the Spirit through faith</u>." We receive <u>all</u> the promises of the Spirit through faith; there's the condition. And it doesn't matter if you call yourself a Christian or if you've shaken a preacher's hand, or gone to an altar, or had an experience with God in the past. The point is, do you believe <u>now</u>? Are you believing now? The benefits of the Kingdom are to those who believe. "These signs will accompany them that <u>believe</u>." We have a right to minister God's deliverance, but on the other hand, Jesus said, *(Mat.8:13) ... As thou hast believed, [so] be it done unto thee.* It's very important that we believe to enter in to the benefits of the blessings of Abraham.

There are some conditions in the Scriptures that make it legal to cast demons out of lost people, but it has to do with the benefits of God's people. *(Act.16:16) And it came to pass, as we were going to the place of prayer, that a certain maid having a <u>spirit</u> of divination....* You may have a footnote that the Greek word there for "spirit" is "python" and Jesus gave us authority to tread upon serpents and scorpions (Luke 10:19). These are kinds of demons. By the way, the serpent has its poison in the head and the scorpion has its poison in the tail. The head has to do a lot of times with knowledge, discernment, prophecy and these kinds of things. These are deceiving spirits and this was a deceiving, false prophecy demon here. *(Act.16:16) And it came to pass, as we were going to the place of prayer, that a certain maid having a <u>spirit of divination</u> met us, who brought her masters much gain by soothsaying.* Now, certainly, this wasn't a child of the Kingdom, right? *(Act.16:17) The same following after Paul and us cried out, saying, These men are servants of the Most High God, who proclaim unto you <u>the way</u> of salvation.* Literally, it says "<u>a way</u> of salvation." Isn't that what the devil preaches, folks? He preaches that there are many different ways of salvation, but Scripture says otherwise: ***(Act.4:12) And in none other is there salvation: for neither is there any other name under heaven, that is given among men, where<u>in</u> we must be saved.*** "There's no other name given among men where<u>in</u> we must be saved." There's only <u>one</u> way; the Lord is very narrow-minded. ***(Mat.7:13) Enter ye in by the <u>narrow</u> gate: for wide is the gate, and broad is the way, that leadeth to destruction, and many are they that enter in thereby. (14) For <u>narrow</u> is the gate, and <u>straitened the way</u>, that leadeth unto life, and few are they that find it.*** He calls it the "straitened way" and "straitened" means "narrow."

Well, this lying demon was perverting the gospel of Paul into "many ways." ***(Act.16:18) And this she did for many days. But Paul, being sore troubled, turned and said to the spirit, I charge thee in the name of Jesus Christ to come out of her. And it came out that very hour.*** (Here's an instance where he said, "Come out in the name of Jesus." That's not a law, but he exercised his authority.) ***(Act.16:19) But when her masters saw that the hope of their gain was gone, they laid hold on Paul and Silas, and dragged them into the marketplace before the rulers.*** So when her masters saw their hope of gain was gone, they started to persecute Paul and Silas. ***(Act.16:20) and when they had brought them unto the magistrates, they said, These men, being Jews, do exceedingly trouble our city, (21) and set forth customs which it is not lawful for us to receive, or to observe, being Romans. (22) And the multitude rose up together against them: and the magistrates rent their garments off them, and commanded to beat them with rods. (23) And when they had laid many stripes upon them, they cast them into prison, charging the jailor to keep them safely: (24) who, having received such a charge, cast them into the inner prison, and made their feet fast in the stocks.*** Now this woman wasn't a Christian and she hadn't heard the Gospel. ***(Rom.1:16) For I am not ashamed of the gospel: for it is the power of God unto salvation to every one that believeth; to the Jew first, and also to the Greek.*** Certainly, what we need to do, if we want to see someone delivered, is preach the Gospel to them first. We need to make sure they are believers in what the Lord accomplished at the cross. He is our sacrifice; He is our blood Covenant. And when we preach the Gospel and when people believe it, there are other things we should cover immediately. We should cover baptism, we should cover being baptized in the Holy Spirit and we should cover deliverance, if there's a deliverance necessary because this poor child of God cannot serve Him very well under the burden of these demons. So you should make sure, first of all, that you're entering through the door, here; that you are first of all offering the Good News, the Gospel to these people. It's like people who want to go out and heal everybody, but they don't offer them the Gospel. Well, the <u>Gospel</u> is the power of God unto salvation to every one who believes it, so we need to be offering the Gospel; we need to be preaching the Gospel.

There was another instance years ago where the Lord showed me it was legal to cast demons out of a lost person and it was in my own home. In Acts 16:16, it was legal to cast out demons from a lost woman because she was hindering the Gospel and Apostle Paul was being tormented by that demon spirit of hers. You see, <u>we're not under the curse</u> and when another person's curse involves bringing us under the curse, then we have authority. We have authority from God not to live under the curse and Paul knew that. I'm sure Paul had in his mind, **(Mat.15:26) ... *It is not meet to take the children's bread and cast it to the dogs*.** He didn't jump quickly to casting this demon out of this woman, but maybe the Lord spoke the same thing to Paul that He spoke to me: "Hey, Paul, you're not under the curse; you don't have to put up with this," and being frustrated with this woman ruining his Gospel message, Paul did what he could. He exercised his authority and broke the power of that demon.

Well, I needed something like that when my mother came to live with me. She was living over in Louisiana while we were living in Florida and there was a good distance between us. We were having trouble because she was on medications for different ailments including some mental conditions and she was writing bad checks and things like that. She was rather old and feeble, and had some of what is called dementia. I decided we couldn't continue to handle the situation over such a distance, so she had to come move in with us. Well, don't you know, she was tormenting us. She would do really weird things, such as go into the refrigerator late at night and just leave the door wide open. That's how we'd find it when we'd enter the kitchen in the morning. Or she'd run up the long distance bill. One time, she even went running down the street, yelling, "Help! Help! Save me from these people!" Thank God the neighbors understood when I went out there and hauled her back home! Anyway, we were having these kinds of torments and I didn't know what to do. I did know that the Lord said it's not right to cast the children's bread to the dogs, but she was in our house and bringing us under the curse by keeping us awake at night and so on. These are the kind of things dementia does to a person.

An interesting thing was that during this time, there was a neighbor lady about a block down the road who was in the same shape as my mom and she died. Well, her children were down there auctioning off all of her things, though my mom didn't know this because it was a block down the road and she never went down there. So when I came home the next day, she was just so sad. I asked her, "What's the matter, Mom?" And she said, "Oh, I just watched them as they sold off all of my stuff. They were selling off all of my stuff and I couldn't do a thing about it. I could only just sit there and watch them." When I heard that, I knew it was the demon talking in her and I realized that the neighbor lady and my mom had the same demonic spirit. And I told her, "Mom, there's nothing wrong with your stuff; everything's intact." Actually, we had arranged for a friend to rent her house over in Louisiana while she was living with us.

Anyway, I beseeched the Lord. I said, "Lord, I know my mom is not a believer and she wouldn't turn loose of her lying dead religion that she was a part of to receive You. But the benefits of the Kingdom are still ours and I am your son, and according to Galatians 3:13, I am not under the curse. Yet, her being in our house has become a curse to us. It's tormenting our family and, Lord, I'm asking Your permission, because we're not under the curse, to cast these demons out of my mom." Well, don't you know, that very night my oldest daughter had a dream. She saw our house and going out through the middle of our roof was this three-story house, which she knew was my mom's house, even though in real-life my mom's house was only one-story. As she observed this, she saw coming out of the second story that there was a plank leading out to the street and there were five chickens walking out this plank to the street. And the first thing that came to my mind was body, soul and spirit, for the three stories of her house, which is made up of body, soul and spirit. The chickens reminded me of the fowls of Revelation 18:2, the unclean spirits. Unclean birds, they were called. And so I knew that the Lord was saying to me, "Okay. Since her house is in your house and this is bringing <u>you</u> under the curse, then <u>you</u> have authority to cast these out." I knew what the Lord was saying to me and I was just rejoicing that the Lord was giving me this answer!

And so, the next night, I was ready when my mom came knocking on our door. My wife and I had gone to bed and my mom came knocking on our door. She called out to us, "I'm going to keep you awake all night long!" Those demons were mean, you know. And I answered her, "Oh, no, you're not!" Then my wife and I got up and we marched into my mom's room and we commenced to commanding these five demons to, "Come out of her in the name of Jesus Christ." Literally, names of the demons were coming to us. I remember one of them was Dementia, though I've forgotten the other ones. But, you don't have to call the demons by their name; you can just call them by what they do and that will work just as well. So, as these five names came to us, we commanded them to, "Come out of her in the name of Jesus Christ," and we didn't stick around. That's been my habit for years. If you tell demons to come out, you don't have to stick around and wrestle with them. You don't have to argue with them. You can just go on about your business. That's the way I've done it for years. You don't have to argue with demons because they'll know if you don't have any authority. And don't wrestle with them because they'll know for sure that you don't have any authority, if you wrestle with them. So we just walked out of there, closed the door, went to bed and had a good night's sleep.

My mom's room was right next to the kitchen. When we woke up the next morning and went into the kitchen, we were noticing how quiet it was in there and how peaceful it felt in the house. So I decided, I'm going to peek through the door a little bit and see what's going on there, and I cracked the door just a little bit and looked in. Wow! Everything was just a wreck in my mom's room. Everything was all over the floor, even the bed clothes. I took a step into the room and looked around, but I didn't see my mom, until she came crawling out from under the bed. She had rolled around with those demons on the floor all night long, but I wasn't rolling around there with them and I didn't even have to worry about it; I'd just gone to bed. So, anyway, she came crawling out from under that bed and, I tell you, I'd never known this lady. I was realizing at this time that she'd had demons all of my life! As a young person and not knowing God, the problems I'd had with mom were because these demons were in her and now she was delivered, folks! This was a new lady! This lady was kind and thoughtful. She would listen and she was submissive. She'd never been submissive, even to my dad; she'd never been submissive. I was just rejoicing that the Lord had delivered <u>my</u> house from these demons, even though she wasn't a believer. Then, at that time, she started picking up Christian books and reading them. And I'd talk to her a little bit about the Lord and a little bit of it went in there. As a matter of fact, we had some awesome instances of total deliverance and healing for her up until the time she died.

One time she decided she wanted to go into an assisted living facility and she lived there for a while, but they started putting her back on drugs for some things and, I tell you, it was a downhill road from there. I'd never seen anything like that. She had a shoe box full of drugs by the time she left that place and they couldn't keep her balanced, so she was just out of her mind again. Then, one day she had some kind of attack. She went into the hospital and they took her off all of those drugs, all of them. She was in the hospital on an oxygen monitor and it was beeping all the time that her brain was not getting enough oxygen. I had three doctors tell me, "David, she's just not going to make it." So my wife and I decided to pray that the Lord would bring her totally through this so that she could have some relationship with her children and, then, if the Lord wanted to take her, so be it.

So we prayed that prayer going to the hospital and we just thanked the Lord for bringing her through this and saving her from it. Sure enough, when we talked to the doctors there, they said, "She's just not going to make it," and one of the doctors was my oldest sister, who is a psychiatrist. She, too, said, "Mom's not going to make it. Not this time." They knew her brain wasn't getting oxygen and, if she came out of it, she wasn't going to be right. But I confessed the Lord in front of them all. I said, "Oh, yes. She's going to make it. She's going to come out of this and she'll be fine." Well, lo and behold, by the grace of God, she did come out of a coma that she'd been in for some time, with the oxygen monitor beeping constantly. And she was perfectly normal. She was on no drugs. She was mobile. She even went back to that assisted living facility and she was talking intelligibly to people. Everybody was just amazed and they looked at her as a miracle. "What happened to her?" Well, the Lord's salvation was involved here and not man's works. They were giving her drugs to counteract the drugs to counteract the drugs and they'd driven the lady crazy, but she was now free. And everyone saw this as an awesome miracle because she was normal. Glory to God, folks! This is the power that <u>God</u> has! Thank You, Father! God bless you, saints.

CHAPTER 12

Authority and Demons!

Greetings, saints. God bless you. Thank you for continuing with us in this Bible study. Father, in the name of Jesus, we ask You for Your grace today for our understanding, for our willingness to obey. We ask You, Lord, to draw us and cause us to run after You. Lord, cause us to walk in the steps of Jesus. Cause us to be <u>true</u> disciples of Christ, Father. Thank You so much, Lord. Teach us, Lord; teach us today. Amen.

Well, brethren, we've been talking about the real Good News and I'd like for us to begin today's study here: ***(Col.1:12) Giving thanks unto the Father, who made us*** <u>***meet***</u> (that means "able") ***to be partakers of the inheritance of the saints in light*** (The <u>Lord</u> made us able to <u>partake</u> of our inheritance.)***; (13) who delivered us out of the power of darkness, and translated us into the kingdom of the Son of his love....*** <u>We have already been delivered</u>. This is the Good News. We know we have a right to cast out demons. We know we have a right to take authority over the power of darkness because the Lord already delivered those who believe. Of course, that's the question in our mind whenever we go to administer God's blessings to people: Do they believe the Gospel? So we share the Gospel with them and when we see if they do believe or if they don't believe, we have authority according to that. If they believe, we can administer the blessings. ***(Col.1:13) Who delivered us out of the power of darkness, and translated us into the kingdom of the Son of his love; (14)*** <u>***in whom***</u> ***we have our redemption, the forgiveness of our sins.*** "Redemption" is "the release of a prisoner in exchange for a sum of money or other payment demanded or paid." You know, the Lord paid the ransom so that we could be set free from bondage. We have been redeemed. Isn't that what a ransom does? He paid the ransom and we don't belong in bondage, saints. And, as believers, we also have the wonderful gift to be able to administer this gift to other believers. The Lord said, ***(Mar.16:17) And these signs shall accompany*** <u>***them that believe***</u>***:*** <u>***in my name shall they cast out demons;***</u> ***they shall speak with new tongues; (18) they shall take up serpents, and if they drink any deadly thing, it shall in no wise hurt them; they shall lay hands on the sick, and they shall recover.*** So it has to be "in my name." The only condition is to be a believer; not necessarily even a mature believer, just a believer. You just have to believe and that means "babies" in the Lord are entitled to these benefits the same as adults. All believers, even from a baby Christian on up, have a <u>right</u> to do all the signs there in Mark 16 and one of those signs is to cast out demons.

The verse says, "in my name." What does it mean to be in God's name? Doesn't it mean to be representing Him? "In His name" means "in His nature, character and authority"; that's what "name" means in the New Testament. So, in God's name, representing Him, we will cast out demons and these signs will accompany those who <u>believe</u>. That's the condition and again I want to say that the believer is not necessarily somebody who is mature in the Lord. You don't have to bring people who are oppressed or possessed to the preacher. In fact, many times the preacher may not know what to do with them. But even as a baby Christian, you can do the work of the Lord. You know, the Bible says something very interesting: ***(Eph.1:17) That the God of our Lord Jesus Christ, the Father of glory, may give unto you a spirit of wisdom and revelation in the knowledge of him; (18) having the eyes of your heart enlightened, that ye may know what is the hope of his calling*** (What is it that God called you for? What has He prepared you for? What has He prepared you to do? What are your orders? You can find some of them, for example, in the Sermon on the Mount of Matthew 5:3-12.), ***what the riches of the glory of his inheritance in the saints*** (He made us meet, He made us able to partake of the inheritance that we have.), ***(Eph.1:19) and what the exceeding greatness of his power to us-ward who believe*** (We need a revelation of the power that God is willing to manifest to all people who believe. Mark 16:17-18 is very plain that these signs will accompany those who believe. "In my name they will cast out demons."), ***according to that working of the strength of his might (Eph.1:20) which he wrought in Christ, when he raised him from the dead, and made him to sit at his right hand in the heavenly [places]***. What else happened when Christ was raised from the dead? ***(1Co.15:22) For as in Adam all die, so also in Christ shall all be made alive.*** When Christ was raised from the dead, who else was raised from the dead? We were, folks! When Adam fell, all mankind fell because the seed of all mankind was in Adam when he fell. But Jesus was the last Adam. He is called, by the way, in the original manuscripts, the "Father of eternity" (Isaiah 9:6). And so, just as all mankind fell when Adam fell, when Christ was resurrected, all of those in Him were also resurrected.

    (Joh.20:21) Jesus therefore said to them again, Peace be unto you: as the Father hath sent me, even so send I you. He sent His disciples with authority, the very same authority over the curse that He had. ***(Eph.1:20) Which he wrought in Christ, when he raised him from the dead, and made him to sit at his right hand in the heavenly [places], (21) far above all rule, and authority, and power, and dominion, and every name that is named*** (So Jesus was made to sit above all authority, all the principalities and powers.), ***not only in this world, but also in that which is to come: (22) and he put all things in subjection under his feet, and gave him to be head over all things to the church, (23) which is his body....*** We see here that Jesus is above; He's the head and all the principalities and powers are under His feet. This means, of course, that God put all the principalities under the very lowest member of the body of Christ. Even if you're the feet of the body, you have dominion over the principalities and powers. ***(Eph.1:23) Which is his body, the fulness of him that filleth all in all.*** All these principalities are under the feet of the body and Christ is the head of the body. That let's you know that even the very lowest, the very least of us, has authority over the devil's kingdom.

    It also brings to mind the revelation in Daniel about the image of the Beast, where the toes represented the end-time kingdom. ***(Dan.2:32) Thou, O king, sawest, and, behold, a great image. This image, which was mighty, and whose brightness was excellent, stood before thee; and the aspect thereof was terrible. (32) As for this image, its head was of fine gold, its breast and its arms of silver, its belly and its thighs of brass, (33) its legs of iron, its feet part of iron, and part of clay. (34) Thou sawest till that a stone was cut out without hands, which smote the image upon its feet that were of iron and clay, and brake them in pieces. (35) Then was the iron, the clay, the brass, the silver, and the gold, broken in pieces together, and became like the chaff of the summer threshing-floors; and the wind carried them away, so that no place was found for them: and the stone that smote the image became a great mountain, and filled the whole earth. (36) This is the dream; and we will tell the interpretation thereof before the king. (37) Thou, O king, art king of kings, unto whom the God of heaven hath given the kingdom, the power, and the strength, and the glory; (38) and wheresoever the children of men dwell, the beasts of the field and the birds of the heavens hath he given into thy hand, and hath made thee to rule over them all: thou art the head of gold. (39) And after thee shall arise another kingdom inferior to thee; and another third kingdom of brass, which shall bear rule over all the earth. (40) And the fourth kingdom shall be strong as iron, forasmuch as iron breaketh in pieces and subdueth all things; and as iron that crusheth all these, shall it break in pieces and crush. (41) And whereas thou sawest the feet and toes, part of potters clay, and part of iron, it shall be a divided kingdom; but there shall be in it of the strength of the iron, forasmuch as thou sawest the iron mixed with miry clay. (42) And as the toes of the feet were part of iron, and part of clay, so the kingdom shall be partly strong, and partly broken. (43) And whereas thou sawest the iron mixed with miry clay, they shall mingle themselves with the seed of men; but they shall not cleave one to another, even as iron doth not mingle with clay.***

According to Jesus, there are only two men in the earth: Christ and Antichrist. The Beast kingdom is all of those in whom the Antichrist lives; it's the body of Antichrist, if you will. ***(Luk.17:34) I say unto you, In that night there shall be two men on one bed; the one shall be taken, and the other shall be left. (35) There shall be two women grinding together; the one shall be taken, and the other shall be left. (36) There shall be two men in the field; the one shall be taken, and the other shall be left.*** So, just as it was in the days of Jesus, in these days, the body of Christ will face-off with the body of Antichrist. And, if you see the body as a type being stretched out over history, as Daniel also did, then you see that we're at the end of history. We're the people who are going to take dominion over the devil's kingdom. We're the people who are going to crush the devil's kingdom and bring it to nought, destroy it. This, according to Daniel, has been given unto the saints, folks. ***(Dan.7:26) But the*** *judgment shall be set, and they shall take away his dominion, to consume and to destroy it unto the end. (27) And the kingdom and the dominion, and the greatness of the kingdoms under the whole heaven, shall be given to the people of the saints of the Most High: his kingdom is an everlasting kingdom, and all dominions shall serve and obey him.* In these days, God's people are going to rise up or, I should say, God is going to rise up in His people and crush the kingdom of the Beast. The seed of the woman is going to crush the serpent's head. *(Gen.3:14) And the Lord God said unto the serpent, Because thou hast done this, cursed art thou above all cattle, and above every beast of the field; upon thy belly shalt thou go, and dust shalt thou eat all the days of thy life: (15) and I will put enmity between thee and the woman, and between thy seed and her seed: he shall bruise thy head, and thou shalt bruise his heel.* In these days, that's going to be fulfilled. You see here clearly that He has put every principality and power under the end-time saints; not that they haven't always been under all of the saints because the body is above the feet, obviously. But in these days, it's going to be manifest. In these days, we're going to see greater works than in Jesus' day in crushing the serpent. Of course, Jesus obviously did it all; it was all accomplished for us, but the body of Christ is going to bring it to pass in these days.

Remember that you don't have to bring people to someone else; you can just exercise your authority. God will use you to cast out demons and here's another confirmation of that: *(Psa.8:1) O Lord, our Lord, How excellent is thy name in all the earth, Who hast set thy glory upon the heavens! (2) Out of the mouth of babes and sucklings hast thou established strength, Because of thine adversaries, That thou mightest still the enemy and the avenger.* "Out of the mouths of babes and sucklings" doesn't sound like you have to be very, very mature, in order to take dominion over the Lord's enemies, does it? *(Psa.8:3) When I consider thy heavens, the work of thy fingers, The moon and the stars, which thou hast ordained....* As you read on, you find a text that was also quoted in Hebrews 2:6 and it reads, *(Psa.8:4) What is man, that thou art mindful of him? And the son of man, that thou visitest him? (5) For thou hast made him but little lower than God* (Or, some versions say, "angels." The word here is *elohim* and it means "mighty ones." In the Old Testament, it's translated many times as "God."), *And crownest him with glory and honor. (6) Thou makest him to have dominion over the works of thy hands; Thou hast put all things under his feet* (There it is, folks! All things! In these days, God's people are going to get the revelation that they're the head and not the tail; they're above and not beneath.)*: (Psa.8:7) All sheep and oxen, Yea, and the beasts of the field, (8) The birds of the heavens, and the fish of the sea, Whatsoever passeth through the paths of the seas. (9) O Lord, our Lord, How excellent is thy name in all the earth!* The curse was the opposite of that, wasn't it? So we see that God's people have been given dominion. God spoke to those who were in His name. Jesus spoke to those who were in His name. He said, "As the Father hath sent me, even so send I you."

This dominion was first spoken of Adam. ***(Gen.1:26) And God said, Let us make man in our image, after our likeness: and <u>let them have dominion</u> over the fish of the sea, and over the birds of the heavens, and over the cattle, and over all the earth, and over every creeping thing that creepeth upon the earth. (27) And God created man in his own image, in the image of God created he him; male and female created he them.*** Adam was given this dominion over the earth, but Adam sinned and everyone in him fell. ***(Rom.5:12) Therefore, as through one man sin entered into the world, and death through sin; and so death passed unto all men, for that all sinned....*** He sinned and they inherited sin, and they fell. ***(6:16) Know ye not, that to whom ye present yourselves [as] servants unto obedience, <u>his servants ye are whom ye obey</u>; whether of sin unto death, or of obedience unto righteousness?*** Well, Adam obeyed the devil and the devil took dominion over the earth, but then Jesus came along, Who is called the "last Adam," to restore that dominion. ***(1Co.15:45) So also it is written, The first man Adam became a living soul. The last Adam became a life-giving spirit.***

When Jesus was led of the Spirit to be tempted of the devil, the devil lost. ***(Mat.4:1) Then was Jesus led up of the Spirit into the wilderness to be tempted of the devil. (2) And when he had fasted forty days and forty nights, he afterward hungered. (3) And the tempter came and said unto him, If thou art the Son of God, command that these stones become bread. (4) But he answered and said, It is written, Man shall not live by bread alone, but by every word that proceedeth out of the mouth of God. (5) Then the devil taketh him into the holy city; and he set him on the pinnacle of the temple, (6) and saith unto him, If thou art the Son of God, cast thyself down: for it is written, He shall give his angels charge concerning thee: and, On their hands they shall bear thee up, Lest haply thou dash thy foot against a stone. (7) Jesus said unto him, Again it is written, Thou shalt not make trial of the Lord thy God. (8) Again, the devil taketh him unto an exceeding high mountain, and showeth him all the kingdoms of the world, and the glory of them; (9) and he said unto him, All these things will I give thee, if thou wilt fall down and worship me. (10) Then saith Jesus unto him, Get thee hence, Satan: for it is written, Thou shalt worship the Lord thy God, and him only shalt thou serve. (11) Then the devil leaveth him; and behold, angels came and ministered unto him.*** Jesus didn't obey the devil, so He retained dominion and He passed that dominion on to His children. Well, who were and who are Jesus' children? They're identified in the Bible as His disciples. As a matter of fact, He called them "children" several times, like in John 21:5, because they were His spiritual children.

Just as when Adam fell, all mankind fell because in his loins was the seed of all mankind; so also, when Christ was resurrected, we were all resurrected because in Him was the seed of all of the body of Christ. And so, this was first spoken of Adam here, about man and the son of man. Adam and his children were given dominion over all the earth. But they lost it. Then Paul, in Hebrews 2:6, applies this verse to the last Adam, Who was the Father of the born-again creation and the last Adam didn't lose dominion. He passed it on to His children, but His children in these days have forgotten that. They don't understand that. They don't have that revelation in their heart. As the body of Christ, we have the same dominion that the first body had, which is another revelation that God is going to bring to His people in these days. We're the feet, folks; we're the end-time body. We're the end-time body that's going to have dominion over all the principalities and powers and rulers of darkness. And notice that it's the children; even the children can do this. ***(Psa.8:2) Out of the mouth of babes and sucklings hast thou established strength, Because of thine adversaries, That thou mightest still the enemy and the avenger.*** And, boy, does it ever! How many times in the Scriptures did God use weak vessels to conquer great, enormous vessels? For example, Israel seemed always to be in the minority whenever they won a battle. God's power was always made perfect in weakness. ***(2Co.12:9) And he hath said unto me, My grace is sufficient for thee: for my power is made perfect in weakness. Most gladly therefore will I rather glory in my weaknesses, that the power of Christ may rest upon me.*** He <u>loves</u> to use children to do things. Some people think, "Well, I'm not mature enough. I'm not wise enough. I don't have enough of the Word in me; therefore, I can't do this. I'll have to bring them to the pastor." Well, I can tell you that in many cases the pastor may be younger than you! It has nothing to do with age in the Lord. It has to do with maturity. It has to do with someone who is a <u>believer</u>. You have to believe in order to cast out demons; that's the condition. You have to believe.

And as believers, there are two things we need: We need authority and we've just discovered that we have authority. God gave us authority. "Yea, I give you authority over all the <u>power</u> of the enemy." "Authority" is the "right to use power." We saw in the Scriptures, as a matter of fact, that the apostle Paul used the power even of the devil. He had the right to use it. He turned a man over to Satan for the destruction of his flesh so that his spirit would be saved in the day of the Lord (1 Corinthians 5:5). He turned Hymenaeus and Alexander over to the devil so that they might be taught not to blaspheme (1Timothy 1:20). And, you know, the devil is a fierce taskmaster. He will *whip you good*. He'll whip you until you're ready to say, "I repent, Lord!" But the devil is working against himself because of what he does to mature the people of God and they're ultimately going to destroy him. ***(Mar.3:24) And if a kingdom be divided against itself, that kingdom cannot stand. (25) And if a house be divided against itself, that house will not be able to stand. (26) And if Satan hath risen up against himself, and is divided, he cannot stand, but hath an end.*** Every kingdom that's divided against itself will not stand. The people of God are going to destroy the devil's dominion. They're going to destroy the Beast kingdom, but God's Kingdom is going to reign forever. When the stone in Daniel 2 rolled down out of the mountain and struck the image of the Beast in the feet, it crumbled the whole thing <u>all the way back to the head</u>, folks. The seed of all those kingdoms is still with us today and God has given us dominion.

I mentioned that there's something else we need besides authority and that's anointing. We need <u>anointing</u>. Now, I'm not saying it's <u>absolutely</u> necessary; the seven sons of Sceva cast out demons and they didn't have the Holy Spirit, did they? What they did have was a Covenant right. But by the time the Lord came and preached the truth, their preaching "Jesus whom Paul preacheth" was not enough. It wasn't enough to preach to someone they didn't know anymore and now God held them responsible. ***(Act.19:13) But certain also of the strolling Jews, exorcists, took upon them to name over them that had the evil spirits the name of the Lord Jesus, saying, I adjure you by Jesus whom Paul preacheth. (14) And there were seven sons of one Sceva, a Jew, a chief priest, who did this. (15) And the evil spirit answered and said unto them, Jesus I know, and Paul I know, but who are ye? (16) And the man in whom the evil spirit was leaped on them, and mastered both of them, and prevailed against them, so that they fled out of that house naked and wounded.*** But the disciples, these ignorant fishermen, weren't trained in Bible schools. They went out there and cast out demons; they did miracles and many mighty works because they knew they had been given authority. Yet, Jesus didn't do one miracle until He received His anointing. ***(Luk.3:22) And the Holy Spirit descended in a bodily form, as a dove, upon him, and a voice came out of heaven, Thou art my beloved Son; in thee I am well pleased.*** And from there, the Holy Spirit led Him into the wilderness. ***(Luk.4:1) And Jesus, <u>full of the Holy Spirit</u>, returned from the Jordan, and was led in the Spirit in the wilderness (2) during forty days, being tempted of the devil....*** In type, the Israelites were baptized in the sea and in the cloud, representing the baptism of the Holy Spirit, after which they were led into their wilderness. ***(1Co.10:1) For I do not want you to be ignorant of the fact, brothers and sisters, that our ancestors were all under the cloud and that they all passed through the sea. (2) They were all baptized into Moses in the cloud and in the sea.***

Folks, we need to be filled with the Holy Spirit. Multitudes, some 90% or more of people who claim a born-again experience, have never been filled with the Holy Spirit and that's a shame because it was a much higher percentage in the early church. Whenever the apostles found a disciple, one of the first things they asked them was, ***(Act.19:2) ... Did ye receive the Holy Spirit when ye believed? And they [said] unto him, Nay, we did not so much as hear whether the Holy Spirit was [given]. (3) And he said, Into what then were ye baptized? And they said, Into John's baptism. (4) And Paul said, John baptized with the baptism of repentance, saying unto the people that they should believe on him that should come after him, that is, on Jesus. (5) And when they heard this, they were baptized into the name of the Lord Jesus. (6) And when Paul had laid his hands upon them, the Holy Spirit came on them; and they spake with tongues, and prophesied.*** It was very <u>common</u> in the early church to be filled with the Holy

Spirit with the <u>evidence of the gifts</u>.

So why was it, then, that Jesus, after receiving this great anointing, had to be led of the Holy Spirit to <u>be</u> tempted of the devil? Notice the Holy Spirit didn't tempt Jesus, but the Holy Spirit <u>led</u> Jesus to be tempted. It's because, **(Rev.2:26)** <u>**And he that overcometh, and he that keepeth my works unto the end, to him will I give authority over the nations**</u>. The Lord had authority to give Jesus, but first Jesus had to overcome the temptation of the devil. Why? Well, you remember what happened to Adam. Adam was tempted; he flunked the test; he lost the dominion. Jesus was tempted, but Jesus beat the devil every time with the sword of the Word of God, until the devil finally backed off for a season. Jesus overcame and God gave Him authority. "To him that overcometh, to him will I give authority." If you overcome the temptations of the devil, God will give you authority. It's not just faith, folks, it's holiness. Again, I'm not saying we have to be perfect in order to exercise authority; nobody would ever get to perfection if that was true, you know. And Jesus said, **(Luk.4:18) The Spirit of the Lord is upon me, Because <u>he anointed me</u> to preach good tidings to the poor: He hath sent me to proclaim release to the captives, And recovering of sight to the blind, To set at liberty them that are bruised**. The anointing is the outpouring of the Holy Spirit. The Bible says the <u>anointing</u> breaks the yoke, the yoke of bondage, the yoke of bondage to the old man, the yoke of bondage to the beast. **(Gal.5:1) For freedom did Christ set us free: stand fast therefore, and be not entangled again in a yoke of bondage.** The <u>anointing</u> does that. The anointing is <u>power</u> from God to give us dominion. **(Act.1:4) And, being assembled together with them, he charged them not to depart from Jerusalem, but to wait for the promise of the Father, which, [said he], ye heard from me: (5) For John indeed baptized with water; but ye shall be baptized in the Holy Spirit not many days hence.** Well, here you have probably the most valuable men on earth, these disciples, who had been trained by the Master Himself, and the Lord said, "No, you don't need to go to Bible school. You just need to wait here and receive the Holy Spirit." Many people come out of Bible school with their certificates and they go straight to work in the church. They don't have to overcome to receive authority. As a matter of fact, the Pharisees had that kind of authority, but it was fleshly authority. It wasn't any kind of authority like Jesus had. **(Mat.7:28) And it came to pass, when Jesus had finished these words, the multitudes were astonished at his teaching: (29) for he taught them <u>as one having authority</u>, and not as their scribes.** Well, He did have authority and it was because Jesus had <u>overcome</u> that He received His authority. And so these disciples, too, had to be filled with the Spirit and go through their own wilderness and overcome and exercise their authority.

There's a really bad demon doctrine today that says whenever you're saved, you automatically receive the Holy Spirit but, evidently, their "holy spirit" is pretty weak because they don't go and do these works. Jesus said these signs will accompany those who believe. He said they'll cast out demons and speak in tongues. He said they'll lay hands on the sick and they'll recover. Let me point out to you that in the Book of Acts and in the Gospels <u>before</u> the Book of Acts, after teaching these disciples for three-and-a-half years, Jesus said, ***(Mat.19:28) ... Verily I say unto you, that <u>ye who have followed me</u>, <u>in the regeneration</u> when the Son of man shall sit on the throne of his glory, ye also shall sit upon twelve thrones, judging the twelve tribes of Israel***. "Regeneration" is a Greek word that means "born again." Speaking to His disciples, He said, "You, who have been born again." So they were born again. And, as a matter of fact, He said, ***(Joh.15:3) Already ye are clean because of the word which I have spoken unto you***. So they were also cleaned up. God spoke the Word that cleaned up their heart. ***(Joh.6:63) It is the spirit that giveth life; the flesh profiteth nothing: <u>the words that I have spoken unto you are spirit</u>, <u>and are life</u>***. "The words that I have spoken unto you are spirit and are life." That Word went into those disciples and cleaned them up. Well, Jesus said that even though they were born again and cleaned up, they didn't have the Holy Spirit. He said, ***(Joh.14:17) Even the Spirit of truth: whom the world cannot receive; for it beholdeth him not, neither knoweth him: ye know him; for he abideth <u>with you</u>, and <u>shall be in you</u>***. And He also said to them, ***(Joh.7:38) He that believeth on me, as the scripture hath said, from within him shall flow rivers of living water. (39) But this spake he of the Spirit, which they that believed on him <u>were to receive</u>: for the Spirit was not yet [given]; because Jesus was not yet glorified***.

You see, if we believe on Him as the Scripture has said, we get the same Spirit. The same mantle that Jesus had comes upon His disciples. We receive that anointing to minister with power. And these important men, as important as they were to the whole world, as needed as they were among the people of God, still had to wait until they received this anointing. ***(Act.1:8) But <u>ye shall receive power</u>, <u>when the Holy Spirit is come upon you</u>: and ye shall be my witnesses both in Jerusalem, and in all Judaea and Samaria, and unto the uttermost part of the earth***. So these people, who <u>were born again</u>, didn't have the Holy Spirit. The Book of Acts is full of examples of people who <u>had</u> been saved and yet had not received the Holy Spirit. Here's one good example: ***(Act.8:12) But when they <u>believed</u> Philip preaching good tidings concerning the kingdom of God and the name of Jesus Christ, they were baptized, both men and women***. These people were believers and were baptized. ***(Mar.16:16) <u>He that believeth and is baptized shall be saved</u>; but he that disbelieveth shall be condemned***. It goes on to say, ***(Act.8:13) And Simon also himself believed: and being baptized, he continued with Philip; and beholding signs and great miracles wrought, he was amazed. (14) Now when the apostles that were at Jerusalem heard that Samaria <u>had received the word of God</u>, they sent unto them Peter and John: (15) who, when they were come down, prayed for them, that they might <u>receive the Holy Spirit</u>: (16) for as yet it was fallen upon none of them: only they had been baptized <u>into the name</u> of the Lord Jesus***. You see, folks, some of you have been lied to; in fact, lots of you have been lied to about this automatic receiving of the Holy Spirit. First of all, if you get what they got, you will do what they did. That anointing is <u>to</u> heal the sick, cast out devils, so on and so forth. "These signs shall accompany them that believe." There are multitudes today who are missing out on their inheritance. We have been given the ability to partake of the inheritance of the <u>saints</u>, the "sanctified ones." <u>We</u> have been given the ability to partake of <u>that</u> inheritance to the sanctified ones (Colossians 1:12). What did Jesus pass on to us? He passed on to us the same authority that Adam was supposed to pass on to his children, but because Adam was tempted of the devil and failed, he didn't. Now Jesus has passed on that authority to us, yet, multitudes of Christians haven't realized what has happened.

If you receive the Holy Spirit and you believe the Word of God, you will have a miraculous life, folks. You will have signs, wonders and miracles happening in your life. When I was a baby Christian and didn't hardly know my right hand from my left, I started casting out demons. At first, I was just stepping out because I saw it in the Word and I didn't know that much about it. But I just stepped out in obedience and the Lord honored my faith with signs and wonders. In fact, one of the first people I cast demons out of was my dad. My dad used to be a chemist and a metallurgical engineer for Exxon; and Exxon doesn't know this, but my dad's passed on, so I guess I can tell you. He built a stainless steel still from Exxon's materials. Of course, my dad didn't know the Lord. So he used this awesome stainless steel still that had copper tubing and all those good things to make some white lightning, which is very high proof homemade whiskey, for those of you who don't know what it is. Now my dad was a real intellectual person; he was a lot smarter than I am. But he just thought, "Well, I'm gonna try this thing," so he did. And my dad and an old friend of his, Uncle Purce, had a little building in Mississippi where they made their white lightning. Well, it ended up as a really sad story. One day, Uncle Purce went into the building that they put the still in and accidentally blew the thing all to pieces. The explosion shattered the whole building and it killed the old man. And my dad was just heartbroken, you know, because of this experiment to make whiskey.

The problem was, he'd been sipping too much of his own white lightning and my dad had become an alcoholic. And even though he had gone to the detox centers and to Alcoholics Anonymous, and he'd gone to just about anybody he could run to for deliverance from this, none of it was doing him any good. Then, one day, after my wife and I had become Christians and we'd been witnessing to him and talking to him about the Lord, my dad was sitting in our living room, just crying one of those drunk cries. He was just crying and bemoaning himself over all the problems he'd brought upon himself. So, as my wife and I were sitting there, praying within ourselves about the situation, suddenly a thought came to me. I said, "Daddy, the Lord delivered you from this and you don't have to walk under this dominion of this alcoholic demon any longer. You can be free because the Lord set you free." You know, it was child-like faith. I believed what the Word said, although I hadn't been seeing much of it in the full-Gospel-type church where I was fellowshipping at the time. They weren't doing much of it there, but I was stretching out my faith for everything. I was trying everything I could see in the Book. But this just came into my heart. I'd been reading the Bible and was full of the Word, so I just told him. I said, "Daddy, we're going to lay our hands on your head and we're going to command this alcoholism to leave you and it has to go." So my wife and I laid hands on my dad and we rebuked that spirit of alcoholism, and the Lord took it from him! I mean, just like that, he was delivered! All the struggling, all the strain, all the works of man had failed him. All of his brilliance, because he was a very brilliant man; all his brilliance had failed him, but the Lord, in a <u>moment</u>, set him free through a couple of baby Christians. Glory to God, folks! "That he might still the enemy and the avenger." "Out of the mouths of babes and sucklings he has perfected strength." All you have to have is faith, folks. Step forward. Obey God in receiving the Holy Spirit because the Holy Spirit will make up for what you don't and can't do. Now my daddy still didn't consider himself a Christian, but after that, he went around and told everybody that <u>God</u> set him free. It was a witness; it was a testimony out of his mouth to tell people that God set him free when nothing else would work. <u>God</u> set him free. Glory be to God!

Even though God has not given the "children's bread" of healing and deliverance to those who are not in Covenant with Him, <u>He can do over and above</u> what He has guaranteed, but <u>He will not do less</u> for those who believe. God was delivering a lost man to show him of His power and love, and then that lost man began to tell others that he had tried and failed to save himself, but God saved him. And God did that work on him, as I said, through a couple of fairly baby Christians who just simply believed on their Father. We have to have that child-like mind. You know, I guess I have a head start on some of you in that department, but I'm kind of child-like. I loved the Word; I devoured the Word. And because I trusted my Father, He acted upon that. He confirmed it with a sign and a wonder.

Let me tell you about one of the first deliverances, well, it was an attempted deliverance, in that same church that I was talking about. No deliverance happened because the people didn't really know what they were doing. Some of them had been in the Lord for many years, but they hadn't been casting out demons, even though they were so-called "Pentecostal" people. So a man came into this church who was just a total mess. He was a total wreck, full of drugs and probably alcohol. And here were these "Pentecostal" guys gathered around this man. Some of them had gone to the same school with me and I'd bumped into them in this church. They'd been there before I was. Well, some of these guys were gathered around this man because they were going to cast demons out of him, but they didn't know the really simple method that God has of just commanding it done in faith.

I'd learned that you just command those demons to come out and they have to obey you. You don't argue with them and you don't stay around waiting to see if they leave. You just command them to come out and go your way. You don't worry about it and you don't wrestle with it all night long. The devil will sit there and he'll wrestle with you when he knows that <u>you</u> don't believe that you have authority because then he knows that he doesn't have to obey. And you're not going to be heard for your "much speaking" (Matthew 6:7). You're not going to be heard by God for your much speaking and you're not going to be heard by the devil for your much speaking. Somebody who stands around just talking, talking, talking, you know they don't have any authority and you know they don't believe they do, either. So these guys were standing around and they were talking, and they were commanding this and they were commanding that, and nothing was really happening. They couldn't <u>see</u> anything happening and, since they couldn't see anything happening, they didn't believe anything <u>was</u> happening. But that's not the way faith works.

Then finally they decided, "We're gonna test this guy." And I'll tell you the truth. I thought, "That's crazy!" Anybody, anybody, could see what was going on with him. You didn't have to have the Holy Spirit to tell this guy was demon-possessed. First of all, he thought he was a woman. Well, that's pretty demon-possessed right there and, second of all, he was reading minds! Some of you who don't think the devil can read minds had better think again; I saw him doing it. It was kind of an interesting story because, in this church, most of the people <u>were</u> filled with the Spirit, but they had a problem with how faith actually worked. Their doctrine about receiving the Holy Spirit was what tripped them up on that. They believed that unless you spoke in tongues, you didn't have the Holy Spirit. Well, I believe tongues is one of the most common signs of the Holy Spirit, but I can't say what the Bible doesn't say. And tongues is a manifestation of the Spirit. You receive the Spirit by faith and the manifestation comes, you see. But they didn't ever believe anything unless they saw it, which is a stumblingblock and that's the reason they had problems casting out demons. They weren't going to believe it until they saw the demon come out. That's not how faith works, folks.

Anyway, they were standing around this guy and somebody came up with the bright idea, "We're gonna test this guy. We'll see if this is the devil." Well, I knew it was a devil. So they picked this verse: ***(1Jn.4:2) Hereby know ye the Spirit of God: every spirit that confesseth that Jesus Christ <u>is come in the flesh</u> is of God: (3) and every spirit that confesseth not Jesus is not of God: and this is the [spirit] of the antichrist, whereof ye have heard that it cometh; and now it is in the world already.*** Well, John was talking about testing the spirits of people; he wasn't talking about testing demon spirits. He was talking about the spirit of a person who is not born of God because he talks about He Who's in you and he who's in the world. ***(1Jn.4:4) Ye are of God, [my] little children, and have overcome them: because greater is <u>he that is in you</u> than he that is in the world.*** That's only two. That's Christ in you and that's Antichrist in the world, so he's talking about testing the spirits of <u>people</u>. He's not talking about demons. But it also says, "every spirit that confesseth that Jesus Christ <u>is come in the flesh</u> is of God," and this means that, if a man's spirit confesses that Jesus Christ <u>is presently in that flesh</u>, then that's the Spirit of God. That's what this is talking about. It doesn't say, "Jesus Christ <u>has</u> come in the flesh," because it wasn't talking about Jesus coming once upon a time in His flesh. This is talking about the Spirit that brings Jesus in your flesh. *(2Jn.7 NENT) **For many deceivers are gone forth into the world, they that confess not Jesus Christ coming in [the] flesh.*** He who is in you is greater than he who is in the world. This is your born-again spirit in the image of the Spirit of Jesus, produced in you and then hopefully empowered by the Spirit of God. *(Rom.8:9) **But ye are not in the flesh but in the Spirit, if so be that the Spirit of God*** (the Holy Spirit) ***dwelleth in you. But if any man hath not the Spirit of Christ*** (your born-again spirit in Christ's image), ***he is none of his. (11) But if the Spirit of him that raised up Jesus from the dead*** (the Holy Spirit) ***dwelleth in you, he that raised up Christ Jesus from the dead shall give life also to your mortal bodies through his Spirit*** (the Holy Spirit) ***that dwelleth in you.*** So you see the Holy Spirit coming to empower your born-again spirit of Christ, to live and do the works of Christ. And this is to then bring Christ in the born-again soul, which is the born-again mind, will and emotions. So, they tested the guy and guess what he said? "Jesus Christ has come in the flesh." And he was still demon-possessed! Well, they were very confused over that, but this is the answer.

Meanwhile, the guy would look around the room and they would ask him, "Whose mind can you read? Can you read that guy's mind?" "Yep." "Can you read that guy's mind?" "Nope." There were people in there whose mind he couldn't read. Now I'm not saying that reading minds has anything to do with the devil having authority over you. You give the devil authority over you. It has nothing to with what the devil knows about you or whether he can read your mind or not, folks. But I tell you, that guy couldn't read the mind of anyone in there who was Spirit-filled. Those people whom he pointed out in the crowd, "I can read that guy," were people who everybody knew weren't filled with the Holy Spirit. But this guy didn't know anybody in the building! He knew nobody! He really was reading their minds. Now, here's what the Lord taught me: It has nothing to do with whether the devil can read your mind or not. You can talk in English; you can say anything you want to, folks. I'm telling you that it makes no difference what the devil knows. It makes a difference what you give him authority to do. If you disagree with God's Word, you bring yourself under the curse. If anyone adds to the Word, God said He would add to that person the curses that are written in this Book. *(Rev.22:18) **I testify unto every man that heareth the words of the prophecy of this book, if any man shall add unto them, God shall add unto him the plagues which are written in this book: (19) and if any man shall take away from the words of the book of this prophecy, God shall take away his part from the tree of life, and out of the holy city, which are written in this book.*** If anyone takes away from the words of this Book, the Lord said He would take away their part in the Tree of Life. And guess who administers the curse? The devil does. So we know that we give the devil authority by disagreeing with God's Word. *(Mat.18:18) **Verily I say unto you, what things soever ye shall bind on earth shall be bound in heaven; and what things soever ye shall loose on earth shall be loosed in heaven.*** We bind and we loose, according to whether we agree with God's Word by faith or not. If you don't agree with God's Word, you permit the devil to take authority over you. If you do agree with God's Word, if you believe and you speak God's Word, you bind the devil. He can do nothing. It makes no difference whether you say, "I bind you devil" or not. You just bind him. Get used to agreeing with God's Word. **(Amo.3:3) Shall two walk together, except they have agreed?** We want the Lord to walk in us, talk in us and do His works in us, and we have to agree with God. Now that's what looses or binds the devil. It has nothing to do with whether the devil knows all of your strategy, folks. It makes no difference. I'm telling you in the name of Jesus, it makes no difference, whatsoever.

Some people say that we speak in tongues so the devil won't know what we're doing. The devil speaks in tongues and he knows the tongues of men and he knows the tongues of angels, so that's ridiculous! He's been around for thousands of years and he and his demons all know tongues. They all speak in tongues, too, folks: "The tongues of men or the tongues of angels," the Bible says (1 Corinthians 13:1). No, the demons can do nothing, unless you give them authority. Remember that we have dominion over all the principalities and powers (Ephesians 1:21-22). So if we have that dominion over them, how do they get it? How did Adam give it away? He disagreed with God. He fell out with God and he lost his dominion. **(Rom.6:16) His servants ye are whom ye obey.** He gave away that dominion. But, like Jesus did when He was tempted of the devil, we overcome so we don't give away that dominion. God empowered Jesus and He said you'll receive power after the Holy Spirit is come upon you (Acts 1:8). What kind of power is that? I can tell you it's power over your flesh, it's power over the devil, it's power over the world. Obey the Word of God. **(Act.2:38) ... Repent ye, and be baptized every one of you in the name of Jesus Christ unto the remission of your sins; and ye shall receive the gift of the Holy Spirit.** Notice it doesn't come at the same time: "and you shall receive the gift of the Holy Spirit." That's God's command. We need God's anointing, we need His authority and we need His wisdom. And, obviously, these guys needed it because they thought they should try the devil. I'll show you another verse. **(2Jn.7) For many deceivers are gone forth into the world, [even] they that confess not that Jesus Christ cometh in the flesh. This is the deceiver and the antichrist.** See, not only is He come in us who have the Holy Spirit of God, but also He is coming in flesh. **(2Co.3:18) But we all, with unveiled face beholding as in a mirror the glory of the Lord, are transformed into the same image from glory to glory, even as from the Lord the Spirit.** He is coming in us as we walk by faith in the true Gospel, the Good News. Do you see Jesus in the mirror? He has authority to cast out demons. Do you see yourself as dead for Christ's sake? Do you see yourself as, **(Gal.2:20) I have been crucified with Christ; and it is no longer I that live, but Christ living in me: and that life which I now live in the flesh I live in faith, the faith which is in the Son of God, who loved me, and gave himself up for me.**

You know what? You are able to partake of the inheritance of the saints, the sanctified ones, in Christ. You're able to partake of that inheritance! You see, you don't have to be perfect to partake of the inheritance of the saints in Christ. You don't have to be perfect to cast out demons or to administer healing, deliverance of <u>any</u> form or any of the other benefits of the Kingdom. The Lord has given us dominion. I've gone on since then to cast out many, many demons up until this day. Some people specialize in doing that and they call it a deliverance ministry. I've never called myself a deliverance ministry because I believe that this gift is for <u>all</u> who believe. Some people can, of course, teach you things about it from their own experience, but the gift is for all who believe. A number of years ago, when Bob Aicardi was talking to a neighbor, Linda, she confessed to him that they'd found cancer in her lung. So he witnessed to her what the Bible has to say about that, which is the real Good News that she'd already been delivered of this. He told her we were going to agree with her that night over at our meeting. She said, "Fine," and she gave the good confession in the sight of witnesses. She said, "I believe the Lord has healed me." When Bob shared the Good News with her, she believed it and she confessed it. That's when you know, folks, that you have authority. People can have many, many problems, but when they believe the Gospel, you have authority. Go ahead and exercise it. So Bob said, "We're gonna agree with you tonight." That was the method he used at that particular time and when he brought the testimony to us, we prayed. I believed the cancer was a spirit of infirmity and I don't know what everybody else said, but I commanded the demon of cancer to come out of her in the name of Jesus. That was about 7:30 in the evening. She gave the testimony to Bob the next day. She said that about 11:30 p.m. she was in bed and she woke up suddenly and smoke was coming out of her nose. It was the demon of cancer coming out of her. And, sure enough, she went and had tests run and the doctor was just awed because the cancer was gone! Well, you know what? That's nothing that baby Christians can't do! This is not for necessarily mature believers, you know. I'm thinking of the Pharisees and the Sadducees, how they went to Bible college for many years. They had all the letters behind their name, but they weren't casting out demons. It was these fishermen who were doing it; the people who walked with Jesus were doing it.

And, by the way, you can walk with Jesus today. You don't have to see Him to walk with Him. You just ask Him to take you by the hand and make you His disciple, and begin to do the things that He commanded you to do in the Book. "These signs shall accompany them that believe...." The Great Commission has never been taken back, folks (Mark 16:15-18). He gave it to <u>us</u>. We've been called to do this work, to spread the Good News and to administer the gift for those who believe. We have dominion over the forces of darkness. Jesus gave it to us. He returned to us the dominion of Adam and his children. ***(Heb.2:5) For not unto angels did he subject the world to come, whereof we speak.*** He's talking about you and me here. ***(Heb.2:6) But one hath somewhere testified, saying, What is man, that thou art mindful of him? Or the <u>son</u> of man, that thou visitest him? (7) Thou madest him a little lower than the angels; Thou crownedst him with glory and honor, And didst set him <u>over the works of thy hands</u>: (8) Thou didst put <u>all things</u> in subjection under his feet.*** What do you think would happen if the Church got this revelation here, folks? ***For*** *in that he subjected all things unto him, <u>he left nothing that is not subject to him. But now we see not yet all things subjected to him</u>.* Why is that? Well, not only was there hardness of heart of the disciples of that day, there was a great falling away that followed and, even today, most of the people of God are in a fallen-away state. They don't <u>do</u> the works of Jesus. They don't believe in receiving the Holy Spirit <u>with</u> the evidence of the gifts. Their leaders have told them it passed away but their leaders can't show them any verses that actually say that because there is no such thing. The devil has tempted the church and they've fallen for it. They've become his servants and they've lost their dominion, exactly as happened to Adam. *(Heb.2:9) But we behold him who hath been made a little lower than the angels, [even] Jesus, because of the suffering of death crowned with glory and honor, that by the grace of God he should taste of death for every [man].*

Jesus is the Father of the born-again creation and <u>His</u> children are not those who merely confess, "Jesus is my Savior." His children are the people who <u>believe</u>. They are birthed of the Word of God. The seed that Jesus sowed as the Sower was not a physical seed like natural Adam sowed. His seed was the Word of God. Do you receive the Word of God in your heart? That's what creates the child of God; it's the Word of God living in you. That person has dominion over all of creation, according to this Word right here. Now even at that time, they didn't yet <u>see</u> this happening. But in these days, it's going to happen because the principalities and powers are under the <u>feet</u> and the feet are in the end-time days of the body of Christ. The Bible says He will come to be glorified in His saints. *(2Th.1:10) when he shall come to be glorified in his saints, and to be marvelled at in all them that <u>believed</u> <u>(because our testimony unto you was believed)</u> in that day.* See, He said, we don't yet <u>see</u> all things subject." What's the hold-up here, folks? It's <u>belief</u>.

In our day, God is going to give grace to people to believe. The feet are going to crush the serpent's head; the feet are going to destroy the Beast's kingdom. There's a One World Order being raised up, folks, but guess what? There's always really been one. It's He Who is in you and he who is in the world. There's been one for the world and one for the Kingdom. We are a One World Order. We have to learn to be connected to the head and we have to let the head be the ruler. We have to let the Word rule in us, the <u>seed</u> that brings forth the <u>sons</u> who do the works. Adam's children were to have dominion over the earth. He was tempted. He lost that dominion. The Lord Jesus brought forth the born-again creation, the real creation that God desired from the foundation of the world. He chose us in Him from the foundation of the world. *(Eph.1:3) Blessed be the God and Father of our Lord Jesus Christ, who hath blessed us with every spiritual blessing in the heavenly places in Christ: (4) even as he chose us in him before the foundation of the world, that we should be holy and without blemish before him in love: (5) having foreordained us unto adoption as sons through Jesus Christ unto himself, according to the good pleasure of his will.* The real creation, folks, is the born-again creation. So step up and take your position as the elect of God and exercise dominion and cast out demons. God bless you, saints! Please pray for us that we're able to continue to share the Good News with multitudes of people, that God will open a door to us. God bless you and the Lord pour out His Spirit upon you, and empower you to walk in <u>all</u> the inheritance that Jesus passed on to you. Receive it, folks. Just receive it. It's the Word of God. You know it is. "As the Father sent me," Jesus said, "so send I you." God bless you.

CHAPTER 13

Act on Faith!

Greetings, saints! God bless you. May the Lord pour out His Holy Spirit on you today and give you His benefits richly. Lord, we ask for all the brethren who are joining us today, that Your mercy and Your grace would be poured out upon them. We ask, Father, that Your benefits would be in their heart and their mind, and coming out of their mouth in their confession toward You, for You have said, **(Rom.10:10) with the heart man believeth unto righteousness; and with the mouth confession is made unto salvation.** And we pray that their good confession will be in the heart and the mouth of the saints of God out there to spread Your wonderful Good News and Your benefits all over this world, Lord. We praise You for it, Father! We praise You in Jesus' name. Bless us today, Lord. Bless us in our study and as we fellowship in sharing the Word. And we thank You, God, that this Word is going into our hearts and creating the life of Christ in us. We thank You that His Word is His seed and that seed can only bring forth Him. And so we praise You for it, Father. We praise You in Jesus' name. Amen.

Well, as we've been continuing to learn about the Gospel, in particular, we've been talking about the deliverance that God gives us in the real Good News. Let's begin by looking at what Jesus said to His disciples when He sent them out, just before they were about to "go solo" because He was about to go home. **(Mat.28:18) And Jesus came to them and spake unto them, saying, All authority hath been given unto me in heaven and on earth. (19) Go ye therefore, and make disciples of <u>all the nations</u>, baptizing them into the name of the Father and of the Son and of the Holy Spirit: (20) <u>teaching them to observe all things</u> whatsoever I <u>commanded you</u>: and lo, I am with you always, even unto the end of the world.** Obviously, Jesus wasn't telling those particular disciples that He was going to be with them that long, right? He was talking about all disciples who go forth at His bidding and who teach others to "observe all things" that He told the first disciples. The word "observe" in this text means "to hold fast to," or "to keep." "To hold fast to"? We haven't done that, have we? Over the last 2,000 years, we have slid about as far as we can slide away from what was written in the Gospels, the Book of Acts and the rest of the New Testament. Yet, now the Lord is bringing His people back to a time when His benefits are going to be known in the earth once more, miraculously and powerfully, but we need to hold fast to the commands that He gave to the first disciples. **(Jud.3) Beloved, while I was giving all diligence to write unto you of our common salvation, I was constrained to write unto you exhorting you to contend earnestly for the faith which was <u>once for all</u> delivered unto the saints.** We need to contend "for the faith which was once delivered unto the saints."

One of those things that He commanded His first disciples, which was passed on to us, is **(Mar.16:17) And these signs shall accompany them that believe: <u>in my</u>**

name shall they cast out demons.... Who did He say that to? He said that to the disciples, so that they would know real disciples. ***(Mar.16:14) And afterward he was manifested unto the eleven themselves as they sat at meat; and he upbraided them with their unbelief and hardness of heart, because they believed not them that had seen him after he was risen. (15) And he said unto them, Go ye into all the world, and preach the gospel to the whole creation.*** They didn't get to do that, did they? Once again, He was obviously talking to more than just the first disciples; He was speaking to us. ***(Mar.16:16) He that believeth and is baptized shall be saved; but he that disbelieveth shall be condemned. (17) And these signs shall accompany them that believe: <u>in my name shall they cast out demons</u>; they shall speak with new tongues; (18) they shall take up serpents, and if they drink any deadly thing, it shall in no wise hurt them; they shall lay hands on the sick, and they shall recover.*** So we see that He taught them how to identify the people who really believed what the disciples said when the disciples were <u>passing on the commandments that Jesus gave unto them</u>.

Do you understand, folks, that we are not to receive anything but the commandments that Jesus gave unto the first disciples? The church has not kept the Word of God. They have not held fast to the commands that were given to the first disciples. ***(Luk.10:16) He that heareth you heareth me; and he that rejecteth you rejecteth me; and he that rejecteth me rejecteth him that sent me.*** Well, I tell you, we have rejected them. We have rejected their word and we have rejected their commands and now we see the trouble that's come of it. The church has not brought forth any deliverance in the earth, as Isaiah 26:18 says, and there has been a great falling away. ***(Luk.10:17) And the seventy returned with joy, saying, Lord, even the demons are subject unto us in thy name.*** They were happy to get this revelation and a lot of people are going to be happy to get this revelation once again, as if it's been hidden. Well, it's been right there all along, folks. Get in your Bible and read your Bible. Make sure that you're not wasting your time. Find out what a <u>real</u> disciple is. They were just overjoyed to see that the demons had to obey them. ***(Luk.10:18) And he said unto them, I beheld Satan fallen as lightning from heaven. (19) Behold, I have given you authority to tread upon <u>serpents and scorpions</u>, and over all the power of the enemy: and nothing shall in any wise hurt you. (20) Nevertheless in this rejoice not, that the <u>spirits</u> are subject unto you*** (So we can see that when He talks about serpents and scorpions, He's talking about spirits.)***; but rejoice that your names are written in heaven.*** He gave them this authority and He commanded them to go out and give this authority to others. He commanded them to teach the disciples to observe, or to hold fast to, everything that He spoke to them. And that's what we're doing today. We have no authority to do anything else but to share with the disciples what the Lord has given us as benefits and as an inheritance. Praise be to God for that!

I'm going to share a little more with you about one of the testimonies in the previous chapter. It's the testimony of Sister Linda, who received her deliverance because she held fast to the confession of the Scriptures. Family before her had died of cancer and she had received the inheritance of her parents. Doctors told her that she had cancer in the lobe of a lung. They said that they were going to have to perform surgery to cut off that lobe. Now, even though she admitted that she was not a bold person, she knew that the Lord was rising up in her and she told the doctor very boldly that the Lord was going to heal her. She confessed that very plainly. And I think it was the next month that she ran into our brother, Bob Acardi, one of our elders. Bob shared the real Good News with her that, not only was Jesus going to heal her, but He had already healed her at the cross. He shared the real Gospel with her and she understood that this was already accomplished. It wasn't something she had to do. It wasn't something the doctors could bring to pass. It was something that she just had to receive by faith as a gift from God. So when she was talking with Bob, she confessed very boldly that she was healed, which is the real truth. You know, **(1Pe.2:24) ... by whose stripes ye were healed.** And as you've been studying along with us, you've learned that many healing issues are demonically motivated. **(Act.10:38) Even Jesus of Nazareth, how God anointed him with the Holy Spirit and with power: who went about doing good, and healing all that were <u>oppressed of the devil</u>; for God was with him.** It is an oppression, or sometimes a possession of the devil. Many of these very bad diseases are spirits of infirmity.

Anyway, Linda boldly confessed her faith and Bob told her, "Hey, we're going to pray tonight. We're going to agree with God tonight and we're going to command your healing tonight, so you expect it." Then Bob brought the message to us that Linda had boldly confessed her healing. So about 7:30 in the evening, we just commanded the spirit of cancer to come out of her, in Jesus' name. Well, you know, it didn't happen immediately at that particular moment, but you know the devil has to obey. And so about 11:30 that night, Linda suddenly woke up and there was smoke coming out of her nose. She knew at that moment that the demon had come out of her and she knew that she was now healed. And proof of that followed very, very quickly. You know, the demon can come out sometimes immediately, but the healing for the damage they do to your body can follow thereafter. First of all, she confessed very boldly to everyone, even the doctor, that she was healed, and when they did their scans, lo and behold, Linda was already healing. She was healing almost instantly and in the days that followed she received a complete, perfect healing because she held fast to her confession. God is faithful, but the Bible says, faith without works is dead. **(Jas.2:26) For as the body apart from the spirit is dead, even so faith apart from works is dead.** Faith without works is incomplete and the Lord has told us to confess Him before men. **(Mat.10:32) Every one therefore who shall confess me before men, him will I also confess before my Father who is in heaven.** Linda did that. She confessed Him before men. She confessed Him before the unbelieving doctors and she stepped out by faith. This is a confirmation of a person's faith, when they are willing to suffer scorn, willing to suffer indignities from others because they believe the Word of God enough to speak it.

The Bible says all that's necessary is to believe with our heart and confess with our mouth. *(Rom.10:8) But what saith it? The word is nigh thee, in thy mouth, and in thy heart: that is, the word of faith, which we preach.* You're not very far from a healing, or a deliverance, or anything you need, folks, and that's what Paul is telling you right here. In the previous text, he tells you, *(Rom.10:6) But the righteousness which is of faith saith thus, Say not in thy heart, Who shall ascend into heaven? (that is, to bring Christ down:) (7) or, Who shall descend into the abyss? (That is, to bring Christ up from the dead.)* "Hey, do you have to go up to Heaven to get it? Does Christ have to come down for you to get it? No! Look! The word is very, very nigh you. It's in your mouth and in your heart. *(Rom.10:8) But what saith it? The word is nigh thee, in thy mouth, and in thy heart: that is, the word of faith, which we preach: (9) because if thou shalt confess with thy mouth Jesus as Lord, and shalt believe in thy heart that God raised him from the dead, thou shalt be saved.* What is Jesus Lord of? What did Jesus do at the cross? What Jesus did at the cross was become <u>Lord over all</u> of the curse, sin and <u>creation</u>. *(Mat.28:18) And Jesus came to them and spake unto them, saying, <u>All authority hath been given unto me in heaven and on earth</u>.* When Jesus walked the earth, He exercised this authority over the curse to set God's people free. *(Isa.61:1) The Spirit of the Lord God is upon me; because the Lord hath anointed me to preach good tidings unto the meek; he hath sent me to bind up the broken-hearted, to proclaim liberty to the captives, and the opening [of the prison] to them that are bound.* Isaiah boldly proclaims that He would set the captives free and open the prison to those who are bound, delivering God's people from bondage to Satan, bondage to the curse and sin, and so on. And we see here that it's very, very simple. Salvation in any form, whether it's salvation of your spirit, soul, body or circumstances, is with your heart you believe the promises of the Word of God and with your mouth you confess them. Faith without works is dead, as the Scripture very plainly tells us. *(Rom.10:10) For with the heart man believeth unto righteousness; and with the mouth confession is made unto salvation. (11) For the scripture saith, <u>Whosoever believeth on him shall not be put to shame</u>.*

(Rom.10:16) But they did not all hearken to the glad tidings. For Isaiah saith, Lord, who hath believed our report? And it is the same way today, folks. Many do not believe and, therefore, do not really confess the good confession in the sight of many witnesses. *(1Ti.6:12) Fight the good fight of the faith, lay hold on the life eternal, whereunto thou wast called, and didst confess the good confession in the sight of many witnesses.* The Greek word "confess" here means "to speak the same as; to speak the same thing." It's *homologeó* and some people translate it as "the same word." "To speak the same as" and "to confess in agreement" with healing, or deliverance, or provision of any form, is to say what the Bible says about it; it's "to speak with the same word" about it. Our Lord Jesus said that if we will confess Him

before men, He will confess us before the Father and before the holy angels. ***(Luk.12:8) And I say unto you, Every one who shall confess me before men, him shall the Son of man also confess before the angels of God.*** And the Bible says the angels are ministering spirits sent forth to do service for them that are heirs of salvation. ***(Heb.1:13) But of which of the angels hath he said at any time, Sit thou on my right hand, Till I make thine enemies the footstool of thy feet? (14) Are they not all ministering spirits, sent forth to do service for the sake of them that shall inherit salvation?*** They serve the heirs of salvation. They're the ones who manifest these precious gifts that we agree with. ***(Psa.103:19) The Lord hath established his throne in the heavens; And his kingdom ruleth <u>over all</u>.*** "Over <u>all</u>!" Folks, that doesn't leave anybody out. It includes the principalities, the powers, the spirit of cancer that had taken dominion, in Linda's case. ***(Psa.103:20) Bless the Lord, ye his <u>angels</u>, That are mighty in strength, that fulfil his word, Hearkening unto the voice of his word. (21) Bless the Lord, all ye his hosts, Ye <u>ministers of his</u>, that do his pleasure.*** See, as ministers of His, we confess Him before men. We "speak the same as"; in other words, we "agree with" the Word of God. Do you know that the angels are waiting for you to agree with the Word of God? Well, it says right here, "they hearken unto the voice of His Word" and "they are mighty in strength, that fulfil His Word." They are waiting for you to agree with the Word of God, so that they can administer the benefits of the Kingdom. They are "ministering spirits sent forth to do service for them that are <u>heirs of salvation</u>." That is us; <u>we who believe</u> are the heirs of salvation.

We have authority to bind or to loose, according to Jesus. ***(Mat.18:18) Verily I say unto you, what things soever ye shall bind on earth shall be bound in heaven; and what things soever ye shall loose on earth shall be loosed in heaven.*** We bind or we loose by agreeing with the Word of God, or disagreeing with the Word of God. We loose the devil to take advantage of us, and to plunder us, if we don't agree with the Word of God. We disagree with the Word of God, if we add to or take away from the words of the Bible. In other words, if we don't "confess" Him, then we don't "speak the same as." If we don't "speak the same as," He said that we're under the curses of this Book. ***(Rev.22:18) I testify unto every man that heareth the words of the prophecy of this book, if any man shall add unto them, God shall add unto him the plagues which are written in this book: (19) and if any man shall take away from the words of the book of this prophecy, God shall take away his part from the tree of life, and out of the holy city, which are written in this book.*** And, also, our name will be taken out of that Book of Life. It behooves us to agree with God's Word so that we can have those benefits. It behooves us to confess Him boldly before men, even men who don't believe. The Lord Jesus wants a testimony in the earth and He wants us to confess Him before men. He said He would confess us before the angels, if we did that. "And I say unto you, Every one who shall confess me before men, him shall the Son of man also confess before the angels of God."

And, of course, then the angels administer the benefits because the Word of God has been spoken. Many believe this only means that the angels listen to what God says. Well, you have it both ways because Jesus said He would confess us before the holy angels, if we confessed Him before men. If we confess Him before men, we are speaking the Word of God before them and so, either way, folks, the angels get the authority from us. "Verily I say unto you, what things soever ye shall bind on earth shall be bound in heaven; and what things soever ye shall loose on earth shall be loosed in heaven." If we don't agree with the Word of God, we loose the devil and we bind God. It's just as when Jesus went to His own hometown. **(Mat.13:58) And he did not many mighty works there because of their unbelief.** You see, their unbelief had bound God.

How could we possibly bind God with our unbelief? Very simply, Scripture says it's because God has bound Himself by His Own Word. Once He has made a promise and once He has made a condition, if He were to disagree with it, or annul it, or not submit to it in any way, He would be a liar. And God is not a liar. **(Num.23:19) God is not a man, that he should lie, Neither the son of man, that he should repent: Hath he said, and will he not do it? Or hath he spoken, and will he not make it good?** So you see, God has bound Himself by His Word, but many times, men would like to get Him to change the Word. They would like to get Him to administer the benefits of the Kingdom to them, while ignoring all the conditions that He put in there. **(Rom.1:16) For I am not ashamed of the gospel: for it is the power of God unto salvation to every one that <u>believeth</u>; to the Jew first, and also to the Greek.** Therefore, that's a condition. The benefits of the Kingdom are for believers because they are Covenant people and not those loosely-called "Christians." We have to be very careful because with our heart and with our mouth we can administer salvation or we can administer the curse. We have authority both ways, positive and negative. If we disagree with God, if we preach the gospel of the devil, or the bad news of the devil, I tell you, that's what we are going to have and God will teach us a lesson.

Well, anyway, I want to get on to the rest of this testimony because it didn't stop there with Linda. She received a wonderful healing and she was very blessed, but then she was really encouraged to believe for her son and so we got to see another miracle. I'm going to read you a little bit of his story; his name is Terri. (My notes are in italics and parentheses.) He said, "I was a lost soul from the Lord. I went under the curse when I was a teenager. It started with a common problem facing many teens: premarital sex, lusts of the flesh and worshiping the almighty dollar. I eventually married an individual whom I was told not to marry and my mother had prayed and prayed every day for my salvation, but I refused to listen and, after five years, the marriage ended in disaster. I ended up having two nervous breakdowns in this relationship. *(I'll reveal at the end of this why he was having these nervous breakdowns.)* A lot of hate for everyone and everything filled my heart for the next seven years. *(You know, folks, unforgiveness and bitterness are destroying many people out there. You can pray all you want; you can pray until you are blue in the face, but if you are full of unforgiveness, bitterness or wrath toward anyone, your prayers won't be answered because Jesus said, if you don't forgive, you won't be forgiven.* **(Mat.6:15) But if ye forgive not men their trespasses, neither will your Father forgive your trespasses.** *You must be forgiven, in order to have the benefits of the Kingdom.* **(Jas.5:14) Is any among you sick? Let him call for the elders of the church; and let them pray over him, anointing him with oil in the name of the Lord: (15) and the prayer of faith shall save him that is sick, and the Lord shall raise him up; and if he have committed sins, <u>it shall be forgiven him</u>.** *You see, you have to be forgiven. God has to be willing to forgive you to give you the benefits, so make sure that you,* **(Mat.6:16) Confess therefore your sins one to another, and pray one for another, that ye may be healed. The supplication of a righteous man availeth much in its working.** *Make sure that you have forgiven everyone, so that the Lord can forgive you and give you His benefits.)* During this time, I did remarry." *(But, I tell you, folks, you are just carrying all that baggage with you, if you get remarried in the midst of a situation like that. And, sooner or later, it's going to catch up with you. The curse is chasing you down. Some of you out there are being chased by the curse and it will catch you, unless you first run to the Lord.)*

"I found happiness again, I thought. This marriage was nice for the first year-and-a-half years or so. However, because of the hate I had toward my ex-wife, I fell deeper into bondage. I had another breakdown on August 28, 1999. This one landed me in a psychiatric hospital. I was given several different medications and I was told that I had several different mental disorders. Of course, I believed everything I was told by this doctor because that's where I had my faith. I started out-patient therapy in September of 1999 and by November I was on Social Security disability. My 'mental condition' *(Obviously, he doesn't believe that was really the problem nowadays, but that's what they called it.)* became worse. My medications were increased and changed numerous times over the next four years. I had become so dependent on these medications that I would almost die, if I missed a dose in a day. My wife and my two kids watched me deteriorate and wither into a broken-down shell of a man and I had to drink a pot to two pots of coffee a day to stay awake to try to take care of my kids.

"Eventually, I became so lethargic that I couldn't even do that. In October of 2002, I had to check back into the hospital. I lost everything this time: my wife, my kids, my home, my car, my possessions. About a week later, I almost lost my life. *(Well, about this time is when Linda came to us and she was very encouraged because God had just healed her of cancer and she was really full of faith. She came to us and she wanted us to pray and agree for Terri to be healed. She wanted us to agree that he would get off those drugs and be delivered of the demons that had filled his life, and so we put our faith together with hers. Now let's read on here a little bit more of the testimony of what happened <u>when we agreed in faith according to the Scripture</u>.* **(Mat.18:19) Again I say unto you, that if two of you shall agree on earth as touching anything that they shall ask, it shall be done for them of my Father who is in heaven.**

And this is in his own words.) I had two people, both vessels of dishonor, approach me in the hospital. The first was my roommate. He would talk to himself and babble utter nonsense all day, but he turned to me and said very clearly, 'Take this Bible and read it.' *(Here's a guy he never heard say anything coherent or intelligible the whole time he'd known him and suddenly he said this very clearly: 'Take this Bible and read it.' Awesome! You know, God can speak to you through a donkey, if He wants to. But nothing can stop God from bringing to pass what you can believe Him for. Nothing! Nothing in this world! It doesn't matter where you are. Terri was where there was no minister of the Gospel to preach to him. His family wasn't there. There was nothing but the same kind of people like that all around him, but that didn't stop God.)* Within minutes, he returned to his old self. The same day, an elderly lady who had, in many ways, the same problems as my roommate, came up to me and gave me about 20 Scriptures to read. She told me she didn't know why she was to give me this message.

"The next day, I wanted to thank my two messengers. *(I mean, Terri had a real experience that night studying the Scriptures. The Lord moved on his heart mightily that particular night and so he wanted to go thank these messengers that the Lord had sent to him.)* But they didn't even know what I was talking about. My roommate said he didn't own a Bible and the lady said she had never even talked to me. Well, this amazed me. *(I can imagine it would have amazed anyone.)* Soon, I was released from the hospital and I went to go live with my sister, but I was still on the medication. I attended the Unleavened Bread Ministries Bible Study and the Lord did something wonderful for me. He laid it on my heart to repent and to confess my sins. The group laid hands on me and prayed for my deliverance from the medication and the evil spirits that had consumed my body, my heart and my soul. The next day, I took a leap of faith and stopped taking my medicine all at once. *(The doctors had told Terri that if he ever did this, it would kill him. They had pretty well convinced him. This brother knew more about medicine than any layman I've run across. He could tell you the name of it, tell you what it did, just everything, you know. He really studied up on this stuff.)* Look, several of these medicines that I took, if you get off of them cold turkey and you don't have the power of God on you, you are just going to die. *(That's what the doctors told him, too.)* But I thank the Lord for that healing every day. *(The Lord gave him a total and complete deliverance.)* Without the Lord's intervention, I would not be alive today. Since then, I've devoted my life to try to understand God's Word with the ability the Lord gives me and I'm very thankful."

You know, the change in this man was sudden and dramatic. You just couldn't imagine it. He was on so many drugs that he couldn't walk straight, talk straight, think straight or keep an intelligible stream of words. He was a mess and the Lord God set him free. It was an awesome miracle. Terri was a very bright, very intelligent man and one of the first jobs he got was with a pool cleaning service. Now he didn't know it and his boss didn't know it, but one of the pools that the company had a contract to clean was at the house of the psychiatrist who had dealt with him at the hospital. And the psychiatrist just couldn't believe that Terri was the same guy. He was just amazed and asked, "What happened to you?" Of course, Terri got to testify of the saving power of the Lord Jesus Christ. You know, the doctors told his wife that he was totally incurable, that he would never be right and he would never come out of an institution. So here's the psychiatrist and he's looking at Terri, who is now intelligent and totally healed, but the psychiatrist is finding out that it wasn't any of his works or any of his medicine that did it. It was just a simple prayer of faith and the Lord Jesus Christ. Boy, oh boy! I tell you, folks, the power that God has invested in those who believe, the power that He's willing to share and willing to administer in His gifts upon the people who believe, is just awesome! Well, it was around this time that Terri had a flashback to his childhood of something that he had repressed, a memory that he hadn't thought about in years. He didn't remember it and it wasn't in his consciousness, but he had this memory flashback. He had been molested by a Catholic priest when he was just a child and, of course, the priest threatened him so that he wouldn't report the situation. This began the demonic possession that brought Terri to a very humble state, so that he would realize his need for the Lord Jesus Christ.

You see, folks, God works all things after the counsel of His will. ***(Eph.1:11) In whom also we were made a heritage, having been foreordained according to the purpose of him who worketh all things after the counsel of his will.*** He knows what we need. He knows we're proud. He knows we have to go through these trials and tribulations. Jesus has been given authority over all the power of the enemy, over all the principalities and powers, and He's given that power to those who believe. As we studied last time, we saw that, just as Adam fell and lost the authority he had over all the creation, the second Adam didn't fall, didn't stumble, didn't give in to the devil and didn't give away His authority. His servant you are whom you obey. ***(Rom.6:16) Know ye not, that to whom ye present yourselves as servants unto obedience, his servants ye are whom ye obey; whether of sin unto death, or of obedience unto righteousness?*** It doesn't matter if you call yourself a Christian or not. You will serve the devil; you will obey him. You will give him <u>your authority over him</u>, if you walk in sin. And so Terri learned very well the message of repentance, faith and deliverance that was given to him. The Lord demonstrated it to him very well. You know, many people have gone through horrendous things in their childhood and they are packing a lot of baggage. This thing snowballs the further down life's trail you go and demons open doors to other demons, and you find yourself totally cursed and in bondage. The nursing homes are full of people who can't function because they're demon-possessed. I don't remember this being the case when I was younger. I'm seeing it worse now because, obviously, we are on the far end of the curse and it is manifesting strongly all around us. But we've been given the answer, folks, by the Gospel. The Lord Jesus has already taken care of this. Most "Christians" are just sitting on their hands and not really doing any of the things that they're commanded, but we, as Christians, are the ones who can bring this revelation to the world.

I'm going to share one more testimony here. This was a brother who came to us right after Terri did and his name is Mike Doty. He had been in a terrible accident when he was riding a horse while he was on drugs. He got out in the middle of a highway and was hit by a truck that killed the horse and came within a fraction of an inch of killing him. His brains were splattered out on the highway, too, and they didn't get them all back. And after they took him to the hospital, they had to cut out some more there. The doctors said that he had irreparable brain and spinal damage and he would never be right. And so they put him on strong drugs which left him with a very short attention span and a very poor memory. He also had poor mobility and pain in his back because he had crushed his spinal column. Mike had a lot of anger from the brain damage and from ongoing pain in his back. Now, when Mike came to our meeting, he became convinced very quickly of the Word of God. You know, you have to understand how simple-minded he is. Not only did he lose an awful lot of his brains, but he was drugged so heavily that he couldn't think very clearly. As I said, one reason they did this was because he was so full of anger that they couldn't trust him around people. Well, the very day he came to visit our assembly, I shared on, **(Mar.11:23) Verily I say unto you, Whosoever shall say unto this mountain, Be thou taken up and cast into the sea; and shall not doubt in his heart, but shall believe that what he saith cometh to pass; he shall have it. (24) Therefore I say unto you, All things whatsoever ye pray and ask for, believe that ye receive them** (Literally, the Greek word is "received them," as I have already shared.) **and ye shall have them.** He became very impressed with that; I tell you, that just stuck in his mind. By the grace of God, it just stuck in his mind and he lit up like a lightbulb. The Lord touched his heart right there because he wasn't saved when he came, but the Lord moved on his heart and he believed on this verse. Mike began to pray this way and he began to agree this way. He asked questions about it and we answered his questions. "What was the meaning of this?" "Why God would do this?" and so on and so forth. We answered a lot of questions for him. He was very hungry but those particular verses stuck in his heart very strongly.

About a month before Mike came to us and came to the Lord, his son, Conner, was diagnosed with epilepsy and Tourette's Syndrome. Conner was having seizures and tics and cursing episodes, and Mike's wife, who was separated from him, was complaining of the great cost of the drugs that they had to buy. Mike began to confess Mark 11:24 and he prayed and believed he had received. He confessed that Conner was healed. He told me one day, "I did just what you said. I commanded the demons to loose Conner and I believe I have received." And I asked Mike if he wanted us to agree with him for Conner and he told me it wasn't necessary. He said, "I've taken care of it." In fact, he told me one time, "I've healed him," so I gently explained to him, "No, the Lord has healed him; you are just the mouthpiece," and he understood that: "Yep! Yep!" So he accepted that but he continued to confess that his son was healed. I was reminded of the Syrophoenician woman (Mark 7:26-30) and the story of the centurion (Luke 7:2-10; Matthew 8:5-13), of how the Lord was just awed at their simple faith and their confession of faith that the Lord was sovereign over this situation. Well, the next week, I had an opportunity to pray over Mike. I believe it was for anger and, while I prayed, I just decided, "I'm just going to agree with Michael on this. I'm going to agree with his faith." So when I got through praying for him, I went on and prayed for Conner and rebuked that Tourette's Syndrome and I rebuked that epilepsy from him. Mike called me the next day or so and he said, "David, he hasn't had one more episode, one more tic, one more falling out!" He said, "All that's gone! My wife is awed!" And then he said, "I'm awed!" Conner has stayed delivered ever since then, too. You know, without Mike's faith and his bold confession, I don't think this would have been possible.

I am always really encouraged and I always feel really good when I hear somebody who is willing to do this. Most people you pray for don't say a thing. They don't confess the deliverance. They think that it's all just in your mind. Well, you know faith without works is incomplete and when we act on our faith, that's the completion of our real faith. A person who doesn't do that doesn't have real faith; it's incomplete. "Fruitless" is the word there used in James, too. So Mike's bold faith fulfilled what Jesus said: **(Mat.8:13) And Jesus said unto the centurion, Go thy way; <u>as thou hast believed</u>, [so] be it done unto thee. And the servant was healed in that hour. (9:29) Then touched he their eyes, saying, <u>According to your faith be it done unto you</u>. (Mar.11:23) Verily I say unto you, Whosoever shall say unto this mountain, Be thou taken up and cast into the sea; and shall not doubt in his heart, but shall believe that what he saith cometh to pass; he shall have it.** So Mike had that child-like faith. If everyone had that, folks, I tell you, it would just be so wonderful to be praying for people. You wouldn't have to worry about them. And Mike began to <u>use</u> his faith. He shared with me one time right after this, how the garage door opener in his mother's house, which was a few blocks down from him, quit working and they thought it was burned up. His mom said, "Well, we'll have to call somebody to work on it," but Mike said, "You don't have to do that. We have the authority to command this thing to be fixed in Jesus' name. Command it to be healed, in Jesus' name." He was just exercising his faith everywhere for everything. He prayed for his cat and God healed his cat. So he commanded that garage door to work in the name of Jesus and, of course, it immediately started working. His child-like faith was powerful to bring the benefits of the Kingdom.

I've been asked, "David, can we cast demons out of ourselves?" Well, of course you can! This happens all the time. I'm not saying it's not good to get the elders to pray over you or to get other people to agree with you. As with Mike, the prayer of agreement brought it to pass very quickly, although there's no doubt in my mind it would have come to pass, the way Mike was holding fast to his faith. But the Bible says one will chase a thousand and two will chase 10,000. You know, combined faith is 10 times more powerful. **(Deu.32:30) How should one chase a thousand, And two put ten thousand to flight, Except their Rock had sold them, And the Lord had delivered them up?** So, when we put our faith together, God brought it to pass. Glory be to God! But, yes, you can. You can cast demons out of yourself. I'm not saying that you don't need to get around God's saints and get them to agree with you. Sometimes God will speak to people and tell them, "Go get somebody to agree with you," even though they have the faith. It's also a powerful thing to do to confess your sins one to another, to humble yourself before God. God gives grace to the humble, but He resists the proud. ***(Jas.4:6) But he giveth more grace. Wherefore the scripture saith, God resisteth the proud, but giveth grace to the humble.*** So confessing your sins, gathering together and getting other people to agree with you and put their faith with yours is powerful. But, at the same time, yes, you can cast demons out of yourself. You can command them to go and they have to obey you. You have authority over all the power of the enemy. You've been given authority over all the demon spirits and many, many diseases are manifested by demon spirits. Sometimes it's an oppression, sometimes it's a possession; it really doesn't make that much difference. You have to deal with it the same way.

I want to say to you moms and dads, husbands and wives, that you have authority in your household. You have authority for those whom you take care of. For example, some of you are taking care of older relatives. In the case of the centurion, it was his servant for whom the centurion was responsible. You have authority in that situation. You don't even have to have a confession of their faith in that situation. If you are taking care of them and they're under your household, or even if you're taking care of them in their household, you have authority in that situation. You can take the authority that Jesus has given to you and just exercise it in the name of Jesus and God will stand behind your words. However, in situations where you are dealing with other people out there, always share the Gospel with them. Don't share deliverance with them. Don't share healing with them. Share the Gospel with them because the Gospel is the power of God unto salvation to the one who believes. ***(Rom.1:16) For I am not ashamed of <u>the gospel</u>: for it is the power of God unto salvation to every one that believeth; to the Jew first, and also to the Greek.*** And when I say the Gospel, I mean the Good News that Jesus has <u>already</u> saved them from their sins, healed their body, delivered them from demons, provided their needs, all these things. Share with them that Jesus has delivered them totally from the curse. Share the good Gospel with them and, if they believe it, they can have it and you can administer it. That's the condition when you are dealing with somebody who's not under your authority. You always have to make sure that they confess in some form, either with their mouth or with their feet, that they are agreeing with the Gospel. When they do that, you know that you have authority. Go forth and share the Gospel. Lift up Jesus and what He has done before men and God's power will be present.

Share the real Good News that Jesus has already delivered them and not the common, weak gospel that we hear nowadays. You know, the gospel that the suffering that you go through is somehow beneficial to you because it humbles you. That's true, but that's not what Jesus preached. He preached <u>deliverance</u>. He was consistent and everyone who was a member of His Kingdom, everyone who was in Covenant with God, was offered this benefit and He expected their faith to reach out for it and receive it. Faith is that substance for the thing hoped for while the evidence is not seen. ***(Heb.11:1) Now faith is assurance of things hoped for, a conviction of things not seen.*** And, of course, when we're in the midst of misery, in some form of bondage to the devil or to the demons or whatever, there's no evidence seen. But faith is that substance. This is the thing you need to send forth. If you are on the receiving end or if you are on the ministering end, it doesn't make any difference; it's what you have to send forth. If any two agree, that can include the one being ministered to and the one ministering. Be sure to share the Gospel with people around you who are in misery and just ask them for a simple agreement with you concerning what the promise is.

It's possible that you can believe part of the Gospel and receive the benefit of that particular part and you can believe another part and receive the benefit of that other particular part. There are many people who believe the Gospel that Jesus bore their sins and that He has forgiven them, and they stop right there. They may die not believing the other part of the Gospel that He's also borne all the curse. You know, if Jesus bore your sin, folks, if He really did that, why would He not bear the penalty of your sin? You are saying that He took away the sin, but He didn't take away the penalty? In other words, "I'm guiltless, but I still have to live under the curse." What kind of justice is that? No! That's not the Gospel. That's not the "full gospel," as Paul called it. ***(Rom.15:18) For I will not dare to speak of any things save those which Christ wrought through me, for the obedience of the Gentiles, by word and deed, (19) in the power of signs and wonders, in the power of the Holy Spirit; so that from Jerusalem, and round about even unto Illyricum, I have <u>fully preached the gospel of Christ</u>; (20) yea, making it my aim so to preach the gospel, not where Christ was already named, that I might not build upon another man's foundation; (21) but, as it is written, They shall see, to whom no tidings of him came, And they who have not heard shall understand.*** He said the full Gospel could only be manifested in signs and wonders and that's absolutely true. We don't have any authority to share half a Gospel by sharing only the part of the Gospel that a person needs. If they're sick, or they have demons, or they have mental problems, we still are to share the full Gospel.

Terri was totally lost and he didn't know God, but we believed that God would save him. We believed that Terri would believe the Gospel and that he would be delivered, and so God brought all that to pass. When he came here the first time, we stood around him and commanded the demons to come out of him in the name of Jesus. The next day, he was off of all of his drugs. There was a sudden change in the man's life. I shudder to think what could have happened if he had gone into an assembly that didn't believe the real Gospel, that sent him back to the psychiatrists. I've seen some so-called "full Gospel" assemblies sending their people to psychiatrists. Can you imagine? We have the benefits of the Kingdom and they are free! They're unmerited! Why would you send a person to somebody who charges? This is not the way that Jesus administered the benefits of the Kingdom. He did it freely; He didn't charge. ***(Mat.10:8) Heal the sick, raise the dead, cleanse the lepers, cast out demons: freely ye received, freely give.*** We are to freely give these benefits. We're not to bring people under the Law or anything like that. All they have to do is very simply agree with the Gospel. For example, "Yes, I agree that by the stripes of Jesus I was healed." *(1Pe.2:24) Who his own self bare our sins in his body upon the tree, that we, having died unto sins, might live unto righteousness; by whose stripes ye were healed.* If they make a confession of any kind, like Linda did, that Jesus had healed them, that's all you need, folks. It's very simple. It's a free gift. Give them a free gift; you have authority to do that. This is the great commission. Every disciple of Christ has these orders to go forth and share with the people around them and administer the benefits of the Kingdom.

How fast the Gospel would spread, if everybody wasn't depending upon their preacher to just do everything for them. You can go out and tell people, "Come to my church." Well, they can come to your church but, in most cases, they're not going to get their deliverance, they're not going to get their healing, they're not going to get their benefit because, in many cases, you are in a dead church and they do not preach the full Gospel. So, you know what, folks? <u>You</u> are to be those evangelists. Evangelism is outside the church; you go outside of the church. You know who's in <u>the</u> Church? <u>Only</u> the people of God are in <u>the</u> Church. Only the true people of God are in the true Church. That's the way it was in the first church. They went out; they evangelized. They brought people into the Kingdom outside of their dead churches. The disciples shared the Gospel with them, they gave them the benefits of the Kingdom and they joined themselves to the believers. You don't want unbelievers to join themselves to the believers. As a matter of fact, in the Book of Acts, they were afraid to join themselves to the believers. Ananias and Sapphira are a good demonstration of what happens if you're half-a-Christian and you join yourself to real believers. *(Act.5:1) But a certain man named Ananias, with Sapphira his wife, sold a possession, (2) and kept back part of the price, his wife also being privy to it, and brought a certain part, and laid it at the apostles' feet. (3) But Peter said, Ananias, why hath Satan filled thy heart to lie to the Holy Spirit, and to keep back part of the price of the land? (4) While it remained, did it not remain thine own? and after it was sold, was it not in thy power? How is it that thou hast conceived this thing in thy heart? thou has not lied unto men, but unto God. (5) And Ananias hearing these words fell down and gave up the ghost: and great fear came upon all that heard it. (6) And it was about the space of three hours after, when his wife, not knowing what was done, came in. (7) And it was about the space of three hours after, when his wife, not knowing what was done, came in. (8) And Peter answered unto her, Tell me whether ye sold the land for so much. And she said, Yea, for so much. (9) But Peter said unto her, How is it that ye have agreed together to try the Spirit of the Lord? behold, the feet of them that have buried thy husband are at the door, and they shall carry thee out. (10) And she fell down immediately at his feet, and gave up the ghost: and the young men came in and found her dead, and they carried her out and buried her by her husband. (11) And great fear came upon the whole church, and upon all that heard these things.* Do you know that there are many people out there who are dead because they tried to join themselves to believers?

See, what you do is you bring the Gospel to them! You go out there and you share it with them and, if they prove themselves to be a beneficiary of the Kingdom because of their belief, you give them the benefit. You just give it to them. That's the job, folks. Don't invite them to your church. Go out there and share with them. Don't bring them to me. The real Good News has to spread geometrically. The manifold gifts of God have to go out through many people. Most ministers make people dependent upon them to pray for the sick, to evangelize, to preach the Gospel. This is not the way, folks! The way is to make disciples and send the disciples. And the disciples go and make disciples, and the disciples go and make disciples, and it's just a geometric progression that is growing and growing! The Nicolaitan error has made people dependent upon preachers and I would say that a whole lot more than half of these are not going to preach the Gospel. So *you* find out what the Gospel is; *you* get filled with God's Holy Spirit; *you* bring the powerful gifts of God to others. You know, Jesus said, **(Act.1:8) But ye shall receive power, when the Holy Spirit is come upon you: and ye shall be my witnesses both in Jerusalem, and in all Judaea and Samaria, and unto the uttermost part of the earth.** Am I saying that you can't do this without the infilling of the baptism of the Holy Spirit? No, I'm not. All you have to do is believe to administer the benefits. I'm just saying that the Holy Spirit comes upon you in power. If you need more power, you need the Holy Spirit.

God bless you, saints. I pray that you will take the Gospel seriously and go forth in the name of Jesus.

CHAPTER 14

Demons Fear the Gospel!

God bless you, folks! We appreciate you so much. We hope you are praying for us. Father, in the name of Jesus, we ask Your grace and Your mercy upon our understanding today. We pray, Lord, that You will have mercy upon us and give us the grace to have the renewed mind of Christ. Oh, Lord, Your Word, Your truth motivates us to run after You, but the deceptions that are out there, Lord, take all that away. The deceptions cause people to be satisfied with the world and with far, far less of You than what You offer. So, Lord, we are just asking You to open our understanding and let us be motivated by the truth. Let Your truth live in us, Lord. Thank You so much. Amen.

Well, we've been learning about the <u>real</u> Good News, as opposed to the false "good news." We've discovered, folks, the real Good News is that the Lord has accomplished all this for us. The works were finished from the foundation of the world and we just enter into those works through faith. **(Heb.4:3) For we who have believed do enter into that rest; even as he hath said, As I sware in my wrath, They shall not enter into my rest: although the works were finished from the foundation of the world.** It's already done. We discovered that the Lord has <u>already</u> healed us; He <u>already</u> took away our sins; He <u>already</u> delivered us from the curse; He <u>already</u> provided our every need. All these things are done, according to the real Good News. You know, one thing that helped me to really respect the real Good News was how much the devil hated it and how much the devil is afraid of it. The Lord has taught me that. The devil hates it, he's afraid of it, he speaks against it and his ministers, whom he fashions as ministers of righteousness, also hate and speak against it. **(2Co.11:14) And no marvel; for even Satan fashioneth himself into an angel of light. (15) It is no great thing therefore if his ministers also fashion themselves as ministers of righteousness, whose end shall be according to their works.** And it's a war going on out there, folks! Years ago, the Lord taught me a lesson and I'm going to share it with you. I was going to be speaking on the Gospel at our meeting that evening and I learned just how much the devil hates the Gospel, and how he's warring against it. Well, a lady joined us who had never been in our meeting before, but she came into the meeting and she sat down right next to me and the microphone because we were recording it. And she started out by asking me, "David, what is this all about tongues?" So I explained to her, "Well, tongues is a gift from God by which the Holy Spirit speaks through us according to the will of God. It's a wonderful gift because the Holy Spirit doesn't know how to ask anything in unbelief. The reason it's in tongues is because, in that way, we don't know what we're saying, so we're not tempted to change it. We're not tempted to make it agree with our theology or our thinking. Many people who prophesy, for instance, have the temptation of prophesying in part. Their theology gets in there because they know what they're saying. But, of course, when you speak in tongues, you don't know what you're saying, so you don't have any motivation to change it. That's the reason for tongues. It's not because you're trying to get something by the devil. It really has nothing to do with that." Anyway, I explained this to her and she accepted that explanation for the moment, but we were just getting ready to start into our meeting.

I began in Romans. ***(Rom.1:16) For I am not ashamed of the gospel*** (which is the Good News)***: for it is the power of God unto salvation to every one that believeth; to the Jew first, and also to the Greek. (17) For therein is revealed a righteousness of God from faith unto faith: as it is written, But the righteous shall live by faith.*** The first thing you want to look at here is, "To whom is God talking? Is He talking to the world or is He talking to His people?" Well, when we back up a little, we read, ***(Rom.1:7) To all that are in Rome, beloved of God, called to be saints: Grace to you and peace from God our Father and the Lord Jesus Christ.*** So we can see that He's not talking to the world. He's not offering this power of God unto salvation to the world. He's offering it to the "beloved of God," the "saints" of God. I know that people have sometimes a very simplistic idea of this verse and they would like it to mean that this is only talking about sinners coming to the Lord. But, actually, we need salvation every day. Many people, who sell God far short and themselves far short, would like salvation to be a little line that you step over when you make some kind of a commitment toward the Lord. And from then on, you always count on the fact that you stepped over that line. It has nothing to do with your motivation to continue to walk in that salvation. Well, the word "salvation," *soteria*, as a Greek man once told me, means "all my needs supplied, like a little baby." In the Bible, it is actually the noun of the verb *sozo*, "save," and it's used to mean "deliverance," "salvation," "preservation," "healing," all those things. They're all part of salvation, according to the Scriptures, and you can go back and review the previous chapters if you want. But all of this is provided in salvation and it is something we need every day.

There are a great many people who see salvation as something that was manifested only when they received salvation. Well, you know, there was something that happened when we were saved. Our spirit was saved, which enabled us to walk in the Kingdom with this renewed spirit. But the Bible teaches that our soul still has need of sanctification. Your soul is born again through your obedience to the truth, as Peter tells us, so that's where we have to bear the fruit, folks. We have to bear fruit in our soul and this is why we need salvation. If you look very closely, it says here, "the power of God unto salvation." The Good News is "the power of God unto salvation" and he's speaking to people who are called "saints," "beloved of God." "Unto salvation" let's you know that there is a manifestation that we're expecting down the road. Now a lot of people don't expect that manifestation. They believe and they confess that they have been saved, that they have been delivered and so on, but they believe that this is manifestly "so," instead of by faith "so." This is a terrible mistake. It's something that the devil has done to deceive the church. It blinds the church to the great glory of God that He wants to give us as we continue to walk in the Gospel. Well, you know, when I got to this point where I spoke about unto salvation, I pointed out that unto salvation is not talking about something in your past; this is something coming down the road. **(1Pe.2:1) Putting away therefore all wickedness, and all guile, and hypocrisies, and envies, and all evil speakings, (2) as newborn babes,** (Obviously, he's talking about somebody who's already born again.) **long for the spiritual milk which is without guile, that ye may grow thereby unto salvation.** Wow! That's interesting; here's somebody who's born again but who needs to grow unto salvation, which is the same thing we read back over in Romans. And notice that we have to "grow thereby." We grow from newborn babes unto salvation, as we put away wickedness, as we put away guile, as we put away hypocrisies, envies and evil speaking.

Some Bible versions don't have "unto salvation" here, but the numeric pattern proves that's the correct translation. As I've explained previously, *Numerics* is a system by which God wrote the Bible. In the languages of the Old and New Testament, the Hebrew and Greek letters are also their numbers. That lets you know the whole Bible has actually been written in numbers, so there is a pattern going through the whole Bible that can be destroyed if you remove one letter or add one letter. And there is a numeric pattern in this text that is broken, unless you put in the words "unto salvation.. Some people are very proud of their own Bible translation, but the point is that "unto salvation" is in the ancient manuscripts and the numeric pattern is proof of that.

So we see here that, even after you're born again as babes, you grow thereby unto salvation. Jesus said, **(Mat.24:13) But he that endureth to the end, the same shall be saved**. Too many people think and they've been taught that they have all they're ever going to get when they received a new spirit, but your spirit is not your soul, folks. Your soul is your mind, will and emotions, and the Lord has planned to manifest His salvation in your soul. **(1Pe.1:5) Who by the power of God** (How does it come? The power of God comes through the Gospel.) **are guarded through faith unto a salvation ready to be revealed in the last time** (or "the latter end.") He also said, **(1Pe.1:9) Receiving the end of your faith, [even] the salvation of [your] souls**. It's not received at the beginning of your faith; it's the end of your faith. The beginning of your faith is the salvation of your spirit, but the Lord sacrificed for us so that we could be born-again spirit, soul and body. Your soul is the area of your life in which you bear fruit, not in your spirit, but in your soul. That's where you are bearing the fruit of the mind, will and emotions of Jesus Christ because He is Salvation. So as I was speaking on these things, this woman suddenly made a kind of gasping sound and when I looked over at her, I could tell that she was suffering. I knew right away that she was being tormented by demon spirits. Then, a few minutes later, as I continued speaking, the same sound came out of her mouth again, just like she was being tormented. I could tell the demons in her were angry that I continued to teach that there is a manifestation of salvation in our life. It's not just receiving it by faith but a manifestation of salvation in our life. In other words, there is a manifestation of deliverance, healing, preservation, all these things that God provided for us. Do you know what teaching the truth of this does? It takes away the shelter of people who are satisfied with the false step-over-the-line "gospel."

(Isa.28:14) Wherefore hear the word of Jehovah, ye scoffers, that rule this people that is in Jerusalem: (15) Because ye have said, We have made a covenant with death, and with Sheol are we at agreement; when the overflowing scourge shall pass through, it shall not come unto us; <u>for we have made lies our refuge</u>, and <u>under falsehood have we hid ourselves</u>: (16) therefore thus saith the Lord Jehovah, Behold, I lay in Zion for a foundation a stone, a tried stone, a precious corner-[stone] of sure foundation: he that believeth shall not be in haste. (17) And I will make justice the line, and righteousness the plummet; and the <u>hail shall sweep away the refuge of lies</u>, and the waters shall overflow the hiding-place. (18) And your covenant with death shall be annulled, and your agreement with Sheol shall not stand; when the overflowing scourge shall pass through, then ye shall be trodden down by it. There are people who shelter themselves from the conviction of God, from the responsibility that truth brings. They do it with lies. It takes away their responsibility to be obedient, to be faithful, to manifest anything past that first initial manifestation of Christ in their life, that born-again spirit. That's why people invent these false doctrines to hide under. People invent them because they take away their responsibility. They don't want to be like Christ. But those who love truth and love Christ and desire to see the fulness of the Good News, those who desire for His salvation to be complete, Christ is able to save "to the uttermost." Those are the people who draw near unto Him. ***(Heb.7:25) Wherefore also he is able to save to the uttermost*** (Or "completely"; it's the same Greek word.) ***them that draw near unto God through him, seeing he ever liveth to make intercession for them.*** We're being saved, spirit, soul and body. We're being saved 30-, 60- and 100-fold, as God's fruit is being borne in us.

But this lady and the spirits that were in her were very angry at what I was saying about salvation being more than just that initial experience with God. She had stepped over the line and she wanted to be justified where she was. She did not want to go on with God and those spirits in her were, of course, deceiving her. As they began manifesting more and more, she started making comments that were disjointed, that didn't fit the text of what I was saying. For instance, some of what she said was, "I'm saved. Christ has cleansed me. The blood of Jesus has cleansed me. Don't dispute the blood!" She spoke these things very harshly, in a very strident manner. I was calm and quiet as I was speaking and sharing the Word, but when I read the verse from Romans, "For I am not ashamed of the gospel: for it is the power of God unto salvation to every one that believeth; to the Jew first, and also to the Greek," she cried out, "Alright, Satan! Enough, accuser!" And, of course, these things were coming out of the mouth of somebody who was demon-possessed. This kind of thing went on for about 13 minutes. She just kept on interrupting and I guess even the most carnal people who were in the room knew that this lady was demon-possessed. These things that the devil was speaking and what the devil wanted her to believe was, "Hey, you've received all you need to receive. There's no manifestation of deliverance of sin. There's no manifestation of the power of salvation in your life. What you have is what you're going to get and that's all you need." You know, people believe that because they're satisfied. They don't want more of Christ. They don't want Him to manifest His salvation.

We all understand that we're saved by <u>faith</u>, but, **(Heb.11:1 KJV) ... <u>faith is the substance of things hoped for, the evidence of things not seen</u>**. That's because, if you had the evidence of your salvation, you know who you would be? Christ would be living in you fully. You'd be delivered of your sins and you'd be walking in the Spirit constantly. That's the manifestation of salvation. But, you see, some people don't believe that's even possible in this life. Instead of receiving salvation by faith, they believe that they've already received salvation by manifestation, which is a very dangerous thing. As long as we're striving for a goal and that goal is Christ-likeness, and we accept it by faith, Christ will empower us to go there. If you don't have any expectation of going there or any hope of going there, then you've been short-circuited by the devil. Anyway, the devil just kept speaking out and intervening through this lady. He gave the greasy-grace gospel that many people hear in their churches: "It's all done; it's all finished; that's all I'm going to receive," and so on and so forth. Finally, after she had been speaking on-and-off for about 16 minutes, I stopped teaching and I bound the demons in her. I forbid them to speak through her or torment her. She had spoken several times about the light burning her eyes and burning her skin. Well, it was the demons talking; they didn't like the light. They didn't like what we were talking about. They hate the Gospel because there's nothing that can really deliver religious or foolish Christian people from his bondage, except the Gospel, so the devil hates it!

The demons don't want to lose their house, folks. They want to dwell in the midst of God's people. **(Isa.14:13) And thou saidst in thy heart, I will ascend into heaven, I will exalt my throne above the stars of God; and I will sit upon the mount of congregation, in the uttermost parts of the north.** They want to exalt their throne over the stars of God. **(Gen.15:5) And he brought him forth abroad, and said, Look now toward heaven, and number the stars, if thou be able to number them: and he said unto him, So shall thy seed be.** And, of course, the stars are the people of God, according to what God told Abraham. The demons want to do this and they don't want to lose their house, so they make war. They put thoughts in the hearts of people that they want to hear anyway. One time, I went to one of the nursing homes where I'd gone quite often to preach the Gospel and in this particular nursing home there was a woman who had Alzheimer's. The Lord told me to pray for her and command the demon to come out of her, so when I did, she spoke for the first time anyone in there had heard her speak. They were all amazed because immediately she started talking intelligibly. She said, "Oh, thank you! I really needed that!" Those were the very first words that came out of her mouth! Everybody just looked at her in amazement and said, "Wow! She's never spoken before!" And she never had. They'd never heard her speak. Well, that was an Alzheimer's demon that had manifested in her.

Now there was another person in that nursing home who had been a preacher and he wasn't all that old, but he also had Alzheimer's. And, normally speaking, he was just big trouble. The staff couldn't handle him. He would wrestle with the nurses and he would just curse. He was really troublesome for them. But, every once in a while, this guy would start preaching and, if you looked in his face, you knew he wasn't doing it with his intelligence. It was demons preaching that old dead gospel out of him and when you heard it, you knew that it was being spoken intelligibly. And he was beyond that, folks! He wasn't able to speak a coherent sentence, let alone carry on a conversation with anybody. But when he started preaching, in-between the cursing, you could stop and listen to him. You could hear what his church always taught and it was coming out of the mouth of demons! And every once in a while, they would intersperse with a bunch of cursings in the midst of the whole thing, then he'd go back to preaching. I asked some of the staff there, "Does he do this often?" They answered, "All the time. And he's a handful, too." I thought, "Wow! Here's the devil preaching a *gospel*." It wasn't the real Gospel, folks, but it was a gospel that you hear in a lot of churches. It was, "You have everything you're going to get."

The devil hates the true Gospel because it's the power of God to save you and me, to bring us into the manifestation of Christ and to deliver us from the curse of this world. He hates that! And he's going to war against it. The devil sent a demon-possessed woman to our Bible study to fight against what he knew I was going to share on that night. But after I bound the demons from tormenting her, or tormenting us by speaking through her, she said a few more words and then she remained quiet for 10 minutes. It took the demons those 10 minutes to figure out a loophole. They figured out that, although they were forbidden to speak, they could still use her to interrupt us by coughing loudly into the microphone. She did that over and over. You know, demons can be really silly sometimes. So I bound that attack, too, and she was quiet for the rest of the teaching. And at the end of that teaching, she started making comments again because I had bound her until I was through speaking. So I just turned to her and asked, "Would you like us to pray for you with those tongues that you were speaking about?" And I'll tell you, demons are not just afraid of the Gospel, they're afraid of you praying over them in tongues! It was like I lit a fire under that woman and she jumped up and ran for the door as fast as she could! I've never seen anybody cross a room that quickly. But she hit that door and she was gone. She said, "No, thank you." She said those three words and by the time she said "you," she was going out the door; it was that fast. Another time we had a different lady who was obviously full of demons come here. She pointed at me and said right off, "I don't want him praying over me!" And I thought to myself, "I know why you don't want me praying over you." The devil hates the prayer of the Holy Spirit. The devil hates the Word of God. The devil hates the true Gospel, but he'll give you an anointing to preach that old, dead, lying gospel. Did you know that? He'll anoint you! He'll actually anoint you to speak that lying gospel because it's a deception. It's an antichrist gospel. The Lord came to conquer this old flesh and live in its place. **(Col.1:27) To whom God was pleased to make**

known what is the riches of the glory of this mystery among the Gentiles, which is <u>Christ in you</u>, <u>the hope of glory</u>. He came to be "Christ in you."

Then there was the time that I had been invited to a meeting up north of Pensacola. When I came in the door, I happened to glance down at a woman who was already seated in the pew. And as she looked up at me, I saw demons in her eyes, but I didn't say anything. I just walked on a little farther and sat down. Now before the meeting started, there was the usual general conversation going on in the audience and so on, and this woman spoke up. She started speaking the same exact things that I knew that demon was and when she got through, she was talking about her problems. So I said to her, "Ma'am, when I walked by you and I looked into your face, I saw demons in you. You need deliverance. This is your problem; you need deliverance." Well, I no more than got that out of my mouth than here comes the preacher, a female preacher. I had stood up as I was speaking because I was going to go over to the woman and try to minister to her, but immediately this lady preacher <u>ran</u> over and stood in-between us! She said something like, "We don't reveal sins here; we cover them," and I thought to myself, "Now what does that have to do with anything that we're doing here?" But, you know, the lady preacher stopped me just long enough for this woman, who was on the other side of her, to jump up and run out the door as fast as she could run out the door. Gone! And suddenly, it was as if this lady preacher got a revelation. She looked at me and she said, "I'm so sorry! Would you like to go after her?" But I answered, "No, I don't think so. I think she has too good a head start on me." She was very convicted, but I knew exactly what had happened. The spirit in this lady preacher was covering for that other woman. It was hindering, in order to protect the house of that other demon, you see. It was possibly a Jezebel spirit or something like that, but a little later, the lady preacher felt convicted yet again and she asked my forgiveness a second time. Well, that's a great example of how demons cover for one another. They'll behave almost like a wolf pack. The demons will fight with one another, but then they'll work together to bring someone down or to hinder the work of God. And what they love to hinder, folks, is the Gospel.

(Act.15:11) But we believe that <u>we shall be saved</u> through the grace of the Lord Jesus, in like manner as they. Now, we're used to saying, "I'm saved," and rightfully so because we're claiming something by faith. We're claiming the deliverance, the healing, the blessing, all of the provision of God that is associated with this salvation. We're not saved, as some people think, <u>to sin</u>; we're saved <u>from sin,</u> folks. We're saved from the curse of sin. We've been delivered out of the power of darkness. ***(Col.1:13) Who delivered us out of the power of darkness, and translated us into the kingdom of the Son of his love.*** We're saved from everything that Deuteronomy 28 speaks of as being the curse that has been put upon this world. But it's God's plan that there is a manifestation of that salvation. Faith is a means to an end; it's not an end in itself. It's "the substance of the thing hoped for," but God wants to give us the thing hoped for. ***(Heb.11:1 KJV) Now faith is the substance of things hoped for, the evidence of things not seen.*** We're not meant to walk by faith in what God has given the rest of our life. It's a means to an end. It's supposed to bring us this manifestation of God's salvation. And so the apostle is saying here to other apostles, who know what he's talking about, "We believe that we shall be saved through the grace of the Lord Jesus." We shall be saved. Do you know that, in the Scriptures, it never says that we are saved, except when it speaks about us being saved by faith. I want to destroy this false doctrine because it's the foundation of bondage for many, many people. It's that lying gospel. **(1Co.15:1) Now I make known unto you brethren, the gospel which I preached unto you, which also ye received, wherein also ye stand, (2) by which also ye are** (Literally, in the Greek it says "being saved.") **saved, if ye hold fast the word which I preached unto you, except ye believed in vain.** There are a lot of people who don't accept that they can believe in vain or that they could have believed in vain. But it's clear here that, if you don't hold fast to the Word that was spoken unto you, the Word of your salvation, the faith of your salvation, then you've just believed for nothing.

And the correct translation here is definitely "being saved," not "saved." "By which also ye are being saved." As a matter of fact, the numeric pattern is in "being saved." If "being" is omitted, then there's a word missing and it ruins the numeric pattern. And for those of you King-James-only folks out there, you go get your Received Text and look it up because the Received Text says the same thing. The King James doesn't say that, but the Received Text does. It says "being saved." Isn't that interesting?

Yes, we are being saved, as we hold fast the Word He preached unto us, not the "word" that we hear nowadays. We are to contend earnestly for the faith which was once delivered unto the saints. **(Jud.3) Beloved, while I was giving all diligence to write unto you of our common salvation, I was constrained to write unto you exhorting you to contend earnestly for the faith which was once for all delivered unto the saints.** As we hold fast to that Gospel, we are being saved. There is coming a manifestation of our deliverance from this curse of sin and death. There is coming a manifestation of Christ in you! **(Col.1:27) To whom God was pleased to make known what is the riches of the glory of this mystery among the Gentiles, which is Christ in you, the hope of glory.** Wow! Yet, some people have no hope whatsoever for this. **(1Co.1:18) For the word of the cross is to them that perish** (literally, "are perishing") **foolishness; but unto us who are** (literally, "are being") **saved it is the power of God.** "To them that are perishing" and "unto us who are being saved" is what it says in the original. Both the Numerics and the Received Text prove that, as does the Nestle's Text. The Nestle's Text is comprised of the three most ancient manuscripts all rolled into one text. Where two or more of those manuscripts agreed, they put it in the text. It was the best way to find a true text until the Numerics came along and superceded it as the best method. So we have all the proof in the world that it doesn't say "we are saved," but that it says, "we are being saved." If you don't have that hope, it can't come to pass. You know why? Let me point out to you what it says in Colossians. The devil knows how to stop the manifestation of salvation. **(Col.1:21) And you,**

being in time past alienated and enemies in your mind in your evil works, (22) yet now hath he reconciled.... The original Greek word there for "reconciled," *apokatallasso*, means "an exchange." There was "an exchange" in Christ's Body. He took our curse upon Himself and He gave us His blessing. He took our nature, crucified it on the cross and He gave us His nature. That was all accomplished. That's what "reconciliation" means. **(Col.1:22) *Yet now hath he reconciled*** ("exchanged") ***in the body of his flesh through death to present you holy and without blemish and unreproveable before him: (23) if*** (And you can circle that "if" there because it is conditional.) ***so be that ye continue in the faith, grounded and stedfast, and not moved away from the hope of the gospel which ye heard, which was preached in all creation under heaven; whereof I Paul was made a minister.*** Notice that both "faith" and "hope" are mentioned here.

"If so be that ye continue in the faith...." That is, calling the things that are not, as though they were, because they were. At the cross, we were delivered from the curse of sin and death. **(Rom.8:2) *For the law of the Spirit of life in Christ Jesus made me free from the law of sin and of death.*** "If so be that ye continue in the faith, grounded and stedfast, and not moved away from the hope of the gospel...." Now that's different. Faith looks back but hope looks forward. "Hope" is "a firm expectation." The people who believe by faith that Christ took away their sins, who believe by faith that He bore their sins in His body, who believe by faith that "by whose stripes ye were healed," the people who believe those past-tense promises also have hope! In other words, they have a firm expectation of something that's coming down the road. See, one looks back and one looks forward. And what the Lord spoke to me one time is everyone who has faith has hope, but not everyone who has hope has faith. Many people hope for something they don't ever expect to get, but this is a firm expectation, this is someone who is believing that something is coming down the road. What is it? It's the fulfillment of the Gospel. We have faith for the Gospel. We accept the Good News that we were crucified with Christ and that we don't live anymore, that the old man has passed away. **(Gal.2:20) *I have been crucified with Christ; and it is no longer I that live, but Christ living in me: and that [life] which I now live in the flesh I live in faith, [the faith] which is in the Son of God, who loved me, and gave himself up for me.*** We accept that Good News, but we also expect it to come to pass. That's where the hope comes in, the hope of the Gospel. **(Php.1:6) *Being confident of this very thing, that he who began a good work in you will perfect it until the day of Jesus Christ.*** We have a firm expectation that the Lord Who began a good work in us will fulfill it unto the day of Jesus Christ. This is the true Gospel, folks. The false gospel is that you received everything you're going to get when you "accepted Jesus as your personal Savior." Have you ever heard that preached? Well, those words are not even in the Bible, by the way, so that's a lying devil right there. You didn't get everything you're going to get; you only received a down payment. **(2Co.1:21) *Now he that establisheth us with you in Christ, and anointed us, is God; (22) who also sealed us, and gave us the***

earnest of the Spirit in our hearts. That's what the Bible says. God's going to finish the good work He started in you, if you give Him the faith.

Let me point out another verse that also uses this terminology. ***(2Co.2:15) For we are a sweet savor of Christ unto God, in them that are <u>saved</u>*** (The original reads "are being saved."), ***and in them that <u>perish</u>*** (The original reads "that are perishing."); ***(16) to the one a savor from death unto death; to the other a savor from life unto life. And who is sufficient for these things?*** The Numerics, the Received Text and the Nestle's Text all agree that this is "them that <u>are perishing</u>" and "them that <u>are being saved</u>." And all three of the most ancient manuscripts agree on this. No place in the Bible does it read "you <u>are</u> saved," except by faith. ***(Mar.11:24) Therefore I say unto you, All things whatsoever ye pray and ask for, believe that ye <u>receive</u> them*** (According to the Numeric, this is also past tense; it's "<u>received</u> them."), ***and ye shall have them.*** And why is it that Jesus says that? It's because we <u>did</u> receive them! We received everything at the cross. We were crucified with Christ and we were resurrected with Christ. It is now Christ Who lives in us. ***(Gal.2:20) I have been crucified with Christ; and it is no longer I that live, but Christ living in me: and that [life] which I now live in the flesh I live in faith, [the faith] which is in the Son of God, who loved me, and gave himself up for me.*** We've received it all! And so anything we pray for, we believe we received. That's what faith is. Faith calls the things that are not as though they were. ***(Rom.4:17) (As it is written, A father of many nations have I made thee) before him whom he believed, even God, who giveth life to the dead, and <u>calleth the things that are not, as though they were</u>.*** Faith is the substance of the thing hoped for, while there's no evidence of it yet. ***(Heb.11:1 KJV) Now faith is the substance of things hoped for, the evidence of things not seen.*** We're justified by our faith and that is because we are receiving our need through giving to God the substance of our faith. God reckons righteousness unto us; that's what "justified" means. He reckons righteousness unto us because we <u>believe</u> that Christ took away our sins and that He delivered us from the curse.

Say, for example, that you've believed for a healing. You asked the Lord to heal you and you walk by faith, and if you continue in your faith, God always does it, right? So, again, faith is the substance while the evidence isn't seen, but faith is a means to an end, the end being the true substance of the thing you're hoping for. It's the same for salvation. When you first come to Christ, let me give you a revelation: you're accepting God's salvation by faith. You say, "Uh-uh, David. I got something." Well, I did, too. I received a new spirit, but Jesus also spoke to His disciples about "regeneration," which means "new birth." ***(Mat.19:28) And Jesus said unto them, Verily I say unto you, that <u>ye who have followed me</u>, <u>in the regeneration</u> when the Son of man shall sit on the throne of his glory, ye also shall sit upon twelve thrones, judging the twelve tribes of Israel.*** The disciples who walked with Jesus were born again, but they didn't have everything the Lord had to give them. They were entering into it as they walked by faith and they were manifesting more and more of the wisdom of Christ which was being sown in their heart. Jesus said, **(Joh.6:63) It is the spirit that giveth life; the flesh profiteth nothing: the words that I have spoken unto you are spirit, and are life.** The Lord's Spirit and life in His words were going into them and recreating Himself in them, first spirit, but then soul and, ultimately, body. Those who bear the fruit of the Spirit in their soul, 30-, 60- and 100-fold, are manifesting the works of Christ. **(Rom.13:11) And this, knowing the season, that already it is time for you to awake out of sleep: <u>for now is salvation nearer to us than when we [first] believed</u>.** Wow! You see, they had to hope for something that was coming down the road, but the <u>fullness</u> of God's salvation is now nearer to us than when we first believed. **(Rom.13:12) The night is far spent, and the day is at hand: let us therefore <u>cast off the works of darkness</u>, and let us put on the armor of light. (13) Let us walk becomingly, as in the day; not in revelling and drunkenness, not in chambering and wantonness, not in strife and jealousy. (14) But <u>put ye on the Lord Jesus Christ</u>, and make not provision for the flesh, to [fulfil] the lusts [thereof].** "Salvation is nearer to us than when we first believed" because we are <u>putting on</u> the Lord Jesus Christ! I know that we've been talking about demons in this book, but I'm tying it together with the direction I'm going in and that is talking about the fullness of Christ in us. I love to think on that because it's my favorite subject!

We had a lady come here one time and one time only. It was another one of those instances where we were talking about the Gospel, as a matter of fact. She was sitting about 15 feet from me and she hit the floor on her knees and ran around a table on her knees! She ran right up to my wife and me, who were sitting next to one another, and her eyes were just glaring with hatred. And she reached her hands out toward my neck, like she wanted to choke me. She looked over at my wife and said, "Don't you know I could just <u>choke</u> your husband to death!" But my wife said, "No, you can't do that." And I said, "No, you can't do that." I've forgotten all I said, but as soon as I refused her, she got back up, as if she was in her right mind and just looked around. Then she walked over and sat back down. Well, you know, the devil hates people who preach the real Gospel. He'll make war on people who preach the real Gospel because he hates this revelation getting out to the church.

You know, the Bible says that the devil is the god of this world. **(2Co.4:4) In whom the god of this world hath blinded the minds of the unbelieving, that the light of the gospel of the glory of Christ, who is the image of God, should not dawn upon them.** And the devil is also the king of Babylon, identified in Isaiah 14:4 as that. He wants to rule. **(Isa.14:13) And thou saidst in thy heart, I will ascend into heaven, I will exalt my throne above the stars of God; and I will sit upon the mount of congregation, in the uttermost parts of the north.** He wants to exalt his throne, as that verse says, over "the stars of God," and he doesn't want anybody <u>plundering him</u>. But the Lord Jesus has given us the authority to plunder the devil's kingdom and the Gospel is the primary means of doing that, of <u>plundering his</u>

kingdom. The Gospel is the power of God unto salvation, and salvation, as we just saw in Romans 13, is the manifestation of Christ in you. We're putting on Christ! That's God's salvation. You look at Jesus and you see what salvation is. The early Christians were called "Christians" because they walked in His steps, they spoke as He spoke, they had power as He had power and they showed they were witnesses of Him. They didn't just witness; they were witnesses. People looked at them and they saw Jesus. They looked at these people and they called them "Christians" because they were Christ-like.

The overwhelming majority of Christianity could never be accused of that nowadays. But the truth is, that's where we're headed back to, folks. The Lord, in these days, is going to do a work that many will not believe. *(Hab.1:5) Behold ye among the nations, and look, and wonder marvellously; for I am working a work in your days, which ye will not believe though it be told you. (Act.13:41) Behold, ye despisers, and wonder, and perish; For I work a work in your days, A work which ye shall in no wise believe, if one declare it unto you.* They certainly didn't believe Jesus when He came the first time. Can you imagine? These demon-possessed people, whom He said were sons of their father, the devil, had the Lord Jesus Christ standing in their midst and they thought He had demons. *(2Th.1:10) When he shall come to be glorified in his saints, and to be marvelled at in all them that believed (because our testimony unto you was believed) in that day.* You know, the Lord is giving special grace in these days to finish His salvation in His people. We're nearer to salvation than when we first believed. This is talking about Jesus coming to be glorified in His saints. *(2Th.1:11) To which end we also pray always for you, that our God may count you worthy of your calling, and fulfil every desire of goodness and [every] work of faith, with power....* See, *(Php.2:13) for it is God who worketh in you both to will and to work, for his good pleasure.* He works in us to will and to do of His good pleasure. This is what salvation is all about in the New Covenant. When you're out from under the Law, this is how it works. He works in you to will. He gives you a desire of goodness and then He works in you to do. He brings it to pass, every desire of goodness and every work of faith. Wow! And Paul wasn't praying an impossible prayer; he was praying something that was according to the will of God because there is a numeric pattern in this, too. *(2Th.1:11) To which end we also pray always for you, that our God may count you worthy of your calling, and fulfil every desire of goodness and [every] work of faith, with power; (12) that the name of our Lord Jesus may be glorified in you, and ye in him, according to the grace of our God and the Lord Jesus Christ.*

Notice that it's "according to the grace of our God"; it's not according to our works. Many people complain that we can never be perfect, we can never manifest Christ. They say we'll always be "sinners saved by grace," which is not according to the Bible. But they say that because the only hope they have is their own power. They just don't seem to understand that it has nothing to do with our power. *(Eph.2:8) For by grace have ye been saved through faith; and that not of yourselves, [it is] the gift of God;*

(9) not of works, that no man should glory. It has to do with God's power. Can you tell God that He's not able to do this? If He's not able to do this, why is Paul praying for it? Does he not have good sense? "That the name of our Lord Jesus may be glorified in you, and ye in him." The Greek word for "name" is *onoma* and it means "nature, character and authority." Paul was praying that the nature, character and authority of Jesus Christ would be glorified in you. That's God's plan and when did he say this was going to happen? Well, if you look at the text from verse 10 on up, you find out that he's talking about the days before the coming of the Lord. These are the days that God's going to do this. These are the days when He's going to finish His creation!

You know, we're still in the creation process here, folks. Some people think that we're in "Plan B" because "Plan A" didn't work. They think God's plan was thwarted when Adam fell, but that's ridiculous! Jesus was the Lamb slain from the foundation of the world, before Adam fell. ***(Rev.13:8) And all that dwell on the earth shall worship him, every one whose name hath not been written from the foundation of the world in the book of life of the Lamb that hath been slain.*** A sacrifice was made for us and God chose us in Him before the foundation of the world, before Adam fell. ***(Eph.1:4) Even as he chose us in him before the foundation of the world, that we should be holy and without blemish before him in love.*** He knew that we needed a Savior and He chose us to be in Him, to be in that Savior. We're not in Plan B. We're in Plan A and God doesn't have a "Plan B"! So God planned for us to be in this state and He planned for there to be a first Adam and a last Adam, called Jesus Christ. ***(1Co.15:45) So also it is written, The first man Adam became a living soul. The last Adam became a life-giving spirit.*** And the last Adam is the Father of the born-again creation, the creation that's born in the image of God, the true image of God. People say, "Well, Adam was born in the image of God." Yes, but that was naturally, not spiritually! Now we're talking about the born-again image of God, the true image of God, the true sons of God. We're awaiting the manifestation of the sons of God! ***(Rom.8:19) For the earnest expectation of the creation waiteth for the revealing of the sons of God. (20) For the creation was subjected to vanity, not of its own will, but by reason of him who subjected it, in hope (21) that the creation itself also shall be delivered from the bondage of corruption into the liberty of the glory of the children of God.***

You see, folks, the manifestation of sonship is what God's interested in. He wants Jesus to be "the firstborn among many brethren." ***(Rom.8:29) For whom he foreknew, he also foreordained to be conformed to the image of his Son, that he might be the firstborn among many brethren.*** Jesus came to be God's *charagma*, His image and, in that case, the word means "a tool to recreate itself." You see, that's what Jesus was. Jesus was God's tool to recreate Himself in us. He is also the Father of the born-again creation, the last Adam. It is God's plan that we come into His image and we've been sold far short by the preachers who just *went and weren't sent*. They were sent by men and not God. They have preached an antichrist *gospel* that is keeping God's people from coming into His image. They are keeping the name of our Lord Jesus from being glorified in His people, but Paul prayed, "that the name of our Lord Jesus may be glorified in you." ***(2Co.3:18) But we all, with unveiled face beholding as in a mirror <u>the glory of the Lord</u>, are <u>transformed into the same image from glory to glory, even as from the Lord the Spirit.</u>*** So we behold as in a mirror, that is, we behold by faith, that we no longer live and that Christ lives in us (Galatians 2:20). And as we hold fast to the faith of this Gospel, the Lord is going to bring us from glory to glory into His image and manifest His name in us. You know, when we went down in the waters of baptism, we took on His name. The Bible says we were baptized "<u>into</u>" His name, not "<u>in</u>" His name. The literal word there is "into" and the Numerics proves it. We're baptized <u>into</u> His name, which means <u>into His nature</u>, <u>character</u> and <u>authority</u>. The plan of the Lord is that we do the greater works in these days, not that we do them, but that He does them through us. When we put our faith in Him, He's going to fulfill in us every desire of goodness and every work of faith with power, so that the name of the Lord Jesus Christ may be glorified in you. God bless you, saints! I hope you're catching hold of this wonderful truth!

CHAPTER 15

All Needs Supplied in Christ!

    Greetings, saints! The Lord be with you and bless you. Father, we're asking for Your grace today, Lord, that we would have eyes and ears, a gift from You, Lord, to understand Your Word, to retain Your Word and to have Your Holy Spirit bring to our remembrance all things that You say unto us. Lord, we thank You for Your grace. We thank You for the awesome privilege of being called of You. And, Lord, we're asking You to finish the good work You started in us and manifest the fruit of Jesus Christ in our lives. Take us by the hand, Father, make disciples of us, God. Make us learners and followers of our Lord Jesus Christ. Thank You, Lord. Amen.

    Well, we're still learning about the real Good News, folks, and I thought I'd share a little bit with you about our provision because so many people are worried about their provision for the days to come. They see how the economies are faltering. Some Christians are realizing that there's a wilderness coming, a place where we're going to have to walk by faith and we all need to understand that. How do we <u>know</u> that God's going to keep us through this? How much of it is our work and how much of it is God's work? Well, folks, it's <u>all God's work</u> through us. The New Covenant is all about learning how to rest in Him and be a vessel through whom He does His will, a vessel through whom He manifests His life. It is "Christ in you, the hope of glory." *(Col.1:27) **To whom God was pleased to make known what is the riches of the glory of this mystery among the Gentiles, which is <u>Christ in you</u>, <u>the hope of glory</u>.*** So, again, how do we <u>know</u> that God is going to do this for us? It's because of these awesome promises that the Lord made to us and, if we call ourselves believers, we should act in accordance with what we know these say. ***(Mat.21:22) And all things, whatsoever ye shall ask in prayer, believing, ye shall receive.*** Where could you go that would get you beyond the grace of God, if you believed a promise like that? I've proven these promises over and over. Many years ago, the Lord told me, "I'm sending you through a wilderness, so you can tell My people I still supply there." And I've had many exciting days in the wilderness, seeing God's hand do miracles for me. Here's another one of those awesome promises: ***(Mar.11:24) Therefore I say unto you, All things whatsoever ye pray and ask for, believe that ye <u>received</u> them*** (past tense)***, and ye shall have them.*** Wow! Where can you go where God's grace, God's provision and God's mercy will not be?

    We also have the awesome promises Apostle Paul gave us. ***(Php.4:19) And my God shall <u>supply every need of yours</u> according to his riches in glory in Christ Jesus.*** How does he know that God is going to supply every need of <u>yours</u>? He's talking to the saints here in Philippians, but how does he know that God is going to do this for <u>you</u>? And, of course, if God is going to do this, why would we even worry about it? Why don't we just rest and trust in Him, instead of running around and trying to be our own savior because we're fearful of the things we see on the horizon? He loves to show His glory and power in our weakness. His power is made perfect in our weakness. ***(2Co.12:9) And he hath said unto me, My grace is sufficient for thee: for [my] power is made perfect in weakness. Most gladly therefore will I rather glory in my weaknesses, that the power of Christ may rest upon me.*** But how does Paul know that, "my God shall supply every need of yours according to His riches in glory in Christ Jesus"? There's a key phrase, right there. You know, it is not necessarily true that everyone will receive all their needs met, but it is definitely true that all their needs are met in Christ Jesus. Let's look at a similar statement concerning this. ***(Eph.1:3) Blessed [be] the God and Father of our Lord Jesus Christ, who hath*** (past tense) ***blessed us with every spiritual blessing in the heavenly [places] in Christ.*** He has already blessed us with every spiritual blessing in heavenly places, in Christ. All of our blessings are in Christ. As we learn to abide in Him, we will learn exactly what Paul said: "And my God shall supply every need of yours according to his riches in glory in Christ Jesus"; and He has blessed us with every spiritual blessing, too, "in the heavenly places in Christ Jesus."

Where is this "in Christ Jesus"? ***(1Jn.2:24) As for you, let that abide in you which ye heard from the beginning. If that which ye heard from the beginning abide in you, ye also shall abide in the Son, and in the Father.*** In other words, we need to "contend earnestly" for the doctrine, the faith, that was given to us from the beginning. ***(Jud.3) Beloved, while I was giving all diligence to write unto you of our common salvation, I was constrained to write unto you exhorting you to contend earnestly for the faith which was once for all delivered unto the saints.*** This is not the fallen faith of our day, but the faith that was "once delivered unto the saints." If we contend for that, if that's what we're putting into our hearts, then we abide in the Son. That's what the Scripture says. And Scripture also says, ***(1Jn.2:6) He that saith he abideth in him ought himself also to walk even as he walked.*** You see, Jesus was our example, not just our sacrifice. He taught us what it was to walk as a disciple and His disciples walked that way after Him. You know, if you put this Word in you that they had in them, you'll do what they did. As I like to say, "If you get what they got, you'll do what they did." And, if you do what they did, if you put the living Word of God in your heart, you'll get what they got. We don't need the apostasy that's in the churches nowadays. We need that original Word that was given unto us and we need to know that God has called us to walk in His steps.

And here's one more point about what it is to abide in Christ: ***(1Jn.3:6) Whosoever abideth in him sinneth not: whosoever sinneth hath not seen him, neither knoweth him.*** Wow! That makes it almost impossible in some people's minds, unless you understand what sin is in the New Testament. ***(Jas.4:17) To him therefore that knoweth to do good, and doeth it not, to him it is sin.*** In the New Testament, it takes knowledge to make sin. "To him that knoweth to do good, and doeth it not, to him it is sin." In other words, you can be ignorant of a lot of things and the blood of Jesus will cover you and you can still abide in Christ, although you abide in Christ at a younger age because you don't know so much about God. But God forgives you because of your ignorance, just like a child who's still growing up. God forgives that child of the foolish things that children do and He's that merciful with us, too. Thank God! Because we are ignorant of a lot of things, but when knowledge comes, He begins to hold us responsible, just like with a child. When the child grows up, you don't treat them like a child anymore. You begin to hold them responsible because they know more. ***(Heb.10:26) For if we sin wilfully after that we have received the <u>knowledge of the truth</u>*** (There it is again, "<u>knowledge</u> of the truth."), ***there remaineth no more a sacrifice for sins, (27) but a certain fearful expectation of judgment, and a fierceness of fire which shall devour the adversaries.*** And John says that there is no sin in Him: ***(1Jn.3:5) And ye know that he was manifested to take away sins; and <u>in him is no sin</u>.*** So, therefore, when you sin, you are not abiding in Christ. ***(1Co.6:18) Flee fornication. <u>Every sin that a man doeth is without the body</u>; but he that committeth fornication sinneth against his own body.*** When you sin, you're not sinning in Christ because there's no sin in Him and sin is based on your <u>knowledge</u> of the truth.

What is it to be "in Christ"? First of all, you are in Christ, if you believe that He took away your sins. You are justified by your faith. ***(Rom.3:28) We reckon therefore that <u>a man is justified by faith</u> apart from the works of the law.*** That's the only thing that puts you in Christ -- justification by faith -- because you believe that you are no longer a sinner. You believe that now He has taken away your sins and that He has imputed to you His righteousness through faith. Therefore, faith and knowledge have everything to do with abiding in Christ. And we just saw that, in Christ, all of your needs are met. Your spiritual needs and physical needs are met. That's why Paul was so sure that He "shall supply every need of yours according to His riches in glory in Christ Jesus." When you qualify with those last few phrases, what you are saying is that those saints who are abiding in Him will have their needs met and it is so, folks; it is so. So that is a very safe statement for Paul to make. We're not talking here about using the Word of God for a fleshly prosperity, using the Word of God to let your flesh live after all the lusts of the world. ***(1Jn.2:15) Love not the world, neither the things that are in the world. If any man love the world, the love of the Father is not in him.*** The love of the world is apostasy and yet many are teaching that. No, we just need our needs met, so that we can do the will of God. Jesus wasn't interested in the world; He wasn't caught up in the world. He had a simple life and His disciples did, too. They didn't want to be distracted by the things of the world. They knew they were here on a very important mission and we are, too. We are to be <u>disciples</u> of Christ. We are to carry on the great commission and we don't want to waste our time living in the luxury of this world, this lascivious lifestyle of the wicked. So don't be deceived by this false gospel that's out there. The true Gospel says, "My God shall supply every need of yours according to His riches in glory in Christ Jesus." <u>Every need</u>! And don't forget that. When you come into the wilderness experiences that are ahead of us, just remember that God has made this promise unto you. And if you can't find a specific promise that applies to your situation, you can always go back to those "super" promises because He said, *(Mat.21:22) And all things, whatsoever ye shall ask in prayer, believing, ye shall receive. (Mar.11:24) Therefore I say unto you, All things whatsoever ye pray and ask for, believe that ye receive them, and ye shall have them.* He said, "All things whatsoever"!

I'm going to give you a little bit of foundation here, so we can know what we have in Christ Jesus and understand why Paul was so confident all our needs will be met. *(Gal.3:11) Now that no man is justified by the law before God, is evident: for, <u>The righteous shall live by faith</u>.* It pleases God that we learn to put our trust in Him and to walk into places where nobody else would go without their own supply. You know what? We don't need to bring our own supply. When Jesus sent out His disciples, He told them, *(Mat.10:9) Get you no gold, nor silver, nor brass in your purses; (10) no wallet for [your] journey, neither two coats, nor shoes, nor staff: for the laborer is worthy of his food.* Why did He send them out like that? It's because He wanted them to be people of faith and He wanted them to know that they had the supply of the Lord. And He still does that today, folks. *(Gal.3:13) Christ <u>redeemed</u> us from the curse of the law....* If you've ever read the Law in Deuteronomy 28, you know that there's every form of lack and every form of evil that the curse there brings upon us and yet we've been redeemed. The Greek word for "redeemed" is *exagorazo* and it means "purchasing a slave with a view to his freedom"; in other words, to buy out a slave in order to set him free from captivity. And every one of us has been a slave to sin, a slave to the curse; and the Lord set us free. *(Gal.3:13) Christ redeemed us from the <u>curse of the law</u>* (meaning the curse that comes upon people who disobey God's law), *having become a curse for us; for it is written, Cursed is every one that hangeth on a tree: (14) that upon the Gentiles might come the blessing of Abraham <u>in Christ Jesus</u>; that we might receive the promise of the Spirit through faith.* Notice that the "blessing of Abraham" is also "in Christ Jesus." There are quite a few of those whom we loosely call "Christians" who don't walk "in Christ Jesus." They don't walk by faith for God to give them the grace in the form of power to walk in obedience to Him. They are not justified by faith. Because of this, they don't receive redemption from the curse of the blessing of Abraham because they are not abiding in Christ Jesus.

What's the blessing of Abraham? *(Gen.24:1) And Abraham was old, [and] well stricken in age. And Jehovah had blessed Abraham in all things.* Abraham was blessed in <u>all things</u> and that's what we need because wherever we go, the blessing of God will be upon us and we won't be subject to the curses of this world. It matters not about the economy, it matters not about the judgments that are falling upon this world; we're under the blessings of Abraham in Christ Jesus in heavenly places. *(Eph.1:3) Blessed [be] the God and Father of our Lord Jesus Christ, who hath blessed* *us with every spiritual blessing <u>in the heavenly [places] in Christ</u>.* You see, <u>we</u> walk in Heaven! We walk in the Kingdom of Heaven while we're on this earth, while the world walks in the world. "That upon the Gentiles might come the blessing of Abraham in Christ Jesus; that we might receive the promise of the Spirit through faith." Wow! The Spirit made a lot of promises, folks! This is not talking about just the promise of <u>receiving</u> the Spirit; it's also talking about the <u>promises of the Spirit</u> that were given to us through the blessing of Abraham. He goes on to explain that the blessing of Abraham has never been made void. *(Gal.3:15) Brethren, I speak after the manner of men: Though it be but a man's covenant, yet when it hath been confirmed, no one maketh it void, or addeth thereto.* In other words, the Covenant that God made with Abraham is still in effect today, but a lot of people don't know that. *(Gal.3:16) Now to Abraham were the <u>promises</u> spoken, and to his seed. He saith not, And to seeds, as of many; but as of one, And to thy seed, which is Christ.* What are these promises? Well, they are many and here's one I'd like to point out to you that's very powerful: *(Rom.4:13) For not through the law was the promise to Abraham or to his seed that <u>he should be heir of the world</u>, but through the righteousness of faith.* Wow! "Heir of the world." This is awesome!

You know, the Bible says, "All things are yours." *(1Co.3:21) Wherefore let no one glory in men. For <u>all things are yours</u>; (22) whether Paul, or Apollos, or Cephas, or the world, or life, or death, or things present, or things to come; <u>all are yours</u>; (23) and ye are Christ's; and Christ is God's.* It also says, "We are joint heirs with Christ." *(Rom.8:16) The Spirit himself beareth witness with our spirit, that we are children of God: (17) and if children, then heirs; heirs of God, and <u>joint-heirs with Christ</u>; if so be that we suffer with him, that we may be also glorified with him.* Well, now let me see, what does Christ own? What dominion was He given when He was resurrected? He was given dominion over <u>all</u> principalities, powers and all rulers in all the earth. *(Eph.1:20) Which he wrought in Christ, when he raised him from the dead, and made him to sit at his right hand in the heavenly [places,] (21) far above all rule, and authority, and power, and dominion, and every name that is named, not only in this world, but also in that which is to come.* Christ has dominion over everything in this world and over that which is to come, and yet, we are joint-heirs with Christ. Why? We are joint-heirs with Christ because we're sons of God through faith. And notice, if the promise given to Abraham that he would be heir of the world sounds very similar to what we've been promised of being joint-heirs with Christ, that's because it is a type and shadow of what we've been promised in the New Testament. *(Rom.4:16) For this cause [it is] of <u>faith</u>, [that it may be] according to grace; to the end that the promise may be sure <u>to all the seed</u>* (So, our access to the promise that's been given to us of being a joint-heir with Christ and the promise of Abraham of being heir of the world is through faith.)*; not to that only which is of the law, but to that also which is of the faith of Abraham, who is the father of us all.* Faith is our access to the promises.

(Gal.3:16) Now to Abraham were the promises spoken, and to his seed. He saith not, And to seeds, as of many; but as of one, And to thy seed, which is Christ. Now we see what he says in Galatians 3:14, "that upon the Gentiles might come the blessing of Abraham in Christ Jesus," because there is no blessing of Abraham outside of Christ Jesus, for He is the seed Who was to inherit the promise. And, "He saith not, And to seeds, as of many; but as of one, And to thy seed, which is Christ." So, Jesus Christ is the only One Who inherits the promise of the Spirit and the only way we can inherit it, folks, is to abide in Him, as we read earlier. John even says, ***(1Jn.5:11) And the witness is this, that God gave unto us eternal life, and this life is in his Son. (12) He that hath the Son hath the life; he that hath not the Son of God hath not the life.*** Some people make a very foolish mistake, thinking that God has given to them eternal life. They think they can live any way they want and still have this eternal life, but that's a lie of the devil. He's given unto us eternal life, but the life is in His Son. And there is no sin in Him. ***(1Jn.3:5) And ye know that he was manifested to take away sins; and in him is no sin. (Heb.4:15) For we have not a high priest that cannot be touched with the feeling of our infirmities; but one that hath been in all points tempted like as [we are, yet] without sin. (Jas.4:17) To him therefore that knoweth to do good, and doeth it not, to him it is sin.*** And, if you sin willfully after you know what the truth is, you have no sacrifice. ***(Heb.10:26) For if we sin wilfully after that we have received the knowledge of the truth, there remaineth no more a sacrifice for sins, (27) but a certain fearful expectation of judgment, and a fierceness of fire which shall devour the adversaries.*** Listen carefully and tremble, you who are walking after your stubborn, self-willed ways. You think that you have these blessings, but you don't. Unless you are a committed disciple of Jesus Christ, there is no promise to you of eternal life or for any of God's provision. So repent and turn away from your stubborn self-will.

(Gal.3:17) Now this I say: A covenant confirmed beforehand by God, the law, which came four hundred and thirty years after, doth not disannul, so as to make the promise of none effect. So, even when the Law came along, it didn't annul the promise of Abraham in Christ Jesus and it's still ours today. We who walk by the faith of Abraham are assured to have the promise of Abraham and even to have the inheritance of all the world. It's all ours! "All things are yours," the apostles said, but we have this through faith. Faith is a sure provision of your needs being met, no matter what happens in this world, folks. That's why Jesus was so sure of this that He sent out His disciples without any of their own provision. ***(1Ti.5:18) For the scripture saith, Thou shalt not muzzle the ox when he treadeth out the corn. And, The laborer is worthy of his hire.*** In other words, "My Father will take care of you. He will pay your wages because you're working for Him in the Kingdom. He will make sure your needs are met." Now, if you're going on your own and you're not in Christ Jesus, and you're not walking as He walked, but you're walking after Babylon, you probably will have to do a little manipulation out there to try to get your needs met because you are not fully abiding in Him. You're doing your own will and many religious leaders are doing that. They aren't sent of God. They're sent by man and ordained of man. They're building their own kingdom and they're thinking that God is going to support their kingdom. Well, when He doesn't do it, they have to manipulate. They have to put you under the Law, they have to condemn you and they have to preach 15-minute "gimmee" sermons after every half-hour of teaching the Word. These people are <u>not</u> sent of God, folks! When you're sent of God, He supplies. And He doesn't send people who are immature in the faith. He created those disciples to be men of faith; He forced them into it. He sent them out without any of their own supplies, so that they would have to learn that God was their provider, their Jehovah-Jireh! If you don't have that relationship with Him, He's not going to send you. So many just go but they aren't sent of God.

But the law didn't annul this wonderful promise of Abraham, this provision of Abraham: ***(Gal.3:18) For if the inheritance is of the law, it is no more of promise: but God hath granted it to Abraham by promise. (19) What then is the law? It was added because of transgressions, till the seed should come to whom the promise hath been made; [and it was] ordained through angels by the hand of a mediator.*** So the Law was just a temporary thing, although some of you think that you're still under the Law. It was a temporary thing, until the seed should come to Whom the promise was due and that was Jesus Christ. ***(Rom.10:4) For <u>Christ is the end of the law</u> unto righteousness to every one that believeth.*** Christ is the end of the Law because He is the seed Who came, to Whom the promise of Abraham was due. Now that Jesus has received the promise of Abraham, it's just as much ours because we are joint-heirs with Him, as we abide in Him. "And if children, then heirs; heirs of God, and joint-heirs with Christ; if so be that we suffer with him, that we may be also glorified with him." We are joint-heirs. What is His is ours. We are sons of God, being manifested in His image as we walk by faith and as we walk in His steps. ***(Gal.3:26) For ye are all sons of God, through faith, in Christ Jesus.***

Well, just as in the New Testament, the Lord Jesus taught His people using parables that had to do with the customs of the time, God chose to use a blood covenant in type and shadow because it was common in that time. As a matter of fact, the blood covenant has been well-known through many cultures all the way up to our day, even though there might have been slight differences in the details. Back when the Europeans first came to America, for instance, they found that the Indians already had a blood covenant here. The Hebrew word for "covenant" is *beriyth* and it means "a cutting." One common blood covenant between two people was that they would kill the animal to be sacrificed and split it right down the middle. Then they would lay the halves of the animal across from each other and walk down between the halves. By doing that, the two people were saying, "God do so unto me, if I don't keep this covenant"; meaning, "This sacrifice of flesh will be my sacrifice, it will be my body, if I don't keep this covenant." Well, that's kind of interesting because the Lord speaks about returning and finding unfaithful people. *(Mat.24:50) The lord of that servant shall come in a day when he expecteth not, and in an hour when he knoweth not, (51) and shall <u>cut him asunder</u>* (Some translations say, "severely chasten him," but this is the Greek word *dichotomeo* and it literally means "to cut into two parts."), *and appoint his portion with the hypocrites: there shall be the weeping and the gnashing of teeth.* And this is talking about God's unfaithful servants. In other words, it's a people who have broken the blood covenant: "God do so unto me, if I don't keep this covenant."

Now, the people who walked down through the middle of the sacrificed animal were making a commitment to one another. They were called the "surety," the "guarantors," of the covenant. They were <u>guaranteeing their part</u> in keeping this covenant. But in this covenant with Abraham there was a good measure of faith and grace involved because it wasn't quite according to the common covenant. You know, the Bible says that <u>Jesus</u> is our surety. *(Heb.7:22) By so much also hath Jesus become the surety of a better covenant.* He is the "guarantor" of the Covenant. We're not; He is! <u>He</u> guarantees this Covenant and it's <u>His power</u> that brings it to pass. In fact, *(Heb.8:6) He is also the mediator of a better covenant, which hath been enacted upon better promises.* So, according to the normal, natural blood covenant between men, they would walk down through the midst of this sacrifice to show that they were guaranteeing their part of the covenant. What kind of covenant was it? Well, they were guaranteeing, with their own life and with their own resources, to come to their brother's help in a time of need, or in a time of an attack by an enemy, or if there was starvation, etc. And if either one was attacked by an enemy, the other guaranteed to preserve him and protect him with his own life. That seemed to be a standard protection and provision covenant back when there was a lot of lawlessness. People would join together like this in order to preserve one another by strength in numbers.

Well, just imagine, God is making a covenant here and He puts Abraham to sleep! Abraham, who would have normally walked down with the Lord between the sacrifice, was asleep when the sacrifice was made. *(Gen.15:12) And when the sun was going down, <u>a deep sleep fell upon Abram</u>; and, lo, a horror of great darkness fell upon him.* And, you know what, folks? That's exactly what Jesus did for us. Jesus is the guarantor of the Covenant; we're not. We're trusting in His guarantee, His provision. What's our provision? What provision do <u>we</u> have to save us from our enemies? Our enemies are many and they are fierce! And they're supernatural, too, by the way. We don't wrestle with flesh and blood, but with principalities and powers. *(Eph.6:12) For our wrestling is not against flesh and blood, but against the principalities, against the powers, against the world-rulers of this darkness, against the spiritual [hosts] of wickedness in the heavenly [places].* What guarantee could we give to anyone? Besides, how would God need any of our guarantee? We can promise nothing to God. We're coming to Him for grace, which is unmerited, unearned favor. We have nothing to add to this Covenant. Even the faith that we receive comes from Him.

What could we add to this Covenant? The faith, the repentance, the power, it all comes from God. He's the sole guarantor; He's the sole surety of this Covenant.

Paul says about Jesus, **(Col.1:19) For it was the good pleasure of the Father that <u>in him</u> should all the fulness dwell....** Some people think, "Hey, this is talking about the fullness of God." No, it's not. It's talking about the fullness of His people abiding <u>in Him</u>. If we back up a few verses, we read, **(Col.1:16) For <u>in him</u> were all <u>things</u>** (The word "things" was not in the original; he is talking about people here. "For in him were all created.") **created, in the heavens and upon the earth, things visible and things invisible, whether thrones or dominions or principalities or powers; all things have been created through him, and unto him; (17) and he is before all things, and in him all things consist. (18) And <u>he is the head of the body</u>** (There it is! He's the head of the body. So where's the body? It's all <u>in Him</u>, right?), **the church: who is the beginning, the firstborn from the dead; that in all things he might have the preeminence. (19) For it was the good pleasure of the Father that <u>in him</u> should <u>all the fulness dwell</u>** (What is he talking about? The verse before it was talking about the <u>Church abiding in Christ</u>.); **should all the fulness dwell. (20) and through him to reconcile all <u>things</u> unto himself** (Again, the word "things" was not in the original. The original says, "all unto him."), **having made peace through the <u>blood of his cross</u>; through him, I say, whether things upon the earth, or things in the heavens.** Here's the blood sacrifice of the Covenant. The blood sacrifice is Christ and what did He do through His sacrifice? He made "reconciliation," *apokatallasso*, and it means "to exchange completely." He made an exchange, meaning that the Lord Jesus, on the cross, made a blood Covenant with us and He is the sole surety, the guarantor, of that Covenant. He is the One guaranteeing its power. He is the One guaranteeing to come to your rescue, no matter what, whether you're in lack or you need protection from enemies, or whatever. He is guaranteeing to do this for you. "Reconciliation," again, is "to exchange." What did He exchange? What did <u>we</u> have to offer? Why could we not be a surety? <u>We</u> have nothing to give to God but the curse, sin and corruption. Well, you know what, folks? That's what He exchanged. He made an exchange of His life, His blessing, His provision, for your curse and your corruption. He made that exchange and now we have what is His. He's the surety and He's given to us His provision, protection and blessing -- the blessing of Abraham in Christ Jesus. And, again, as we see here, it is <u>in Christ Jesus</u>. We found out that to abide in Christ Jesus is to walk by faith, to walk in His steps, to have that in you which you heard from the beginning and to walk not living in sin. **(1Jn.2:24) As for you, let that abide in you which ye heard from the beginning. If that which ye heard from the beginning abide in you, ye also shall abide <u>in the Son</u>, and in the Father.** That's what it says! That's what it is to be in Christ Jesus. We have a really good deal, folks, because living in sin in the New Testament is walking in willful disobedience.

(Gen.15:12) And when the sun was going down, a deep sleep fell upon

Abram; and, lo, a horror of great darkness fell upon him. (13) And he said unto Abram, Know of a surety that thy seed shall be sojourners in a land that is not theirs, and shall serve them; and they shall afflict them four hundred years; (14) and also that nation, whom they shall serve, will I judge: and afterward shall they come out with great substance. Folks, this is a type and shadow for our day. We're much in bondage in this world. God's people are crying out in bondage in this world, but the Lord is going to save His people out of the land of Egypt once again. He's going to bring them into a wilderness experience. He's going to teach them how to walk by faith, so that they learn what it is to abide in Christ and have all of this provision in the wilderness. *(Gen.15:15) But thou shalt go to thy fathers in peace; thou shalt be buried in a good old age. (16) And in the fourth generation they shall come hither again; for the iniquity of the Amorite is not yet full.* Well, here we are in the days, folks, when the iniquity of the Amorite is becoming full and, once again, God is going to be calling His people out of bondage in Egypt to serve Him. He's bringing judgments upon the world in order for His people to be motivated to come out and for the Egyptians to be motivated to turn them loose. *(Gen.15:17) And it came to pass, that, when the sun went down, and it was dark, behold, a smoking furnace, and a flaming torch that passed between these pieces.* Why was that? We see that the Lord Himself is the One Who passed between them as a "smoking furnace, and a flaming torch."

You know, the Bible says in both the Old and New Testament that God is a "consuming fire." *(Deu.4:24) For the Lord thy God is a devouring fire, a jealous God. (Heb.12:29) For our God is a consuming fire.* And what does He consume? His plan, His promise, is to consume the old man. *(Mal.3:2) But who can abide the day of his coming? and who shall stand when he appeareth? for <u>he is like a refiner's fire</u>, and like fuller's soap: (3) and he will sit as a refiner and purifier of silver, and he will purify the sons of Levi* (That is the priesthood and we are all priests unto God.)*, and refine them as gold and silver; and they shall offer unto the Lord offerings in righteousness. (4) Then shall the offering of Judah and Jerusalem be pleasant unto the Lord, as in the days of old, and as in ancient years.* Part of our Covenant, folks, is the sacrifice of the old man. The Lord is the consuming fire that we go through to accomplish that. It's like the three Hebrew children who were thrown into the midst of the fiery furnace and the only thing they lost were their bonds. Only their bonds were burned off. *(Dan.3:20) And he commanded certain mighty men that were in his army to bind Shadrach, Meshach, and Abed-nego, and to cast them into the burning fiery furnace. (21) Then these men were bound in their hosen, their tunics, and their mantles, and their other garments, and were cast into the midst of the burning fiery furnace. (22) Therefore because the king's commandment was urgent, and the furnace exceeding hot, the flame of the fire slew those men that took up Shadrach, Meshach, and Abed-nego. (23) And these three men, Shadrach,*

Meshach, and Abed-nego, fell down bound into the midst of the burning fiery furnace. (24) Then Nebuchadnezzar the king was astonished, and rose up in haste: he spake and said unto his counsellors, Did not we cast three men bound into the midst of the fire? They answered and said unto the king, True, O king. (25) He answered and said, Lo, I see four men loose, walking in the midst of the fire, and they have no hurt; and the aspect of the fourth is like a son of the gods. (26) Then Nebuchadnezzar came near to the mouth of the burning fiery furnace: he spake and said, Shadrach, Meshach, and Abed-nego, ye servants of the Most High God, come forth, and come hither. Then Shadrach, Meshach, and Abed-nego came forth out of the midst of the fire. What is it that keeps us in bondage? It's the old Egyptian, the old man keeps the spiritual man in bondage. The old man doesn't permit the spiritual man to be free to serve God as he should. The Lord has promised more than just all of Abraham's provision. He's promised to be a consuming fire to set the spiritual man free from bondage, to burn those bonds asunder.

We can see this in type when Moses spoke to the people. *(Deu.9:1) Hear, O Israel: thou art to pass over the Jordan this day, to go in to dispossess nations greater and mightier than thyself, cities great and fortified up to heaven....* These were the Canaanites whom they were dispossessing. The Canaanites were the "old man" who lived in the land. The Israelites, as the spiritual man, were to conquer them and take their land and live in their house. In fact, Hebrews calls us "the tilled land that brings forth." *(Heb.6:7) For the land which hath drunk the rain that cometh oft upon it, and bringeth forth herbs meet for them for whose sake it is also tilled, receiveth blessing from God.* And 1 Corinthians calls us "the land in which the Lord will give the increase," which is the spiritual man's fruit. *(1Co.3:7) So then neither is he that planteth anything, neither he that watereth; but God that giveth the increase. (8) Now he that planteth and he that watereth are one: but each shall receive his own reward according to his own labor. (9) For we are God's fellow-workers: ye are God's husbandry, God's building.* Now let's go back to our verse. *(Deu.9:1) Hear, O Israel: thou art to pass over the Jordan this day, to go in to dispossess nations greater and mightier than thyself, cities great and fortified up to heaven, (2) a people great and tall, the sons of the Anakim, whom thou knowest, and of whom thou hast heard say, Who can stand before the sons of Anak?* Those were giants. They represented that old flesh that we think sometimes is unconquerable, so much bigger than ourselves; and yet, what does God say? *(Deu.9:3) Know therefore this day, that the Lord thy God is he who goeth over before thee <u>as a devouring fire</u>; he will destroy them, and he will bring them down before thee: so shalt thou drive them out, and make them to perish quickly, as the Lord hath spoken unto thee.* So, the smoking furnace here is the Lord Himself. <u>He</u> will drive them out as a "devouring fire" or, as Deuteronomy 4 calls Him, "a smoking furnace, and a flaming torch."

A torch is, of course, a light. "For the Lord thy God is a devouring fire, a jealous God." Jesus is our light, too, isn't He? ***(Psa.119:105) Thy <u>word</u> is a lamp unto my feet, And light unto my path.*** Who is the Word? The Lord is the Word! So we're seeing that <u>God</u> passed between the sacrifice; He's the guarantor and He's going to set us free from bondage. He's going to deliver us from our enemies. Who's the biggest enemy we have? Go look in the mirror! That's the biggest enemy you have! Well, God's promised to deliver us out of the hand of those giants. He's promised to deliver us out of the hand of the Egyptians. See, this is part of the promise, too. Some people don't like this part of the promise because they don't want to lose their old life in this world. They don't want to lose that "old man." They would rather serve the old man, but these people are not proven to be sons of Abraham. Sure, they are receiving Christianity, but they're keeping their old life; they're just accepting Christianity on top of their old life. But that's not an acceptable sacrifice to God. He won't receive it. We have a continual burnt offering just like the Jews did because we are New Testament spiritual Jews. We have a continual burnt offering and that is to offer up this old body as a living sacrifice unto God. ***(Rom.12:1) I beseech you therefore, brethren, by the mercies of God, to present your bodies a living sacrifice, holy, acceptable to God, which is your spiritual service.*** And the Lord has promised to bring this to pass for us; He's the furnace; He's the torch. He will give us the light of His Word so that we will be able to walk this walk in His steps and bring to pass the death of the "old man," the burning up of the flesh.

(Gen.15:18) In that day the Lord made a covenant (a *beriyth*) ***with Abram, saying, Unto thy seed have I given this <u>land</u>, from the river of Egypt unto the great river, the river Euphrates.*** I mentioned that it says in Hebrews that we are the "land" and here's another place where it clearly tells us the same thing: ***(Mal.3:11) And I will rebuke the devourer for your sakes, and he shall not destroy the fruits of your ground; neither shall your vine cast its fruit before the time in the field, saith the Lord of hosts. (12) And all nations shall call you happy; for <u>ye shall be a delightsome land</u>, saith the Lord of hosts.*** You know, this land that we live in here, folks, is inhabited by both the Canaanite and the Israelite, the carnal man and the spiritual man. God has given us authority to take the "sword of the spirit, which is the Word of God," and go through this land and put to death our enemies. ***(Eph.6:17) And <u>take</u> the helmet of salvation, and <u>the sword of the Spirit, which is the word of God</u>.*** He's given us this authority but, as a matter of fact, the Lord has already done it. ***(Gal.2:20) <u>I have been crucified with Christ; and it is no longer I that live, but Christ living in me: and that [life] which I now live in the flesh I live in faith, [the faith] which is in the Son of God, who loved me, and gave himself up for me.*** We have been crucified with Christ. So we have this sacrifice to make that's pleasing unto the Lord: a continual burnt offering, a fiery trial that we go through every day to deny this old man. The provision that we have from God, as heirs of the world, was accomplished by our surety, Who is Jesus Christ. Everything we need to conquer and be delivered from the power of our enemies has been given to us. ***(1Pe.1:3) Seeing that his divine power <u>hath granted unto us all things</u> that pertain unto life and godliness, through the knowledge of him that called us by his own glory and virtue.*** Everything! Everything has been given to us through Jesus Christ. Abraham was heir of the world, heir of everything, and we have that, too.

So how do we know that the Lord will provide for us in these days to come? Well, there are some things that the Lord asks of us. He asks that we abide in Him, based on the knowledge that we have of His will. You cannot rebel against the known will of God and still claim you are abiding in Him! The Bible says we ought to walk even as He walked, right? So look at what Jesus says to us: ***(Mat.6:19) Lay not up for yourselves treasures upon the earth, where moth and rust consume, and where thieves break through and steal....*** Here it is again, folks. Once again, as with the disciples, the Lord demands that we don't take our own provision, but that we trust in His provision, since He's promised everything. He wants us to walk by faith. He wants us to have the experience of Him providing for us and I'm going to share with you some of the testimonies that the Lord has given to me, as He led me through the wilderness. ***(Mat.6:19) Lay not up for yourselves treasures upon the earth, where moth and rust consume, and where thieves break through and steal: (20) but lay up for yourselves treasures in heaven, where neither moth nor rust doth consume, and where thieves do not break through nor steal: (21) for where thy treasure is, there will thy heart be also.*** In other words, if your treasure is on the earth, that's where your heart will be. If your treasure is in Heaven, that's where your heart will be. How do we get our treasures in Heaven? Well, we know that we have "every spiritual blessing in the heavenly places in Christ," and as we walk in His steps and we abide in Him, we store up our blessings in Heaven. ***(Luk.12:33) Sell that which ye have, and give alms; make for yourselves purses which wax not old*** (In other words, not storing up your own provision.), ***a treasure in the heavens that faileth not, where no thief draweth near, neither moth destroyeth. (34) For where your treasure is, there will your heart be also.*** Sell that which you have and give alms. Meet the needs of the brethren around you. John asks, ***(1Jn.3:17) But whoso hath the world's goods, and beholdeth his brother in need, and shutteth up his compassion from him, how doth the love of God abide in him?*** So we see how we can store up treasures in Heaven.

We can also learn from the story of the rich young ruler: ***(Mat.18:18) And a certain ruler asked him, saying, Good Teacher, what shall I do to inherit eternal life? (19) And Jesus said unto him, Why callest thou me good? none is good, save one, even God. (20) Thou knowest the commandments, Do not commit adultery, Do not kill, Do not steal, Do not bear false witness, Honor thy father and mother. (21) And he said, All these things have I observed from my youth up. (22) And when Jesus heard it, he said unto him, One thing thou lackest yet: sell all that thou hast, and distribute unto the poor, and thou***

shalt have <u>treasure in heaven</u>: and come, follow me. Wouldn't you like to have an eternal treasure in Heaven, rather than these trinkets that you love down here? Well, God knows you have need and that you are a steward for Him, and that what He puts in your hands should be used for the Kingdom. In other words, what once was used by you for yourself, what once was used for the "old man," the Egyptian, is now to be used for the spiritual man. When the Israelites, who represented the spiritual man, came out of bondage in Egypt, they plundered the Egyptians. ***(Exo.12:35) And the children of Israel did according to the word of Moses; and they asked of the Egyptians jewels of silver, and jewels of gold, and raiment. (36) And the Lord gave the people favor in the sight of the Egyptians, so that they let them have what they asked. And they despoiled the Egyptians.*** They took the goods out of the hand of the old man and put them in the hand of the new man, the Kingdom man. This is the man who is serving God. This is the man who is walking through this life in order to promote the Kingdom of God. ***(Mat.6:33) But seek ye first his kingdom, and his righteousness; and all these things shall be added unto you.*** Let's back up and read a little bit more. ***(21) For where thy treasure is, there will thy heart be also. (22) The lamp of the body is the eye: if therefore thine eye be single, thy whole body shall be full of light. (23) But if thine eye be evil*** (If your eye is on the lusts of the world, the things of the world ...), ***thy whole body shall be full of darkness. If therefore the light that is in thee be darkness, how great is the darkness! (24) No man can serve two masters; for either he will hate the one, and love the other; or else he will hold to one, and despise the other. Ye cannot serve God and mammon.*** In other words, the old man can hold on to what belongs to the new man, what belongs to God! What belongs to the Kingdom people! The old man can consider it his! But we're a thief if that happens because the Lord told us, ***(Luk.14:33) So therefore whosoever he be of you that renounceth not <u>all</u> that he hath, he cannot be my disciple.*** We have to renounce ownership of all that belongs to God.

It doesn't say anything about tithing in the New Testament, folks. Jesus told the Jews, ***(Mat.23:23) Woe unto you, scribes and Pharisees, hypocrites! <u>for ye tithe mint and anise and cummin</u>, <u>and have left undone the weightier matters of the law</u>, <u>justice</u>, <u>and mercy</u>, <u>and faith</u>: but these ye ought to have done, and not to have left the other undone.*** He called tithing <u>of the Law</u>. Folks, Jesus said, "Except you renounce <u>everything</u> you have." We are now stewards of 100%, not 10%. God puts everything into our hands to serve His Kingdom. The Egyptian is being plundered by the spiritual man, the Israelite, as he goes into the wilderness to walk by faith. He takes that gold and silver from the Egyptians, and goes and walks by faith to promote the Kingdom of God. "Ye cannot serve God and mammon." Well, *mammonas* was just a common Aramaic term for "riches" or "treasure." And what does the Lord say? He says you cannot serve God and mammon. ***(Mat.6:25) Therefore I say unto you, be not anxious for your life, what ye shall eat, or what ye shall drink; nor yet for*** *your body, what ye shall put on. Is not the life more than the food, and the body than the raiment? (26) Behold the birds of the heaven, that they sow not, neither do they reap, nor gather into barns; and your heavenly Father feedeth them.* Is He talking about laziness here, not sowing, not reaping, not working? No, but there is going to come a time when you won't be able to buy or sell in this world. And guess what? God still promises to provide for you and He's going to do it. That's exactly what this is talking about. *Are not ye of much more value then they? (Mat.6:27) And why are ye anxious concerning raiment? Consider the lilies of the field, how they grow; they toil not, neither do they spin* (There it is again! They're not having to work to provide for themselves here. There's a time coming, folks, when you won't be able to do it; you'll only be able to work for the Kingdom. And, as a matter of fact, disciples will once more take on the Great Commission of going forth and sharing the Gospel and God's going to provide for them.)*: (Mat.6:29) yet I say unto you, that even Solomon in all his glory was not arrayed like one of these. (30) But if God doth so clothe the grass of the field, which to-day is, and to-morrow is cast into the oven, [shall he] not much more [clothe] you, O ye of little faith?* The Lord is going to feed us, He's going to clothe us, He's going to be our provision. It's only unbelief or anxiety that causes us to worry about these things. *(Mat.6:31) Be not therefore anxious, saying, What shall we eat? or, What shall we drink? or, Wherewithal shall we be clothed? (32) For after all these things do the Gentiles seek; for your heavenly Father knoweth that ye have need of all these things. (33) But seek ye first his kingdom, and his righteousness; and all these things shall be added unto you.* I wish that everybody would understand that. Just seek first His Kingdom, His righteousness and God will make sure all the rest comes to you. Many people haven't tried God on this, but it is a sure promise; it works. *(Mat.6:34) Be not therefore anxious for the morrow: for the morrow will be anxious for itself. Sufficient unto the day is the evil thereof.* Don't be worried about tomorrow, folks. Don't be storing up in barns. Just put your trust in God because in the places where you're going, you can't bring barns with you. And God is going to be our provider and our savior in all things. Lord, we thank You, in Jesus' name.

CHAPTER 16

Treasures in Heaven!

Greetings, friends! God bless you! Thank you for joining us. As we continue our study, we invite our Lord Jesus to be with us today and His grace to be with us, and His anointing to be with us. Lord, we just pray that You'll be a blessing to our brethren out there. That You will encourage them in the trials that they're going through now and that they will put their trust in You, Lord. Lord, You've been teaching us about our provision and how You have already provided all of our needs, according to the promises of Your Word. And through these awesome promises, we are able to enter into Your rest, God. Thank You, Father. Thank You for blessing us with rest and peace in You, as any believer would have, Lord, who believes Your awesome promises. So, Father, work in us to will and to do of Your good pleasure and help us to be true disciples of Jesus. In Jesus' name. Amen.

Well, we've been finding out what the real Good News is concerning our provision from God and in the previous chapter we learned about the sacrificial foundation for our provision. We learned that it was all given in Christ. Everything is in Christ. *(Eph.1:3) **Blessed [be] the God and Father of our Lord Jesus Christ, who hath blessed us with every spiritual blessing in the heavenly [places]** in Christ.* So many times Scripture adds those two little words, "in Christ," at the end of a great promise. That's because, as we learn to abide in Him by faith, we know that we're able to partake of all those benefits that were so abundantly provided for us at the cross. It's a great privilege. Well, folks, if you know the background of the time of Jesus and His disciples, you know that they were headed into great tribulation. ***(Heb.10:32) But call to remembrance the former days, in which, after ye were enlightened, ye endured a great conflict of sufferings....*** Of course, when these Jews came to Christ, they were persecuted heavily by their brethren and some of them, including the disciples, lost their lives. As you know, the disciples did; they lost their lives because of it. Many people don't realize it, but the things that happened in the Gospels, the Book of Acts and the epistles parallel our day. The Lord told me that very specifically. Everything that happened there in the Gospels and in Acts is going to happen again in our day, except the cast of characters is multiplied many times over. As a matter of fact, now it will be worldwide. ***(Heb.10:32) But call to remembrance the former days, in which, after ye were enlightened, ye endured a great conflict of sufferings; (33) partly, being made a gazingstock both by reproaches and afflictions; and partly, becoming partakers with them that were so used.*** In other words, suffering with the saints. ***(Heb.10:34) For ye both had compassion on them that were in bonds, and took joyfully the spoiling of you possessions, knowing that ye have for yourselves a better possession and an abiding one.*** That sounds as if they were headed into tribulation and, yet, let me share with you some advice that the Lord gave to them about provision.

I'm going to go back to where we left off in our last teaching and take a deeper look at what Jesus said to us. ***(Mat.6:19) Lay not up for yourselves treasures upon the earth, where moth and rust consume, and where thieves break through and steal: (20) but lay up for yourselves treasures in heaven, where neither moth nor rust doth consume, and where thieves do not break through nor steal.*** Well, it's interesting that the Lord would give them this command at a time when they were headed toward tribulation. The carnal man's natural inclination when facing tribulation, terrible lack and possibly even starvation in the world is to prepare a place of safety. But it is carnally-minded people who think this way and it shows a total lack of trust in God. We just read that the saints were being plundered by their own brethren; they couldn't buy or sell, similar to what's coming in our day. Why would God tell them to store up for the tribulation to come, if it was all just going to be stolen? No. He told them, <u>don't store up your treasures</u>. Don't lay up for yourselves treasures upon the earth. He wanted them to trust. He brought them to that place in order that they would learn to put their trust in Him Who is totally dependable. Nothing that we do to prepare for ourselves is dependable. Looking at the Israelites as a type and shadow, when they were coming out of Egypt and getting ready to go into their own tribulation, they called it the "wilderness." By the way, Revelation tells us that the "wilderness" is "tribulation." ***(Rev.12:6) And the woman fled into the wilderness, where she hath a place prepared of God, that there they may nourish her a thousand two hundred and threescore days. (17) And the dragon waxed wroth with the woman, and went away to make war with the rest of her seed, that keep the commandments of God, and hold the testimony of Jesus.*** And God taught those Israelites a lesson about storing up. ***(Exo.12:35) And the children of Israel did according to the word of Moses; and they asked of the Egyptians jewels of silver, and jewels of gold, and raiment. (36) And the Lord gave the people favor in the sight of the Egyptians, so that they let them have what they asked. And they <u>despoiled</u> the Egyptians.*** The Israelites plundered Egypt, but that wasn't God's method to save them in the wilderness. Storing up of gold was not His method and, don't you know, they immediately made an idol out of that gold and God made them destroy it. ***(Exo.32:20) And he took the calf which they had made, and burnt it with fire, and ground it to powder, and strewed it upon the water, and made the children of Israel drink of it.*** He wanted them to see that none of their provision was going to save them in the wilderness. And so they got out there where there was no water and they had to have God do a miracle; they got out there where there was no food and God had to do another miracle. <u>He provided for them out of Heaven</u>! That represented their seven years of famine, like in the prophecy of Joseph. Well, I think we're going through our seven years of plenty right now and we're headed toward seven years of famine, in a fulfillment in our day of the prophecy of Joseph.

I've heard a lot of people say, "Maybe we ought to do what Joseph did. Maybe we ought to store up and get ready for the times to come." Well, I want to share a little something with you about that. First of all, if the Lord wanted us to do that, He certainly wouldn't have had Jesus give us the command to "Lay not up for yourselves treasures upon the earth." He gave us this command because He expects us, as disciples, to obey it. If you are thinking you are going to save your money by storing it up in gold or silver or any other thing, it's ultimately going to fail you. God's going to prove it. Any idol that people trust in for their salvation they will fail, just exactly like the Israelites did in the wilderness. However, Jesus said, but do "lay up for yourselves treasures in Heaven." And there's a reason for that. *(Luk.12:31) Yet seek ye his kingdom, and these things shall be added unto you.* In other words, God said, "I'll take care of it. You just seek the Kingdom and I'll take care of the rest." *(Luk.12:32) Fear not, little flock; for it is your Father's good pleasure to give you the kingdom.* Why are we so anxious and troubled? Remember what Jesus told us. *(Mat.6:25) Therefore I say unto you, be not anxious for your life, what ye shall eat, or what ye shall drink; nor yet for your body, what ye shall put on. Is not the life more than the food, and the body than the raiment? (26) Behold the birds of the heaven, that they sow not, neither do they reap, nor gather into barns; and your heavenly Father feedeth them. Are not ye of much more value than they?* He tried to take away that anxiety, but people have unbelief, they have a doubt that God is going to provide for them out there in that wilderness. They think that somehow God just might let them down.

Well, we're supposed to be <u>believers</u> and the Lord is not going to let us down. He's planned this whole tribulation to show us His power and to reveal to us His plan of provision. So He commands us, *(Luk.12:33) Sell that which ye have, and give alms; make for yourselves purses which wax not old,* <u>*a treasure in the heavens that faileth not*</u>*, where no thief draweth near, neither moth destroyeth.* In other words, God is saying, "If you put your treasures in Heaven, they will not fail you. You will be able to get them when you need them and where you need them." But, if you think you are going to pack them on your back, you are not going to make it very far. First of all, there's always somebody who will "knock you in the head" for it in a time of trouble. Everybody is not a Christian, you know. I'm thinking about the Mormons, who have been taught to store up in barrels and so on. Of course, when trouble comes, everybody's going to be looking for a Mormon. People are not stupid. Well, God is bringing us to a place where our provision will come out of Heaven! Where did the provision come from for the Israelites who went into the wilderness? It came out of Heaven. It was supernatural; it was God's work. So, let's see now, if it's coming out of Heaven and God tells us to store it up in Heaven and it won't fail us, then He wants us to put it in Heaven in the first place, right? That's the point He's making here. "A treasure in the heavens that faileth not."

Now, this comes right on the heels of a parable Jesus gave about a man who tore down his barns and built bigger, so he could store up his grain and all of his goods and eat, drink and be merry. *(Luk.12:16) And he spake a parable unto them, say-*

ing, The ground of a certain rich man brought forth plentifully: (17) and he reasoned within himself, saying, What shall I do, because I have not where to bestow my fruits? (18) And he said, This will I do: I will pull down my barns, and build greater; and there will I bestow all my grain and my goods. (19) And I will say to my soul, Soul, thou hast much goods laid up for many years; take thine ease, eat, drink, be merry. (20) But God said unto him, Thou foolish one, this night is thy soul required of thee; and the things which thou hast prepared, whose shall they be? (21) So is he that layeth up treasure for himself, and is not rich toward God. What is it to be "rich toward God"? It's when you're laying up your treasures in Heaven. He tells us here, "Sell that which ye have, and give alms." Is He saying to sell your home that you're living in right now? Or is He talking about selling your investments in the earth, your provisions for the future? Obviously, He's talking about your provisions for the future -- those idols that you're trusting in for your salvation. Everybody needs a roof over their head and when you lose that, folks, God's going to take care of you. Don't worry about it. God has a method. *(Luk.6:38) Give, and it shall be given unto you; good measure, pressed down, shaken together, <u>running over</u>, shall they give into your bosom. For with what measure ye mete it shall be measured to you again.* That's His method and it will gain you God's provision anywhere, even when you have very little. Remember the woman with the two mites. *(Luk.21:1) And he looked up, and saw the rich men that were casting their gifts into the treasury. (2) And he saw a certain poor widow casting in thither two mites. (3) And he said, Of a truth I say unto you, This poor widow cast in more than they all: (4) for all these did of their superfluity cast in unto the gifts; but she of her want did cast in all the living that she had.* She gave more than all those rich Pharisees, according to the way God saw things. What do you think her reward was? I can guarantee you that it was much greater than theirs and she only had two mites.

There's another verse I'd like to point out to you before I leave this part of the Bible. *(Luk.18:22) And when Jesus heard it, he said unto him, One thing thou lackest yet* (He's talking about the rich young ruler.)*: sell all that thou hast, and distribute unto the poor, and thou shalt have treasure in heaven: and come, follow me.* Amen. Notice, He didn't say, "sell what you have and give it to the fatcat preachers." No. He didn't say that; He said to give it to the poor. In other words, make sure the needs among God's people are met. You know, when Jesus sent out His disciples, He wanted them to learn that He was always going to be their provider. *(Mat.10:7) And as ye go, preach, saying, The kingdom of heaven is at hand. (8) Heal the sick, raise the dead, cleanse the lepers, cast out demons: <u>freely ye received, freely give</u>.* Folks, <u>this</u> is God's economy. <u>You freely received it from God</u>, <u>so freely give it</u>. *(Luk.6:23) Give, and it shall be given unto you; good measure, pressed down, shaken together, running over, shall they give into your bosom.* God's economy is not buying and selling, as God said they would be doing in the days of Noah and the days of Lot. *(Luk.17:26) And as it came to pass in the days of Noah, even so shall it be also in the days of the Son of man. (27) They ate, they drank, they married, they were given in marriage, until the day that Noah entered into the ark, and the flood came, and destroyed them all. (28) Likewise even as it came to pass in the days of Lot; they ate, they drank, they bought, they sold, they planted, they builded; (29) but in the day that Lot went out from Sodom it rained fire and brimstone from heaven, and destroyed them all: (30) after the same manner shall it be in the day that the Son of man is revealed.* God's economy is not the buying and selling that much of the church does; it's giving and receiving. You get a reward for that and it gets multiplied back, according to the Scriptures. When you're buying and selling, you only receive equal value for equal value. That's not as good a deal. God has a better deal and even in a wilderness God's economy works. So Jesus said, *(Mat.10:8) Heal the sick, raise the dead, cleanse the lepers, cast out demons: freely ye received, freely give. (9) Get you no gold, nor silver, nor brass in your purses; (10) no wallet for [your] journey, neither two coats, nor shoes, nor staff: for the laborer is worthy of his food.* Jesus sent them without any of their own provision. And, by the way, He asked them a question when they came back. *(Luk.22:35) And he said unto them, When I sent you forth without purse, and wallet, and shoes, lacked ye anything? And they said, Nothing.*

Of course, some people jump in there immediately and they say, "Well, read on, David." *(Luk.22:36) And he said unto them, But now, he that hath a purse, let him take it, and likewise a wallet; and he that hath none, let him sell his cloak, and buy a sword. (37) For I say unto you* (Now here come the words that reverse the point these people are trying to make.), *that this which is written must be fulfilled in me, <u>And he was reckoned with transgressors</u>: for that which concerneth me hath fulfilment.* Who was He saying were transgressors? Those who took their own provision and those who took the sword were transgressors. They were transgressors against the Kingdom, transgressors against discipleship, transgressors against the Lord. So the point is very firm that He sent them out without their own provision and when they went out they lacked nothing because they learned that God is their provider. God wanted to shift their focus away from their own ability to save themselves and onto Him. And they learned what I've learned, that God is a faithful Savior in all things. The Lord sent me out many years ago and He told me, "I'm sending you through a wilderness, so you can tell My people that I still supply there." I learned that I didn't have to make my own way and I learned that all I had to do was to give and God would give to me. The Lord always preserved and kept me.

Maybe you're one of those people who thinks, "You know, David, you're missing that point about Joseph. Joseph stored up and it saved many people alive because of what he did." Well, I'd like to look at that for just a minute. There are some really good points I'd like to make there about who Joseph represented. But first of all, no type, no shadow, can trump what the Lord Jesus told us in black and white in our Covenant. You cannot make the Word fight against itself. The Lord Jesus said, "Don't lay up treasures upon the earth," not talking about your immediate needs, your home and so on, unless your home is your treasure. Obviously, some people have a lot more than what they need and others have needs. But what the Lord is saying is that we should not lay up our treasurers upon the earth because He wants us to learn to trust in Him. *(Heb.10:38) But <u>my righteous one shall live by faith</u>: And if he shrink back, my soul hath no pleasure in him.* When His disciples went out, they learned to walk by faith and they learned that God was faithful. It was quite encouraging to them to know that anywhere they went, God was there ahead of them.

So what does the story of Joseph represent? Well, I'm going to point out to you that Joseph represented Jesus and there are some really awesome promises in here of God's provision for us in the coming times. *(Gen.37:14) And he said to him, Go now, see whether it is well with thy brethren, and well with the flock; and bring me word again.* This sounds very similar to one of Jesus' parables about Him being sent of the Father to collect the fruits from His vineyard (Matthew 21:33-41; Mark 12:1-9; Luke 20:9-16). And what did Jesus find when He came to collect the fruits? He found some very jealous brethren who fought against Him. As a matter of fact, if we back up a few verses, we see, *(Gen.37:11) And his brethren envied him; but his father kept the saying in mind.* Joseph's brothers were jealous of him and so were the Pharisees with Jesus. As we read on here, you're going to see Joseph is the clearest type of Jesus in the Bible. As a matter of fact, this is a prophecy of Jesus' life, death, resurrection and provision for us, if we look at the story of Joseph in the spirit. *(2Co.3:6) Who also made us sufficient as ministers of a new covenant; not of the letter, but of the spirit: for <u>the letter killeth</u>, <u>but the spirit giveth life</u>.* If the only thing you see is Joseph storing up for the people during the seven years of plenty, in order to restore it in the seven years of famine, you've missed the whole point because when you figure out who Joseph is, it makes my point very clearly. And it doesn't contradict what is clearly stated already in the New Testament: "Lay not up for yourselves treasures upon the earth." And the story continues here talking about Joseph's brethren: *(Gen.37:18) And they saw him afar off, and before he came near unto them, they conspired against him to slay him.* Wow! This is exactly what happened to Jesus. *(Joh.1:11) He came unto his own, and they that were his own received him not.* His own <u>brethren</u> did not receive Him; they were jealous. *(Gen.37:19) And they said one to another, Behold, this dreamer cometh. (20) Come now therefore, and let us slay him, and cast him into one of the pits, and we will say, An evil beast hath devoured him: and we shall see what will become of his dreams.* Well, an evil beast did devour Jesus; it was the Roman Beast, right? And Jesus was betrayed into the hands of this Gentile Roman Beast by His own brethren, so the type and shadow is very clear here of who Joseph represents. He represents Jesus Christ.

By the way, Joseph also had a coat of many colors on him, which represents the righteousness of Christ. ***(Gen.37:23) And it came to pass, when Joseph was come unto his brethren, that they stripped Joseph of his coat, the coat of many colors that was on him.*** A prism separates light into the seven colors of the rainbow and they are the seven different attributes of light. Who is Jesus? ***(Joh.1:4) In him was life; and the life was the <u>light</u> of men. (9) There was the true <u>light</u>, even the light which lighteth every man, coming into the world.*** Jesus Christ is the light. And we are commanded to be partakers of these seven different attributes. ***(2Pe.1:4) Whereby he hath granted unto us his precious and exceeding great promises; that through these ye may become partakers of the divine nature, having escaped from the corruption that is in that world by lust. (5) Yea, and for this very cause adding on your part all diligence in your faith, supply virtue; and in [your] virtue knowledge; (6) and in [your] knowledge self-control; and in [your] self-control patience; and in [your] patience godliness; (7) and in [your] godliness brotherly kindness; and in [your] brotherly kindness love.*** These are the different attributes of the righteousness of Christ in us. You can see from this that Joseph represented a righteous person; he was the different manifestations of the light.

As we keep reading, we see that Judah, Joseph's brother, says, ***(Gen.37:27) Come, and let us sell him to the Ishmaelites, and let not our hand be upon him; for he is our brother, our flesh. And his brethren hearkened unto him.*** Joseph's own brothers sold him into the hands of the Gentiles, just as it was with Jesus. There is type after type that proves exactly who Joseph represents. ***(Gen.37:28) And there passed by Midianites, merchantmen; and they drew and lifted up Joseph out of the pit, and sold Joseph to the Ishmaelites for twenty pieces of silver. And they brought Joseph into Egypt.*** His brothers sold Joseph for 20 pieces of silver and we know that Jesus was also sold for silver, wasn't He? ***(Mat.26:14) Then one of the twelve, who was called Judas Iscariot, went unto the chief priests, (15) and said, What are ye willing to give me, and I will deliver him unto you? And they weighed unto him thirty pieces of silver.*** Then we read that Joseph's father said, "A beast hath devoured him." ***(Gen.37:31) And they took Joseph's coat, and killed a he-goat, and dipped the coat in the blood; (32) and they sent the coat of many colors, and they brought it to their father, and said, This have we found: know now whether it is thy son's coat or not. (33) And he knew it, and said, It is my son's coat: <u>an evil beast hath devoured him</u>; Joseph is without doubt torn in pieces.*** And it was true of Jesus, also. The Roman Beast devoured Him. You know, Pilate really didn't want anything to do with Jesus. His arm was being twisted by the Jews and they were using their political power with him to bring this to pass. ***(Mat.27:22) Pilate saith unto them, What then shall I do unto Jesus who is called Christ? They all say, Let him be crucified. (23) And he said, Why, what evil hath he done? But they cried out exceedingly, saying, Let him be crucified. (24) So when Pilate saw that he prevailed*** *nothing, but rather that a tumult was arising, he took water, and washed his hands before the multitude, saying, I am innocent of the blood of this righteous man; see ye [to it].* And we see the type and shadow of this from Joseph's life here. *(Gen.37:36) And the Midianites sold him into Egypt unto Potiphar, an officer of Pharaoh's, <u>the captain of the guard</u>.* In the Hebrew, it says, "the chief of the executioners." Well, who was "the chief of the executioners" who worked for the Beast and represented the Beast in Jesus' day? It was Pontius Pilate, wasn't it? Once again, the types and the shadows just keep on unfolding here.

The story of Joseph is continued in chapter 39, after Chapter 38 talks about Judah's children by Tamar and so on. We know that Joseph was bought by Potiphar, the officer of Pharaoh, and that he was in Potiphar's household. Potiphar, I believe, represents Pilate, the representative of the Roman Beast; and Potiphar's wife, I believe, represents the Harlot. In the Book of Revelation, the Harlot comes in riding the Beast (Revelation 17:3). Ahab and Jezebel also represent the Beast and the Harlot; therefore, in type, the Beast and Harlot are married here, so to speak. Anyway, Potiphar's wife tried to tempt Joseph. *(Gen.39:12) And she caught him by his garment, saying, Lie with me: and he left his garment in her hand, and fled, and got him out.* The Harlot, who was married to the Beast, tried to tempt Joseph; or, in type, tried to tempt Jesus. *(1Co.6:15) Know ye not that your bodies are members of Christ? shall I then take away the members of Christ, and make them members of a harlot? God forbid. (16) Or know ye not that he that is joined to a harlot is one body? for, The twain, saith he, shall become one flesh. (17) But he that is joined unto the Lord is one spirit. (18) Flee fornication....* Well, that's exactly what Joseph was doing: he was fleeing fornication. Jesus was fleeing fornication, too: spiritual fornication. The Bible says that anyone who is joined unto a harlot becomes a member of that body and spiritual fornication is to be a member of the body of the Harlot. Do you know what the religious system was attempting to do with Jesus when He came? They were attempting to assimilate Him into their body, so that they would not be convicted by all these things He was saying. They were trying to browbeat Him into believing and acting the way they did. You know what? He was being tempted, spiritually-speaking, to have relations with a harlot! He knew they were a harlot and He didn't give in to them. He said they were guilty of the blood of the saints. *(Mat.23: 34) Therefore, behold, I send unto you prophets, and wise men, and scribes: some of them shall ye kill and crucify; and some of them shall ye scourge in your synagogues, and persecute from city to city: (35) that upon you may come all the righteous blood shed on the earth, from the blood of Abel the righteous unto the blood of Zachariah son of Barachiah, whom ye slew between the sanctuary and the altar.* That's exactly what it says about the Harlot in Revelation: *(Rev.18:24) And in her was found the blood of prophets and of saints, and of all that have been slain upon the earth.* So, once again, we see a type of the wife of the Beast tempting Jesus to assimilate into her body.

However, since Jesus didn't give in and since Joseph didn't give in, the Harlot lied about them. *(Gen.39:17) And she spake unto him according to these words, saying, The Hebrew servant, whom thou hast brought unto us, came in unto me to mock me: (18) and it came to pass, as I lifted up my voice and cried, that he left his garment by me, and fled out.* Joseph, or Jesus in type here, was falsely accused by a lying harlot, but we're leading up to some good news here, some really good news. *(Gen.39:20) And Joseph's master took him, and put him into the prison, the place where the king's prisoners were bound: and he was there in the prison.* Wow! Because the harlot lied about him, he was cast into prison; he was devoured by the Beast. What is "prison"? *(1Pe.3:19) In which also he went and preached unto the spirits in prison.* Jesus went and preached to the spirits in prison which, in that case, was "Sheol." "Sheol" in the Old Testament, or "Hades" in the New Testament, depending on how you want to look at it, was also the "pit"; and, remember, Joseph was cast into the pit. "Come now therefore, and let us slay him, and cast him into one of the pits." Both Sheol and Hades were also called the pit. So, Jesus went and preached to the souls in prison; or, in other words, He died and He went to the place of the departed dead.

In the Old Testament, or even when Jesus first came, Sheol was the place of all the departed dead. We have the parable about the rich man and the beggar, Lazarus: *(Luk.16:19) Now there was a certain rich man, and he was clothed in purple and fine linen, faring sumptuously every day: (20) and a certain beggar named Lazarus was laid at his gate, full of sores, (21) and desiring to be fed with the crumbs that fell from the rich man's table; yea, even the dogs came and licked his sores. (22) And it came to pass, that the beggar died, and that he was carried away by the angels into Abraham's bosom: and the rich man also died, and was buried. (23) And in Hades he lifted up his eyes, being in torments, and seeth Abraham afar off, and Lazarus in his bosom. (24) And he cried and said, Father Abraham, have mercy on me, and send Lazarus, that he may dip the tip of his finger in water, and cool my tongue; for I am in anguish in this flame. (25) But Abraham said, Son, remember that thou in thy lifetime receivedst thy good things, and Lazarus in like manner evil things: but now here he is comforted and thou art in anguish. (26) And besides all this, between us and you there is a great gulf fixed, that they that would pass from hence to you may not be able, and that none may cross over from thence to us.* The rich man was in Hades and Lazarus was in "Abraham's bosom," a part of Hades. But Jesus went there to preach the Gospel because the faithful Old Testament Jews had to have a method for entering into the Kingdom. Jesus had already said to Nicodemus that nobody would enter the Kingdom, unless they were first born again (John 3:3). So Jesus went to preach the Gospel to them and, of course, we know the righteous accepted it, but those in Hades did not. *(Eph.4:8) Wherefore he saith, When he ascended on high, he led captivity captive, And gave gifts unto men. (9) (Now this, He ascended, what is it but that he also descended into the lower parts of the earth?* So we know that after Jesus preached to them, He took those who were righteous and those who were captive to Heaven with Him. Jesus told *the thief on the cross, (Luk.23:43) ... Today shalt thou be with me in Paradise.*

(Gen.39:22) And the keeper of the prison committed to Joseph's hand all the prisoners that were in the prison; and whatsoever they did there, he was the doer of it. In type and shadow, Joseph was the Lord in the prison, just as Jesus was the Lord in the prison of the departed dead. Jesus was the Lord and Joseph was the Lord. The story of the butler and baker confirms that. *(Gen.40:9) And the chief butler told his dream to Joseph, and said to him, In my dream, behold, a vine was before me; (10) and in the vine were three branches: and it was as though it budded, and its blossoms shot forth; and the clusters thereof brought forth ripe grapes: (11) and Pharaoh's cup was in my hand; and I took the grapes, and pressed them into Pharaoh's cup, and I gave the cup into Pharaoh's hand. (12) And Joseph said unto him, This is the interpretation of it: the three branches are three days; (13) within yet three days shall Pharaoh lift up thy head, and restore thee unto thine office: and thou shalt give Pharaoh's cup into his hand, after the former manner when thou wast his butler. (14) But have me in thy remembrance when it shall be well with thee, and show kindness, I pray thee, unto me, and make mention of me unto Pharaoh, and bring me out of this house: (15) for indeed I was stolen away out of the land of the Hebrews: and here also have I done nothing that they should put me into the dungeon. (16) When the chief baker saw that the interpretation was good, he said unto Joseph, I also was in my dream, and, behold, three baskets of white bread were on my head: (17) and in the uppermost basket there was of all manner of baked food for Pharaoh; and the birds did eat them out of the basket upon my head. (18) And Joseph answered and said, This is the interpretation thereof: the three baskets are three days; (19) within yet three days shall Pharaoh lift up thy head from off thee, and shall hang thee on a tree; and the birds shall eat thy flesh from off thee. (20) And it came to pass the third day, which was Pharaoh's birthday, that he made a feast unto all his servants: and he lifted up the head of the chief butler and the head of the chief baker among his servants. (21) And he restored the chief butler unto his butlership again; and he gave the cup into Pharaoh's hand: (22) but he hanged the chief baker: as Joseph had interpreted to them. (23) Yet did not the chief butler remember Joseph, but forgat him.*

When Joseph interpreted their dreams, the dream actually said that in three days one of them would be resurrected out of that prison to stand before Pharaoh. And Pharaoh was considered to be the "god" of the earth at that time. Some people think that the Lord doesn't use a negative person, like Pharaoh, as a type of God, but in the Book of Esther we see God using Ahasuerus to represent Him in type. Ahasuerus married Esther, the bride who was chosen out of all the fair virgins of the kingdom, and God is using Ahasuerus, a pagan king, to represent Him in this wonderful revelation of the end time. We're going to see later on in this text that Joseph was second only to Pharaoh. So when he translated these two dreams, the butler represented the people whom Jesus took captive up out of the prison. The baker, of course, represented those who were condemned to stay there. They are going to lose their position. In both cases, it was after three days that this happened. Now let me point out something to you. What happened after three days when Jesus went to prison? He came out and He took captivity captive, right? It was after three days, which is exactly what we see in this type, so once again, we see that this is talking about Jesus. And where did Jesus go after three days? He took captivity captive and He went to Heaven. Well, there's something very interesting in the next chapter. *(Gen.41:1) And it came to pass at the end of two full years, that Pharaoh dreamed: and, behold, he stood by the river. (2) And, behold, there came up out of the river seven kine, well-favored and fat-fleshed; and they fed in the reed-grass. (3) And, behold, seven other kine came up after them out of the river, ill-favored and lean-fleshed, and stood by the other kine upon the brink of the river. (4) And the ill-favored and lean-fleshed kine did eat up the seven well-favored and fat kine. So Pharaoh awoke. (5) And he slept and dreamed a second time: and, behold, seven ears of grain came up upon one stalk, rank and good. (6) And, behold, seven ears, thin and blasted with the east wind, sprung up after them. (7) And the thin ears swallowed up the seven rank and full ears. And Pharaoh awoke, and, behold, it was a dream.* Pharaoh had this dream about the seven years of plenty and the seven years of famine, but Joseph was left in the prison for two full years before he was remembered by the chief butler. Then the chief butler told Pharaoh about this man who could give the revelation of dreams and so Pharaoh brought him up out of the prison. What? After two full years? Well, that didn't happen with Jesus! What's wrong here? Usually the types are pretty accurate. We know, *(Mat.12:40) for as Jonah was three days and three nights in the belly of the whale; so shall the Son of man be three days and three nights in the heart of the earth.* Jesus was three days and three nights in the bowels of the earth. What's wrong here? Why only two years?

I'll tell you what I believe and what the Lord spoke to me. The two full years here represent 2000 years. It's talking about the fifth day and the sixth day, in type. Jesus was born after four days or 4000 years. *(2Pe.3:8) But forget not this one thing, beloved, that one day is with the Lord as a thousand years, and a thousand years as one day.* At the end of 4000 years from the creation, Jesus was born. And then, the next two days, the fifth and the sixth days, are 2000 years leading up to the seventh day, which we are now in and which are the beginning of the seven years of plenty; and then the seven years of famine. So, why is it that Joseph, as Jesus in type, was not coming up out of that prison for two full years, which I say represents 2000 years? Well, I'm going to point something out to you. Many people don't know that the Bible is very clear about Jesus coming again, but not just in the sky. The Bible also teaches an *epiphaneia*, a coming of the Lord <u>in</u> His people before He comes <u>for</u> His people, a *parousia*. Those are two different words with two different meanings, though some Bible versions have translated them as the same word. The *epiphaneia* is "the shining forth from"; meaning, of course, the Lord is coming to shine forth from His people. **(2Co.2:18) But we all, with unveiled face beholding as in a mirror the <u>glory</u> of the Lord, are transformed into the same image from glory to glory, even as from the Lord the Spirit.** That glory is the shining forth of Jesus Christ in us. Paul said, **(Gal.2:20) I have been crucified with Christ; and it is no longer I that live, but <u>Christ living in me</u>: and that life which I now live in the flesh I live in faith, the faith which is in the Son of God, who loved me, and gave himself up for me.** And Paul spoke about the resurrection life: **(Php.3:10) That I may know him, and the power of his resurrection, and the fellowship of his sufferings, becoming conformed unto his death; (11) if by any means I may attain unto the resurrection from the dead.** That's <u>the resurrection life of Christ in us</u>, meaning that Christ is being resurrected in His people.

(Ecc.1:9) That which hath been is that which shall be; and that which hath been done is that which shall be done: and there is no new thing under the sun. History just keeps repeating. The first-fruits in the time God's people were in bondage in Egypt was Moses. He came out of Egypt and went to the mountain of God; then he came back to bring God's people to the mountain of God. In this case that we're looking at now, Joseph was the first-fruits. And in Jesus' day, of course, He was the first-fruits. These are all types of the Man-child, so to speak, in the Bible. And Jesus told us about another Man-child. In fact, He told the disciples, **(Joh.16:16) A little while, and ye behold me no more; and again a little while, and ye shall see me. (21) Verily, verily, I say unto you, that ye shall weep and lament, but the world shall rejoice: ye shall be sorrowful, but your sorrow shall be turned into joy. (21) A woman when she is in travail hath sorrow, because her hour is come: but when she is delivered of the child, she remembereth no more the anguish, for the joy that a man is born into the world. (22) And ye therefore now have sorrow: but I will see you again, and your heart shall rejoice, and your joy no one taketh away from you.** He said that the Church was a woman and that <u>born</u> to this woman would be a man-child, and at that time, <u>He would see them again</u>. The Lord is coming as a Man-child. You see, when we bear the fruit of Jesus Christ, that's "Christ in you, the hope of glory" (Colossians 1:27). So, <u>who</u> is being resurrected 2000 years later in the image of Christ? The Man-child of Revelation is being resurrected. **(Rev.12:1) And a great sign was seen in heaven: a woman arrayed with the sun, and the moon under her feet, and upon her head a crown of twelve stars; (2) and she was with child; and she crieth out, tra-**

vailing in birth, and in pain to be delivered. And, if you think that's Jesus, you're wrong! ***(4:1) After these things I saw, and behold, a door opened in heaven, and the first voice that I heard, [a voice] as of a trumpet speaking with me, one saying, Come up hither, and <u>I will show thee the things which must come to pass hereafter</u>.*** That was <u>after</u> the revelation that John saw in 96 A.D. You can't be Jesus personally; he's talking about Jesus coming in a body. He's talking about Jesus manifested in His people, which He promised to do!

So history keeps repeating. We have man-child after man-child who keep bringing God's people out of bondage and providing for them, and so on and so forth. Jesus provided as a man-child. He provided in the "wilderness," which is the word translated "desert" in the New Testament. He provided for them miraculously, like Moses did, like Joseph did and now, in the end time, we have another provision coming along exactly like this, except this Man-child is a corporate Man-child. You see, when Jesus stepped over into the New Testament, because of the sacrifice of His blood, He became a corporate body called the body of Christ. The Man-child is the first-fruits of those to come in to His image. So now you see a resurrection of Him two full years later, or 2000 years later. Let me give you proof of that. Pharaoh had a dream, a revelation, and how did Joseph interpret it? ***(Gen.41:29) Behold, there come seven years of great plenty throughout all the land of Egypt: (30) and there shall arise after them seven years of famine; and all the plenty shall be forgotten in the land of Egypt....*** We're coming to that in our day, folks, 2000 years later! Jesus was raised after three days, but now He's being raised again, resurrected in the earth in His people. And the first-fruits of those are the Man-child corporate body, who is also going to raise up the woman in the wilderness who comes into that fruit. ***(Gen.41:30) And there shall arise after them seven years of famine; and all the plenty shall be forgotten in the land of Egypt; (31) and the plenty shall not be known in the land by reason of that famine which followeth; for it shall be very grievous.*** We read in the Book of Revelation about that famine. And we're coming to the famine after the seven years of plenty, which we are in <u>right now</u>. So we see in type Joseph representing Jesus in his time and Joseph representing the Man-child in our time. And we see Joseph storing up during the seven years of plenty for the seven years of famine. But the question is, <u>where</u> did Joseph store up the seven years of plenty? Jesus in Joseph was storing up in the <u>Kingdom of Heaven</u>. We're not taking anything away from Jesus. Whatever God does in us, it's God in us. It's "Christ in you," right? We're not taking anything away from God; He just uses flesh, right? He even used the flesh of Jesus Who was born of the virgin Mary. ***(Rom.1:3) Concerning his Son, who was born <u>of the seed of David according to the flesh</u>.*** That's right; Jesus, the living Son of God, was <u>in</u> the son of man and today He's <u>in</u> the son of man, too! He's manifesting in the son of man. He is God with us! ***(Mat.1:23) Behold, the virgin shall be with child, and shall bring forth a son, And they shall call his name <u>Immanuel</u>; <u>which is</u>, <u>being interpreted</u>, <u>God with us</u>.*** We are to store up under the hand of Jesus.

What happened to Jesus in Joseph when he was brought up out of that prison? Pharaoh, who was considered to be the sun god over the earth and who was worshipped by the people as such, said to him, *(Gen.41:40)* <u>**Thou shalt be over my house**</u>, *and according unto thy word shall all my people be ruled: only in the throne will I be greater than thou.* Well, if you're talking about Jesus, you can see very plainly that He's second only to God. It's exactly what Jesus said when He was resurrected: *(Mat.28:18) And Jesus came to them and spake unto them, saying,* <u>**All authority**</u> *hath been given unto me in heaven and on earth.* Wow! And that happened when? It happened when He was resurrected. And how does the Lord manifest His authority? He manifests authority in His people. When Jesus sent out His disciples, He said, *(Mat.28:19) Go ye therefore, and make disciples of all the nations, baptizing them into the name of the Father and of the Son and of the Holy Spirit: (20) teaching them to observe all things whatsoever I commanded you: and lo, I am with you always, even unto the end of the world.* He was giving them authority. Jesus was delegating His authority. He told them, *(Mat.18:18) Verily I say unto you, what things soever ye shall bind on earth shall be bound in heaven; and what things soever ye shall loose on earth shall be loosed in heaven. (Mat.21:22) And all things, whatsoever ye shall ask in prayer, believing, ye shall receive.* So He exercises His authority through His body on the earth.

You know, even when the Father performed the great signs in Egypt, He did it through Moses and Aaron. He does it through people. The Father preserved and provided for His people through Jesus, the first New Testament Man-child. *(Gen.41:41) And Pharaoh said unto Joseph, See, I have set thee over all the land of Egypt.* In type, Egypt represents the whole world. *(42) And Pharaoh took off his signet ring from his hand, and put it upon Joseph's hand, and arrayed him in vestures of fine linen, and put a gold chain about his neck; (43) and he made him to ride in the second chariot which he had;* <u>*and they cried before him,*</u> *Bow the knee: and he set him over all the land of Egypt.* You see, Jesus is the head and before Joseph's chariot, they cried, "Bow the knee! Bow the knee!" What does the Bible say about that? It says very plainly that every knee shall bow unto Jesus Christ. *(Rom.14:11) For it is written, As I live, saith the Lord,* <u>*to me every knee shall bow*</u>, *And every tongue shall confess to God. (Gen.41:44) And Pharaoh said unto Joseph, I am Pharaoh, and without thee shall no man lift up his hand or his foot in all the land of Egypt.* Under God Almighty, under the Father, is Jesus Christ. He is taking up during the seven years of plenty that which He is going to restore in the seven years of famine. <u>Our opportunity is today</u>, folks. We need to be storing up for ourselves in Heaven.

(Gen.41:45) And Pharaoh called Joseph's name <u>Zaphenath-paneah</u>.... Josephus, the famous Jewish historian, says that this means "the revealer of secrets." This is interesting because Jesus was a revealer of secrets and the Man-child will be a

revealer of secrets. Steindorf, another translator, says that this means "the God speaks and He lives." Wow! Who is it who's speaking through Joseph here? It is "God with us," "Emmanuel." God speaks and He lives, and He married a Gentile bride! *(Gen.41:45) And Pharaoh called Joseph's name Zaphenath-paneah; and he gave him to wife Asenath, the daughter of Poti-phera priest of On.* Once again, we see everything following the pattern of this type and shadow being Jesus. *(Gen.41:46) And Joseph went out from the presence of Pharaoh, and went throughout all the land of Egypt. (47) And in the seven plenteous years the earth brought forth by handfuls. (48) And he gathered up all the food of the seven years which were in the land of Egypt, and laid up the food in the cities: the food of the field, which was round about every city, laid he up in the same.* Yet, Jesus said, *(Mat.6:19) Lay not up for yourselves treasures upon the earth, where moth and rust consume, and where thieves break through and steal.* So what does this mean? It means that we have to store up under Jesus, Who is second in the Kingdom only to the Father. We store up under His hand; or, in other words, we store up our treasures in Heaven. Where did the treasures come back from in the time of the wilderness? When the Israelites were driven into the wilderness, their provision came out of Heaven.

I'd like to make a few more points here. *(Gen.41:56) And the famine was over all the face of the earth: and Joseph opened all the store-houses, and sold unto the Egyptians; and the famine was sore in the land of Egypt.* These are the heavenly storehouses. We are storing up in the Kingdom of Heaven. When you give to the poor, He said you're storing up your treasures in Heaven and it is a treasure that "faileth not." In other words, anywhere you go, it will be there to meet your needs because it's stored up in the Kingdom of Heaven, not on the earth. And we see something else interesting here about His manifestation in the first-fruits because Joseph was gathering from the Gentiles. *(Gen.42:7) And Joseph saw his brethren, and he knew them, but made himself strange unto them....* How is it that when the Lord comes in His man-child, He's going to be strange unto them? It's because He's going to look like a Gentile to them. They looked on Joseph and he looked like an Egyptian: he was dressed like an Egyptian and he spoke the language of the Egyptians. The Lord has a people, He has a remnant of Jews, who are waiting to come into the Kingdom, but the Kingdom right now is a mostly Gentile Kingdom. The Man-child of our day is going to go first to the lost sheep of New Testament spiritual Israel, who are Gentiles, and so the Man-child is going to be raised up among the Gentiles. And, once again, the brethren of Jesus aren't going to recognize Him. Jesus is going to be manifested in a Gentile church first. Remember what He said: *(Mat.20:16) So the last shall be first, and the first last.* We're coming to that time when the first people in the Kingdom are going to be the Gentile church. *(Rom.11:25) For I would not, brethren, have you ignorant of this mystery, lest ye be wise in your own conceits, that a hardening in part hath befallen Israel, until the fulness of the Gentiles be come in.* And then, when the fullness of the Gentiles is come in, God is going to turn back to the natural Jews and bring a remnant of them into the Kingdom.

Here's another point I want you to see: **(Gen.42:25) Then Joseph commanded to fill their vessels with grain....** That is, his brethren, who were first coming to him to be preserved in this time of famine. His brethren who were coming out of Canaan's land, out of the land near Israel. They were coming as Jews to him who appeared to be a Gentile and so they didn't recognize him as their brother. **(Gen.42:25) Then Joseph commanded to fill their vessels with grain, and to restore every man's money into his sack, and to give them provisions for the way: and thus was it done unto them. (26) And they laded their asses with their grain, and departed thence. (27) And as one of them opened his sack to give his ass provender in the lodging-place, he espied his money; and, behold, it was in the mouth of his sack. (28) And he said unto his brethren, My money is restored; and, lo, it is even in my sack: and their heart failed them, and they turned trembling one to another, saying, What is this that God hath done unto us?** Now this is interesting. They brought their money and they thought their money would buy them salvation from this famine, but God <u>gave</u> them back their money and He <u>gave</u> them the grain. It's grace, you see. The way God is going to save His people during this famine is not going to be by how much money they've stored up anywhere. Neither was it when the children of Israel came out of Egypt with their gold. That gold didn't save them a bit. That gold was an idol and had to be destroyed. So their money wasn't saving them here. God was freely giving it to them. And, once again, folks, in the coming seven years of famine, we're storing up in Heaven that which is going to come back to us and it's going to be by grace. It's going to be like the grace Joseph's brothers received when they were explaining why it was they had all their money and they had their grain, too. **(Gen.43:19) And they came near to the steward of Joseph's house, and they spake unto him at the door of the house, (20) and said, Oh, my lord, we came indeed down at the first time to buy food: (21) and it came to pass, when we came to the lodging-place, that we opened our sacks, and, behold, every man's money was in the mouth of his sack, our money in full weight: and we have brought it again in our hand. (22) And other money have we brought down in our hand to buy food: we know not who put our money in our sacks. (23) And he said, Peace be to you, fear not: your God, and the God of your father, hath given you treasure in your sacks: I had your money....** You know what? The Lord is going to freely give, freely provide for His people in this coming tribulation. **(Gen.44:1) And he commanded the steward of his house, saying, Fill the men's sacks with food, <u>as much as they can carry</u>, and put every man's money in his sack's mouth.**

Once again, the Lord's going to take care of His people. It's going to be free. It's going to be grace. It's going to be through faith and not through our works. It's not going to be what we've stored up on Earth. It's what we've stored up in Heaven that's going to come back to us. "A treasure that faileth not" is stored up under the hand of Jesus in the Kingdom of Heaven. It's in a place where no one can steal it, no moth can devour it, nothing can destroy it. At this time, by the way, Joseph revealed himself to them as his brother and it was two years into that famine. ***(Gen.45:6) <u>For these two years hath the famine been in the land</u>: and there are yet five years, in which there shall be neither plowing nor harvest.*** Two years into the seven years of famine, the Lord is going to reveal Himself to the remnant. That's very clear. There's a final point I'd like to make here: ***(Gen.45:20) Also <u>regard not your stuff; for the good of all the land of Egypt is yours</u>.*** Pharaoh even sent forth his wagons to bring God's people into the Kingdom of God, to bring that remnant of Jews into the Kingdom of God, in this parable. You know, folks, people are thinking, "I'm going to try to have me a little hideaway where I can keep everything that I have." It isn't going to happen! It isn't going to happen, whether it's talking about the natural Jewish remnant that's coming in or the spiritual Jews, those who are grafted into the olive tree. God is going to supply your needs. <u>Don't worry about a thing</u>! Just store up your treasures in Heaven and be prepared for the coming seven years of famine.

God bless you, friends, in Jesus' name.

CHAPTER 17

Tithing: Renounce Ownership!

Greetings, saints! Thank you so much for joining us. We bless you in Jesus' name. We've been studying the real Good News and I have some more I'd like to share with you. We were looking at the story of Joseph and the seven years of plenty and the seven years of famine. I'd like to take up from there and share some things that could <u>hinder</u> God's supply to us in the seven years of famine. We wouldn't want that, right? ***(Gen.41:49) And Joseph laid up grain as the sand of the sea, very much, until he left off numbering; for it was without number.*** Now I've said that Joseph was very clearly a type of Jesus Christ. He was sold into bondage, he went into prison to preach to the souls in prison and he decided who was to go up and who was to go down. When Joseph, as a type of Jesus Christ, came out of prison at the end of three spiritual days of death, burial and resurrection, he became ruler. ***(Gen.41:39) And Pharaoh said unto Joseph, Forasmuch as God hath showed thee all of this, there is none so discreet and wise as thou: (40) thou shalt be over my house, and according unto thy word shall all my people be ruled: only in the throne will I be greater than thou.*** Of course, this is a Word of God Almighty. So this Joseph, who represented Jesus, "laid up grain as the sand of the sea." For what? He laid up for the coming seven years of famine. Folks, the Lord has <u>greatly</u> prepared for what's coming. We shouldn't fear, we shouldn't doubt, we shouldn't even have to worry about it ourselves at all. God's Word says very plainly in this parable what's prepared for us.

(Gen.41:50) And unto Joseph were born two sons before the year of famine came.... And, you know, that's true: the Lord has had two sons. ***(Hos.11:1) When Israel was a child, then I loved him, and called my son out of Egypt.*** He said He called His son out of Egypt, speaking of natural Israel, so notice that these two sons were born before the year of famine came. ***(Gen.41:50) And unto Joseph were born two sons <u>before the year of famine came</u>, whom Asenath, the daughter of Poti-phera priest of On, bare unto him. (51) And Joseph called the name of the first-born Manasseh: For, [said he,] God hath made me forget all my toil, and all my father's house. (52) And the name of the second called he Ephraim: For God hath made me <u>fruitful</u> in the land of my affliction.*** "Ephraim" means "fruitful," but also we are told of Ephraim that he would be greater than Manasseh "and his seed shall become a multitude of nations." ***(Gen.48:19) And his father refused, and said, I know it, my son, I know it. He also shall become a people, and he also shall be great: howbeit his younger brother shall be greater than he, and his seed shall become a <u>multitude</u> of nations.*** The Hebrew word for "multitude" is literally "the fullness," "the fullness of nations." So here you have Joseph, as Jesus in type, having two sons before the year of famine and the second one represents "the fullness of nations." Wow! That could only mean the Church.

God is bringing a people out of the nations to be His people. In fact, He's almost through doing that. We're very close to that point in time.

Well, after the second son, Ephraim, was born, we're told, **(Gen.41:53) And the seven years of plenty, that was in the land of Egypt, came to an end.** Think about that. When the fullness of nations has come forth, that means the seven years of plenty is coming to an end. It's very interesting, folks, because this is where we are today. **(Gen.41:54) And the seven years of famine began to come, according as Joseph had said: and there was famine in <u>all lands</u>; but in all the land of Egypt there was bread.** You know, many people are coming to believe that we're headed toward a very bad economic decline here in the United States, but I can tell you, folks, it's not going to stop here in the United States. According to the Word, it's going to be in "<u>all lands</u>." Some are trying to reconcile how America could be the head of the nations all the way through the tribulation period and, yet, have this terrible economic decline at the beginning. I can tell you it's because God is going to bring down all nations and all lands are going to be in the midst of this famine. This is not just talking about a physical famine, either; it's a famine in many ways, including a <u>famine of the Word in the midst of the apostate people of God</u>. "But in all the land of Egypt there was bread." In other words, God has made provision in His Kingdom. In this particular instance, Egypt represents His Kingdom and Joseph, as a type of Jesus, was second in this kingdom only to Pharaoh, as a type of the Most High God. **(Gen.41:55) And when all the land of Egypt was famished, the people cried to Pharaoh for bread: and Pharaoh said unto all the Egyptians, Go unto Joseph; what he saith to you, do. (56) And the famine was over all the face of the earth: <u>and Joseph opened all the store-houses</u>, and sold unto the Egyptians; and the famine was sore in the land of Egypt. (57) And all countries came into Egypt to Joseph to buy grain, because the famine was sore in all the earth.** The provision is going to be given to God's people and I want you to know that multitudes of people are going to come into the Kingdom because of the provision God's going to be giving to His people. It's going to be awesome and many are not expecting this, but it's going to be a great revival.

Why does he say, "<u>buy</u> grain"? What is it we have that's of value that we can trade for the provision that God has provided? Well, stop and think about it, folks. **(Heb.11:1 KJV) Now faith is the <u>substance</u> of things hoped for, the evidence of things not seen.** The one thing that Jesus demanded before He administered the benefits of the Kingdom was faith. **(Mat.9:29) Then touched he their eyes, saying, <u>According to your faith be it done unto you</u>. (Mar.9:23) And Jesus said unto him, If thou canst! <u>All things are possible to him that believeth</u>.** That means nothing is impossible to "him that believeth." The constant theme in the New Testament is that, if you have faith, you can have the benefits of the Kingdom. So faith is what we have of value that we can trade for the benefits of the Kingdom. And, remember, Jesus also told us, **(Luk.12:32) Fear not, little flock; for it is your Father's good pleasure to give you the kingdom. (33) Sell that which ye have, and give alms; make** *for yourselves purses which wax not old, a treasure in the heavens that faileth not, where no thief draweth near, neither moth destroyeth. (34) For where your treasure is, there will your heart be also.* The Lord wants us to give up our provision so that we can see His provision. Why is that? *(2Co.12:9) And he hath said unto me, My grace is sufficient for thee: for <u>my power is made perfect in weakness</u>. Most gladly therefore will I rather glory in my weaknesses, that the power of Christ may rest upon me.* <u>His power</u> is made perfect in <u>our weakness</u>. As long as we provide for ourselves, we have no need of His provision. God sent Israel into a wilderness to run out of their own provisions, so that they could see God's provision. This is God's plan for His people to learn to walk by faith. And this great provision that's been stored up has everything to do with what <u>we're giving</u> into the hand of Jesus. You know, Joseph was taking up in the seven years of plenty, out of the hand of the Egyptians, that which he restored. Joseph represents Jesus and what did Jesus say? We're storing up our treasures in "the heavens that faileth not"!

Also, I'd like us to read this warning: *(1Ti.6:17) Charge them that are rich in this present world, that they be not highminded, nor have their hope set on the uncertainty of riches* (A big problem is that many people trust in their riches and they think that's what going to save them. God's not going to permit it.)*, but on God, who giveth us richly all things to enjoy* (Put your faith in God; your supply is coming from Him.)*; (18) that they do good, that they be rich in good works, that they be ready to distribute....* In other words, the rich better be ready to give because in giving is how it will be given unto you. *(Luk.6:38) <u>Give, and it shall be given unto you</u>; good measure, pressed down, shaken together, running over, shall they give into your bosom. For with what measure ye mete it shall be measured to you again.* This is God's method. *(1Ti.6:18) That they do good, that they be rich in good works, that they be ready to distribute, willing to <u>communicate</u>* (meaning "share")*; (19) <u>laying up in store</u>* (There it is again, folks!) *<u>for themselves a good foundation against the time to come</u>* (That's very clear. That's exactly what we're seeing over there in Genesis.)*, that they may lay hold on the life which is [life] indeed.* O, Praise God!

Well, I believe this storehouse is spoken of here and, if you'll please bear with me, I'd like for us to read this first, then I'd like to come back and explain it. *(Mal.3:8) Will a man rob God? yet ye rob me. But ye say, Wherein have we robbed thee? In tithes and offerings. (9) Ye are cursed with the curse; for ye rob me, even this whole nation. (10) Bring ye the whole tithe into the store-house, that there may be food in my house, and prove me now herewith, saith the Lord of hosts, if I will not open you the <u>windows of heaven</u>* (That's awesome!)*, and pour you out a blessing, that there shall not be room enough [to receive it].* Can He do that? Of course! *(11) And I will rebuke the devourer for your sakes, and he shall not destroy the fruits of your ground* (In other words, the curse just devours and plunders, things break, you become sick and so on and so forth.)*; neither* *shall your vine cast its fruit before the time in the field, saith the Lord of hosts.* So when we're storing up in the storehouse, He says that the "windows of heaven" will be open and He will send forth a blessing. Is that going to happen for everyone? Is that going to happen for <u>all Christians</u>? No. Not at all. There are conditions, just as there were in Jesus' day, and I'll give you a "for instance" here: *(2Ki.6:24) And it came to pass after this, that Benhadad king of Syria gathered all his host, and went up, and besieged Samaria. (25) And there was a great famine in Samaria: and, behold, they besieged it, until an ass's head was sold for fourscore [pieces] of silver, and the fourth part of a kab of dove's dung for five [pieces] of silver.* The Beast of that time, the enemy of God's people, the world, if you will, had caused a famine by besieging the people of God. And then a prophet came on the scene. *(2Ki.7:1) And Elisha said, Hear ye the word of the Lord: thus saith the Lord, To-morrow about this time shall a measure of fine flour be sold for a shekel, and two measures of barley for a shekel, in the gate of Samaria. (2) Then the captain on whose hand the king leaned answered the man of God, and said, Behold, if the Lord should make <u>windows in heaven</u>, might this thing be? And he said, Behold, thou shalt see it with thine eyes, but shalt not eat thereof.* Now here's a guy who <u>doubted</u> that God had windows in Heaven, but we see from God's own testimony in Malachi that He does have these windows in Heaven.

You know, there are a lot of people in Christianity today who don't believe that God can supply their needs out of Heaven. They're full of doubt and unbelief, and they speak against the promises of God. They speak against the provision of God, but we've studied the foundation for the provision of God that has been given to us. It's sure, folks! It's as sure as God's Word! It's as sure as His promise that He has provided everything for us. Paul said, *(Php.4:19) And my God shall supply every need of yours according to his riches in glory in Christ Jesus.* He was very confident that God had already taken care of our provision, but this "captain on whose hand the king leaned" is like an awful lot of Christians today. They're full of doubt and unbelief. And what does the Bible say about that? *(Jas.1:7) For let not that man think that he shall receive anything of the Lord; (8) a doubleminded man, unstable in all his ways.* Well, if we skip down a few verses, the story goes on. *(2Ki.7:17) And the king appointed the captain on whose hand he leaned to have the charge of the gate: and the people trod upon him in the gate, and he died as the man of God had said, who spake when the king came down to him. (18) And it came to pass, as the man of God had spoken to the king, saying, Two measures of barley for a shekel, and a measure of fine flour for a shekel, shall be to-morrow about this time in the gate of Samaria; (19) and that captain answered the man of God, and said, Now, behold, if the Lord should make windows in heaven, might such a thing be? and he said, Behold, thou shalt see it with thine eyes, but shalt not eat thereof: (20) it came to pass even so unto him; for the people trod upon him in the gate, and he died.* Folks, there are a lot of people who aren't going to see this provision because they're just unbelievers in the midst of the Church. They claim to be believers but they don't know what believers are. They don't know that they have to believe the Word of the living God. So you see, though the treasure might be there for some people, it won't do them any good because they don't believe, just like in Jesus' day. *(Mat.13:58) And he did not many mighty works there because of their unbelief.*

Well, back in Malachi, there are some things he says that I'd like to qualify just a little bit. *(Mal.3:8) Will a man rob God? yet ye rob me. But ye say, Wherein have we robbed thee? In tithes and offerings. (9) Ye are cursed with the curse; for ye rob me, even this whole nation. (10) Bring ye the whole tithe into the store-house, that there may be food in my house.* You know, in the days of the Old Covenant, when God's people who were faithful and did according to the Law, and gave the tithe, God blessed them by opening the windows of Heaven. How much more would it be for us, who have a better Covenant based on better promises? *(Heb.7:18) For there is a disannulling of a foregoing commandment because of its weakness and unprofitableness (19) (for the law made nothing perfect), and a bringing in thereupon of a better hope, through which we draw nigh unto God. (20) And inasmuch as it is not without the taking of an oath (21) (for they indeed have been made priests without an oath; but he with an oath by him that saith of him, The Lord sware and will not repent himself, Thou art a priest for ever); (22) by so much also hath Jesus become the surety of a better covenant.* How much better would it be for us? What they received was a letter; it was a type and a shadow. How much more would it be for us who are keeping our Covenant? You know, many deceived people are going back under the Old Covenant, but I believe I can prove to you that it is a Covenant that doesn't exist with the New Testament people of God. The Lord says in the Old Testament book of Malachi, "You rob Me by not bringing the whole tithe into the storehouse." Well, we hear this being taught today, as though it's New Testament, but I'm going to show you that it's not. We're told that we're supposed to be bringing the whole tithe into the storehouse and we're told the storehouse is our particular religion or it's some building. But, in the Old Testament, the storehouse was the treasury and the treasury was in the Temple. And we know what the New Testament teaches about the Temple, which is that God has no respect for buildings made with man's hands. The Temple that He is building is a building not made with man's hands and it is the temple of the body of Christ. Well, according to the Old Testament type and shadow, the treasury, or the "storehouse," was in the midst of the Temple. You know what, folks? It's still that way today, except the temple is the body of Christ. We, the people of God, are the storehouse; we are God's treasury. When people want to meet the needs of the Levitical Priesthood, then they have to put it into the people of God. Now we're not talking about keeping somebody's apostate religious kingdom going because they don't trust God and they don't have any faith, so they manipulate people. They drag people back under the Old Testament Law, but this storehouse in the New

Testament is God's people.

When Jesus comes back, He speaks about gathering the nations before Him and judging them according to how they treated His people. ***(Mat.25:34) Then shall the King say unto them on his right hand, Come, ye blessed of my Father, inherit the kingdom prepared for you from the foundation of the world: (35) for I was hungry, and ye gave me to eat; I was thirsty, and ye gave me drink; I was a stranger, and ye took me in; (36) naked, and ye clothed me; I was sick, and ye visited me; I was in prison, and ye came unto me. (37) Then shall the righteous answer him, saying, Lord, when saw we thee hungry, and fed thee? or athirst, and gave thee drink? (38) And when saw we thee a stranger, and took thee in? or naked, and clothed thee? (39) And when saw we thee sick, or in prison, and came unto thee? (40) And the King shall answer and say unto them, Verily I say unto you, Inasmuch as ye did it unto one of these my brethren, even these least, ye did it unto me. (41) Then shall he say also unto them on the left hand, Depart from me, ye cursed, into the eternal fire which is prepared for the devil and his angels: (42) for I was hungry, and ye did not give me to eat; I was thirsty, and ye gave me no drink; (43) I was a stranger, and ye took me not in; naked, and ye clothed me not; sick, and in prison, and ye visited me not. (44) Then shall they also answer, saying, Lord, when saw we thee hungry, or athirst, or a stranger, or naked, or sick, or in prison, and did not minister unto thee? (45) Then shall he answer them, saying, Verily I say unto you, Inasmuch as ye did it not unto one of these least, ye did it not unto me. (46) And these shall go away into eternal punishment: but the righteous into eternal life.*** Did you feed them? Did you clothe them? Did you visit them in prison? It was all according to how the nations treated His people, His temple, you see. The Lord had no respect for the physical Temple of God, the physical building. He pointed out to His disciples, ***(Mat.24:2) But he answered and said unto them, See ye not all these things? verily I say unto you, There shall not be left here one stone upon another, that shall not be thrown down.*** And, of course, they were shocked. They thought this was a holy building, when it was just a type and shadow of the holy building that God is in the midst of building right now.

Well, let me point out something to you. If it was robbing God in the Old Testament to not bring in the tithe, since now we have a greater Covenant based on better promises, what would be robbing God in the New Testament? Look at what Jesus said: ***(Luk.14:33) So therefore whosoever he be of you that renounceth not all that he hath, he cannot be my disciple.*** In other words, what Jesus made us in the New Testament, and the only thing we are ever called in the New Testament, are "stewards." A steward is someone who handles material things for their master and we do that. We have been bought with a price. ***(1Co.6:19) Or know ye not that your body is a temple of the Holy Spirit which is in you, which ye have from God?***

and ye are not your own; (20) for ye were bought with a price: glorify God therefore in your body. (1Co.7:23) Ye were bought with a price; become not bondservants of men. We are not our own, neither does anything under our hand belong to us. If we do not renounce ownership of the other 90%, then we are robbing God. <u>We have to totally become stewards</u>. It's, "Yes, Lord! What do You want to do with this, Lord?" Always! Now, don't worry. God's not going to leave you destitute. The New Testament teaches that very plainly. He's going to supply your every need. But, He does demand that He has the authority over you and over everything you have. "So therefore whosoever he be of you that renounceth not all that he hath, he cannot be my disciple." It's very plain. As a matter of fact, when Jesus was observing the rich Pharisees bringing their tithes and dropping them into the treasury, He saw there a widow with two mites. *(Luk.21:1) And he looked up, and saw the rich men that were casting their gifts into the treasury. (2) And he saw a certain poor widow casting in thither two mites. (3) And he said, Of a truth I say unto you, This poor widow cast in more than they all: (4) for all these did of their superfluity cast in unto the gifts; but she of her want did cast in <u>all</u> the living that she had.* And He pointed out to His disciples that this widow, who gave out of her need, gave everything she had. He made no mention of these Pharisees giving their tithes, folks. Well, in the New Testament, we have the Spirit of God, which they didn't have, and we're not under the Law; we're under the law of the Spirit. And we have been given the law of the Spirit in order to know what to do next with God's money, to know how much to give, to know where to give, and so on. All those things are determined by the Spirit of God. Why did they have a Law in the Old Testament? It was because they didn't have the Spirit of God and they needed to know what to do next. The Law was a "meantime thing." *(Gal.3:19) What then is the law? It was added because of transgressions, <u>till the seed should come to whom the promise hath been made</u> ... (23) But before faith came, we were kept in ward under the law, shut up unto the faith which should afterwards be revealed. (24) So that the law is become our tutor to bring us unto Christ, that we might be justified by faith. (25) But now that faith is come, we are no longer under a tutor.* And the "seed" was Christ and those who abide in Christ. Galatians 3 is very clear about that.

Now I want to show you what is going to <u>rob</u> a lot of people of the great treasure that they should be storing up in Heaven and some of you might be shocked. *(Mat.23:23) Woe unto you, scribes and Pharisees, hypocrites* (Obviously, Jesus is not talking to His disciples here; He's talking to the Jews.)*! for ye tithe mint and anise and cummin, and have left undone the weightier matters of the law* (So He's saying that tithing is of the Law and that they were ignoring the most important, "heavier" parts of the Law. And who was He talking to? He wasn't talking to His people; He was talking to the Pharisees, so see what He says next.)*, <u>justice, and mercy, and faith: but these ye ought to have done, and not to have left the other undone</u>.* He was talking to the Jews about the way it was under their Covenant. "These you ought to have done." The word is past tense here, no matter if you look in the *Texus Receptus*, which is the *Received Text*, or whether you look in the ancient manuscripts, or whether you look at the numeric pattern. It's always past tense. Always! Some versions don't translate it as past tense, but there's no manuscript that doesn't have it past tense. "These you ought to have done." He was not talking to His disciples and telling them what they should do. This time, He was talking to these Pharisees under the Law, about what they had done. "These things you ought to have done, and not to have left the others undone." ***(Mat.23:24) Ye blind guides, that strain out the gnat, and swallow the camel!*** Meaning, of course, that they made things that were not heavy and not important a priority. And the things that were important, they ignored. They strained out a gnat and swallowed a camel. But we see Jesus clearly said that tithing was of the Law.

Also, let me point out to you what the Apostle Paul says about tithing: ***(Heb.7:4) Now consider how great this man was, unto whom Abraham, the patriarch, gave a tenth out of the chief spoils. (5) And they indeed of the sons of Levi that receive the priest's office have commandment to take tithes of the people according to the law*** (It was the Law that commanded to take tithes.)***, that is, of their brethren, though these have come out of the loins of Abraham.*** Melchizedek, who received a tenth from Abraham, never demanded a tenth. He never made it a law, He never made it a command, He never said anything about it. It was a freewill offering from Abraham to give a tenth to Melchizekek. Some people use that to say, "Well, tithing was before the Law." No, it wasn't! The Bible says only that Abraham gave a tithe to Melchizekek and not that it was demanded of him. He gave it as a freewill offering. If you think Abraham gave the tenth because tithing was before the Law, remember that animal sacrifice was before the Law, too. We don't still do that, do we? In fact, God would be very insulted if we did, wouldn't He? So we can see once again that tithing, according to the apostle Paul, is of the Law. ***(Heb.7:5) And they indeed of the sons of Levi that receive the priest's office have commandment to take tithes of the people according to the law, that is, of their brethren*** (that is, the people under the Law)***, though these have come out of the loins of Abraham: (6) but he whose genealogy is not counted from them hath taken tithes of Abraham, and hath blessed him that hath the promises. (7) But without any dispute the less is blessed of the better. (8) And here men that die*** (still speaking of the Levitical priesthood) ***receive tithes; but there one, of whom it is witnessed that he liveth.*** What is the point that Paul is trying to make here? ***(Heb.7:11) Now if there was perfection through the Levitical priesthood (for under it hath the people received the law), what further need [was there] that another priest should arise after the order of Melchizedek, and not be reckoned after the order of Aaron?*** And that priest, of course, is Jesus. Paul is saying that if there was any kind of perfection through the Levitical priesthood and the Law, then God would not have decided to have a new Priest and a new order.

And, first of all, what did this Priest demand? Jesus said, "So therefore whosoever he be of you that renounceth not all that he hath, he cannot be my disciple." Notice that not one time did Jesus demand a tithe. Not one time did any of His disciples demand a tithe. You see, everything has to be founded on our Covenant, out of the mouth of two or three witnesses, and we don't have even one witness. It's just not there. ***(Heb.7:12) For the priesthood being changed, there is made of necessity a change also of the law.*** Wow! Some people insist, "Well, the Law can't be changed. Every jot and every tittle cannot pass away until it's all fulfilled." They like to quote, ***(Mat.5:18 KJV) For verily I say unto you, Till heaven and earth pass, one jot or one tittle shall in no wise pass from the law, till all be fulfilled.*** Yes, that's fulfilling the Law. The Law was going to be fulfilled, but we're not under the Law. You have to reconcile those two statements. Now, let me ask you this question: If a person gave all into the hand of God and totally became a steward, not an owner of the 90% or the 10%, would they not be fulfilling the law of the 10%? Yes! Of course they would and that's the whole point! But, if a person went back under the Law, when their Covenant has delivered them from the Law, would they not be going back under a law that's not even theirs? Would they not be going back under a law that does not exist? Yes! Of course! If the devil can get you out from under the Covenant of grace and under the Covenant of Law, then you will be rebelling against your Lord and you will not be keeping the Covenant that He made with you. ***(Heb.7:18) For there is a disannulling of a foregoing commandment because of its weakness and unprofitableness. (19) (for the law made nothing perfect)....*** See, the Law could not perfect, so God did away with it. Did He do away with it as the letter, as a parable? No. It's a shadow of the good things to come. It's still a shadow and it's still a parable. But God doesn't expect us to go back and keep the shadow or the parable. He wants us to fulfill it in the New Testament. That's the difference. ***(Heb.7:19) (For the law made nothing perfect), and a bringing in thereupon of a better hope, through which we draw nigh unto God. (Heb.8:4) Now if he were on earth, he would not be a priest at all, seeing there are those who offer the gifts according to the law.*** That's right! The Bible says that there's a veil upon the face of the Jews because they don't know that the Law was done away in Christ. ***(2Co.3:12) Having therefore such a hope, we use great boldness of speech, (13) and [are] not as Moses, [who] put a veil upon his face, that the children of Israel should not look stedfastly on the end of that which was passing away: (14) but their minds were hardened: for until this very day at the reading of the old covenant the same veil remaineth, it not being revealed [to them] that it is done away in Christ.*** They are blinded.

And this doesn't mean just the Jews, but it means everybody, the Christians, too, who are under the Law. It says there's a veil upon their face; they're blinded. The god of this world has blinded the minds of the unbelieving. ***(2Co.4:3) And even if our gospel is veiled, it is veiled in them that perish: (4) in whom the god of this world hath blinded the minds of the unbelieving, that the light of the gospel of the glory of Christ, who is the image of God, should not dawn [upon them].***

And because of that, <u>they serve a copy and shadow of the heavenly things</u>. *(Heb.8:5) Who serve [that which is] a copy and shadow of the heavenly things, even as Moses is warned [of God] when he is about to make the tabernacle: for, See, saith he, that thou make all things according to the pattern that was showed thee in the mount. (13) In that he saith, A new [covenant] he hath made the first old. But that which is becoming old and waxeth aged is nigh unto vanishing away. (Heb.9:1)* <u>*Now even a first* [covenant] *had ordinances*</u> (Notice that. It passed away, folks. There is no covenant for you in the Old Covenant. There is a type and shadow that must be fulfilled, and <u>every jot and tittle of it will be fulfilled</u>.) *of divine service, and its sanctuary, [a sanctuary] of this world.*

Since we've determined that tithing is of the Law and some people are diligently giving their tithes to their religion, are you going to receive the benefits from that? Are you going to get the benefits of the New Covenant from that, like the people who give by grace under the New Covenant receive? Let's look and see. *(Gal.4:21) Tell me, ye that desire to be under the law, do ye not hear the law? (22) For it is written, that Abraham had two sons, one by the handmaid, and one by the freewoman. (23) Howbeit the [son] by the handmaid is born after the flesh; but the [son] by the freewoman [is born] through promise. (24) Which things contain an allegory* (or a parable, or the fulfillment of a type and a shadow)*: for these [women] are two covenants; one from mount Sinai* (the Law)*, bearing children unto bondage, which is Hagar.* Wow! He's saying that the Jews' Covenant under the Law makes you a son of the handmaid. *(Gal.4:25) Now this Hagar is mount Sinai in Arabia and answereth to the Jerusalem that now is* (Uh-oh! You mean natural Jerusalem, whose people are under the Law and were under the Law in the time of the Galatians, were actually sons of the handmaid? That's what it says.)*: for she is in bondage with her children. (Gal.4:26)* <u>*But the Jerusalem that is above is free*</u>*,* <u>*which is our mother*</u>*. (30) Howbeit what saith the scripture? Cast out the handmaid and her son: for the son of the handmaid shall not inherit with the son of the freewoman.* So if you are free from the Law, you are sons of the freewoman. If you're under the Law, you are sons of the handmaid. <u>You do not inherit the benefits of the freewoman</u>. You can be doing a lot of giving under the Law and it doesn't benefit you as a son of the freewoman.

(Gal.5:1) <u>*For freedom did Christ set us free*</u> (Paul is talking about freedom from the Law.)*: stand fast therefore, and be not entangled again in a yoke of bondage. (2) Behold, I Paul say unto you, that, if ye receive circumcision, Christ will profit you nothing.* It doesn't matter if it's circumcision or whether it's any other part of the Law. If you're going back under the Law, "Christ will profit you nothing." The Bible says that the Law was done away in Christ. *(2Co.3:14) But their minds were hardened: for until this very day at the reading of the old covenant the same veil remaineth, it not being revealed [to them] that it is* <u>*done away in Christ*</u>*.* Those who have a veil on their face don't know this yet. *(Gal.5:3)*

Yea, I testify again to every man that receiveth circumcision, that he is a debtor to do the whole law. You see, if you seek to be justified by just one part of the Law, you have to keep the whole Law. What a curse! And totally impossible to do! In fact, ***(Gal.3:10) For as many as are of the works of the law....*** This includes all the works of the Law, any one of them you want to pick, and not only circumcision, as we just read. You can substitute any other work of the Law in there for circumcision and it would be the same story. ***(Gal.3:10)*** <u>***For as many as are of the works of the law are under a curse***</u> (You see, when preachers who don't know any better bring you under the Law, they bring you under a curse. And what is that curse?)***:*** <u>***for it is written, Cursed is every one who continueth not in all things that are written in the book of the law,***</u> ***to do them.*** In other words, here is the curse. If you want to be justified by one part of the Law, you have to keep the whole Law. If you can't keep the whole Law, you're dead, folks! There's no way you can make it into the Kingdom because the son of the handmaid will not inherit with the son of the freewoman. You see, those preachers are plundering you, in order to fill their pockets. They're plundering the people of God because those preachers have no faith that God will supply their needs. They condemn you and put you back under the Law to supply their needs because under grace you have to listen to the Holy Spirit. Under grace, you are under the law of the Spirit. Do you think the Holy Spirit is going to have you support a bunch of people who are dragging you under a curse? No. The Lord doesn't send people to do that. The New Testament tells us as much by what is not said and not done, as by what is said and what is done. Jesus never one time taught tithing to the Christians, nor did any of His disciples. Not one time! I'll tell you something else they didn't do. They didn't take up offerings for themselves. These guys walked by faith. You can't find one time that any of Jesus' disciples took up an offering for themselves, saying, "Bring the tithe into the storehouse." It's not there, folks! And if we read the very next verse, ***(Gal.3:11) Now that no man is justified by the law before God, is evident: for, The righteous shall live by faith.*** It is evident that you can never be justified by the Law. You can't keep enough of it to be righteous because you have to keep all of it to be righteous. ***(Gal.5:3)*** <u>***Yea, I testify again to every man that receiveth circumcision, that he is a debtor to do the whole law.***</u> You have to do the <u>whole Law</u>! And if you put tithing in there, you still have to do the <u>whole Law</u>! If you put the Old Testament Sabbath in there, you have to do the <u>whole Law</u>! (God has a better Sabbath in the New Testament, folks. I'm not saying it's Saturday, Sunday or any one day; I'm just saying a better Sabbath, but it's not part of this study and I won't get into that here.) So, if anybody is seeking to be justified by one part of the Law, <u>the curse is that you have to keep the whole Law</u>. That's rough! The Jews couldn't do it and you can't, either.

There's something else that being under the law of tithing does. ***(Gal.5:4) Ye are severed from Christ, ye would be justified by the law; ye are fallen away from <u>grace</u>.*** Well, what is grace? Grace is God's favor! You don't benefit from the Kingdom under the Law, like you do under grace. "You are severed from Christ, you who would be justified by the law." I learned something about this. I was about a year old in the Lord when I discovered that I was not supposed to be under the Law. As a matter of fact, I was doubly a Pharisee because I would give 20%. And the Lord told me one day, "You're still a Pharisee; you're still living by the Law." So I asked, "What do you mean, Lord? I give 20%. I thought that would be better than 10%." And He answered, "You're under a law that's not even a law of the Old Covenant. You're under a law of your own making and you're seeking to be justified by it." Well, I didn't want to be cut off from Christ by going under a Covenant that was not mine and that God never made with me. He only made it with the Jews and He refused to make it with the Gentiles. The Lord taught me, "Look at what I said in the New Testament. Look at the commands I gave in the New Testament." **(Mat.5:42) Give to him that asketh thee, and from him that would borrow of thee turn not thou away. (1Jn.3:17) But whoso hath the world's goods, and beholdeth his brother in need, and shutteth up his compassion from him, how doth the love of God abide in him?**

Look at the commands. He didn't say, "Bring your tithes into the storehouse." So what are you doing? If you have in your mind to "bring your tithe into the storehouse," which is an Old Testament command of the Law, and you're ignoring what Jesus did say in the New Testament, then you've departed from your Covenant and entered into a Covenant that God never made with you. You've entered into a Covenant that does not exist. That's dangerous! It means that now you don't have a Covenant! Well, it says very plainly, you are severed from Christ, if you would be justified by the Law. You've fallen away from grace and, if there's anything we need in the seven years of famine, folks, it's grace. **(Gal.5:5) For we through the Spirit by faith wait for the hope of righteousness. (6) For in Christ Jesus neither circumcision availeth anything, nor uncircumcision; but faith working through love. (7) Ye were running well; who hindered you that ye should not obey the truth? (8) This persuasion [came] not of him that calleth you.** Amen to that! Then Paul pronounces a curse against the Judaizers who were putting them under this law. **(Gal.5:12) I would that they that unsettle you would even go beyond circumcision.**

Well, let's see how can you store up in the Kingdom and get it back when you need it: **(2Co.9:6) But this [I say,] He that soweth sparingly shall reap also sparingly; and he that soweth bountifully shall reap also bountifully.** Now, folks, that's not tithing. You can't see a percentage in there anywhere. God is just saying, the more you give, the more He'll give to you. And here it is again: **(Luk.6:38) Give, and it shall be given unto you; good measure, pressed down, shaken together, running over, shall they give into your bosom.** The more you give, the more He'll give to you. **For with what measure ye mete it shall be measured to you again.** Where does Jesus ever put a 10% in there? He doesn't. You have to renounce all you have, all ownership, to be a disciple. So you see here that this is not at all what the Law says, but <u>this is the command that we do have in our Covenant</u>. **(2Co.9:7) [Let] each man [do] according as he hath <u>purposed in his heart</u>....** Wow! That's not

10%! Under the Law, you'd better not make up your own rules. What is "purposed in your heart"? It's what your conscience tells you. God is relieving us of this Old Testament Law and He's saying, "Okay, it's the law of the Spirit now. You hear My Spirit, you follow Him." **(2Co.9:7) [Let] each man [do] according as he hath <u>purposed in his heart</u>: not grudgingly, or of necessity....** That's not the Law there! It was a necessity of the Law to give the 10%. If you're under the tithe, you have to give the 10%. You are bound by the Law and, according to Galatians 3 and 4, you are in bondage to the Law. So, once again, we see the New Testament does not teach the law of tithing. **(2Co.9:7) [Let] each man [do] according as he hath <u>purposed in his heart</u>: not grudgingly, or of necessity: for God loveth a cheerful giver.** God wants people to give from the heart and not just to their local assembly, but to their brother in need down the block. He wants them to give to the people whom they know are in need around them and to people who ask of them. But some people are ignoring the commands of Jesus in order to take <u>His money</u> and sow it into a kingdom of man. You know why I know that? Because it's man that puts you back under the Law. It's man that builds his kingdom and has to have you under the Law, in a form of manipulation and extortion, in order to support their kingdom. You know, these disciples, they just walked by faith. They freely gave, they freely received. They didn't put anybody under the Law, they didn't charge anybody anything. They didn't even take up collections for themselves.

Now I want to say, they did take-up collections for saints in need. We have an example of that. **(2Co.8:1) Moreover, brethren, we make known to you the grace of God which hath been given in the churches of Macedonia; (2) how that in much proof of affliction the abundance of their joy and their deep poverty abounded unto the riches of their liberality. (3) For according to their power, I bear witness, yea and beyond their power, [they gave] of their own accord, (4) beseeching us with much entreaty in regard of this grace and the fellowship in the ministering to the saints: (5) and [this], not as we had hoped, but first they gave their own selves to the Lord, and to us through the will of God. (6) Insomuch that we exhorted Titus, that as he made a beginning before, so he would also complete in you this grace also.** They took up for the saints in Jerusalem because they were being persecuted and plundered by the Jews. And another example is here: **(2Co.9:1) For as touching the ministering to the saints, it is superfluous for me to write to you: (2) for I know your readiness, of which I glory on your behalf to them of Macedonia, that Achaia hath been prepared for a year past; and your zeal hath stirred up very many of them. (3) But I have sent the brethren, that our glorying on your behalf may not be made void in this respect; that, even as I said, ye may be prepared: (4) lest by any means, if there come with me any of Macedonia and find you unprepared, we (that we say not, ye) should be put to shame in this confidence. (5) I thought it necessary therefore to entreat the brethren, that they would go before unto you, and make up beforehand your afore-**

promised bounty, that the same might be ready as a matter of bounty, and not of extortion. So they did take it up for other people who were in need, but they never took it up for themselves, not on any occasion that we can find. They just walked by faith. They trusted that God, moving through people, would meet their needs. You can't argue with it because you're not going to find any verses that say anything different.

So, God loves a cheerful giver and here's the promise, but the promise is not to the one who's under the Law. The promise is to the one who is under grace. ***(2Co.9:8)*** <u>***And God is able to make all grace abound unto you;***</u> ***that ye,*** <u>***having always all sufficiency in everything….***</u> Wow! There it is right there, folks! What do you need in the seven years of famine? You need that promise right there fulfilled for you. I don't know of a more inclusive promise in all the Bible than that. That's awesome! If you have that one in your pocket, you have something! You can walk out into the wilderness. God will supply your needs. And it's not for those who are under the Law. You know, the Lord Jesus told us, ***(Mat.5:20) For I say unto you, that except your righteousness shall exceed [the righteousness] of the scribes and Pharisees, ye shall in no wise enter into the kingdom of heaven.*** The people who are living under the Law are not living in the Kingdom. Now, if your righteousness has to exceed theirs, that must mean that the tithe wasn't enough <u>and it's not enough</u>. The Lord wants it all! He demands it all! Does that mean you have to give up your house, your car and walk away from them and just be penniless? No. It means you are handling it for Him and, if He tells you to give it, you have to give it because you are now just a steward, you see. Thank God He wants to supply our needs, not our "greeds," but our needs. Thank God He wants to do that and He will do that, and He's promised to do that. ***(2Co.9:9) As it is written, He hath scattered abroad, he hath given to the poor; His righteousness abideth for ever. (10) And he that supplieth seed to the sower and bread for food*** (Wouldn't you like to have bread for food in the days to come?), ***shall supply and multiply your seed for sowing, and increase the fruits of your righteousness.*** God promises to meet your needs, if you'll come out from under the Law, not be separated from Christ in grace, and enter in to what the New Covenant <u>does</u> say about giving. You have a Covenant and that's the one the Lord wants you to keep. It's the only one He made with you. ***(2Co.9:11) Ye being enriched in everything unto all liberality, which worketh through us thanksgiving to God.*** Wow!

So what's God's plan? The Lord told me one time that the things that happened in the Gospels and in the Book of Acts are going to happen again in the end time, except with much larger groups of people. History just repeats with more and more people as it goes along. Well, in the days of the Book of Acts, which represents our day, folks, God put it in the hearts of those people to make sure everybody's needs were met. And that's been commanded of us in the Bible ever since; it's just that it hasn't been obeyed. When the Holy Spirit fell upon them in the Book of Acts, it empowered them to make sure that everybody's needs were met. There was equality. That grace is coming once again by the power of the Holy Spirit and there will be equality. The Holy Spirit will empower us to bring this to pass in the days to come. ***(2Co.8:13) For [I say] not [this] that others may be eased [and] ye distressed; (14) but by equality*** (This is what God demands: equality.)***: your abundance [being a supply] at this present time for their want, that their abundance also may become [a supply] for your want; that there may be equality: (15) as it is written, He that [gathered] much had nothing over; and he that [gathered] little had no lack.*** See, if you gather much, you don't need to have anything over. <u>You only need your needs supplied</u>. Why are you holding onto it? Is it because that's what you're trusting in? "For where thy treasure is, there will thy heart be also," is what the Bible says. Don't tell me you can have it and not trust in it. The fact that you have it while people around you are in need tells you that you're trusting in it; you're holding onto it. Either that or you don't love the brethren. Well, folks, the Holy Spirit is going to change the hearts of His people. This latter rain is going to be poured out and there's going to be equality. "He that had little will have no lack, and he that had much will have nothing over," because you'll need to walk by faith. What did Jesus tell them? "Sell that which ye have, and give alms; make for yourselves purses which wax not old, a treasure in the heavens that faileth not, where no thief draweth near, neither moth destroyeth." You see, the people who have much are going to be able to meet the needs of the people who have little and sometimes it will be turned around.

Years ago, when I first started thinking about these things and I went to the 20% instead of the 10%, God showed me that I was still a Pharisee. I began to diligently search the Scriptures to find out, "Lord, what do You say about this? I was wrong, I was deceived. I listened to man and I don't want to do this again. Please show me the truth." Well, I did some searching and I found that ministries didn't take up collections. I've never taken one up and I've never been without, folks. The Lord has always supplied my needs. Nor have I gone around charging people the tithe. It's "freely you have received, freely give." Nor have I told everybody my needs; I've never had to do that. I found out that in my weakness, <u>God is made strong</u>. God sent those disciples out. He told them <u>not</u> to take all their own provision and when they came back, He asked, "Did you lack anything?" They said, "No, Lord." Why did He tell them not to take their own provision? It was because God wanted to prove Himself strong and to miraculously meet the needs of His people. He wanted to prove Himself. Now, in these days, He's going to do the same thing. The ministers He's raising up are going to be people of faith. You'll know that they are sent by God because they are people of faith. They are not back under the Babylonish attitudes of religion. They're not, by graft and extortion, dragging the money out of the people. They are totally trusting God. They are not worried about what people do with their money, nor are they going to preach any sermons to get people to give them money. They don't have to do that because they know that they're sent by God and they believe in their God Who said, "The laborer is worthy of his hire." That's what He told us.

Folks, you will know them by their fruits. ***(Mat.7:15) Beware of false prophets, who come to you in sheep's clothing, but inwardly are ravening wolves.***

(16) By their fruits ye shall know them. Do [men] gather grapes of thorns, or figs of thistles? (17) Even so every good tree bringeth forth good fruit; but the corrupt tree bringeth forth evil fruit. (18) A good tree cannot bring forth evil fruit, neither can a corrupt tree bring forth good fruit. (19) Every tree that bringeth not forth good fruit is hewn down, and cast into the fire. (20) Therefore by their fruits ye shall know them. What is the fruit of one who is a disciple of Jesus Christ? It's faith. It's a walk of faith. It's a life of faith. The Bible says, "The righteous shall live by faith." When did Jesus ever preach a "gimmee" sermon? When did His disciples ever do that? It really wasn't necessary, was it? He knew His Father. And He shared His Father's beliefs with us, like the sparrows who didn't store up in barns and like the flowers who didn't have to spin their clothing. It was freely given by God. We need to know our God that way. We need to know that it's His plan, it's His love to provide for us. **(Luk.12:32)** <u>**Fear not, little flock; for it is your Father's good pleasure to give you the kingdom**</u>**.** He's going to <u>give</u> it to you.

So, store up willingly from the heart in the Kingdom of God. Let the Holy Spirit tell you who to give to, how much to give, where to give, all this things, because He is the Lord and you're not. And the Law is not. The Law was just a tutor to bring us to Christ. It was a meantime thing because of sin, "Till the seed should come to whom the promise hath been made." Thank God that He has a better plan and He wants to manifest Jesus Christ in us. We will be walking in His steps, fulfilling His will and the world will look at us and call us "Christians" because we walk in His steps. It's going to be an exciting time! And the people who walk by faith are not going to have to worry about receiving the grace, nor worry about being separated from Jesus Christ because they haven't gone under a Covenant that is not His. Do you understand? Why obey a word that He did not speak to disobey a Word that He did? Some of you are breaking your Covenant because you've been deceived by these preachers and they are plundering you. They're bringing you under a curse because what you are giving is under the Law. You're wondering, "Why is it not coming back to me like they tell me it will come back to me?" When I first started tithing, I learned that because I was now giving, God was giving back to me. But I didn't stay a baby in these things and the further I went, the more the Lord expected me to find out about the New Testament. Some of you have been in the Lord for many, many years and you haven't found out what the New Testament says about this. I tell you, God is holding you responsible. You're wondering why you're not being blessed the way the preachers tell you you're supposed to be blessed and it's because those promises do not apply to those under the Law. The promises apply to those under grace and you've yet to come under grace; you're seeking to be justified by the Law.

God bless you, saints. I hope that, from now on, what He puts in your hands will be stored up in the Kingdom of Heaven. Praise God! The Lord bless you.

CHAPTER 18

Provision: Receiving it Multiplied!

Greetings, saints! The Lord bless you and be with you today. Thank you so much for joining us. Let's go to the Father and ask His grace for us today. O, precious Father, thank You, thank You, Lord. Thank You for this opportunity for us to join together in Your Presence and enjoy Your Word, to learn to love You and to learn to walk in the steps of our Lord Jesus. Thank You, Father. Thank You for drawing us. Thank You for giving us a hunger and a thirst after righteousness. Thank You, Lord, for opening our spiritual eyes and ears to perceive Your ways. Thank You for working in us to will and to do of Your good pleasure. Thank You for manifesting Your Son in us, Lord. Thank You. And now, Lord, let us have Your anointing today, God, and let Your Words go forth in power. Please encourage the brethren, Lord. In Jesus' name, amen.

Well, once again we're studying the real Good News and especially as it concerns God's provision for His people, not only in these days, but in the days to come. The Lord says, *(Mat.21:22) And all things, whatsoever ye shall ask in prayer, believing, ye shall receive.* We've discovered that because of the sacrificial provision of Christ, all those promises are guaranteed to "every one that believeth." *(Rom.1:16) For I am not ashamed of the <u>gospel: for it <u>is the power of God unto salvation to every one that believeth</u>; to the Jew first, and also to the Greek.</u>* The good news! We have real Good News, folks, and because of that, the Apostle Paul said, *(Php.4:19) And my God shall supply every need of yours according to his riches in glory in Christ Jesus.* We know we can abide in Christ through our faith. We know we are accounted righteous through our faith. We have these benefits because of our faith and what happened at the cross. And we're told, "Forget not all his benefits." *(Psa.103:2) Bless the Lord, O my soul, And forget not all his <u>benefits</u>: (3) Who forgiveth all thine iniquities; Who healeth all thy diseases; (4) Who redeemeth thy life from destruction; Who crowneth thee with lovingkindness and tender mercies; (5) Who satisfieth thy desire with good things, [so that] thy youth is renewed like the eagle. (6) The Lord executeth righteous acts, And judgments for all that are oppressed.* Well, by the grace of God, I am what I am and you are what you are, and we really can't claim anything. It is by the grace of God working in us and through us, through the faith He has given unto us, praise be to God! And, you know, it may sound kind of strange, but I've really enjoyed for many, many years, walking in what the Lord has shown me is a wilderness. It's really just a wilderness of man's ability. The wilderness for Israel wasn't a place where they could provide for themselves, but they got to see the awesome provision of God and, once again, folks, we're going to see the awesome provision of God. I tell you, to be a Christian is to have a miraculous life. It's a life of realizing your weakness in the wilderness, but receiving God's power. As He said, His power is made perfect in our weakness. *(2Co.12:9) And he hath said unto me,*

My grace is sufficient for thee: for [my] power is made perfect in weakness. Most gladly therefore will I rather glory in my weaknesses, that the power of Christ may rest upon me. We're learning how to trust in Him. ***(Heb.10:38) But my righteous one shall live by faith: And if he shrink back, my soul hath no pleasure in him.*** We're learning how to live by faith and trust in Him.

You know, I learned about this wilderness not long after I came to the Lord and I learned that walking by faith is fun! I loved to see God's personal care manifested in my life and the things around me. I loved to see signs and wonders, healings, miracles and deliverances. Of course, I started out young in the faith and immature in my walk, but the Lord helped me continue to grow. I've had many years of seeing God's provision before coming to the place I am today. In those early years, I stored up treasures in Heaven. I lost all real interest in the world and the things of the world. ***(1Jn.2:15) Love not the world, neither the things that are in the world. If any man love the world, the love of the Father is not in him.*** Many of the things that I had treasured when I was in the world now meant nothing to me and I started getting rid of them. I used them to plunder Egypt for the benefit of the Kingdom. That's what I called it because it was like what the Israelites did when they went into the wilderness. I did that a lot. I enjoyed and still do enjoy walking into places where I didn't bring my own provision. It's what Jesus did with His disciples when He commanded them to, ***(Mat.10:9) Get you no gold, nor silver, nor brass in your purses; (10) no wallet for [your] journey, neither two coats, nor shoes, nor staff: for the laborer is worthy of his food.*** In other words, they went without their own provision as disciples of Christ, going forth to do His work, to carry on the great commission, and the Lord was always there. He said, "The laborer is worthy of his food," so the Lord was always there and He's always been there for me, too. Many times, in obedience to the Lord, I found myself in a wilderness. You know, if you obey God's Word, you're automatically in the wilderness. If you do what God tells you to do, it puts you in a wilderness.

I remember a brother and his family who were in need and at the time I made a really good living but I didn't keep it. I tried to find the need around me and meet the need. I was storing up my treasures in Heaven, storing up in the seven years of plenty for the seven years of famine, as we've looked at. Well, the Lord sent me a trial. I knew that I wasn't going to have a paycheck for another two weeks, but I gave what I had to this brother's family. As the Bible asks, ***(1Jn.3:17) But whoso hath the world's goods, and beholdeth his brother in need, and shutteth up his compassion from him, how doth the love of God abide in him?*** So I went ahead and gave him what I had. I didn't store up my treasures on earth at the time; we didn't bother to do that. Jesus commanded us not to do that and there were always plenty of needs around me. Anyway, the next thing you know, the shaft on the water pump of my truck started wobbling and I've never really seen one go that bad without the water pump's seal going out on it. And when I saw that, I prayed, "Well, Lord, I just ask You to keep this water pump going until my next paycheck." That's what I felt to do at the time, but I've prayed over water pumps before and God's healed them; and prayed over alternators and God's healed them. God still does that! But at the time, that's what I felt to do and I learned a lesson through that. The lesson is, be careful what you ask of God and be very specific. I had asked God to make the water pump and the seal last until I got my next paycheck. And it was about 40 miles round-trip to work, so over the next two weeks I put a lot of miles on that truck, the whole time with the shaft actually moving around, jumping around in there because it was really bad.

Praise God! The Lord answered my prayer perfectly and exactly! Two weeks later, when I pulled into the bank drive-thru in town to get some money from my paycheck, right at the teller window, my water pump seal blew out onto the ground. And that's what I had asked God, to just make it last until I got my next paycheck. So, before all the water ran out, I wheeled across the road to the auto parts store. I parked the truck, went in, bought the water pump seal, borrowed some tools and put it in right there. I was a pretty good mechanic and it wasn't long before I had it in and was back on the road again and went home. You know what? If you store up your treasures in Heaven, they're always there for you. <u>The Lord is always going to provide for you</u>! He's going to meet your needs. **(2Co.8:13) For [I say] not [this] that others may be eased [and] ye distressed; (14) but by equality: your abundance [being a supply] at this present time for their want, that their abundance also may become [a supply] for your want; that there may be <u>equality</u>: (15) as it is written, He that [gathered] much had nothing over; and he that [gathered] little had no lack.** You never know down the road when the Lord will cause you to reap what you have sown, but we can't take any credit for anything. It's the Lord's grace working in us. Because of our faith, God continues to give us the desire and the ability to do what He wants done and to do signs and wonders that can be used to glorify Him.

After quite a few years of my own trials like that and being in the ministry part-time, the Lord decided to answer my prayer to go into the ministry full-time. And leading up to that, for about seven years before we moved from Louisiana to Pensacola, Florida, the Lord started giving us dreams about that. One brother in particular, a teenager named Ricky, was given a dream about us moving to Florida. In the dream, he had shown up at my neighbor's house and my neighbor had pointed over toward our house and said, "Look over there!" And he looked over and we had a U-Haul backed up to our door. Then, in his dream, he walked across and met me over in the yard and we were packing up the U-Haul because we were moving to Florida. Ricky said that I told him, "I'm never going to work for man again," and he said I showed him some papers. He looked at the papers and he saw there was a word that started with the letter "P" on them. So after Ricky told me the dream, I asked him, "Was it the word 'pension'?" Remember, this was seven years before it actually happened. And Ricky answered, "Yeah! That's the word, 'pension.'" Seven years after this, it turned out to be a severance pension of a year's pay. It wasn't really enough to help us out much, but there were a lot of other things that came in at that time to meet our needs. Well, anyway, for seven years I told everybody that I was going

Provision: Receiving it Multiplied!

to retire as a young person and finally the time came when the company decided to get rid of company labor. They were paying out a lot of benefits and wanted to hire contract labor instead. And they decided to do it as early retirement for anybody who would volunteer for that. Well, I already knew I was leaving, so the decision was made as soon as they made the offer.

Of course, I knew that wasn't enough for us to live on. There was myself, my wife and five children, so I knew that wasn't enough. Where I was in Louisiana, I had everything paid for -- my house, my car, everything. Now the Lord had already told us that we were going to give our house away, but my car was getting a little old and so I asked the Lord, "Lord, I'm asking you to <u>give</u> me a house and <u>give</u> me a car in Pensacola." I told my children, "The Lord's going to give us a house and give us a car." I confessed it to them and you know how kids are -- they went and confessed it to all the relatives. They told all the relatives, "God's going to give us a house and a car in Pensacola, Florida." And, of course, you know how relatives are, especially unbelieving relatives. They said, "Oh, no! No way! You're crazy!" Even my dad told them, "God's not going to do that!" Well, God did do that! He did it exactly, as a matter of fact! And I hadn't seen Ricky in years, but seven years later, he showed up at my neighbor's house and my neighbor pointed him over toward us and we had a U-Haul backed up to the door. So when he came over to see me, I told him about the papers and I told him, "Sure enough, Ricky, I'm never going to work for man again." That really put me into the wilderness, the revelation that I'm not going to work for man anymore. The Lord showed me that I was going to work full-time in the ministry, but I wasn't supported by some big organization. As a matter of fact, I was one of those guys who was a "come-outer." I was getting delivered of religion and I really didn't want to be in any bondage to it. So I knew God had spoken and that God was doing this miracle. At the time, we actually had a church out at Exxon and I agreed with the brethren there that the Lord was going to <u>give</u> me a house and a car because I was totally out of debt where I was. And the Lord revealed to us that we were going to give our house away, then a little later He revealed to me that I was going to give my car away. So the Lord put us in a position of being in a wilderness because we really didn't have any provision of our own. We were giving up the provision that we had.

My wife asked me one day, "Do you think we are going to sell our house and buy over there?" So I asked the Lord and the Lord said, "No, you're going to give your house away," which is exactly what we did. So, once again, we needed God to come through and He came through awesomely. **(Mat.18:19) Again I say unto you, that if two of you shall agree on earth as touching anything that they shall ask, it shall be done for them of my Father who is in heaven. (20) For where two or three are gathered together in my name, there am I in the midst of them.** And just one week after we agreed in faith, God answered the prayer. Now, it probably isn't the way I would have chosen, but God had His own plans. One week after that, my wife and my oldest daughter got in a wreck on one of the main roads going through Baton Rouge, Louisiana. My wife was driving a Toyota and coming up behind a Cadillac. It was at

Christmas time and the man behind her was in a big Lincoln. He was sightseeing, looking from one side to the other, not paying any attention, and when the car in front of my wife stopped, he plowed right into the back of them and squashed this little Toyota Corolla between a Cadillac and a Lincoln. It didn't leave much of my Toyota Corolla. They had to use the jaws-of-life to get my wife and daughter out of the car; they were slightly injured but it was nothing that the Lord couldn't handle. Anyway, someone came up alongside the car and told my wife, "Don't worry; that guy has good insurance," and then they just left. We don't know who it was or how they could have known that, though later we had a thought that it was an angel.

Well, we found out that the man who ran into the back of her car had something like 100/300/100 insurance and also that he was self-insured. And he was just so repentant. He kept telling my wife that he was so sorry this happened, that it was all his fault, "But don't worry about it, we're going to take care of you." To make a long story short, they did take care of us. They bought us a new Toyota Corolla and we ended up buying a big, new Chevy station wagon because I had five kids that you can't get into a Toyota Corolla. And we knew it was time to move because we had been asking the Lord and the Lord had given us visions about being in our house over in Pensacola, with a little baby girl on my hip, walking through the house. Our little girl had now become "hip-sized" and we knew it was time to move. All these things started coming together at one time. Of course, we needed enough money to come over here and buy a house outright because we weren't in debt. The Lord had taught us many years before to get out of debt and to never go back there, and we did that. We obeyed the Lord. We prayed and asked Him to do it and He got us totally out of debt. Everything we bought was in cash. Even though we didn't save up, God always came through at the right moment for us. We've never been in debt since that day, since maybe a year after I came to the Lord, and I suggest getting out of debt to every one of you. **(Pro.22:7) The rich ruleth over the poor; <u>And the borrower is servant to the lender</u>.** You don't take what God puts under your hand as a steward and put it in bondage. That's totally unscriptural.

You ask, "Well, how is God going to get me a house, unless I go into debt?" I tell you, if you don't ever go into the wilderness place of your own weakness, folks, you never get to see God's strength. His power is made perfect in weakness. God can do everything and He will! He will supply your every need according to His riches in glory. Even in the coming wilderness, God's going to provide shelter for His children. Anyway, through that wreck, God provided for us handsomely. He provided both cars, as a matter of fact, and our house. It wasn't a fancy house, but I'm not a fancy person. It was totally paid for, it was in a very nice area that we really liked and it had everything we needed. The Lord showed me a vision of it before I came to Pensacola to find it. I saw it under great big oak trees and loved the place. It was an old house, solid as a rock and met all of our needs. God wondrously provided for us through that accident. And He showed us who to give our house in Lousiana to. It was something these people needed because they had just lost their company house and their company car, and God miraculously came through for them, too. I remember that my wife was a little bit uneasy because she didn't know for sure if I'd heard from the Lord about giving our house away, but I asked the Lord to give her a sign. The sign was, I believe, six heads in a row, and so she asked and I confidently affirmed that it was going to come up that way and it did; we got six heads in a row. So the answer confirmed to her that we were going in the right direction and she was confident about that. **(Pro18:18) The lot causeth contentions to cease, And parteth between the mighty.** In other words, if somebody is not totally convinced, God can clear up their doubts.

That's how our full-time ministry began. I was walking into a wilderness because, in the previous years that I'd ministered, the Lord taught me some things that I had abided by in the Scriptures. I told you a little bit about how the Lord showed me that neither He nor His disciples took up collections for themselves, so I never did it either. I never took up collections during the years of my part-time ministry and I've never taken up collections since I started full-time ministry. And here I was coming to a new town and didn't know anybody, and wasn't receiving any support, but Exxon gave me a year's salary and we had this wreck, so I came here with enough to buy our house and car. And we were starting out with no debt, which was neat, but we had no visible means of support, either. Some principles the Lord had put in my heart, which I had already been obeying, were that we didn't take up any collections and we didn't receive any government money or anything like that. Basically, we were going into a wilderness, folks, a place where God would have to supply supernaturally.

Another thing I've shared with you is that I didn't teach the tithe. I did not bring God's people under the law of the Old Covenant tithe. I didn't teach giving to me, either, as a matter of fact. I didn't talk about giving to me and I haven't until this day talked about giving to me. I never talked about it in our meetings and, once in a while, people would come up to me and give me money, which was fine. But I never talked about what my needs were because I felt that wasn't faith. I felt it was more like extortion. I had a neighbor, a brother who was into a prosperity movement, and he told me how people would get up and tell everything that they were believing the Lord for. So, of course, somebody out there would feel like they had to answer that brother's need. Well, that isn't faith in God. It is manipulation. And I'm remembering where Paul wasn't taking up a collection for himself or his ministry, but he <u>was</u> taking up a collection for the Macedonian Christians who were in great need. He wrote to Corinth to ask them to make this collection before he arrived so he wouldn't look bad to any Macedonians who might be coming with him. He didn't want it to be a case of, "We've brought these needy people and now you <u>have</u> to give to them because we've stuck them up in front of you." He said, **(2Co.9:5) I thought it necessary therefore to entreat the brethren, that they would go before unto you, and make up beforehand your aforepromised bounty, that the same might be ready as a matter of bounty, and not of <u>extortion</u>**. In other words, Paul didn't want to force gain from the Corinthians by putting them in a position where they had to give because the Scripture commanded them to give. He called it extortion. Some Bible versions use the word "covetousness" there, but according to the numeric pattern, the correct word is "extortion." It's using your position to manipulate people out of their money. I learned that if you have a need, bring it to God. You just ask God and that's the way of faith. Don't be telling everybody your needs. You are putting yourself into a position of being an extortionist and manipulating people, like a lot of religions and a lot of the religious leaders do. God's not pleased with that!

So here I was. I didn't take up collections, didn't take any government money, didn't command the tithe, didn't make people pay. "Freely you received, freely give," the Bible says. I just freely gave and didn't tell people my needs, and I was put in this position of being in a wilderness, trusting in God. Since I didn't talk about money, there were actually people I had ministered to for months and months who would come along and ask me, "By the way, David, how do you make your living?" They didn't even know. I just don't talk about it. I figured God's people hear so much of this manipulation that they need an example. They need to <u>not</u> hear all this begging which brings disrepute to the Gospel. Jesus sent out the disciples without their own way of providing for themselves. **(1Ti.5:18) ... *The laborer is worthy of his hire*.** In other words, God said, "I'm going to take care of you." **(Mat.10:8) *Heal the sick, raise the dead, cleanse the lepers, cast out demons: <u>freely ye received, freely give</u>. (9) <u>Get you no gold, nor silver, nor brass in your purses</u>; (10) <u>no wallet for your journey, neither two coats</u>, <u>nor shoes</u>, <u>nor staff</u>: <u>for the laborer is worthy of his food</u>.*** "I'm going to take care of you." And I tell you, I have found over the years, since I've been in the full-time ministry, that God's <u>never</u> failed to take care of us.

Now, we haven't lived richly because I don't believe in that, personally. I believe everyone needs to sacrifice, to live a sacrificial life. We're not here to please ourselves or our flesh; we're here to please the Lord. This old man doesn't <u>need</u> everything he <u>wants</u>! **(Php.4:19) *And my God shall supply every need of yours according to his riches in glory in Christ Jesus.*** A need is a need and we do have needs. God knows it and He will provide them. In fact, He'll even provide our wants sometimes. We can ask and we can receive because He is a very good and generous God. He gives us richly everything that we need. When I first started learning how to walk with the Lord, I had plenty of income, but I didn't keep it, so I was in a wilderness basically of my own making. After we moved to Florida, about the end of the first year, we ran out of the money that we had. Of course, we gave to people's needs all that time. We met the needs that we saw because we weren't saving our money or anything, but within about a year we had run out of everything. Well, we were learning to walk by faith and we lived basically on the edge of a cliff, and like the eagles that live on the side of the cliff, we always saw the edge. We couldn't trust in our money in the bank because the Lord didn't give us a whole bunch of money to put in the bank. He wanted us to walk by faith. **(Heb.10:38) *But my righteous one <u>shall live by faith</u>: And if he shrink back, my soul hath no pleasure in him.*** He taught us to live by faith, day-by-day. **(Mat.6:34) *Be not therefore anxious for the morrow: for the morrow will be anxious for***

itself. Sufficient unto the day is the evil thereof. We learned how not to worry about tomorrow.

As we gave what we had, God multiplied it and that's the way God brought us through. He taught us to give what we had, even if we didn't have enough to meet our own bills that we had at the end of the month. Many times, the Lord would tell me to "Go and give what you have" and yet it wouldn't leave me any money to meet my bills, if I gave it. But I knew that God said, **(Luk.6:38) *Give, and it shall be given unto you; good measure, pressed down, shaken together, running over, shall they give into your bosom. For with what measure ye mete it shall be measured to you again.*** And so I gave. We gave out of our need many, many times, but the Lord never, ever failed us. We came up to the edge of the cliff, but we never fell off. God always took care of us and it was fun watching God come through, one way and then another, because we didn't have a large income. We always walked by faith. He took care of our bodies and the Lord always healed us. Of course, He always did it before then, but He always healed us when we stood by faith, when we endured the trial. The Lord took care of things that would normally break. We prayed for our vehicles and God healed them because we didn't want to waste any of our precious income on things like that. So we would pray over our cars, our water pumps and so on and God would fix them, folks. God would fix them!

When you're in a position in the wilderness of being weak, that's where God is strong. "His power is made perfect in weakness." So we got to see many, many miracles like that. I've forgotten more miracles than many people ever see. I remember one time I decided, "Well, I'm going to plant a little garden," but somewhere back in my mind I was thinking, "I'll kind of help God out." So I planted some tomatoes in five-gallon buckets because our yard was overshadowed by these great big oak trees and I needed to move the plants around a bit to keep them in the sun. I put these buckets out there and, sure enough, the tomato plants sprouted and grew really well. They blossomed and produced lots of tomatoes. Then, right about the time the tomatoes started turning the right color, the birds came and just plundered them until they were completely gone. It was a miracle of God. I thought, "Wow! That's awesome!" And then the Lord spoke to me. He said, "I didn't call you here to plant tomatoes. I called you here to study the Word and to share with My people, and you'd best be getting about the business that I sent you to do." I said, "Yes, Sir! Thank You, Lord!" Well, I gave up on the tomato idea and you know what happened? God spoke to a lady about that time. She didn't know anything about this situation because I didn't tell people about these kind of things, but she knew us. She went to a local farm where you pick your own tomatoes and while she was out there, the Lord spoke to her. He told her, "I want you to pick a couple of sacks of tomatoes and bring them to David." And I'm talking about big sacks of beautiful, vine-ripened beefsteak tomatoes. So she showed up right after this situation with the Lord and she and I had a really good laugh about it. I know the Lord was showing me, "Look, son, I can take care of that. I can take care of you. You just take care of Me. You just take care of My children and I'll take care of you! You just be about your Father's business." **(Mat.6:33) *But seek ye first***

his kingdom, and his righteousness; and all these things shall be added unto you. He was teaching me, "Don't you worry about the supply; I'll take care of that."

I remember when the new Chevrolet station wagon that the Lord had given me had maybe 35,000 or 40,000 miles on it, I found out about "Slick 50," an automotive lubricant, and I was really sold on it. I'd seen a demonstration of an engine running on Slick 50 and, after dumping all the oil out, the thing kept running. I said, "Wow! This is a really good lubricant." You know, it was a really awesome demonstration, so I wanted to put some of that in my car, even though I felt like the Lord really just wanted me to trust in Him for that car, to keep the engine running and keep it in good shape and so on. But I put Slick 50 in there and, actually, I put it in there before they recommended it. They recommend that you get some miles on the car because they say you can break rings if you put it in there with the engine too tight and it's too tight when it's new and only at 35,000 or 40,000 miles. Anyway, after I got some of this stuff and put it in there, we were called to Texas to preach in an assembly over there. So we got all the kids in the car and we got out on the road, and I remember looking up in the rearview mirror and seeing this cloud of smoke pouring out the back of my car. I said, "What's wrong? This is a new car! Why would this be happening?" I got out and checked the PCV, checked to see if it was overfilled, checked everything, but it wasn't any of the simple things that could normally cause the crankcase to suck oil over into the combustion chamber. Well, knowing a little bit about engines as I did, I realized I had busted some rings. And so, here we were. We had to make it from Florida all the way to Texas and preach, stay a week and then come back. I poured a quart of oil in that thing and commanded that engine to be healed in the name of Jesus. I think I ended up pouring about two quarts of oil in before it stopped using it and it never gave us a bit more trouble. It wasn't over-filled either. I'm telling you, I had checked everything; I knew it wasn't over-filled and it wasn't the PCV plugged-up. Of course, this was a new engine, so it had just broken some rings and God fixed that engine. He put that thing back together. And for as long as we had that car, we never had a bit more trouble with the rings or the engine. It never used anymore oil. It was just an awesome thing that God did! I was depending on <u>my idea</u> about how God was going to preserve this engine, but God wouldn't have it. His power was made perfect in <u>my</u> weakness.

And there were many other educational lessons the Lord gave me. I got to see instant miracles of commanding water pump seals to stop leaking in the name of Jesus and God just sealed them up, and commanding alternators to be healed and God would heal them, and things like that. I called it "healing" because early in my Christian walk, I figured if God can heal a body, He can heal an engine. Or He can heal a washing machine, or He can heal a refrigerator, or He can heal an air conditioner, or whatever. I would pray over things like that and God would heal them. I always just called it healing. I remember we bought a brand new washing machine because we basically gave away the washer and the dryer, refrigerator, and all those kind of appliances; we gave them away with the house. So we came to Florida and bought a new washing machine. It's very sandy and my kids were always out in the sand, and walking and tracking it into the house. And if you get a lot of sand in the water pump seal, the seal will go out. That's what happened. The water pump's seal went out on this thing and we had a brother in the small assembly that we had who found out about it. He said, "I just went through George Stone. It's a local technical vocation school. I can take this washing machine over there and we can train on it. We'll fix it and bring it back and all it will cost you is parts." I said, "That's great!" I was in the position where I needed it fixed. Now I'd prayed over washing machines and I even had my children pray over washing machines before and God fixed them. I sent my two oldest boys to pray over our washing machine before we left Louisiana. It wouldn't run and we couldn't make it run. They laid hands on it and commanded it to run in Jesus' name and that thing took off, and we never had anymore trouble with it. So we did those kind of things and we liked doing them, but the brother wanted to train on it, so I sent him on off with it.

He called me the next day and said, "Well, we got it fixed and the parts are only $70." He was going to bring it by that night, but I didn't have the money to pay for the parts. As a matter of fact, I had only $20 at the time. Then, suddenly, it came to me, as I was standing in front of the picture window in our house. I pointed at the mailbox and said, "$50 is coming in that mailbox today!" That's just what came into my mind; it just came right out of my mouth. Well, we weren't used to getting money in the mail. We were used to getting money from individuals who would offer it to us. So, after the mailman came through, I walked out to the mailbox and, sure enough, there was an envelope in there from a brother who had moved from up north. I opened the envelope and there was a check in it for $50! I had no idea it was coming, other than speaking the Word, and then the Lord impressed me to look at the postmark on the envelope. It was postmarked two months before this day. It had been hung up in the mail for two months, waiting on me to say, "$50 is coming in that mailbox today." It had been floating around for two months! And the letter said, "It's past midnight, but the Lord won't let me go to bed until I write this check and get it in the mail." I thought, "Lord, You did that just to show me that You can coordinate things perfectly on time." It was an emergency for this guy to get it in the mail, so it could float around out there for two months and finally show up at my mailbox the exact day I had to have it. You know, <u>we have an omnipotent God</u>, folks! He can meet out needs anytime, anyway. He's looking for somebody to speak the word of faith; that's what He's waiting on -- somebody to speak the word of faith. Well, I got the washing machine and paid the brother right on time.

After a few years, the washing machine started leaking again, but this time the Lord wanted me to do it the easy way, so I did. I commanded that thing to be healed in the name of Jesus and God healed it. And, you know, that was kind of a trial because a few months later, my wife told me, "This washing machine is leaking again." I said, "No, it's not." And in a day or two it wasn't leaking anymore. Then a month or two later, when my wife went back to the laundry area, she said, "Hey, this washing machine is leaking a bit again. I see a little dampness on the floor." I said, "No, it's not." And you know what?

The Lord sealed it up after that and we never had anymore trouble with that washing machine. But it was getting kind of old and I asked the Lord for another one and what happened is astounding. I mean, the washing machine was still holding up and everything; I just asked the Lord to give me another one. Well, a neighbor lady who had a Cadillac drove up in her garage and didn't stop in time. In the front of her garage was her washer and dryer. She drove up in her garage and hit her brand new washing machine. So her husband got the insurance company to buy her a new washing machine. And one day he said to me, "David, I have a washing machine over here that's brand new. The only thing is, the box is wrinkled on it a little bit. Will you come over and look at it?" Sure enough, when I went over and looked at it, there was nothing wrong with the washing machine. Only the box was wrinkled where his wife's bumper hit it and he was just going to haul this thing off. He asked me, "Would you like to have this thing?" And I said, "Well, sure! I would like to have it." So we ended up with a new free washing machine. God has so many ways of coming through for you.

The Lord taught me, **(Mat.9:29) ... According to your faith be it done unto you.** It's however you can believe that God can do it. I asked God to heal my teeth one time and He did. He didn't put fillings in; He healed them. I had two molars with terrible cavities and He healed them.

We prayed for our neighbor. She asked for a filling. We prayed and God put a filling in her tooth. But I asked God to <u>heal</u> my teeth. It's according to your faith. "According to your faith be it done unto you"; it's however you can believe.

We've prayed over air conditioners. I had a neighbor who couldn't afford to get his air conditioner worked on and I said, "Well, let's just pray over it and command it to be healed." And we commanded it to be healed and God healed it. One time, when my own air conditioner had gone out, even though I didn't know much about air conditioners, I walked out there to look at it. I took the cover off of it and I looked around for a burnt wire or something simple because I'm not all that big on electrical things, but I didn't know what to do with it. So I walked back into the house and my wife said, "Well, what are you going to do about the air conditioner?" I said, "Nothing. God's going to send somebody to fix it." She said, "Oh, yeah?" and I said, "Yep."

And after a few minutes, I looked out my back window and my neighbor from behind the house was walking through my yard. So I walked back out there. Now this guy was very introverted. I'd never been able to strike up a conversation with him because he just wasn't a talkative guy at all. If he answered me, it was one or two words and that was it. He really wasn't fond of me whatsoever, but anyway, here's this guy walking through my yard, so I went out there to see what it was all about. He said, "I saw you looking at your air conditioner. I just went through school to learn how to work on air conditioners." That was already more than he'd ever said to me in his whole life. Then he asked, "Would you like me to look at it? It would be a good time for me to use some of my training." I said, "Well, sure!" He went right to the problem and told me, "All you have to do is go get this part right here." It was a capacitor. I told him, "Well, thank you!" He said, "No problem." He was just as joyous as could be. So I went and got the capacitor, and stuck it in and, sure enough, that was the problem; it cranked right up and everything worked fine. Later, his wife called me and asked, "What did he want?" I said, "Well, my air conditioner broke and he was kind enough to come over and show me what was wrong with it." And she replied, "He's never done anything like that for anybody. I've never seen him do something like that." I answered, "Well, I was believing God to send someone to fix my air conditioner for me." And she agreed with me, "Well, it had to be God!" I said, "Well, God sent him." God worked in this man a desire and a will to come over. God came through! He fixed our air conditioner and it was very, very cheap for the part and my neighbor didn't want any money.

You know, when you're in that position of being weak, God just performs miracles. I've prayed over my refrigerator, our children, our teeth; it doesn't make any difference. When you're in a position of weakness, folks, you're in the wilderness and sometimes you just put yourself there by obedience to God's Word. If He tells you, "All things whatsoever ye pray and ask for, believe that ye receive them, and ye shall have them," do you really believe that? Or do you believe it passed away with the apostles? Well, if you really believe it, you won't worry about going anywhere, you won't even worry about storing up your treasures on earth for a "rainy day." People used to call it "storing up for a rainy day." Well, let me tell you what the Lord taught me about rainy days. If you store up for a rainy day, a rainy day's coming. If you store up in case you might need it, you'll need it! If you trust in insurance instead of assurance, you'll need it! But if you don't worry about it, if you just "seek ye first His Kingdom," when the day comes that you have a need, God will meet it. <u>Trust in His assurance</u>! His assurance is in His Word. He will meet your need. He'll do it miraculously. He's done it for us many, many times over many years. It really didn't matter what the need was. Our tires seemed to last forever. If something went wrong with our car, we would pray for our car. If you're thinking, "Well, David, are you sure you weren't causing your children to go through rather harsh trials?" My kids never lacked for anything. I prayed with them and everything they prayed for, toys or whatever, would come miraculously.

One time, my daughter came to me and she said, "Daddy, the swimming pool is rotted and it doesn't hold water anymore." That was when we had a little wading pool. I said, "Now, you know where we get swimming pools, don't you?" She said, "Yeah." So we prayed and agreed that God was going to send her a swimming pool. Now, at that time, my little boys had their own business. They would go out and cut grass and they were just happy as a lark because God would give them all the money they needed for toys and things that they wanted. And so they cut grass for this lady who lived about four or five blocks down the road. Then one day we got a knock on the door and it was this lady, whom we had never actually met. She said, "I'm looking for a couple of little boys who came down and cut my grass." My son Nathan poked his head around the corner and she said, "Oh, I see I've found the right place." I guess the boys had told her where they lived. Anyway, she said, "Listen, if you would come down and cut my grass again, I have a swimming pool I'd like to give you that I bought for exercising in and I'm not going to use it." This was only a week after we had agreed for my daughter's swimming pool. And, as we found out, it was one of those four-foot deep pools with the filter, ladder and everything. Well, the boys went down there and cut her grass a couple of times and she just gave us this brand new pool that was still in the box. We set it up and, of course, they <u>all</u> had fun with that for a few years and my daughter got to see God come through for her. We didn't have any money to buy a swimming pool. My boys got to see God come through and answer her prayers, too. They all got to see over and over that God would answer our prayers. I had told her, "You know, honey, you know where we go to get these things. We go to God, right?" And she had answered, "Yeah." So we joined hands and prayed the prayer of agreement. **(Mat.18:19) Again I say unto you, that if two of you shall agree on earth as touching anything that they shall ask, it shall be done for them of my Father who is in heaven.** We prayed the prayer of agreement and God came through a week later.

I remember when my boys were young and they decided that they wanted a certain motorcycle. I said, "Okay, let's pray." And, you know what? I don't think it was two weeks before they had that motorcycle. A neighbor who lived behind us and worked on them had one in his yard. He offered them a really good deal on it, a deal they couldn't refuse. And they didn't go around telling people about their needs; they did the same thing we did. We prayed, we believed God, we confessed it before Him, we thanked Him for it and so on. God's just awesome, folks! I tell you, you can't out-give God! You can "make a living by giving." I just pray that the Lord will encourage you and fill you with His faith, and boldness to walk by faith, because there are days coming down the road when that's going to be necessary. God bless you and walk with Jesus. God bless you!

CHAPTER 19

Provision: Receiving it in the Wilderness!

Greetings, saints! God bless you. Thank you for joining us. Let's go to the Lord and ask for His grace today. Dear Father, Lord, we praise You. We give thanks unto You for Your mercy toward us. Lord, we ask You to prepare us for the days to come. We ask that Your mercy, in the form of grace for faith, is poured out upon us, that we might walk in the steps of Jesus Christ; that we might be a witness to this world unto Him; that we might be called Christians truly by this world that looks upon us. Lord, we ask in Jesus name, that You give us the grace to stand as the sons of God and to manifest Jesus Christ in this world, and to do Your work to finish Your Kingdom, Lord. We know that once again, Lord, You're raising up Your New Jerusalem Kingdom and raising up new leadership for Your people. We know that, once again, Lord, You're going to cause those people to walk in the steps of the Lord Jesus Christ and He, in them, is going to be a witness to this world. He, in them, is going to deliver this fallen creation, that is, the elect of this world. Thank You, Father, for this opportunity for us to come together and study Your Word, and just enjoy You, Lord. Thank You! Thank You! Amen.

I've been talking about how we can obtain the supernatural provision of God in these coming days. I've been talking about the real Good News of what the Lord has already accomplished for us and will accomplish through us. What we have by faith <u>will</u> be manifested, folks; it will be manifested before this world and it will be manifested in God's elect. Many times, the Lord brings His people to a state of weakness, so that they have to put their faith in Him, for His power is made perfect in weakness. ***(2Co.12:9) And he hath said unto me, My grace is sufficient for thee: <u>for [my] power is made perfect in weakness</u>. Most gladly therefore will I rather glory in my weaknesses, that the power of Christ may rest upon me.*** And the Lord is bringing about a situation in this world whereby God's people will be very weak and incapable by any strength of man, any wisdom of man, any money, any political power, or any such thing from saving themselves. The Lord is bringing us into this situation, because the righteous "shall live by faith." ***(Heb.10:38) But <u>my righteous one shall live by faith</u>: And if he shrink back, my soul hath no pleasure in him.*** I believe that we're coming to a war here very quickly, a war and another strike on the United States that will motivate the people of the United States to do things like they did after 9/11. We're going to see a terrible war in the Middle East that's going to bring about a situation where the world is going to fear. The world is going to be willing to put together this New World Order, which is already designed and ready, waiting in the wings. But people have not yet been willing to give up their sovereignty, nor their benefits, in order to see this thing happen. Well, it's coming. It's on its way and a wilderness is going to come from this. There are going to be natural catastrophes at the same time and between them and the war, the economy will collapse. We're headed toward a real wilderness, folks. God is going to bring forth earthquakes, volcanoes and tsunamis, even hitting America with tsunamis and great shakings.

All of this, I believe, is to bring us to the place of our wilderness experience, a place of weakness where God can show Himself strong on our behalf and be our Savior. The Lord told me many years ago that He was bringing me through a wilderness, so that I could tell His people that He still supplies there. I shared with you in the previous chapter how the Lord wonderfully supplied for my family a house and a car, at no expense to us, when He moved us to Florida. It was our prayer of agreement that the Lord would supply these things because everything we had was paid for, but He told us to give it away. We asked the Lord to supply these things so that we wouldn't be in debt because the Lord had taught us that He didn't want us to be in debt. The only thing He didn't supply at that time was a visible means of support. We had an <u>invisible</u> means of support, but we didn't have a <u>visible</u> means of support. And to make things even better, the Lord had given me a conviction that He didn't want me to ask for money in this ministry that He was putting me in. He never had let me do it before and He wouldn't let me take any government benefits or anything like that, either -- not that I ever had any desire to. I didn't take up collections, and I didn't take up offerings for myself. I didn't reveal my needs to people. All these restrictions put me into a wilderness because, once again, there was no planned visible means of support. That put me in a position where I was trusting God, month-by-month, to be my Savior and He didn't let me down! It was a wonderful experience and I wouldn't have traded it for anything in the world.

You know, our God is "the same yesterday and today, and forever." *(Heb.13:5) Be ye free from the love of money; content with such things as ye have: for himself hath said, I will in no wise fail thee, neither will I in any wise forsake thee.* Meaning, of course, that you don't have to store up and put your trust in the things of this world, the money of this world, because God said He's going to take care of us. *(Heb.13:6) So that with good courage we say, The Lord is my helper; <u>I will not fear</u>* (When you get into a position where you have no way to provide for yourself, nothing that you can see around you that you can trust in, you're tempted to fear, but God comforts us that He will in no wise fail us, nor forsake us.)*: What shall man do unto me? (Heb.13:7) Remember them that had the rule over you, men that spake unto you the word of God; and considering the issue of their life, imitate their faith.* We have just such demonstrations in the Scriptures of men who had the rule over us, our spiritual forefathers, the apostles and the people who followed them. These people gave us a demonstration of what it is to walk by faith. They gave us a demonstration of what it is to lose any kind of ambition in this world. They showed us what it is to have no love of money and to have no trust in the things of this world. This is what God loves in His people and He will have it again. And then, God comforts us with this fact: *(Heb.13:8) Jesus Christ [is] the same yesterday and to-day, [yea] and for ever.* Wow! So the Jesus Who's with <u>us</u> is just like the Jesus Who was with <u>them</u>. We have a mighty Savior and He is with us all the time. We have to walk by faith.

We can't walk by sight. They saw Him, they touched Him and they saw a demonstration of His power. We read the Scriptures and we see these things. We see that they have been passed on to His apostles and we who believe the Word of God are beginning to see these signs, wonders and miracles in our day. We are encouraged that, no matter where we go, we don't have to trust in the world. We have a mighty Savior! "Jesus Christ is the same yesterday and today, yea and forever."

The same Jesus Who walked with them walks with us. Where can we possibly go to get out from under His comforting hands? Where can we go that He can't reach down and touch us? He asked, **(Isa.50:2) ... Is my hand shortened at all, that it cannot redeem? or have I no power to deliver?** Well, is His arm so short that He can't save? The Bible has an answer to that question. And every time I study this text, I receive a little more understanding from it and the Lord shows me how it applies in my own life. Our Jesus is the same Jesus Who multiplied the fishes and the loaves, and He's just as much with us as He was with them. Look at what happened with His disciples: **(Mat.16:5) And the disciples came to the other side and forgot to take bread.** Notice here, they had no bread whatsoever. Now they had known this Jesus Who twice before had multiplied the fishes and the loaves, but here they didn't have anything to multiply. They had never yet known a Jesus Who would multiply something out of nothing, but the Lord was about to give them a revelation here. **(Mat.16:6) And Jesus said unto them, Take heed and beware of the leaven of the Pharisees and Sadducees.** What did that have to do with the disciples forgetting to bring bread with them? Well, they were counting upon what they could supply, what they could provide, to be their confidence. And He's warning them to beware of the "leaven," which He later tells them is the teaching of the Pharisees and the Sadducees. So what was it about the Pharisees and Sadducees that the disciples needed to beware of? It was that they taught salvation by works. They taught salvation by the works of the Law, salvation by self-effort. That's what the Law was all about. God had given them the Law and if they didn't obey it or failed to obey it by their own effort, then they had to have a sacrifice. Jesus wanted His disciples not to depend upon themselves, nor their own supply, nor anything they could do to save themselves. And here they were without any bread whatsoever. They had known a Jesus who could multiply the fishes and the loaves, but you have to have fishes and loaves before you can multiply them.

So Jesus warned them that salvation is not by their works, it is by God's promise. **(Gal.3:19) What then is the law? It was added because of transgressions, till the seed should come to whom the promise hath been made.... (29) And if ye are Christ's, then are ye Abraham's seed, heirs according to promise.** We are the seed of the promise that the New Testament said was coming. **(Mat.16:7) And they reasoned among themselves, saying, We took no bread. (8) And Jesus perceiving it said, O ye of little faith, why reason ye among yourselves, because ye have no bread? (9) Do ye not yet perceive, neither remember the five loaves of the five thousand, and how many baskets ye took**

up? Well, it happened to be 12 baskets that they picked up afterward. Five loaves fed 5000 and there were 12 baskets left over. ***(Mat.16:10) Neither the seven loaves of the four thousand, and how many baskets ye took up?*** There were seven baskets that time. So, they had seven loaves and they fed 4000, but there were only seven baskets left over. Notice the difference in the miracle here. When they put in less of their own supply, when they put in five loaves, God fed 5000 and there was much more left over. When they put in more of their own supply, when they put in seven loaves, it only fed 4000. The more they put in, the less of a miracle God did. The less God saved! The less God provided! And there was less left over! See, the more of their own works they put in, the less of God's works were put in. God said His power is made perfect in our weakness, so the weaker they were, the bigger the miracle. ***(Mat.16:11) How is it that ye do not perceive that I spake not to you concerning bread? But beware of the leaven of the Pharisees and Sadducees. (12) Then understood they that he bade them not beware of the leaven of bread, but of the teaching of the Pharisees and Sadducees.*** In other words, they got the revelation that the Lord was saying, "It isn't by your works. The more of your works you put in, the less of My works will be put in."

The Lord showed me in my own life what happens when you come to the place that you have nothing to multiply. According to the relationship the Lord is showing here, between the five loaves and the 5000, and the seven loaves and the 4000, the <u>less you put in, the greater the miracle</u>. Well, I had this happen to me. For instance, when the Lord sent us into the wilderness, He wouldn't let us tell anybody our needs. And we were very careful not to let people understand what we were doing. Most of the time, God provided for us well and He blessed us, although we were always tried. But there were times when we ran out of everything and that's when we were tried the most. It did happen a few times that we ran out of everything in the house to eat, for instance. One of those times, I remember that the last thing we had that we could make in the whole house was a large pot of spaghetti. My wife cooked it up on the stove and when she was through, we ate about half of that pot. And, of course, we prayed over it, we blessed it and we commanded it to be multiplied because it was the last thing we had in the house to eat. So when we were through eating, we just took the whole pot and shoved it into the refrigerator. We didn't have much else in there to get in its way. And the next day, that was what we pulled out to eat. Mary pulled the pot out of the refrigerator, set it on the stove and lifted the lid off of it. Both of us were looking into the pot when she lifted the lid and the pot was full again. Everything that we had left from the day before was multiplied. God doubled what was in there. Here we were looking at this and I said to Mary, "This pot was down to here yesterday!" She said, "Yeah, I know!" Praise God! We were having a good time in the Lord! So the Lord supplied again. Of course, after that, the Lord met our needs many more times. That was an instance where God multiplied what we put in.

Then there was another time where we were just like the disciples, where we didn't have any "bread." We didn't have anything to multiply. But, you see, the relationship here is, the less you put in, the more God puts in. The more you're weak, the more God is strong. Why is that? It's because God has made the promise that He's going to supply your every need; therefore, it doesn't matter how much you put in; He has to make up the difference. **(Php.4:19) And my God shall supply every need of yours according to his riches in glory in Christ Jesus.** He's going to supply your every need "according to His riches in glory." You want to see a bigger miracle? Walk out into the wilderness, folks! The wilderness is a place of the lack of your own supply and we were in that place where we didn't have any "bread"; we had nothing! My wife was very ingenious and she had cooked up the last things we could find around the house to throw together, though some of it didn't taste all that great. But, we were trusting the Lord, we were confessing that the Lord was going to come through, confessing that He was going to miraculously supply for us. So my wife asked me, "What are we going to do?" I said, "Well, I think you ought to set the table," and that's what she did. Then she, our five young children and I sat around the table with a bunch of empty plates staring back at us, and I prayed a prayer. It was just what came to my mind. I hadn't rehearsed it or thought about it whatsoever; I just knew I was going to pray. So I sat down and I said, "Well, Lord, You sent us here. Now we're asking You to fill our plates or fill our tummies." That was all there was to it. I didn't get anymore out of my mouth. But it was a prayer of faith because, when you know God sent you and you know He's supported you with everything you can see in the Word of God, when you know that you've obeyed Him with everything you can see that He's commanded you, then you know you're in right standing for His benefits. Not that you have to be perfectly obedient to receive something from God. He is merciful and He doesn't want any of His children to starve before they grow up, so that's not the foundation of our benefits. The foundation of our benefits is grace. But we had been obedient. The Lord had sent us and He had made us promises of provision, and He hadn't failed us up until that time.

So I prayed that prayer and my oldest son, who could eat like a horse, said, "Dad, I'm full. I don't need to eat." And he stood up and walked away from the table. I looked around at my other children and they were all of the same opinion. They started getting up and walking away from the table, saying, "I don't need to eat." And as I got my attention off of them, I realized that I wasn't hungry anymore either. I realized that I was full, too! That was an instance where we just didn't have anything to multiply, but it didn't make any difference, since God said He would supply our every need. He had to make up the difference, so we got to see a bigger miracle. The wilderness is a place of miracles -- mighty, mighty miracles! That's where we're headed, folks. The whole world, the economy, everything is going down the drain and God's people are going to learn to walk by faith because that's what God loves. **(Heb.10:38) But my righteous one shall live by <u>faith</u>: And if he shrink back, my soul hath no pleasure in him. (11:6) And without faith it is impossible to be well-pleasing [unto him;] for <u>he that cometh to God must believe that he is, and [that] he is a rewarder of them that seek after him</u>.** The Lord desires faith in His people. He says the righteous shall live from faith. Now, in order to live from faith, you have to get to a place where you have to go to God by faith to get your needs met. You have to get to a place where you have to depend upon Him. And He is mighty! He is mighty to bring these things to pass. He's going to teach us what it is to be disciples of Jesus Christ and what it is to live well-pleasing unto Him. We trust Him for righteousness and He imputes righteousness to us. We trust Him for our provision and He provides. We trust Him for protection and He does that, too. There isn't anything that God won't supply to meet our needs and so we trust in those past tense promises that we call the real Good News, the real Gospel!

Well, there was a time where God tried us a little more than that because, you see, over all those years of raising our children, my children had never missed a meal; they'd never had the utilities disconnected. The Lord had been faithful. And I'm not saying that the Lord can't try you even beyond that point, to see if you're going to continue to obey and submit to Him. I don't know where the Lord can take people; I just know where He's taken me. At any rate, once again, this was a time when we had run out of everything. I'm not trying to tell you that this happened all the time, because it didn't, but this was another time that we had run out of every bit of food in the house. And yet, we just continued having Bible studies with people, but we didn't put out a "tin cup" or "pass the hat," or do anything like that. There were people who, after meeting with us for months, would ask, "David, how do you make your living?" They didn't know and we didn't say; we didn't talk about those things. We just studied the Bible. We just shared the Bible. We just shared the Word; that's all we did. **(Luk.6:38) Give, and it shall be given unto you; good measure, pressed down, shaken together, running over, shall they give into your bosom. For with what measure ye mete it shall be measured to you again.** That's what the Bible commands. There's to be no manipulation. There's to be no tear-jerking, no crying-on-the-shoulder, none of these things to manipulate. But we'd run out of everything. This was the first time and the only time ever in all of those years that my kids had missed a meal. The only time they ever fasted was that particular day and my wife had prayed, "Lord, I'm asking that You show them the end of this trial." And, wow! God answered that! Let me tell you what happened. A lady called us and said, "I'm leaving town and before I go, I'd like to cook a meal and bring it to you guys." Well, she didn't know we were out of everything in the whole house.

So the lady came over to our house in the morning with a couple of bags of dinner rolls. That's all, just a couple bags of dinner rolls, because she was going to bring the meal for that evening, but for some reason, she showed up in the morning with the dinner rolls. Well, she set them on the counter. We didn't say a word, nobody said anything, but my kids were all looking over there at those dinner rolls because they had missed a meal. They were all looking at those dinner rolls when she left. And my wife commented to me, "That's exactly what I'd prayed. God let them see the end of this trial." So since there were two bags of these rolls, we told them, "Each of you take a roll out and eat a roll," and so we "fudged" a little bit on the fast. Anyway, the lady showed up that evening with a real nice meal and we thanked her, and we never said a word, even afterwards, about the shape we were in. You know, folks, I've fasted for weeks on purpose and it's not a bad thing. It's actually very, very good for you, both physically and spiritually. It didn't hurt my kids a bit; there was no child abuse going on there. The Lord brought us through this trial and He gave us the answer. And, of course, after this, the Lord supplied our needs, but we got to see the end of it and the answer came through. Praise God! He tempted us even beyond that point of missing a meal that one time, but He answered.

Quite often, we prayed for certain things and told nobody, told not a soul, not even the kids. Mary and I would pray and we wouldn't tell a soul, and the very things we'd prayed for would arrive. I remember one time we were very, very specific. I believe that we should be specific with God because then we give Him an opportunity to do things that are miraculous and provide a great demonstration of Who He is. God wants to demonstrate His power. He wants to make His power known, Scripture says. God hardened Pharaoh's heart so that He had to do wondrous miracles to set the people of God free from Egypt. God did it on purpose to prove His power. So sometimes when we needed things, even if we had the money, we would ask God to do it, just to see Him do a miracle. In this particular instance, my wife and I prayed in the morning for mayonnaise, cheese and poultry; that's what we prayed for. And between that day and the next morning, all that stuff came to us. One lady called me and said, "David, I'm on my way out of town and I have this great big jar of mayonnaise in my refrigerator and I just don't want it to go to waste." You know, what God puts in people's minds doesn't have to be reasonable; it just has to work, right? And I thought to myself, "Mayonnaise doesn't go bad that quickly." But this was in her mind, so she brought over this great big jar of mayonnaise. **(Php.2:13) For it is God who worketh in you both to will and to work, for his good pleasure.** It doesn't even have to be reasonable; even when He does it through the lost, it doesn't have to be reasonable. So she brought over this jar of mayonnaise. Then, the next morning, somebody else just happened by and they brought us cheese and a turkey. The Lord supplied mayonnaise, cheese and poultry -- everything we had prayed for.

I don't even remember most of the times the Lord did this, but the Lord constantly did this for us because we prayed. We did what Jesus said: **(Mar.11:24) Therefore I say unto you, All things whatsoever ye pray and ask for, believe that ye received them, and ye shall have them.** You know, that's how you enter into the "rest" of God because you believe you received. You believe He's heard. You believe the answer is finished; it's done and so you don't have to worry about it anymore. You believe you've received, you cease from your works and you enter into the rest. That's our New Testament spiritual Sabbath. So we learned to enter into the rest; we prayed for everything we needed. You know, if people would just pray before automatically going to their money, many times they would find out that they don't have to spend their money. Your money belongs to the Lord; we've already discussed that. We have to renounce ownership of everything we have, according to what Jesus said to His disciples, so we need to be good stewards. Anyway, we prayed for coats for the kids and God would come through with the coats; some hand-me-downs would be given to us in perfect shape. We would pray for food and we would pray for miracles that the electric bill wouldn't be high. We prayed over equipment constantly, over washers, dryers, refrigerators and air conditioners. We prayed over them and God would heal them.

There was one time I'll never forget because it was just an awesome thing the Lord did. My boys were going on a camping trip and they took the last bag of potato chips in the house. And my youngest daughter, Jennifer, ran into the washroom where Mary was and she said, "Oh, Mama! They're taking the last of the chips we have in the house! I want some potato chips!" So Mary told her, "Well, you know how to take care of that. You go pray," and Mary pushed her out the door. You know, my children had learned to walk by faith, they learned to pray. And before Jennifer got into the dining room, she had prayed. Well, right then someone knocked on the front door and before Jennifer went to the door to see who was there, she started shouting, "That's my potato chips! It's here! It's here! My potato chips are here!" And Mary came out of the washroom and put her hand over Jennifer's mouth, saying, "Hush! You don't even know who that is!" Well, we went to the door and there stood our neighbor, who lived back behind our house. The neighbors just loved the way Mary cooked cornbread, so she had cooked a pan of cornbread for the neighbor and he was returning the pan, which had aluminum foil over it. And, lo and behold, he walked in and he handed the pan to Jennifer. And when she peeled the foil off, there was a bag of potato chips! Praise be to God! God's awesome! Jennifer had said with her child's faith, "That's my potato chips! It's here! It's here! My potato chips are here!" You know, that's the kind of faith we have to have: the faith of a child. The faith of a child, "It's here! It's here!" And so the Lord did another awesome miracle, as He loves to do.

If you don't put yourself in a position of being weak or you're afraid to put yourself in a position of being weak, and you try to insulate yourself from any chance of coming into a position of weakness, you won't see miracles because you don't <u>need</u> a miracle. <u>You don't need miracles until you need miracles</u>. Therefore, you have to put yourself into a position to need a miracle. And if you just obey the Word of God, you'll end up getting into that position because the Word of God is <u>designed</u> to put you in a wilderness. We've studied that the Bible tells us not to store up our treasures on Earth, but to store them up in Heaven (Matthew 6:19-20). That doesn't leave you much to fall back on for a rainy day, does it? Many of you already know that whatever you put away for a rainy day, somehow gets eaten up when you have a rainy day. But what about the people who don't store up for a rainy day because they have the <u>assurance</u> of God, rather than the <u>insurance</u> of man? What do they do? Well, most often, nothing really happens to them. According to His promise, God has to supply their every need, so if something does happen, He has to miraculously meet that need. That is, He has to meet that need, if they are people who believe that He is *Jehovah-Jireh*, "The Lord, our Provider." You see, none of these promises in the Bible are automatic. They only happen for believers. So, number one, you have to be in a position to need. And, number two, you have to walk by faith. So these promises are for believers in need. You see, that's what the promises are there for.

"And my God shall supply every need of yours according to his riches in glory in Christ Jesus." When we studied the benefits of the Blood Covenant, we learned that when you make a blood covenant with someone, they are guaranteeing to meet your needs, should you come into a position of lack; they are guaranteeing to defend you against your enemies. All these things are actually what a blood covenant meant in those days. And, so, I put myself in that position quite often because I do believe.

I can remember one time I had to go to the Exxon refinery in Baton Rouge very early in the morning because I needed to set up something for the workers. It was a large refinery along the Mississippi River and it was about a 20-mile ride from where I lived. Well, I took off, planning to get some gas in my truck when I reached the interstate because I had no gas in my truck. I'd never been at the station there that early and I didn't realize that the station wouldn't be open yet. I would have had to wait until it was too late for me to get to the plant on time. I realized there wasn't any way I was going to get any gas, but it came into my heart, "Well, just go. Ask God to fill your tank and just go." That's what I did. I just got on the interstate and the tank was on empty. I had driven from my house to the gas station and, you know how gas gauges are -- sometimes they take a while to climb, but this time the gauge was where it was going to stay. So I got on the interstate and I just prayed, "God, I have to go to work. You know I have to be there, so I'm asking You to put gas in my tank." I prayed and I commanded it after I prayed. Then I watched the needle on the gas gauge just start climbing. It climbed and climbed and stopped short of being on full. I asked, "Lord, why didn't You fill my tank?" And the Lord said, "Well, I always give you what you need, not necessarily what you want, but what you need." I knew that was true because that's all I needed and I didn't fill the tank going there or coming back because I had plenty of gas in my tank.

But, other times, the Lord had me walk by total faith because the needle wouldn't move at all. It wouldn't show any gas in the tank at all. And I would be called upon to just keep on driving. One time, after we'd moved to Florida, I didn't have any gas for my tank and I didn't have any money to put gas in my tank, but everybody was calling upon me to do things for them. One of those people was Brother Curt. Curt had slipped off the road in his vehicle and he was stuck there. This was while I still had that big Chevrolet station wagon, which was just a big gas hog in the first place, but I had five kids I needed to cart around. So Curt called me and asked, "David, can you come pull me out?" I thought, "Well, I still don't have any gas in the car, but the Bible says, **(Mat.5:42) Give to him that asketh thee....**" That's the verse that came to me, so it didn't matter if I didn't have any gas. He just said <u>give</u>, so I jumped in the car and took off. I'd been driving the car for a week like that -- on empty. As a matter of fact, it was down <u>below</u> the empty mark, below the last line on the gauge but I just kept on driving it for a week like that. I didn't say a word to Curt. I kept on going like that, until the Lord supplied the money I needed to fill the tank. But God never gave me any encouragement in that whole trial. As far as seeing the gas gauge go up, I didn't see it. It didn't happen. I just drove it with the gas gauge on empty. The Lord wants to try you and He will. You can't put the rules on

Him. He doesn't always want to comfort you by what you see because He doesn't want you trusting in what you see. He wants you to trust in "Thus sayeth the Lord." He wants you to put your faith in what He said.

In the days to come, Christians are going to need to know that, although you may have a dead battery in your car, although you may have no gas in your tank, "Jesus Christ is the same yesterday and today, yea and forever." And He said, "I will in no wise fail thee, neither will I in any wise forsake thee." He is encouraging us to know that He's there all the time and He's the same with us as He was in those days. When He walked with those disciples, it didn't matter what the need was, He met it! He met it by the power of God and He met it through faith. And, today, He lives in us to do the same thing. Praise be to God! We just need to put our total trust in Him. ***(Psa.78:13) He clave the sea, and caused them to pass through*** (That was the Israelites when they were coming out of Egypt.)***; And he made the waters to stand as a heap. (14) In the day-time also he led them with a cloud, And all the night with a light of fire. (15) He clave rocks in the wilderness, And gave them drink abundantly as out of the depths.*** I don't know if you've ever seen the place, and it seems very likely that it is the place, where people claim the rocks brought forth the water out in the middle of the wilderness. It's very rocky territory and there's a hill there where water had actually come out of a crack in a rock on the <u>top</u> of this hill, way above ground level. This isn't the kind of ground that you can get water to travel through, but somehow, that water went up through that hill, came out of that rock on the top and washed all the way down the side of that hill. And here God tells you that it was a lot of water. You're talking about enough water for probably three or four million people, plus their livestock. So it wasn't just a little creek that we're talking about here; it was a lot of water! ***(Psa.78:15) He clave rocks in the wilderness, And gave them drink abundantly as out of the depths. (16) He brought streams also out of the rock, And caused waters to run down like rivers.*** There it is, "like rivers"! What's the point? The point is, "If I can bring you water out of a rock, I can get you water anywhere."

Remember, God did that for Sampson. When Sampson had finished a battle with the Philistines and he was about to die of thirst, the Lord brought forth water for him (Judges 15:14-19). ***(Psa.78:17) Yet went they on still to sin against him, To rebel against the Most High in the desert. (18) And they tempted God in their heart By asking food according to <u>their</u> desire.*** The Lord wanted to feed them with the manna, which was Jesus. Jesus said, ***(Joh.6:51)*** <u>***I am the living bread which came down out of heaven***</u>***: if any man eat of this bread, he shall live for ever: yea and the bread which I will give is my flesh, for*** <u>***the life of the world.***</u> Jesus was the Man Who came down out of Heaven Who gives life to the world. The actual word there is the word "man." "Manna" was a transliteration; the word is actually "man" and the "man" was Jesus Christ, <u>the Word of God</u>. He wanted to feed them with the Word of God, but they wanted flesh to eat. They wanted to partake of the flesh. They wanted to run after the flesh and God was angry because that was a type and shadow that He fulfilled through them for us. **(Psa.78:19) Yea, <u>they spake against God; They said, Can God prepare a table in the wilderness</u>?** Wow! God doesn't want to be questioned about that, does He? It's offensive to Him for you to question, "Can He do this? Can He meet my needs anywhere? Can He bring water out of a rock?" What <u>can't</u> He do, if He can bring water out of a rock? We shouldn't question God.

There are people who say, "Nah! That Red Sea was only a foot or so deep." They give all kinds of carnal reasons why God was able to do this miracle because they really don't believe in a God of miracles. They're very liberal in their interpretation of Scriptures and they don't have a childlike faith to believe exactly what it says. **(Psa.78:20) Behold, he smote the rock, so that waters gushed out, And streams overflowed; Can he give bread also? Will he provide flesh for his people? (21) Therefore the Lord heard, and was wroth** (The Lord was angry because they questioned His ability to provide for them.)**; And a fire was kindled against Jacob, And anger also went up against Israel; (22) Because they believed not in God, And trusted not in his salvation.** Do <u>we</u>? Do we believe in God? Do we trust in His salvation? He has promises to cover every possible lack you could conceivably have. Do we trust Him? Will we speak for Him? Will we confess Him before men, so that "the High Priest of our confession" (Hebrews 3:1) may confess us before the Father? Will we do that? **(Psa.78:23) Yet he commanded the skies above, And opened the doors of heaven; (24) And he rained down manna upon them to eat, And gave them food from heaven. (25) Man did eat the bread of the mighty: He sent them food to the full. (26) He caused the east wind to blow in the heavens; And by his power he guided the south wind. (27) He rained flesh also upon them as the dust.** This is awesome! He blew them with the east wind, then He blew them with the south wind and He brought those quail to those Israelites. God guided the winds to bring those quail to the Israelites. You wonder, when you read the story, "How could God have found that many quail?" **(Num.11:31) And there went forth a wind from the Lord, and brought quails from the sea** (He brought these quail all the way from the sea, out into the middle of the wilderness.)**, and let them fall by the camp, about a day's journey on this side, and a day's journey on the other side, round about the camp, and about two cubits above the face of the earth.** Wow! "A day's journey in every direction." That's a lot of quail, folks! He must have swept up every quail from all around that wilderness to bring it out there like that.

I used to be a big hunter before I came to the Lord. And if you go hunting, whether you're quail hunting or not, you can walk right up on a quail. They hunker down and they wait until you're a step from them, then they explode in a flurry of their wings. They are three or four times louder than any other bird when they take off. They just explode. And they scare you half to death because they do it right there at your feet. They are such a fat little bird that they have to flap their wings really fast in order to get off the ground. The name in Hebrew is *selav* and it has a meaning of "slowness in speed because of weight." That's the way they are, so they don't fly very fast. If you want to go hunting and you want to hit something, you go for quail. Quail are fat and dumpy, and they take off slowly, even though they're flapping their wings as fast as they can.

Well, it says the quail were "two cubits above the face of the earth" all around the camp, and you think, "That has to be wrong." No. God's never wrong. The Word is telling the truth here. I don't know whether the Lord had the quail multiplied greatly that year for that reason, but it doesn't make any difference. He did it. He supplied their need in a place where it was impossible. He did it with the east wind and He did it with the south wind. He swept them this way and then He swept them that way. And those little quails, if they went very far, were dead when they got there because a quail expends all of its energy just to stay up in the air. They don't fly very far when they do fly. God was keeping those quail up in the air and He swept them across that wilderness to the right and then north, and from the south. He swept them all the way out into the middle of that wilderness. Nothing can stop a God Who can bring water out of a rock, quail across the wilderness, manna out of the sky and a coin out of a fish's mouth. Nothing can stop a God who can multiply the fishes and the loaves, or fill your stomach when you haven't eaten anything. <u>Nothing can stop Him from meeting your needs, if you will boldly confess Him before men</u>! Nothing can stop Him! **(Psa.78:28) And he let it fall in the midst of their camp, Round about their habitations. (29) So they did eat, and were well filled; And he gave them their own desire.** And He goes on to talk about the type and shadow of them desiring flesh. Well, God gave them flesh. He gave them more than they could stand. They went out for a day-and-a-half and gathered up these quail, probably until they started stinking. They gathered them up and they probably did every kind of thing they could to preserve all those quail. But God gave them quail until it came out of their noses. Awesome! **(Num.11:20) But a whole month, until it come out at your nostrils, and it be loathsome unto you; because that ye have rejected the Lord who is among you, and have wept before him, saying, Why came we forth out of Egypt?** In other words, "Why did we ever get saved, if we came out here in this wilderness just to eat this old manna! We're tired of this manna!"

God's people were tired of the Word of God. They would rather please their old flesh and God knew that. So He said, "Okay. I'll give you more than you can stand." You've heard the story of the dad who catches his son smoking, so he says, "Okay, son, I want you to smoke the rest of that pack." In other words, "You go ahead and smoke them until they make you sick and maybe that will teach you a lesson." The only thing is, these people did it but they never learned their lesson. They died because they ran after the flesh. **(Num.11:34) And the name of that place was called Kibroth-hattaavah, because there they buried the people that lusted.** *Kibroth-hattaavah* means "the graves of lust." See, they'd rather follow their flesh than follow after the manna, which was the Word out of Heaven. Jesus said He was the bread that came out of Heaven. **(Joh.6:31) Our fathers ate the manna in the wilderness; as it is written, He gave them bread out of heaven to eat. (32) Jesus therefore said unto them, Verily, verily, I say unto you, It was not Moses that gave you the bread out** *of heaven; but my Father giveth you the true bread out of heaven. (33) For the bread of God is that which cometh down out of heaven, and giveth life unto the world. (34) They said therefore unto him, Lord, evermore give us this bread. (35) Jesus said unto them. I am the bread of life: he that cometh to me shall not hunger, and he that believeth on me shall never thirst.* The Lord wants us to live by His Word. He wants us to <u>trust</u> in His Word, not to partake of fleshly methods, not to walk by fleshly eyesight and fleshly hearing, but to speak by faith and walk in the Spirit. Do you know what "walking in the Spirit" is? "Walking in the Spirit" is when you're not walking according to your carnal senses, or your carnal understanding, or your own ability to save yourself, or your own ability to provide for yourself. You know the old saying, "God helps those who help themselves." Well, that's a very unbelieving thing and it's not in the Scriptures. It's not there and, in fact, the opposite is true there. God helps those who can't help themselves and He does it miraculously. He provides miraculously for those people who put their trust and faith in Him. He can multiply the gas in your car, He can multiply the gas in your house, He can multiply the water, He can multiply the money for the bills; He can do all those things!

Don't put anything beyond Him. Don't limit Him. *(Psa.78:41KJV) Yea, they turned back and tempted God, and <u>limited the Holy One of Israel</u>.* <u>Don't limit God</u>! We need childlike faith, like my little daughter. She prayed in the few steps between the washroom and the dining room, and she was already confessing she had received. She was so convinced, "It's my potato chips!" And, sure enough, God answered her prayer. Awesome! That's what God wants in His people. When God says He parted the Red Sea to bring His people across, to show them a mighty miracle, He did exactly what He said. *(Exo.14:21) And Moses stretched out his hand over the sea; and the Lord caused the sea to go back by a strong east wind all the night, and made the sea dry land, and the waters were divided. (22) And the children of Israel went into the midst of the sea upon the dry ground: and the waters were a wall unto them on their right hand, and on their left. (30) Thus the Lord saved Israel that day out of the hand of the Egyptians; and Israel saw the Egyptians dead upon the sea-shore. (31) And Israel saw the great work which the Lord did upon the Egyptians, and the people feared the Lord: and they believed in the Lord, and in his servant Moses.* It was a mighty miracle! God was being very careful to prove Himself to His people.

Again, in these days, God is going to prove Himself to His people who can't provide for themselves. There is a day coming, folks, when the judgment of the Book of Revelation arrives. God's people are going to be dependent upon Him and He likes it that way. He will come through and He will answer.

God bless you! May the Lord be with you in your faith walk with Him. May He manifest to you His wondrous provision in everything. He wants to prove Himself to you, so put your trust in Him totally and He will come through, and don't limit Him! He said, *(Isa.50:2) Is my hand shortened at all, that it cannot redeem? or have I no*

power to deliver? Is His arm so short that He can't answer? Is His arm so short that He can't save? No. Not on your life! The Lord is going to miraculously come through for you and you will get to see miracles. He wants to show Himself strong on behalf of those whose heart is perfect toward Him. ***(2Ch.16:9) For the eyes of the Lord run to and fro throughout the whole earth, to show himself strong in the behalf of them whose <u>heart is perfect toward him</u>.*** And what is He talking about? He's talking about the people who walk by faith, that childlike faith toward Him. Don't lose that! Read this Word in wondrous awe, folks. He's a mighty Savior! God bless you.

CHAPTER 20

Assurance, Not Insurance!

Greetings, saints! Thank you so much for joining us. The Lord be with you! Dear Father, we thank You for this day and we thank You for Your wonderful goodness toward us, Lord. We thank You for pouring out Your Holy Spirit on us, Lord. We thank You that You are anointing us today, Lord, to do Your work and to be Your vessels through whom You can speak, and through whom we can hear You. Lord, hear for us and speak for us. Lord, we can do all things through Christ Who strengthens us, so we thank You so much for Your grace, Lord. Amen.

Folks, I believe the Lord is preparing His people for what He's about to bring to pass on this earth because we're <u>all</u> going to need to walk in the steps of Jesus Christ in the days to come. And we've been learning what it is to "walk in the Spirit." Many people want to know, "What does it mean to 'walk in the Spirit'?" Well, I'll tell you what it is <u>not</u>. It is to <u>not</u> be ruled by the carnal senses, to <u>not</u> walk according to our senses. That's the mind of the flesh. But walking in the Spirit is the opposite of that. Walking in the Spirt is to walk according to the renewed mind of Jesus Christ. One of the biggest problems in the church today, folks, is idolatry. I know a lot of people don't really see it for what it is, but it's idolatry! People will protest that, "Christians don't worship false gods." But they do. Many worship a false Jesus that's not of the Bible. And they have things in their life that are much more important to them, so they serve them rather than serving God. The Lord says, ***(Exo.20:3) Thou shalt have no other gods before me***. The word "gods" is *Elohim* and it means "great or mighty ones." God is the Great One! God is the Mighty One! He is our Savior in all things, but most Christians choose the salvation of the world. They choose to run to man, his methods and salvation. The world to them is the "mighty one." ***(Exo.20:4) Thou shalt not make unto thee a graven image*** (a carved or hewn man-made image), ***nor any likeness [of any thing] that is in heaven above, or that is in the earth beneath, or that is in the water under the earth. (5) Thou shalt not bow down thyself unto them, nor serve them, for I the LORD thy God am a jealous God, visiting the iniquity of the fathers upon the children, upon the third and upon the fourth generation of them that hate me.*** Wow! You know, idolatry can cause a curse to travel through your family for many generations and idolatry is really common today, even though people who read only the letter don't understand that.

We get our English word for "idolatry" from the Greek word *eidololatreia*. It means "a servant to an image" or "a servant to, or a worshipper of, that which is seen." In other words, "an image servant," someone who serves the physical, someone who serves the things that are seen. Well, multitudes of Christians serve the things that are seen, the things that are in this world. ***(1Jn.2:16) For all that is in the world, the lust of the flesh and the lust of the eyes and the vain glory of life, is not of the Father,*** *but is of the world.* Idolatry is like the lusts of the flesh, the lusts of the eyes and the pride of life. Many people serve the physical and I want to share a parable with you concerning that, which may help us to identify what idolatry is. ***(1Sa.4:3) And when the people were come into the camp, the elders of Israel said, Wherefore hath the Lord smitten us to-day before the Philistines? Let us fetch the ark of the covenant of the Lord out of Shiloh unto us, that it may come among us, and save us out of the hand of our enemies.*** The Israelites and the Philistines had been at war and, at this particular time, Israel had forgotten the Ark of the Covenant. They were losing the battle, so they brought the Ark of the Covenant on the scene and it really struck fear in the hearts of the Philistines to see the Ark of the Covenant come onto the scene. ***(1Sa.4:5) And when the ark of the covenant of the Lord came into the camp, all Israel shouted with a great shout, so that the earth rang again. (6) And when the Philistines heard the noise of the shout, they said, What meaneth the noise of this great shout in the camp of the Hebrews? And they understood that the ark of the Lord was come into the camp. (7) And the Philistines were afraid, for they said, God is come into the camp. And they said, Woe unto us! for there hath not been such a thing heretofore. (8) Woe unto us! who shall deliver us out of the hand of these mighty gods? these are the gods that smote the Egyptians with all manner of plagues in the wilderness.*** But the Philistines actually won the battle and took the Ark of the Covenant captive. ***(10) And the Philistines fought, and Israel was smitten, and they fled every man to his tent: and there was a very great slaughter; for there fell of Israel thirty thousand footmen. (11) And the ark of God was taken; and the two sons of Eli, Hophni and Phinehas, were slain.***

At that particular time, Eli was the judge of Israel and his daughter-in-law was about to give birth. ***(1Sa.4:19) And his daughter-in-law, Phinehas' wife, was with child, near to be delivered: and when she heard the tidings that the ark of God was taken, and that her father-in-law and her husband were dead, she bowed herself and brought forth; for her pains came upon her. (20) And about the time of her death the women that stood by her said unto her, Fear not; for thou hast brought forth a son. But she answered not, neither did she regard it. (21) And she named the child Ichabod, saying, The glory is departed from Israel; because the ark of God was taken, and because of her father-in-law and her husband. (22) And she said, The glory is departed from Israel; for the ark of God is taken.*** Now think about it, folks. The Ark of God represents the vessel in which the presence of God was. We are vessels of God. We are vessels of God's presence, but we are also spiritual man and carnal man. And the parable here is that Israel, the spiritual man, was to conquer the Promised Land, which is this land in which we live. ***(Heb.6:7) For the land which hath drunk the rain that cometh oft upon it, and bringeth forth herbs meet for them for whose sake it is also tilled, receiveth blessing from God: (8) but if it beareth thorns and*** *thistles, it is rejected and nigh unto a curse; whose end is to be burned.* This land that we live in is supposed to bear the fruit of the Lord and, if it doesn't, it's good for nothing but to be cast out and burned. Well, the daughter-in-law of Eli bore fruit, but the fruit was Ichabod because the Ark of God had now been taken by the Philistines. The carnal man had captured the vessel of the presence of God and taken it away. Do you know that when you walk in the flesh, that's exactly what's happening? The carnal man has captured the Ark of the presence of God and is taking it where he wants to go, walking in the lust of the flesh, the lust of the eyes and the pride of life. That's what the Philistine represented and there is no glory in that. We're here to manifest the glory of the Lord. *(2Co.3:18) But we all, with unveiled face beholding as in a mirror the glory of the Lord, are transformed into the same image from glory to glory, even as from the Lord the Spirit.* So when we walk by faith, we behold "as in a mirror the glory of the Lord." By faith we see God's glory manifested in us. *(Col.1:27) ... Christ in you, the hope of Glory*. But when you walk in the flesh willfully, you know you're not fulfilling the will of God and the Glory of God is not growing in you.

Well, this is the story of the man of flesh taking possession of the vessel, the man of flesh ruling the vessel of the presence of God. *(1Sa.5:1) Now the Philistines had taken the ark of God, and they brought it from Eben-ezer unto Ashdod. (2) And the Philistines took the ark of God, and brought it into the house of Dagon, and set it by Dagon.* An Israelite would never bring another "god" in and set it up next to the Ark of God because they believed in one God. But the Philistines believed in many gods and they believed that Dagon was the god of gods, that he was the god over all of the gods. And when you read the story, you see that they also believed in Jehovah and they feared Jehovah as just one more of many gods. *(1Sa.5:3) And when they of Ashdod arose early on the morrow, behold, Dagon was fallen upon his face to the ground before the ark of the Lord.* Yes, we know! Because he's not the God of gods, is he? The God of gods is the One whose presence is in the Ark of the Covenant and He's the God of all false gods. *(1Sa.5:3) And when they of Ashdod arose early on the morrow, behold, Dagon was fallen upon his face to the ground before the ark of the Lord. And they took Dagon, and set him in his place again. (4) And when they arose early on the morrow morning, behold, Dagon was fallen upon his face to the ground before the ark of the Lord* (He was submitting to the Lord, bowing to the Lord.)*; and the head of Dagon and both the palms of his hands lay cut off upon the threshold; only the stump of Dagon was left to him.* This is very symbolic. You know, the Bible speaks about the Word of God being manifested in our hand and in our forehead, between our eyes. *(Exo.13:16) And it shall be for a sign upon thy hand, and for frontlets between thine eyes: for by strength of hand the Lord brought us forth out of Egypt.* And the Israelites would literally bind the Word of God between their eyes, upon their forehead and upon the backs of their hands. *(Deu.11:18) Therefore shall ye lay up these my words in your heart and in your soul; and ye shall bind* *them for a sign upon your hand, and they shall be for frontlets between your eyes.*

The same chapter and verse in Revelation speaks about having the mark of the Beast or the number of his name. **(Rev.13:16) And he causeth all, the small and the great, and the rich and the poor, and the free and the bond, that there be given them a mark on their right hand, or upon their forehead.** Well, the mark of the Beast is the opposite of the mark of God. The mark of the Beast is to walk after the mind of the flesh and do the works of the flesh because the hand symbolizes our works. But Deuteronomy 11:18 and Exodus 13:16 speak about the mark of God. The Jews would put Scriptures written on tiny parchments into little boxes and wear them between their eyes, and bind them onto their hand and forearm. This symbolizes the Word of God manifested in our mind, which is the renewed mind of Christ, and it symbolizes the Word of God manifested in our works. Here, Dagon represents what the carnal man worships because idolatry is the worship of a man-made god, but when the Ark of the Covenant of the Lord was placed next to Dagon, it proved that Dagon was no god. So we see that <u>God is going to judge all gods</u> that stand next to Him. In these days, <u>anything</u> that man worships, anything that man is a servant of that is seen, anything that he prizes, anything that he counts on to save him, is ultimately going to <u>fail</u>. Even Christians trust in many things to save them, but God is offended. God has His own methods of salvation. Just remember, folks, the Beast wants to "save" you from God, but God wants to save you from the Beast.

The world does offer salvation. The world offers methods of salvation, but these methods of salvation don't cause you to walk in the steps of Jesus Christ. These methods are the works of man and they cause you to trust in the power of man. As a matter of fact, **(Jer.17:5) Thus saith the Lord: Cursed is the man that trusteth in man, and maketh flesh his arm....** Meaning the <u>strength</u> by which you do your works. The hand symbolizes your works and the arm symbolizes the strength by which you do your works. Well, the strength by which many people do their works is the arm of flesh. **(Jer.17:5) Thus saith the Lord: Cursed is the man that trusteth in man, and maketh flesh his arm, and whose heart departeth from the Lord. (6) For he shall be like the heath in the desert** (like a tumbleweed in the desert)**, and shall not see when good cometh, but shall inhabit the parched places in the wilderness, a salt land and not inhabited.** The wilderness, of course, represents the Tribulation (Revelation 12, 17), and many of us are in tribulation now, but the Lord is telling you that, if you trust in the arm of the flesh, you're going to be cursed. You're going to be walking under the curse. Multitudes of people don't know what the curse is. They live under it and they think it's normal. They think it's the normal Christian life to not have the blessing of God on the things that they do, on their provision, on their life. They don't understand that they're trusting in a "mighty one" that is not the Mighty One of God! They are trusting in the works of the flesh and the mind of the flesh, which is what? The mind of the flesh is the mark of the Beast on their forehead. They're trusting in the nature, character and authority of the flesh. The Greek word for "name" is *onoma* and it means "nature, character and authority." In Revelation, the Bible speaks of having God's name in the foreheads of His righteous people. ***(Rev.14:1) And I saw, and behold, the Lamb standing on the mount Zion, and with him a hundred and forty and four thousand, having his name, and the name of his Father, written on their foreheads.***

So you see, folks, there are people who are idolaters. They're trusting in, they're worshipping, they're serving that which is seen. They could be serving religious systems, or they could be counting on armies to be their protection, or they could be counting on insurance to bail them out of trouble, if it comes. Where we live, many people have become very discouraged concerning insurance because insurance didn't come through after all those hurricanes made landfall a while back. Many people are still suffering and still in desperate need because they found out their false god, the thing that they had put their hope in, didn't come through. Some people have their hope in their bank account, even though the Lord Jesus said not to store up your treasures upon the earth. Some people have their hope in doctors, some have their hope in lawyers. Many people have idolatrous relationships with the world, with the Beast system, and they don't understand that. Well, the Lord is a very jealous God. ***(Exo.34:14) For thou shalt worship no other god: for the Lord, whose name is Jealous, is a jealous God.*** And He is coming to save us from this idolatry that we, as Christians, have become mixed up in. Christians are very much like the world and they don't see anything wrong with that, so God is going to judge these idols. Anything that His people trust in and, in a way, worship more than Him, He's going to judge. We're going to see armies fail! We're going to see insurance fail! We're going to see bank accounts fail! Because of the system God's bringing onto the scene, everything that men and everything that His people trust in is going to fail them. Everything is going to fail them, just like Dagon failed the Philistines, and the strength of their own works and their mind of the flesh is going to be lost.

You know, everywhere the Philistines took the Ark of the Covenant, it brought a curse upon them. ***(1Sa.5:6) But the hand of the Lord was heavy upon them of Ashdod, and he destroyed them, and smote them with tumors, even Ashdod and the borders thereof. (7) And when the men of Ashdod saw that it was so, they said, The ark of the God of Israel shall not abide with us; for his hand is sore upon us, and upon Dagon our god. (8) They sent therefore and gathered all the lords of the Philistines unto them, and said, What shall we do with the ark of the God of Israel? And they answered, Let the ark of the God of Israel be carried about unto Gath. And they carried the ark of the God of Israel thither. (9) And it was so, that, after they had carried it about, the hand of the Lord was against the city with a very great discomfiture: and he smote the men of the city, both small and great; and tumors brake out upon them. (10) So they sent the ark of God to Ekron. And it came to pass, as the ark of God came to Ekron, that the Ekronites cried out, say-***

ing, They have brought about the ark of the God of Israel to us, to slay us and our people. (11) They sent therefore and gathered together all the lords of the Philistines, and they said, Send away the ark of the God of Israel, and let it go again to its own place, that is slay us not, and our people. For there was a deadly discomfiture throughout all the city; the hand of God was very heavy there. (12) And the men that died not were smitten with the tumors; and the cry of the city went up to heaven. You see, when the carnal man takes the vessel of God where he wants it to go, it brings a curse on the carnal man. Every time the old man takes the vessel of God's presence where he wants it to go, that's walking in the flesh, that's walking after the mind of the flesh, that's walking after the works of the flesh, and that <u>will</u> bring a curse on you. That's why we need to repent. If we trust in the arm of the flesh, it's a curse. If we put God's name on man's works, like we commonly do with religion, with the Beast system, with patriotism, it's a curse. Our nation is the spiritual nation of New Testament Israel and we are not to worship any of the fallen nations. Every place we put our trust in as a savior that's not *the* Savior, there's a curse on it.

Remember that an idolater is "a worshipper or a servant of that which is <u>seen</u>"; that is, the works of man, the physical. <u>We</u> serve, we trust as our Savior, in the things that are <u>not seen</u>, the Bible says. *(Heb.10:38) But my righteous one shall live by <u>faith</u>: And if he shrink back, my soul hath no pleasure in him.* God desires earnestly a people who live by faith. *(Heb.10:39) But we are not of them that shrink back unto perdition* (or "destruction"); *but of them that have faith unto the saving of the soul.* We want the soul of Christ in us, not just the Spirit of Christ, but the soul of Christ. *(Heb.11:1) Now faith is <u>assurance</u>* (i.e., the assurance is that you have received the <u>substance</u> [KJV] of what you ask) *of [things] hoped for, <u>a conviction of things not seen</u>.* Faith puts its hope in the things that are not seen; whereas, an idolater puts his hope and his faith in the things that are seen. What does this mean? *(1Co.1:28) And the base things of the world, and the things that are despised, did God choose, [yea] and the <u>things that are not</u>, that he might bring to nought the things that are....* And we wonder, "What is He talking about? He chose things that <u>are not</u>, to bring to nothing the things <u>that are</u>?" Yes. The promises of God, all of them, <u>are not</u>. When you see the promise of God but you're under the curse, you're in lack, you're in need, you're in sickness, you're in oppression, and so on and so forth, then that promise is one of the "<u>things that are not</u>." God chose for us to take that promise and to use it "to bring to nought the things that are." We take the promise of God's protection, God's provision, God's salvation, and so on and so forth, and use it "to bring to nought the things that are," which is the curse. But the natural man doesn't do that; he chooses the things that can be seen to save him. That's an idolater.

Many Christians today like to put God's name on <u>their</u> works. They say, "Nowadays, God does it this way," or "Nowadays, God uses doctors," and suchlike. Well, the Scripture says, *(Heb.13:8) Jesus Christ [is] the same yesterday and to-day, [yea] and for ever.* He's the same! He hasn't changed His methods one bit. But it's comfortable for the flesh to say that, "Now God does it our way. He uses the things that are to bring to naught the things that are." No. The Bible doesn't say that. ***(Rom.4:17) (As it is written, A father of many nations have I made thee) before him whom he believed, [even] God, who giveth life to the dead, and <u>calleth the things that are not, as though they were</u>.*** In other words, God just speaks things into existence. He calls things that be not, as though they were. God <u>agrees</u> with the promises of God. He speaks these promises and He wants us, as sons of God, to speak these promises into existence. He doesn't want us to set about salvation by our own works, or a salvation that comes through the things that are seen in the world. It's not God's method and, as a matter of fact, He proves this: ***(Heb.11:1) Now faith is assurance of [things] hoped for, a conviction of things <u>not seen</u>.*** In the promises of God, you have the assurance of things that are not seen. ***(Heb.11:2) For therein the elders had witness borne to them. (3) By faith we understand that the worlds have been framed by the word of God, so that what is <u>seen</u> hath <u>not</u> been made out of things <u>which appear</u>.*** To say it another way, they haven't been made out of the natural. They haven't been made out of things that man has created. Everything man has created is a "graven image," a thing that is seen, whether it be insurance or medicine or any such attempt at salvation. He serves it because he thinks it will save him and, ultimately, it won't. In these days, God's had enough. God is going to judge every idol that men lean upon to save, preserve and provide for themselves. He's going to judge them all.

But <u>we</u> choose the things that are not, to bring to nothing the things that are. We choose these promises, which are the things that are not seen. We don't try to save ourselves by using the things that are seen. We do what God commanded us to do. Jesus merely spoke the Word of God. He trusted in the Word of God. The Bible says, "Faith is the assurance of things hoped for." It's an assurance, so why do men need insurance? Well, because they don't believe in assurance. Insurance is thinking, "In case I get myself in a position where God won't save me or can't save me. We have these great big insurance institutions that have a lot of money behind them and, if a hurricane takes my home away, I'll put my trust in them to restore it." But when you trust in the arm of the flesh, you're much more likely for a hurricane to destroy your home because the Bible says you're cursed; therefore, it's a self-perpetuating thing. Also, let me tell you that there are multitudes of people who didn't get their home replaced. So you see, God is judging the idols of man. Things that men thought were insurance are being judged. Some of those insurance companies are moving out of the state and many of them moved out a long time ago because of the hurricanes. You couldn't go to them for insurance in this state and other states are losing insurance companies, too.

Anyway, God would rather we have His assurance and trust in His assurance, than in insurance. A few years ago, we had a little lesson at UBM about that. Kevin and Holly Rea, who produce videos for us, had a large external hard drive and it had a lot of our videos that we have put together for television on it. So, I get a call on the telephone, but there's almost nothing but a broken whisper on the other end. I'm thinking, "Who is this? I don't recognize the voice," and it was Kevin. He spoke a little louder the next time and he said, "We need a miracle." I asked, "What happened, Kevin?" because his voice was just kind of broken, you know. He said, "All those videos on that hard drive are gone. It's gone out. It's burnt up. David, I know hard drives and I know these things, I've been doing this for many, many years. When a computer won't even recognize that the hard drive is there, that's bad." I said, "Okay, I'll take your word for it. I'm not a techie." And I told Kevin, "Well, we'll just command it to be healed in the name of Jesus." Then, even worse, Kevin said, "You know, I hadn't backed up any of those videos. I had no back-up for any of those videos that we had on that large external hard drive because they really weren't ready to send out to Access TV or regular TV or anything." Since there were final things that needed to be done to them, he didn't want to back them up too soon. He had no insurance, did he? None whatsoever. The only One Who was going to save us in this situation was God Almighty! He's the only One who <u>could</u> save us! And since there was no place else to go, we went to God. Kevin and Holly laid hands on that hard drive and I spoke on my end of the phone. I just commanded it, in the name of the Lord Jesus Christ, to be healed. I commanded it to be restored in Jesus' name. Well, they were evidently late to be somewhere at this particular moment, but because of this emergency they had called me and they immediately took off after we had prayed. I didn't hear anything from them for maybe an hour or so. When they came back, Kevin called me and he said, "David, as soon as I brought the computer up, the hard drive was there and everything was on it! Everything was totally restored!" Of course, we rejoiced and we praised our mighty Savior! Our mighty God! Our mighty One! He was the One Who saved us when there wasn't anything else that could save us. We didn't have any insurance. We didn't trust in any insurance, but God was our assurance. You see, God wanted to do this, so God saved these.

Of course, we could have leaned on the arm of the flesh and, if we had a back-up, we could have restored them. But we would have had to go out and buy this big hard drive and then we wouldn't have had a witness, either. We wouldn't have had a good testimony before God. The glory of God would have departed because the old fleshly man would have been in control, saving himself. We wouldn't have gotten to see the glory of God. You know, you get to see miracles when you put yourself in a position to see miracles. In that particular case, we had no insurance; all we had was assurance. According to the Lord Jesus, **(Mar.11:23) Verily I say unto you, Whosoever shall say unto this mountain, Be thou taken up and cast into the sea; and shall not doubt in his heart, but shall believe that what he saith cometh to pass; he shall have it.** Glory to God! Now <u>that's living by the things that are not</u>, folks! That's living by the things that are not seen. None of the methods that you could use by the things that are seen would give glory to God. None of them would cause you to grow up in God. None of them would cause you to walk in the steps of Jesus. None of them would cause you to bring a testimony of His power before the brethren. "But my righteous one shall live by faith, and if he shrink back, my soul hath <u>no pleasure in him</u>." God is pleased with us glorifying His great name and we should be about our Father's business, glorifying His great name before men.

I've shared with you how the Lord gave us a house and two cars. We had agreed in faith one week earlier that God was going to give us a house and cars for free because we didn't have any money. We weren't storing up our treasures on earth and we didn't have any way to pay for them. And God told us to give away our house and car, so we couldn't sell them to get the money. He put us in a position of needing a miracle, you see. We were moving five hours away and we needed a house and car. Well, the way God chose to do it was a way in which we had been honoring Him. I didn't mention it before, but we had no insurance on our car. You see, in those days, it wasn't a law that we had to have automobile insurance and so we didn't have insurance because we trusted in God to be our assurance. And I tell you, we've never been put to shame in this, folks. What happened was that a car ran into my wife and daughter in our car, slammed her into the car in front and just totaled our car. But the man who caused the accident was self-insured and had something like 100/300/100 coverage. He was the president of a big warehouse corporation and they took good care of us. They bought us a house and they bought us a new, larger car to replace the car that was wrecked. We had five kids and we couldn't all pile into a Toyota Corolla. Praise be to God! We had no insurance, we couldn't have replaced that car, but God caused this accident and He used it to plunder the insurance companies, like plundering Egypt. He blessed us! We put our trust in Him and He never has failed us. It's much better to have the assurance of God and depend upon it, and trust in it. It's much better to trust in the things that cannot be seen in the physical realm, than it is to trust in the arm of the flesh because the arm of the flesh always brings a curse.

When I first got that conviction to drop our insurance, I'd already been walking for many years trusting in God for healing. I'd never trusted in the arm of the flesh. I would just pray and believe God. We raised five kids like that and God healed them all; it didn't matter what they had. He healed them. He performed wondrous miracles the whole time. So I was putting my trust in Him and trusting in the things that cannot be seen, like the Bible says. And one of those things was healing. **(1Pe.2:24) Who his own self bare our sins in his body upon the tree, that we, having died unto sins, might live unto righteousness; <u>by whose stripes ye were healed</u>.** Well, you can't see that when you're sick. That's one of those things that is not and we call the things that are not as though they were. In other words, they're just done. "God said it, I believe it and that settles it," as the saying goes. So I asked myself, "Why am I paying so much for this insurance, when God has already told me He's going to supply my every need? Why am I paying for insurance when God has told me that He's going to send His angel to hold me up, lest I even dash my foot against a stone?" **(Psa.91:11) For he will give his angels charge over thee, To keep thee in all thy ways. (12) They shall bear thee up in their hands, Lest thou dash thy foot against a stone.** He's promised us protection and provision, and He says, **(Mat.21:22) And all things, whatsoever ye shall ask in prayer, believing, ye shall receive.** I thought, "Why should I trust in these big banks and these big insurance companies to be my salvation in case things go bad? Isn't that like planning by faith for things to go bad?" Well, that's exactly what it is. Now, I'm not putting anybody under any law, just, **(Mat.9:29) *According to your faith be it done unto you.*** I'm not condemning anybody. I'm just sharing with you what the Lord taught me. So I decided, "Okay, Lord, I see what You're saying." And the Lord convicted me to get rid of my insurance. You may be thinking, "Oh, David, that's foolish because look what can happen." But it will happen, if you trust in insurance. Trusting in the arm of the flesh brings the curse along with it, so I called my insurance man. As a matter of fact, he came to my house and I told him that I wanted to drop the insurance on my house and car. I was going to put my trust in God. Well, the guy was a Christian of sorts, but he tried to talk me out of it. I said, "No, I know what God has spoken to me and I'm going to put my trust in Him." So, don't you know, a week later I had a severe trial, but it was a miracle because I put my trust in God and, you see, He always honors that.

Well, a week later I drove our relatively new Datsun station wagon over to a convenience store. That was back when Nissans were Datsuns which, of course, dates this story. Again, keep in mind that a week before, I had dropped all insurance on this car. So I went inside and I was walking up and down the aisles, picking out a few things. Then I hear this "Kaboom!" And I look out the window to see that a car had just slammed into my car so hard that it shook the plate glass across the front of this store. In fact, I saw dust falling onto the floor off the little sill that went over the top of the window. He just slammed right into the back corner of my Datsun station wagon. Now a Datsun station wagon isn't much. You could probably take your elbow and knock a dent in it anywhere you wanted to and this guy who hit me was in a big, old heavy Buick. I hurried down the aisle and walked outside, and the guy had backed the car up just about a foot or so. He got out and walked around his car, and we met right there where his car had hit my car. My car had V'd in the front of his car! The whole front of his car was V'd-in. The hood, the grill and the bumper were all busted. His bumper, where it hit the corner of this "tin box" Datsun station wagon, was busted. This was an old Buick. They're built like a tank! It's all steel; it's not plastic. This guy's jaw was falling open and mine was, too. He looked at this and he said, "Boy, they sure make them a lot better than they used to!" Well, that was about the stupidest statement I believe I've ever heard in that kind of a situation. But my car had knocked a notch right in the middle of the front of his car. I reached over where his hood had hit the corner of my car and, with my thumbnail, scratched the paint from his hood off the plastic tail lens on the back left corner of my car. And after I took the paint off that plastic tail lens, there wasn't anything you could see on my car. Not a scratch. It was a miracle from God. I mean, his car hit mine right in the middle of that plastic tail lens and there was not a scratch on my car. It was supernatural protection from God. I had no insurance and God left the paint on my tail lens there just to prove that the guy actually hit it.

Do you think that confirmed what God was doing in my life? Some people say, "That's a foolish thing to do, David." No. I don't think putting my faith in God is ever a foolish thing to do, but He certainly confirmed with a miracle that He approved of my faith. Of course, I'm not taking any credit because, **(Eph.2:8) For by grace have ye been saved through faith; and that not of yourselves, [it is] the gift of God; (9) not of works, that no man should glory.** God gives us the faith, He does the miracle and too often we get the credit for it, but it's not of works, lest any man should boast. We have nothing to brag about, folks. It's the mercy and the grace of God. If you want a miracle, you have to step out there where miracles are made. You have to put yourself in a position to come into a place of weakness. **(2Co.12:9) And he hath said unto me, My grace is sufficient for thee: for <u>my power is made perfect in weakness</u>. Most gladly therefore will I rather glory in my weaknesses, that the power of Christ may rest upon me.** God's power "is made perfect in weakness." There was nothing I could have done to save my little Datsun station wagon. If I had kept my insurance and he would have hit it, his Buick would have badly damaged my car. I would have had to wait for them to fix it or for them to total it out and give me another car, but then God wouldn't have received any glory from it.

Well, he told me his brakes went out. I don't know if that's true or not, but at any rate, he wasn't looking at what he was doing and he slammed right into my Datsun and ruined the front of his car. So he didn't even bother to go into the store; it just shook him up so much that he had hit my car. He got in his Buick and he took off. Then it occurred to me, "David, you just missed the best chance you've ever had of witnessing to somebody!" So I jumped in my car and I took off, and I caught him down at the railroad crossing. There was a light there and it had blocked the traffic, and I had some tracts that I kept in my glove compartment. I reached in there and I grabbed them, jumped out and ran up to him. I said, "Mister, that was a miracle!" And he looked at me and said, "It has to be." I said, "Let me tell you, I had gotten rid of all my insurance. I didn't have any insurance and I was trusting in God to keep my car." You know what he said? He said, "It has to be a miracle!" Anyway, I shoved those tracts in his hand and he took off and I never saw him again, but I had an awesome testimony that I've been sharing with people ever since. The glory and the power of God can keep your vehicle. It can keep your shoes from wearing out walking in the wilderness, can't it? **(Deu.29:5) And I have led you forty years in the wilderness: your clothes are not waxen old on you, and your shoe is not waxen old on your foot.** God can protect, He can preserve. I guarantee you, there must have been an angel's hand right there on the corner of my car. Plastic usually gives way to steel, but that steel didn't even crack the plastic. Left not a scratch on it! Almighty God wanted to prove Himself strong on behalf of them whose heart is perfect toward Him. **(2Ch.16:9) For the eyes of the Lord run to and fro throughout the whole earth, to show himself strong in the behalf of them whose heart is perfect toward him....** What did He say in Jeremiah? "Thus saith the Lord: Cursed is the man that trusteth in man, and maketh flesh his arm, and whose heart departeth from the Lord." You see, when you're trusting in the arm of the flesh, it's because your heart is departing from the Lord. God loves those people who believe and trust in Him. That's why He brought Israel into the wilderness. He wanted them to trust in Him as their mighty God, their Savior.

Well, we love insurance because it appears to insulate us from the possibility of any bad things happening, but folks, lots of bad things are coming toward God's people and insurance isn't going to save them, armies aren't going to save them, bankers aren't going to save them and doctors aren't going to save them. God is deciding that none of these things are going to work for His people because He wants them now to learn to walk by faith. There are more Christians alive today than have ever lived throughout history. Now is the time to teach them to walk by faith, in order to bring them into the Kingdom, in order to bring about a glorious revival throughout this world. God is going to do awesome, wonderful things!

I remember one time I was going to work in my Toyota pickup truck and I still didn't have any insurance. I was about 20 miles from Exxon, where I worked, and I was driving over the middle of a bridge. There was a car that was stopped on the bridge and the car in front of me suddenly hit that stopped car in front of them. They slammed right into it. Well, I was slowing because I saw what happened, but the guy behind me was looking down the river and he scooped me up and slammed me into the car in front of me. So it was four cars in a row. Boom! Boom! Boom! When I got out of my car, I saw the guy in front of me was slumped over his steering wheel and I said, "Uh, oh. That guy's hurt." So I went over and looked in on the passenger's side. I opened the door and there was blood just gushing out of the guy's mouth and nose, and he was incoherent because his head had been slammed into the steering wheel. So I reached in and took him out and laid him on the concrete, with his head on the bridge embankment. Blood was coming out of his nose and pooling on the ground like jelly underneath his head, and the guy was still incoherent. I was trying to talk to him, but he wasn't responding, and so I knelt down and I prayed for him right there. I didn't know if he was a Christian or not; I couldn't get any response out of him, but I prayed for him right there. Now, this was an interstate highway and lots of the people who worked at the Exxon plant and who knew me took it to work. Well, I had blood all over my hands from getting this guy out of the car and a Baptist brother I had been witnessing to at the plant pulled up right alongside me. He said, "Man, you better get to the hospital." He was looking at this blood on my hands, you know. I told him, "There's nothing wrong with me; I'm fine." And then he screamed it, "You better get to the hospital!" He thought I was speaking faith.

Then an ambulance came and picked this guy up and took him to the hospital. I asked them where they were going to take him and, as soon as I got back home, I called the hospital. I asked them about this man who was brought in from a wreck. It was a small town there, Denham Springs, and they knew who I was talking about. They said, "Yeah, we treated the guy and we actually couldn't find anything wrong with him. We turned him loose and sent him home." I said, "Ma'am, if you'd seen that pile of blood out there on the highway, you'd know that there would be something wrong with him. There was blood gushing out of his face." She said, "Well, maybe something happened in his nose, but we couldn't find anything wrong with him and we sent him home." Glory to God!

So I went back out to work and as soon as I walked into the big six-acre central mechanical building, I noticed that everybody was looking at me. And I thought, "That guy's come in here and told everybody, 'David was in a terrible wreck and he's dying,'" or something. They came over looking at me, staring at my arms and I told them, "Look, I was telling the truth; I didn't get hurt. The other guy got hurt and I just prayed for him." Well, I got a good kick out of that, but they still thought, "This guy is talking faith again." You know the world: they don't really believe in faith, do they? Anyway, to make a long story short, my Toyota truck was crumpled, just crumpled. And I didn't have any insurance on it, but I ended up getting my truck fixed, including a paint job that it needed. And I ended up with $1500 in my pocket, which was really neat. I've been blessed like that every time I put my trust in the Lord. There have been times when He totally protected my car, like the Datsun station wagon, and there were other times when it was more advantageous for me to have some money in my pocket and to get a paint job, <u>and</u> to get a miracle because God healed that guy. Glory be to God! God is awesome! We need to put our trust and our faith in Him.

We get to see these miracles, folks, when we put ourselves in a position to see miracles. His power is made perfect in weakness, but we don't want to be weak. We're afraid that, if we're weak, something bad will happen and wipe us out, but when you trust in the arm of the flesh, something bad <u>will</u> happen. Now you might not get wiped out, but it's still a curse. Almighty God has given His assurance to believers. I know that many people don't believe them and they are weak in the faith. But we have promises like, **(Mat.21:22) And all things, whatsoever ye shall ask in prayer, believing, ye shall receive.** Instead of believing that, we do like the world does and we insure ourselves, we try to insulate ourselves from any possibility of bad things coming down the road. What we're actually doing is planning for these bad things to happen and they do! There have been many times when I was totally, supernaturally protected by God from getting in a wreck. There were other times when God blessed me abundantly because I was in a wreck. There are other times when He totally protected my vehicle when other cars slammed into it. God has an abundance of ways and methods to protect us and bless us. He's promised that, if we put our faith in Him, He will bless us. Praise be to God! Well, I just know that God is pleased with those whose heart is perfect toward Him, with those who decide to walk by faith. Very soon, folks, very soon, we're going to have to walk this way because there won't be anything in the world to lean upon. God is going to judge everything, all the gods of Egypt. Father, we thank You so much. We thank You so much for being our Savior in all things. We put our trust in You, Lord. We worship You, we praise You, we trust in You and we thank You. God bless you, saints!

CHAPTER 21

Protection!

God bless you, saints! Thank you for joining us. May the Lord be with you. Let's go to the Lord and ask for His grace and His help, since I'm not much of a teacher without Him. Thank You, Father. Father, we ask for Your grace today, Your wisdom today, Your anointing today. Lord, we just want You to share something with the brethren that will encourage them and build them up, and prepare them for the days to come. Show them what You have provided for them through Jesus Christ. Lord, we all sell You too short, Father. You have done an awesome work. You have provided everything that we need through the sacrifice of Christ; help us to understand this, Lord. Help us to discern what Your Word is saying and we thank You so much, Lord, in Jesus' name. Amen.

Well, some know Jesus as Savior and, of course, they receive salvation; and some know Him as healer and they receive healing. Some know Him as the Passover Lamb and they receive protection and they get blessed. And that's really what I'd like to share with you today, what the Lord has provided for His people as far as protection in the days to come. ***(Hos.4:6)*** <u>***My people are destroyed for lack of knowledge***</u>***: because thou hast rejected knowledge, I will also reject thee, that thou shalt be no priest to me: seeing thou hast forgotten the law of thy God, I also will forget thy children.*** Of course, we can see that the opposite of this is true, too, that if we do not forget the Law of God, the Lord will remember our children and we won't be destroyed in our ignorance. The Lord has given us understanding very openly in the Word; He's not hidden it very deeply for those who are seeking the truth. He's given us understanding concerning the great provision that He has for us and yet the overwhelming majority of Christianity denies what the Bible clearly says concerning this. We have Psalm 91, yet we have preachers saying that's for the Millennium, although they can't prove that whatsoever from Scripture. But many Christians are partaking of the benefits of Psalm 91 here and now, so they know better. As the saying goes, "The man with an experience is never at the mercy of the man with an argument." The preachers can argue all they want, but if you see the Lord provide for you because you believe, then you don't have to worry about their arguments. Jesus said, ***(Mat.9:29) According to your faith be it done unto you***, and ***(8:13) As thou hast believed, [so] be it done unto thee.*** It's very important that we believe, but it's also very important <u>what</u> we believe and that's what knowledge is all about. You don't know what to exercise faith in, unless you have an understanding of what God has done for you. He has provided richly for us everything that we need. ***(Php.4:19) And my God shall supply every need of yours according to his riches in glory in Christ Jesus.***

I'd like to lay a little foundation here of why God could be so merciful to us because of what Jesus did for us when He became our sacrifice. ***(Lev.16:6) And Aaron shall present the bullock of the sin-offering, which is for himself, and make atone-***

ment for himself, and for his house. (7) And he shall take the two goats, and set them before Jehovah at the door of the tent of meeting. (8) And Aaron shall cast lots upon the two goats; one lot for Jehovah, and the other lot for Azazel. "Azazel" means "removal" and it's the word many times also used for "escape" -- "escape" goat. One lot was for the goat that identified the Lord and the other lot was for the scapegoat, the "removal." So to find out which goat was to be sacrificed, the High Priest would draw a lot. *(Lev.16:9) And Aaron shall present the goat upon which the lot fell for the Lord, and offer him for a sin-offering.* You know, that's what happened, folks. The Lord Jesus came as God's sin-offering and what does it say about this other goat? *(Lev.16:10) But the goat, on which the lot fell for Azazel* (that is "removal" or "scapegoat")*, shall be set alive before the Lord, to make atonement for him, to send him away for Azazel* ("removal") *into the wilderness.* The High Priest sacrificed the goat upon which the Lot of the Lord fell and the other goat was set free to go into the wilderness.

You see, we're supposed to go into the wilderness and I shared with you previously that it's God's plan for one of us to go into a wilderness just as soon as we get saved. As soon as we go through our Red Sea baptism and the <u>old man</u> is put to death, the wilderness is there, but God's people refuse to go into the wilderness because they don't like depending totally upon God. They would rather do it the way they've always done it. They would rather do it the way they did it in Egypt where they depended upon the arm of the flesh, but God's not pleased with that. So here we are, folks, about to go into a wilderness -- a corporate, worldwide wilderness. And God is preparing His people, but we have a sacrifice. The lot of the Lord fell upon the Lord Jesus Christ. God sacrificed Him so that we could be "set alive," free to go into the wilderness. That's the reason that Psalm 91 is true today. *(Gal.3:13) Christ redeemed us from the curse of the law, having become a curse for us; for it is written, Cursed is every one that hangeth on a tree.* Christ became a curse for us so that we might have Abraham's blessings. The Lord put <u>our</u> curse upon the Lord Jesus Christ and we were set free. So now it's, "As you have believed, so shall it be done unto you," as Jesus said. If you don't want to believe any particular part of Christianity, you don't have to have it. It's that simple. What part of the Lord's Word you do believe, you will have. The part you won't believe, you won't have. What I'm pointing out to you is that God's protection is there for us. *(Psa.91:1) He that dwelleth in the secret place of the Most High Shall abide under the shadow of the Almighty.* "The secret place of the Most High" is abiding in Christ through belief in His Word, through faith in His Word. We abide in Him. In fact, we read, *(Psa.90:1) Lord, thou hast been our dwelling-place In all generations.* So we know that it's <u>the Lord Himself</u> in Whom we abide.

(Psa.91:2) <u>I will say</u> of the Lord, He is my refuge and my fortress; My God, in whom I trust. This is what we have to say of the Lord because salvation doesn't come when you merely believe in your heart: *(Rom.10:10) For with the heart man believeth unto righteousness; and <u>with the mouth confession is</u>*

made unto salvation. Whatever situation you find yourself in, if you need the protection and deliverance of the Lord, you need to say it. You need to confess it. "With the mouth confession is made unto salvation." Many people miss out on a miracle because they won't agree with God's Word with their mouth, and with their feet, and with their actions. And here He tells us, "I will say of the Lord, He is my refuge and my fortress; My God, in whom I trust." ***(Psa.91:3) For he will deliver thee from the snare of the fowler, And from the deadly pestilence. (4) He will cover thee with his pinions, And under his wings shalt thou take refuge: His truth is a shield and a buckler. (5) Thou shalt not be afraid for the terror by night, Nor for the arrow that flieth by day; (6) For the pestilence that walketh in darkness, Nor for the destruction that wasteth at noonday. (7) A thousand shall fall at thy side, And ten thousand at thy right hand; But it shall not come nigh thee. (8) Only with thine eyes shalt thou behold, And see the reward of the wicked. (9) For thou, O Lord, art my refuge! Thou hast made the Most High thy habitation.*** You see, when you do confess the Lord as your refuge, you make Him your habitation because "with the mouth confession is made unto salvation." And that's salvation in spirit, soul, body and circumstances; salvation covers all of those things. It's not just getting to go to Heaven when you die, folks. Religion is selling us short on what salvation is all about. Salvation actually means "all my needs supplied, like a little baby," and we have lots of needs.

(Psa.91:10) There shall no evil befall thee, Neither shall any plague come nigh thy tent. (11) For he will give his angels charge over thee, To keep thee in all thy ways. (12) They shall bear thee up in their hands, Lest thou dash thy foot against a stone. (13) Thou shalt tread upon the lion and adder: The young lion and the serpent shalt thou trample under foot. (14) Because he hath set his love upon me, therefore will I deliver him: I will set him on high, because he hath known my name. This is what we're studying for; we're studying to know His name! What does His name mean? What does His nature, character, and authority mean? Both the Hebrew and Greek word for "name" means "nature, character and authority." ***(Psa.91:15) He shall call upon me, and I will answer him; I will be with him in trouble: I will deliver him, and honor him. (16) With long life will I satisfy him, And show him my salvation.*** Wow! That's awesome! You know some people say, "It's too good to be true." Well, unless you believe it, it's something you'll never see in your life because every benefit we receive of the Kingdom of God comes through faith. That means you accept it. You accept the good report of God's Word. You don't accept what you see, you don't accept what you feel, you don't accept what you hear. You don't accept the bad report. Those people who accepted the bad report, by the way, died in the wilderness. We don't want to be there, do we? So the Lord is our sacrificial goat. He bore the curse of our sins. He made atonement for us as our sin offering. "Atonement" is like "at oneness." He made us "at one" with God because of His sacrifice. He didn't only bear the sin, He bore the curse. That's what most of Christianity denies. They say, "He bore the sin and I'm forgiven, but that's it. That's the best I can do down here." Well, the Lord has constantly proven them wrong, by people receiving the awesome benefits they do not deserve. We don't deserve this, folks! We don't deserve it because Jesus was sacrificed. He bore our curse and He is being merciful toward us. He paid the debt we could not pay.

Jesus has been sacrificed as our Passover Lamb. This is why we can have protection. This is why we can believe Psalm 91 in the days to come, when tremendous things are going to be happening on this earth. ***(Exo.12:3) Speak ye unto all the congregation of Israel, saying, In the tenth [day] of this month they shall take to them every man a lamb, according to their fathers' houses, a lamb for a household: (4) and if the household be too little for a lamb, then shall he and his neighbor next unto his house take one according to the number of the souls; according to every man's eating ye shall make your count for the lamb. (5) Your <u>lamb shall be without blemish</u>*** (Well, that's our Lord; that's why He came.)***, a male a <u>year</u> old....*** The Lord spoke to me one time when I was reading this and He said, "A 'year' means 'death, burial and resurrection.'" I thought, "Why is that, Lord?" Well, it's because every year the seasons go through death, burial and resurrection. Spring is resurrection, isn't it? And death is winter, right? So this Lamb is One Who went through death, burial and resurrection for us. ***(Exo.12:5) Your lamb shall be without blemish, a male a year old: ye shall take it from the sheep, or from the goats: (6) and ye shall keep it until the fourteenth day of the same month; and the whole assembly of the congregation of Israel shall kill it at even. (7) And they shall take of the blood, and put it on the two side-posts and on the lintel, upon the houses wherein they shall eat it.*** So they sacrificed their lamb and there are people today who tell you that we should still be keeping this feast. Of course, they say it's just a ceremony, but if you understand what the Passover is about, you know the ceremony is really not pleasing to God. It's a waste of time. Paul tells us very plainly that this part of the ceremony has already been accomplished, and we should believe and confess that. We should be thanking God for this and giving honor to Jesus Christ. The parable has been fulfilled and we don't need to go back and do the parable again; we need to partake of the fulfillment.

When the Apostle Paul finds a man who has his father's wife, he chides the church because they haven't done anything about this man and he's in their midst, polluting their assembly. ***(1Co.5:1) It is actually reported that there is fornication among you, and such fornication as is not even among the Gentiles, that one [of you] hath his father's wife. (2) And ye are puffed up, and did not rather mourn, that he that had done this deed might be taken away from among you. (3) For I verily, being absent in body but present in spirit, have already as though I were present judged him that hath so wrought this thing, (4) in the name of our Lord Jesus, ye being gathered together, and my spirit, with the power of our Lord Jesus, (5) to deliver such a one unto Satan for*** *the destruction of the flesh, that the spirit may be saved in the day of the Lord Jesus.* In other words, he turns him over to the devil for a spanking, so that the man might repent. *(1Co.5:6) Your glorying is not good. Know ye not that a little leaven leaveneth the whole lump?* I guess they were glorying in their grace, but they had a wrong perception of grace, just as many do today. They have a cheap, "greasy" grace that doesn't deliver from sin. This is not grace, folks! <u>Grace delivers from sin</u>. In the church, when there are willfully disobedient people, you're to throw them out. You're not to forgive them, according to what this text tells us very plainly. And, in fact, they're not forgiven by God. *(Heb.10:26) For if we sin wilfully after that we have received the knowledge of the truth, there remaineth <u>no more a sacrifice</u> for sins....* There's no grace there, if we sin willfully after we've received the knowledge of the truth; there remains no sacrifice for sin. *(Heb.10:26) For if we sin wilfully after that we have received the knowledge of the truth, there remaineth no more a sacrifice for sins, (27) but a certain fearful expectation of judgment, and a fierceness of fire which shall devour the adversaries.* Walking in willful disobedience is when you <u>know</u> what you're doing is wrong, but you're going to do it anyway. And if you're sinning with the will, then you're going to run into a chastening from God. Everybody should receive that warning right up front. It will save you from going through an awful lot of misery. We've been lied to about what grace covers. There is a blood covering and it's for our mistakes, and it's for our foolishness, and our childishness and our failures. The blood covering is for all these things, but it's not for willful disobedience. *(1Co.5:6) Your glorying is not good. Know ye not that a little leaven leaveneth the whole lump?* In other words, "Don't let this man sit in your assembly and continue to pollute you." If it's permissible for him to sin, then it's permissible for you to sin and people begin to see that. They begin to think, "Yeah, okay. I might as well sin a little bit, so the Lord will be pleased and give me some grace." No. That's willful sin and it will bring judgment upon you and upon your house.

(1Co.5:7) Purge out the old leaven, that ye may be a new lump, even as ye are unleavened. For our passover also hath been sacrificed, [even] Christ. So we see the first part of Exodus 12 has already been fulfilled. Christ was sacrificed for us and the Lamb has taken our punishment and He's taken our curse. But Paul says, "Purge out the old leaven," because, along with the sacrifice of the lamb, the Israelites had to eat unleavened bread. They had to partake of unleavened bread. And Paul said, *(1Co.10:17) Seeing that we, who are many, are one bread, one body: for we are all partake of the one bread.* In other words, "You are all one loaf. We are bread." We gather together to break bread and share it with one another, but we don't want leaven in that bread. Jesus Christ is the "loaf." He's the body and we abide in Him, and we don't want leaven in there. Leaven is put into bread to make bread palatable for the flesh, to make it pleasing to the flesh, but we don't want to please the flesh in anything. And as we're going to read in Exodus, the Israelites ate the lamb with bitter herbs because He's sweet in the mouth but bitter in the belly. You know, when you partake of Jesus, He's death to the old

man. It's not a pleasant thing to the old man to be partaking of God; it's a pleasant thing to the new man; he's growing up.

Well, Paul says, "Purge out the old leaven, that ye may be a new lump, even as ye are unleavened. For our passover also hath been sacrificed, even Christ: *(1Co.5:8) wherefore let us keep the feast, not with old leaven, neither with the leaven of malice and wickedness, but with the unleavened bread of sincerity and truth.* Then he goes on to say that he's not talking about the people of the world; he's talking about the people of the Kingdom. Don't have company with these people who claim to be Christians yet who walk in immorality. *(1Co.5:9) I wrote unto you in my epistle to have no company with fornicators; (10) not at all [meaning] with the fornicators of this world, or with the covetous and extortioners, or with idolaters; for then must ye needs go out of the world: (11) but as it is, I wrote unto you not to keep company, if any man that is named a brother be a fornicator, or covetous, or an idolater, or a reviler, or a drunkard, or an extortioner; with such a one no, not to eat. (12) For what have I to do with judging them that are without? Do not ye judge them that are within? (13) But them that are without God judgeth. Put away the wicked man from among yourselves.* And, of course, it will give them a reason to repent, if you don't accept them in their sins. You're not supposed to accept willful, disobedient people in their sins. The church is very confused about that.

Now let's go back and read a little more in Exodus. We see that the Lamb has already been sacrificed, but there are still some things left for us to do concerning this Passover feast. *(Exo.12:7) And they shall take of the blood, and put it on the two sideposts and on the lintel, upon the houses wherein they shall eat it.* And we know, of course, that the blood represents the sacrifice. *(Isa.53:12) Therefore will I divide him a portion with the great, and he shall divide the spoil with the strong; because he poured out his soul unto death, and was numbered with the transgressors: yet he bare the sin of many, and made intercession for the transgressors.* He poured out His life unto death, meaning, *(Lev.17:11) For the life of the flesh is in the blood; and I have given it to you upon the altar to make atonement for your souls: for it is the blood that maketh atonement by reason of the life.* When Jesus poured out His life, He was giving us life. He sacrificed His life for us. He made an exchange and He gave us His blood for our blood. "The life of the flesh is in the blood," or, "the soul of the flesh is in the blood." Our soul has been polluted because of the sinful nature that's been passed on to us through the blood. Now the Lord Jesus has given us His blood. He's made an exchange, "a reconciliation," and He's given us His blood. He's now our Father. We are born again and we are adopted by Him. So the Israelites were to put this blood upon the doorpost and we're told, *(Deu.28:1) And it shall come to pass, if thou shalt hearken diligently unto the voice of the Lord thy God, to observe to do all his commandments which I command thee this day, that the Lord thy God will set thee on high* *above all the nations of the earth: (2) and all these blessings shall come upon thee, and overtake thee, if thou shalt hearken unto the voice of the Lord thy God. (6) Blessed shalt thou be when thou <u>comest in</u>, and blessed shalt thou be when thou <u>goest out</u>.* If you hearken unto His Word, He'll bless you going in and He'll bless you coming out. And then He says, *(Deu.28:15) But it shall come to pass, if thou <u>wilt not hearken unto the voice of the Lord thy God</u>, to observe to do all his commandments and his statutes which I command thee this day, that all these curses shall come upon thee, and overtake thee. (19) Cursed shalt thou be when thou comest in, and cursed shalt thou be when thou goest out.* It's kind of a simple way to tell you, that whether you're coming or going, you're going to be under the curse, if you don't hearken. "Hearken" means "to hear <u>and</u> obey," and we know that through faith, we receive power from God to obey. But not if we walk in willful rebellion: *(Heb.10:26) ... if we sin wilfully after that we have received the knowledge of the truth, there remaineth no more a sacrifice for sins.* And so He says, whether we're going in or whether we're going out, we're walking under the blood.

(Exo.12:8) And they shall eat the flesh in that night, roast with fire, and unleavened bread; with bitter herbs they shall eat it. This is the part that we have to partake of. The Lord has sacrificed His life. He was the offering and now we have to partake of Who He is, what He is. This is what it represented to eat the flesh in that night. And it was to be roasted with fire because fire purifies things. Well, the flesh and the unleavened bread both represent Christ. He was the Word made flesh. *(Joh.1:14) And <u>the Word became flesh</u>, and dwelt among us (and we beheld his glory, glory as of the only begotten from the Father), full of grace and truth.* And He was also the bread that came down out of Heaven; that was the manna. *(Joh.6:48) I am the bread of life. (49) Your fathers ate the manna in the wilderness, and they died. (50) This is the bread which cometh down out of heaven, that a man may eat thereof, and not die. (51) <u>I am the living bread which came down out of heaven</u>: if any man eat of this bread, he shall live for ever: yea and the bread which I will give is my flesh, for the life of the world.* So when you partake of the manna, you're partaking of the Word; and when you partake of the Word made flesh, you're partaking of the Word. He said to <u>eat</u> the flesh and <u>eat</u> the unleavened bread. What you eat goes into you and it becomes who you are. To partake of the Word is to put it into your life to where <u>you</u> become the Word made flesh. He's sowing the Word in you, so that <u>you</u> become the living Word on this earth, the body of Christ.

If the body of Christ in Jesus' day was the Word made flesh, what could the body of Christ be today? Well, we're called the body of Christ. Who lives in the body of Christ? He does. So who has to die, in order for Him to live there? <u>We do</u>. We have to sacrifice the old fleshly life and Jesus accomplished this for us. We were crucified with Christ and we don't live anymore, as the Apostle Paul said: *(Gal.2:20) I have been crucified with Christ; and it is no longer I that live, but Christ living in me: and that*

[life] which I now live in the flesh I live in faith, [the faith] which is in the Son of God, who loved me, and gave himself up for me. It's Christ Who lives in us. His sacrifice was a sacrifice for us. ***(1Co.15:22) For as in Adam all die, so also in Christ shall all be made alive.*** I thought about that and the Lord helped me to understand that, in the loins of Adam, the seed of all mankind fell, but Christ was the last Adam and His seed wasn't a physical seed. According to Matthew 13, His seed was the Word of God. Therefore, His seed brings forth His fruit in us and, if we receive of His seed and bear His fruit, we are what? We are the Word made flesh. He says to, ***(Exo.12:9) Eat not of it raw, nor boiled at all with water, but roast with fire; its head with its legs and with the inwards thereof.*** In other words, eat the <u>whole</u> lamb. When the children of Israel were in the wilderness, God said He was going to try them, to test them, with the manna. They got a day's portion every day and they had to eat all of it. And it's the same with us today, folks. We should be partaking of all of what the Lord is through His Word.

Some people pick this piece of the Word and they pick that piece of the Word, and another piece of the Word, but those pieces that you're ignoring don't give you the benefits of God because you're not believing them and acting upon them. You're not <u>eating</u> them. To "partake" of them is to bring them into yourself, so they become who you are. You eat food and that food becomes who you are. You've heard the saying, "You are what you eat." Well, that's a spiritual saying and it's the truth. We're to partake of the head; that is the renewed mind of Christ. We're to partake of His legs; that is the walk of Christ. And we're to partake of His inward parts; that is the heart and the desire of Christ. We're to partake of all of Christ. This is our part to do and we are to partake of that through the Word of God. We eat this Word every day, just like the Israelites had to eat that manna that came in the wilderness every day. We have to put it into action in our life; it has to be the walk. We have to put it into action in our minds; it has to be the thoughts. And it has to be the desire of our hearts. ***(Exo.12:10) And ye shall let nothing of it remain until the morning*** (The same command was given about the manna.)***; but that which remaineth of it until the morning ye shall burn with fire.*** The same thing was said about the manna. It bred worms when they tried to save it for the next day. See, you're supposed to get your portion of Christ today and you're not to save it up for tomorrow. You won't be able to have it tomorrow. The portion of Christ that He gives to you today is only for today and the manna is the same way. You get the manna and you partake of that manna that day; you can't save it for tomorrow. Tomorrow has its own manna. He's telling us to begin to find out what this Word says, begin to walk in it, begin to speak it, begin to act upon it. This is what's going to prepare people for the Passover.

(Exo.12:11) And thus shall ye eat it: with your loins girded, your shoes on your feet, and your staff in your hand (In other words, when you start eating God's Word, you have to be ready to start walking out of Egypt.)***; and ye shall eat it in haste: it is the Lord's passover.*** Glory to God! ***(12) For I will go through the***

land of Egypt in that night, and will smite all the first-born in the land of Egypt, both man and beast; and against all the gods of Egypt I will execute judgments: I am the Lord. (13) And the blood shall be to you for a token upon the houses where ye are: and when I see the blood, I will pass over you, and there shall <u>no plague be upon you</u> to destroy you, when I smite the land of Egypt. No plague, folks. Now, when you go back and look at the plagues that God cast upon Egypt, a "plague" didn't represent a pestilence. Every single judgment was called a plague: the plague of the thick darkness, the plague of the hail, the plague of the murrain of the cattle, the plague of the locusts and so on. In other words, <u>the curse is called the plague</u>. And who bore the curse? The Lord Jesus did; He bore the penalty. And whose fault was it? Well, we're the ones who sacrificed the lamb. See, He told each house to sacrifice the lamb. It's our fault. We sacrificed the Lamb. He died for all of us and He delivered us from this curse. And it has to be just the Lamb and nothing added, no leaven. *(Rev.22:18) I testify unto every man that heareth the words of the prophecy of this book, if any man shall add unto them, God shall add unto him the plagues which are written in this book.* "And the blood shall be to you for a token upon the houses where ye are: and when I see the blood, I will pass over you, and there shall no plague be upon you to destroy you, when I smite the land of Egypt." If you partake only of what Christ is, without adding anything, "there shall no plague be upon you to destroy you, when I smite the land of Egypt."

It's very important that we make sure it's the Word. Only the Word brings forth Christ. It's the seed and it brings forth Him. If you add to that seed or take away from that seed, it's not Christ anymore. And religion is famous for doing that. *(Rev.22:19) And if any man shall take away from the words of the book of this prophecy, God shall take away his part from the tree of life, and out of the holy city, which are written in this book.* Wow! Most people don't think it's that important if they "fudge" a little on the Word here and there, but God is saying that you're not going to get by with that. It's very important for you to make sure that you're fellowshipping with people who are not just leaven in your life. In other words, they're not just polluting you with their thinking and their ideas because it has to be the Word. You need to study the Word. It will bring forth the life of Christ in you and it will give you a passover of the death angel, or "destroyer," as he's called. The destroyer is loosed in the Book of Revelation and his name is Apollyon, which means "destroyer." *(Rev.9:11) They have over them as king the angel of the abyss: his name in Hebrew is Abaddon, and in the Greek [tongue] he hath the name Apollyon.* He is loosed from his prison and gathers the demons to come against humanity in the Tribulation period. He is "the destroyer" once more, loosed to bring death and destruction to those <u>who do not have a Passover</u>. See, the Passover Lamb has been sacrificed, but you had to eat all of that lamb before morning. And you had to eat unleavened bread. *(Mat.16:6) And Jesus said unto them, Take heed and <u>beware of the leaven of the Pharisees and Sadducees</u>.* Jesus said, "Beware." Why did He say that? It's because you won't have a Passover. In fact, He tells us very plainly here, *(Exo.12:15) Seven days shall ye eat unleavened bread; even the first day ye shall put away leaven out of your houses: for <u>whosoever eateth leavened bread</u> from the first day until the seventh day* (the Tribulation period, the 70th week of Daniel), *that soul <u>shall be cut off from Israel</u>*. And then He says the same thing again: *(Exo.12:19) Seven days shall there be no leaven found in your houses: for <u>whosoever eateth that which is leavened</u>, that soul <u>shall be cut off from the congregation of Israel</u>, whether he be a sojourner, or one that is born in the land.* And what is the Passover? *(23) For the Lord will pass through to smite the Egyptians; and when he seeth the blood upon the lintel, and on the two side-posts, the Lord will <u>pass over</u> the door, and will not suffer the destroyer to come in unto your houses to smite you.* He will "pass over."

We, as Christians, have a Passover. You are either partaking of the curse, "the death angel," or he's passing over. But, in order to get him to pass over you, you have to eat the unleavened bread, you have to walk under the blood and you have to eat all of the Lamb. And He says, "there shall no plague be upon you." The word "plague" here just means "a blow, an affliction, a smiting." He said, "I will smite the land of Egypt." The Lord says He's doing it, but notice that He says He won't let the "death angel," the "destroyer," come into your houses to smite you, "when I smite the land of Egypt." In other words, He has the destroyer on a short leash, folks. The Lord is the One Who permits him or doesn't permit him, you see, and He doesn't permit him to come against you, if you are a believer in the Passover Lamb. See, if you're a believer that the Lord Jesus Christ bore your curse, you get the benefit of that. If you don't believe that the Lord Jesus Christ bore you curse, you don't get the benefit of that. And if you're sitting in a church that doesn't believe that, you need to get out of there quickly because that's <u>leaven</u>, and "a little leaven leaveneth the whole lump." If you're leavened, you're not partaking of the Passover. Christians live under the curse and they think it's normal. It's not. The Lord delivered us from the curse. He bore the curse, He took our chastening for us and now it's up to us to believe that because Jesus said, "According to <u>your</u> faith be it done unto you."

I'll give you a good example of the protection of the Lord. You remember the story in Daniel that Nebuchadnezzar made an image of gold, the image of the Beast, which is actually made up of all nations. And Babylon, the great eagle, was the head. It's exactly what we have today. The great eagle is at the head of all nations. And in Revelation 13, this composite of all nations in the image of a man is called the Beast. Well, the <u>preachers</u> commanded the people to bow down to this image of the Beast. *(Dan.3:4) Then the <u>herald</u> cried aloud, To you it is commanded, O peoples, nations, and languages, (5) that at what time ye hear the sound of the cornet, flute, harp, sackbut, psaltery, dulcimer, and all kinds of music, ye fall down and worship the golden image that Nebuchadnezzar the king hath set up; (6) and whoso falleth not down and worshippeth shall the same hour be cast into the midst of a burning fiery furnace.* The word "herald" there is a Greek word in the text and it means "preacher." It's the same word in the New Testament. So he's commanding all the peoples and the nations to bow down to this image of the Beast when they hear the sound of the music; and guess who didn't bow down? Only the three Hebrew children, Shadrach, Meshach and Abednego, didn't bow down, but all the peoples and all the nations and languages bowed down to the image of the Beast. So this small group of people represents the faithful in our day who will not bow down to the image of the Beast.

Well, they told Nebuchadnezzar about this. ***(Dan.3:8) Wherefore at that time certain Chaldeans came near, and brought accusation against the Jews. (13) Then Nebuchadnezzar in his rage and fury commanded to bring Shadrach, Meshach, and Abed-nego. Then they brought these men before the king. (14) Nebuchadnezzar answered and said unto them, Is it of purpose, O Shadrach, Meshach, and Abed-nego, that ye serve not my god, nor worship the golden image which I have set up? (15) Now if ye be ready that at what time ye hear the sound of the cornet, flute, harp, sackbut, psaltery, and dulcimer, and all kinds of music, ye fall down and worship the image which I have made, [well:] but if ye worship not, ye shall be cast the same hour into the midst of a burning fiery furnace; and <u>who is that god that shall deliver you out of my hands</u>? (16) Shadrach, Meshach, and Abed-nego answered and said to the king, O Nebuchadnezzar, we have no need to answer thee in this matter. (17) If it be [so], <u>our God whom we serve is able to deliver us</u> from the burning fiery furnace; <u>and he will deliver us out of thy hand</u>, O king. (18) But if not, be it known unto thee, O king, that we will not serve thy gods, nor worship the golden image which thou hast set up.*** He will deliver you, too.

(Dan.3:19) Then was Nebuchadnezzar full of fury, and the form of his visage was changed against Shadrach, Meshach, and Abed-nego: therefore he spake, and commanded that they should heat the furnace <u>seven times</u> more than it was wont to be heated. So the king heated the furnace seven times hotter. The Book of Revelation uses "time" as a year and "a time, and times, and half a time" is three-and-a-half years. That means "seven times" is seven years. He heats the furnace seven times. That's the Tribulation period. When the great eagle rules over all nations, there's a persecution against the saints. And so, these three refused to bow down to the image of the Beast or take the mark of the Beast. ***(Dan.3:20) And he commanded certain mighty men that were in his army to bind Shadrach, Meshach, and Abed-nego, and to cast them into the burning fiery furnace. (21) Then these men were bound in their hosen, their tunics, and their mantles, and their other garments, and were cast into the midst of the burning fiery furnace. (22) Therefore because the king's commandment was urgent, and the furnace exceeding hot, the flame of the fire slew those men that took up Shadrach, Meshach, and Abed-nego.*** In other words, God started destroying the Beast army that was throwing these men into the furnace. ***(23) And these three men, Shadrach, Meshach, and Abed-nego, fell down bound into the midst of the burning fiery furnace. (24) Then Nebuchadnezzar the king was astonished, and rose up in haste: he spake and said unto his counsellors, Did not we cast three men bound into the midst of the fire? They answered and said unto the king, True, O king. (25) He answered and said, Lo, <u>I see four men loose</u>, walking in the midst of the fire, and they have no hurt; and the aspect of the fourth is like a son of the gods.*** The furnace didn't do anything but burn off their bonds and they were not touched. They were partaking of the Passover. Nebuchadnezzar called them "servants of the Most High God" when he saw this. The Most High God. You know, he believed in many gods, but he was most impressed with "Jehovah God" at this particular time. And then it says, ***(Dan.3:27) ... the fire had no power upon their bodies, nor was the hair of their head singed, neither were their hosen changed, nor had the smell of fire passed on them.***

These three men found the boldness and the wisdom not to bow down to the image of the Beast. And, not only that, they partook of the Passover. The fire and heat literally went over them when they were being thrown into the furnace, but destroyed the men throwing them in there. The three weren't touched. They weren't even singed! And I'll tell you why that happened: ***(Dan.1:8) But Daniel purposed in his heart that he would not defile himself with the king's dainties, nor with the wine which he drank.*** And then we see down in verse 11 that it was not only Daniel, it was Hananiah, Mishael and Azariah -- "Shadrach, Meshach and Abednego" -- who did not partake of the king's dainties. So they were the only ones who didn't partake of this food of Babylon and they're the only ones who didn't bow down; and they're the only ones who didn't get burnt. We see that they partook of the benefits of the Passover. Why? Because they wouldn't eat the food that was polluted. They were going to partake only of what their God commanded. They weren't going to partake of the "leaven of Herod." Jesus said, ***(Mar.8:15) ... Take heed, beware of the leaven of the Pharisees and the leaven of Herod***. Who was Herod? He was the king and they weren't going to partake of the king's dainties.

You know, there are many people who are in idolatry with their nation, their kingdom and men. But we don't belong to this world. Our Kingdom is not of this world and that's the Kingdom we belong to, although we submit to this world. We submit to rulers and we pray for them, that we lead a peaceable life, as Paul tells us to do. ***(1Ti.2:2) I exhort therefore, first of all, that supplications, prayers, intercessions, thanksgivings, be made for all men; (2) for kings and all that are in high place; that we may lead a tranquil and quiet life in all godliness and gravity.*** We are not of this world and we don't worship them. We don't agree with their principles, which pollute Christians, because they don't know where the edge of the Kingdom of God is and where the world starts. They're polluted with the leaven, the teaching, of the Pharisees and the Sadducees, and they're polluted with the leaven of Herod, patriotism and so on.

We don't want any leaven; we want only the pure Word, the thinking of God, the walk of God, the heart of God. This is what we're partaking of when we partake of this Word, when we desire after the One who wrote this Book. We want this Word living in us and we can partake of this Passover. Multitudes are going to do it, but multitudes are going to pass away because, **(Hos.4:6) My people are destroyed for lack of knowledge: <u>because thou hast rejected knowledge</u>, <u>I will also reject thee</u>, <u>that thou shalt be no priest to me</u>: seeing thou hast forgotten the law of thy God, I also will forget thy children.** God says, "If you've rejected knowledge, I'm going to reject you from being a Priest unto Me and your children." Even if you don't go to some dead church, it's important that you read the Book. It's important that you put this Word in your heart. It will deliver you. It will put confidence in you.

I've partaken of this particular Passover, back when I worked at Exxon Refinery in Baton Rouge, Louisana. You know, I just loved the Word of God and I was devouring it day and night at that time. I was reading the Word and I was, and still am, simple-minded, but I didn't have a lot of religious education to pollute my mind. I was raised in a church that didn't read the Bible at all. So, when I started reading the Bible, I just said, "Wow! Look at this! This is <u>food</u>!" I was just gobbling it up, you know, in my childlike mind. And I was just beginning to walk in it and do it, and people told me, "That all passed away." Well, it was working for me, so I didn't pay attention to them. Anyway, I was a volunteer fireman for Exxon and I was a machinist for them for a while, and I was a supervisor for a while. They had a fire team out there, in case they had an industrial fire, and so I was on their fire team, and I received some really good education. I went to Texas A&M University over several years for a week at a time. And I went through their fire training course at Louisiana State University. But, one day we had a fire on the Number Nine Pipe Still, which is a mass of pipes, pumps, drivers and a tower that's several stories tall. They had an oil spill that caught this whole thing on fire and the flames were just going up to heaven, you know. So they called us out and they sent the pumper over there. We pulled the hoses off and hooked them up to the pumper. Then we pulled a three-inch hose off and we got about five of us guys on it. And the first thing we saw was that there were pipes leading through this unit that were about to melt and drop a lot more fuel down in the midst of this problem. The whole unit was on fire, but the process people told us, "Look, you need to save those pipes right there because they are going to dump this whole tower right out here on the ground and we're going to have a lot worse fire than we have now!"

So we were taking this three-inch line and it takes about five people to hold a three-inch line. It will push on you, especially when the pumper turns the pressure up and it's really pushing back like a rocket on you. We had about five of us and we walked in through the burning oil, and we had laid down a foam blanket. The foam cut off the oxygen to the oil and it stopped the fire. So we laid down this foam blanket and we were walking through the foam with our helmets and our bunker coats, and our boots and equipment. We walked out there where we could get a shot at these pipes and we were really putting a heavy stream on these pipes to keep them from melting and dropping their liquid down into the rest of it. These were some big pipes and there was no telling what was going through them. This was a pipe still, so something between oil and jet fuel was going through them, but whatever it was, we didn't want a bigger fire, so we were training the hose on this pipe and we were doing pretty well. We had a safety crew over on the side, in case the foam blanket broke down. They were there to put the fog nozzle on us to keep us from burning up. You can open these things up into a fog and it will just put light water all over you to keep you from burning up. So, anyway, the guys on the safety team are trained not to ever turn fog down into the blanket and wash the blanket away because then you just have boiling oil there that's going to flame right up and you're standing in this flame.

Well, they started seeing the blanket breaking down in front of us because it will do that after a while. You have burning oil and you put the foam blanket out there, and after a while it will start breaking it down and the fire will start burning through it. So they got excited when they saw that it was coming back on us and the guy that was on the line swung his hose around there and unintentionally just washed our foam blanket away. When he did that, the fire was all over us. I mean, we were standing in the middle of burning crude. And there were two guys in front of me. The guy in the front, the face shield on his helmet just melted right off of it and he took off running. And then the guy who was in front of me stepped forward to hold the nozzle and the same thing happened to him, so he took off running. Those two guys went to the hospital because you can't run through burning crude very well. It splashes all over you; everywhere you throw oxygen down there into it makes it a whole lot worse. It's just an inferno. Anyway, the safety guys knew what they did wrong. They backed it off and they put the fog up in the air and they backed off a little bit. So I stepped forward, but now there were only three of us holding this three-inch line and you can't hold a three-inch line very long like that. There's too much force against you, so the pumper had to cut down on the pressure. Well, I stepped forward and grabbed the nozzle, and then, before I knew it, the guys behind me took off, too, because this fire was all around us. I felt the fire coming up under my bunker coat and I knew it was coming up under my coat, but I didn't feel any heat from it. I just felt a little warmth and I thought, "Well, I"m just going to stay here as long as I can."

So I stayed there and held that nozzle on those pipes, for I don't know how long, but it was quite a few minutes past that point that I stayed out there. That fire was all up under my shield but my shield didn't melt and I wasn't afraid. I'll tell you one thing: the Lord can put His boldness in you. People are afraid; it's just natural for them to be afraid because they don't know where they're going when they die. They don't know where they're going and they don't know who their God is. They don't trust in Him. Even though I was young in the Lord, I was full of God and full of the Word. It was exciting to me, so I just stuck around. I stayed there for quite a while and when I decided to turn the nozzle off and walk out, I still really wasn't feeling the heat. I really wasn't feeling burnt at all. But when I decided to turn it off, it wouldn't turn off because it had rocks in it. The pumping system had probably picked up some rocks in the system and put them into the nozzle and jammed it. You can't put a flowing nozzle like that down in burning oil because it takes off like a rocket behind you and it throws all that oil right back on you. You can't even put it down because, if you put it down and you let it go, first thing you know, you're getting hit in the back with burning crude. So I couldn't put it down. I worked with it a little bit and they turned the pumper down when they saw I was having problems. I worked with it a little bit and I finally got it closed off enough to where I could lay it down without it taking off. And then I just walked on out. I walked through the crude and some of it was burning, but I didn't run and I didn't even stir it up; I just walked out. I had the confidence of the peace of the Lord the whole time. As a matter of fact, I was kind of enjoying it. It's just amazing that the grace of the Lord upon His people, to not only think right in a situation like that, but to protect His people.

We have the protection of God, folks. We have it, but the world won't have it; they'll be burnt up in a situation like that. You know, there are times coming and, if it's not this, it's something else for which you're going to need the protection of God. That's what the Passover is all about. The Lord Jesus bore our curse. We're not under the curse of this world. The whole world is under a curse and you can't go by the statistics because they're all under the curse. The only people who are not under the curse are the people who <u>believe</u> in the Passover Lamb. They believe that He bore this curse, so that they would not have to bear the penalty for their own sins. We have to believe that! "According to your faith be it done unto you." One time I was with a good friend of mine and there was a fire on the Coker Unit. It wasn't crude; it was lighter stuff and it was just burning everywhere. Someone had pulled a blind out of a six-inch line and the valve was partially opened, and when they pulled the blind out, it just started dumping that stuff and it found a source and ignited. Well, the whole unit went up in flames. There was this guy on the line with me, whom I'd been witnessing to about the Lord. His name was Bruce and I'd been telling him about the Lord. Of course, we did all this training and practicing, and one thing they taught us is that in a fire, you don't go near any piece of equipment that has a fuel tank on it. Because, if that fuel tank lets go, it will take you with it. So, we were walking in there and it was so black and smoky that we couldn't see very well. We got real close to this valve and we saw the hydrocarbon just coming out underneath the valve, where the blind had been pulled out. It was flashing out and there were flames everywhere. We set our nozzles on a fog pattern. We had the two of them side-by-side, which kind of pushed the fire back. So I looked over and I saw a crane, and the fire was all up underneath this crane, but we had to hold our nozzle on this pressurized hydrocarbon that was coming at us on fire. So I said, "Hey, Bruce, look over there! Look at that crane! I wonder if that tank's blown yet, Bruce? This would be a good time for you to know the Lord, Bruce!" He said, "I'm trying, David! I'm trying!" I said, "You'd better do more than that! Bruce, if that tank lets go, you're going with it. You know that don't you? This is a good time for you to know the Lord, Bruce!" Anyway, we got up closer to the valve. We had two fogs overlapping and we pulled right up on the valve, and a guy came up between us and closed the valve off. The fire was allowed to burn out whatever hydrocarbons were left on the ground and it eventually went out.

(Pro.28:1) The wicked flee when no man pursueth; But the righteous are bold as a lion. When you know who you are in Jesus Christ, you can stand your ground. When you know what He's done for you, you can stand your ground and you don't have to be afraid. The worst thing you have to fear in any situation is fear itself, as one president loudly proclaimed. And it's the truth because you know what fear is? It's faith in reverse; it's faith in the curse. If you permit yourself to fear, there isn't anything God can do for you because He's bound Himself by His Word and He said, "According to your faith be it done unto you." ***(Rom.1:16) For I am not ashamed of the gospel: for it is the power of God unto salvation to every one that believeth; to the Jew first, and also to the Greek.*** The Gospel is the power of God to save the one who believes. So giving in to fear is the worst thing you can do, whether it's a disease epidemic, or any kind of plague, or any kind of judgment. If you have faith in the Passover Lamb, then you're believing in all the Gospel because you've eaten all the Lamb. You see, there are a lot of half-Gospel churches out there and they don't believe in this part. They believe they'll be forgiven, but they don't believe that He bore the curse. ***(Gal.3:13) Christ redeemed us from the curse of the law, having become a curse for us; for it is written, Cursed is every one that hangeth on a tree.*** So, you know what? They're not going to partake of this. They're going to pass away in the midst of it. Am I saying that they won't go to Heaven? Not necessarily, but I'm saying that they're not going to partake of this benefit because it is, "According to your faith be it done unto you."

The Good News of the Gospel is the good news of His salvation in spirit, soul, body and in circumstances. Salvation is not just so you get to go to Heaven. If you don't believe this part, you don't receive it. If you give in to fear, you've lost. You need to fight. You need to resist fear because, when you get into a situation like that, you can't think you're just like everybody else out here. You're not like everybody else; you're not like the world. Statistics don't mean anything to you. You see, you're a very small percentage of planet Earth and they don't gather any statistics on you. If they went to the churches, they still wouldn't get any statistics on you because those are mostly unbelievers, too. There is only a remnant of people who want to believe. They want to eat the head, legs and inwards of Jesus Christ. They want to partake of all of Who He is and everything that He has given unto them, and so they are exercising their faith in all of the Gospel. They are partaking of all of the Lamb. They are not leaving any of the manna until the morning. That's the way it needs to be with us, folks. Get in the Word and find out who you are, find out what God has done for you, so that you can stand in the evil days and the great tribulations that are coming. God bless you! The Lord be with you. May His faith be yours and may you get into this Word and not depart from it, in Jesus' name. Amen.

CHAPTER 22

Safety in Zion!

Greetings, saints! God bless you and thank you for being with us today. Father, we ask You in Jesus' name to bless all the brethren who are joining us today, to please pour out Your Holy Spirit upon them and to bless them with discernment, understanding and wisdom for the days to come. Lord, we want to see all of Your people abiding in the protection of the Passover Lamb, all of Your people abiding in the protection of Mt. Zion. We're asking, Lord, that You give wisdom to Your people, to hide in You in these coming days. Lord, we just praise You! We know that You are getting this revelation out to the brethren and that You are being a blessing unto them. We ask You, God, in Jesus' name, to bless our study today. Amen. Thank You, Father!

Again, I'm going to talk about receiving protection and safety from the Lord in the days to come. I'd like to share a vision with you that I received which I believe was in 1996. I was caught up high above the Gulf of Mexico and viewed the United States stretched out before me. As I looked up above the United States, I saw a veil stretched over the whole United States. And up above the veil, in this vision, I saw a bomb hanging there. It was a <u>tremendous bomb</u>, almost as big as the United States. I looked up above it and, believe it or not, it was hanging from a piece of string with a bow knot in it. So, I looked back down past the veil upon the United States stretched out before me, and the outer perimeter of the nation was a wall. It was kind of like an above-ground swimming pool would be, with a wall that goes around the outside edge and there was water on the inside. And swimming all around inside the United States were fish. Then I realized that I had a fishing pole in my hand and I looked at the fishing pole and the fish. And after this, the Lord began to give me the revelation of what this was, although I didn't get the full revelation for two more years. But, I got a partial revelation that the fish couldn't see the bomb because of this veil stretched above them. They didn't know that judgment was on its way because this veil was between them and the bomb. The Lord gave me the wisdom to know that, if I caught the fish, then from my perspective, they could see that judgment was imminent. Many of God's people don't know that; I didn't know that back then. By the way, in those days, there were a lot of prophets and a lot of people getting dreams and visions about judgment coming to the United States around 1999. Many people think those were wrong, but they were not wrong; they were just "Jonah" prophecies.

In 1998, God gave me another piece of the revelation that had been hidden from me. When I saw the United States as a pool with fish in it, God was showing me that the United States was Nineveh in the Scriptures. Nineveh was a type of the United States because Nineveh was the head of the Beast empire, the Assyrian Beast empire; and now, folks, the United States is the head of a one-world Beast empire. God has raised up every Beast empire in a time when His people were apostate. So I got this revelation that America was Nineveh and that the judgment the prophets were speaking against America was not going to come to pass because when Jonah preached to Nineveh, God delayed the judgment. As I began to tell people about that, they realized that I was speaking the truth and a lot of them stopped preaching about imminent judgment coming. However, the Lord didn't let me release that until about four months before the end of 1999. He let those prophets keep preaching until then, in order to bring people to repentance because He wanted some repentance, in order to delay the judgment. And, you know, He did get some repentance, not from America itself, but from the elect. I realized something else, too. There are matching war cycles between the United States and Israel. From the foundation of the United States, there have been 15 wars that were 17 years apart. Israel had the same cycles before the Assyrian Empire, whose head was Nineveh, conquered the northern 10 tribes. Israel also had 15 wars that were 17 years apart. So at the end of this cycle, when it broke, we were expecting a judgment on the United States but God delayed it.

Actually, the Bible Code speaks of two judgments on the United States: one in 2000 and one in 2006. And in the matrix for each of them is the word "Delayed." So in 2000 and 2006, America was looking for great judgment and it was delayed. Why did God delay judgment on America? Well, the Lord showed me that the same story was in Jonah. When Jonah preached to Nineveh and God delayed judgment, God was doing something there that a lot of people don't know about and understand. It wasn't just because they repented; it was because He had a use for Nineveh. As a matter of fact, if God hadn't delayed the judgment on Nineveh, Nineveh would have been conquered and destroyed at that time and there would have been no one there to chasten God's people and bring them to repentance. All the prophets who were Jonah's contemporaries had been speaking that Nineveh, at the head of the Assyrian Empire, was going to conquer His people. Jonah didn't want that. And for that reason, Jonah was angry when the Lord decided to have mercy. He knew that Assyria would be used by God to judge Israel. The delaying of the judgment made it possible that Assyria could now conquer Israel, which they did. And then afterward, God would judge Nineveh. That's exactly what happened. God moved the Tribulation, the judgment of America, from before the Tribulation of God's people to after the Tribulation of God's people. He showed me the proof of that all through the Scriptures. I'm talking about the ultimate judgment of America, a nuclear war with Russia and China, and so on.

At the end of the 17-year war cycle for Israel, something happened. **(2Ki.18:9) And it came to pass in the fourth year of king Hezekiah, which was the seventh year of Hoshea son of Elah king of Israel, that Shalmaneser king of Assyria came up against Samaria, and besieged it.** Samaria was the northern 10 tribes. They had been worshipping the "golden calf" and they had been making priests that were not of the Levites. In other words, the priests were not ordained of God, just like many ministers today are not ordained of God. Samaria called their golden calf "Yahweh," and they called it "Elohim," just like the Israelites when they made the first golden calf in the wilderness. **(Exo.32:4) And he received it at their hand, and fashioned it** *with a graving tool, and made it a molten calf: and they said, <u>These are thy gods</u>, O Israel, which brought thee up out of the land of Egypt.* They were again saying, "This is the real Yahweh," which was a lie. Or, "This is the real Jehovah," which was a lie. So, Assyria conquered Samaria, the northern 10 tribes, in their apostate state. *(2Ki.18:10) And at the end of three years they took it: in the sixth year of Hezekiah, which was the ninth year of Hoshea king of Israel, Samaria was taken. (11) And the king of Assyria carried Israel away unto Assyria, and put them in Halah, and on the Habor, the river of Gozan, and in the cities of the Medes, (12) because they obeyed not the voice of the Lord their God, but transgressed his covenant, even all that Moses the servant of the Lord commanded, and would not hear it, nor do it. (13) Now in the fourteenth year* (that was eight years later) *of king Hezekiah did Sennacherib king of Assyria come up against all the fortified cities of Judah, and took them.* The Beast was conquering and bringing God's people into bondage.

However, the very interesting thing to me is that there was one group of people that the Beast wasn't able to conquer. When the Assyrian Empire invaded Judah, as they were taking Judah, the people were fleeing from before the Beast to Jerusalem. *(2Ki.19:30) And the remnant that is escaped of the house of Judah shall again take root downward, and bear fruit upward. (31) For out of Jerusalem shall go forth a remnant, and out of mount Zion they that shall escape: the zeal of the Lord shall perform this.* The people of Judah were fleeing into Jerusalem, to get behind the broad walls of Jerusalem for safety. *(2Ki.19:32) Therefore thus saith the Lord concerning the king of Assyria, He shall not come unto this city, nor shoot an arrow there, neither shall he come before it with shield, nor cast up a mound against it. (33) By the way that he came, by the same shall he return, and he shall not come unto this city, saith Jehovah. (34) For I will defend this city to save it, for mine own sake, and for my servant David's sake. (35) And it came to pass that night, that the angel of the Lord went forth, and smote in the camp of the Assyrians a hundred fourscore and five thousand* (185,000)*: and when men arose early in the morning, behold, these were all dead bodies.* So God jealously defended Zion. The people of God went to hide in Zion and God jealously defended them. The Beast conquered all the other so-called "people of God" and brought them into bondage and some into death. But these people escaped the bondage and they escaped death because they were in Jerusalem.

What does Jerusalem, or "Zion," represent? That's the thing that we need to know because, just as Nineveh was the head of the Assyrian Empire that conquered the people of God, America at the head of a one-world empire is going to come against the saints. They will persecute the saints. It is the Word of the Lord and it's in many more places than in this text that we're looking at. They're going to very much turn against the saints and you're going to see it, so get ready to do what the Word of the Lord says, right here. There's a remnant that shall escape and the reason is they're going to be behind the broad walls of Zion. So what in the world does Zion represent? *(Mic.4:8) And thou, O tower of the flock, the hill of the daughter of Zion, unto thee shall it come, yea, the former dominion shall come, the kingdom of the daughter of Jerusalem.* What is that? Well, these were the people who escaped. In fact, he's warning people to flee inside the walls of Zion, to escape from this judgment. *(Mic.5:1) Now shalt thou gather thyself in troops, O daughter of troops: he hath laid siege against us; they shall smite the judge of Israel with a rod upon the cheek.* And Micah calls it the "tower of the flock." You can imagine Zion being a city with a broad wall around it at the top of the hill, looking like a tower, with the people fleeing into it for safety. *(Pro.18:10) The name of the Lord is a strong tower; The righteous runneth into it, and is safe* (Hebrew: "set on high."). Once again, we see that the people who escaped did so because they ran to Zion. God used this as a motivating factor to bring them to a place of safety. And not only a place of safety, but a place of holiness because "The name of the Lord is a strong tower." The Hebrew word for "name" means "nature, character and authority." When you're in the name of the Lord, when you're abiding in His "nature, character and authority," there is safety. *(Pro.11:4) Riches profit not in the day of wrath; But righteousness delivereth from death.* Abiding in the name is abiding in righteousness. The apostle Paul said, *(Col.3:17) And whatsoever ye do, in word or in deed, do all in the name of the Lord Jesus, giving thanks to God the Father through him.* Meaning, of course, that you do everything to represent Him on this earth. You are an ambassador for Christ. When people see you, they see Him. So we are to abide in that name and that is the place of safety.

Now, we have a witness to that here: *(Jer.4:5) Declare ye in Judah, and publish in Jerusalem; and say, Blow ye the trumpet in the land: cry aloud and say, Assemble yourselves, and let us go into the fortified cities. (6) Set up a standard toward Zion: flee for safety.* They were fleeing from a Beast kingdom that wanted to conquer and bring an end to them. In the end-time, for us as spiritual Jews, this has to do more with losing this battle that we fight for our souls, than just losing a physical kingdom. Zion in the New Testament is not talking about physical Zion, but born-again spiritual Zion, which we have forsaken. Paul said, *(Heb.12:18) For ye are not come unto [a mount] that might be touched....* Meaning that it's not a physical mountain we're talking about; it's a spiritual mountain. We're spiritual Jews and we have a spiritual kingdom on earth. The Israelite kingdom was a type and shadow of our spiritual kingdom. *(Heb.12:22) But ye are come unto mount Zion, and unto the city of the living God, the heavenly Jerusalem* (not the natural Jerusalem), *and to innumerable hosts of angels, (23) to the general assembly and church of the firstborn who are enrolled in heaven.* Now you see what Zion was in that day. It represented the holy people of God, the people in whom the Lord dwelt. The physical type-and-shadow Temple was in Jerusalem, but in the New Testament, the temple is God's people. Our job is to climb Mount Zion and to go into the presence of the Lord. The Church, or "the called-out ones," were called "Zion" in that day because they were keeping the orders of the Lord. They were being obedient. They were full of the Spirit of God and they had the gifts of the Holy Spirit. There was a mighty revival in their midst as they were walking with God and God called them "the heavenly Jerusalem." By the way, Revelation says the same thing about God's Bride. ***(Rev.21:2) And I saw the holy city, new Jerusalem, coming down out of heaven of God, made ready as a bride adorned for her husband.***

Since that time, God's people have departed from the original God-ordained doctrine that was given unto the saints; they have not held fast to it. ***(Jud.3) Beloved, while I was giving all diligence to write unto you of our common salvation, I was constrained to write unto you exhorting you to <u>contend earnestly for the faith which was once for all delivered unto the saints</u>.*** They've gone off into Babylonish bondage. Now God is calling His people back out of Babylon to rebuild Zion, to re-establish the original Covenant that was given unto us, with the original principles and the original commandments. That's why God is warning His people, "Flee! Go to Zion! It's a place of safety." If you don't flee Babylon, you'll be conquered,. ***(Jer.4:6) Set up a standard toward Zion: flee for safety, stay not; for I will bring evil from the north, and a great destruction. (7) A lion is gone up from his thicket, and a destroyer of nations; he is on his way, he is gone forth from his place, to make thy land desolate, that thy cities be laid waste, without inhabitant. (8) For this gird you with sackcloth, lament and wail; for the fierce anger of the Lord is not turned back from us. (9) And it shall come to pass at that day, saith the Lord, that the heart of the king shall perish, and the heart of the princes; and the priests shall be astonished, and the prophets shall wonder. (10) Then said I, Ah, Lord God! surely thou hast greatly deceived this people and Jerusalem, saying, Ye shall have peace; whereas the sword reacheth unto the life.*** And, folks, it's the same today. Many people are saying "peace and safety" because they believe they're all going to "fly away." They believe there aren't going to be any problems because they'll never see the Beast, but it's never happened in history that God's people haven't gone under the dominion of the Beast. The Beast was raised up by God to bring His people back to Zion, to motivate them to run to a place of safety.

There is no safe place but Zion. Zion represents "abiding in the presence of the Lord," just as the Lord dwelt in the Temple in Zion, where David was king. As you know, David was a type of Jesus, and in our day, the corporate man-child is a type of David. So, once again, God is calling His people to come out of Babylon and return to Zion. He's saying, "Come back to the way it was; <u>return</u> to the faith that was once delivered unto the saints." That's the story of Jeremiah 3. ***(Jer.3:17) At that time they shall call Jerusalem the throne of the Lord; and all the nations shall be gathered unto it, to the <u>name</u> of the Lord, to Jerusalem....*** Jerusalem is the name of the Lord; Jerusalem is the nature, character and authority of the Lord. And notice that He's calling the <u>nations</u>. He's not calling the Jews. He's calling the nations, which are the Gentiles. You see, the

Church has a Jerusalem that is a place of safety. That place of safety represents abiding in the name of the Lord, doing everything in the name of the Lord. It is a place of safety. ***(Jer.3:17) At that time they shall call Jerusalem the throne of the Lord; and all the nations shall be gathered unto it, to the name of the Lord, to Jerusalem: neither shall they walk any more after the stubbornness of their evil heart.*** And what does He say to them? He says, "neither shall they walk any more after the stubbornness of their evil heart." Wow! That's talking about being born-again, folks, and abiding in the doctrine that was once given unto the saints. ***(Jer.3:19) But I said, How I will put thee among the children, and give thee a pleasant land, a goodly heritage of the hosts of the nations! and I said, Ye shall call me My Father, and shall not turn away from following me.*** He says you will "call me My Father." Now, the Jews don't do that; they don't call Him their "Father." The Judaized Christians don't call Him "Father," either; they have their own Old Testament names they like to put on Him. But in the New Testament, God's people have always called Him "Father" and Jesus, Himself, called Him, over and over, "My Father." He taught His disciples to call Him "my Father" and He is our Father. We have this relationship with Him.

These days, we are being called to once again run to the place of holiness. Remember, "righteousness delivereth from death." The Beast is not able to conquer a righteous people. The reason the Beast is able to bring judgment against God's people is because they aren't sanctified. The word "saint" means "sanctified one." They aren't saints and they aren't the Church. Paul said that those who were a part of the Heavenly Jerusalem, which was on earth, by the way, were called "the Church." The Church is only "the called-out ones." God's people are being called-out, and in that day they were being called-out of apostate Judaism. Now they're being called out of apostate Christianity. It's apostate because it doesn't reflect the truth and it doesn't reflect what was given to us in the beginning. ***(1Jn.2:24) As for you, let that abide in you which ye heard from the beginning. If that which ye heard from the beginning abide in you, ye also shall abide in the Son, and in the Father.*** So, if you abide in Christ, then "that which you heard from the beginning will abide in you." If we're really going to abide in the place of safety in that name, then what we heard in the beginning has to be our teaching, our doctrine, our renewed mind. How can you walk as Jesus walked, unless you agree with His doctrine? God is calling us to come back into agreement with Jesus Christ, to renew our minds. ***(Rom.12:2) And be not fashioned according to this world: but be ye transformed by the renewing of your mind, and ye may prove what is the good and acceptable and perfect will of God.*** Folks, there's no curse on a person who's walking in the good, acceptable, perfect will of God. The judgments of the Beast have always been against God's people because they've been in apostasy, which means "backslidden." They've been quite content to live a worldly life, but now God is calling us to be separate, calling us to be "a peculiar people," separate from the world. ***(Deu.14:2 KJV) For thou [art] an holy people unto the LORD thy God, and the LORD hath chosen thee to be a peculiar people unto himself, above all*** *the nations that [are] upon the earth.* He's drawing us back to Zion, to the way it was under King David in the presence of the Lord.

We can't make our own "golden calves" anymore. The churches are full of golden calves that they think are Jesus Christ, yet we know that the Scriptures describe the only true Jesus Christ. And you can't abide in His name -- His nature, character and authority -- unless you really know Who He is. We are coming to know Who He is and learning to walk as He walked. The Bible says you don't abide in Him unless, *(1Jn.2:6) He that saith he abideth in him ought himself also to walk even as he walked.* Let everyone who says that they abide in Him walk as He walked. Well, in the apostate Christian church world, people don't even think that it's possible to walk as He walked, but the Bible says you don't even abide in Him, unless you do that. Remember those disciples; they were just men like us, they were of "like passions." *(Act.14:15) And saying, Sirs, why do ye these things? We also are men of like passions with you, and bring you good tidings, that ye should turn from these vain things unto a living God, who made the heaven and the earth and the sea, and all that in them is.* But the grace of God worked in them because they believed the promises of Jesus Christ. His Words went into them and recreated in them the life of Jesus Christ. That's what we need, folks, because grace is powerful, but grace comes when you have faith in the <u>real</u> promises of God. Grace comes when you haven't recreated Christianity in your own likeness and according to your own will.

Well, abiding in Zion represents all those awesome, wonderful provisions of the promises, dominion over enemies and a place of safety. There are people in these days who are going to escape the coming Beast kingdom. I know a lot of people think that they're going to fly away, but the truth will be known; that's not going to happen. *(Ecc.1:9) That which hath been is that which shall be; and that which hath been done is that which shall be done: and there is no new thing under the sun.* Every time a Beast kingdom came, God's people didn't escape it. The only ones who escaped it were those who were holy. Psalm 125 tells us what it is to abide in Zion. *(Psa.125:1) <u>They that trust in the Lord</u> Are as mount Zion, which cannot be moved, but abideth for ever.* In other words, it's a place of safety for "they that trust in the Lord." You know, there are few Christians who are walking by faith in the Lord, very few, who really believe those promises that Jesus gave us. *(Mat.21:22) And all things, whatsoever ye shall ask in prayer, believing, ye shall receive.* That's awesome! We hear of miracles when people get this renewed in their mind that the Lord really meant what He said. People are working signs and wonders all around them because they're returning to the faith of our spiritual Fathers, the apostles and Jesus Christ. *(Psa.125:2) As the mountains are round about Jerusalem, So the Lord is round about his people From this time forth and for evermore.* Wouldn't you like the Lord to be around you? *(34:7) The angel of the Lord encampeth round about them that fear him, And delivereth them.*

(Psa.125:3) For the <u>sceptre</u> of wickedness shall not rest upon the lot of

the righteous.... The sceptre, meaning "the authority of the Beast kingdom," will not rest upon the righteous, that is, the people who are walking with the Lord through faith. Their faith is in the Lord. They believe He took away their sins; they believe that He gave them His life through reconciliation; they believe that they no longer live and that Christ lives in them. This revelation of faith, which is the Gospel that lives in them, causes God to call them His children and to call them righteous. And because they believe the Gospel, the Lord's going to bring it to pass. "The sceptre of wickedness shall not rest upon the lot of the righteous." So you can see that "righteousness delivereth from death" at the hands of the Beast, at the hands of the Harlot, at the hands of this end-time corrupt society, which is going to hate Christians with a passion. Jesus said, ***(Mat.24:9) Then shall they deliver you up unto tribulation, and shall kill you: and ye shall be hated of all the nations for my name's sake.*** And He meant it. It's coming now very quickly. ***(Psa.125:3) For the sceptre of wickedness shall not rest upon the lot of the righteous; That the righteous put not forth their hands unto iniquity. (4) Do good, O Lord, unto those that are good,*** (And God will certainly bring this prayer to pass!) ***And to them that are upright in their hearts. (5) But as for such as turn aside unto their crooked ways, the Lord will lead them forth with the workers of iniquity. Peace be upon Israel.*** And as the New Covenant says, "upon the Israel of God." ***(Gal.6:16) And as many as shall walk by this rule, peace be upon them, and mercy, and upon the Israel of God.*** That is, of course, the people who are grafted in to the olive tree called "all Israel" through their faith in Jesus Christ (Romans 11). Those are the only Israelites in the New Testament, folks; that's what the Bible says. Psalm 125 is very plain about what it is to dwell in Zion.

I also like, in particular, Psalm 15. ***(Psa.15:1) Lord, who shall sojourn in thy tabernacle? Who shall dwell in thy holy hill?*** And Zion is the holy hill. ***(Psa.15:2) He that walketh uprightly, and worketh righteousness, And speaketh truth in his heart; (4) He that slandereth not with his tongue, Nor doeth evil to his friend, Nor taketh up a reproach against his neighbor; (5) In whose eyes a reprobate is despised, But who honoreth them that fear the Lord; He that sweareth to his own hurt, and changeth not; (6) He that putteth not out his money to interest, Nor taketh reward against the innocent. He that doeth these things shall never be moved.*** Wow! God has a place of protection, right? ***(24:3) Who shall ascend into the hill of the Lord? And who shall stand in his holy place? (4) He that hath clean hands, and a pure heart; Who hath not lifted up his soul unto falsehood, And hath not sworn deceitfully.*** You know, the overwhelming majority of Christianity has done the same thing as the overwhelming majority of Judaism; they've lifted up their souls to falsehood. Why, saints, would you accept anybody's word for anything, when you have this New Covenant to read and study, so that you can come into the image of our Lord Jesus Christ? This is what God has called us to do. Those who add to or take away from the Word are under a curse. ***(Rev.22:18) I testify unto every man that heareth the words of***

the prophecy of this book, if any man shall add unto them, God shall add unto him the plagues which are written in this book: (19) and if any man shall take away from the words of the book of this prophecy, God shall take away his part from the tree of life, and out of the holy city, which are written in this book. They have changed the Covenant and caused God's people to depart from the very thing that will protect them in the days to come.

But I believe that when multitudes of God's people realize that there is no safety outside of abiding in the Word of God, Who is Jesus Christ, that many people are going to be running for the safety of Mount Zion. Others are lifting up their soul unto falsehood. They're deceived. They proclaim that they've been born again, that they're saved, that they're children of God, that they have eternal life, but they will persecute you at the drop of a hat and think nothing of it. As a matter of fact, they'll think they're doing God a favor (John 16:2), just like so-called "God's people" throughout history have done to the true people of God. The closer we draw to Christ, the more enemies we're going to make in the religious Christian world. That's normal and it's been that way throughout history because many of God's people have lifted up their souls to falsehood. They've heard what sounds good, what's ear-tickling, what permits them to live the way they want to live. They've heard it and they like it. They want the flesh to live, but God says, "No. You are to be a burnt offering. Your old fleshly life, your old beastly life, has to be sacrificed." Jesus said, ***(Mat.16:25) For whosoever would save his life shall lose it: and whosoever shall lose his life for my sake shall find it. (10:39) He that findeth his life shall lose it; and he that loseth his life for my sake shall find it.*** If you don't lose your life, you won't gain your life. And those who love the things of the world in this life, naturally, will accept a doctrine that permits them to keep living the way they want to live.

But He says, ***(Psa.24:5) He shall receive a blessing from the Lord*** (That is, those who don't lift up their souls to falsehood will receive a blessing.)***, And righteousness from the God of his salvation.*** Wow! Thank You, Father. You know, over and over, God makes this promise about those who will abide in that secret place of Zion. Paul said you couldn't even touch that mountain because it wasn't a physical place. It was a spiritual place because we are spiritual Jews, spiritual people. The Jews and their kingdom were a type and shadow of our Kingdom today. ***(1Co.10:11) Now these things happened unto them by way of <u>example</u>; and they were written for our admonition, upon whom the ends of the ages are come.*** They were "in the letter" but we're "in the Spirit." Paul said, ***(1Co.15:46) Howbeit that is not first which is spiritual, but that which is natural; then that which is spiritual.*** The natural comes first and then the spiritual. Parables are like that. They are first fulfilled literally, then they are fulfilled spiritually. Now, there is a Kingdom just like the Jew's kingdom on this earth today, but it's in the Spirit. And Zion, once again, is that place of safety, where God is going to protect the lives of His people.

You remember that the Beast lost 185,000 men when they tried to attack Zion. Well, the percentages today will be much higher than that. The United States itself is going to suffer <u>great</u> destruction at the hands of the judgment of God, and from other nations, because of the persecution of the saints. The more this world persecutes the saints, the more judgments will fall upon this world to make them release the saints. It's going to be exactly like it was with Egypt, folks. The more the Egyptians brought the Israelites into deeper bondage, the more God brought judgment upon them. Ultimately, God brought the Passover judgment, which killed all the firstborn of Egypt. And you know who the firstborn of Egypt is, don't you? It's the flesh! As Paul told us, that which is first is natural and then that which is spiritual. The fleshly man is the first-born and the spiritual man is the second-born. When the Israelites went through the "Red Sea baptism," as Paul called it, the old man, the first-born of Egypt, died there. That's why we're going through an end-time baptism of death, so that the old man will die and the spiritual man will come up out of that water on the other side and be washed, cleansed and ready for the Kingdom. Praise be to God!

Well, I'd like to share something else with you. I had a vision of a tower in the early 1980s. This was when I lived in Baton Rouge, Louisiana. And in this vision, I suddenly found myself standing on top of a mountain in front of a vast castle, which I think probably represented the "New Jerusalem." The vast doors that were in front of me opened and standing there in front of me was the king, dressed regally. He waved his hand and ushered me into this vast castle, and we went to a place inside there where he showed me something that I realized since then was the ministry the Lord was giving to me. What he showed me was a tower that was being built in the midst of this New Jerusalem setting. And we saw from Micah that the tower is Zion itself. God is rebuilding Zion in these days. But what I saw was a log-type tower and the logs were stacked like a log cabin would be, crossing at the corners, and this tower became narrower and narrower as it neared the top. All the way at the top, there was a place to stand inside the top. Well, I was looking at this thing and, at that time, I didn't know what this was. But the Lord showed me later that this was the kind of tower that the Israelites built to protect them in case of an enemy invasion, and that's what this represented. The Lord also showed me later that the logs represented His people because at the corners they made a cross and they were all joined together by those crosses. The tower of the flock was Zion and Zion also represents His holy people. And even in Revelation 21 we see the New Jerusalem coming down, called "the Bride," so it represents a holy people unto the Lord, a people who have borne their cross.

You know, in a vision God makes characters any way He wants; He makes towers and buildings and anything else the way He wants. So here I was looking at this tower, wondering about it and thinking about it, and the king said to me, "Because my Son died in the ministry, I want you to have this," and He was talking about this tower. Then He handed me a payment book of what He was going to pay me in this ministry and I saw the amount on there. It wasn't a tremendous amount, according to the world, but it was all I would need because God was going to take care of everything else, which He did. I remember two years after He moved us from Baton Rouge, we went back and averaged our income and it was within $20 of what the Lord told us right there. And I'm sure the error was ours and not His. At any rate, He said, "Because my son died in the ministry, I want you to have this," and He was talking about this tower. You know, everything that Jesus sacrificed, He sacrificed so that we could have something. He gave up something, so that we could have it. He bore our stripes, He took the curse upon Himself, so that we could be blessed, so that we could be healed. He bore our sins, so that we could be blessed, so that we could be delivered from bondage. And He gave up a ministry, so that we could have one. Everything that He lost through sacrifice, we gained. He made a reconciliation, "an exchange." The Lord has reminded me of this many times since then. I said, "Lord, I'm just not worthy that You should do this with me." He said, "It has nothing to do with that. It's because My Son died in the ministry, that you have this ministry." It's grace, folks. Whatever God gives us, it's grace, the unmerited favor of God.

So, anyway, at that time, I didn't really understand this tower too much, but then the next night, the Lord caught me up above Baton Rouge in another vision and I looked down the interstate and saw that tower in Florida. The Lord had been revealing to us, via a series of dreams and visions, that we were going to move to Florida. Well, I realized the Lord was showing me that my ministry was to build that tower. My ministry was to cause God's people to find a place of safety. They built these towers in the wilderness and they built them in the small cities. They built them as a place of protection and safety from other Beast kingdoms that would come to invade -- from thieves that would come to steal the flocks and different things like that. And so I began to look on this tower as something that we were to build, in order to have a place of safety for the troubles that were coming upon the world. The tower is built by causing people to abide in the name of the Lord, teaching them to walk in the name of the Lord, which is His nature, character and authority.

In other words, it's teaching them to walk as Jesus walked. We take His name in baptism. We accept that when we go down into that water that we don't live anymore, and when we come up, the One Who lives in us is Jesus Christ. That's how we take His name in baptism (Romans 6:3; Galatians 3:27). It doesn't have anything to do with exactly what you say over someone, so much as it is being baptized <u>into</u> the name. That's what the word is; it's "<u>into</u> the name" and not "<u>in</u> the name." We are baptized <u>into</u> His nature, character and authority, you see. When the Lord began to reveal to me what this tower represented, I saw it as a place of safety. We come to that place of safety through searching the Word, through putting the Word to work in our life and through renewing our mind with the Word of God. As we learn to walk in the way Jesus walked, we're coming to this place of safety, this place of the name, this city called "the Heavenly Jerusalem" that those early saints had come to. Folks, when we begin to walk as they walked and as Jesus walked, we will be <u>abiding</u> in the name, we will be abiding in that city; that's the place of safety. All of the 10 tribes and all of Judah that didn't escape into Zion were conquered by the Beast kingdom. And, as you can see from the sequence of events that I've laid out here, that was a prophecy about us, at this time, including the 17-year war cycle.

In building my little part of the tower, because I know that God has many people building it, I want to tell you that we need to cast down all imaginations. ***(2Co.10:3) For though we walk in the flesh, we do not war according to the flesh (4) (for the weapons of our warfare are not of the flesh, but mighty before God to the casting down of strongholds), (5) <u>casting down imaginations</u>, and every high thing that is exalted against the knowledge of God, and bringing every thought into captivity to the obedience of Christ.*** We need to cast out all doctrine that we received from religion. We need to start from scratch, to read the New Testament and find out what our Covenant is about. We need to not add to it or take away from it, under penalty of the curse that the Bible speaks about in Revelation. "I testify unto every man that heareth the words of the prophecy of this book, if any man shall add unto them, God shall add unto him the plagues which are written in this book: and if any man shall take away from the words of the book of this prophecy, God shall take away his part from the tree of life, and out of the holy city, which are written in this book." We don't add to His Word and we don't take away from His Word. If you take away from the Book, you will <u>not</u> be abiding in the Holy City. In the Holy City, there is peace, safety, wisdom and the presence of the Lord. That's where we need to be in these days.

Well, the Lord began to show me many things about this tower. For instance, I realized that Abimelech, who was the head of the kingdom, had made an agreement with the men of Shechem to kill the 70 sons of Gideon, so that he would be ruler (Judges 9:1-6). Sounds familiar, doesn't it? That's exactly what happens every time. That's history repeating; it just repeats on a larger and larger scale. You see, the head of the kingdom is going to agree with the Harlot of this day to, once again, crucify the saints for the sake of the Harlot. God did the same thing with Abimelech that He's going to do in these days. He sent demons between the men of Shechem and Abimelech to cause division between them (Judges 9:22) and, as you know, the Beast devoured the Harlot (Revelation 17:16). Well, Abimelech and his men decided to make war against Shechem, which represents the Harlot in type and the people fled to <u>their tower</u>, the tower of Shechem. And, as you know, Abimelech and his men burned it down with all the people in it because the tower of Shechem represents the <u>Harlot</u> tower (Judges 9:46-49). He devoured the Harlot with fire, exactly like Revelation says. You know, the worldly religions think that they're building their own kingdom of safety, but it's not going to save anybody, folks. It never has, all through the scriptures. Safety doesn't come in numbers, it doesn't come in money, it doesn't come with prestige and it doesn't come with favors of the Beast. It doesn't come with any of those things. It comes only from God Almighty. And it comes only from being holy. "Righteousness delivereth from death."

But that wasn't the end of the story. ***(Jdg.9:50) Then went Abimelech to Thebez, and encamped against Thebez, and took it.*** Well, "Thebez" means "whiteness," and it represents the tower of God's people. ***(51) But there was a strong tow-***

er within the city, and thither fled all the men and women, and all they of the city, and shut themselves in, and gat them up to the roof of the tower. In the vision, that's the little thing I saw on the top and these towers were normally built out of logs. *(Jdg.9:52) And Abimelech came unto the tower, and fought against it, and drew near unto the door of the tower to burn it with fire. (53) And a certain woman cast an upper millstone upon Abimelech's head, and brake his skull. (54) Then he called hastily unto the young man his armorbearer, and said unto him, Draw thy sword, and kill me, that men say not of me, A woman slew him. And his young man thrust him through, and he died.* So, the Beast will devour the Harlot and then the Beast itself will be destroyed. But Thebez was still there. God had preserved the city called "Whiteness" in their tower because it was a place of safety. And so it is in our day. All the righteous ministers of the Lord are putting the truth of the Word of God in the minds of God's people and that will cause them to walk in the steps of Jesus Christ. They will accept every Word that He says. They will not cast down or disrespect any of the Word of God for the sake of any religion.

The Pharisees and the Sadducees warred against Jesus because they liked the little kingdom that they had built. They didn't want this upstart, this guy who hadn't gone through their Bible school, to come and tear it down, but that's exactly what He was doing by speaking the truth of the Kingdom. History is going to repeat and in these days the exact same thing is going to happen. God is raising up a Man-child ministry to go forth and do the exact same things that Jesus did. They are the first-fruits. They are a new leadership to bring the people back to the way it was, bring them back to Heavenly Jerusalem, back to Mount Zion, the place of safety. God is going to do that again in these days, starting with the beginning of the Tribulation period; and right now, folks, we need to be running to Zion, the city of our God. We need to be running to Zion because it's the only place of safety. It's the place where God is going to preserve His people through a terrible time, a terrible seven years of famine and destruction. Not only is God going to save His people from the Beast kingdom, but He's going to save them from famines, destructions, earthquakes, from all these things. You know, folks, there is a curse upon the people who depart from the Word, who add to the Word or who take away from the Word, but there is no curse upon the people who are <u>abiding in Christ</u>. He is the secret place of the Most High and He is the fulfillment of Psalm 91.

Read all the provisions of God's protection in Psalm 91. There are people saying that it's not for today, but it is. It's God's safety; it is the secret place of the Most High. Zion is a secret place because it's not a physical place anymore. There's nothing holy about that city over in the Middle East, folks. They have departed from God. They're antichrist and they are in big trouble. God is going to bring a remnant of them to Christ. He's going to give them the born-again experience and they are the remnant that God is going to save. *(Zec.14:1) Behold, a day of the Lord cometh, when thy spoil shall be divided in the midst of thee. (2) For I will gather all nations against Jerusalem to battle; and the city shall be taken, and the houses rifled, and the women*

ravished; and half of the city shall go forth into captivity, and the residue of the people shall not be cut off from the city. And only then is God going to go forth to defend that city because of a remnant, a "residue," of God's people. Only then is He going to go forth and defend those people. They are going to be in the real Zion. So many people have their eyes on the physical today, but God has hidden the truth in a parable. ***(Mat.11:25) At that season Jesus answered and said, I thank thee, O Father, Lord of heaven and earth, that thou didst <u>hide these things from the wise and understanding</u>, and <u>didst reveal them unto babes</u>.*** And that is, those who are simple-minded enough to accept everything He tells them and everything He shows them from His Word.

Folks, we need to get in the tower of Thebez; it's a place of safety and God's preservation. God has provided everything for these days. Very soon, you're going to see people who are being preserved supernaturally, provided for supernaturally, healed supernaturally, delivered supernaturally. The mighty miracles that happened in the days of Jesus are coming now. The beginning of the Tribulation is right around the corner and that is also the beginning of the Man-child ministry. It's the beginning of Jesus' ministry on this earth again. Jesus abiding in His people will be doing signs, wonders and miracles to preserve the elect. Jesus abiding in His people will heal, cast out devils, bring holiness, sanctification, preservation, everything. Oh, thank You, Father! Lord, we ask that You would put it in the hearts of everyone reading this to have an awesome desire for Your Word to be manifested in them, for Your life to be manifested in them. Father, we ask You to draw the brethren into the Word, into the love of the Jesus Christ of the Word. We ask You to renew their mind with the Word, Lord, that they would accept no longer anything that man says to them that would lead them astray from what they see written there. And, Lord, like the Apostle Paul warned in 1 Corinthians 4:6, that they would "learn not to go beyond the things which are written." Amen.

Folks, if you can't break free any other way, stay home and read the Word. Find out what it says, so that you can have the preservation that it talks about. Come to realize and recognize what the real Church looks like, so that you can recognize those people when you are around them and so that you won't be deceived with all the golden calves that are out there. God bless you, saints! And the Lord be with you, in Jesus' name.

CHAPTER 23

God's Disclaimer and Ours!

Hello, saints! God bless you and thank you so much for joining us. Let's ask our Father for His grace. Father, in Jesus' name, we thank You for all of Your precious promises, Lord. We ask, Lord, that Your Holy Spirit bring to remembrance all things that You have said unto us, to defend us against the works of the devil, the curses of this world. Father, we thank You that You put this Word in our hearts to defend us, that it's a shield of faith and a sword of the Spirit, which is the Word of God. Thank You, Lord, for helping us to fight the good fight of the faith and to lay hold on life that is life indeed. Thank You, Lord! Lord, please continue to guide us through Your Word and draw us as Your disciples into the image of Jesus Christ. Thank You, Lord! Amen.

I'm going to share with you what I felt like the Lord told me was His "<u>disclaimer</u>." God has a disclaimer and, as a matter of fact, it's supposed to be our disclaimer, too. We know that the Gospel is the basis for everything that we have in God. It's the "Good News" of the promises and the benefits of Jesus Christ that were given to us through His crucifixion. ***(Rom.1:16) For I am not ashamed of the gospel: for <u>it is the power of God unto salvation to every one that believeth</u>; to the Jew first, and also to the Greek. (17) For therein is revealed a righteousness of God from faith unto faith: as it is written, <u>But the righteous shall live by faith</u>***. "Living by faith" is living by faith in the Gospel. Our access to the promises of the Good News has been given unto us through faith. We have <u>no</u> other access to these benefits. And I believe that is God's disclaimer because many people want the benefits of the Kingdom, but they do not want to "fight the good fight of faith" to lay hold of these benefits. ***(1Ti.6:12) <u>Fight the good fight of the faith</u>. Take hold of the eternal life to which you were called when you made your good confession in the presence of many witnesses.*** There's <u>no</u> promise in the Scriptures for receiving the benefits without that, folks; no promise at all.

Let me read to you what *Vine's Expository Dictionary* says the Greek word for "salvation" -- *soteria* -- actually means. It means "salvation" of course, but salvation in so many different ways. "Soteria denotes deliverance, preservation and salvation. Salvation is used in the New Testament of material and temporal deliverance from danger and apprehension." And then another one is, "Salvation is used in the New Testament of the spiritual and eternal deliverance granted immediately by God to those who accept His conditions of repentance and faith in the Lord Jesus, in Whom, alone, it is to be obtained." Another example is, "Salvation is used in the New Testament of the present experience of God's power to deliver from the bondage of sin." The next one is, "Of the future deliverance of believers at the *parousia* of Christ for His saints." *Parousia* is the coming of Christ <u>for</u> His saints. *Epiphaneia* is the coming of Christ <u>in</u> His saints. And another is, "Of the deliverance of the nation of Israel, at the second advent of Christ, at the time of the *epiphaneia* and of His *parousia*," and so on. You can see that salvation is extremely big, compared to what the normal church idea of salvation is.

This has been afforded to us, this has been given to us, only through our faith and everyone doesn't have faith. The Bible says, "to each has been given a measure of faith," meaning, of course, Christians. ***(Rom.12:3) For I say, through the grace that was given me, to every man that is among you, not to think of himself more highly than he ought to think; but to think as to think soberly, according as <u>God hath dealt to each man a measure of faith</u>.*** But Paul also said, "for all have not faith." ***(2Th.3:1) Finally, brethren, pray for us, that the word of the Lord may run and be glorified, even as also it is with you; (2) and that we may be delivered from unreasonable and evil men; <u>for all have not faith</u>.*** And even among those we call "Christians," there are many people who don't have faith or are not willing to fight the good fight of the faith, to lay hold of the benefits of the Kingdom. And God's condition, all the way through the Scriptures, is that we do fight this good fight of the faith to receive the awesome benefits. ***(Eph.1:1) Paul, an apostle of Christ Jesus through the will of God, to the saints that are at Ephesus, and <u>the faithful in Christ Jesus</u>*** (Notice this was the only time he said "the faithful in Christ Jesus."): ***Grace to you and peace from God our Father and the Lord Jesus Christ.*** The faithful receive grace: ***(Eph.2:8) For <u>by grace have ye been saved through faith</u>; and that not of yourselves, it is the gift of God....***

Then Paul begins to say what the faithful have in the form of grace. ***(Eph.1:3) Blessed [be] the God and Father of our Lord Jesus Christ, who hath blessed us with <u>every spiritual blessing</u> in the heavenly [places] <u>in Christ</u>.*** He has blessed us with every spiritual blessing in Heavenly places in Christ and who is that addressed to? The faithful. You know, when God sent the Israelites into the wilderness, it was to try them to see who was going to be the faithful. It was to see who was going to fight the good fight of faith and believe what He said. Folks, life is a tribulation and He is proving us now to see who is a believer and a true disciple of Christ. ***(Mat.22:14) For many are called, but few chosen. (Heb.10:38) But my righteous one shall live by faith: And if he shrink back, my soul hath no pleasure in him.*** "The righteous shall live by faith" is God's condition for all of the benefits of Christ, all throughout the Scriptures, and it is here, too. In fact, he said, "who hath blessed us with every spiritual blessing in the heavenly places <u>in Christ</u>." The blessings are in Christ. ***(1Jn.2:24) As for you, let that abide in you which ye heard from the beginning. If that which ye heard from the beginning abide in you, ye also shall abide in the Son, and in the Father.*** In other words, it's not faith in just any religious doctrine that we have today. It's faith in the Word as it's been passed on down to us through the apostles and writers of the New Testament. It's very important to know <u>what</u> to have faith in. Going to some church and hearing two, maybe three verses in a 30-minute sermon isn't how you learn the Word. You learn the Word by studying the Word for yourself and putting the Word down in your heart. Only if that which you heard from the beginning abides in you, <u>then</u> you abide in the Son. And all this spiritual blessing in Heavenly places is in Christ. The condition here is you have to be among the faithful because <u>knowing</u> what you have in Christ is not enough. You have to actually fight the good fight of faith and <u>lay hold</u> on it.

(Heb.11:1) Now faith is <u>assurance</u> (i.e., the assurance is that you have received the <u>substance</u> [KJV] of what you ask) **of things hoped for, a conviction of things not seen.** Are you assured of what you hope for? Do you have the assurance of the promises that have been given unto you, just like you have the assurance of your salvation? Are you convicted of the things that are not seen? Are you convinced of the things that are not seen? Well, that's what faith is. Faith is when you're <u>convinced</u> of something, even though you don't <u>see</u> it, and that's what Hebrews 11:1 tells us. Actually, the numeric pattern backs up this particular translation: "assurance of things hoped for, a conviction of things not seen." We are to be convinced that we have all those things that we have in Christ; we are to be convinced that they are ours. As a matter of fact, we have a pretty close version of that here. **(2Pe.1:2) ... <u>Grace to you and peace be multiplied</u> in the knowledge of God and of Jesus our Lord.** Grace is multiplied. The more you know about God, the more of Him you put into you, the more your grace is multiplied. Grace is the favor of God to be what He wants you to be. **(2Pe.1:3) Seeing that his divine power hath granted unto us all things that pertain unto life and godliness, through the knowledge of him that called us by his own glory and virtue.** "Seeing that his divine power hath granted unto us all things that pertain unto life and godliness" through that knowledge of God I was just sharing. So, the more we know about Him, the more faith we should have that He has already given us "all things that pertain unto life and godliness." And knowing this, we should understand that we have been called to fight the good fight of faith.

We don't always automatically receive an instant miracle, an instant healing, an instant deliverance or an instant provision. Many times we are called to fight this battle with the forces of darkness that are trying constantly to talk us out of the benefit. This is our trial. Have we decided that we're going to be a disciple of Jesus Christ and to walk as a son of God? Have we decided to walk and fight the battle as a son of God would fight? Well, that's exactly what the Lord has us in training for and that's why we go through our wilderness experiences. It's so that we prove to be the people who walk by faith. "The righteous shall live by faith," the Bible says. That's God's condition for all of His benefits in the Kingdom. In fact, <u>He tells us we have to fight</u> that good battle. **(Mat.11:12) And from the days of John the Baptist until now the kingdom of heaven suffereth violence, and men of violence take it by force.** You see, folks, we're not waiting on God to just bring everything to us. We've been given authority to fight this battle. The Lord told the Israelites, "You take up your sword and you go into that land, and you take that land, and I will be with you" (Joshua 1:1-9). **(Rom.8:13) For if ye live after the flesh, ye must die; but if by the Spirit ye put to death the deeds of the body, ye shall live.** We who have faith are endued with power by God's Spirit to do this. Faith is what brings us that power. We have to take up our sword and we have to conquer our enemy.

Of course, our sword is the sword of the Spirit, which is the Word of God (Ephesians 6:17). Our sword comes out of our mouth against our enemies. We confess Him before men; we confess His Word concerning the promises and the benefits that He has given to us in Christ Jesus. You see, we have to fight for what has been given us in Christ Jesus. If we don't fight, we won't win the battle. Some people are just very lazy; they want to be fed like a baby all of their life. But the truth is, as we grow up, God expects us to get into this battle and to fight it, just as when He sent those Israelites in there to put to death the old man that lived in the land and to take that property. He's telling us to do the same thing with this land that we live in; we are to take over this property by the sword of the Spirit. And it's a violent warfare in the spiritual realm. He said the Kingdom of Heaven suffers violence and that violent men take it by force. We're not taking it away from God. He's giving it to us, but He's told us to take up our Sword and fight this battle, and He will be with us.

You know, God justifies us when we fight this battle. ***(Rom.3:4) God forbid: yea, let God be found true, but every man a liar; as it is written, That thou mightest be justified in thy words, And mightest prevail when thou comest into judgment.*** Well, we see judgment all around us. And we are learning to fight the curse and come out from under the curse by holding fast to God's Word. That's the battle. He says, "let God be found true, but every man a liar." If a thought that's not according to God's Word comes into our mind, we cast it down in order to fight this battle and be found qualified to receive the benefits of the Kingdom. And he said, "that you might prevail when you come into judgment." We are constantly coming into judgment, folks. You see, because of our sins and because of our actions, we rightly are under the curse of judgment, but that curse has been taken by the Lord Jesus Christ. Jesus bore our curse and we accept that free gift from Him. That's one of the benefits we have to agree with, in order to come out from under the curse. But we're justified as we fight this battle by faith. We are accounted righteous because we fight this battle by faith. If you don't fight this battle by faith, you're not entitled to the benefits of the Kingdom and that's God's disclaimer. "The righteous shall live by faith." It's our disclaimer, too. Jesus laid down faith as a condition for receiving the benefits and so must we.

(Rom.4:16) For this cause [it is] of faith, that [it may be] according to grace; to the end that the promise may be sure to all the seed.... Why does the promise have to be of faith so it will be by grace? It's because we're trained to save ourselves by our own works. And yet, the Lord expects us to deny ourselves. He expects us to take up our cross, follow Him and, instead, accept His works. And as we do that, of course, the salvation comes by grace, unmerited, unearned and not by man's works. This is the only way God will accept it. That's why it has to be by faith. That's why God demands that the righteous live from faith. ***(Rom.4:16) For this cause [it is] of faith, that [it may be] according to grace; to the end that the promise may be sure***

to all the seed; not to that only which is of the law, but to that also which is of the faith of Abraham, who is the father of us all. We prove that Abraham is our father by walking in his steps, right? If we don't walk in his steps, then he's not really our father. *(Rom.4:17) (as it is written, A father of many nations* ["Gentiles"] *have I made thee) before him whom he believed, [even] God, who giveth life to the dead, and <u>calleth the things that are not</u>, <u>as though they were</u>.* And this is something, of course, that the world can't do. This is another identification of what faith really is: it's "calling the things that are not, as though they were." We can do that because it was all given to us at the cross and we were blessed with every spiritual blessing in Heavenly places in Christ. *(Rom.4:18) Who in hope believed against hope, to the end that he might become a father of many nations, according to that which had been spoken, So shall thy seed be.* In many cases, when we believe for the benefits of God, we're having to believe in hope against any hope that we can see with our eyes. In other words, we have no hope of help from the world, of help from man. Instead, we believe in God's promise and we call the things that are not, as though they were.

(Rom.4:19) And without being weakened in faith he considered his own body now as good as dead (he being about a hundred years old), and the deadness of Sarah's womb; (20) yet, looking unto the promise of God, he wavered not through unbelief.... Now, this is what we struggle with, folks: the demons of unbelief, depression and despair, concerning not having the things that the Lord has promised. These demons war against us with this evil heart of unbelief. *(Heb.3:12) Take heed, brethren, lest haply there shall be in any one of you an evil heart of unbelief, in falling away from the living God.* Unbelief is one of those things that will cause someone to be in the lake of fire. *(Rev.21:8) But for the fearful, and <u>unbelieving</u>, and abominable, and murderers, and fornicators, and sorcerers, and idolaters, and all liars, their part [shall be] in the lake that burneth with fire and brimstone; which is the second death.* <u>God considers unbelief as evil in His sight</u>. Abraham had plenty of reason to waiver because it was not a possibility for them to bring forth the seed that brought forth the nations, but it says, "looking unto the promise of God, <u>he wavered not through unbelief</u>." This is our fight, to hold fast to the Word and we're justified when we do this. We're justified when we let God be true and every man a liar.

(Rom.4:20) Yet, looking unto the promise of God, he wavered not through unbelief, but waxed strong through faith, giving glory to God. We glorify God by holding fast to His Word and being a witness to the people around us as <u>believers</u>. *(Rom.4:21) And being fully assured that what he had promised, he was able also to perform. (22) Wherefore also it was reckoned unto him for righteousness. (23) Now it was not written for his sake alone, that it was reckoned unto him; (24) but for our sake also, unto whom it shall be reckoned, who believe on him that raised Jesus our Lord from the dead,*

(25) who was delivered up for our trespasses, and was raised for our justification. (5:1) Being therefore justified by faith, we have peace with God through our Lord Jesus Christ. Yes, we are justified through our faith in God's promises and not by what we see naturally in the mirror. It's our faith that Christ is the One Who lives in us now and that He has healed us, He has delivered us, He has provided for us and that He will supply our every need, according to His riches in glory. All of this brings justification, as when Abraham was justified because he believed against all odds the promise that God was going to give him an heir. God's power is made perfect in weakness. *(2Co.12:9) And he hath said unto me, My grace is sufficient for thee: for my power is made perfect in weakness. Most gladly therefore will I rather glory in my weaknesses, that the power of Christ may rest upon me.* And Abraham was in a position of weakness. He had no way to bring forth this fruit anymore than we do. We have no way to bring forth the fruit of Jesus Christ, the Heir, but we do it against all the odds that we see around us. We hold fast to the Word and we're justified because of that. *(Rom.5:1) Being therefore justified by faith, we have peace with God through our Lord Jesus Christ; (2) through whom also, we have had our access by faith into this grace wherein we stand* (Notice that faith is our only access to the grace to bring forth the promises.)*; and we rejoice in hope of the glory of God.* Praise God!

Where does faith come from? How do we get more faith? Well, one answer to that is prayer. We can pray and ask God to give us more faith and He will do it. *(Mat.21:22) And all things, whatsoever ye shall ask in prayer, believing, ye shall receive.* And I challenge you to be diligent about praying for all things that you need. But praying the prayer of faith, we need His faith to do that, right? *(Rom.10:16) But they did not all hearken to the glad tidings....* Or the "Good News," which is that God has provided every need of ours in Christ. *(Rom.10:16) But they did not all <u>hearken</u>* ("to hear and obey or act upon") *to the glad tidings. For Isaiah saith, Lord, who hath believed our report?* Isaiah asked that about God's people and it's still true today: "who hath believed our report?" Such a small percentage of Christianity has any interest in walking by faith for things that they don't see. Most of God's people live in the flesh, they live according to their mind and they don't live by faith, other than believing that they're saved because they have "accepted Jesus as their personal Savior." But they don't know what "saved" is. We've discovered that "saved" is very, very big. The Greek word for "saved" is *sozo*, which is the verb of *soteria*, meaning "salvation." So, "Lord, who hath believed our report?" The cry is just that today, "Who is believing the Word of the Lord?" This is what God is going to find out before the end. *(Rom.10:17) So belief [cometh] of hearing, and hearing by the word of Christ.* Do you see why we have to put the Word of God in our hearts, folks? It's because it gives us ears to hear the Spirit of God. As we become familiar with His voice, His voice overcomes all those other voices that are in our minds. His voice overcomes the voices that are from our flesh. His voice overcomes the voices from the principalities and powers. Folks, the demons around us are attempting to discourage us so we will just give up and not hold fast to the Word until we see it come to pass. Many people don't endure until the end to see the promise come to pass, but God's Word in our heart is powerful to give us faith. If you want faith, if it's something that you really, truly and honestly desire after, then put the Word of God in your heart. Find the promises concerning the things that you need and begin to stand upon them. As your faith begins to get stronger and stronger, and you begin to speak the Word of the Spirit and the words of your promise, you will conquer your enemies. It's a battle that we're called to fight. God wants us to do this because He wants us to manifest the same sonship that Jesus had when He was on this earth.

 The Lord said to us, *(Joh.15:7) If ye abide in me, and <u>my words abide in you, ask whatsoever ye will</u>, and it shall be done unto you.* Ask whatever you will. Wow! How can the Lord trust us with that kind of responsibility? A major problem is that our will is contrary to His, until we receive the renewed mind of the Spirit. Then we become stable, we become someone whom God can trust and we become someone who can really speak the words of faith because then His will is our will. "If my words abide in you." We discovered that, *(1Jn.2:24) As for you, let that abide in you which ye heard from the beginning. <u>If that which ye heard from the beginning abide in you</u>, ye also shall abide in the Son, and in the Father*. "If <u>that which ye heard from the beginning</u> abide in you," that is, the <u>true</u> Gospel, the <u>true</u> Word of God. If you have the true Word of God in your heart, if His Words abide in you, then you can ask whatever you will and it shall be done unto you. You are a faithful servant of God, you have renewed your mind with the Word, you are trustworthy and God can use that. Now the true Sword of the Spirit is coming out of your mouth and this is God's plan. Again, His disclaimer is that you have to have <u>faith</u> in the <u>true</u> Word of God. If you don't, He doesn't have to keep any promise in this Book. If the people to whom we minister don't have faith in the true Word of God, there's no guarantee that we can help them. As a matter of fact, Jesus Himself couldn't help them. He went to His hometown, *(Mat.13:58) And he did not many mighty works there because of their unbelief.* Jesus put the same condition of having faith in the true Word on everybody who came to Him and He was very impressed with the centurion. *(Mat.8:10) And when Jesus heard it, he marvelled, and said to them that followed, Verily I say unto you, I have not found so great <u>faith</u>, no, not in Israel.* Isn't it amazing that He had to go to a Gentile to find somebody with faith? New believers coming out of the world have way more faith than a lot of Christians who've been with the Lord for many, many years, and that's really sad because they are not bearing the fruit of Christ. A very wise brother once told me about a vision he had of babies with beards. He said, "Christians are babies with beards. They've been with the Lord a long, long time, but they still haven't grown up." *(Mat.8:13) And Jesus said unto the centurion, Go thy way; as thou hast believed, [so] be it done unto thee.* Notice that Jesus put <u>upon the centurion</u> this responsibility for what he was going to receive.

 You ask me, "David, wasn't it important that Jesus have faith?" Well, yes, of course, because "these signs shall accompany them that believe." *(Mar.16:17) And these signs shall accompany them that believe: in my name shall they cast out demons; they shall speak with new tongues; (18) they shall take up serpents, and if they drink any deadly thing, it shall in no wise hurt them; they shall lay hands on the sick, and they shall recover.* The minister has to have faith. That's a condition to be able to administer the benefits of the Kingdom. But a condition to administer these benefits of the Kingdom to people who are in need of them is their own faith. We cannot make God break His Word; this is His condition; this is God's disclaimer. If you don't have faith, He doesn't promise you anything. "As thou hast believed, so be it done unto thee." This centurion was living by faith. The benefit he received for his servant was coming from his own faith. Jesus demanded this from the people who came to Him and, if He demands it, we must demand it. We're disciples of Christ because we're learners and followers. We're studying Him, we're walking in His steps, we're saying what He said and we're doing what He did. He's our example in all things. So when we offer this to other people, we have to make sure that we give them the disclaimer here, folks. The condition is that you receive according to your faith; as you have believed, so it will be done unto you. *(Mat.9:2) And behold, they brought to him a man sick of the palsy, lying on a bed: and Jesus seeing their faith said unto the sick of the palsy, Son, be of good cheer; thy sins are forgiven.* And, of course, further down, He says, *(6) ... Arise, and take up thy bed, and go up unto thy house.* "Seeing their faith." You know, one of our shortcomings is that we don't see as clearly as Jesus sees.

I believe that soon multitudes of God's people will see just as Jesus sees. They will see in the Spirit, with His eyes. And when they see faith in people, then they will be able to bestow the benefits upon them. Even as Jesus did, we have a compassion for people and we want to see the benefits bestowed upon them, whether they have faith or not. Jesus knew that if you did try to give the benefits to someone who didn't have faith, it would just bring disrepute to the promises of God. But when we know that people have faith, then we can act on that and they do receive the benefits. I'm not saying they receive them instantly, but they will receive the benefits. And this, of course, brings glory to the Word of God because people see that they can trust the Word. We need the eyes that Jesus has. We need to be able to see as He sees and I'm convinced He's going to bestow that upon us in these coming days. So, "seeing their faith," He just spoke out His own faith. His faith was conditional upon their faith. When they believed and He saw it and He knew it, He acted. And again, our disclaimer here is that, if you don't believe, you're not entitled to the benefits of the Kingdom.

(Mat.9:20) And behold, a woman, who had an issue of blood twelve years, came behind him, and touched the border of his garment: (21) for she said within herself, If I do but touch his garment, I shall be made whole. (22) But Jesus turning and seeing her said, Daughter, be of good cheer; thy faith hath made thee whole. And the woman was made whole from that

hour. Well, it certainly wasn't Jesus' faith that made her whole because He didn't know what was happening until after it had happened. She spoke her faith, even if it was only in her heart. She spoke her faith and she acted on her faith, and it was her faith that saved her. It's not a matter of convincing Jesus, as you can see from this text, because He didn't know about it. The power went forth from Him and healed her. ***(Mat.9:27) And as Jesus passed by from thence, two blind men followed him, crying out, and saying, Have mercy on us, thou son of David. (28) And when he was come into the house, the blind men came to him: and Jesus saith unto them, Believe ye that I am able to do this? They say unto him, Yea, Lord. (29) Then touched he their eyes, saying, According to <u>your</u> faith be it done unto you.*** So this is consistent. Jesus put this condition upon the person who was in need; they had to have faith <u>before</u> He bestowed the benefit. According to <u>your</u> faith, be it done unto you. And, of course, we can say this to anyone who is asking for the benefits of the Kingdom, whether it's healing, deliverance, provision or anything that God has provided, which is "all things," as we've discovered. We can say this to anyone else: "according to <u>your</u> faith, be it done unto you." That's our condition, that's our disclaimer. You know, we can pray for people and even if God puts their faith together with our faith so that we have a mustard seed to bring forth their need, if that person doesn't <u>continue</u> in their faith, they will lose the benefit that they just received. Faith is still a condition in that case, too.

The devil comes to steal the seed which has been sown in the heart. He doesn't want people to have testimonies and he comes to rob their faith. He's "blinded the minds of the unbelieving." ***(2Co.4:4) In whom the god of this world hath blinded the minds of the unbelieving, that the light of the gospel of the glory of Christ, who is the image of God, should not dawn [upon them].*** As a matter of fact, sometimes you need to bind the devil from blinding the minds of the unbelieving because he has that authority, but we have authority over him. He fights against us because he knows every testimony is something that's going to destroy and plunder his kingdom, and he doesn't want us to have the victory. We have to "fight the good fight of the faith" and "lay hold on the life eternal." ***(Mat.21:22) And all things, whatsoever ye shall ask in prayer, <u>believing</u>, ye shall receive.*** "All things whatsoever." That's hard for a lot of people to believe because of our natural mind, which is incredulous that the Lord would answer in such a way. The devil is able to take advantage of the fallen nature of our natural mind, of the old man, and use that to drag us down and rob from us, plunder us of the benefits of the Kingdom. And we see again that the condition here is, of course, "believing." You know, the Lord has put this authority in our hands by promises such as this one, and also, ***(Mat.18:18) Verily I say unto you, what things soever ye shall bind on earth shall be bound in heaven; and what things soever ye shall loose on earth shall be loosed in heaven.*** The Lord has put authority in <u>us</u>, folks. The Lord won't go around us and do something other than what He has said. In other words, if our unbelief is binding Him from doing something, <u>He won't break</u> His Word and go around it. You can't <u>make</u> God break His Own Word. He's made the condition and He has to abide by it.

What pleases God is <u>believers</u>. We are entering into His Kingdom, which is Jesus Christ. We are partaking of all of our benefits which, as we discovered, are in Christ Jesus. We partake of these benefits because we exercise this authority of binding and loosing. We can bind the devil and loose the devil. We can bind God because of unbelief and we can loose Him because of our belief. The condition, the disclaimer, is "according to <u>your</u> faith, be it done unto you." We may sometimes desire to go around the authority for their own faith that He has put in other people, but we shouldn't. We should learn not to because, again, we only bring disrepute to the great promises of God, if we do that. Jesus wouldn't go around them and we shouldn't, either. ***(Mat.13:58) And he did not many mighty works there because of <u>their unbelief</u>.*** As a matter of fact, the corresponding section of Mark says, ***(Mar.6:5) And he could there do no mighty work, save that he laid his hands upon a few sick folk, and healed them.*** If Jesus cannot, then we cannot. Jesus Christ, with all of His faith, <u>could not</u> give the benefits of the Kingdom to these people because of their unbelief. We don't want to spread disrepute upon the Gospel by trying to give something to someone who is double-minded and full of unbelief. I tell you, folks, even if Jesus Christ gives you a gift, you can lose it by unbelief because He has no authority to give you something by breaking His Own Word.

Let's look at a really good example: ***(Mat.14:28) And Peter answered him and said, Lord, if it be thou, bid me come unto thee upon the waters. (29) And he said, Come. And Peter went down from the boat, and walked upon the waters to come to Jesus. (30) But when he saw the wind, he was afraid; and beginning to sink, he cried out, saying, Lord, save me.*** Notice he got his eyes off of the Word, off of the command to "come." The command of the Lord Jesus Christ to "come" gave Peter the authority to do it, but he got his eyes off of that and onto the wind. So Peter began to be afraid and <u>he began to doubt because he was afraid</u>. He started to sink and he cried out to the Lord. Now, you would think, "Hey, if the Lord is in this, His faith would hold Peter up." But, did you notice, ***(Mat.14:31) And immediately Jesus stretched forth his hand, and took hold of him....*** Well, Jesus' faith wasn't holding him up; Jesus' <u>hand</u> was holding him up. God would <u>not</u> accept Jesus' faith to hold Peter up, nor did Jesus <u>try</u> to exercise His faith to hold Peter up when Peter's <u>own</u> faith wasn't holding him up. Peter became double-minded because of what he was looking at, what he had his eyes on. ***(Mat.14:31) And immediately Jesus stretched forth his hand, and took hold of him, and saith unto him, O thou of little faith, wherefore didst thou doubt?*** Well, Peter doubted because he got his eyes on the circumstances and not on the Lord.

And another good example of this is here: ***(Jas.1:2) Count it all joy, my brethren, when ye fall into manifold temptations.*** Temptation is not sin, folks. Temptation is the particular place where you just need to make a decision about whether you're going to believe God or believe the circumstances. So, temptation is not sin, but the devil tells people that it is. **(2) Count it all joy, my brethren, when ye fall into manifold temptations; (3) Knowing that the proving of your faith worketh patience. (4) And let patience have [its] perfect work, that ye may be perfect and entire, lacking in nothing.** We need patience in our faith. That's why sometimes we don't get answers immediately and sometimes we do, and that's nice. But sometimes, when there is a delay in the answer, we're tempted of the devil with all of his sly ideas. He'll tell you something like, "You're not good enough." Well, we can never be good enough. And Scripture says, "For this cause it is of faith, that it may be according to grace." Or the devil will say, "There's something you're not remembering here; there's something that you've done that you don't know about." But the Bible clearly says, **(Jas.4:17) To him therefore that knoweth to do good, and doeth it not, to him it is sin.** So, it has to be something that you know about; it can't be something you don't know about. The devil's pretty sly in his tactics.

Jesus didn't have a lot of conditions for receiving the benefits. All through the Gospels, it was, "Do you believe?" And, "If you do believe, prove it!" Prove it by speaking your faith or prove it by doing something to show your faith. So he says, "the proving of your faith worketh patience, and let patience have its perfect work." If a person is patient in their faith, they will receive the benefit and they will keep it. And that's what God wants -- stable sons of God, "perfect and entire, lacking in nothing." In other words, a person who is patient in their faith is going to receive everything that they need from God and they're going to be perfected in God. But the next part is also very important: **(Jas.4:5) But if any of you lacketh wisdom** (And that's all of us, isn't it?)**, let him ask of God, who giveth to all liberally and upbraideth not** (In other words, it's God's desire to give to us. He's not holding back. He desires earnestly to give to us and He desires our faith to do that.)**; and it shall be given him. (6) But let him ask in faith, nothing doubting: for he that doubteth is like the surge of the sea driven by the wind and tossed. (7) For let not that man think that he shall receive anything of the Lord; (8) a doubleminded man, unstable in all his ways.** Think not that you will receive anything from the Lord. Wow! Folks, we need to avoid this double-mindedness at all costs and it's a fight. It's a battle to cast down the vain imaginations that the devil fires at us concerning the things that we've desired of God, concerning the benefits that are ours. He's very sly and he tries everything. He tries to get us into salvation by works and he tries to get us under legalism. In every kind of way, he tries to make us depart a determination to "let God be true and every man a liar." The devil tries to shake us from our faith.

Consider it a given that, when you believe God for anything, the devil is going to come at you with every kind of reason to try to shake your faith because faith is the condition to receive. This trial is not sin. The fact that you hear all these doubts in your mind, these thoughts in your mind, these questionings in your mind, that's not sin. It's only when you decide that you're going to entertain these thoughts, that it becomes sin. **(Jas.1:12) Blessed is the man that endureth temptation....** What is temptation? That's when you hear those voices, those thoughts in your mind that are contrary to God's Word. You have to be patient in enduring this, patient in casting down those vain imaginations, so that you may be perfect and entire, lacking in nothing. *(Jas.1:12) Blessed is the man that endureth temptation; for when he hath been approved, he shall receive the crown of life, which [the Lord] promised to them that love him.* See, some people say, "Well, when Jesus prayed, He pretty well had instantaneous miracles." In some places it wasn't that way, but, yes, most of the time it was instantaneous. And we're coming to that time, too, but until then, we're going to be tried in our faith and we're going to endure in patience to see the end result. God wants us to do this. He wants us to <u>learn</u> to cast down everything that's contrary to the Word of God. *(2Co.10:5) Casting down imaginations, and every high thing that is exalted against the knowledge of God, and bringing every thought into captivity to the obedience of Christ.* In doing this, we become very stable, not moved by what we see or by the circumstances around us. We're only moved by, "Thus sayeth the Lord." We let God be true and every man a liar, and so we're justified when we come into a place of judgment.

(Jas.1:13) Let no man say when he is tempted, I am tempted of God; for God cannot be tempted with evil, and he himself tempteth no man: (14) but each man is tempted, when he is drawn away by his own lust, and enticed. These thoughts that come into our minds are to raise up lusts in us to overcome us, but we haven't sinned, as long as we've cast them down. <u>We haven't sinned</u>. In fact, we're called to be tempted of the devil, just like Jesus was led of the Spirit into the wilderness to be tempted of the devil. The Holy Spirit led Jesus to be tempted of the devil. He leads us to be tempted of the devil because we have to be <u>approved</u>. "When he hath been approved, he shall receive the crown of life." So, each man is tempted when he's drawn away by his own lusts, then enticed. *(Jas.1:15) Then the lust, when it hath conceived, beareth sin* (Only when you give in to the thoughts, when you give them a home and you accept them as your thoughts, that's when it becomes sin.)*: and the sin, when it is fullgrown, bringeth forth death. (16) Be not deceived, my beloved brethren.* So we're warned, "Don't be deceived." *(Heb.10:23) Let us hold fast the confession of our hope that it waver not* (Like Abraham, who wavered not through unbelief.)*; for he is faithful that promised.* And He is faithful, as long as we are faithful. If you give up the battle, if you give up fighting the good fight of the faith, you won't see the answer. But if you fight, if you you cast down these imaginations, you become approved of God in your trial and the answer will come. *(Heb.10:36) For ye have need of patience, that, having done the will of God* (That is, holding fast to the Word of God.)*, ye may receive the promise.* We need to be patient to receive the promise. Multitudes of people start out by faith, but then they're talked out of it by the devil and they never see the answer. Of course, that's the way it was for the Israelites in the wilderness. All they saw around them was lack and need, but it was God Who brought them into this place of lack and need to try their faith and see who was go-

ing to be a true believer. "For many are called, but few chosen" and "the righteous shall live by faith."

(Heb.10:37) For yet a very little while, He that cometh shall come, and shall not tarry. I believe this is talking about the Lord coming in us because, if we learn to walk by faith, guess Who's coming to be manifested in us? *(Heb.10:38) But <u>my righteous one</u>....* Some versions say, "the righteous one," but there's no numeric pattern in that. The numeric pattern is in "my righteous one." *(Heb.10:38) But my righteous one shall live by faith....* In other words, this is not talking about just the coming of Jesus; it's talking about Jesus manifesting in you. And God says "my righteous one" is the one who lives by faith. *(Heb.10:38) But my righteous one shall live by faith: And if he <u>shrink back</u>....* I remember looking this up one time and thought, "let's down sail." You know, we are catching the wind of God's Spirit. It is His power that drives us on and, if you shrink back, if you give up your faith, then, in other words, you're letting down sail. You no longer catch the wind of the Spirit. In fact, the Greek word for "wind" is the same Greek word for "spirit," and the Hebrew word for "wind" is the same Hebrew word for "spirit." *(Heb.10:38) But my righteous one shall live by faith: And if he shrink back, my soul hath no pleasure in him. (39) But we are not of them that shrink back unto perdition; but of them that have faith unto the saving of the soul.* Do you know what the saving of the soul is? It's Christ in you. It's His nature and it's His faith, and it's His walk in you. "Now faith is the assurance of things hoped for, a conviction of things not seen." Are you assured, not in your carnal man but in your spiritual man? I know that the devil uses your carnal man to talk to you all the time and reason with you all the time, but the Word is clear. If by the Spirit we put to death the deeds of the body, we shall live. We deny the works of the flesh and that includes casting down all the thoughts that come through our mind of the flesh. We have the assurance, we have the conviction that we have what God has said, even though we don't see it. It's ours and we receive it.

And I especially like, *(Eph.6:10) Finally, be strong in the Lord, and in the strength of his might.* We would love that, wouldn't we? Well, it's ours! It was given to us at the cross. *(Eph.6:11) Put on the whole armor of God, that ye may be able to stand against the wiles of the devil.* The devil is very sneaky, folks. The only way we can stand up to him is with the wisdom of God in our heart. *(Eph.6:12) For our wrestling is not against flesh and blood, but against the principalities, against the powers, against the world-rulers of this darkness, against the spiritual [hosts] of wickedness in the heavenly [places]. (13) Wherefore take up the whole armor of God, that ye may be able to withstand in the evil day, and, having done all, to stand. (14) Stand therefore, having girded your loins with truth, and having put on the breastplate of righteousness, (15) and having shod your feet with the preparation of the gospel of peace; (16) withal taking up the shield of faith, wherewith ye shall be able to quench all the fiery darts of the evil [one]. (17) And take the helmet of*

salvation, and the sword of the Spirit, which is the word of God. We need to fight this battle, folks, and believing the Word of God is the key to everything we see here. Hold fast to the Word of God, saints, and the Lord be with you in this battle.

CHAPTER 24

Beware of Condemnation!

Greetings, saints. God bless you and thank you for being with us today. We bless you in Jesus' name. Dear Father, we love You and we appreciate You. We thank You for the gift You have given to us in Jesus Christ and especially Your precious Word through Him. And we love the way Your Word lives in our hearts, Lord. It shows us the path of life and righteousness, Lord. Thank You for bringing to our remembrance every day, Lord, the things that You have spoken to us, to protect us and give us discernment to heighten our faith and cause us to be able to partake of Your blessings. Thank You, Father. Help us to see the things that hinder, Lord. We know there are things that hold us back from entering fully into Your presence and into Your ways, and walking in Your steps. We ask You to give us discernment of those, Father, and to deliver us from them, in the name of the Lord Jesus Christ. Thank You, Lord. Thank You.

I've been sharing the real Good News and have explained God's "disclaimer," which is our "disclaimer," also. Well, I'd like to share with you of another "disclaimer" that I think hinders an awful lot of people and that is legalism. You know, there's only one way to the benefits of Christ and it's faith, but many people want to take another route. They want to be justified by something that they do, they want to be justified by their works, in order to partake of the benefits of Christ and it's a lying deception of the devil. *(Rom.1:16) For I am not ashamed of the gospel* ("Gospel" means "Good News," the Good News of the New Testament promises that God has given unto us.)*: for it is the power of God unto salvation to every one that believeth; to the Jew first, and also to the Greek.* The condition is believing. And, of course, the condition Jesus mentioned almost every time was faith. Faith is what gives us the power of God unto salvation. The Greek word for "salvation" is *soteria*, and the verb of that is *sozo*, which we've discovered is translated differently in many places, even though it's always the word *sozo*. It's translated as God saving us through deliverance, salvation, preservation, healing, provision and so on. *Sozo* is used to mean salvation through all of those ways. Now we're told in this text here, that Paul said, "I'm not ashamed of the Gospel, for it's the power of God unto all of that provision of God, to everyone that believeth." So, the condition for us to partake of the benefits of God, is first of all, faith. The devil tries to sidetrack us from that faith because we are justified by our faith. We're not justified by our works, but people try to earn the benefits of the Kingdom, or they try to condemn people into working for the benefits of the Kingdom, none of which will work. Many people have been hurt and separated from Christ through such things.

The text goes on to say, *(Rom.1:17) For therein is revealed a righteousness of God from faith unto faith: as it is written, But the righteous shall live by faith* (Or, literally, "from faith."). Our life comes from faith. The benefits that we receive, that come through the grace of God, all come from faith. We are to grow from "faith unto faith" because "the righteous shall live from faith." Our benefits of the Kingdom come that way. *(Rom.5:1) Being therefore justified by faith....* That means "accounted righteous by faith." Many people are attempting to circumvent this by accounting that their righteousness comes through something that they believe or something that they do and they think they're going to receive the benefits of God because they believe this certain thing, or they do this certain thing. But really, it's just faith in the promises of God that justifies us or accounts us righteous. In order to have the benefits of God, you have to be <u>accounted righteous first</u>. Therefore, after repentance, the very first thing that we need is <u>faith</u>. *(Mar.1:14) Now after John was delivered up, Jesus came into Galilee, preaching the gospel of God, (15) and saying, The time is fulfilled, and the kingdom of God is at hand: <u>repent ye</u>, <u>and believe in the gospel</u>.* So it says, *(Rom.5:1) Being therefore justified by faith, we have peace with God through our Lord Jesus Christ*. It's just because we <u>believe</u>. Just because we believe, we are accounted righteous, justified and we have peace with God. Even <u>before</u> we're fully obedient, even before we're walking in perfection, we have peace with God. *(Rom.5:1) Being therefore justified by faith, we have peace with God through our Lord Jesus Christ; (2) through whom also <u>we have had our access by faith into this grace</u> wherein we stand; and we rejoice in the hope of the glory of God.* See, our access to the grace of God, which is God's favor to provide for us all these benefits that we've been learning about, comes through grace. It all comes through God's favor and God's favor comes through <u>faith</u>. We have our access into this grace through our faith; nothing else will give that to us.

Well, somewhere along the line, most all of us have probably been caught up in seeking to be justified by a doctrine, and I remember when I was caught up into that, too. Denominations seem to work that way. They teach that you are justified because of something you believe or something that you do that most other people don't. That's a silly trap. It's a silly trap of the devil to keep you from receiving the benefits of God. You <u>cannot</u> grow in that way. You've basically been separated from the body of Christ. *(Gal.5:19) Now the <u>works of the flesh</u> are manifest, which are [these:] fornication, uncleanness, lasciviousness, (20) idolatry, sorcery, enmities, <u>strife</u>, jealousies, wraths, <u>factions</u>, <u>divisions</u>, parties, (21) envyings, drunkenness, revellings, and such like; of which I forewarn you, even as I did forewarn you, that they who practise such things shall not inherit the kingdom of God.* Paul said a sect, or a division, or a strife, is a work of the flesh. You've been divided away from the people of God because you're self-righteous about something that you do, but, of course, the other denominations have something that they do and you don't. So, it just depends on what denomination you're in, or what non-denominational denomination you're in, concerning the foolishness with which the devil has deceived you, right? I've been there. I know what it feels like and I know what deliverance from it feels like. Our access is through <u>faith</u>.

What is faith? As we've studied, Jesus said, *(Mar.11:24) Therefore I say unto you, All things whatsoever ye pray and ask for, believe that ye receive* (The literal translation is "received.") *them, and ye shall have them.* Most of your Bibles have a footnote down at the bottom of the page that "receive" is past tense: "received" or "have received." And no matter which of the ancient manuscripts you look at, the word "receive" is always past tense. So faith is believing you have something on the grounds that God says you have it, not because you see it. He's telling you to "believe you have received" it before you even see it. That's what faith is and we're accounted righteous because we believe something solely on the grounds that God said so. And, of course, that faith gives us access to grace. What is grace? Grace is God fulfilling that benefit or that promise to you, by His power, since you have no way to do it yourself. As a matter of fact, this gift of faith totally negates any way that you would use to get that benefit or promise because faith is believing you've already received it; therefore, you can't go out and get it. You can't use your methods to get it. *(Heb.11:1 KJV) Now faith is the substance* (i.e., the assurance [ASV] that you have what you asked for) *of things hoped for, the evidence of things not seen.* Since faith is the substance of the thing hoped for, while there's no evidence seen, you're merely claiming this gift on the grounds that it's already been given to you. For instance, if "by whose stripes you were healed," what can you do to go get it? If you try to go get it by your own methods, by your money, by your intelligence, or whatever, you prove that you do not believe the verse because God says it's already yours. *(1Pe.2:24) Who his own self bare our sins in his body upon the tree, that we, having died unto sins, might live unto righteousness; by whose stripes ye were healed. (Eph.2:8) For by grace have ye been saved through faith; and that not of yourselves, [it is] the gift of God; not of works, that no man should glory.* As we have seen, salvation in all forms has already been provided. All we have to do is believe and rest (Hebrews 4:1-11), and let God bring the manifestation.

God is a miraculous God, as you who are entering into this rest know. His provision is everywhere. You can't go into the deepest wilderness without receiving His provision, even if it comes out of the sky. Even if it comes out of a rock. Even if it comes out of a fish's mouth. You cannot get away from God's provision, if you will accept it by faith. But, if you attempt to get God's grace any other way, you will fail. Notice the verse reads, "We have had our access by faith into this grace wherein we stand." That's the way grace comes and you can't talk God out of it. That's His method. Many people want to make rules and regulations, which they say you have to keep in order for you to be justified. They want you to keep a part of the Law, or they want you to keep a part of man's law, or they want you to do something in order to be justified before God, so that God can answer your prayers. Justification isn't by works of the Law, or works of man, or special beliefs that you might have. Justification doesn't come that way; justification comes only through faith in the promises of God. Faith! And faith is believing that you've received something that you haven't yet manifestly received. Paul makes it pretty plain. He says, *(Rom.4:1) What then shall we say that Abraham, our forefather, hath*

found according to the flesh? (2) For if Abraham was <u>justified by works</u>, he hath whereof to glory; but not toward God. Of course, if Abraham had been trying to be justified by his works and his works had failed him, then he would have been condemned. And many people do that; they trust in themselves, they trust in their own works to save them and they fall under condemnation when those works fail. Well, there are ministries, and ministers, and doctrines that attempt to get people to change through the method of condemnation. Their method is to condemn you into doing something, in order to be justified by God, so He can give you a benefit, but there's only one way to obtain grace and that is through <u>faith</u>. And faith is the <u>opposite</u> of condemnation.

One of the most common things that we see is where preachers will command their groups to stay away from doctors and medicine, so that they will receive healing from God. But that's getting the cart before the horse. You're attempting to get God to do something for you <u>by your works</u>. The <u>faith</u> has to come <u>first</u>. If your works come first, that's not faith. ***(Eph.2:8) For by grace have ye been saved through faith; and that not of yourselves, [it is] the gift of God; (9) <u>not of works</u>, that no man should glory. (10) For we are his workmanship, created in Christ Jesus <u>for good works</u>, which God afore prepared that we should walk in them.*** You see, there are <u>your</u> works and there are <u>God's</u> works. God's works come on the other end of faith and grace, and your works come <u>before</u> faith and grace. When it's your works, you're attempting to be accepted by God and to receive some benefit from God by something that <u>you do</u>. So when you hear a legalistic command like that, just remember it's coming from the devil. He wants to supplant the real method of God in your life; he wants to supplant the only method that works. <u>Faith</u> gives grace and <u>grace</u> gives the benefit. These apostate preachers are saying, "No, if you do this, God will do this." In other words, <u>you're buying the benefits of God</u>, as if He didn't pay a big enough price when He sacrificed Jesus Christ. That doesn't make any sense, does it? And then there are other apostate leaders who want to put you under works of the Law, in order for you to be justified. In other words, they say you have to keep the feasts, keep the Sabbath, abstain from certain meats, pay tithes and on and on. And they tell you that you're not justified unless you <u>do</u> these things. These are deceivers, every one of them. They want to obtain the benefits of God by receiving justification through the works of the Law, but it doesn't matter whether it's the works of the Law or the commands of men. It makes no difference because it's the same lie. The truth is, <u>you're only justified by faith</u>. And, if you're not justified, you don't get the benefit.

In fact, ***(Rom.3:4) God forbid: yea, let God be found <u>true</u>, but every man a liar*** (In other words, you're believing the truth, you're believing the Word of God.)***; as it is written, That thou mightest be justified in thy words, And mightest prevail when thou comest into judgment***. We definitely always want to <u>prevail</u> when we come into judgment. We want God's salvation there, whatever that need might be. If we need health, or if we need deliverance, or if we need a provision, all of it comes because of God's grace, <u>and all of that grace comes</u> because of <u>His</u> faith, which

He puts into us. And so, he tells you here that you can prevail when you come into judgment, if you just agree with God's Word. Just believe what God says; don't add to it and don't take away from it. Let every man be a liar, but let God be true. *(Rom.4:2) For if Abraham was justified by works, he hath whereof to glory; but not toward God. (3) For what saith the scripture? And Abraham believed God, and it was reckoned unto him for righteousness.* That's it, folks. Believe God. It's not as if you are able to save yourself. It's not as if you're able to do the works of God. Remember, there are two different kinds of works. *(Eph.2:8) For by grace have ye been saved through faith; and that not of yourselves, it is the gift of God; (9) not of works* (These are your works.), *that no man should glory. (10) For we are his workmanship, created in Christ Jesus for good works* (These are God's works.)*, which God afore prepared that we should walk in them.* See, faith gives you grace and grace gives you God's works. *(Php.2:13) For it is God who worketh in you both to will and to work* (or "to do" KJV)*, for his good pleasure.* God works in us to will and to do of His good pleasure. That's one way His grace is manifested in us. He works in us to will and to do. You see, it's God's works. Salvation is God's works. And what causes God to do that in us? Faith, bringing grace, causes God to do that in us. None of your works will cause Him to do it. You cannot buy off God with any of your works. It's "Not of works, lest any man should boast," for in Christ Jesus were we created for good works; and again, these are God's works. When you abide in Him, you walk as He walked, and that means His works are moving through you. So, basically, salvation is God putting His will in us.

You know, you don't have any problems when your will is the will of God because you get everything you want. God does everything He wants to do, doesn't He? Our problem is that we have a will contrary to God, so there's a war, but God puts His will in us and He gives us the capability to bring His will to pass. He works in us to will and to do, or to work, you see. That's God working in us and it's not our works at all, so we're not justified by our works, anymore than Abraham was. We're justified by faith. *(Rom.4:4) Now to him that worketh, the reward is not reckoned as of grace, but as of debt.* This is talking about a person who has to go do something in order to please God, so that God can give them their benefit. *(Rom.4:4) Now to him that worketh, the reward* (or the answer to your need) *is not reckoned as of grace, but as of debt.* In other words, you're going around grace, or you think you're going around grace. You really can't go around grace because, without God's favor, you are only what you are and you can't do anything more than what you are. You do what you are. But, God's grace enables us to do what He is and not what we are. Because of our own nature, God has to reach in from the outside and change us from the outside. What causes Him to do that? Your faith. Your faith brings His favor to do that. "The reward is not reckoned as of grace, but as of debt." God is not going to be our debtor. We are not going to be able to buy Him off, no matter what we do. No matter what we believe. No matter what kind of a law we go back under. The Law was righteousness through works, justification through works.

God rejected that. *(Rom.3:20) Because <u>by the works of the law shall no flesh be justified in his sight</u>; for through the law cometh the knowledge of sin.* So, by the works of the Law shall no man be justified. *(Rom.4:5) But to him that worketh <u>not</u>, but believeth on him that justifieth the ungodly, his faith is reckoned for righteousness.* Oh, praise the Lord! That's the hope; that's the "Good News" right there: "to him <u>that worketh not</u>." In other words, we don't have to be something that we're not. We can rest in God and His grace will bring us the manifestation and make us something that we're not. His grace will bring *(Col.1:27) ... Christ in you, the hope of glory*.

We've studied "reconciliation," which means "an exchange." Jesus has made reconciliation; He has exchanged His life for my life. What do I have to do to be like Jesus? All I have to do is look in the mirror and see Him. All I have to do is accept by faith that this person I see, is <u>now</u> Jesus living in me. I no longer live, but Christ now lives in me. *(Gal.2:20) I have been crucified with Christ; and <u>it is no longer I that live, but Christ living in me</u>: and that life which I now live in the flesh I live in faith, the faith which is in the Son of God, who loved me, and gave himself up for me.* By faith, you're accepting the sacrifice of Jesus. And Who's going to bring that to pass? <u>God</u> is going to bring that to pass by His grace because you've given Him the faith. "Faith is the substance of the things hoped for, the evidence of things not seen." You're giving God a substance that He will use to make into the answer to your need and that substance is <u>faith</u>. And because you were chosen by Him even before you knew Him, He gave you the grace to receive the very first faith, from which you continue to receive grace. *(Psa.65:4) Blessed is the man whom thou choosest, and <u>causest to approach unto thee</u>, That he may dwell in thy courts....* This is grace to do and be whatever you need to be because we know He has saved us. As a Christian, if you need faith, ask Him for it, for salvation in all forms is not by your works but by His works in you. *(Rom.4:6) Even as David also pronounceth blessing upon the man, unto whom God reckoneth righteousness apart from works, (7) [saying,] Blessed are they whose iniquities are forgiven, And whose sins are covered. (8) Blessed is the man to whom, the Lord will not reckon sin.* Praise be to God for that blessing!

Well, I would like for us to study a man who was having just that problem. Paul was feeling condemned because of his works and, since he was condemned, he had no faith. Since he had no faith, he had no grace. It's a terrible rut you'll be in until you lay hold on faith. And he says, *(Rom.7:14) For we know that the law is spiritual: but I am carnal, sold under sin.* In other words, because of his very nature, he wasn't able to partake of the benefit of God. He was not <u>capable</u> of partaking of the benefit of God. He was telling us his problem here and he comes to the solution a little further down. *(Rom.7:15) For that which I do I know not: for not what I would, that do I practise; but what I hate, that I do.* To put it simply, Paul was saying, "I'm doing what I don't want to do and I don't know how to be saved from this circumstance."

He hated his sin, but he was in it and it was overcoming him. And he wasn't getting grace from God because he was feeling condemned. Do you know why? It's because when you're feeling condemned, what you're saying is, "I could do better and I'm not." Think about it. When you're under condemnation, you're thinking, "I could do better," or, "I should have done better and I'm not." Well, you're reckoning that you are capable of pleasing God and, really, it's only God Who's capable of pleasing God. His nature is the only thing that pleases Him. Our nature doesn't please Him. When you have condemnation, you do not feel justified by faith and that's the problem. If you're justified by faith, you don't have condemnation. Condemnation only has one particular good use: **(Heb.10:26) For if we sin wilfully after that we have received the knowledge of the truth, there remaineth no more a sacrifice for sins, (27) but a certain fearful expectation of judgment, and a fierceness of fire which shall devour the adversaries.** Condemnation comes from willful disobedience. Paul was saying, "The good that I would do, I do not. The good that I will to do, I do not, and the evil which I will not to do, that I am doing." You see, his will was totally set against his sin, so it wasn't a willful disobedience, but he hadn't figured out the key to receiving the power from God to overcome.

What is the key? The key is faith. It's not justification by works and Paul was proving that he was trying to be justified by works because of the condemnation he was feeling. He was proving that he was under the Law, which was justification by works, but in the New Testament, we have no access to God or His benefits that way. And so the Judaizers who want to bring you back under the Law and the legalists who want to bring you under their church laws or their doctrines are all separating you from Christ and from the benefits of God. There's no way for you to be any better than you are; you do what you are because it's your nature. We need the nature of God to be given to us through grace and we don't get grace, except by faith. Paul needed to know that he was justified by faith because he was condemning himself, proving that he thought he was justified by works. **(Rom.7:16) But if what I would not, that I do, I consent unto the law that it is good.** He was saying, "The Law's good and I'm bad." But the New Testament teaches us that we're not bad anymore. **(Rom.6:11) Even so reckon ye also yourselves to be dead unto sin, but alive unto God in Christ Jesus.** God made an exchange, your life for His life, and you don't live anymore. Christ now lives in you. See, as long as you're going to call yourself "a sinner saved by grace," you're going to be a sinner. The truth is, that old sinner's dead. That's what Paul commanded us to believe in Romans 6. "The old man is dead and now Jesus lives in us." Now watch how your faith causes God to give you grace to bring it to pass. Something you could never, ever do, God will do. He will do it for you as a gift. He will give it to you as a gift. You couldn't work your way to it! Never! If you were here a million years, you would never get it, but God will give it to you as a gift. He will not allow you to reach it any other way because He's not going to be your debtor.

(Rom.7:17) So now it is no more I that do it, but sin which dwelleth in me.

He's saying, "Since my will is against it," that proves that there are two entities here. "My will is against this, but my flesh is doing it." He says, "Now it is no more I that do it, but sin which dwelleth in me." Wow! We are schizophrenic when we desire to serve God and yet we walk in the flesh. ***(Rom.7:18) For I know that in me, that is, in my flesh, dwelleth no good thing: for to will is present with me, but to do that which is good [is] not. (19) For the good which I would I do not: but the evil which I would not, that I practise.*** In other words, "The evil which I desire not to do, or wish not to do, or will not to do, that's what I practice." ***(Rom.7:20) But if what I would not, that I do, it is no more I that do it, but sin which dwelleth in me.*** Therefore, "I, the one who wills not to sin, I am a son of God. I am righteous." That's the spiritual man who wills not to sin. But since Paul was continuing to sin because of his flesh, he said, "It is no more I that do it, but the sin which dwelleth in me." Paul received the understanding that when he desired to do right, God separated him from the sinful man. God separated the righteous spiritual man from the sinful man of flesh. ***(1Co.15:50) Now this I say, brethren, that flesh and blood cannot inherit the kingdom of God; neither doth corruption inherit incorruption.*** You know, the "old man" has to die here; you're not trying to save the old man and he can't be saved anyway. It's your spiritual man who's saved, the one who is an eternal son of God. That spiritual man is growing in you; as the outer man is decaying, that inner man is being renewed day-by-day. ***(2Co.4:16) Wherefore we faint not; but though our outward man is decaying, yet our inward man is renewed day by day.*** That spiritual inner man is taking the territory. The Israelite is going in, taking the territory away from the Canaanite, the old man. The spiritual man is conquering the old man with the edge of the sword, taking his land and our old life is his land. As we walk by faith in God, this is what's happening because God is doing this in us. God said, "I'm going to go before you. You go, you take up your Sword, but I will conquer your enemies for you and I will give them into your hands." And that's what the Lord is doing. He's giving this old life into the hand of the spiritual man and his sword is the Word of God. ***(Eph.6:17) And take the helmet of salvation, and the sword of the Spirit, which is the word of God.***

(Rom.7:21) I find then the law, that, to me who would do good, evil is present. (22) For I delight in the law of God after the inward man: (23) but I see a different law in my members, warring against the law of my mind, and bringing me into captivity under the law of sin which is in my members. (24) Wretched man that I am! who shall deliver me out of the body of this death? And he goes on to say, ***(25) I thank God through Jesus Christ our Lord.*** Or, as the numeric pattern reads, "But thanks to God through Jesus Christ our Lord." Paul is crying out, "Who's going to deliver me?" He's looking for a savior and that's Jesus; that's His job. Thanks be to God! He's already done this for us! It's already accomplished! Paul receives the revelation here that the sacrifice of Jesus already delivered him and, when you read on, you can see that. He says, ***(Rom.7:25) I thank God through Jesus Christ our Lord. So then I of myself with the mind, indeed,***

serve the law of God; but with the flesh the law of sin. So faith in this revelation that the Lord has already delivered him out of the body of that death, already delivered him from his bondage to the sinful man, is what's going to give Paul the grace he needs to walk away from that old man and to walk as Jesus walked.

It's like the serpent on the pole in the wilderness. You remember the story: **(Num. 21:5) And the people spake against God, and against Moses, Wherefore have ye brought us up out of Egypt to die in the wilderness? for there is no bread, and there is no water; and our soul loatheth this light bread. (6) And the Lord sent fiery serpents among the people, and they bit the people; and much people of Israel died. (7) And the people came to Moses, and said, We have sinned, because we have spoken against the Lord, and against thee; pray unto the Lord, that he take away the serpents from us. And Moses prayed for the people. (8) And the Lord said unto Moses, Make thee a fiery serpent, and set it upon a standard: and it shall come to pass, that every one that is bitten, when he seeth it, shall live. (9) And Moses made a serpent of brass, and set it upon the standard: and it came to pass, that <u>if a serpent had bitten any man</u>, <u>when he looked unto the serpent of brass</u>, <u>he lived</u>.** And the solution came when anyone who had been bitten got their eyes off of the bite and onto the serpent on the pole; then they were healed. They got their eyes off the problem and on the solution. They quit looking inward and started looking upward. Well, folks, we've been snake-bit. That's the problem. This old man is a serpent and he is the son of the serpent. We've been snake-bit and the poison of that serpent is in us. The solution is for us to see that Jesus, Who became sin for us, was crucified on that pole, on that cross, and now we're free. We died with Him. We <u>were</u> delivered, we <u>were</u> healed, we <u>were</u> provided for because all the things that are included in salvation <u>were</u> given to us at the cross.

So we have to get our eyes off the problem and on the solution, but what does condemnation do, instead? Condemnation gets your eyes on <u>yourself</u> and it separates you from God. As I mentioned, condemnation does have one good use and that's when you're in willful disobedience. But when you're like Paul and you're not in willful disobedience, when you desire the power of God and you just don't know the way to reach it, then condemnation is detrimental to your life because it separates you from Christ. Condemnation tells you, "You should have done better." It's the very opposite of, "Look at Jesus; He's already done it for you." And, as a matter of fact, Paul goes on to say, **(Rom. 8:1) There is therefore now no condemnation to them that are in Christ Jesus.** Using condemnation to force a person to change is called legalism and is doomed to failure. If you are under condemnation, you will receive no power from God to change. Condemnation is the opposite of faith. Faith gives grace and grace gives the benefit. But, again, if you are under condemnation, it's either because you feel justified by works or you feel not justified by works. You have a wrong relationship with God. Instead of a relationship of faith, it's a relationship of self-works. Some of you are trying to change people through condemnation, but it won't work. And you ministers out there trying to use condemnation to make people change, all you're going to do is make Pharisees. If you want people to change, there's only one thing that will work. You have to put faith in a person's heart. Condemnation will cause them to look inward. Condemnation will cause them to get their eyes off the serpent on the pole and back on the snake bite, and the only thing they'll ever have there is the curse. But if you put faith in that person's heart, they will have grace and they will have the benefit of the Kingdom. So what we have to do is put faith in their heart. We have to speak encouragement to people. We have to speak the promises of the Word of God to people. We have to help them accept, freely, who they are in Christ Jesus. Once they accept that they are righteous in Christ because they are justified through <u>faith</u>, then they can receive the benefit as a gift.

Paul continues, ***(Rom.8:2) For the law of the Spirit of life <u>in</u> Christ Jesus made me free from the law of sin and of death.*** <u>What put Paul in Christ Jesus</u>? The only thing you can see from the text is that Paul <u>believed</u> Jesus was the solution and, of course, that's true. Jesus was the solution and Jesus is the solution. He's already given us the benefit. ***(Gal.2:16) Yet knowing that <u>a man is not justified by the works of the law</u> but through faith in Jesus Christ, even we believed on Christ Jesus, that we might be justified by faith in Christ, and <u>not by the works of the law</u>: because <u>by the works of the law shall no flesh be justified</u>.*** He's saying the same thing over and over there, isn't he? Paul wants this to come across because this is very, very important. People are seeking to be justified by various self-works of keeping Sabbaths, or paying tithes, or keeping the feasts, or abstaining from certain meats, and so on and so forth. And I mentioned one fallacy that is very detrimental and destructive, and that is, "Well, if I don't go to the doctor, God will heal me. If I don't take my medicine, God will heal me." No! You're getting the cart before the horse. That is justification by <u>your</u> works. You're saying God will give you the grace because of your works, but He's not going to do that. It has to be <u>faith</u>. Have you already been healed? Of course. That's what the Bible says, so if you believe that you've <u>already</u> been healed, that is faith. And what do you receive for that? Grace. And what does the grace do? It causes you to <u>walk</u> in the benefit. If you want to walk in the benefit, the grace for the ability to do that has to come from God.

Remember, there are two kinds of works. There are your works, which come <u>before</u> faith, and there are God's works, which are a <u>fruit</u> of faith. God's works in you are what will cause you to walk in perfection before the Lord. James spoke about faith being made perfect through works. ***(Jas.2:22) Thou seest that faith wrought with his works, and <u>by works was faith made perfect</u>.*** What works was he talking about? ***(Php.2:13) For <u>it is God who worketh in you</u> both to will and to work, for his good pleasure.*** James was talking about <u>God's works</u>. ***(Eph.2:8) For by grace have ye been saved through faith; and that not of yourselves, [it] is the gift of God; (9) <u>not of works</u>*** (This is referring to <u>your</u> works.), ***that no man should glory. (10) For we are his workmanship, created <u>in Christ Jesus for good</u>***

works, which God afore prepared that we should walk in them. In other words, these works are His works because you are in Him. So he says here, ***(Php.2:13) For it is <u>God who worketh in you</u>*** (It's <u>God</u> working in you and that's grace!), ***both to will and to work, for his good pleasure.*** That's what we need. That's real salvation. <u>All those other things</u> people tell you that you can do in order to receive the benefits of God are just a cheap substitute and they don't work. No, it has to be <u>faith</u>.

(Gal.3:10) For as many as are of the works of the law.... How do you know if something is a work of the Law? You know it's a work of the Law because there's condemnation involved. ***(Gal.3:10) For as many as are of the works of the law are under a curse....*** See, you can't get out from under the curse when you're seeking to be justified by your works. There's no way out. You're under the curse of the Law. It doesn't matter if it's the Old Testament Law, or man's law, or your law; you're under a curse because your works are coming before your faith. ***(Gal.3:10) For as many as are of the works of the law are under a curse: for it is written, Cursed is every one who continueth not in <u>all</u> things that are written in the book of the law, to do them.*** So if you want to seek to be justified by anything you <u>do</u>, you have to <u>do everything</u> God wants. That's the only way you <u>could</u> be justified and that's not possible. It's not possible because your fallen nature won't permit that. We need grace, we need unmerited favor from God, to make us into something that <u>we're not</u>. You can only do what you are and so God has to make you into something else, and only faith brings the grace for that. ***(Gal.3:11) Now that no man is justified by the law before God, is evident: for, The righteous shall <u>live</u> by <u>faith</u>....*** Notice that there's only one way to have God's life and that is to live by faith. That life is a free gift from God through faith and He doesn't give that gift to just anybody. He only gives that gift to people who <u>believe</u>; that's the condition. ***(Mat.9:29) ... According to your faith be it done unto you***, and ***(Mat.8:13) ... As thou hast believed, [so] be it done unto thee***, as Jesus said. For all of God's benefits, that is the condition. If a person doesn't believe, they won't receive and will go on in their self-works and die under the curse. You see, "The righteous shall live by (or, literally 'from') faith," ***(Gal.3:12) and the law is not of faith*** (There is no law that man can put you under to make you righteous because none of that is faith.)***; but, He that doeth them shall live in them. (13) Christ redeemed us from the curse of the law, having become a curse for us....*** See, the Lord put <u>our</u> curse upon Jesus. We're not under the curse of the Law. We don't have to obey the Law in order to be justified. Now, if we walk by faith, God will give us grace and that grace will cause the Law to be fulfilled in us. Fulfilling the Law is not the same as being <u>under the Law</u>; <u>to be under the Law is to be under a curse</u>. ***(Gal.3:10) <u>For as many as are of the works of the law are under a curse: for it is written, Cursed is every one who continueth not in all things that are written in the book of the law, to do them.</u>*** The Law is the letter, a parable, and only the Spirit fulfills the letter. It is being fulfilled in Spirit in you who walk by faith in Him.

For example, I don't have to worry about tithing. I give plenty because God puts it in my heart to give plenty. In other words, God fulfills it naturally and I'm not under a rule or regulation. This is a totally different relationship with God, the one He wants. ***(Gal.3:19) What then is the law? It was added because of transgressions, till the seed should come to whom the promise hath been made; and it was ordained through angels by the hand of a mediator.*** So the Law was only a meantime thing, until the seed should come to whom the promise was due. God never wanted the relationship that the Law commanded of righteousness by works, "because by the works of the law shall no flesh be justified." Some people think that's a superior relationship and they can go back under the Law, but they're separated from Christ, as it says here: ***(Gal.5:1) For freedom did Christ set us free*** (Free from what? Free from that relationship.)***: stand fast therefore, and be not entangled again in a yoke of bondage.*** Most of Galatians 3 and 4 is about that. It's rebuking Christians for following the Judaizers and going back under the Law. ***(Gal.5:2) Behold, I Paul say unto you, that, if ye receive circumcision....*** Or you could say paying the tithe, or you could say keeping the feasts, or abstaining from meats, or whatever. These things are just a type and shadow of the things to come (Colossians 2:16-17; Hebrews 10:1), Paul said. They are not the fulfillment. They're not important. ***(Gal.5:2) Behold, I Paul say unto you, that if ye receive circumcision*** (Or, again, this could be any other works of the Law, or anything you think you can do to be acceptable by God, to buy His benefit. If you receive this thing, whatever it is, then)***, Christ will profit you nothing. (3) Yea, I testify again to every man that receiveth circumcision*** (or any of those other things)***, that he is a debtor to do the whole law. (4) Ye are severed from Christ, ye who would be justified by the law*** (meaning "by the works of the law," as in Galatians 2:16)***; ye are fallen away from grace.*** And you're a debtor to do the whole Law, he says. See, this is very, very dangerous. You're severed from Christ because you're seeking your own righteousness and there has to be repentance and a return to justification by faith. You are fallen away from grace because there's no other way to get to grace, except through faith. You have to hold onto faith. Your works cannot impress God enough to get Him to give you grace. You cannot do it. ***(Gal.5:5) For we through the Spirit by faith wait for the hope of righteousness. (6) For in Christ Jesus neither circumcision availeth anything, nor uncircumcision; but faith working through love.*** Yes! ***(Gal.3:18) For if the inheritance is of the law, it is no more of promise: but God hath granted it to Abraham by promise.*** There's no other way to receive the inheritance.

(Jas.2:14) What doth it profit, my brethren, if a man say he hath faith, but have not works? Now, what works are these? These are the works that come from faith, not the works that come before faith; those are your works. When you believe, God gives grace for you to do His works. Some people want to take the Book of James out of their Bible. They insist that it's a false doctrine because they say, "No! We're not justified by works!" They don't understand that there are two kinds of works. There are God's works, which are the fruit of faith, and there are your works, which are not acceptable.

(Jas.2:14) What doth it profit, my brethren, if a man say he hath faith, but have not works? can that faith save him? (15) If a brother or sister be naked and in lack of daily food, (16) and one of you say unto them, Go in peace, be ye warmed and filled; and yet ye give them not the things needful to the body; what doth it profit? (17) Even so faith, if it have not works, is dead in itself. If God's works don't come from your faith, then your faith is not His faith. There is a mental assent which is not God's faith and doesn't believe you have already received. Faith is calling "the things that are not, as though they were." Faith is believing you have received. People say, "I believe! I believe! I believe!" But when you ask them if they believe they <u>have</u> received, you find out that they don't because their actions prove that they don't believe they have received and their words prove that they don't believe they have received, so it's not faith. That kind of faith can't bring forth God's works. It's not faith at all. There's an old saying that goes, "Faith that fizzles out at the finish had a flaw in it from the first." The truth is that it's not faith, if it's not bringing forth God's works. ***(Jas.2:18) Yea, a man will say, Thou hast faith, and I have works: show me [thy] faith apart from thy works, and I by my works will show thee [my] faith.*** You know, people do think that they can show you their works apart from their faith, but the works of God manifested through man only come because of true faith and that faith comes only by His grace. Nobody can brag. Nobody!

And he goes on to say, ***(Jas.2:19) Thou believest that God is one; thou doest well: the demons also believe, and shudder. (20) But wilt thou know, O vain man, that faith apart from works is <u>barren</u>*** (or, "unfruitful")***?*** True faith will give you the works of Jesus as a free gift. ***(21) Was not Abraham our father justified by works, in that he offered up Isaac his son upon the altar? (22) Thou seest that faith wrought with his works, and <u>by works was faith made perfect</u>.*** <u>Faith is made perfect by works</u>. When you have faith, are you justified <u>before</u> the works? Yes. As we've previously studied in Romans 4, you're justified, you're accounted righteous. See, when you have faith, even <u>before</u> the works perfect the faith, you are accounted righteous. And when you're accounted righteous, then you're entitled to the benefit that grace brings. So, faith brings grace and grace brings the works of God in your life. It's just so neat the way God has it planned! People like to turn that around and put the cart before the horse, but God won't accept it. You're separated from Jesus and you're separated from grace, if you do that.

What do we need to do for people to enable them to overcome? We need to put <u>faith</u> in them, not condemnation. And how do you put faith in them? <u>You speak the Word of God</u>. ***(Rom.10:17 KJV) Faith [cometh] of hearing, and hearing by the Word of God.*** You speak the Word of God to them and you ***(4:17) calleth the things that are not, as though they were***. Don't attribute their failures to them. Don't attribute their stumbling to them. Help them to take their eyes off of themselves and get their eyes on the Lord. Help them to see that He already took away that sinful nature and nailed it to the cross, and now they have His nature. <u>This</u> will cause a person to overcome. If, instead of putting faith in them and letting that faith bring them the grace to change, you put them under condemnation to force them to change, the only thing that you're going to make there is a Pharisee. They will feel that they're justified, that they're righteous because of something that they've done, or something that they believe. We are righteous because of something God did. We are righteous because we believe in something He already accomplished, not in something that we could do.

Well, faith is the foundation for salvation, but we're going to be judged by our works. Every place in the Bible where Jesus talks about coming back and judging His people, He's judging them for their works. Why? It's because your works are proof of your faith. If you don't have the works of God, it proves that you have not been walking in the faith of God. So, is God judging our faith? Yes. He's judging our faith by our works. He said, "And I by my works will show thee my faith." What we need to do, above all things, is encourage one another. We need to share with one another what the Lord has done and not what we need to do. If you get your eyes on yourself, you may become withdrawn and feel rejected, but if you get your eyes off of yourself and on the Savior, you become someone who walks by faith. You walk by faith in what He has accomplished on that cross. You walk by faith in what He has given to you by bearing your curse. That's what delivered Paul out from under his problem with condemnation. He said, "There is therefore now no condemnation to them that are in Christ Jesus." No condemnation. You would think there would be condemnation, if, "I'm sinning and I'm failing," but not if you're justified by faith. See, God wants to give righteousness to you as a free gift. You don't deserve it. Condemnation comes because you think you should deserve it or, in other words, "I have to do better, so God will accept me." No, the only One Who can do better is God Himself. He wants to give it to you as a free gift and He wants you to know it's a free gift. It's not of yourself, "lest any man should boast." He will not accept your buying any of His benefits. The condemnation that comes through legalism separates God's people from Him, from His power and from His benefits. It separates us from grace, His unmerited favor.

Oh, praise God! Father, give us Your grace freely, that You have given us in Christ Jesus. Give it to us through the faith that You put in our heart. Lord, we ask You to fill us with Your gift of faith, so that we may have Your grace to walk in the steps of our Lord, Jesus Christ. Father, thank You for freely giving us the gift of righteousness, as You called it in Romans, a "gift," a free gift of righteousness. Lord, we can't earn it because of our fallen nature, but we can receive it as a gift. Lord, we thank You for this gift. Thank You for teaching us how to help our brethren by speaking faith into their hearts, into their lives, when they are failing, Lord, and getting their eyes off themselves and getting their eyes on You, Lord. Help us to do that, too! Thank You, Father, in the name of Jesus. Amen.

UBM BOOKS

www.ubmbooks.com

- *Sovereign God For Us and Through Us* by David Eells
- *Hidden Manna For the End Times* by David Eells
- *The Man-child and Bride Prophecy* by David Eells
- *Perfection Through Christ* by David Eells
- *How Shall We Die?* by David Eells
- *Destructive Demon Doctrines* by David Eells
- *The Tongue Conquers the Curse* by David Eells
- *Are You Following a Wolf?* by David Eells
- *Speak Grace, Not Condemnation* by David Eells
- *What Has Been Shall Be: The Man-child Returns* by David Eells
- *The Curse of Unforgiveness* by David Eells
- *Weakness, the Way to God's Power* by David Eells
- *Salvation: Instant and Progressive* by David Eells
- *Numeric English New Testament* by Ivan Panin and UBM (also available for e-Sword)
- *Numeric English New Testament - Contemporary Version* by Ivan Panin and UBM

Audio/Video Teachings Available For Free at www.ubm1.org